A
SURVEY OF LONDON

WRITTEN IN THE YEAR 1598

BY

J O H N   S T O W

CITIZEN OF LONDON

WITH AN INTRODUCTION BY

A N T O N I A   F R A S E R

EDITED BY

HENRY MORLEY, LLD

SUTTON PUBLISHING

First published in 1598, revised edition 1603

This facsimile edition taken from Routledge & Sons Ltd edition of 1912
First published in this edition in the United Kingdom in 1994 by Alan
Sutton Publishing Limited, an imprint of Sutton Publishing Limited
Phoenix Mill · Thrupp · Stroud · Gloucestershire · GL5 2BU

Reprinted 1997

ISBN 0-7509-0827-0

The publisher wishes to thank Mark Latus of W. & G. Foyle Ltd,
London, for his valauble help in the preparation of this book

Acknowledgements
Oxford University Press for permission to reproduce the portrait of
John Stow; the Guildhall Library, London, for permission to reproduce
the map 'City of London in Parishes and Wards'.

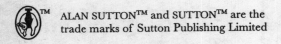

Printed in Great Britain by
The Guernsey Press Company Limited,
Guernsey, Channel Islands.

CONTENTS

INTRODUCTION

Antonia Fraser

I wish I had known John Stow and been able to wander with him on his historical journeyings. He must have been a wonderfully diverting companion to anyone interested in the past, and in spite of his encyclopaedic knowledge, never dull or Dryasdust (Carlyle's dismissive phrase for pedants). Even in his final years – he died in 1605 at the age of eighty – Stow was described as 'the merry old man'. The only flaw to such companionable expeditions might have been Stow's combination of inexhaustible energy and ineradicable poverty. This meant that he could never afford to go by horse or coach, but travelled the country investigating cathedrals, tombs, monuments and so forth, always on foot. On second thoughts, perhaps we are fortunate to enjoy the fruits of Stow's labours, nearly four hundred years later, from our armchairs as it were, and find them as freshly invigorating and instructive as ever.

The *Survey of London* was Stow's last book. It was first published in 1598, and reprinted in a revised version in 1603 (the year in which Elizabeth I died). Stow's other works are also well worth consulting – his *Annales* for example is still used as a source by historians – but the *Survey* has a particularly important place in the bibliography of British history. This is for two reasons. First of all, no-one before Stow had attempted a comprehensive study of London, already in the sixteenth century a great capital city. A population of roughly a quarter of a million in 1600 may not sound vast by the standards of our own day, but as a proportion of the national population – under four million – it was of course enormous. Certainly the London which John Stow knew was considered to be an enormous sprawling octopus of a place, and he was the first man to catalogue the tentacles of the octopus.

Stow worked meticulously. Historians of his own day and the

age immediately following paid tribute to his painstaking methods, his reliable conclusions. We can be confident that if Stow notes the presence of a particular monument or reports some peculiar topographic detail, such a note and such a report owe nothing to his imagination. Stow for his part prided himself on his honesty: he never accepted bribes, never wrote out of 'malice, fear or favour' but purely to establish the truth.

There is a second reason for studying the *Survey* today. Stow himself, born in the reign of Henry VIII and dying at the beginning of the reign of James I, lived through one of the most tumultuous centuries in our history. At the time of Stow's birth – in the district now known as the City of London, near the present Bank of England – Henry VIII still cherished Catherine of Aragon as his consort. He had not yet fallen fatally in love with Anne Boleyn, let alone set in train those events which would culminate in the reformation of religion in England, and his own establishment at the head of the English Church, replacing the Pope. The Henrician reformation, which still retained most Catholic practices and rituals, was followed by the hardline Protestantism of the reign of Edward VI (when Stow was in his twenties) and then again by the restoration of Catholicism under Henry's daughter Mary.

Although the accession of Henry's second daughter Elizabeth would lead to a permanent Anglican settlement, this was a development which could not necessarily have been predicted in 1558: Elizabeth's nearest relative and potential successor was a Catholic – Mary Queen of Scots. Certainly Stow himself retained strong sympathies for the old religion and its ways – like so many of his contemporaries – although it is not quite clear whether this was genuine 'Romanism' or simply a love of the past for its own sake. He certainly had no reason to love the Reformers. Stow tells us of the encroachment of Henry VIII's minister Thomas Cromwell upon his father's garden, leaving the deprived Stow still paying the same rent for the truncated space. Stow reflects grimly that 'the sudden rising of some men causeth them in some manner to forget themselves', and immediately a past when the great men tyrannized the weak with impunity is brought back to life.

If Stow's picture of London is comprehensive, it is also conveyed with a host of vivid detail. This is a city of tradesmen, from the bakers of Stratford-atte-Bowe bringing 'divers long carts loaded with bread' to sell in Cheapside, to the butchers of Pudding Lane, whose way with offal led to the naming of the street. (Just as Houndsditch got its name from the numerous dead dogs found floating there . . .) It is a city of sports: skaters on the 'fens' to the north of London in the hard winters characteristic of those times, or spectators at the various bear-gardens where bulls as well as bears awaited their fate with mastiffs 'in several kennels nourished to bait them'. It is a city of vice, with 'stew-houses' (brothels) abounding, and a special Single Woman's Churchyard for those of their inhabitants who did not manage to make a deathbed repentance. It is a city of sickness – Stow gives us details of the Lazar Houses for 'Leprous People'. And of course there is the recurrent danger of plague, although Stow emphasizes that fire was the real danger, in a largely wooden city: the two great plagues of his day, he notes, are 'immoderate quaffing amongst fools' and casualties as a result of fires. All this is in addition to his careful, scholarly notification of churches and monuments which can still be studied today with profit.

'I have painfully (to my great cost and charges) out of old hidden histories and records of Antiquity brought the same to light', wrote Stow at the end of the sixteenth century. Towards the end of the twentieth century, we can still be grateful that he did so.

Antonia Fraser
London, July 1994

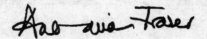

A portrait of John Stow [from the Gentleman's Magazine *or 1837], contained in J. Stow,* Survey of London, *ed. C. L. Kingsford (2 vols., 1908, reprinted 1971, Oxford University Press). Reproduced by permission of Oxford University Press*

JOHN STOW.

———

JOHN STOW was a patriotic Londoner who lived throughout the whole reign of Elizabeth, and into the reign of James the First. He was born in 1525, in the year of the Battle of Pavia, where Francis the First of France was taken prisoner. He was four years old when Wolsey and Cardinal Campeggio presided over a Court at Blackfriars to consider the question of the divorce of Catherine of Aragon by Henry the Eighth. He was eleven years old when the first edition of a complete English Bible was produced by Miles Coverdale, and a copy of it was ordered to be placed in every church in England. He was twenty-two years old when Henry the Eighth died.

In the reign of Edward the Sixth, John Stow, who had been born in the parish of St. Michael, Cornhill, the son (and grandson) of a tailor, completed his apprenticeship to the family business in the year 1549.

In the days of the divorce of Queen Catherine, Stow had been a boy in a simple City household, many a time fetching halfpenny-worths of milk from the farm at the nunnery of the Franciscan sisters, who were called not Minorites, but Minoresses, whence, by abbreviation, Minories. Forty or fifty milch-kine were then fed on the meadows there, and a halfpenny was the price, in summer, of three pints, in winter, of two pints, of new milk hot from the cow. The boy's way to fetch milk was only along Leadenhall Street to the City gate, known as Aldgate, between Bevis Marks and Crutched Friars. Just outside that gate the house and farm of the Minories lay to the right of him.

A story told by Stow of his young days enables us to determine very nearly where his father the tailor lived. It must have been in Threadneedle Street, old tailors' quarters; for he has an illustration of the high-handed dealing of great men in the days of Henry the Eighth, that touched his father's house. Thomas Cromwell—Wolsey's Cromwell—when, after Wolsey's fall, he had risen high in the king's favour, bought some old tenements in Throgmorton Street, which he pulled down, to build upon their site a large house for himself. When the new house was built there was a fair space for garden to the south of it which met the ends of the gardens running northward from Threadneedle Street. But Thomas Cromwell, as his garden was not large enough to please him, without payment offered or leave asked, simply pulled down the palings that were his neighbours' landmarks to the north, pushed his own garden limit twenty-two feet southward into the gardens of his neighbours, and then built them out with a high brick wall. Stow says that his father had a house— probably a summer house—at the end of his garden, and the great man had it taken up and moved on rollers, off the ground he had annexed, into that half of his garden which was left to Mr. Stow. But Mr. Stow had to go on paying the rent of the whole for the half that was left him, "because no man durst go to argue the matter." The surveyors of the work had no answer to expostulations but that "Sir Thomas commanded them to do so." The ground here in question was very close to, if not actually on, the site of the present Stock Exchange. This sort of procedure was afterwards more restricted to commons, enclosures, and the blocking up of rights of way; a practice against which Shakespeare battled at Stratford in his latter days. The gardens invaded by Sir Thomas Cromwell must, of course, have run back from houses in Threadneedle Street, and as the date must have been 1531 or 1532 when Cromwell is known to have put new buildings on the ground of two messuages taken on a ninety-nine years' lease from the Austin Friars, this was a home incident of the time when the author of the "Survey of London" was a child of six or seven.

At four and twenty, when his apprenticeship was at an end, and John Stow had himself become a master tailor, he was not living in Threadneedle Street, but near the well within Aldgate; for he records incidentally that in 1549, when he was living there, the bailiff of Romford "was executed upon the pavement of my door, where I then kept house."

John Stow must have lived by his occupation as a tailor for the next fourteen or sixteen years. But he was born to take a patriotic interest in the annals of his native country and his native city, and at the beginning of the reign of Queen Elizabeth, when his age was thirty-three, he had gathered books about him for aid to his diligent search into the history of the past. He was then beginning to compile for himself, and he published in 1561, at the age of thirty-six, "A Summarie of Englysh Chronicles." Of this volume in its first edition there is but one copy extant, which belongs to the Grenville Collection in the British Museum. It is in 120 leaves, but without the title page. Its date is determined by the text on the last page but one, where the Chronicle stands at the second year of the reign of Elizabeth. There was a second edition of Stow's Summary of English Chronicles in 1565, and other editions in 1566, 1570, 1573, 1575, 1579, 1584, 1587, 1590, 1598, and 1604; that is to say, there were eleven editions in the author's lifetime, the last of them published in the year before his death, and brought down by himself to 1604, the date of issue. John Stow's digest of the Chronicles was, therefore, in Elizabeth's reign one of the accepted short guides to a knowledge of the History of England. Elizabethan school-boys learnt their history by committing to memory the Latin verses in which Christopher Ocland set forth "Anglorum Prælia" from 1327 to 1558, followed by "Elizabetha; De Pacatissimo Angliæ statu imperante Elizabetha."

The friendly acceptance of his Summary, and his own strong bent towards such research, led John Stow, about the time when he was preparing for its first reprint, and when his age was about forty, to give up his business, that he might devote himself exclusively to the research in which he found the true use and enjoyment of his life. In the edition of his "Summarie" produced in 1573, he wrote—"It is now eight years since I, seeing the confused order of our late English Chronicles, and the ignorant handling of ancient affairs, *leaving mine own peculiar gains*, consecrated myself to the search of our famous antiquities." This indication, nearest to the time of giving up his trade for the one all absorbing pursuit, may be taken as best marking the time of that bold change, by which, for the love of intellectual research, he risked the coming of what really at last came, old age with poverty. In later editions he so counted the time since his first devoting himself to historical studies, that according to the edition of 1587 it was in 1564, according to the edition of 1598 it was in 1562, and in his last edition, that of 1604, the old man wrote—"It is now nigh forty-five years since I, seeing the confused order of our late English Chronicles, and the ignorant handling of ancient affairs, as also by occasion being persuaded by the Earl of Leicester," &c.—and adds in a sidenote to this—"I gave him a book compiled by his grandfather, Edward Dudley." These forty-five years "now nigh" would bring us to the end of 1559 or the beginning of 1560, and so evidently dated from the time when he began first to prepare the "Summarie of Englysh Chronicles," with the fact now added that he was encouraged to do so by the Earl of Leicester.

Writers in Elizabeth's time—except the dramatists—depended for support rather on patronage than on the money earned. John Stow, when he withdrew from his trade to give the rest of his life wholly to research, had, no doubt, a little store of means, inherited and saved from his past earnings, that would enable him to work steadily on until that further support came which he had right, if not reason, to expect. But his research cost money, he accumulated books, he paid no servile suit for patronage, his life reached to the age of eighty, and he was left in his last years very poor.

Meanwhile, in the midway of his life, at the age of forty, he put away needle and thread, and devoted himself to the preparation of a fuller record of the Annals of England.

A man surrounded with old books, who loved the past and

studied it incessantly, exposed himself to criticism of the crowd who, as Chaucer observed, "demen gladly to the badder end." He was regarded as a suspicious character. Two or three years after he had begun to give his whole life to his work, he was reported to Queen Elizabeth's Council as "a suspicious person with many dangerous and superstitious books in his possession." Edmund Grindal was then Bishop of London, by himself and through his chaplain one of the official licensers of books; they were days also of active search for "recusants," who remained Roman Catholics outside the English Church as it had been by law established. Grindal ordered his chaplain and two others to make search in John Stow's study, and report on what they found there. As John Strype tells us, the chaplain reported concerning Stow "that he had great collections of his own for the English Chronicles wherein he seemed to have bestowed much travail. They found also a great sort * of old books printed; some fabulous, as of Sir Degorie, Triamour, &c., and a great parcel of old MS. Chronicles, both in parchment and paper. And that besides he had miscellaneous tracts touching physic, surgery, and herbs; and also others, written in old English, in parchment. But another sort of books he had, more modern; of which the said Searchers thought fit to take an Inventory, as likely most to touch him; and they were books lately set forth in the realm or beyond sea in defence of Papistry. Which books, as the Chaplain said, declared him a great fautor † of that religion." It was not permitted by the law of that day to prove all things as a security for holding fast that which was good. A loyally religious Englishman was expected by the government to be of one side without knowing what was said upon the other.

Stow's catholicity, as student of the past, brought him into trouble also at other times. He had a younger brother who abused the trust put in him when employed in the business, and once brought him into peril by false witness against him.

---

* *Sort.* This is an old use of the word in the sense of an assemblage, a company of persons or things of like character, as in Shakespeare's Richard III., "a sort of vagabonds, rascals and runaways."

† *Fautor*, favourer.

While John Stow was at work upon his "Annals," he was disputing with a rival chronicler on behalf of his "Summarie of the Chronicles." The passage from Latin Monastic Chronicles to Histories in English began with a Londoner, Robert Fabyan, if we leave out of account such early work as the rhymed Chronicle of England written at the end of the thirteenth century by Robert of Gloucester, for recitation to the people, or the rhyming Chronicles of John Harding, who fought at Agincourt, and Andrew of Wyntoun. Robert Fabyan was a prosperous London draper, member of the Drapers' Company, and Alderman for the Ward of Farringdon without. He resigned his Alderman's gown in the year 1502 to avoid the expense of the Mayoralty, for, although well-to-do, his wife presented him with sixteen children, of whom six were living when their father died in 1512. Fabyan was a zealous student of the past, well versed in French and Latin, and a modest student of good literature. He wrote a "Concordance of Histories," afterwards called "New Chronicles of England and France," opened with a Prologue in Chaucer's Stanza which represented its author as one who prepared material, for the skilled artist or historian who should come after him to perfect what he had rudely shaped. The Prologue ended with an invocation to the Virgin for help; and the seven parts of the prose Chronicle, which brought the history from the mythical founder of Britain to the year 1504, ended with seven metrical epilogues, entitled the Seven Joys of the Blessed Virgin. Fabyan also translated into English rhyme such Latin verses as he cited. Robert Fabyan's Chronicle was first printed in 1516, four years after its author's death, and nine years before Stow was born.

The next English chronicler was Edward Hall, a Shropshire man, who after education both at Cambridge and Oxford entered at Gray's Inn, was called to the bar, became Common Serjeant and Under-Sheriff of London, and was in 1540 one of the judges of the Sheriffs' Court. He died in 1547, while still at work upon his history of "The Union of the Two Noble and Illustre Families of Lancastre and Yorke." This work, known as Hall's Chronicle, is of high value.

Richard Grafton was a Londoner, who signed himself in 1550, in the reign of Edward the Sixth, Printer to the King's Majesty. Edward Hall's Chronicle was in his hands, and he published it in 1548, the year after its author's death, with some completions of his own, which he undertook, he said, Hall dying, and "being in his latter time not so painful and studious as he ought to have been." The first edition, therefore, of Hall's Chronicle appeared when John Stow's age was three and twenty. There was a second issue of it in the same year, and a fourth was reached in 1550; but in 1555, during the persecutions under Philip and Mary, the book was prohibited by Act of Parliament.

Richard Grafton produced at the end of February 1563, "An Abridgement of the Chronicles of England, gathered by Richard Grafton, Citizen of London." Stow's "Summarie of English Chronicles" had first appeared in 1561. Grafton's was, therefore, a rival book, of which there was a second edition in 1564, followed in 1565 by a still further abridgement into "A Manuell of the Chronicles of Englande from the Creacion of the Worlde to this Yere of our Lorde 1565. Abridged and collected by Richard Grafton." This was a little book of a hundred leaves in 24mo, beginning with a Calendar in which the evil and unfortunate days, and such as are not altogether so evil, are noted, and ending with a List of Fairs. It was followed by two folio volumes, in 1568 and 1569, of "A Chronicle at large, and meere History of the Affayres of Englande, and Kinges of the same." There was a second edition of this within the year, and of the "Abridgement" (not the "Manuell") another edition then followed in 1572, which was dedicated as the first had been, to Robert Dudley, who had been Earl of Leicester since the end of September 1564. Grafton sought to discredit Stow's work. Stow declared that Grafton's "Manual" was "new scoured or cleanly altered" from Grafton's "Abridgement," after the buying of Stow's "Summary." The controversy included little elegancies, such as Grafton's play on the name of Stow when he condemned the "memories of superstitions, foundations, fables, and lies foolishly *Stowed* together," or such as Stow's hope that his work would not be defaced and overthrown "through the thundering noise of empty *tonnes* and unfruitful *graftes* of Momus' offspring."

Grafton's "Chronicle at large" in the two folios of 1568 and 1569 was not followed until 1580 by the result of John Stow's larger research in "Annales, or a Generall Chronicle of England, from Brute unto this present Year of Christ, 1580." This was a quarto of 1215 pages, followed by an account of our Universities upon eight pages more, and it was dedicated to the Earl of Leicester. There was a second edition of it in 1592, another in 1601, and another in 1605, continued to the 26th of March, within ten days of its author's death. There were also two editions after Stow's death, "continued and augmented by Edmond Howes," which were published in 1615 and 1631, the edition of 1631 being again continued to date.

But Stow had left completed at his death a yet larger Chronicle, which is now lost, and to which he refers in the edition of his "Annales" published in 1605. "Thus, good reader, I desire thee to take these and other my labours in good part, like as I have painfully (to my great cost and charges) out of old hidden histories and records of Antiquity brought the same to light, and for thy great commodity bestowed them upon thee; so shalt thou encourage me, if God permit me life" [he was then eighty years old], "to publish or leave to posterity a far larger volume, long since by me laboured, at the request and commandment of the Reverend Father, Matthew Parker, Archbishop of Canterbury; but he then deceasing, my work was prevented, by printing and reprinting (without warrant or well-liking) of Raigne Wolfe's Collection, and other late comers, by the name of Raphael Holinshed his Chronicle." Archbishop Parker died in 1575, and the first edition of Holinshed's Chronicle appeared in 1577, the second in 1586 and 1587. Holinshed's was one of the two histories that Shakespeare used; the other was Hall's Chronicle.

The death of Archbishop Parker had deprived Stow of his one strong supporter. Parker was a devoted student of antiquity, with especial reference to the subject of his own main work, a folio published in Latin, in 1572, on the Antiquity of the Church of Britain. Archbishop Parker required all servants in his house, when they had nothing else to do, to bind books, print from MSS., or engrave on copper. He caused Anglo-Saxon types to be cut, and cultivated study of the Anglo-Saxon Homilies as evidence of doctrine in the Early Church. He paid costs of the printing of four old historians, Matthew Paris, Matthew of Westminster, Thomas Walsingham, and Asser's Life of Alfred ; and except Asser all of them were published at the suggestion and with the aid of John Stow ; Matthew of Westminster in 1567, Matthew Paris in 1571, and Thomas Walsingham in 1574, the year before the Archbishop's death.

It was not till the next reign that John Speed, another patriotic tailor, thirty years younger than John Stow, published his fifty-four maps of England and Wales, and in 1611 his " History of Great Britain under the Conquests of the Romans, Saxons, Danes, and Normans."

So much for Stow's place among the Annalists of Britain, at a time when the rising forces of the nation gave new interest to study of its past. Stow's researches into the History of England were followed by a concentration of his energies upon the book now under the reader's eyes, a study of the present and past state of London. Here he could work without a rival at his large collections. He was the one Londoner who, in the reign of Elizabeth, made thorough study of his native city, and resolved to set down all he knew of its past history and present state. His "Survey of London," of which the first edition was published in 1598, and the second, with revisions, in 1603, was the first of its kind, and even grows in interest by course and change of time.

While engaged upon his record of London itself, Stow was engaged also in cherishing the memory of the greatest of all Londoners, the poet Chaucer. " His works," Stow tells us in this volume, " were partly published in print by William Caxton, in the reign of Henry VI. ; increased by William Thynne, esquire, in the reign of Henry VIII. ; corrected and twice increased through mine own painful labours, in the reign of Queen Elizabeth, to wit, in the year 1561, and again, beautified with notes by me collected out of divers records and monuments, which I delivered to my loving friend, Thomas Speght ; and he having drawn the same into a good form and method, as also explained the old and obscure words, &c., hath published them in anno 1597." The edition of Chaucer by William Thynne, chief clerk of the kitchen to Henry the Eighth, was published in 1532, and was the first attempt at a complete Chaucer. It was reprinted in 1542 with addition of "The Plowman's Tale," which was not written by Chaucer. The next edition was that of 1561, and John Stow was its only editor. He added to the volume Lydgate's "Story of Thebes." Next came the edition in 1597 or 1598 by Thomas Speght, to whom Stow gave his additional materials, including "Chaucer's Dream" and the "Flower and the Leaf," which were then first printed. Afterwards came in 1602, printed by Adam Islip, a new edition of Speght's Chaucer, with further additions. There was no demand for a reprint of that until 1687, and no other edition of Chaucer's Works until Urry's in 1721. Thus the impulse given by John Stow, and communicated to his friend Speght, represented all that was done to bring Chaucer home to English readers from 1542 to 1721, that is to say, during a period of one hundred and seventy-nine years. Much honour to John Stow !

We are told of Stow, by the friend who edited his " Annales " not long after his death, that he was tall, lean, with small clear eyes and a pleasant cheerful face, that he was " very sober, mild, and courteous to any who required his instructions ; and retained the true use of his senses unto the day of his death, being of an excellent memory. He always protested never to have written anything either for malice, fear, or favour, nor to seek his own particular gain and vain glory ; and that his only pains and care was to write truth." He had written, indeed, this rhyming caution in 1565—

> " Of smooth and flattering speech remember to take heed :
> For Truth in plain words may be told ; of craft a Lie hath need."

He travelled much on foot to cathedrals and other places in search of records. He lived peacefully, and "was very careless of scoffers, backbiters, and detractors."

But Stow "annaled for ungrateful men." In his old age, after he had spent all the powers of his mind and all his worldly goods in service of his country, he was at the age of seventy-nine rewarded by his Sovereign with—a license to beg. The date of the license, March 8th, 1603, being before the 25th of the month, when 1604 officially began, was, according to the present way of reckoning, March 8th, 1604. Stow died of stone colic, and was buried on the 8th of April 1605 in his parish church of St. Andrew's Undershaft, where his widow set up as monument a terra-cotta figure of him reading in his chair.

Some men in those days got Patents of Nobility for serving a king in his meaner pleasures. For his nobler service to his country John Stow was rewarded with the Patent of Beggary which closes this short record of a kindly, busy, earnest life, made happy by the work it loved.

𝕵𝖆𝖒𝖊𝖘, 𝖇𝖞 𝖙𝖍𝖊 𝕲𝖗𝖆𝖈𝖊 𝖔𝖋 𝕲𝖔𝖉, 𝕶𝖎𝖓𝖌 𝖔𝖋 𝕰𝖓𝖌𝖑𝖆𝖓𝖉, 𝕾𝖈𝖔𝖙𝖑𝖆𝖓𝖉, 𝕱𝖗𝖆𝖓𝖈𝖊, 𝖆𝖓𝖉 𝕴𝖗𝖊𝖑𝖆𝖓𝖉, 𝕯𝖊𝖋𝖊𝖓𝖉𝖊𝖗 𝖔𝖋 𝖙𝖍𝖊 𝕱𝖆𝖎𝖙𝖍, &c.

To all our well-beloved Subjects greeting.

"𝖂𝖍𝖊𝖗𝖊𝖆𝖘 our loving subject, John Stowe (a very aged and worthy member of our City of London), this five and forty years hath to his great charge, and with neglect of his ordinary means of maintenance (for the general good, as well of posteritie as of the present age) compiled and published diverse necessary bookes and Chronicles; and 𝖙𝖍𝖊𝖗𝖊𝖋𝖔𝖗𝖊 𝖂𝖊, in recompense of these his painful labours, and for encouragement to the like, have in our royal inclination been pleased to graunt our 𝕷𝖊𝖙𝖙𝖊𝖗𝖘 𝕻𝖆𝖙𝖊𝖓𝖙 under our Great Seale of England, dated the eighth of March, 1603, thereby authorizing him, the sayd John Stowe, and his deputies, to collect amongst our loving subjects theyr voluntary contribution and kinde gratuities, as by the sayd Letters Patents more at large may appeare.　Now, seeing that our sayd Patents (being but one in themselves) cannot be shewed forth in diverse places or parishes at once (as the occasions of his speedy putting them in execution may require) we have therefore thought expedient in this unusuall manner to recommend his cause unto you ; having already, in our own person, and of our speciall grace, begun the largesse for the example of others.　Given at our palace at Westminster."

With what sum his Majesty headed the list, when he took this unusual way of starting a subscription for which the solicitation was to be left to the old man himself, history does not record. It was in the following year, 1605, that Francis Bacon laid at the feet of James the First his " Two Books of the Advancement of Learning."　But towards the Advancement of Learning may we not believe that this poor Tailor did more than the King ?

This volume of Stow's "Survey of London" gives the text of the author's second edition, read with the first.　Much was added in the second edition, and whatever was added to the text in 1603 is here included.　Here and there I have retained a little fact worth keeping that Stow had written in his first edition and omitted from his second.

The first edition having been in 1598, the second in 1603, within the author's lifetime ; there was a third in 1618 ; a fourth, in one folio volume, in 1633, enlarged by Anthony Munday and Henry Dyson, with a map of London and Westminster by T. Porter ; a fifth, in 1720, in two folio volumes, edited by John Strype, with a two-sheet plan of the City of London, Westminster, and Southwark, a map of London in Elizabeth's time, and 41 plates.　Strype's volumes were re-edited in a sixth edition of the "Survey," published with 132 plates in two folios in 1754 and 1755.　These later editions overlaid the text with new matter. In 1842 Mr. William J: Thoms produced an edition of the original text in royal 8vo, with valuable notes. This was re-published in 1876.

Stow's frequent citations of Fitzstephen caused him to append to his Survey the Latin text of Fitzstephen's account of London in the twelfth century. "The said author being rare, as to my knowledge not extant out of mine own custody, I have," he wrote, " in this place thought good by impression to impart the same to my loving friends, the learned Antiquaries, as the author wrote it in the Latin tongue." I give it here in English.

WILLIAM FITZSTEPHEN,

who died about the year 1190, was a trusted clerk in the service of Thomas à Becket, and was present at his murder. He wrote the Life of his great chief, and prefaced it with this

DESCRIPTION OF THE MOST NOBLE CITY OF LONDON.

Of the Site thereof.

Among the noble cities of the world that Fame celebrates, the City of London of the Kingdom of the English, is the one seat that pours out its fame more widely, sends to farther lands its wealth and trade, lifts its head higher than the rest. It is happy in the healthiness of its air, in the Christian religion, in the strength of its defences, the nature of its site, the honour of its citizens, the modesty of its matrons; pleasant in sports; fruitful of noble men. Let us look into these things separately.

Of the Mildness of the Air.

If the clemency of the skies there softens minds, it is not so that they corrupt in Venus, but that they be not fierce and bestial, rather benign and liberal.

Of Religion.

There is in the church there the Episcopal Seat of St. Paul; once it was Metropolitan, and it is thought will again become so if the citizens return into the island, unless perhaps the archiepiscopal title of Saint Thomas the Martyr, and his bodily presence, preserve to Canterbury. where it now is, a perpetual dignity. But as Saint Thomas has made both cities illustrious,

London by his rising, Canterbury by his setting, in regard of that saint, with admitted justice, each can claim advantage of the other. There are also, as regards the cultivation of the Christian faith, in London and the suburbs, thirteen larger conventual churches, besides lesser parish churches one hundred and twenty-six.

Of the Strength of the City.

It has on the east the Palatine Castle, very great and strong, of which the ground plan and the walls rise from a very deep foundation, fixed with a mortar tempered by the blood of animals. On the west are two towers very strongly fortified, with the high and great wall of the city having seven double gates, and towered to the north at intervals. London was walled and towered in like manner on the south, but the great fish-bearing Thames river which there glides, with ebb and flow from the sea, by course of time has washed against, loosened, and thrown down those walls. Also upwards to the west the royal palace is conspicuous above the same river, an incomparable building with ramparts and bulwarks, two miles from the city, joined to it by a populous suburb.

Of Gardens.

Everywhere outside the houses of those living in the suburbs are joined to them, planted with trees, the spacious and beautiful gardens of the citizens.

Of Pasture and Tilth.

Also there are, on the north side, pastures and a pleasant meadow land, through which flow river streams, where the turning wheels of mills are put in motion with a cheerful sound. Very near lies a great forest, with woodland pastures, coverts of wild animals, stags, fallow deer, boars and wild bulls. The tilled lands of the city are not of barren gravel but fat plains of Asia, that make crops luxuriant, and fill their tillers' barns with Ceres' sheaves.

Of Springs.

There are also about London, on the north side, excellent suburban springs, with sweet, wholesome, and clear water that flows rippling over the bright stones; among which Holy Well, Clerken Well, and Saint Clements are held to be of most note; these are frequented by greater numbers, and visited more by scholars and youth of the city when they go out for fresh air on summer evenings. It is a good city indeed when it has a good master.

Of Honour of the Citizens.

That City is honoured by her men, adorned by her arms, populous with many inhabitants, so that in the time of slaughter of war under King Stephen, of those going out to a muster twenty thousand horsemen and sixty thousand men on foot were estimated to be fit for war. Above all other citizens, everywhere, the citizens of London are regarded as conspicuous and noteworthy for handsomeness of manners and of dress, at table, and in way of speaking.

Of Matrons.

The City matrons are true Sabine women.

Of Schools.

In London three principal churches have by privilege and ancient dignity, famous schools; yet very often by support of some personage, or of some teachers who are considered notable and famous in philosophy, there are also other schools by favour and permission. On feast days the masters have festival meetings in the churches. Their scholars dispute, some by demonstration, others by dialectics; some recite enthymemes, others do better in using perfect syllogisms. Some are exercised in disputation for display, as wrestling with opponents; others for truth, which is the grace of perfectness. Sophists who feign are judged happy in their heap and flood of words. Others paralogize. Some orators, now and then, say in their rhetorical speeches something apt for persuasion, careful to observe rules of their art, and to omit none of the contingents. Boys of different schools strive against one another in verses, and contend about the principles of grammar and rules of the past and future tenses. There are others who employ in epigrams, rhymes, and verses the old trifling banter, and with Fescennine license freely pull their comrades to pieces, without giving their names, fling at them scoffs and sarcasms, touch the faults of schoolfellows or perhaps of greater people with Socratic salt, or bite harder with Theonine tooth. The hearers ready to laugh much

"Ingeminant tremulos naso crispante cachinnos.*

Of the Ordering of the City.

Those engaged in the several kinds of business, sellers of several things, contractors for several kinds of work, are distributed every morning into their several localities and shops. Besides, there is in London on the river bank, among the wines in ships and cellars sold by the vintners, a public cook shop; there eatables are to be found every day, according to the season, dishes of meat, roast, fried and boiled, great and small fish, coarser meats for the poor, more delicate for the rich, of game, fowls, and small birds. If there should come suddenly to any of the citizens friends, weary from a journey and too hungry to like waiting till fresh food is bought and cooked, with water to their hands comes bread,† while one runs to river bank, and there is all that can be wanted. However great the multitude of soldiers or travellers entering the city, or preparing to go out of it, at any hour of the day or night,—that these may not fast too long and those may not go out supperless,—they turn hither, if they please, where every

* Fitzstephen is quoting Persius.
† Fitzstephen here quotes Virgil's Æneid—
  "Dant famuli manibus lymphas, Cereremque canistris
    Expediunt,"
shortening the last clause to "panesque."

man can refresh himself in his own way; those who would care
for themselves luxuriously, when set before the delicacies there to
be found, would not desire sturgeon nor the bird of Africa nor
the Ionian godwit.   For this is the public kitchen, very convenient to the city, and part of its civilisation; hence we read in
the Gorgias of Plato that next to medicine the office of the
cooks, as the adulation of imitators, makes the fourth part of
civility.*   Outside one of the gates there, immediately in the
suburb, is a certain field, smooth (Smith) field in fact and name.
Every Friday, unless it be a higher day of appointed solemnity,
there is in it a famous show of noble horses for sale.   Earls,
barons, knights, and many citizens who are in town, come to see
or buy.   It is pleasant to see the steppers in quick trot going
gently up and down, their feet on each side alternately rising and
falling.   On this side are the horses most fit for esquires, moving
with harder pace yet swiftly, that lift and set down together, as
it were, the opposite fore and hind feet; on that side colts of fine
breed who not yet well used to the bit

"Altius incedunt, et mollia crura reponunt."†

In that part are the sumpter horses, powerful and spirited;
here costly chargers, elegant of form, noble of stature, with ears
quickly tremulous, necks lifted, haunches plump.   In their step-

---

* Quotation of Plato by a writer of the reign of Henry the Second is worth
noting.   Socrates in Gorgias is reasoning that there are two Acts, each in two
parts, one Politic, pertaining to the Soul, which he subdivides into Legislation and
Justice, and one without a name of its own, pertaining to the Body, which he subdivides into Gymnastic and Medicine.   Since these are four, the Adulatory Power,
which does not seek what is best, but is concerned only with what is pleasant, hunts
after folly, and makes its own fourfold division.   Cookery here takes the place of
Medicine, and feigns that it knows what is best ; Allurements of Outward Form re-
place Gymnastic ; the Sophistic takes the Legislative Power, and Rhetoric sup-
plants Justice : Rhetoric, as an Art of Adulation, being to Justice, what Cookery,
as Art of Adulation, is to Medicine.   All this is referred to by Fitzstephen, whose
text in different copies, is varied with many corruptions,—in this passage "Hinc
est quod legitur in Gorgia Platonis, Juxta medicinam esse coquorum officium,
simulantium et adulationem quartæ particulæ civilitatis."

† Virgil's Georgics—
                    " Continuo pecoris generosi pullus in arvis
                    Altius ingreditur, et mollia crura reponit."

ping, the buyers first try for the gentler, then the quicker pace, which is by the fore and the hind feet moving in pairs together. When a race is ready for such thunderers, and perhaps for others of like kind, powerful to carry, quick to run, a shout is raised, orders are given that the common horses stand apart. The boys who mount the wing-footed by threes or twos according to the match, prepare themselves for contest; skilled to rule horses, they restrain the mouths of the untamed with bitted bridles. For this chiefly they care, that no one should get before another in the course. The horses rise too in their own way to the struggle of the race; their limbs tremble, impatient of delay they cannot keep still in their place; at the sign given their limbs are stretched, they hurry on their course, are borne with stubborn speed. The riders contend for the love of praise and hope of victory, plunge spurs into the loose-reined horses, and urge them none the less with whips and shouts. You would think with Heraclitus everything to be in motion, and the opinion to be wholly false of Zeno, who said that there was no motion and no goal to be reached. In another part of the field stand by themselves the goods proper to rustics, implements of husbandry, swine with long flanks, cows with full udders, oxen of bulk immense, and woolly flocks. There stand the mares fit for plough, dray, and cart, some big with foal, and others with their young colts closely following. To this city from every nation under heaven merchants delight to bring their trade by sea—

> " Aurum mittit Arabs ; species et thura Sabæus ;
> Arma Scythes ; oleum palmarum divite sylva
> Pingue solum Babylon ; Nilus lapides preciosos ;
> Norwegi, Russi, varium grisium, sabelinas ;
> Seres, purpureas vestes ; Galli sua vina." *

London is, on the faith of the chroniclers, a much older city than Rome, for by the same Trojan forefathers this was founded by Brutus before that by Romulus and Remus. Whence it is

---

* The Arabian sends gold; Sabæan, spice and incense; Scythian, arms; from its rich wood fat soil of Babylon sends oil of palms ; Nile, precious stones; Norwegians, Russians, **many furs and sables** ; Seres, her purple clothing ; Gaul, her wines.

that they still have the same laws established in common. This city, like that, is divided into wards, has annual sheriffs for its consuls, has senatorial and lower magistrates, sewers and aqueducts in its streets, its proper places and separate courts for cases of each kind, deliberative, demonstrative, judicial; has assemblies on appointed days. I do not think there is a city with more commendable customs of church attendance, honour to God's ordinances, keeping sacred festivals, almsgiving, hospitality, confirming betrothals, contracting marriages, celebration of nuptials, preparing feasts, cheering the guests, and also in care for funerals and the interment of the dead. The only pests of London are the immoderate drinking of fools and the frequency of fires. To this may be added that nearly all the bishops, abbots, and magnates of England are, as it were, citizens and freemen of London; having there their own splendid houses, to which they resort, where they spend largely when summoned to great councils by the king or by their metropolitan, or drawn thither by their own private affairs.

Of Sports.

[*The whole of this section has been translated by Stow with unbroken continuity, and will be found placed at the beginning of his chapter on " Sports and Pastimes of old time used in this City." The translation is there closed with the words " Thus far Fitzstephen of Sports." After this Fitzstephen's description of London ends as follows :*]

The Londoners, then called Trinovantes, repulsed Caius Julius Cæsar, who had pleasure only in paths wet with blood. Whence Lucan

"Territa quæsitis ostendit terga Britannis." *

The City of London has brought forth some men who made many kingdoms and the Roman Empire subject to themselves; and many others, lords over the world, whom virtue lifted to the skies, as was promised in Apollo's oracle to Brutus—

To the sought Britons showed backs turned in fear.

" Brutus, far west, beyond the realms of Gaul,
An island that the Ocean waves enfold,

.   .   .   .   .   .

Seek thou ; for ever it shall be thy seat,
Another Troy to thy posterity :
Their kings shall be thy offspring and shall hold
The round of all the earth in sovereignty."

In Christian times London brought forth that noble Emperor
Constantine, who gave the City of Rome and all the insignia of
the Empire to God and Saint Peter, and to Pope Silvester, whom
he served in office of a stirrup-holder, rejoicing not to be called
Emperor, so much as Defender of the Holy Roman Church : and
lest his presence should cause noise of secular affairs to break the
peace of our lord the Pope, he departed from the city given by
him to our lord the Pope and built for himself the city of Byzan-
tium. London also in modern times has produced illustrious
and magnificent rulers, the Empress Matilda, King Henry III.,*
and Saint Thomas, the Archbishop, glorious martyr of Christ,
than whom it bore none purer, and there was none more bound
to whatever is good in all the Roman world.

[Here ends the prelude of Fitzstephen to his life of Thomas à
Becket.]

* Whose name, as reigning sovereign, was put in after the death of Fitzstephen.

LONDON

UNDER ELIZABETH.

> But now behold,
> In the quick forge and working-house of thought,
> How London doth pour out her citizens !
> —SHAKESPEARE.

A SURVEY OF LONDON

Containing the Original, Antiquity, Increase, Modern Estate, and Description of that City.

AS the Roman writers, to glorify the city of Rome, derive the original thereof from gods and demi-gods, by the Trojan progeny, so Geoffrey of Monmouth, the Welsh historian, deduceth the foundation of this famous city of London, for the greater glory thereof, and emulation of Rome, from the very same original. For he reporteth that Brute, lineally descended from the demi-god Æneas, the son of Venus, daughter of Jupiter, about the year of the world 2855, and 1108 before the nativity of Christ, built this city near unto the river now called Thames, and named it Troynovant, or Trenovant. But herein, as Livy, the most famous historiographer of the Romans, writeth, antiquity is pardonable, and hath an especial privilege, by interlacing divine matters with human, to make the first foundation of cities more honourable, more sacred, and, as it were, of greater majesty.

King Lud, as the aforesaid Geoffrey of Monmouth noteth, afterwards not only repaired this city, but also increased the same with fair buildings, towers, and walls, and after his own name called it Caire-Lud, as Lud's town; and the strong gate which he built in the west part of the city he likewise, for his own honour, named Ludgate.

This Lud had issue two sons, Androgeus and Theomantius, who being not of age to govern at the death of their father, their uncle Cassibelan took upon him the crown; about the eighth year of whose reign, Julius Cæsar arrived in this land with a great power of Romans to conquer it; the manner of which conquest I will summarily set down out of his own Commentaries, which are of far better credit than the relations of Geoffrey Monmouth.

The chief government of the Britons, and ordering of the wars, was then by common advice committed to Cassibelan, whose seigniory was separated from the cities towards the sea-coast by the river called Thames, about fourscore miles from the sea. This Cassibelan, in times past, had made continual war upon the cities adjoining; but the Britons being moved with the Roman invasion, had resolved in that necessity to make him their sovereign, and general of the wars, which continued hot between the Romans and them. But in the meanwhile the Troynovants, which was then the strongest city well near of all those countries, and out of which city a young gentleman, called Mandubrace, upon confidence of Cæsar's help, came unto him into the mainland of Gallia, now called France, and thereby escaped death, which he should have suffered at Cassibelan's hand, sent their ambassadors to Cæsar, promising to yield unto him, and to do what he should command them, instantly * desiring him to protect Mandubrace from the furious tyranny of Cassibelan, and to send him into their city with authority to take the government thereof upon him. Cæsar accepted the offer, and appointed them to give unto him forty hostages, and withal to find him grain for his army; and so sent he Mandubrace unto them.

When others saw that Cæsar had not only defended the Trinobants against Cassibelan, but had also saved them harmless from the pillage of his own soldiers, then did the Conimagues, Segontians, Ancalits, Bibrokes, and Cassians, likewise submit themselves unto him; and by them he learned that not far from thence was Cassibelan's town, fortified with woods and marsh ground, into the which he had gathered a great number both of men and cattle.

For the Britons call that a town, saith Cæsar, when they have fortified a cumbersome wood with a ditch and rampart, and thither they resort to abide the approach of their enemies. To this place therefore marched Cæsar with his legions. He found

* *Instantly*, urgently.

it excellently fortified, both of nature and by man's advice. Nevertheless, he resolved to assault it in two several places at once, whereupon the Britons, being not able to endure the force of the Romans, fled out at another part, and left the town unto him. A great number of cattle he found there, and many of the Britons he slew, and others he took in the chase.

Whilst these things were doing in these quarters, Cassibelan sent messengers into Kent, which lieth upon the sea, in which there reigned then four particular kings, named Cingetorex, Caruill, Taximagull, and Segonax, whom he commanded to raise all their forces, and suddenly to set upon and assault the Romans in their trenches by the seaside; the which, when the Romans perceived, they sallied out upon them, slew a great sort of them, and taking Cingetorex their noble captain prisoner, retired themselves to their camp in good safety.

When Cassibelan heard of this, and had formerly taken many other losses, and found his country sore wasted, and himself left almost alone by the defection of the other cities, he sent ambassadors by Comius of Arras to Cæsar, to entreat with him concerning his own submission; the which Cæsar did accept, and taking hostages, assessed the realm of Britain to a yearly tribute, to be paid to the people of Rome, giving strait charge to Cassibelan that he should not seek any revenge upon Mandubrace or the Trinobantes, and so withdrew his army to the sea again.

Thus far out of Cæsar's Commentaries concerning this history, which happened in the year before Christ's Nativity, 54. In all which process there is for this purpose to be noted, that Cæsar nameth the city of Trinobantes, which hath a resemblance with Troynova, or Trinobantum, having no greater difference in the orthography than changing *b* into *v*, and yet maketh an error whereof I will not argue. Only this I will note, that divers learned men do not think "*civitas Trinobantum*" to be well and truly translated, "the city of the Trinobantes;" but it should rather be the state, commonalty, or seigniory of the Trinobantes; for that Cæsar in his Commentaries useth the word *civitas*, only for a people living under one and the self-same prince and law; but certain it is that the cities of the Britons were in those days neither artificially built with houses, nor strongly walled with

stone, but were only thick and cumbersome woods, plashed *
within and trenched about. And the like in effect do other
the Roman and Greek authors directly affirm, as Strabo, Pom-
ponius Mela, and Dion, a senator of Rome, which flourished
in the several reigns of the Roman emperors, Tiberius, Claudius,
Domitian, and Severus; to wit, that before the arrival of the
Romans the Britons had no towns, but called that a town which
had a thick entangled wood, defended, as I said, with a ditch
and bank; the like whereof, the Irishmen, our next neighbours,
do at this day call Fastness. But after that these hither parts
of Britain were reduced into the form of a province by the
Romans, who sowed the seeds of civility over all Europe; this
city, whatever it was before, began to be renowned, and of fame.
For Tacitus, who first of all authors nameth it Londinum, saith,
that in the 62nd year after Christ, it was, albeit no colony of the
Romans, yet most famous for the great multitude of merchants,
provision, and intercourse. At which time, in that notable revolt
of the Britons from Nero, in which 70,000 Romans and their
confederates were slain, this city, with Verulam, near St. Albans,
and Maldon, in Essex, then all famous, were ransacked and
spoiled. For Suetonius Paulinus, then lieutenant for the Romans
in this isle, abandoned it, as not then fortified, and left it to the
spoil.

Shortly after, Julius Agricola, the Roman lieutenant, in the
time of Domitian, was the first that by adhorting the Britons
publicly, and helping them privately, won them to build houses
for themselves, temples for the gods, and courts for justice, to
bring up the noblemen's children in good letters and humanity,
and to apparel themselves Roman like, whereas before, for the
most part, they went naked, painting their bodies, &c., as all the
Roman writers have observed.

True it is, I confess, that afterwards many cities and towns in
Britain, under the government of the Romans, were walled with
stone, and baked bricks or tiles, as Richborough or Ryptacester,
in the Isle of Thanet, until the channel altered his course, beside
Sandwich in Kent; Verulamium, beside St. Albans, in Hertfordshire; Silchester, in Hampshire; Wroxeter, in Shropshire; Ken-

---

* *Plashed*, with branches half-cut to be bent and platted among those left
growing, and so form a denser fence.

chester, in Herefordshire, three miles from Hereford town; Ribchester, seven miles above Preston, on the water of Ribble; Aldborough, a mile from Boroughbridge, or Watling Street, on Ure river, and others. And no doubt but this city of London was also walled with stone, in the time of the Roman government here, but yet very lately, for it seemeth not to have been walled in the year of our Lord 296, because in that year, when Alectus the tyrant was slain in the field, the Franks easily entered London, and had sacked the same, had not God, of his great favour, at the very instant, brought along the river of Thames certain bands of Roman soldiers, who slew those Franks in every street of the city.

In few years after, as Simeon of Durham, an ancient writer, reporteth, Helen, the mother of Constantine the Great, was the first that inwalled this city, about the year of Christ, 306. But however those walls of stone might have been built by Helen, yet the Britons, I know, had no skill of building with stone, as it may appear by that which followeth, about the year of Christ 399, when Arcadius and Honorius, the sons of Theodosius Magnus, governed the empire, the one in the east, the other in the west. For Honorius having received Britain, the city of Rome was invaded and destroyed by the Goths, after which time the Romans left * to rule in Britain, as being employed in defence of their territories nearer home; whereupon the Britons, not able to defend themselves against the invasions of their enemies, were many years together under the oppression of two most cruel nations, the Scots and Picts, and at the length were forced to send their ambassadors with letters and lamentable supplications to Rome, requiring aid and succour from thence, upon promise of their continual fealty so that the Romans would rescue them out of the hands of their enemies. Hereupon the Romans sent unto them a legion of armed soldiers, which coming into this island, and encountering with the enemies, overthrew a great number of them, and drove the rest out of the frontiers of the country; and so setting the Britons at liberty, counselled them to make a wall, extending all along between the two seas, which might be of force to keep out their evil neighbours, and then returned home with great triumph. The Britons, wanting masons,

* *Left*, left off, ceased.

built that wall not of stone as they were advised, but made it of turf, and that so slender that it served little or nothing at all for their defence ; and the enemy perceiving that the Roman legion was returned home, forthwith arrived out of their boats, invaded the borders, overcame the country, and, as it were, bore down all that was before them.

Whereupon ambassadors were eftsoon despatched to Rome, lamentably beseeching that they would not suffer their miserable country to be utterly destroyed. Then again another legion was sent, which coming upon a sudden, made a great slaughter of the enemy, and chased him home even to his own country. These Romans, at their departure, told the Britons plainly, that it was not for their ease or leisure to take upon them any more such long and laborious journeys for their defence, and therefore bade them practise the use of armour and weapons, and learn to withstand their enemies, whom nothing else did make so strong as their faint heart and cowardice. And for so much as they thought that it would be no small help and encouragement unto their tributary friends whom they were forced now to forsake, they built for them a wall of hard stone from the west sea to the east sea, right between those two cities which were there made to keep out the enemy, in the self-same place where Severus before had cast his trench, the Britons also putting-to their helping hands as labourers.

This wall they built eight feet thick in breadth, and twelve feet in height, right, as it were by a line, from east to west, as the ruins thereof remaining in many places until this day do make to appear. Which work, thus perfected, they give the people strait charge to look well to themselves, they teach them to handle their weapons, and they instruct them in warlike feats. And lest by the seaside southwards, where their ships lay at harbour, the enemy should come on land, they made up sundry bulwarks, each somewhat distant from the other, and so bid them farewell, as minding no more to return. This happened in the days of the Emperor Theodosius the younger, almost 500 years after the first arrival of the Romans here, about the year after Christ's incarnation, 434.

The Britons after this, continuing a lingering and doubtful war with the Scots and Picts, made choice of Vortigern to be their

king and leader, which man, as saith Malmesbury, was neither
valorous of courage, nor wise of counsel, but wholly given over
to the unlawful lusts of his flesh. The people likewise, in short
time, being grown to some quietness, gave themselves to gluttony
and drunkenness, pride, contention, envy, and such other vices,
casting from them the yoke of Christ. In the mean season, a
bitter plague fell among them, consuming in short time such a
multitude, that the quick were not sufficient to bury the dead ;
and yet the remnant remained so hardened in sin, that neither
death of their friends, nor fear of their own danger, could cure
the mortality of their souls. Whereupon a greater stroke of vengeance ensued upon the whole sinful nation. For being now
again infested with their old neighbours the Scots and Picts, they
consult with their king Vortigern, and send for the Saxons, who
shortly after arrived here in Britain, where, saith Bede, they were
received as friends ; but as it proved, they minded to destroy the
country as enemies. For after that they had driven out the Scots
and Picts, they also drove the Britons, some over the seas, some
into the waste mountains of Wales and Cornwall, and divided the
country into divers kingdoms amongst themselves.

These Saxons were likewise ignorant of building with stone
until the year 680; for then it is affirmed that Benet, Abbot of
Wearmouth, master to the Reverend Bede, first brought artificers
of stone houses and glass windows into this island amongst the
Saxons, arts before that time unto them unknown, and therefore
used they but wooden buildings. And to this accordeth Policronicon, who says, "that then had ye wooden churches, nay
wooden chalices and golden priests, but since golden chalices
and wooden priests." And to knit up this argument, King Edgar
in his charter to the abbey of Malmesbury, dated the year of
Christ 974, hath words to this effect : "All the monasteries in
my realm, to the outward sight, are nothing but worm-eaten and
rotten timber and boards, and that worse is, within they are
almost empty, and void of Divine service."

Thus much be said for walling, not only in respect of this city,
but generally also of the first within the realm. Now to return
to our Trinobant (as Cæsar hath it), the same is since by Tacitus,
Ptolemæus, and Antoninus, called Londinium, Longidinum ; of
Ammiamus, Lundinum and Augusta, who calleth it an ancient

city; of our Britons, Lundayne; of the old Saxons, Lunden-ceaster, Lundenbrig, Londennir; of strangers, Londra and Lon-dres; of the inhabitants, London; whereof you may read a more large and learned discourse, and how it took the name, in that work of my loving friend, Master Camden, now Clarenceux, which is called "Britannia." *

This city of London having been destroyed and burnt by the Danes and other Pagan enemies, about the year of Christ 839, was by Alfred, king of the West Saxons, in the year 886, repaired, honourably restored, and made again habitable. Who also com-mitted the custody thereof unto his son-in-law, Ethelred, Earl of Mercia, unto whom before he had given his daughter Ethelfled.

And that this city was then strongly walled may appear by divers accidents, whereof William of Malmesbury hath, that about the year of Christ 994, the Londoners shut up their gates, and defended their king Ethelred within their walls against the Danes.

In the year 1016, Edmund Ironsides reigning over the West Saxons, Canute the Dane bringing his navy into the west part of the bridge, cast a trench about the city of London, and then attempted to have won it by assault, but the citizens repulsed him, and drove them from their walls.

Also, in the year 1052, Earl Goodwin, with his navy, sailed up by the south end of the bridge, and so assailed the walls of this city.

William Fitzstephen, in the reign of King Henry II., writing of the walls of this city, hath these words: "The wall is high and great, well towered on the north side, with due distances between the towers. On the south side also the city was walled and towered, but the fishful river of Thames, with his ebbing and flowing, hath long since subverted them."

By the north side, he meaneth from the river of Thames in the east to the river of Thames in the west, for so stretched the wall in his time, and the city being far more in length from east to west than in breadth from south to north, and also narrower at both ends than in the midst, is therefore compassed with the wall

---

* William Camden's "Britannia, sive florentissimorum Regnorum Angliæ, Scotiæ, Hiberniæ, et Insularum adjacentium ex intima Antiquitate Chorographica Descriptio" was first published in 1586. There were eight editions of it between 1586 and 1590. Camden was made Clarenceux King of Arms in 1597.

on the land side, in form of a bow, except denting in betwixt
Cripplegate and Aldersgate; but the wall on the south side, along
by the river of Thames, was straight as the string of a bow, and
all furnished with towers or bulwarks, as we now term them, in
due distance every one from other, as witnesseth our author, and
ourselves may behold from the land side. This may suffice for
proof of a wall, and form thereof, about this city, and the same to
have been of great antiquity as any other within this realm.

And now touching the maintenance and repairing the said
wall. I read, that in the year 1215, the 16th of King John, the
barons, entering the city by Aldgate, first took assurance of the
citizens, then brake into the Jews' houses, searched their coffers
to fill their own purses, and after with great diligence repaired
the walls and gates of the city with stones taken from the Jews'
broken houses. In the year 1257, Henry III. caused the walls
of this city, which were sore decayed and destitute of towers, to
be repaired in more seemly wise than before, at the common
charges of the city. Also in the year 1282, King Edward I.
having granted to Robert Kilwarby, Archbishop of Canterbury,
license for the enlarging of the Blackfriars' Church, to break and
take down a part of the wall of the city, from Ludgate to the
river of Thames; he also granted to Henry Wales, mayor, and
the citizens of London, the favour to take, toward the making of
the wall and enclosure of the city, certain customs or toll, as
appeareth by his grant. This wall was then to be made from
Ludgate west to Fleet Bridge along behind the houses, and along
by the water of the Fleet unto the river of Thames. Moreover,
in the year 1310, Edward II. commanded the citizens to make
up the wall already begun, and the tower at the end of the same
wall, within the water of Thames near unto the Blackfriars, &c.
In 1328, the 2nd of Edward III., the walls of this city were repaired. It was also granted by King Richard II. in the tenth year
of his reign, that a toll should be taken of the wares sold by land
or by water for ten years, towards the repairing of the walls, and
cleansing of the ditch about London. In the 17th of Edward IV.
Ralph Joceline, mayor, caused part of the wall about the city of
London to be repaired; to wit, betwixt Aldgate and Aldersgate.
He also caused Moorfield to be searched for clay, and brick
thereof to be made and burnt; he likewise caused chalk to be

brought out of Kent, and to be burnt into lime in the same Moorfield, for more furtherance of the work. Then the Skinners, to begin in the east, made that part of the wall betwixt Aldgate and Bevis Marks, towards Bishopsgate, as may appear by their arms in three places fixed there : the mayor, with his company of the Drapers, made all that part betwixt Bishopsgate and Allhallows Church, and from Allhallows towards the postern called Moorgate. A great part of the same wall was repaired by the executors of Sir John Crosby, late alderman, as may appear by his arms in two places there fixed : and other companies repaired the rest of the wall to the postern of Cripplegate. The Goldsmiths repaired from Cripplegate towards Aldersgate, and there the work ceased. The circuit of the wall of London on the land side, to wit, from the Tower of London in the east unto Aldgate, is 82 perches ; from Aldgate to Bishopsgate, 86 perches ; from Bishopsgate in the north to the postern of Cripplegate, 162 perches ; from Cripplegate to Aldersgate, 75 perches ; from Aldersgate to Newgate, 66 perches ; from Newgate in the west to Ludgate, 42 perches ; in all, 513 perches of assize. From Ludgate to the Fleet Dike west, about 60 perches ; from Fleet Bridge south to the river Thames, about 70 perches ; and so the total of these perches amounteth to 643, every perch consisting of five yards and a half, which do yield 3536 yards and a half, containing 10,608 feet, which make up two English miles, and more by 608 feet.

Of Ancient and Present Rivers, Brooks, Bourns, Pools, Wells, and Conduits of Fresh Water, serving the City, as also of the Ditch compassing the Wall of the same for Defence thereof.

ANCIENTLY, until the Conqueror's time, and two hundred years after, the city of London was watered, besides the famous river of Thames on the south part, with the river of Wells, as it was then called, on the west ; with the water called Walbrook running through the midst of the city in the river of Thames, serving the heart thereof ; and with a fourth water or bourn, which ran within the city through Langbourne Ward, watering that part in the east. In the west suburbs was also another great water, called

Oldbourne, which had its fall into the river of Wells; then were there three principal fountains, or wells, in the other suburbs; to wit, Holy Well, Clement's Well, and Clerks' Well. Near unto this last-named fountain were divers other wells, to wit, Skinners' Well, Fags' Well, Tode Well, Loder's Well, and Radwell. All which said wells, having the fall of their overflowing in the aforesaid river, much increased the stream, and in that place gave it the name of Well. In West Smithfield there was a pool, in records called Horsepool, and one other pool near unto the parish church of St. Giles without Cripplegate. Besides all which, they had in every street and lane of the city divers fair wells and fresh springs; and after this manner was this city then served with sweet and fresh waters, which being since decayed, other means have been sought to supply the want, as shall be shown. But first of the aforenamed rivers and other waters is to be said, as following :—

Thames, the most famous river of this island, beginneth a little above a village called Winchcombe, in Oxfordshire; and still increasing, passeth first by the University of Oxford, and so with a marvellous quiet course to London, and thence breaketh into the French Ocean by main tides, which twice in twenty-four hours' space doth ebb and flow more than sixty miles in length, to the great commodity of travellers, by which all kind of merchandise be easily conveyed to London, the principal store-house and staple of all commodities within this realm. So that, omitting to speak of great ships and other vessels of burthen, there pertaineth to the cities of London, Westminster, and borough of Southwark, above the number, as is supposed, of 2000 wherries and other small boats, whereby 3000 poor men, at the least, be set on work and maintained.

That the river of Wells, in the west part of the city, was of old so called of the wells, it may be proved thus :—William the Conqueror, in his charter to the College of St. Martin le Grand, in London, hath these words : " I do give and grant to the same church all the land and the moor without the postern which is called Cripplegate, on either part of the postern ; that is to say, from the north corner of the wall, as the river of the Wells, there near running, departeth * the same moor from the wall, unto the

* *Departeth.* divides,

running water which entereth the city." This water hath long since been called the river of the Wells, which name of river continued; and it was so called in the reign of Edward I., as shall be shown, with also the decay of the said river. In a fair book of Parliament Records, now lately restored to the Tower, it appeareth that a parliament being holden at Carlisle in the year 1307, the 35th of Edward I., "Henry Lacy, Earl of Lincoln, complained, that whereas in times past the course of water, running at London under Oldbourne Bridge and Fleet Bridge into the Thames, had been of such breadth and depth, that ten or twelve ships' navies at once, with merchandise, were wont to come to the foresaid bridge of Fleet, and some of them to Oldbourne Bridge: now the same course, by filth of the tanners and such others, was sore decayed; also by raising of wharfs; but especially, by a diversion of the water made by them of the new Temple for their mills standing without Baynards Castle, in the first year of King John, and divers others impediments, so as the said ships could not enter as they were wont, and as they ought: wherefore he desired that the mayor of London, with the sheriffs and other discreet aldermen, might be appointed to view the course of the said water; and that by the oaths of good men, all the aforesaid hindrances might be removed, and it to be made as it was wont of old. Whereupon Roger le Brabason, the constable of the Tower, with the mayor and sheriffs, were assigned to take with them honest and discreet men, and to make diligent search and enquiry how the said river was in old time, and that they leave nothing that may hurt or stop it, but keep it in the same state that it was wont to be." So far the record. Whereupon it followed that the said river was at that time cleansed, these mills removed, and other things done for the preservation of the course thereof, notwithstanding it was never brought to the old depth and breadth; whereupon the name of river ceased, and it was since called a brook, namely, Turnmill or Tremill Brook, for that divers mills were erected upon it, as appeareth by a fair register-book, containing the foundation of the priory at Clerkenwell, and donation of the lands thereunto belonging, as also by divers other records.

This brook hath been divers times since cleansed, namely, and last of all to any effect, in the year 1502, the 17th of Henry VII., the whole course of Fleet Dike, then so called, was scoured, I say, down to the Thames, so that boats with fish and fuel were rowed to Fleet Bridge, and to Oldbourne Bridge, as they of old time had been accustomed, which was a great commodity to all the inhabitants in that part of the city.

In the year 1589 was granted a fifteenth, by a common council of the city, for the cleansing of this brook or dike; the money, amounting to a thousand marks, was collected, and it was undertaken, that by drawing divers springs about Hampstead Heath into one head and course, both the city should be served of fresh water in all places of want; and also, that by such a follower, as men call it, the channel of this brook should be scoured into the river of Thames; but much money being therein spent, the effect failed, so that the brook, by means of continual encroachments upon the banks getting over the water and casting of soilage into the stream, is now become worse cloyed and choken than ever it was before.

The running water, so called by William the Conqueror in his said charter, which entereth the city, &c. (before there was any ditch) between Bishopsgate and the late made postern called Moorgate, entered the wall, and was truly of the wall called Walbrook, not of Gualo, as some have far fetched. It ran through the city with divers windings from the north towards the south into the river of Thames, and had over the same divers bridges along the streets and lanes through which it passed. I have read in a book entitled the Customs of London, that the prior of the Holy Trinity within Aldgate ought to make over Walbrook in the ward of Broadstreet, against the stone wall of the city, viz., the same bridge that is next the Church of All Saints, at the wall. Also that the prior of the new hospital, St. Mary Spital without Bishopsgate, ought to make the middle part of one other bridge next to the said bridge towards the north: and that in the twenty-eighth year of Edward I. it was by inquisition found before the mayor of London, that the parish of St. Stephen upon Walbrook ought of right to scour the course of the said brook, and therefore the sheriffs were commanded to distrain the said parishioners so to do, in the year 1300. The keepers of those bridges at that time were William Jordan and John de Bever. This water-course, having divers bridges, was afterwards vaulted over with brick, and paved level with the streets and lanes wherethrough it passed ; and since that, also houses have been built thereon, so that the course of Walbrook is now hidden under ground, and thereby hardly known.

Langbourne Water, so called of the length thereof, was a great stream breaking out of the ground in Fenchurch Street, which ran down with a swift course, west, through that street athwart Grastreet, and down Lombard Street, to the west end of St. Mary Wolnoth's Church, and then turning the course down Sharebourne Lane, so termed of sharing or dividing, it brake into divers rills or rillets to the river of Thames : of this bourn that ward took the name, and is till this day called Langbourne Ward. This bourn also is long since stopped up at the head, and the rest of the course filled up and paved over, so that no sign thereof remaineth more than the names aforesaid.

Oldbourne, or Hilbourne, was the like water, breaking out about the place where now the bars do stand, and it ran down the whole street till Oldbourne Bridge, and into the river of the Wells, or Turnmill Brook. This bourn was likewise long since stopped up at the head, and in other places where the same hath broken out, but yet till this day the said street is there called High Old-bourne Hill, and both the sides thereof, together with all the grounds adjoining that lie betwixt it and the river of Thames, remain full of springs, so that water is there found at hand, and hard to be stopped in every house.

There are (saith Fitzstephen) near London, on the north side, special wells in the suburbs, sweet, wholesome, and clear ; amongst which Holy Well, Clerkes' Well, and Clement's Well, are most famous, and frequented by scholars and youths of the city in summer evenings, when they walk forth to take the air.

The first, to wit, Holy Well, is much decayed and marred with filthiness purposely laid there, for the heightening of the ground for garden-plots.

The fountain called St. Clement's Well, north from the parish church of St. Clements, and near unto an inn of Chancery called Clement's Inn, is fair curbed square with hard stone, kept clean for common use, and is always full.

The third is called Clerkes' Well, or Clerkenwell, and is curbed about square with hard stone, not far from the west end of

Clerkenwell Church, but close without the wall that incloseth it. The said church took the name of the well, and the well took the name of the parish clerks in London, who of old time were accustomed there yearly to assemble, and to play some large history of Holy Scripture. And for example of later time, to wit, in the year 1390, the 14th of Richard II., I read, the parish clerks of London, on the 18th of July, played interludes at Skinners' Well, near unto Clerkes' Well, which play continued three days together; the king, queen, and nobles being present. Also in the year 1409, the 10th of Henry IV., they played a play at the Skinners' Well, which lasted eight days, and was of matter from the creation of the world. There were to see the same the most part of the nobles and gentles in England, &c.

Other smaller wells were many near unto Clerkes' Well, namely, Skinners' Well, so called for that the skinners of London held there certain plays yearly, played of Holy Scripture, &c. In place whereof the wrestlings have of later years been kept, and is in part continued at Bartholomew tide.

Then there was Fagges Well, near unto Smithfield by the Charterhouse, now lately dammed up, Tode Well, Loder's Well, and Radwell, all decayed, and so filled up, that their places are hardly now discerned.

Somewhat north from Holy Well is one other well curved square with stone, and is called Dame Annis the Clear, and not far from it, but somewhat west, is also one other clear water called Perilous Pond, because divers youths, by swimming therein, have been drowned; and thus much be said for fountains and wells.

Horsepool, in West Smithfield, was some time a great water; and because the inhabitants in that part of the city did there water their horses, the same was in old records called Horsepool; it is now much decayed, the springs being stopped up, and the land water falling into the small bottom remaining, inclosed with brick, is called Smithfield Pond.

By St. Giles' Churchyard was a large water called a Pool. I read in the year 1244 that Anne of Lothbury was drowned therein; this pool is now for the most part stopped up, but the spring is preserved, and was coped about with stone by the executors of Richard Whittington.

The said river of the Wells, the running water of Walbrook,

the bourns aforenamed, and other the fresh waters that were in and about this city, being in process of time, by incroachment for buildings and heightenings of grounds, utterly decayed, and the number of citizens mightily increased, they were forced to seek sweet waters abroad; whereof some, at the request of King Henry III., in the twenty-first year of his reign, were, for the profit of the city, and good of the whole realm thither repairing, to wit, for the poor to drink, and the rich to dress their meat. granted to the citizens and their successors, by one Gilbert Sanforde, with liberty to convey water from the town of Tybourne by pipes of lead into their city.

The first cistern of lead, castellated with stone, in the city of London, was called the great Conduit in West Cheap, which was begun to be built in the year 1285, Henry Wales being then mayor. The watercourse from Paddington to James Head hath 510 rods; from James Head on the hill to the Mewsgate, 102 rods; from the Mewsgate to the Cross in Cheap, 484 rods.

The tun upon Cornhill was cisterned in the year 1401; John Shadworth thèn being mayor.

Bosses of water at Belinsgate, by Paul's Wharf, and by St. Giles' Church without Cripplegate, made about the year 1423.

Water conveyed to the gaols of Newgate and Ludgate, 1432.

Water was first procured to the Standard in West Cheap about the year 1285, which Standard was again new built by the executors of John Welles, as shall be shown in another place. King Henry VI. in the year 1442 granted to John Hatherley, mayor, license to take up two hundred fodders * of lead for the building of conduits, of a common garnery, and of a new cross in West Cheap, for the honour of the city.

The Conduit in West Cheape, by Powle's Gate, was built about the year 1442; one thousand marks were granted by Common Council for the building thereof, and repairing of the other conduits.

The Conduit in Aldermanbury, and the Standard in Fleet Street, were made and finished by the executors of Sir William Eastfield in the year 1471; a cistern was added to the Standard in Fleet Street, and a cistern was made at Fleet Bridge, and one other without Cripplegate, in the year 1478.

* A fodder of lead was 19½ cwt.

Conduit in Grastreet, in the year 1491.

Conduit at Oldbourne Cross about 1498; again new made by William Lambe 1577.

Little Conduit by the Stocks Market, about 1500.

Conduit at Bishopsgate, about 1513.

Conduit at London wall, about 1528.

Conduit at Aldgate without, about 1535.

Conduit in Lothbury, and in Coleman Street, 1546.

Conduit of Thames water at Dowgate, 1568.

Thames water, conveyed into men's houses by pipes of lead from a most artificial forcier standing near unto London Bridge, and made by Peter Moris, Dutchman, in the year 1582, for service of the city, on the east part thereof.

Conduits of Thames water, by the parish churches of St. Mary Magdalen, and St. Nicolas Colde Abbey, near unto old Fish Street, in the year 1583.

One other new forcier was made near to Broken Wharf, to convey Thames water into men's houses of West Cheap, about Paul's, Fleet Street, &c., by an English gentleman named Bevis Bulmer, in the year 1594. Thus much for waters serving this city; first by rivers, brooks, bourns, fountains, pools, &c.; and since by conduits, partly made by good and charitable citizens, and otherwise by charges of the commonalty, as shall be shown in description of wards wherein they be placed. And now some benefactors to these conduits shall be remembered.

In the year 1236 certain merchant strangers of cities beyond the seas, to wit, Amiens, Corbie, and Nesle, for privileges which they enjoyed in this city, gave one hundred pounds towards the charges of conveying water from the town of Tybourne. Robert Large, mayor, 1439, gave to the new water conduits then in hand forty marks, and towards the vaulting over of Walbrook, near to the parish church of St. Margaret, in Lothbury, two hundred marks.

Sir William Eastfield, mayor, 1438, conveyed water from Tybourne to Fleet Street, to Aldermanbury, and from Highbury to Cripplegate.

William Combes, sheriff, 1441, gave to the work of the conduits ten pounds.

Richard Rawson, one of the sheriffs, 1476, gave twenty pounds.

Robert Revell, one of the sheriffs, 1490, gave ten pounds.

John Mathew, mayor, 1490, gave twenty pounds.

William Bucke, tailor, in the year 1494, towards repairing of conduits, gave one hundred marks.

Dame Thomason, widow, late wife to John Percivall Taylor, mayor, in the year 1498 gave toward the conduit in Oldbourne twenty marks.

Richard Shore, one of the sheriffs, 1505, gave to the conduit in Oldbourne ten pounds.

The Lady Ascue, widow to Sir Christopher Ascue, 1543, gave towards the conduits one hundred pounds.

David Wodrooffe, sheriff, 1554, gave towards the conduit at Bishopsgate twenty pounds.

Edward Jackman, one of the sheriffs, 1564, gave toward the conduits one hundred pounds.

Barnard Randulph, common sergeant of the city, 1583, gave to the water conduits nine hundred pounds.

Thus much for the conduits of fresh water to this city.

The Town Ditch without the Wall of the City.

THE ditch, which partly now remaineth, and compassed the wall of the city, was begun to be made by the Londoners in the year 1211, and was finished in the year 1213, the 15th of King John. This ditch being then made of 200 feet broad, caused no small hindrance to the canons of the Holy Trinity, whose church stood near unto Aldgate; for that the said ditch passed through their ground from the Tower of London unto Bishopsgate. This ditch, being originally made for the defence of the city, was also long together carefully cleansed and maintained, as need required; but now of late neglected and forced either to a very narrow, and the same a filthy channel, or altogether stopped up for gardens planted, and houses built thereon, even to the very wall, and in many places upon both ditch and wall houses be built; to what danger of the city, I leave to wiser consideration, and can but wish that reformation might be had.

In the year of Christ 1354, the 28th of Edward III., the ditch of this city flowing over the bank into the Tower ditch, the king commanded the said ditch of the city to be cleansed. and so ordered that the overflowing thereof should not force any filth into the Tower ditch.

Anno 1379, John Philpot, mayor of London, caused this ditch to be cleansed, and every householder to pay five pence, which was for a day's work towards the charges thereof. Richard II., in the 10th of his reign, granted a toll to be taken of wares sold by water or by land, for ten years, towards repairing of the wall and cleansing of the ditch.

Thomas Falconer, mayor, 1414, caused the ditch to be cleansed.

Ralph Joceline, mayor, 1477, caused the whole ditch to be cast and cleansed, and so from time to time it was cleansed, and otherwise reformed. Namely,* in 1519, the 10th of Henry VIII., for cleansing and scouring the common ditch between Aldgate and the postern next the Tower ditch, the chief ditcher had by the day seven pence, the second ditcher six pence, the other ditchers five pence, and every vagabond (for so were they termed) one penny the day, meat and drink, at charges of the city, £95, 3s. 4d.

In my remembrance also the same was cleansed, namely, the Moor ditch, when Sir William Hollies was mayor, in the year 1540, and not long before, from the Tower of London to Aldgate.

It was again cleansed in the year 1549, Henry Amcotes being mayor, at the charges of the companies. And again. 1569, the 11th of Queen Elizabeth, for cleansing the same ditch between Aldgate and the postern, and making a new sewer, and wharf of timber, from the head of the postern into the town ditch, £814, 15s. 8d. Before the which time the said ditch lay open, without wall or pale, having therein great store of very good fish, of divers sorts, as many men yet living, who have taken and tasted them, can well witness; but now no such matter: the charge of cleansing is spared, and great profit made by letting out the banks, with the spoil of the whole ditch.

I am not ignorant of two fifteenths granted by a common council in the year 1595, for the reformation of this ditch, and that a small portion thereof, to wit, betwixt Bishopsgate and the postern called Moorgate, was cleansed, and made somewhat broader; but filling again very fast, by reason of overraising the ground near adjoining, therefore never the better: and I will so leave it, for I cannot help it.

Bridges of this City.

THE original foundation of London Bridge, by report of Bartholomew Linsted, *alias* Fowle, last prior of St. Mary Overies

* *Namely*, especially.

Church in Southwark, was this : A ferry being kept in place where now the bridge is built, at length the ferryman and his wife deceasing, left the same ferry to their only daughter, a maiden named Mary, which with the goods left by her parents, and also with the profits arising of the said ferry, built a house of Sisters, in place where now standeth the east part of St. Mary Overies Church, above the choir, where she was buried, unto which house she gave the oversight and profits of the ferry. But afterwards the said House of Sisters being converted into a College of Priests, the priests built the bridge, of timber, as all the other the great bridges of this land were, and from time to time kept the same in good reparations, till at length, considering the great charges of repairing the same, there was, by aid of the citizens of London, and others, a bridge built with arches of stone, as shall be shown.

But first of the timber bridge, the antiquity thereof being great, but uncertain; I remember to have read that, in the year of Christ 994, Sweyn, King of Denmark, besieging the city of London, both by water and by land, the citizens manfully defended themselves, and their king Ethelred, so as part of their enemies were slain in battle, and part of them were drowned in the river of Thames, because in their hasty rage they took no heed of the bridge.

Moreover, in the year 1016, Canute the Dane, with a great navy, came up to London, and on the south of the Thames caused a trench to be cast, through the which his ships were towed into the west side of the bridge, and then with a deep trench, and straight siege, he compassed the city round about.

Also, in the year 1052, Earl Goodwin, with the like navy, taking his course up the river of Thames, and finding none that offered to resist on the bridge, he sailed up the south side of the said river. Furthermore, about the year 1067, William the Conqueror, in his charter to the Church of St. Peter at Westminster, confirmed to the monks serving God there, a gate in London, then called Botolph's Gate, with a wharf which was at the head of London Bridge.

We read likewise, that in the year 1114, the 14th of Henry I., the river of Thames was so dried up, and such want of water there, that between the Tower of London and the bridge, and under the bridge, not only with horse, but also a great number of men, women, and children did wade over on foot.

In the year 1122, the 22nd of Henry I., Thomas Arden gave the monks of Bermondsey the Church of St. George, in Southwark, and five shillings rent by the year, out of the land pertaining to London Bridge.

I also have seen a charter under seal to the effect following :— " Henry king of England, to Ralfe Bishop of Chichester, and all the ministers of Sussex, sendeth greeting, know ye, &c. I command by my kingly authority, that the manor called Alcestone, which my father gave, with other lands to the abbey of Battle, be free and quiet from shires and hundreds, and all other customs of earthly servitude, as my father held the same, most freely and quietly, and namely, from the work of London Bridge, and the work of the castle at Pevensey ; and this I command upon my forfeiture. Witness, William de Pontlearche, at Byrry." The which charter, with the seal very fair, remaineth in the custody of Joseph Holland, gentleman.

In the year 1136, the 1st of King Stephen, a fire began in the house of one Aylewarde, near unto London Stone, which consumed east to Aldgate, and west to St. Erkenwald's Shrine, in Paul's Church ; the bridge of timber over the river of Thames was also burnt, &c., but afterwards again repaired. For Fitzstephen writes, that in the reign of King Stephen and of Henry II., when pastimes were showed on the river of Thames, men stood in great number on the bridge, wharfs, and houses, to behold.

Now in the year 1163, the same bridge was not only repaired, but newly made of timber as before, by Peter of Cole Church, priest and chaplain.

Thus much for the old timber bridge, maintained partly by the proper lands thereof, partly by the liberality of divers persons, and partly by taxations in divers shires, have I proved for the space of 215 years before the bridge of stone was built.

Now touching the foundation of the stone bridge, it followeth : —About the year 1176, the stone bridge over the river of Thames, at London, was begun to be founded by the aforesaid Peter of Cole Church, near unto the bridge of timber, but somewhat more towards the west, for I read, that Botolph Wharf was, in the Conqueror's time, at the head of London Bridge. The king assisted this work: a cardinal then being legate here; and Richard, Archbishop of Canterbury, gave one thousand marks towards the foundation. The course of the river, for the time, was turned another way about, by a trench cast for that purpose, beginning, as is supposed, east about Radriffe, and ending in the west about Patricksey, now termed Battersea. This work, to wit, the arches, chapel and stone bridge, over the river of Thames, at London, having been thirty-three years in building, was in the year 1209 finished by the worthy merchants of London, Serle Mercer, William Almaine, and Benedict Botewrite, principal masters of that work, for Peter of Cole Church deceased four years before, and was buried in the chapel on the bridge, in the year 1205.

King John gave certain void places in London to build upon, the profits thereof to remain towards the charges of building and repairing the same bridge. A mason, being master workman of the bridge, builded from the foundation the large chapel on that bridge of his own charges, which chapel was then endowed for two priests, four clerks, &c., besides chantries since founded for John Hatfield and other. After the finishing of this chapel, which was the first building upon those arches, sundry houses at times were erected, and many charitable men gave lands, tenements, or sums of money, towards maintenance thereof, all which was sometime noted and in a table fair written for posterity, remaining in the chapel, until the same chapel was turned into a dwelling house, and then removed to the Bridge House, the effect of which table I was willing to have published in this book, if I could have obtained the sight thereof. But making the shorter work, I find by the account of William Mariner and Christopher Eliot, wardens of London Bridge from Michaelmas, in the 22nd of Henry VII. unto Michaelmas next ensuing, by one whole year, that all the payments and allowances came to £815, 17s. 2¼d., as there is shown by particulars; by which account then made, may be partly guessed the great charges and discharges of that bridge at this day, when things be stretched to so great a price. And now to actions on this bridge.

The first action to be noted was lamentable; for within four years after the finishing thereof, to wit, in the year 1212, on the

10th of July, at night, the borough of Southwark, upon the south side the river of Thames, as also the Church of our Lady of the Canons there, being on fire, and an exceeding great multitude of people passing the bridge, either to extinguish and quench it, or else to gaze at and behold it, suddenly the north part, by blowing of the south wind, was also set on fire, and the people which were even now passing the bridge, perceiving the same, would have returned, but were stopped by fire; and it came to pass, that as they stayed or protracted time, the other end of the bridge also, namely, the south end, was fired, so that the people thronging themselves between the two fires, did nothing else but expect present death; then came there to aid them many ships and vessels, into the which the multitude so unadvisedly rushed, that the ships being drowned, they all perished. It was said, that through the fire and shipwreck there were destroyed about three thousand persons, whose bodies were found in part, or half burnt, besides those that were wholly burnt to ashes, and could not be found.

About the year 1282, through a great frost and deep snow, five arches of London Bridge were borne down and carried away.

In the year 1289, the bridge was so sore decayed for want of reparations, that men were afraid to pass thereon, and a subsidy was granted towards the amendment thereof, Sir John Britain being custos of London. 1381, a great collection or gathering was made of all archbishops, bishops, and other ecclesiastical persons, for the reparations of London Bridge. 1381, Wat Tyler, and other rebels of Kent, by this bridge entered the city, as ye may read in my Summary and Annals.

In the year 1395, on St. George's Day, was a great jousting on London Bridge, betwixt David Earl of Crawford of Scotland, and the Lord Wells of England; in the which the Lord Wells was at the third course borne out of the saddle: which history proveth, that at that time the bridge being coped on either side, was not replenished with houses built thereupon, as it hath since been, and now is. The next year, on the 13th of November, the young Queen Isabel, commonly called the Little, for she was but eight years old, was conveyed from Kennington besides Lambhithe, through Southwark to the Tower of London, and such a multitude of people went out to see her, that on London Bridge nine persons were crowded to death, of whom the prior of Tiptree, a place in Essex, was one, and a matron on Cornhill was another.

The Tower on London Bridge at the north end of the drawbridge (for that bridge was then readily to be drawn up, as well to give passage for ships to Queenhithe, as for the resistance of any foreign force) was begun to be built in the year 1426, John Rainwell being mayor.

Another tower there is on the said bridge over the gate at the south end towards Southwark, whereof in another place shall be spoken.

In the year 1450, Jack Cade, and other rebels of Kent, by this bridge entered the city: he struck his sword on London Stone, and said himself then to be lord of the city, but they were by the citizens overcome on the same bridge, and put to flight, as in my Annals.

In the year 1471, Thomas, the bastard Falconbridge, besieged this bridge, burnt the gate, and all the houses to the drawbridge, that time thirteen in number.

In the year 1481, a house called the common siege on London Bridge fell down into the Thames; through the fall whereof five men were drowned.

In the year 1553, the 3rd of February, Sir Thomas Wyat, and the Kentish men, marched from Deptford towards London; after knowledge whereof, forthwith the drawbridge was cut down, and the bridge gates shut. Wyat and his people entered Southwark, where they lay till the 6th of February, but could get no entry of the city by the bridge, the same was then so well defended by the citizens, the Lord William Howard assisting, wherefore he removed towards Kingston, &c, as in my Annals.

To conclude of this bridge over the said river of Thames, I affirm, as in other my descriptions, that it is a work very rare, having with the drawbridge twenty arches made of squared stone, of height sixty feet, and in breadth thirty feet, distant one from another twenty feet, compact and joined together with vaults and cellars; upon both sides be houses built, so that it seemeth rather a continual street than a bridge; for the fortifying whereof against the incessant assaults of the river, it hath overseers and officers, viz., wardens, as aforesaid, and others.

Fleet Bridge in the west without Ludgate, a bridge of stone, fair coped on either side with iron pikes; on the which, towards the south, be also certain lanthorns of stone, for lights to be placed in the winter evenings, for commodity of travellers. Under this bridge runneth a water, sometimes called, as I have said, the river of the Wells, since Turnmill Brook, now Fleet Dike, because it runneth by the Fleet, and sometime about the Fleet, so under Fleet Bridge into the river of Thames. This bridge hath been far greater in times past, but lessened, as the water course hath been narrowed. It seemeth this last bridge to be made or repaired at the charges of John Wels, mayor, in the year 1431, for on the coping is engraven Wels embraced by angels, like as on the standard of Cheap, which he also built. Thus much of the bridge: for of the watercourse, and decay thereof, I have spoken in another place.

Oldbourne Bridge, over the said river of the Wells more towards the north, was so called, of a bourn that sometimes ran down Oldbourne Hill into the said river. This bridge of stone, like as Fleet Bridge from Ludgate west, serveth for passengers with carriage or otherwise, from Newgate toward the west and by north.

Cowbridge, more north, over the same water by Cowbridge Street or Cowlane: this bridge being lately decayed, another of timber is made somewhat more north, by Chick Lane, &c.

Bridges over the town ditch there are divers; to wit, without Aldgate, without Bishopsgate, the postern called Moorgate, the postern of Cripplegate without Aldersgate, the postern of Christ's Hospital, Newgate, and Ludgate; all these be over paved likewise with stone level with the streets. But one other there is of timber over the river of Wells, or Fleet Dike, between the precinct of the Black Friars, and the house of Bridewell.

There have been of old time also, divers bridges in sundry places over the course of Walbrook, as before I have partly noted, besides Horseshoe Bridge, by the Church of St. John Baptist, now called St. John's upon Walbrook. I read, that of old time every person having lands on either side of the said brook, should cleanse the same, and repair the bridges so far as their lands extended. More, in the 11th of Edward III. the inhabitants upon the course of this brook were forced to pile and wall the sides thereof. Also, that in the 3rd of Henry V.

this watercourse had many bridges, since vaulted over with bricks, and the streets wherethrough it passed so paved, that the same watercourse is now hardly discerned. For order was taken in the 2nd of Edward IV., that such as had ground on either side of Walbrook, should vault and pave it over, so far as his ground extended. And thus much for bridges in this city may suffice.

Gates in the Wall of this City.

GATES in the wall of this city of old time were four; to wit, Aldgate for the east, Aldersgate for the north, Ludgate for the west, and the Bridgegate over the river of Thames for the south; but of later times, for the ease of citizens and passengers, divers other gates and posterns have been made, as shall be shown.

In the reign of Henry II. (saith Fitzstephen) there were seven double gates in the wall of this city, but he nameth them not. It may, therefore, be supposed, he meant for the first, the gate next the Tower of London, now commonly called the Postern, the next be Aldgate, the third Bishopsgate, the fourth Aldersgate, the fifth Newgate, the sixth Ludgate, the seventh Bridgegate. Since the which time hath been builded the postern called Moorgate, a postern from Christ's Hospital towards St. Bartholomew's Hospital in Smithfield, &c. Now of every of these gates and posterns in the wall, and also of certain water-gates on the river of Thames, severally, somewhat may and shall be noted, as I find authority, or reasonable conjecture to warrant me.

For the first, now called the postern by the Tower of London, it showeth by that part which yet remaineth, to have been a fair and strong arched gate, partly built of hard stone of Kent, and partly of stone brought from Caen in Normandy, since the Conquest, and foundation of the high tower; and served for passengers on foot out of the east, from thence through the city to Ludgate in the west. The ruin and overthrow of this gate and postern began in the year 1190, the 2nd of Richard I., when William Longchamp, Bishop of Ely, Chancellor of England, caused a part of the city wall, to wit, from the said gate towards the river of Thames to the white tower, to be broken down, for the enlarging of the said tower, which he then compassed far wide about with a wall embattled, and is now the outer wall.

He also caused a broad and deep ditch to be made without the same wall, intending to have derived the river of Thames with her tides to have flowed about it, which would not be. But the south side of this gate, being then by undermining at the foundation loosened and greatly weakened; at length,—to wit, after two hundred years and odd,—the same fell down in the year 1440, the 18th of Henry VI., and was never since by the citizens re-edified. Such was their negligence then, and hath bred some trouble to their successors, since they suffered a weak and wooden building to be there made, inhabited by persons of lewd life, oft times by inquest of Portsoken Ward presented, but not reformed; whereas of former times the said postern was accounted of as other gates of the city, and was appointed to men of good credit. Amongst other, I have read, that in the 49th of Edward III., John Cobbe was admitted custos of the said postern, and all the habitation thereof, for term of his life, by William Walworth, then mayor of London, &c. More, that John Credy, Esq., in the 21st of Richard II., was admitted custos of the said postern and appurtenances by Richard Whittington, mayor, the aldermen, and commonalty, &c.

The next gate in the east is called Aldgate. Of the antiquity or age thereof: this is one and the first of the four principal gates, and also one of the seven double gates, mentioned by Fitzstephen. It hath had two pair of gates, though now but one; the hooks remaineth yet. Also there hath been two portcullisses; the one of them remaineth, the other wanteth, but the place of letting down is manifest. For antiquity of the gate: it appeareth by a charter of King Edgar to the knights of Knighten Guild, that in his days the said port was called Aldgate, as ye may read in the ward of Portsoken. Also Matilda the queen, wife to Henry I., having founded the priory of the Holy Trinity within Aldgate, gave unto the same church, to Norman the first prior and the canons that devoutly served God therein, the port of Aldgate and the soke * or franchises thereunto belonging, with all customs as free as she held the

* Soke, first English *sóc*, formed from the verb "seek," meant first the lord's right of judicial search or inquiry into causes, levying fines, &c.; then the lands over which the right was exercised, and then gives its name to a free tenure in chief, *socage.*

same; in the which charter she nameth the house Christ's Church, and reporteth Aldgate to be of his domain.

More, I read in the year 1215, that in the civil wars between King John and his barons, the Londoners assisted the barons' faction, who then besieged Northampton, and after came to Bedford Castle, where they were well received by William Beauchamp, captain of the same; and having then also secret intelligence that they might enter the city of London if they would, they removed their camp to Ware. From thence in the night coming to London, they entered Aldgate, and placing guardians or keepers of the gates, they disposed of all things in the city at their pleasure. They spoiled the friars' houses, and searched their coffers; which being done, Robert Fitzwalter, Geffry Magnavile, Earl of Essex, and the Earl of Glocester, chief leaders of the army, applied all diligence to repair the gates and walls of this city with the stones taken from the Jews' broken houses, namely, Aldgate being then most ruinous (which had given them an easy entry) they repaired, or rather newly built, after the manner of the Normans, strongly arched with bulwarks of stone from Caen in Normandy; and small brick, called Flanders tile, was brought from thence, such as hath been here used since the Conquest, and not before.

In the year 1471, the 11th of Edward IV., Thomas, the bastard Falconbridge, having assembled a riotous company of shipmen and others in Essex and Kent, came to London with a great navy of ships, near to the Tower; whereupon the mayor and aldermen, by consent of a common council, fortified all along the Thames side, from Baynard's Castle to the Tower, with armed men, guns, and other instruments of war, to resist the invasion of the mariners, whereby the Thames side was safely preserved and kept by the aldermen and other citizens that assembled thither in great numbers. Whereupon the rebels, being denied passage through the city that way, set upon Aldgate, Bishopsgate, Cripplegate, Aldersgate, London Bridge, and along the river of Thames, shooting arrows and guns into the city, fired the suburbs, and burnt more than threescore houses. And further, on Sunday the eleventh of May, five thousand of them assaulting Aldgate, won the bulwarks, and entered the city; but the portcullis being let down, such as had entered were slain, and Robert Basset, alderman of Aldgate Ward, with the recorder, commanded in the name of God to draw up the portcullis; which being done, they issued out, and with sharp shot, and fierce fight, put their enemies back so far as St. Botolph's Church, by which time the Earl Rivers, and lieutenant of the Tower, was come with a fresh company; which joining together, discomfited the rebels, and put them to flight, whom the said Robert Basset, with the other citizens, chased to the Mile's End, and from thence, some to Poplar, some to Stratford, slew many, and took many of them prisoners. In which space the Bastard, having assayed other places upon the water side and little prevailed, fled toward his ships. Thus much for Aldgate.

The third, and next toward the north, is called Bishopsgate, for that, as it may be supposed, the same was first built by some Bishop of London, though now unknown when, or by whom. But true it is, that the first gate was first built for ease of passengers toward the east, and by north, as into Norfolk, Suffolk, Cambridgeshire, &c.; the travellers into which parts, before the building of this gate were forced, passing out at Aldgate, to go east till they came to the Mile's End, and then turning on the left hand to Bethenhall Green to Cambridge Heath, and so north, or east, and by north, as their journey lay. If they took not this way, by the east out at Aldgate, they must take their way by the north out at Aldersgate, through Aldersgate Street and Goswell Street towards Iseldon, and by a cross of stone on their right hand, set up for a mark by the north end of Golding Lane, to turn eastward through a long street, until this day called Alder Street, to another cross standing, where now a smith's forge is placed by Sewer's-ditch Church, and then to turn again north towards Tottenham, Endfield, Waltham, Ware, &c. The eldest note that I read of this Bishopsgate, is that William Blund, one of the sheriffs of London, in the year 1210, sold to Serle Mercer, and William Almaine, procurators or wardens of London Bridge, all his land, with the garden, in the parish of St. Botolph without Bishopsgate, between the land of Richard Casiarin, towards the north, and the land of Robert Crispie towards the south, and the highway called Bearwards Lane on the east, &c.

Next I read in a charter, dated the year 1235, that Walter Brune, citizen of London, and Rosia his wife, having founded the priory or new hospital of our blessed Lady, since called St. Mary Spital without Bishopsgate, confirmed the same to the honour of God and our blessed Lady, for canons regular.

Also in the year 1247, Simon Fitzmarie, one of the sheriffs of London, the 29th of Henry III., founded the Hospital of St. Mary, called Bethlem without Bishopsgate. Thus much for the antiquity of this gate.

And now for repairing the same, I find that Henry III. confirmed to the merchants of the Hanse, that had a house in the city called Guildhalla Teutonicorum, certain liberties and privileges. Edward I. also confirmed the same; in the tenth year of whose reign it was found that the said merchants ought of right to repair the said gate called Bishopsgate; whereupon Gerard Marbod, alderman of the Hanse and other, then remaining in the city of London, for themselves, and all other merchants of the said Hanse, granted two hundred and ten marks sterling to the mayor and citizens; and covenanted that they and their successors should from time to time repair the same gate. This gate was again beautifully built in the year 1479, in the reign of Edward IV., by the said Hanse merchants.

Moreover, about the year 1551, these Hanse merchants, having prepared stone for that purpose, caused a new gate to be framed, there to have been set up, but then their liberties. through suit of our English merchants, were seized into the king's hand; and so that work was stayed, and the old gate yet remaineth.

Touching the next postern, called Moorgate, I find that Thomas Falconer, mayor, about the year 1415, the third of Henry V., caused the wall of the city to be broken near unto Coleman Street, and there built a postern, now called Moorgate, upon the moor side where was never gate before. This gate he made for ease of the citizens, that way to pass upon causeys into the field for their recreation: for the same field was at that time a parish. This postern was re-edified by William Hampton, fishmonger, mayor, in the year 1472. In the year also, 1511, the third of Henry VIII., Roger Acheley, mayor, caused dikes and bridges to be made, and the ground to be levelled, and made more commodious for passage, since which time the same hath been heightened: so much that the ditches and bridges are covered and seemeth to me that if it be made level with the battlements of the city wall. yet will it be little the drier, such is the moorish nature of that ground.

The next is the postern of Cripplegate, so called long before the Conquest. For I read in the history of Edmond, king of the East Angles, written by Abbo Floriacensis, and by Burchard, sometime secretary to Offa, king of Mercia, but since by John Lydgate, monk of Bury, that in the year 1010, the Danes spoiling the kingdom of the East Angles, Alwyne, Bishop of Helmeham, caused the body of King Edmond the Martyr to be brought from Bedrisworth (now called Bury St. Edmondes), through the kingdom of the East Saxons, and so to London in at Cripplegate; a place, saith mine author, so called of cripples begging there: at which gate, it was said, the body entering. miracles were wrought, as some of the lame to go upright, praising God. The body of King Edmond rested for the space of three years in the parish church of St. Gregorie, near unto the cathedral church of St. Paul. Moreover, the charter of William the Conqueror, confirming the foundation of the college in London, called St. Martin the Great, hath these words: "I do give and grant to the same church and canons, serving God therein, all the land and the moore without the postern, which is called Cripplegate, on either side the postern." More I read, that Alfune built the parish church of St. Giles, nigh a gate of the city, called Porta Contractorum, or Cripplegate, about the year 1099.

This postern was sometime a prison, whereunto such citizens and others, as were arrested for debt or common trespasses, were committed, as they be now to the compters, which thing appeareth by a writ of Edward I. in these words: "*Rex vic. London. salutem: ex graui querela B. capt. & detent. in prisona nostra de Criples gate pro x. l. quas coram Radulpho de Sandwico tunc custod. ciuitatis nostræ London. & I. de Blackwell ciuis recognit. debit. &c.*" This gate was new built by the brewers of London in the year 1244, as saith Fabian's manuscript. Edmond Shaw, goldsmith, mayor in the year 1483, at his decease appointed by his testament his executors, with the cost of four hundred marks, and the stuff of the old gate, called Cripplegate, to build the same gate of new, which was performed and done in the year 1491.

The next is Ældresgate, or Aldersgate, so called not of Aldrich or of Elders, that is to say, ancient men, builders thereof; not of Eldarne trees, growing there more abundantly than in other places, as some hath fabled, but for the very antiquity of the gate itself, as being one of the first four gates of the city, and serving for the northern parts, as Aldgate for the east; which two gates, being both old gates, are for difference sake called, the one Aldgate, and the other Aldersgate. This is the fourth principal gate, and hath at sundry times been increased with buildings; namely, on the south, or inner side, a great frame of timber hath been added and set up, containing divers large rooms and lodgings; also on the east side is the addition of one great building of timber, with one large floor, paved with stone or tile, and a well therein kerbed with stone, of a great depth, and rising into the said room, two stories high from the ground; which well is the only peculiar note belonging to that gate, for I have not seen the like in all this city to be raised so high. John Day, stationer, a late famous printer of many good books, in our time dwelt in this gate, and built much upon the wall of the city towards the parish church of St. Anne.

Then is there also a postern gate, made out of the wall on the north side of the late dissolved cloister of Friars Minors, commonly of their habit called Grey friars, now Christ's Church and Hospital. This postern was made in the first year of Edward VI. to pass from the said hospital of Christ's Church unto the hospital of St. Bartholomew in Smithfield.

The next gate on the west, and by north, is termed Newgate, as latelier built than the rest, and is the fifth principal gate. This gate was first erected about the reign of Henry I. or of King Stephen, upon this occasion. The cathedral church of St. Paul, being burnt about the year 1086, in the reign of William the Conqueror, Mauritius, then bishop of London, repaired not the old church, as some have supposed, but began the foundation of a new work, such as men then judged would never have been performed; it was to them so wonderful for height, length, and breadth, as also in respect it was raised upon arches or vaults, a kind of workmanship brought in by the Normans, and never known to the artificers of this land before that time. After Mauritius, Richard Beamore did wonderfully advance the work of the said church, purchasing the large streets and lanes round about, wherein were wont to dwell many lay people, which grounds he began to compass about with a strong wall of stone and gates. By means of this increase of the church territory, but more by inclosing of ground for so large a cemetery or churchyard, the high and large street stretching from Aldgate in the east until Ludgate in the west, was in this place so crossed and stopped up, that the carriage through the city westward was forced to pass without the said churchyard wall on the north side, through Paternoster Row ; and then south, down Ave Mary Lane, and again west, through Bowyer Row to Ludgate ; or else out of Cheap, or Watheling Street, to turn south, through the old Exchange ; then west through Carter Lane, again north by Creed Lane, and then west to Ludgate : which passage, by reason of so often turning, was very cumbersome and dangerous both for horse and man ; for remedy whereof a new gate was made, and so called, by which men and cattle, with all manner of carriages, might pass more directly (as afore) from Aldgate, through West Cheap by Paul's, on the north side ; through St. Nicholas Shambles and Newgate Market to Newgate, and from thence to any part westward over Oldbourne Bridge, or turning without the gate into Smithfield, and through Iseldon to any part north and by west. This gate hath of long time been a gaol, or prison for felons and trespassers, as appeareth by records in the reign of King John, and of other kings ; amongst the which I find one testifying, that in the year 1218, the 3rd of King Henry III., the king writeth unto the sheriffs of London, commanding them to repair the gaol of Newgate for the safe keeping of his prisoners, promising that the charges laid out should be allowed unto them upon their account in the Exchequer.

Moreover, in the year 1241, the Jews of Norwich were hanged for circumcising a Christian child ; their house called the Thor was pulled down and destroyed ; Aaron, the son of Abraham, a Jew, at London, and the other Jews, were constrained to pay twenty thousand marks, at two terms in the year, or else to be kept perpetual prisoners in Newgate of London, and in other prisons. In 1255, King Henry III. lodging in the Tower of London, upon displeasure conceived towards the city of London, for the escape of John Offrem, a prisoner, being a clerk convict. out of Newgate, which had killed a prior that was of alliance to the king, as cousin to the queen: he sent for the mayor and sheriffs to come before him to answer the matter. The mayor laid the fault from him to the sheriffs, forasmuch as to them belonged the keeping of all prisoners within the city; and so the mayor returned home, but the sheriffs remained there prisoners by the space of a month and more. And yet they excused themselves, in that the fault chiefly rested in the bishop's officers; for whereas the prisoner was under custody, they at his request had granted license to imprison the offender within the gaol of Newgate, but so as the bishop's officers were charged to see him safely kept. The king, notwithstanding all this, demanded of the city three thousand marks for a fine.

In the year 1326, Robert Baldock, the king's chancellor, was put in Newgate, the third of Edward III. In the year 1337, Sir John Poultney gave four marks by the year to the relief of prisoners in Newgate. In the year 1385, William Walworth gave somewhat to relieve the prisoners in Newgate, so have many others since. In the year 1414, the gaolers of Newgate and Ludgate died, and prisoners in Newgate to the number of sixty-four. In the year 1418, the parson of Wrotham, in Kent, was imprisoned in Newgate. In the year 1422, the first of Henry VI., license was granted to John Coventry, Jenken Carpenter, and William Grove, executors to Richard Whittington, to re-edify the gaol of Newgate, which they did with his goods.

Thomas Knowles, grocer, sometime mayor of London, by license of Reynold, prior of St. Bartholomew's, in Smithfield, and also of John Wakering, master of the hospital of St. Bartholomew, and his brethren, conveyed the waste of water at the cistern near to the common fountain and chapel of St. Nicholas (situate by the said hospital) to the gaols of Newgate and Ludgate, for the relief of the prisoners. Tuesday next after Palm Sunday, 1431, all the prisoners of Ludgate were removed into Newgate by Walter Chartesey, and Robert Large, sheriffs of London; and on the 13th of April the same sheriffs (through the false suggestion of John Kingesell, gaoler of Newgate) sent from thence eighteen persons free men, and these were led to the compters, pinioned as if they had been felons; but on the sixteenth of June, Ludgate was again appointed for free men, prisoners for debt; and the same day the said free men entered by ordinance of the mayor, aldermen, and commons, and by them Henry Deane, tailor, was made keeper of Ludgate prison. In the year 1457, a great fray was in the north country between Sir Thomas Percie, Lord Egremont, and the Earl of Salisbury's sons, whereby many were maimed and slain ; but, in the end, the Lord Egremont being taken, was by the king's counsel found in great default, and therefore condemned in great sums of money, to be paid to the Earl of Salisbury, and in the meantime committed to Newgate. Not long after, Sir Thomas Percie, Lord Egremont, and Sir Richard Percie his brother, being in Newgate, broke out of prison by night, and went to the king ; the other prisoners took the leads of the gate, and defended it a long while against the sheriffs and all their officers, insomuch that they were forced to call more aid of the citizens, whereby they lastly subdued them, and laid them in irons : and this may suffice for Newgate.

In the west is the next, and sixth principal gate, and is called Ludgate, as first built, saith Geoffry Monmouth, by King Lud, a Briton, about the year before Christ's nativity, 66. Of which building, and also of the name, as Ludsgate, or Fludsgate, hath been of late some question among the learned ; wherefore I overpass it, as not to my purpose, only referring the reader to that I have before written out of Cæsar's Commentaries, and other Roman writers, concerning a town or city amongst the Britons. This gate I suppose to be one of the most ancient ; and as Aldgate was built for the east, so was this Ludsgate for the west. I read, as I told you, that in the year 1215, the 17th of King John, the barons of the realm, being in arms against the king, entered this city, and spoiled the Jews' houses; which being done, Robert Fitzwater and Geffrey de Magnavilla, Earl of Essex, and the Earl of Gloucester, chief leaders of the army, applied all diligence to repair the gates and walls of this city, with the stones of the Jews' broken houses, especially, as it seemeth, they then repaired, or rather new built Ludgate. For in the year 1586, when the same gate was taken down to be newly built, there was found couched within the wall thereof a stone taken from one of the Jews' houses, wherein was graven in Hebrew characters these words following : זה מצב הדי משה די ה־בן יצחק. *Hæc est statio Rabbi Mosis, filii insignis Rabbi Isaac :* which is to say, this is the station or ward of Rabbi Moyses, the son of the honourable Rabbi Isaac, and had been fixed upon the front of one of the Jews' houses, as a note or sign that such a one dwelt there. In the year 1260, this Ludgate was repaired and beautified with images of Lud, and other kings, as appeareth by letters patent, of license given to the citizens of London, to take up stone for that purpose, dated the 25th of Henry III. These images of kings, in the reign of Edward VI. had their heads smitten off and were otherwise defaced by such as judged every image to be an idol; and in the reign of Queen Mary were repaired, as by setting new heads on their old bodies, &c. All which so remained until the year 1586, the 28th of Queen Elizabeth, when the same gate being sore decayed, was clean taken down; the prisoners in the meantime remaining in the large south-east quadrant to the same gate adjoining; and the same year the whole gate was newly and beautifully built, with the images of Lud and others, as afore, on the east side, and the picture of Her Majesty Queen Elizabeth on the west side: all which was done at the common charges of the citizens, amounting to fifteen hundred pounds or more.

This gate was made a free prison in the year 1378, the 1st of Richard II., Nicholas Brember being mayor. The same was confirmed in the year 1382, John Northampton being mayor, by a common council in the Guildhall; by which it was ordained that all freemen of this city should, for debt, trespasses, accounts, and contempts, be imprisoned in Ludgate, and for treasons, felonies, and other criminal offences, committed to Newgate, &c. In the year 1431, the 10th of King Henry VI., John Wells being mayor, a court of Common Council established ordinances (as William Standon and Robert Chicheley, late mayors, before had done), touching the guard and government of Ludgate and other prisons.

Also in the year 1463, the 3rd of Edward IV., Mathew Philip being mayor, in a Common Council, at the request of the well-disposed, blessed, and devout woman, Dame Agnes Forster. widow, late wife to Stephen Forster, fishmonger, sometime mayor, for the comfort and relief of all the poor prisoners, certain articles were established. Imprimis, that the new works then late edified by the same Dame Agnes, for the enlarging of the prison of Ludgate, from thenceforth should be had and taken as a part and parcel of the said prison of Ludgate; so that both the old and new work of Ludgate aforesaid be one prison, gaol keeping, and charge for evermore.

The said quadrant, strongly built of stone by the before-named Stephen Forster and Agnes his wife, containeth a large walking-place by ground of thirty-eight feet and a half in length; besides the thickness of the walls, which are at the least six foot, makes all together forty-four feet and a half; the breadth within the walls is twenty-nine feet and a half, so that the thickness of the walls maketh it thirty-five feet and a half in breadth. The like room it hath over it for lodgings, and over it again fair leads to walk upon, well embattled, all for fresh air and ease of prisoners, to the end they should have lodging and water free without charge, as by certain verses graven in copper, and fixed on the said quadrant, I have read in form following :—

> " Devout souls that pass this way,
>   For Stephen Forster, late mayor, heartily pray;
>   And Dame Agnes his spouse to God consecrate,
>   That of pity this house made for Londoners in Ludgate.
>   So that for lodging and water prisoners here nought pay,
>   As their keepers shall all answer at dreadful doomsday."

This piece, and one other, of his arms, three broad arrow-heads, taken down with the old gate, I caused to be fixed over the entry of the said quadrant; but the verses being unhappily turned inward to the wall, procured the like in effect to be graven outward in prose, declaring him to be a fishmonger, because some upon a light occasion (as a maiden's head in a glass window) had fabled him to be a mercer, and to have begged there at Ludgate, &c. Thus much for Ludgate.

Next this is there a breach in the wall of the city, and a bridge of timber over the Fleet Dike, betwixt Fleet Bridge and Thames, directly over against the house of Bridewell. Thus much for gates in the wall.

Water-gates on the banks of the river Thames have been many, which being purchased by private men, are also put to private use, and the old names of them forgotten; but of such as remain, from the west towards the east, may be said as followeth :—

The Black-friars Stairs, a free landing-place.

Then a water-gate at Puddle Wharf, of one Puddle that kept a wharf on the west side thereof, and now of Puddle Water, by means of many horses watered there.

Then Paul's Wharf, also a free landing-place with stairs, &c.

Then Broken Wharf, and other such like.

But Ripa Regina, the Queen's bank or Queen hithe, may well be accounted the very chief and principal water-gate of this city, being a common strand or landing-place, yet equal with, and of old time far exceeding, Belins gate, as shall be shown in the ward of Queen hithe.

The next is Downgate, so called of the sudden descending or down-going of that way from St. John's Church upon Walbrook unto the river of Thames, whereby the water in the channel there hath such a swift course, that in the year 1574, on the fourth of September, after a strong shower of rain, a lad, of the age of eighteen years, minding to have leapt over the channel, was taken by the feet, and borne down with the violence of that narrow stream, and carried toward the Thames with such a violent swiftness, as no man could rescue or stay him, till he came against a cart-wheel that stood in the water-gate, before which time he was drowned and stark dead.

This was sometime a large water-gate, frequented of ships and other vessels, like as the Queen hithe, and was a part thereof, as doth appear by an inquisition made in the 28th year of Henry III., wherein was found, that as well corn as fish, and all other things coming to the port of Downgate, were to be ordered after the customs of the Queen's hithe, for the king's use ; as also that the corn arriving between the gate of the Guildhall of the merchants of Cologne (the Stilyard), which is east from Down-gate, and the house then pertaining to the Archbishop of Canterbury, west from Baynard's Castle, was to be measured by the measure, and measurer of the Queen's soke, or Queen hithe. I read also, in the 19th of Edward III., that customs were then to be paid for ships and other vessels resting at Downgate, as if they rode at Queen hithe, and as they now do at Belingsgate. And thus much for Downgate may suffice.

The next was called Wolf's gate, in the ropery in the parish of Allhallows the Less, of later time called Wolf's Lane, but now out of use; for the lower part was built on by the Earl of Shrewsbury, and the other part was stopped up and built on by the chamberlain of London.

The next is Ebgate, a water-gate, so called of old time, as appeareth by divers records of tenements near unto the same adjoining. It standeth near unto the Church of St. Laurence Pountney, but is within the parish of St. Martin Ordegare. In place of this gate is now a narrow passage to the Thames, and is called Ebgate Lane, but more commonly the Old Swan.

Then is there a water-gate at the bridge foot, called Oyster gate, of oysters that were there of old time commonly to be sold, and was the chiefest market for them and for other shell-fishes. There standeth now an engine or forcier, for the winding up of water to serve the city, whereof I have already spoken.

The next is the Bridge gate, so called of London Bridge, whereon it standeth. This was one of the four first and principal gates of the city, long before the Conquest, when there stood a bridge of timber, and is the seventh and last principal gate mentioned by W. Fitzstephen; which gate being new made when the bridge was built of stone, hath been oftentimes since repaired. This gate, with the tower upon it, in the year 1436 fell down, and two of the farthest arches southwards also fell therewith, and no man perished or was hurt therewith. To the repairing whereof, divers wealthy citizens gave large sums of money; namely, Robert Large, sometime mayor, one hundred marks; Stephen Forster, twenty pounds; Sir John Crosbye, alderman, one hundred pounds, &c. But in the year 1471, the Kentish mariners, under the conduct of bastard Falconbridge, burned the said gate and thirteen houses on the bridge, besides the beer houses at St. Katherine's, and many others in the suburbs.

The next is Botolph's gate, so called of the parish church of St. Botolph, near adjoining. This gate was sometime given or confirmed by William Conqueror to the monks of Westminster in these words: "W. rex Angliæ, &c. William, king of England, sendeth greeting to the sheriffes and all his ministers, as also to all his loving subjectes, French and English, of London: Know ye that I have granted to God and St. Peter of Westminster, and to the abbot Vitalis, the gift which Almundus of the port of S. Botolph gave them, when he was there made monk : that is to say, his Lords court with the houses, and one wharf, which is at the head of London Bridge, and all other his lands which he had in the same city, in such sort as King Edward more beneficially and amply granted the same ; and I will and command that they shall enjoy the same well and quietly and honourably, with sake and soke, &c."

The next is Belins gate, used as an especial port, or harbour, for small ships and boats coming thereto, and is now most frequented, the Queen's hithe being almost forsaken. How this gate took that name, or of what antiquity the same is, I must leave uncertain, as not having read any ancient record thereof, more than that Geoffrey Monmouth writeth, that Belin, a king of the Britons, about four hundred years before Christ's nativity, built this gate, and named it Belin's gate, after his own calling ; and that when he was dead, his body being burnt, the ashes, in a vessel of brass. were set upon a high pinnacle of stone over the same gate. But Cæsar and other Roman writers affirm, of cities, walls, and gates, as ye have before heard ; and therefore it seemeth to me not to be so ancient, but rather to have taken that name of some later owner of the place, happily named Beling, or Billing, as Somar's Key, Smart's Key, Frosh Wharf, and others, thereby took their names of their owners. Of this gate more shall be said when we come to Belin's gate ward.

Then you have a water-gate, on the west side of Wool Wharf, or Customer's Quay, which is commonly called the water-gate, at the south end of Water Lane.

One other water-gate there is by the bulwark of the Tower, and this is the last and farthest water-gate eastward on the river of Thames, so far as the city of London extendeth within the walls ; both which last-named water-gates be within the Tower Ward.

Besides these common water-gates, were divers private wharfs and quays, all along from the east to the west of this city, on the bank of the river of Thames ; merchants of all nations had landing places, warehouses, cellars, and stowage of their goods and merchandises, as partly shall be touched in the wards adjoining to the said river. Now, for the ordering and keeping these gates of this city in the night time, it was appointed in the year of Christ 1258, by Henry III., the 42nd of his reign, that the ports of England should be strongly kept, and that the gates of London should be new repaired, and diligently kept in the night, for fear of French deceits, whereof one writeth these verses :

> " Per noctem portæ clauduntur Londoniarum,
> Mœnia ne forte fraus frangat Francigenarum."

Of Towers and Castles.

"THE city of London (saith Fitzstephen) hath in the east a very great and a most strong palatine Tower, whose turrets and walls do rise from a deep foundation, the mortar thereof being temperey with the blood of beasts. In the west part are two most strong castles, &c." To begin therefore with the most famous Tower of London, situate in the east, near unto the river of Thames : it hath been the common opinion, and some have written—but of none assured ground—that Julius Cæsar, the first conqueror of the Britons, was the original author and founder, as well thereof as also of many other towers, castles, and great buildings within this realm ; but (as I have already before noted) Cæsar remained not here so long, nor had he in his head any such matter, but only to dispatch a conquest of this barbarous country, and to proceed to greater matters. Neither do the Roman writers make mention of any such buildings created by him here ; and therefore leaving this, and proceeding to more grounded authority, I find in a fair register-book, containing the acts of the Bishops of Rochester, set down by Edmond de Hadenham, that William I., surnamed Conqueror, built the Tower of London ; to wit, the great white and square tower there, about the year of Christ 1078, appointing Gundulph, then Bishop of Rochester, to be principal surveyor and overseer of that work, who was for that time lodged in the house of Edmere, a burgess of London ; the very words of which mine author are these : " *Gundulphus Episcopus mandato Willielmi Regis magni præfuit operi magnæ Turris London. quo tempore hospitatus est apud quendam Edmerum Burgensem London. qui dedit unum* were *Ecclesiæ Rofen.*"

Ye have before heard that the wall of this city was all round about furnished with towers and bulwarks, in due distance every one from other ; and also that the river Thames, with his ebbing and flowing, on the south side, had subverted the said wall and towers there.   Wherefore King William, for defence of this city, in place most dangerous, and open to the enemy, having taken down the second bulwark in the east part of the wall from the Thames, built this tower, which was the great square tower, now called the White Tower, and hath been since at divers times enlarged with other buildings adjoining, as shall be shown.   This tower was by tempest of wind sore shaken in the year 1090, the 4th of William Rufus, and was again by the said Rufus and Henry I. repaired.   They also caused a castle to be built under the said tower, namely, on the south side towards the Thames, and also incastellated the same round about.

Henry Huntington, libro sexto, hath these words : " William Rufus challenged the investure of prelates ; he pilled and shaved the people with tribute, especially to spend about the Tower of London and the great hall at Westminster."

Othowerus, Acolinillus, Otto, and Geoffrey Magnaville, Earl of Essex, were four the first constables of this Tower of London, by succession ; all which held by force a portion of land that pertained to the priory of the Holy Trinity within Aldgate ; that is to say, East Smithfield, near unto the Tower ; making thereof a vineyard, and would not depart from it till the 2nd year of King Stephen, when the same was abridged and restored to the church. This said Geoffrey Magnaville was Earl of Essex, constable of the Tower, sheriff of London, Middlesex, Essex, and Hertfordshire, as appeareth by a charter of Maude the empress, dated 1141.   He also fortified the Tower of London against King Stephen ; but the king took him in his court at St. Albans, and would not deliver him till he had rendered the Tower of London, with the castles of Walden and Plashey in Essex.   In the year 1153 the Tower of London and the Castle of Windsor were by the king delivered to Richard de Lucie, to be safely kept.   In the year 1155, Thomas Becket, being Chancellor to Henry II., caused the Flemings to be banished out of England, their castles lately built to be pulled down, and the Tower of London to be repaired.

About the year 1190, the 2nd of Richard I., William Long-champ, Bishop of Ely, Chancellor of England, for cause of dissension betwixt him and Earl John, the king's brother that was rebel, inclosed the tower and castle of London with an outward wall of stone embattled, and also caused a deep ditch to be cast about the same, thinking, as I have said before, to have environed it with the river of Thames. By the making of this enclosure and ditch in East Smithfield, the Church of the Holy Trinity in London lost half a mark rent by the year, and the mill was removed that belonged to the poor brethren of the Hospital of St. Katherine, and to the Church of the Holy Trinity aforesaid, which was no small loss and discommodity to either part; and the garden which the king had hired of the brethren, for six marks the year, for the most part was wasted and marred by the ditch. Recompense was often promised, but never performed, until King Edward coming after, gave to the brethren five marks and a half for that part which the ditch had devoured, and the other part thereof without he yielded to them again, which they hold : and of the said rent of five marks and a half, they have a deed, by virtue whereof they are well paid to this day.

It is also to be noted, and cannot be denied but that the said enclosure and ditch took the like or greater quantity of ground from the city within the wall; namely one, of that part called the Tower Hill, besides breaking down of the city wall from the White Tower to the first gate of the city called the Postern ; yet have I not read of any quarrel made by the citizens, or recompense demanded by them for that matter, because all was done for good of the city's defence thereof, and to their good likings. But Matthew Paris writeth that, in the year 1239, King Henry III. fortified the Tower of London to another end, wherefore the citizens, fearing lest that were done to their detriment, complained ; and the king answered, that he had not done it to their hurt, but, saith he, I will from henceforth do as my brother doth, in building and fortifying castles, who beareth the name to be wiser than I am. It followed in the next year, saith mine author, the said noble buildings of the stone gate and bulwark, which the king had caused to be made by the Tower of London, on the west side thereof, were shaken as it had been with an earthquake, and fell down, which the king again commanded to be built in better sort than before, which was done. And yet again, in the year 1247, the said wall and bulwarks that were newly built, wherein the king had bestowed more than twelve thousand marks, were irrecoverably thrown down, as afore. For the which chance the citizens of London were nothing sorry, for they were threatened that the said wall and bulwarks were built, to the end that if any of them would contend for the liberties of the city, they might be imprisoned; and that many might be laid in divers prisons, many lodgings were made that no one should speak with another: thus much Matthew Paris for this building. More of Henry III. his dealings against the citizens of London we may read in the said author, in 1245, 1248, 1249, 1253, 1255, 1256, &c. But, concerning the said wall and bulwark, the same was finished, though not in his time; for I read that Edward I., in the second of his reign, commanded the treasurer and chamberlain of the Exchequer to deliver out of his treasury unto Miles of Antwerp two hundred marks, of the fines taken out of divers merchants or usurers of London, for so be the words of the record, towards the work of the ditch then new made about the said bulwark, now called the Lion Tower. I find also recorded, that Henry III., in the 46th of his reign, wrote to Edward of Westminster, commanding him that he should buy certain perie plants,* and set the same in the place without his Tower of London, within the wall of the said city, which of late he had caused to be enclosed with a mud wall, as may appear by this that followeth: the mayor and commonalty of London were fined for throwing down the said earthen wall against the Tower of London, the 9th of Edward II. Edward IV. in place thereof built a wall of brick. But now for the Lion Tower and lions in England, the original, as I have read, was thus.

Henry I. built his manor of Woodstock, with a park, which he walled about with stone, seven miles in compass, destroying for the same divers villages, churches, and chapels; and this was the first park in England. He placed therein, besides great store of deer, divers strange beasts to be kept and nourished, such as were brought to him from far countries, as lions, leopards, lynxes, porpentines,† and such other. More, I read that in the year 1235, Frederick the emperor sent to Henry III. three leopards, in token of his regal shield of arms, wherein three leopards were pictured;

---

* *Perie plants*, young pear trees.
† *Porpentines*, porcupines.

since the which time those lions and others have been kept in a part of this bulwark, now called the Lion Tower, and their keepers there lodged. King Edward II., in the 12th of his reign, commanded the sheriffs of London to pay to the keepers of the king's leopard in the Tower of London sixpence the day for the sustenance of the leopard, and three-halfpence a day for diet of the said keeper, out of the fee farm of the said city. More, in the 16th of Edward III., one lion, one lioness, one leopard, and two cat lions, in the said Tower, were committed to the custody of Robert, the son of John Bowre.

Edward IV. fortified the Tower of London, and enclosed with brick, as is aforesaid, a certain piece of ground taken out of the Tower Hill, west from the Lion Tower, now called the bulwark. His officers also, in the 5th of his reign, set upon the said hill both scaffold and gallows, for the execution of offenders; whereupon the mayor and his brethren complained to the king, and were answered that the same was not done in derogation of the city's liberties, and thereof caused proclamation to be made, &c., as shall be shown in Tower Street.

Richard III. repaired and built in this tower somewhat. Henry VIII., in 1532, repaired the White Tower, and other parts thereof. In the year 1548, the 2nd of Edward VI., on the 22nd of November, in the night, a Frenchman lodged in the round bulwark, betwixt the west gate and the postern or drawbridge called the warders' gate, by setting fire on a barrel of gunpowder blew up the said bulwark, burnt himself, and no more persons. This bulwark was forthwith again new built.

And here, because I have by occasion spoken of the west gate of this tower, the same, as the most principal, is used for the receipt and delivery of all kinds of carriages; without the which gate are divers bulwarks and gates, towards the north, &c. Then near within this west gate, opening to the south, is a strong postern for passengers by the ward-house, over a drawbridge let down for that purpose. Next on the same south side, toward the east, is a large water-gate, for receipt of boats and small vessels, partly under a stone bridge from the river of Thames. Beyond it is a small postern, with a drawbridge, seldom let down but for the receipt of some great persons, prisoners. Then towards the east is a great and strong gate, commonly called the Iron gate, but not usually opened. And thus much for the foundation, building, and repairing of this tower, with the gates and posterns, may suffice. And now somewhat of accidents in the same shall be shown.

In the year 1196, William Fitzosbert, a citizen of London, seditiously moving the common people to seek liberty, and not to be subject to the rich and more mighty, at length was taken and brought before the Archbishop of Canterbury in the Tower, where he was by the judges condemned, and by the heels drawn thence to the Elms in Smithfield, and there hanged.

In 1214, King John wrote to Geoffrey Magnaville to deliver the Tower of London, with the prisoners, armour, and all other things found therein belonging to the king, to William, Archdeacon of Huntingdon. In the year 1216, the 1st of Henry III., the said Tower was delivered to Lewis of France and the barons of England.

In the year 1206 pleas of the crown were pleaded in the Tower; likewise in the year 1220, and likewise in the year 1224, and again in the year 1243, before William of York, Richard Passelew, Henry Brahe, Jerome of Saxton, justices.

In the year 1222, the citizens of London having made a tumult against the Abbot of Westminster, Hubert of Burgh, chief-justice of England, came to the Tower of London, called before him the mayor and aldermen, of whom he inquired for the principal authors of that sedition; amongst whom one, named Constantine Fitz Aelulfe, avowed that he was the man, and had done much less than he ought to have done : whereupon the justice sent him with two other to Falks de Brent, who with armed men brought them to the gallows, where they were hanged.

In the year 1244, Griffith, the eldest son of Leoline, Prince of Wales, being kept prisoner in the Tower, devised means of escape, and having in the night made of the hangings, sheets, &c., a long line, he put himself down from the top of the Tower, but in the sliding, the weight of his body, being a very big and a fat man, brake the rope, and he fell and brake his neck withal.

In the year 1253, King Henry III. imprisoned the sheriffs of London in the Tower more than a month, for the escape of a prisoner out of Newgate, as you may read in the chapter of Gates.

In the year 1260, King Henry, with his queen (for fear of the barons), were lodged in the Tower. The next year he sent for his lords, and held his parliament there.

In the year 1263, when the queen would have removed from the Tower by water towards Windsor, sundry Londoners got them together to the bridge, under the which she was to pass, and not only cried out upon her with reproachful words, but also threw mire and stones at her, by which she was constrained to return for the time. But in the year 1265, the said citizens were fain to submit themselves to the king for it, and the mayor, aldermen, and sheriffs were sent to divers prisons, and a custos also was set over the city; to wit, Othon, constable of the Tower, &c.

In the year 1282, Leoline, Prince of Wales, being taken at Builth Castle, Roger Lestrange cut off his head, which Sir Roger Mortimer caused to be crowned with ivy, and set it upon the Tower of London.

In the year 1290, divers justices, as well of the bench as of the assizes, were sent prisoners to the Tower, which with great sums of money redeemed their liberty. Edward II., the 14th of his reign, appointed for prisoners in the Tower, a knight twopence the day, an esquire one penny the day, to serve for their diet.

In the year 1320, the king's justices sat in the Tower, for trial of matters; whereupon John Gifors, late mayor of London, and many others, fled the city, for fear to be charged of things they had presumptuously done.

In the year 1321, the Mortimers yielding themselves to the king, he sent them prisoners to the Tower, where they remained long, and were adjudged to be drawn and hanged. But at length Roger Mortimer, of Wigmore, by giving to his keepers a sleepy drink, escaped out of the Tower, and his uncle Roger, being still kept there, died about five years after.

In the year 1326, the citizens of London won the Tower, wresting the keys out of the constable's hands, delivered all the prisoners, and kept both city and Tower to the use of Isabel the queen, and Edward her son.

In the year 1330, Roger Mortimer, Earl of March, was taken and brought to the Tower, from whence he was brought to the Elms, and there hanged.

In the year 1344, King Edward III., in the 18th of his reign, commanded florences of gold to be made and coined in the Tower; that is to say, a penny piece of the value of five shillings and eightpence, the halfpenny piece of the value of three shillings and fourpence, and a farthing piece worth twenty pence; Percevall de Port of Lake being then master of the coin. And this is the first coining of gold in the Tower whereof I have read, and also the first coinage of gold in England. I find also recorded, that the said king in the same year ordained his exchange of money to be kept in Serne's Tower, a part of the king's house in Bucklesbury. And here to digress a little, by occasion offered, I find that, in times before passed, all great sums were paid by weight of gold or silver, as so many pounds or marks of silver, or so many pounds or marks of gold, cut into blanks, and not stamped, as I could prove by many good authorities which I overpass. The smaller sums also were paid in sterlings, which were pence so called, for other coins they had none. The antiquity of this sterling penny usual in this realm is from the reign of Henry II., notwithstanding the Saxon coins before the Conquest were pence of fine silver the full weight, and somewhat better than the latter sterlings, as I have tried by conference of the pence of Burghrede, king of Mercia, Alfred, Edward, and Edelred, kings of the West Saxons, Plegmond, Archbishop of Canterbury, and others. William the Conqueror's penny also was fine silver of the weight of the easterling, and had on the one side stamped an armed head, with a beardless face—for the Normans wore no beards—with a sceptre in his hand. The inscription in the circumference was this: "Le Rei Wilam;" on the other side, a cross double to the ring, between four rowals of six points.

King Henry I. his penny was of the like weight, fineness, form of face, cross, &c.

This Henry, in the 8th year of his reign, ordained the penny, which was round, so to be quartered by the cross, that they might easily be broken into halfpence and farthings. In the 1st, 2nd, 3rd, 4th, and 5th of King Richard I. his reign, and afterwards, I find commonly easterling money mentioned, and yet ofttimes the same is called argent, as afore, and not otherwise.

The first great sum that I read of to be paid in easterlings was in the reign of Richard I., when Robert, Earl of Leicester, being prisoner in France, proffered for his ransom a thousand marks easterlings, notwithstanding the easterling pence were long before. The weight of the easterling penny may appear by divers statutes, namely, of weights and measures, made in the 51st of Henry III., in these words: "Thirty-two graines of wheat, drie and round, taken in the middest of the eare, shoulde be the weight of a starling penie, 20 of those pence should waye one ounce, 12 ounces a pound Troy." It followeth in the statute eight pound to make a gallon of wine, and eight gallons a bushel of London measure, &c. Notwithstanding which statute, I find, in the 8th of Edward I., Gregorie Rokesley, mayor of London, being chief master or minister of the King's Exchange, or mints, a new coin being then appointed, the pound of easterling money should contain as afore twelve ounces; to wit, fine silver, such as was then made into foil, and was commonly called silver of Guthurons Lane, eleven ounces, two easterlings, and one ferling or farthing, and the other seventeen pence to be alloy. Also, the pound of money ought to weigh twenty shillings and threepence by account; so that no pound ought to be over twenty shillings and threepence, nor less than twenty shillings and twopence by account; the ounce to weigh twenty pence, the penny weight twenty-four grains (which twenty-four by weight then appointed were as much as the former thirty-two grains of wheat), a penny force twenty-five grains and a half, the penny deble or feeble twenty-two grains and a half, &c.

Now for the penny easterling, how it took that name I think good briefly to touch. It hath been said, that Numa Pompilius, the second king of the Romans, commanded money first to be made. of whose name they were called *nummi ;* and when copper pence, silver pence. and gold pence were made, because every silver penny was worth ten copper pence, and every gold penny worth ten silver pence, the pence therefore were called in Latin. denarii, and oftentimes the pence are named of the matter and stuff of gold or silver. But the money of England was called of the workers and makers thereof, as the florin of gold is called of the Florentines, that were the workers thereof, and so the easterling pence took their name of the Easterlings which did first make this money in England,* in the reign of Henry II.

Thus have I set down according to my reading in antiquity of money matters, omitting the imaginations of late writers, of whom some have said easterling money to take that name of a star, stamped in the border or ring of the penny; other some of a bird called a star or starling stamped in the circumference; and other, more unlikely, of being coined at Strivelin or Sterling, a town in Scotland, &c.

Now concerning halfpence and farthings, the account of which is more subtle than the pence, I need not speak of them more than that they were only made in the Exchange at London, and nowhere else: first appointed to be made by Edward I. in the 8th of his reign; and also at the same time the said king coined some few groats of silver, but they were not usual. The King's Exchange at London was near unto the cathedral church of St. Paul, and is to this day commonly called the Old Change, but in evidences the Old Exchange.

The king's exchanger in this place was to deliver out to every other exchanger throughout England, or other the king's dominions, their coining irons, that is to say, one standard or staple, and two trussels or punchons; and when the same was spent and worn, to receive them with an account what sum had been coined, and also their pix or bore of assay, and deliver other irons new graven, &c. I find that in the 9th of King John, there was besides the mint at London, other mints at Winchester, Excester, Chichester, Canterbury, Rochester, Ipswich, Norwich, Lynn, Lincoln, York, Carlisle, Northampton, Oxford, St. Edmondsbury, and Durham. The exchanger, examiner, and trier buyeth the silver for coinage, answering for every hundred pounds of silver bought in bullion or otherwise, ninety-eight pounds fifteen shillings, for he taketh twenty-five shillings for coinage.

King Edward I., in the 27th of his reign, held a parliament at

---

* Camden says, "In the time of King Richard I., money coined in the east parts of Germany began to be of especial request in England for the purity thereof, and was called Easterling money, as all the inhabitants of those parts were called Easterlings; and shortly after, some of that country, skilful in mint matters and alloys, were sent for into this realm to bring the coin to perfection, which since that time was called of them Sterling or Easterling."

Stebenheth, in the house of Henry Waleis, mayor of London, wherein amongst other things there handled, the transporting of sterling money was forbidden.

In the year 1351, William Edington, Bishop of Winchester, and treasurer of England, a wise man, but loving the king's commodity more than the wealth of the whole realm and common people, saith mine author, caused a new coin, called a groat and a half-groat, to be coined and stamped, the groat to be taken for fourpence, and the half-groat for twopence, not containing in weight according to the pence called easterlings, but much less, to wit, by five shillings in the pound; by reason whereof, victuals and merchandises became the dearer through the whole realm. About the same time also, the old coin of gold was changed into a new; but the old florin or noble, then so called, was worth much above the taxed rate of the new, and therefore the merchants engrossed up the old, and conveyed them out of the realm, to the great loss of the kingdom. Wherefore a remedy was provided by changing of the stamp.

In the year 1411, King Henry IV. caused a new coin of nobles to be made, of less value than the old by fourpence in the noble, so that fifty nobles should be a pound troy weight.

In the year 1421 was granted to Henry V. a fifteenth, to be paid at Candlemas and at Martinmas, of such money as was then current, gold or silver, not overmuch clipped or washed; to wit, that if the noble were worth five shillings and eightpence, then the king should take it for a full noble of six shillings and eightpence, and if it were less of value than five shillings and eightpence, then the person paying that gold to make it good to the value of five shillings and eightpence, the king always receiving it for a whole noble of six shillings and eightpence. And if the noble so paid be better than five shillings and eightpence, the king to pay again the surplusage that it was better than five shillings and eightpence. Also this year was such scarcity of white money, that though a noble were so good of gold and weight as six shillings and eightpence, men might get no white money for them.

In the year 1465, King Edward IV. caused a new coin both of gold and silver to be made, whereby he gained much; for he made of an old noble a royal, which he commanded to go for ten shillings. Nevertheless, to the same royal was put eightpence of alloy, and so weighed the more, being smitten with a new stamp, to wit, a rose. He likewise made half-angels of five shillings, and farthings of two shillings and sixpence, angelets of six shillings and eightpence, and half-angels of three shillings and fourpence. He made silver money of threepence, a groat, and so of other coins after that rate, to the great harm of the commons. W. Lord Hastings, the king's chamberlain, being master of the king's mints, undertook to make the moneys under form following, to wit—of gold, a piece of eight shillings and fourpence sterling, which should be called a noble of gold, of the which there should be fifty such pieces in the pound weight of the Tower; another piece of gold of four shillings and twopence sterling, and to be of them an hundred such pieces in the pound; and a third piece of gold, of two shillings and one penny sterling, two hundred such pieces in the pound; every pound weight of the Tower to be worth twenty pounds, sixteen shillings, and eightpence, the which should be twenty-three carats, three grains and a half fine, &c., and for silver, thirty-seven shillings and sixpence; the piece of fourpence to be one hundred and twelve groats and twopence in the pound weight.

In the year 1504, King Henry VII. appointed a new coin, to wit, a groat, and half-groat, which bare but half faces; the same time also was coined a groat which was in value twelve pence, but of those but a few, after the rate of forty pence the ounce.

In the year 1526, the 18th of Henry VIII., the angel noble being then the sixth part of an ounce troy, so that six angels were just an ounce, which was forty shillings sterling, and the angel was also worth two ounces of silver, so that six angels were worth twelve ounces of silver, which was forty shillings, a proclamation was made on the sixth of September, that the angel should go for seven shillings and fourpence, the royal for eleven shillings, and the crown for four shillings and fourpence. And on the fifth of November following, again by proclamation, the angel was enhanced to seven shillings and sixpence, and so every ounce of gold to be forty-five shillings, and the ounce of silver at three shillings and ninepence in value.

In the year 1544, the 35th of Henry VIII. on the 16th of

May, proclamation was made for the enhancing of gold to forty-eight shillings, and silver to four shillings the ounce. Also the king caused to be coined base moneys, to wit, pieces of twelve pence, sixpence, fourpence, twopence, and a penny, in weight as the late sterling, in show good silver, but inwardly copper. These pieces had whole, or broad faces, and continued current after that rate till the 5th of Edward VI., when they were on the 9th of July called down, the shilling to ninepence, the groat to threepence, &c., and on the 17th of August from ninepence to sixpence, &c. And on the 30th of October was published new coins of silver and gold to be made, a piece of silver five shillings sterling, a piece of two shillings and fivepence, of twelve pence, of sixpence, a penny with a double rose, half-penny a single rose, and a farthing with a portcullis. Coins of fine gold : a whole sovereign of thirty shillings, an angel of ten shillings, an angelet of five shillings. Of crown gold : a sovereign twenty shillings, half-sovereign ten shillings, five shillings, two shillings and sixpence, and base moneys to pass as before, which continued till the 2nd of Queen Elizabeth, then called to a lower rate, taken to the mint, and refined, the silver whereof being coined with a new stamp of her Majesty, the dross was carried to foul highways, to heighten them. This base money, for the time, caused the old sterling moneys to be hoarded up, so that I have seen twenty-one shillings current given for one old angel to gild withal. Also rents of lands and tenements, with prices of victuals, were raised far beyond the former rates, hardly since to be brought down. Thus much for base moneys coined and current in England have I known. But for leather moneys, as many people have fondly talked, I find no such matter. I read, that King John of France, being taken prisoner by Edward the Black Prince at the battle of Poictiers, paid a ransom of three millions of florences, whereby he brought the realm into such poverty, that many years after they used leather money, with a little stud or nail of silver in the middle thereof. Thus much for mint and coinage, by occasion of this Tower, under correction of others more skilful, may suffice. And now to other accidents there.

In the year 1360, the peace between England and France being confirmed, King Edward came over into England, and straight to the Tower, to see the French king then prisoner there, whose ransom he assessed at three millions of florences, and so delivered him from prison, and brought him with honour to the sea.

In the year 1381, the rebels of Kent drew out of the Tower where the king was then lodged, Simon Sudbury, archbishop of Canterbury, lord chancellor, Robert Hales, prior of St. John's, and treasurer of England, William Appleton, friar, the king's confessor, and John Legg, a sergeant of the king's, and beheaded them on the Tower Hill, &c.

In the year 1387, King Richard held his feast of Christmas in the Tower; and in the year 1399, the same king was sent prisoner to the Tower.

In the year 1414, Sir John Oldcastle brake out of the Tower. And the same year, a parliament being holden at Leicester, a porter of the Tower was drawn, hanged, and headed, whose head was sent up, and set over the Tower gate, for consenting to one Whitlooke, that brake out of the Tower.

In the year 1419, Friar Randulph was sent to the Tower, and was there slain by the parson of St. Peter's in the Tower.

In the year 1428, there came to London a lewd fellow, feigning himself to be sent from the Emperor to the young King Henry VI., calling himself Baron of Blakamoore, and that he should be the principal physician in this kingdom; but his subtlety being known, he was apprehended, condemned, drawn, hanged, headed, and quartered, his head set on the Tower of London, and his quarters on four gates of the city.

In the year 1458, in Whitsun week, the Duke of Somerset. with Anthony Rivers, and other four, kept jousts before the queen in the Tower of London, against three esquires of the queen's, and others.

In the year 1465, King Henry VI. was brought prisoner to the Tower, where he remained long.

In the year 1470, the Tower was yielded to Sir Richard Lee, mayor of London, and his brethren the aldermen, who forthwith entered the same, delivered King Henry of his imprisonment, and lodged him in the king's lodging there; but the next year he was again sent thither prisoner, and there murdered.

In the year 1478, George, Duke of Clarence, was drowned with malmsey in the Tower; and within five years after King Edward V., with his brother, were said to be murdered there.

In the year 1485, John, Earl of Oxford, was made constable of the Tower, and had custody of the lions granted him.

In the year 1501, in the month of May, was a royal tourney of lords and knights in the Tower of London before the king.

In the year 1502, Queen Elizabeth, wife to Henry VII., died of childbirth in the Tower.

In the year 1512, the chapel in the high White Tower was burnt. In the year 1536, Queen Anne Bullein was beheaded in the Tower. 1541, Lady Katherine Howard, wife to King Henry VIII., was also beheaded there.

In the year 1546, the 27th of April, being Tuesday in Easter week, William Foxley, potmaker for the Mint in the Tower of London, fell asleep, and so continued sleeping, and could not be wakened with pricking, cramping, or otherwise burning whatsoever, until the first day of the term, which was full fourteen days and fifteen nights, or more, for that Easter term beginneth not before seventeen days after Easter. The cause of his thus sleeping could not be known, though the same was diligently searched after by the king's physicians, and other learned men; yea, the king himself examining the said William Foxley, who was in all points found at his awakening to be as if he had slept but one night. And he lived more than forty years after in the said Tower, to wit, until the year of Christ 1587, and then deceased on Wednesday in Easter week.

Thus much for these accidents: and now to conclude thereof in summary. This Tower is a citadel to defend or command the city; a royal palace for assemblies or treaties; a prison of state for the most dangerous offenders; the only place of coinage for all England at this time; the armoury for warlike provision; the treasury of the ornaments and jewels of the crown; and general conserver of the most reco..'s of the king's courts of justice at Westminster.

The next tower on the river of Thames is on London Bridge, at the north end of the drawbridge. This tower was newly begun to be built in the year 1426. John Reynwell, mayor of London, laid one of the first corner stones in the foundation of this work, the other three were laid by the sheriffs and bridgemasters; upon every of these four stones was engraven in fair Roman letters the name of "Ihesus." And these stones I have seen laid in the bridge storehouse since they were taken up, when that tower was of late newly made of timber. This gate and tower was at the first strongly built up of stone, and so continued until the year 1577, in the month of April, when the same stone arched gate and tower being decayed, was begun to be taken down, and then were the heads of the traitors removed thence, and set on the tower over the gate at the bridge-foot towards Southwark. This said tower being taken down, a new foundation was drawn, and Sir John Langley, lord mayor, laid the first stone in the presence of the sheriffs and bridgemasters, on the 28th of August; and in the month of September, in the year 1579, the same tower was finished—a beautiful and chargeable piece of work, all above the bridge being of timber.

Another tower there is on London Bridge, to wit, over the gate at the south end of the same bridge towards Southwark. This gate, with the tower thereupon, and two arches of the bridge, fell down, and no man perished by the fall thereof, in the year 1436; towards the new building whereof divers charitable citizens gave large sums of money; which gate, being then again newly built, was, with seventeen houses more on the bridge, in the year 1471 burnt by the mariners and sailors of Kent, Bastard Falconbridge being their captain.

In the west of this city, saith Fitzstephen, are two most strong castles, &c. Also Gervasius Tilbury, in the reign of Henry II., writing of these castles, hath to this effect:—"Two castles," saith he, "are built with walls and rampires, whereof one is, in right of possession, Baynardes; the other the Barons of Mountfichet." The first of these castles, banking on the river Thames, was called Baynard's Castle, of Baynard a nobleman, that came in with the Conqueror, and then built it, and deceased in the reign of William Rufus; after whose decease Geoffrey Baynard succeeded, and then William Baynard, in the year 1111, who by forfeiture for felony, lost his barony of Little Dunmow, and King Henry gave it wholly to Robert, the son of Richard, the son of Gilbert of Clare, and to his heirs, together with the honour of Baynard's Castle. This Robert married Maude de Saint Licio, lady of Bradham, and deceased 1134; was buried at St. Neots by Gilbert of Clare, his father. Walter his son succeeded him; he took to wife Matilde de Bocham, and after her decease, Matilde, the daughter and co-heir of Richard de Lucy, on whom he begat Robert and other: he deceased in the year 1198, and was buried at Dunmow; after whom succeeded Robert Fitzwalter, a valiant knight.

About the year 1213 there arose a great discord between King John and his barons, because of Matilda, surnamed the Fair, daughter to the said Robert Fitzwalter, whom the king unlawfully loved but could not obtain her, nor her father would consent thereunto, whereupon, and for other like causes, ensued war through the whole realm. The barons were received into London, where they greatly endamaged the king; but in the end the king did not only therefore banish the said Fitzwalter, amongst other, out of the realm, but also caused his castle called Baynard, and other his houses, to be spoiled; which thing being done, a messenger being sent unto Matilda the Fair about the king's suit, whereunto she would not consent, she was poisoned; Robert Fitzwalter, and other, being then passed into France, and some into Scotland, &c.

It happened in the year 1214, King John being then in France with a great army, that a truce was taken betwixt the two kings of England and France for the term of five years; and a river, or arm of the sea, being then between either host, there was a knight in the English host, that cried to them of the other side, willing some one of their knights to come and joust a course or twain with him; whereupon, without stay, Robert Fitzwalter, being on the French part, made himself ready, ferried over, and got on horseback, without any man to help him, and showed himself ready to the face of his challenger, whom at the first course he struck so hard with his great spear, that horse and man fell to the ground; and when his spear was broken he went back to the King of France. Which when the king had seen, "By God's tooth," quoth he, after his usual oath, "he were a king indeed that had such a knight." The friends of Robert, hearing these words, kneeled down, and said—"O king, he is your knight; it is Robert Fitzwalter." And thereupon, the next day he was sent for, and restored to the king's favour; by which means peace was concluded, and he received his livings, and had license to repair his castle of Baynard, and other castles.

The year 1216, the 1st of Henry III., the castle of Hertford being delivered to Lewis the French prince, and the barons of England, Robert Fitzwalter requiring to have the same, because the keeping thereof did by ancient right and title pertain to him, was answered by Lewis, "that Englishmen were not worthy to have such holds in keeping, because they did betray their own lord," &c. This Robert deceased in the year 1234, and was buried at Dunmow, and Walter his son that succeeded him. 1258, his barony of Baynard was in the ward of King Henry, in the nonage of Robert Fitzwalter. This Robert took to his second wife Eleanor, daughter and heir to the Earl of Ferrars, in the year 1289; and in the year 1303, on the 12th of March, before John Blondon, mayor of London, he acknowledged his service to the same city, and sware upon the Evangelists, that he would be true to the liberties thereof, and maintain the same to his power, and the counsel of the same to keep, &c.

The rights that belonged to Robert Fitzwalter, chastelian of London, lord of Wodeham, were these :—

The said Robert and his heirs ought to be and are chief bannerers of London, in fee of the chastellerie, which he and his ancestors had by Castle Baynard, in the said city. In time of war the said Robert, and his heirs, ought to serve the city in manner as followeth : that is, The said Robert ought to come, he being the twentieth man of arms on horseback, covered with cloth, or armour, unto the great west door of St. Paul, with his banner displayed before him of his arms ; and when he is come to the said door, mounted and apparelled, as before is said, the mayor with his aldermen and sheriffs armed in their arms, shall come out of the said Church of St. Paul, unto the said door, with a banner in his hand, all on foot, which banner shall be gules, with the image of St. Paul, gold, the face, hands, feet, and sword, of silver ; and as soon as the said Robert shall see the mayor, aldermen, and sheriffs come on foot out of the church, armed with such a banner, he shall alight from his horse and salute the mayor, and say to him—" Sir mayor, I am come to do my service, which I owe to the city." And the mayor and aldermen shall answer—" We give to you, as our bannerer of fee in this city, this banner of this city to bear and govern to the honour and profit of the city to our power." And the said Robert and his heirs shall receive the banner in his hands, and shall go on foot out of the gate with the banner in his hands; and the mayor, aldermen, and sheriffs shall follow to the door, and shall bring a horse to the said Robert worth twenty pounds, which horse shall be saddled with a saddle of the arms of the said Robert, and shall be covered with sendals* of the said arms. Also they shall present to him twenty pounds sterling money, and deliver it to the chamberlain of the said Robert for his expenses that day. Then the said Robert shall mount upon the horse which the mayor presented to him, with the banner in his hand, and as soon as he is up, he shall say to the mayor, that he cause a marshal to be chosen for the host, one of the city; which marshal being chosen, the said Robert shall command the mayor and burgesses of the city to warn the commoners to assemble together, and they shall all go under the banner of St. Paul, and the said Robert shall bear it himself unto Aldgate, and there the said Robert and mayor shall deliver the said banner of St. Paul from thence, to whom they shall assent or think good. And if they must make any issue forth of the city, then the said Robert ought to choose two forth of every ward, the most sage personages, to foresee to the safe keeping of the city after they be gone forth. And this council shall be taken in the priory of the Trinity near unto Aldgate. And before every town or castle which the host of London besiege, if the siege continue a whole year, the said Robert shall have for every siege of the commonalty of London an hundred shillings for his travail, and no more. These be the rights that the said Robert hath in the time of war.—Rights belonging to Robert Fitzwalter, and to his heirs in the city of London, in the time of peace, are these : that is to say, the said Robert hath a soken or ward in the city, that is, a wall of the canonry of St. Paul, as a man goeth down the street before the brewhouse of St. Paul unto the Thames, and so to the side of the mill, which is in the water that cometh down from the Fleet Bridge, and goeth so by London walls, betwixt the Friars preachers and Ludgate, and so returneth back by the house of the said Friars unto the said wall of the said canonry of St. Paul,

---

* *Sendals*, pieces of a rich thin silk. The word was in Greek and in Low Latin σινδών, *cendalum*, derived from Sindhu the Indus, and the country by the Indus from which these fine fabrics of silk or linen were first brought.

that is, all the parish of St. Andrew, which is in the gift of his ancestors by the said seigniority. And so the said Robert hath appendant unto the said soken all these things underwritten—that he ought to have a sokeman, and to place what sokeman he will, so he be of the sokemanry, or the same ward ; and if any of the sokemanry be impleaded in the Guildhall, of anything that toucheth not the body of the mayor that for the time is, or that toucheth the body of no sheriff, it is not lawful for the sokeman of the sokemanry of the said Robert Fitzwalter to demand a court of the said Robert ; and the mayor, and his citizens of London, ought to grant him to have a court, and in his court he ought to bring his judgments, as it is assented and agreed upon in this Guildhall, that shall be given them. If any, therefore, be taken in his sokemanry, he ought to have his stocks and imprisonment in his soken ; and he shall be brought from thence to the Guildhall before the mayor, and there they shall provide him his judgment that ought to be given of him ; but his judgment shall not be published till he come into the court of the said Robert, and in his liberty. And the judgment shall be such, that if he have deserved death by treason, he to be tied to a post in the Thames at a good wharf where boats are fastened, two ebbings and two flowings of the water. And if he be condemned for a common thief, he ought to be led to the Elms, and there suffer his judgment as other thieves. And so the said Robert and his heirs hath honour that he holdeth a great franchise within the city, that the mayor of the city and citizens are bound to do him of right, that is to say, that when the mayor will hold a great council, he ought to call the said Robert, and his heirs, to be with him in council of the city, and the said Robert ought to be sworn to be of council with the city against all people, saving the king and his heirs. And when the said Robert cometh to the hustings in the Guildhall of the city, the mayor, or his lieutenant, ought to rise against him, and set him down near unto him ; and so long as he is in the Guildhall, all the judgment ought to be given by his mouth, according to the record of the recorders of the said Guildhall ; and so many waifs as come so long as he is there, he ought to give them to the bailiffs of the town, or to whom he will, by the counsel of the mayor of the city. These be the franchises that belonged to Robert Fitzwalter in London, in time of peace; which for the antiquity thereof I have noted out of an old record.

This Robert deceased in the year 1305, leaving issue Walter Fitzrobert, who had issue Robert Fitzwalter, unto whom, in the year 1320, the citizens of London acknowledged the right which they ought * to him and his heirs for the Castle Baynard; he deceased 1325; unto whom succeeded Robert Fitzrobert, Fitzwalter, &c. More of the Lord Fitzwalter may ye read in my Annals in 51st of Edward III. But how this honour of Baynard's Castle, with the appurtenances, fell from the possession of the Fitzwalters, I have not read; only I find, that in the year 1428, the 7th of Henry VI., a great fire was at Baynard's Castle, and that same Humphrey, Duke of Gloucester, built it of new. By his death and attainder, in the year 1446, it came to the hands of Henry VI., and from him to Richard, Duke of York, of whom we read, that in the year 1457 he lodged there, as in his own house. In the year 1460, the 28th of February, the Earls of March and of Warwick, with a great power of men, but few of name, entered the city of London, where they were of the citizens joyously received; and upon the 3rd of March, being Sunday, the said earl caused to be mustered his people in St. John's field, where unto that host was showed and proclaimed certain articles and points wherein King Henry, as they said, had offended; and thereupon it was demanded of the said people, whether the said Henry was worthy to reign as king any longer or not: whereunto the people cried Nay. Then it was asked of them, whether they would have the Earl of March for their king; and they cried, Yea, yea. Whereupon certain captains were appointed to bear report thereof unto the said Earl of March, then being lodged at his castle of Baynard. Whereof when the earl was by them advertised, he thanked God and them for their election; notwithstanding he showed some countenance of insufficiency in him to occupy so great a charge, till by exhortation of the Archbishop of Canterbury, the Bishop of Excester, and certain noblemen, he granted to their petition; and on the next morrow at Paul's he went on procession, offered, and had *Te Deum* sung. Then was he with great royalty conveyed to Westminster, and there, in the great Hall, set in the king's seat, with St. Edward's sceptre in his hand.

* *Ought*, owed.

Edward IV. being dead, leaving his eldest son Edward, and his second son Richard, both infants, Richard, Duke of Gloucester, being elected by the nobles and commons in the Guildhall of London, took on him the title of the realm and kingdom, as imposed upon him in this Baynard's Castle, as ye may read penned by Sir Thomas More, and set down in my Annals.

Henry VII., about the year 1501, the 16th of his reign, repaired, or rather new built this house, not embattled, or so strongly fortified castle like, but far more beautiful and commodious for the entertainment of any prince or great estate. In the 17th of his reign, he, with his queen, were lodged there, and came from thence to Paul's Church, where they made their offering, dined in the bishop's palace, and so returned. The 18th of his reign he was lodged there, and the ambassadors from the King of the Romans were thither brought to his presence, and from thence the king came to Paul's, and was there sworn to the King of the Romans, as the said king had sworn to him.

The 20th of the said king, he with his knights of the order, all in their habits of the Garter, rode from the Tower of London, through the city, unto the cathedral church of St. Paul's, and there heard evensong, and from thence they rode to Baynard's Castle, where the king lodged; and on the next morrow, in the same habit they rode from thence again to the said Church of St. Paul's, went on procession, heard the divine service, offered, and returned. The same year the King of Castile was lodged there.

In the year 1553, the 19th of July, the council, partly moved with the right of the Lady Mary's cause, partly considering that the most of the realm were wholly bent on her side, changing their mind from Lady Jane, lately proclaimed queen, assembled themselves at this Baynard's Castle, where they communed with the Earl of Pembroke, and the Earl of Shrewsbury, and Sir John Mason, clerk of the council, sent for the lord mayor, and then riding into Cheap to the Cross, where Garter King at Arms, trumpet being sounded, proclaimed the Lady Mary, daughter of King Henry VIII. and Queen Katherine, Queen of England, &c.

This castle now belongeth to the Earl of Pembroke.

Next adjoining to this castle was sometime a tower, the name whereof I have not read; but that the same was built by Edward II.

is manifest by this that followeth. King Edward III., in the second year of his reign, gave unto William de Ros, of Hamolake, in Yorkshire, a tower upon the water of Thames, by the castle of Baynard in the city of London, which tower his father had built; he gave the said tower and appurtenances to the said William Hamolake, and his heirs, for a rose yearly, to be paid for all service due, &c. This tower, as seemeth to me, was since called Legat's Inn, the 7th of Edward IV.

The next tower or castle, banking also on the river of Thames, was, as is afore showed, called Montfichett's Castle, of a nobleman, Baron of Montfichett, the first builder thereof, who came in with William the Conqueror, and was since named Le Sir Montfichett. This castle he built in a place not far distant from Baynard's, towards the west. The same William Montfichett lived in the reign of Henry I., and was witness to a charter then granted to the city for the sheriffs of London. Richard Montfichett lived in King John's time; and in the year 1213 was by the same king banished the realm into France, when peradventure King John caused his castle of Montfichett, amongst other castles of the barons, to be overthrown; the which after his return might be by him again re-edified; for the total destruction thereof was about the year 1276, when Robert Kilwarby, Archbishop of Canterbury, began the foundation of the Friars Preachers Church there, commonly called the Black Friars, as appeareth by a charter the 4th of Edward I., wherein is declared that Gregory de Rocksley, mayor of London, and the barons of the same city, granted and gave unto the said Archbishop Robert, two lanes or ways next the street of Baynard's Castle, and the tower of Montfichett, to be applied for the enlargement of the said church and place.

One other tower there was also situate on the river of Thames near unto the said Black Friars Church, on the west part thereof built at the citizens' charges, but by license and commandment of Edward I. and of Edward II., as appeareth by their grants; which tower was then finished, and so stood for the space of three hundred years, and was at the last taken down by the commandment of John Shaw, mayor of London, in the year 1502.

Another tower, or castle, also was there in the west part of the city pertaining to the king. For I read, that in the year 1087,

the 20th of William I., the city of London, with the Church of
St. Paul, being burned, Mauritius, then Bishop of London, afterward began the foundation of a new church, whereunto King
William, saith mine author, gave the choice stones of this castle
standing near to the bank of the river of Thames, at the west end
of the city. After this Mauritius, Richard his successor purchased
the streets about Paul's Church, compassing the same with a wall
of stone and gates. King Henry I. gave to this Richard so much
of the moat or wall of the castle, on the Thames side to the south,
as should be needful to make the said wall of the churchyard,
and so much more as should suffice to make a way without the
wall on the north side, &c.

This tower or castle thus destroyed, stood, as it may seem,
where now standeth the house called Bridewell. For notwithstanding the destruction of the said castle or tower, the house
remained large, so that the kings of this realm long after were
lodged there, and kept their courts; for until the 9th year of
Henry III. the courts of law and justice were kept in the king's
house, wheresoever he was lodged, and not elsewhere. And that
the kings have been lodged, and kept their law courts, in this
place, I could show you many authors of record, but for plain
proof this one may suffice. "*Hæc est finalis concordia, facta in
Curia Domini regis apud Sanct. Bridgid. London. a die Sancti
Michaelis in* 15 *dies, Anno regni regis Johannis* 7. *coram G. Fil.
Petri. Eustachio de Fauconberg, Johanne de Gestlinge, Osbart filio
Hervey, Walter De Crisping Justiciar. et aliis baronibus Domini
regis.*" More, as Matthew Paris hath, about the year 1210, King
John, in the 12th of his reign, summoned a parliament at St.
Bride's in London, where he exacted of the clergy and religious
persons the sum of one hundred thousand pounds; and besides
all this, the white monks were compelled to cancel their privileges, and to pay forty thousand pounds to the king, &c. This
house of St. Bride's of latter time being left, and not used by
the kings, fell to ruin, insomuch that the very platform thereof
remained for great part waste, and, as it were, but a laystall of
filth and rubbish; only a fair well remained there. A great part
of this house, namely, on the west, as hath been said, was given
to the Bishop of Salisbury; the other part towards the east
remaining waste until King Henry VIII. built a stately and

beautiful house thereupon, giving it to name Bridewell, of the parish and well there. This house he purposely built for the entertainment of the Emperor Charles V., who in the year 1522 came into this city, as I have showed in my Summary, Annals, and large Chronicles.

On the north-west side of the city, near unto Redcross Street, there was a tower, commonly called Barbican, or Burhkenning; * for that the same being placed on a high ground, and also built of some good height, was in old time as a watch-tower for the city, from whence a man might behold and view the whole city towards the south, and also into Kent, Sussex, and Surrey, and likewise every other way, east, north, or west.

Some other burhkennings, or watch-towers, there were of old time in and about the city, all which were repaired, yea, and others new built, by Gilbert de Clare, Earl of Gloucester, in the reign of King Henry III., when the barons were in arms, and held the city against the king; but the barons being reconciled to his favour in the year 1267, he caused all their burhkennings, watch-towers, and bulwarks, made and repaired by the said earl, to be plucked down, and the ditches to be filled up, so that nought of them might be seen to remain; and then was this burhkenning, amongst the rest, overthrown and destroyed; and although the ditch near thereunto, called Hound's Ditch, was stopped up, yet the street of long time after was called Hound's Ditch; and of late time more commonly called Barbican. The plot or seat of this burhkenning, or watch-tower, King Edward III., in the year 1336, and the 10th of his reign, gave unto Robert Ufford, Earl of Suffolk, by the name of his manor of Base Court, in the parish of St. Giles without Cripplegate, of London, commonly called the Barbican.

Tower Royal was of old time the king's house. King Stephen was there lodged; but sithence called the Queen's Wardrobe. The princess, mother to King Richard II. in the 4th of his reign was lodged there; being forced to fly from the Tower of London when the rebels possessed it. But on the 15th of June (saith Froissart), Wat Tyler being slain, the king went to this lady

---

* *Barbican.*—Stow's etymology will not explain the existence of the word in Old French, Old Spanish, and Low Latin. Its origin is doubtful, but it is usually derived from the Arabic.

princess his mother, then lodged in the Tower Royal, called the Queen's Wardrobe, where she had tarried two days and two nights; which tower (saith the Record of Edward III., the 36th year) was in the parish of St. Michel de Paternoster, &c. In the year 1386, King Richard, with Queen Anne his wife, kept their Christmas at Eltham, whither came to him Lion, King of Ermony, under pretence to reform peace betwixt the kings of England and France; but what his coming profited he only understood; for besides innumerable gifts that he received of the king and his nobles, the king lying then in this Tower Royal, at the Queen's Wardrobe in London, granted to him a charter of a thousand pounds by year during his life. He was, as he affirmed, chased out of his kingdom by the Tartarians. More concerning this tower shall you read when you come to Vintry Ward, in which it standeth.

Sernes Tower in Bucklesbury was sometime the king's house. Edward III., in the 18th of his reign, appointed his exchange of moneys therein to be kept; and in the 32nd, he gave the same tower to his free chapel of St. Stephen at Westminster.

Of Schools and other Houses of Learning.

"In the reign of King Stephen and of Henry II.," saith Fitz-stephen, "there were in London three principal churches, which had famous schools, either by privilege and ancient dignity, or by favour of some particular persons, as of doctors which were accounted notable and renowned for knowledge in philosophy. And there were other inferior schools also. Upon festival days the masters made solemn meetings in the churches, where their scholars disputed logically and demonstratively; some bringing enthymems, other perfect syllogisms; some disputed for show, other to trace out the truth; cunning sophisters were thought brave scholars when they flowed with words; others used fallacies; rhetoricians spake aptly to persuade, observing the precepts of art, and omitting nothing that might serve their purpose; the boys of diverse schools did cap or pot verses, and contended of the principles of grammar; there were some which on the other side with epigrams and rymes, nipping and quipping their fellows, and the faults of others, though suppressing their names, moved thereby much laughter among their auditors." Hitherto Fitzstephen, for schools and scholars, and for their exercises in the city in his days; sithence the which time, as to me it seemeth, by the increase of colleges and students in the universities of Oxford and Cambridge, the frequenting of schools, and exercises of scholars in the city, as had been accustomed, hath much decreased.

The three principal churches which had these famous schools by privileges, must needs be the cathedral church of St. Paul for one; seeing, that by a general council, holden in the year of Christ 1176, at Rome, in the patriarchy of Lateran, it was decreed, that every cathedral church should have his school-master to teach poor scholars, and others as had been accustomed, and that no man should take any reward for license to teach. The second, as most ancient, may seem to have been the monastery of St. Peter's at Westminster, whereof Ingulphus, Abbot of Croyland, in the reign of William the Conqueror,* writeth thus:—"I, Ingulphus, an humble servant of God, born of English parents, in the most beautiful city of London, for to attain to learning, was first put to Westminster, and after to study of Oxford," &c. And writing in praise of Queen Edgitha, wife to Edward the Confessor: "I have seen her," saith he, "often when being a boy, I came to see my father dwelling in the king's court, and often coming from school, when I met her, she would oppose me, touching my learning and lesson; and falling from grammar to logic, wherein she had some knowledge, she would subtilly conclude an argument with me, and by her hand-maiden give me three or four pieces of money, and send me unto the palace where I should receive some victuals, and then be dismissed."

The third school seemeth to have been in the monastery of St. Saviour, at Bermondsey in Southwark; for other priories, as of St. John by Smithfield, St. Bartholomew in Smithfield, St. Mary Overies in Southwark, and that of the Holy Trinity by Aldgate, were all of later foundation, and the friaries, colleges, and hospitals, in this city, were raised since them in the reigns

* The Chronicle ascribed to Ingulphus was forged in the beginning of the fifteenth century.

of Henry III., Edward I., II., and III., &c. All which houses had their schools, though not so famous as these first named.

But touching schools more lately advanced in this city, I read, that King Henry V., having suppressed the priories aliens, whereof some were about London; namely, one hospital, called Our Lady of Rouncivall, by Charing Cross; one other hospital in Oldbourne; one other without Cripplegate; and the fourth without Aldersgate; besides other that are now worn out of memory, and whereof there is no monument remaining, more than Rouncivall converted to a brotherhood, which continued till the reign of Henry VIII. or Edward VI.; this, I say, and other their schools being broken up and ceased, King Henry VI., in the 24th of the reign, by patent, appointed that there should be in London grammar schools, besides St. Paul's, at St. Martin's le Grand, St. Mary le Bow in Cheap, St. Dunstan's in the west, and St. Anthony's. And in the next year, to wit, 1394, the said king ordained by parliament that four other grammar schools should be erected, to wit, in the parishes of St. Andrew in Oldbourne, Allhallows the Great in Thames Street, St. Peter's upon Cornhill, and in the hospital of St. Thomas of Acons in West Cheap; since the which time as divers schools, by suppressing of religious houses, whereof they were members, in the reign of Henry VIII., have been decayed, so again have some others been newly erected, and founded for them; as namely Paul's School, in place of an old ruined house, was built in most ample manner, and largely endowed, in the year 1512, by John Colet, Doctor of Divinity, Dean of Paul's, for one hundred and fifty-three poor men's children, for which there was ordained a master, surmaster or usher, and a chaplain. Again, in the year 1553, after the erection of Christ's Hospital, in the late dissolved house of the Gray Friars, a great number of poor children being taken in, a school was also ordained there at the citizens' charges. Also, in the year 1561, the Merchant Taylors of London founded one notable free grammar school, in the parish of St. Laurence Poultney by Candlewick Street, Richard Hils, late master of that company, having given five hundred pounds towards the purchase of a house, called the Manor of the Rose, sometime the Duke of Buckingham's, wherein the school is kept. As for the meeting of the schoolmasters on festival days, at festival churches, and the disputing of their scholars logically, &c., whereof I have before spoken, the same was long since discontinued; but the arguing of the schoolboys about the principles of grammar hath been continued even till our time; for I myself, in my youth, have yearly seen, on the eve of St. Bartholomew the Apostle, the scholars of divers grammar schools repair unto the churchyard of St. Bartholomew, the priory in Smithfield, where upon a bank boarded about under a tree, some one scholar hath stepped up, and there hath opposed and answered, till he were by some better scholar overcome and put down; and then the overcomer taking the place, did like as the first; and in the end the best opposers and answerers had rewards, which I observed not but it made both good schoolmasters, and also good scholars, diligently against such times to prepare themselves for the obtaining of this garland. I remember there repaired to these exercises, amongst others, the masters and scholars of the free schools of St. Paul's in London, of St. Peter's at Westminster, of St. Thomas Acon's Hospital, and of St. Anthony's Hospital; whereof the last named commonly presented the best scholars, and had the prize in those days.

This priory of St. Bartholomew being surrendered to Henry VIII., those disputations of scholars in that place surceased; and was again, only for a year or twain, in the reign of Edward VI., revived in the cloister of Christ's Hospital, where the best scholars, then still of St. Anthony's School, were rewarded with bows and arrows of silver, given to them by Sir Martin Bowes, goldsmith. Nevertheless, however the encouragement failed, the scholars of Paul's, meeting with them of St. Anthony's, would call them Anthony pigs, and they again would call the other, pigeons of Paul's, because many pigeons were bred in St. Paul's Church, and St. Anthony was always figured with a pig following him; and mindful of the former usage, did for a long season disorderly in the open street provoke one another with, "*Salve tu quoque, placet tibi mecum disputare ?*" "*Placet.*" And so proceeding from this to questions in grammar, they usually fell from words to blows with their satchels full of books, many times in great heaps, that they troubled the streets and passengers; so that finally they were restrained, with the decay of St. Anthony's School. Out of this school have sprung divers famous persons, whereof although time hath buried the names of many, yet in mine own remembrance may be numbered these following :—Sir Thomas More, knight, Lord Chancellor of England ; Dr. Nicholas Heath, sometime Bishop of Rochester, after of Worcester, and lastly Archbishop of York and Lord Chancellor of England ; Doctor John Whitgift, Bishop of Worcester, and after Archbishop of Canterbury, &c.

Of later time, in the year of Christ 1582, there was founded a public lecture on chirurgery, to be read in the College of Physicians in Knightriders Street, to begin in the year 1584, on the sixth of May, and so to be continued for ever, twice every week, on Wednesday and Friday, by the honourable Baron, John Lord Lombley, and the learned Richard Caldwell, doctor in physic, the reader whereof to be Richard Forster, doctor of physic, during his life.

Furthermore, about the same time there was also begun a mathematical lecture, to be read in a fair old chapel, built by Simon Eyre, within the Leaden Hall ; whereof a learned citizen born, named Thomas Hood, was the first reader. But this chapel, and other parts of that hall, being employed for stowage of goods taken out of a great Spanish carrack, the said lecture ceased any more to be read, and was then in the year 1588 read in the house of Master Thomas Smith in Grass Street, &c.

Last of all, Sir Thomas Gresham, knight, agent to the queen's highness, by his last will and testament made in the year 1579, gave the Royal Exchange, and all the buildings thereunto appertaining ; that is to say, the one moiety to the mayor and commonalty of London and their successors, upon trust that they perform as shall be declared ; and the other moiety to the mercers in like confidence. The mayor and commonalty are to find four to read lectures of divinity, astronomy, music, and geometry, within his dwelling-house in Bishopsgate Street, and to bestow the sum of two hundred pounds ; to wit, fifty pounds the piece, &c. The mercers likewise are to find three readers, that is, in civil law, physic, and rhetoric, within the same dwelling-house, the sum of one hundred and fifty pounds ; to every reader, fifty pounds, &c. : which gift hath been since that time confirmed by parliament, to take effect and begin after the decease of the Lady

Anne Gresham, which happened in the year 1596, and so to continue for ever. Whereupon the lecturers were accordingly chosen and appointed to have begun their readings in the month of June 1597; whose names were, Anthony Wootton, for divinity; Doctor Mathew Gwynne, for physic; Doctor Henry Mountlow, for the civil law; Doctor John Bull, for music; Brerewood, for astronomy; Henry Briggs, for geometry; and Caleb Willis, for rhetoric. These lectures are read daily, Sundays excepted, in the term times, by every one upon his day, in the morning betwixt nine and ten, in Latin; in the afternoon, betwixt two and three, in English; save that Dr. Bull is dispensed with, to read the music lecture in English only upon two several days, Thursday and Saturday, in the afternoons, betwixt three and four of the clock.

Houses of Students in the Common Law.

BUT besides all this, there is in and about this city a whole University, as it were, of students, practisers or pleaders, and judges of the laws of this realm, not living of common stipends, as in other universities it is for the most part done, but of their own private maintenance, as being altogether fed either by their places or practice, or otherwise by their proper revenue, or exhibition of parents and friends; for that the younger sort are either gentlemen or the sons of gentlemen, or of other most wealthy persons. Of these houses there be at this day fourteen in all; whereof nine do stand within the liberties of this city, and five in the suburbs thereof; to wit:

Within the liberties.

Sergeants' Inn in Fleet Street, Sergeants' Inn in Chancery Lane; for judges and sergeants only.

The Inner Temple, the Middle Temple, in Fleet Street; houses of court.

Clifford's Inn in Fleet Street, Thavies Inn in Oldborne, Furnival's Inn in Oldborne, Barnard's Inn in Oldborne, Staple Inn in Oldborne; houses of Chancery.

Without the liberties.

Gray's Inn in Oldborne, Lincoln's Inn in Chancery Lane by the old Temple ; houses of court.

Clement's Inn, New Inn, Lyon's Inn ; houses of Chancery, without Temple Bar, in the liberty of Westminster.

There was sometime an inn of sergeants in Oldborne, as you may read of Scrop's Inn over against St. Andrew's Church.

There was also one other inn of Chancery, called Chester's Inn for the nearness to the Bishop of Chester's house, but more commonly termed Strand Inn, for that it stood in Strand Street, and near unto Strand Bridge without Temple Bar, in the liberty of the duchy of Lancaster. This inn of Chancery, with other houses near adjoining, were pulled down in the reign of Edward VI. by Edward Duke of Somerset, who in place thereof raised that large and beautiful house, but yet unfinished, called Somerset House.

There was, moreover, in the reign of King Henry I., a tenth house of Chancery, mentioned by Justice Fortescue in his book of the laws of England, but where it stood, or when it was abandoned, I cannot find, and therefore I will leave it, and return to the rest.

The Houses of Court be replenished partly with young students, and partly with graduates and practisers of the law ; but the Inns of Chancery, being, as it were, provinces, severally subjected to the Inns of Court, be chiefly furnished with officers, attorneys, solicitors, and clerks, that follow the courts of the King's Bench or Common Pleas ; and yet there want not some other being young students, that come thither sometimes from one of the universities, and sometimes immediately from grammar schools ; and these having spent some time in studying upon the first elements and grounds of the law, and having performed the exercise of their own houses (called Boltas Mootes,* and putting of cases), they proceed to be admitted, and become students in some of these four houses or inns of court, where continuing by

---

* *Boltas Mootes*, meetings for disputation, that is, for bolting or sifting a case put for argument. So in Coriolanus, iii. 1 :—

> " He is ill-schooled
> In bolted language ; meal and bran together
> He throws without distinction."

the space of seven years or thereabouts, they frequent readings, meetings, boltings, and other learned exercises, whereby growing ripe in the knowledge of the laws, and approved withal to be of honest conversation, they are either, by the general consent of the benchers or readers, being of the most ancient, grave, and judicial men of every inn of the court, or by the special privilege of the present reader, there selected and called to the degree of utter barristers, and so enabled to be common counsellors, and to practise the law, both in their chambers and at the bars.

Of these, after that they be called to a further step of preferment, called the Bench, there are twain every year chosen among the benchers of every Inn of Court to be Readers there, who do make their readings at two times in the year also; that is, one in Lent, and the other at the beginning of August.

And for the help of young students in every of the Inns of Chancery, they do likewise choose out of every one Inn of Court a Reader, being no bencher, but an utter barrister there, of ten or twelve years' continuance, and of good profit in study. Now, from these of the said degree of counsellors, or utter barristers, having continued therein the space of fourteen or fifteen years at the least, the chiefest and best learned are by the benchers elected to increase the number, as I said, of the bench amongst them; and so in their time do become first single, and then double, readers to the students of those houses of court; after which last reading they be named apprentices at the law, and, in default of a sufficient number of sergeants at law, these are, at the pleasure of the prince, to be advanced to the places of sergeants; out of which number of sergeants also the void places of judges are likewise ordinarily filled; albeit, now and then some be advanced, by the special favour of the prince, to the estate, dignity, and place, both of sergeant and judge, as it were in one instant. But from thenceforth they hold not any room in those inns of court, being translated to one of the said two inns, called Sergeant's Inns, where none but the sergeants and judges do converse.

Of Orders and Customs.

OF orders and customs in this city of old time, Fitzstephen saith as followeth: "Men of all trades, sellers of all sorts of wares,

labourers in every work, every morning are in their distinct and
several places : furthermore, in London, upon the river side,
between the wine in ships and the wine to be sold in taverns,
is a common cookery, or Cooks' Row ; there daily, for the season
of the year, men might have meat, roast, sod, or fried ; fish, flesh,
fowls, fit for rich and poor.   If any come suddenly to any citizen
from afar, weary, and not willing to tarry till the meat be bought
and dressed, while the servant bringeth water for his master's
hands, and fetcheth bread, he shall have immediately from the
river's side all viands whatsoever he desireth : what multitude
soever, either of soldiers or strangers, do come to the city, whatsoever hour, day or night, according to their pleasures may refresh
themselves ; and they which delight in delicateness may be satis-
fied with as delicate dishes there as may be found elsewhere.
And this Cooks' Row is very necessary to the city ; and, according
to Plato in Gorgias, next to physic is the office of cooks, as part
of a city.

"Without one of the gates is a plain field, both in name * and
deed, where every Friday, unless it be a solemn bidden holy day,
is a notable show of horses to be sold ; earls, barons, knights,
and citizens repair thither to see or to buy ; there may you of
pleasure see amblers pacing it delicately ; there may you see
trotters fit for men of arms, sitting more hardly ; there may you
have notable young horses, not yet broken ; there may you have
strong steeds, well limbed geldings, whom the buyers do specially
regard for pace and swiftness ; the boys which ride these horses,
sometime two, sometime three, do run races for wagers, with a
desire of praise, or hope of victory.   In another part of that field
are to be sold all implements of husbandry, as also fat swine,
milch kine, sheep, and oxen ; there stand also mares and horses
fit for ploughs and teams, with their young colts by them.   At
this city, merchant strangers of all nations had their quays and
wharfs ; the Arabians sent gold ; the Sabians spice and frank-
incense ; the Scythian armour, Babylon oil, Indian purple
garments, Egypt precious stones, Norway and Russia amber-
gris and sables, and the Frenchmen wine.   According to the
truth of Chronicles, this city is ancienter than Rome, built of the
ancient Troyans and of Brute, before that was built by Romulus

* Smooth field, Smithfield.

and Remus ; and therefore useth the ancient customs of Rome. This city, even as Rome, is divided into wards ; it hath yearly sheriffs instead of consuls ; it hath the dignity of senators in aldermen. It hath under officers, common sewers, and conduits in streets ; according to the quality of causes, it hath general courts and assemblies upon appointed days. I do not think that there is any city wherein are better customs, in frequenting the churches, in serving God, in keeping holy days, in giving alms, in entertaining strangers, in solemnizing marriages, in furnishing banquets, celebrating funerals, and burying dead bodies.

" The only plagues of London are immoderate quaffing among the foolish sort, and often casualties by fire. Most part of the bishops, abbots, and great lords of the land have houses there, whereunto they resort, and bestow much, when they are called to parliament by the king, or to council by their metropolitan, or otherwise by their private business."

Thus far Fitzstephen, of the estate of things in his time, whereunto may be added the present, by conference whereof the alteration will easily appear.

Men of trades and sellers of wares in this city have oftentimes since changed their places, as they have found their best advantage. For whereas mercers and haberdashers used to keep their shops in West Cheap, of later time they held them on London Bridge, where partly they yet remain. The goldsmiths of Gutheron's Lane and Old Exchange are now for the most part removed into the south side of West Cheap, the pepperers and grocers of Soper's Lane are now in Bucklesbury, and other places dispersed. The drapers of Lombard Street and of Cornhill are seated in Candlewick Street and Watling Street ; the skinners from St. Mary Pellipers, or at the Axe, into Budge Row and Walbrook ; the stockfishmongers in Thames Street ; wet fishmongers in Knightriders Street and Bridge Street ; the ironmongers, of Ironmongers' Lane and Old Jury, into Thames Street ; the vintners from the Vintry into divers places. But the brewers for the more part remain near to the friendly water of Thames ; the butchers in East Cheap, St. Nicholas Shambles, and the Stocks Market ; the hosiers, of old time in Hosier Lane, near unto Smithfield, are since removed into Cordwainer Street, the upper part thereof by Bow Church, and last of all into Birch-overies Lane by Cornhill; the shoemakers and curriers of Cord-wainer Street removed, the one to St. Martin's le Grand, the other to London Wall near unto Moorgate; the founders remain by themselves in Lothbury; cooks, or pastelers, for the more part in Thames Street, the other dispersed into divers parts; poulterers of late removed out of the Poultry, betwixt the Stocks and the great conduit in Cheap, into Grass Street and St. Nicholas shambles; bowyers, from Bowyers' Row by Ludgate into divers places, and almost worn out, with the fletchers; pater-noster makers of old time, or bede-makers, and text-writers, are gone out of Paternoster Row, and are called stationers of Paul's Churchyard; patten-makers, of St. Margaret, Pattens' Lane, clean worn out; labourers every work-day are to be found in Cheap, about Soper's Land End; horse-coursers and sellers of oxen, sheep, swine, and such like, remain in their old market of Smithfield, &c.

That merchants of all nations had their quays and wharfs at this city, whereunto they brought their merchandises before and in the reign of Henry II., mine author wrote of his own know-ledge to be true, though for the antiquity of the city he took the common opinion. Also that this city was in his time and afore divided into wards, had yearly sheriffs, aldermen, general courts, and assemblies, and such like notes by him set down, in commendation of the citizens, whereof there is no question, he wrote likewise of his own experience, as being born and brought up amongst them.

And to confirm his opinion, concerning merchandises then hither transported, whereof happily may be some argument, Thomas Clifford (before Fitzstephen's time), writing of Edward the Confessor, saith to this effect: "King Edward, intending to make his sepulchre at Westminster; for that it was near to the famous city of London, and the river of Thames, that brought in all kind of merchandises from all parts of the world, &c." And William of Malmesbury, that lived in the reign of William I. and II., Henry I., and King Stephen, calleth this a noble city, full of wealthy citizens, frequented with the trade of merchandises from all parts of the world. Also I read, in divers records, that of old time no woad was stowed or harboured in this city, but all was presently sold in the ships, except by licence purchased of the sheriffs, till of more later time; to wit, in the year 1236, Andrew Bokerell, being mayor, by assent of the principal citizens, the merchants of Amiens, Nele, and Corby, purchased letters insealed with the common seal of this city, that they when they come might harbour their woads, and therefore should give the mayor every year fifty marks sterling; and the same year they gave one hundred pounds towards the conveying of water from Tybourn to this city. Also the merchants of Normandy made fine for license to harbour their woads till it was otherwise provided, in the year 1263, Thomas Fitz Thomas being mayor, &c., which proveth that then as afore, they were here amongst other nations privileged.

It followeth in Fitzstephen, that the plagues of London in that time were immoderate quaffing among fools, and often casualties by fire. For the first—to wit, of quaffing—it continueth as afore, or rather is mightily increased, though greatly qualified among the poorer sort, not of any holy abstinence, but of mere necessity, ale and beer being small, and wines in price above their reach. As for prevention of casualties by fire, the houses in this city being then built all of timber, and covered with thatch of straw or reed, it was long since thought good policy in our forefathers wisely to provide, namely, in the year of Christ 1189, the first of Richard I., Henry Fitzalwine being then mayor, that all men in this city should build their houses of stone up to a certain height, and to cover them with slate or baked tile; since which time, thanks be given to God, there hath not happened the like often consuming fires in this city as afore.

But now in our time, instead of these enormities, others are come in place no less meet to be reformed; namely, purpres-tures, or encroachments on the highways, lanes, and common grounds, in and about this city; whereof a learned gentleman and grave citizen hath not many years since written and ex-hibited a book to the mayor and commonalty; which book, whether the same have been by them read and diligently con-sidered upon, I know not, but sure I am nothing is reformed since concerning this matter.

Then the number of cars, drays, carts, and coaches, more than hath been accustomed, the streets and lanes being straitened, must needs be dangerous, as daily experience proveth.

The coachman rides behind the horse tails, lasheth them, and looketh not behind him; the drayman sitteth and sleepeth on his dray, and letteth his horse lead him home. I know that, by the good laws and customs of this city, shod carts * are forbidden to enter the same, except upon reasonable cause, as service of the prince, or such like, they be tolerated. Also that the fore horse of every carriage should be led by hand; but these good orders are not observed. Of old time coaches were not known in this island, but chariots or whirlicotes, then so called, and they only used of princes or great estates, such as had their footmen about them; and for example to note, I read that Richard II., being threatened by the rebels of Kent, rode from the Tower of London to the Mile's End, and with him his mother, because she was sick and weak, in a whirlicote, the Earls of Buckingham, Kent, Warwick, and Oxford, Sir Thomas Percy, Sir Robert Knowles, the Mayor of London, Sir Aubrey de Vere, that bare the king's sword, with other knights and esquires attending on horseback. But in the next year, the said King Richard took to wife Anne, daughter to the King of Bohemia, that first brought hither the riding upon side-saddles; and so was the riding in whirlicotes and chariots forsaken, except at coronations and such like spectacles; but now of late years the use of coaches, brought out of Germany, is taken up, and made so common, as there is neither distinction of time nor difference of persons observed; for the world runs on wheels with many whose parents were glad to go on foot.

Last of all, mine author † in this chapter hath these words: "Most part of the bishops, abbots, and great lords of the land, as if they were citizens and freemen of London, had many fair houses to resort unto, and many rich and wealthy gentlemen spent their money there." And in another place he hath these words: "Every Sunday in Lent a fresh company of young men comes into the fields on horseback, and the best horseman conducteth the rest; then march forth the citizen's sons, and other young men, with disarmed lances and shields, and practise feats of war; many courtiers likewise and attendants of noble-men repair to this exercise, and whilst the hope of victory doth

* *Shod carts*, carts bound with iron.
† Fitzstephen.

inflame their minds, they do show good proof how serviceable they would be in martial affairs, &c." Again he saith : " This city, in the troublesome time of King Stephen, showed at a muster twenty thousand armed horsemen and forty thousand footmen, serviceable for the wars, &c." All which sayings of the said author, well considered, do plainly prove that in those days the inhabitants and repairers to this city, of what estate soever, spiritual or temporal, having houses here, lived together in good amity with the citizens, every man observing the customs and orders of the city ; and those to be contributary to charges here, rather than in any part of the land wheresoever, this city, being the heart of the realm, the king's chamber and prince's seat, whereunto they made repair, and showed their forces, both of horses and of men ; which caused in troublesome time, as of King Stephen, the musters of this city to be so great in number.

And here, to touch somewhat of greater families and house-holds kept in former times by noblemen, and great estates of this realm, according to their honours or dignities, I have seen an account made by H. Leicester, cofferer to Thomas Earl of Lancaster, for one whole year's expenses in the earl's house, from the day next after Michaelmas, in the seventh year of Edward II., until Michaelmas in the eighth year of the same king, amounting to the sum of £7957, 13s. 4½d. as followeth :

To wit, in the pantry, buttery, and kitchen, £3405, &c. ; for one hundred and eighty-four tuns, one pipe of red or claret wine, and one tun of white wine bought for the house, £104, 17s. 6d.

For grocery ware, £180, 17s.

For six barrels of sturgeon, £19.

For six thousand eight hundred stock-fishes, so called for dried fishes of all sorts, as lings, haberdines,* and other, £41, 6s. 7d.

For one thousand seven hundred and fourteen pounds of wax, with vermilion and turpentine to make red wax, £314, 7s. 4¼d.

For two thousand three hundred and nineteen pounds of tallow candles for the household, and one thousand eight hundred and seventy of lights for Paris candles, called perchers,† £31, 14s. 3d.

---

* *Haberdine*, salt cod.
† *Percher*, a large wax candle, such as was placed on altars.

Expenses on the earl's great horses, and the keeper's wages, £486, 4s. 3¼d.

Linen cloth for the earl and his chaplains, and for the pantry, £43, 17s.

For one hundred and twenty-nine dozen of parchment, with ink, £4, 8s. 3¼d.

Sum, £5230, 17s. 7¼d.

Item, for two cloths of scarlet for the earl against Christmas, one cloth of russet for the Bishop of Angew, seventy cloths of blue for the knights (as they were then termed), fifteen cloths of medley for the lord's clerks, twenty-eight cloths for the esquires, fifteen cloths for officers, nineteen cloths for grooms, five cloths for archers, four cloths for minstrels and carpenters, with the sharing and carriage for the earl's liveries at Christmas, £460, 15s.

Item, for seven furs of variable miniver (or powdered ermine), seven hoods of purple, three hundred and ninety-five furs of budge * for the liveries of barons, knights, and clerks, one hundred and twenty-three furs of lambs for esquires, bought at Christmas, £147, 17s. 8d.

Item, sixty-five cloths, saffron colour, for the barons and knights in summer, twelve red cloths, mixed, for clerks, twenty-six cloths, ray, for esquires, one cloth, ray, for officers' coats in summer, and four cloths, ray, for carpets in the hall, for £345, 13s. 8d.

Item, one hundred pieces of green silk for the knights, fourteen budge furs for surcoats, thirteen hoods of budge for clerks, and seventy-five furs of lambs for the lord's liveries in summer, with canvas and cords to truss them, £72, 19s.

Item, saddles for the lord's liveries in summer, £51, 6s. 8d.

Item, one saddle for the earl of the prince's arms, 40s.

Sum, £1079, 18s. 3d.

Item, for things bought, whereof cannot be read in my note, £241, 14s. 1¼d.

For horses lost in service of the earl, £8, 6s. 8d.

Fees paid to earls, barons, knights, and esquires, £623, 15s. 5d.

In gifts to knights of France, the Queen of England's nurses, to the Countess of Warren, esquires, minstrels, messengers, and riders, £92, 14s.

Item, one hundred and sixty-eight yards of russet cloth, and

---

* *Budge*, fine lambskin, with the wool dressed outwards.

twenty-four coats for poor men, with money given to the poor on Maundy Thursday, £8, 16s. 7d.

Item, twenty-four silver dishes, so many saucers and so many cups for the buttery, one pair of paternosters, and one silver coffin, bought this year, £103, 5s. 6d.

To divers messengers about the earl's business, £34, 19s. 8d.

In the earl's chamber, £5.

To divers men for the earl's old debts, £88, 16s. 0¾d.

Sum, £1207, 7s. 11¾d.

The expenses of the countess at Pickering for the time of this account, as in the pantry, buttery, kitchen, and other places, concerning these offices, £285, 13s. 0½d.

In wine, wax, spices, cloths, furs, and other things for the countess' wardrobe, £154, 7s. 4½d.

Sum, £439, 8s. 6¼d.

Sum total of the whole expenses, £7957, 13s. 4½d.

Thus much for this Earl of Lancaster.

More I read, that in the 14th of the same Edward II., Hugh Spencer the elder (condemned by the commonalty) was banished the realm ; at which time it was found by inquisition that the said Spencer had in sundry shires, fifty-nine manors : he had twenty-eight thousand sheep, one thousand oxen and steers, one thousand two hundred kine with their calves, forty mares with their colts, one hundred and sixty drawing horses, two thousand hogs, three hundred bullocks, forty tuns of wine, six hundred bacons, eighty carcases of Martinmas beef, six hundred muttons in larder, ten tuns of cider ; his armour, plate, jewels, and ready money, better than £10,000, thirty-six sacks of wool, and a library of books. Thus much the record, which provision for household showeth a great family there to be kept.

Nearer to our time, I read, in the 36th of Henry VI., that the greater estates of the realm being called up to London.

The Earl of Salisbury came with five hundred men on horseback, and was lodged in the Herber.

Richard, Duke of York, with four hundred men, lodged at Baynard's Castle.

The Dukes of Exeter and Somerset, with eight hundred men.

The Earl of Northumberland, the Lord Egremont, and the Lord Clifford, with fifteen hundred men.

Richard Nevill, Earl of Warwick, with six hundred men, all in red jackets, embroidered with ragged staves before and behind, and was lodged in Warwick Lane; in whose house there was oftentimes six oxen eaten at a breakfast, and every tavern was full of his meat: for he that had any acquaintance in that house might have there so much of sodden and roast meat as he could prick and carry upon a long dagger.

Richard Redman, Bishop of Ely, 1500, the 17th of Henry VII., besides his great family, housekeeping, alms dish, and relief to the poor, wheresover he was lodged, in his travelling, when at his coming or going to or from any town, the bells being rung, all the poor would come together, to whom he gave every one sixpence at the least.

And now to note of our own time somewhat. Omitting in this place, Thomas Wolsey, Archbishop of York, and cardinal, I refer the reader to my Annals, where I have set down the order of his house and household, passing all other subjects of his time. His servants, daily attending in his house, were near about four hundred, omitting his servants' servants, which were many.

Nicholas West, Bishop of Ely, in the year 1532, kept continually in his house an hundred servants, giving to the one half of them 53s. 4d. the piece yearly; to the other half each 40s. the piece; to every one for his winter gown four yards of broadcloth, and for his summer coat three yards and a half: he daily gave at his gates, besides bread and drink, warm meat to two hundred poor people.

The housekeeping of Edward, late Earl of Derby, is not to be forgotten, who had two hundred and twenty men in check roll: his feeding aged persons twice every day, sixty and odd, besides all comers, thrice a week, appointed for his dealing * days, and every Good Friday two thousand seven hundred, with meat, drink, and money.

Thomas Audley, lord chancellor, his family of gentlemen before him, in coats guarded † with velvet, and chains of gold; his yeomen after him in the same livery, not guarded.

William Paulet, lord great master, Marquis of Winchester,

---

* *Dealing*, distributing, as in whist.
　† *Guarded*, embroidered.　So Bassanio orders that Lancelot Gobbo shall have "a livery more guarded than his fellows'."

kept the like number of gentlemen and yeomen in a livery of Reading tawny, and great relief at his gate.

Thomas Lord Cromwell, Earl of Essex, kept the like or greater number in a livery of grey marble; the gentlemen guarded with velvet, the yeomen with the same cloth, yet their skirts large enough for their friends to sit upon them.

Edward, Duke of Somerset, was not inferior in keeping a number of tall and comely gentlemen and yeomen, though his house was then in building, and most of his men were lodged abroad.

The late Earl of Oxford, father to him that now liveth, hath been noted within these forty years to have ridden into this city, and to his house by London Stone, with eighty gentlemen in a livery of Reading tawny, and chains of gold about their necks, before him, and one hundred tall yeomen, in the like livery, to follow him without chains, but all having his cognisance of the blue boar embroidered on their left shoulder.

These, as all other of their times, gave great relief to the poor. I myself, in that declining time of charity, have oft seen at the Lord Cromwell's gate in London more than two hundred persons served twice every day with bread, meat, and drink sufficient; for he observed that ancient and charitable custom, as all prelates, noblemen, or men of honour and worship, his predecessors, had done before him; whereof somewhat to note for example, Venerable Bede writeth, that prelates of his time having peradventure but wooden churches, had notwithstanding on their board at their meals one alms dish, into the which was carved some good portion of meat out of every other dish brought to their table; all which was given to the poor, besides the fragments left, in so much as in hard time, a poor prelate wanting victuals, hath caused his alms dish, being silver, to be divided among the poor, therewith to shift as they could, till God should send them better store.

Such a prelate was Ethelwald, Bishop of Winchester, in the reign of King Edgar, about the year of Christ 963 : he in a great famine sold away all the sacred vessels of his church for to relieve the almost starved people, saying that there was no reason that the senseless temples of God should abound in riches, and lively temples of the Holy Ghost to lack it.

Walter de Suffield, Bishop of Norwich, was of the like mind; about the year 1245. in a time of great dearth, he sold all his plate, and distributed it to the poor every pennyworth.

Robert Winchelsea, Archbishop of Canterbury, about the year 1293, besides the daily fragments of his house, gave every Friday and Sunday, unto every beggar that came to his gate, a loaf of bread sufficient for that day, and there more usually, every such alms day, in time of dearth, to the number of five thousand, and otherwise four thousand, at the least; more, he used every great festival day to give one hundred and fifty pence to so many poor people, to send daily meat, bread, and drink, to such as by age or sickness were not able to fetch his alms, and to send meat, money, and apparel to such as he thought needed it.

I read, in 1171, that Henry II., after his return into England, did penance for the slaughter of Thomas Becket, of whom (a sore dearth increasing) ten thousand persons, from the first of April till new corn was inned, were daily fed and sustained.

More, I find recorded, that in the year 1236, the 20th of Henry III., William de Haverhull, the king's treasurer, was commanded, that upon the day of the Circumcision of our Lord, six thousand poor people should be fed at Westminster, for the state of the king, queen, and their children. The like commandment the said King Henry gave to Hugh Gifford and William Browne, that upon Friday next after the Epiphany, they should cause to be fed in the great half at Windsor, at a good fire, all the poor and needy children that could be found, and the king's children being weighed and measured, their weight and measure to be distributed for their good estates. These few examples for charity of kings may suffice.

I read, in the reign of Edward III., that Richard de Bury, Bishop of Durham, did weekly bestow for the relief of the poor eight quarters of wheat made into bread, besides his alms dish, fragments of his house, and great sums of money given to the poor when he journeyed. And that these alms dishes were as well used at the tables of noblemen as of prelates, one note may suffice in this place.

I read, in the year 1452, that Richard, Duke of York, then claiming the crown, the Lord Rivers should have passed the sea about the king's business, but staying at Plymouth till his money was spent, and then sending for more, the Duke of Somerset sent him the image of St. George in silver and gold, to be sold, with the alms dish of the Duke of Gloucester, which was also of great price, for coin had they none.

To end of orders and customs in this city, also of great families kept by honourable persons thither repairing, and of charitable alms of old times given, I say, for conclusion, that all noble persons, and other of honour and worship, in former times lodging in this city, or liberties thereof, did without grudging bear their parts in charges with the citizens, according to their estimated estates, as I have before said, and could prove by examples ; but let men call to mind Sir Thomas Cromwell, then lord privy seal and vicar-general, lying in the City of London ; he bare his charges to the great muster there in A.D. 1539 ; he sent his men in great number to the Mile's End, and after them their armour in cars, with their coats of white cloth, the arms of this city ; to wit, a red cross, and a sword, on the breast and back ; which armour and coats they ware amongst the citizens, without any difference, and marched through the city to Westminster.

Sports and Pastimes of old Time used in this City.

"Let us now," saith Fitzstephen, "come to the sports and pastimes, seeing it is fit that a city should not only be commodious and serious, but also merry and sportful ; whereupon in the seals of the popes, until the time of Pope Leo, on the one side was St. Peter fishing, with a key over him, reached as it were by the hand of God out of heaven, and about it this verse :

' Tu pro me navem liquisti, suscipe clavem.'

And on the other side was a city, and this inscription on it : ' *Aurea Roma.*' Likewise to the praise of Augustus Cæsar and the city, in respect of the shows and sports was written :

' Nocte pluit tota, redeunt spectacula mane,' &c.

' All night it raines, and shows at morrow tide returne again,
And Cæsar with almighty Jove hath matcht an equal raign.'

"But London, for the shows upon theatres, and comical pastimes, hath holy plays, representations of miracles, which holy confessors have wrought, or representations of torments wherein the constancy of martyrs appeared. Every year also at Shrove Tuesday, that we may begin with children's sports, seeing we all have been children, the schoolboys do bring cocks of the game to their master, and all the forenoon they delight themselves in cock-fighting : after dinner, all the youths go into the fields to play at the ball.

"The scholars of every school have their ball, or baton, in their hands ; the ancient and wealthy men of the city come forth on horseback to see the sport of the young men, and to take part of the pleasure in beholding their agility. Every Friday in Lent a fresh company of young men comes into the field on horseback, and the best horseman conducteth the rest. Then march forth the citizens' sons, and other young men, with disarmed lances and shields, and there they practise feats of war. Many courtiers likewise, when the king lieth near, and attendants of noblemen, do repair to these exercises ; and while the hope of victory doth inflame their minds, do show good proof how serviceable they would be in martial affairs.

"In Easter holidays they fight battles on the water ; a shield is hung upon a pole, fixed in the midst of the stream, a boat is prepared without oars, to be carried by violence of the water, and in the fore part thereof standeth a young man, ready to give charge upon the shield with his lance ; if so be he breaketh his lance against the shield, and doth not fall, he is thought to have performed a worthy deed ; if so be, without breaking his lance, he runneth strongly against the shield, down he falleth into the water, for the boat is violently forced with the tide ; but on each side of the shield ride two boats, furnished with young men, which recover him that falleth as soon as they may. Upon the bridge, wharfs, and houses, by the river's side, stand great numbers to see and laugh thereat.

"In the holidays all the summer the youths are exercised in leaping, dancing, shooting, wrestling, casting the stone, and practising their shields ; the maidens trip in their timbrels, and dance as long as they can well see. In winter, every holiday before dinner, the boars prepared for brawn are set to fight, or else bulls and bears are baited.

"When the great fen, or moor, which watereth the walls of the city on the north side, is frozen, many young men play upon the ice; some, striding as wide as they may, do slide swiftly; others make themselves seats of ice, as great as millstones; one sits down, many hand in hand to draw him, and one slipping on a sudden, all fall together; some tie bones to their feet and under their heels; and shoving themselves by a little picked staff, do slide as swiftly as a bird flieth in the air, or an arrow out of a cross-bow. Sometime two run together with poles, and hitting one the other, either one or both do fall, not without hurt; some break their arms, some their legs, but youth desirous of glory in this sort exerciseth itself against the time of war. Many of the citizens do delight themselves in hawks and hounds; for they have liberty of hunting in Middlesex, Hertfordshire, all Chiltern, and in Kent to the water of Cray." Thus far Fitzstephen of sports.

These, or the like exercises, have been continued till our time, namely, in stage plays, whereof ye may read in anno 1391, a play by the parish clerks of London at the Skinner's Well besides Smithfield, which continued three days together, the king, queen, and nobles of the realm being present. And of another, in the year 1409, which lasted eight days, and was of matter from the creation of the world, whereat was present most part of the nobility and gentry of England. Of late time, in place of those stage plays, hath been used comedies, tragedies, interludes, and histories, both true and feigned; for the acting whereof certain public places, as the Theatre, the Curtain, &c., have been erected. Also cocks of the game are yet cherished by divers men for their pleasures, much money being laid on their heads, when they fight in pits, whereof some be costly made for that purpose. The ball is used by noblemen and gentlemen in tennis courts, and by people of meaner sort in the open fields and streets.

The marching forth of citizens' sons, and other young men on horseback, with disarmed lances and shields, there to practise feats of war, man against man, hath long since been left off, but in their stead they have used on horseback to run at a dead mark, called a quintain; for note whereof I read, that in the year of Christ 1253, the 38th of Henry III., the youthful citizens, for an exercise of their activity, set forth a game to run at the quintain; and whoever did best should have a peacock, which they had prepared as a prize. Certain of the king's servants, because the court lay then at Westminster, came, as it were, in spite of the citizens, to that game, and giving reproachful names to the Londoners, which for the dignity of the city, and ancient privilege which they ought to have enjoyed, were called barons, the said Londoners, not able to bear so to be misused, fell upon the king's servants, and beat them shrewdly, so that upon complaint to the king he fined the citizens to pay a thousand marks. This exercise of running at the quintain was practised by the youthful citizens as well in summer as in winter, namely, in the feast of Christmas, I have seen a quintain set upon Cornhill, by the Leadenhall, where the attendants on the lords of merry disports have run, and made great pastime; for he that hit not the broad end of the quintain was of all men laughed to scorn, and he that hit it full, if he rid not the faster, had a sound blow in his neck with a bag full of sand hung on the other end. I have also in the summer season seen some upon the river of Thames rowed in wherries, with staves in their hands, flat at the fore end, running one against another, and for the most part, one or both overthrown, and well ducked.

On the holy days in summer the youths of this city have in the field exercised themselves in leaping, dancing, shooting, wrestling, casting of the stone or ball, &c.

And for defence and use of the weapon, there is a special profession of men that teach it. Ye may read in mine Annals how that in the year 1222 the citizens kept games of defence, and wrestlings, near unto the hospital of St. Giles-in-the-Field, where they challenged, and had the mastery of the men in the suburbs, and other commoners, &c. Also, in the year 1453, of a tumult made against the mayor at the wrestling besides Clerke's Well, &c. Which is sufficient to prove that of old time the exercising of wrestling, and such like, hath been much more used than of later years. The youths of this city also have used on holy days after evening prayer, at their masters' doors, to exercise their wasters and bucklers; and the maidens, one of them playing on a timbrel, in sight of their masters and dames, to dance for garlands hung athwart the streets; which open pastimes in my youth being now suppressed, worse practices within doors are to be feared. As for the baiting of bulls and bears, they are to this day much frequented, namely, in Bear gardens, on the Bank's side, wherein be prepared scaffolds for beholders to stand upon. Sliding upon the ice is now but children's play; but in hawking and hunting many grave citizens at this present have great delight, and do rather want leisure than goodwill to follow it.

Of triumphant shows made by the citizens of London, ye may read, in the year 1236, the 20th of Henry III., Andrew Bockwell then being mayor, how Eleanor, daughter to Reymond, Earl of Provence, riding through the city towards Westminster, there to be crowned Queen of England, the city was adorned with silks, and in the night with lamps, cressets, and other lights without number, besides many pageants and strange devices there presented; the citizens also rode to meet the king and queen, clothed in long garments embroidered about with gold, and silks of divers colours, their horses gallantly trapped to the number of three hundred and sixty, every man bearing a cup of gold or silver in his hand, and the king's trumpeters sounding before them. These citizens did minister wine, as bottlers, which is their service, at their coronation. More, in the year 1293, for victory obtained by Edward I. against the Scots, every citizen, according to their several trade, made their several show, but especially the fishmongers, which in a solemn procession passed through the city, having, amongst other pageants and shows, four sturgeons gilt, carried on four horses; then four salmons of silver on four horses; and after them six and forty armed knights riding on horses, made like luces of the sea; and then one representing St. Magnus, because it was upon St. Magnus' day, with a thousand horsemen, &c.

One other show, in the year 1377, was made by the citizens for disport of the young prince, Richard, son to the Black Prince, in the feast of Christmas, in this manner:—On the Sunday before Candlemas, in the night, one hundred and thirty citizens, disguised, and well horsed, in a mummery, with sound of trumpets, sackbuts, cornets, shalmes, and other minstrels, and innumerable torchlights of wax, rode from Newgate, through Cheap, over the bridge, through Southwark, and so to Kennington beside Lambhith, where the young prince remained with his mother and the Duke of Lancaster his uncle, the Earls of Cambridge, Hertford, Warwick, and Suffolk, with divers other lords. In the first rank did ride forty-eight in the likeness and habit of esquires, two and two together, clothed in red coats and gowns of say or sandal, with comely visors on their faces; after them came riding forty-eight knights in the same livery of colour and stuff; then followed one richly arrayed like an emperor; and after him some distance, one stately attired like a pope, whom followed twenty-four cardinals, and after them eight or ten with black visors, not amiable, as if they had been legates from some foreign princes. These maskers, after they had entered Kennington, alighted from their horses, and entered the hall on foot; which done, the prince, his mother, and the lords, came out of the chamber into the hall, whom the said mummers did salute, showing by a pair of dice upon the table their desire to play with the prince, which they so handled that the prince did always win when he cast them. Then the mummers set to the prince three jewels, one after another, which were a bowl of gold, a cup of gold, and a ring of gold, which the prince won at three casts. Then they set to the prince's mother, the duke, the earls, and other lords, to every one a ring of gold, which they did also win. After which they were feasted, and the music sounded, the prince and lords danced on the one part with the mummers, which did also dance; which jollity being ended, they were again made to drink, and then departed in order as they came.

The like was in Henry IV., in the 2nd of his reign, he then keeping his Christmas at Eltham, twelve aldermen of London and their sons rode in a mumming, and had great thanks.

Thus much for sportful shows in triumphs may suffice. Now for sports and pastimes yearly used.

First, in the feast of Christmas, there was in the king's house, wheresoever he was lodged, a lord of misrule, or master of merry disports. and the like had ye in the house of every nobleman of honour or good worship, were he spiritual or temporal. Amongst the which the mayor of London, and either of the sheriffs, had their several lords of misrule, ever contending, without quarrel or offence, who should make the rarest pastimes to delight the beholders. These lords beginning their rule on Alhollon eve, continued the same till the morrow after the Feast of the Purification, commonly called Candlemas Day. In all which space there were fine and subtle disguisings, masks, and mummeries, with playing at cards for counters, nails, and points, in every house, more for pastime than for gain.

Against the feast of Christmas every man's house, as also the parish churches, were decked with holm, ivy, bays, and whatsoever the season of the year afforded to be green. The conduits and standards in the streets were likewise garnished; amongst the which I read, in the year 1444, that by tempest of thunder and lightning, on the 1st of February, at night, Paule's Steeple was fired, but with great labour quenched; and towards the morning of Candlemas Day, at the Leadenhall in Cornhill, a standard of tree being set up in midst of the pavement, fast in the ground, nailed full of holm and ivy, for disport of Christmas to the people, was torn up, and cast down by the malignant spirit (as was thought), and the stones of the pavement all about were cast in the streets, and into divers houses, so that the people were sore aghast of the great tempests.

In the week before Easter had ye great shows made for the fetching in of a twisted tree, or with, as they termed it, out of the woods into the king's house; and the like into every man's house of honour or worship.

In the month of May, namely, on May-day in the morning, every man, except impediment, would walk into the sweet meadows and green woods, there to rejoice their spirits with the beauty and savour of sweet flowers, and with the harmony of birds, praising God in their kind; and for example hereof, Edward Hall hath noted, that King Henry VIII., as in the 3rd of his reign, and divers other years, so namely, in the 7th of his reign, on May-day in the morning, with Queen Katherine his wife, accompanied with many lords and ladies, rode a-maying from Greenwich to the high ground of Shooter's Hill, where, as they passed by the way, they espied a company of tall yeomen, clothed all in green, with green hoods, and bows and arrows, to the number of two hundred; one being their chieftain, was called Robin Hood, who required the king and his company to stay and see his men shoot; whereunto the king granting, Robin Hood whistled, and all the two hundred archers shot off, loosing all at once; and when he whistled again they likewise shot again; their arrows whistled by craft of the head, so that the noise was strange and loud, which greatly delighted the king, queen, and their company. Moreover, this Robin Hood desired the king and queen, with their retinue, to enter the greenwood, where, in harbours made of boughs, and decked with flowers, they were set and served plentifully with venison and wine by Robin Hood and his men, to their great contentment, and had other pageants and pastimes, as ye may read in my said author.

I find also, that in the month of May, the citizens of London of all estates, lightly in every parish, or sometimes two or three parishes joining together, had their several mayings, and did fetch in maypoles, with divers warlike shows, with good archers, morris dancers, and other devices, for pastime all the day long; and toward the evening they had stage plays, and bonfires in the streets. Of these mayings we read, in the reign of Henry VI., that the aldermen and sheriffs of London, being on May-day at the Bishop of London's wood, in the parish of Stebunheath, and having there a worshipful dinner for themselves and other commoners, Lydgate the poet, that was a monk of Bury, sent to them, by a pursuivant, a joyful commendation of that season, containing sixteen staves of metre royal, beginning thus :—

> " Mightié Flora ! goddess of fresh flowers,—
> 　　Which clothéd hath the soyle in lustie greene,
> Made buddés springen, with her sweeté showers,
> 　　By the influence of the sunne shine.
> To doen pleasance of intent full cleane,
> 　　Unto the Statés which now sitten here,
> Hath Ver down sent her owné daughter deare.
>
> Making the vertue, that dare in the roote,
> 　　Calléd of clarkes the vertue vegitáble,
> For to transcend, most holsome and most soote,
> 　　Into the crop, this season so agreáble,
> The bawmy liquor is so commendáble,
> 　　That it rejoiceth with his fresh moystúre,
> Man, beast, and fowle, and every creatúre," &c.

These great mayings, and May-games, made by the governors and masters of this city, with the triumphant setting up of the great shaft (a principal maypole in Cornhill, before the parish church of St. Andrew therefore called Undershaft,) by means of an insurrection of youths against aliens on May-day, 1517, the 9th of Henry VIII., have not been so freely used as afore, and therefore I leave them, and will somewhat touch of watches, as also of shows in the night.

Of Watches in this City, and other Matters commanded, and the Cause why.

WILLIAM CONQUEROR commanded that in every town and village, a bell should be nightly rung at eight o'clock, and that all people should then put out their fire and candle, and take their rest; which order was observed through this realm during his reign, and the reign of William Rufus. But Henry I., restoring to his subjects the use of fire and lights, as afore; it followeth, by reason of wars within the realm, that many men also gave themselves to robbery and murders in the night; for example whereof in this city Roger Hoveden writeth thus :— "In the year 1175, a council was kept at Nottingham ; in time of which council a brother of the Earl Ferrers being in the night privily slain at London, and thrown out of his inn into the dirty street, when the king understood thereof, he swore that he would be avenged on the citizens. For it was then (saith mine author) a common practice in the city, that a hundred or more in a company, young and old, would make nightly invasions upon houses of the wealthy, to the intent to rob them ; and if they found any man stirring in the city within the night that were not of their crew, they would presently murder him, insomuch that when night was come no man durst adventure to walk in the streets. When this had continued long, it fortuned that as a crew of young and wealthy citizens, assembling together in the night, assaulted a stone house of a certain rich man, and breaking through the wall, the good man of that house, having prepared himself with others in a corner, when he perceived one of the thieves named Andrew Bucquint to lead the way, with a burning brand in one hand and a pot of coals in the other, which he essayed to kindle with the brand, he flew upon him, and smote off his right hand, and then with a loud voice cried 'Thieves !' at the hearing whereof the thieves took their flight, all saving he that had lost his hand, whom the good man in the next morning delivered to Richard de Lucie, the king's justice. This thief, upon warrant of his life, appeached his confederates, of whom many were taken, and many were fled. Among the rest that were apprehended, a certain citizen of great countenance, credit, and wealth, named John Senex, who for as much as he could not acquit himself by the water doem, as that law was then he offered to the king five hundred pounds of silver for his life; but forasmuch as he was condemned by judgment of the water, the king would not take the offer, but commanded him to be hanged on the gallows, which was done, and then the city became more quiet for a long time after." But for a full remedy of enormities in the night, I read, that in the year 1253, Henry III. commanded watches in the cities and borough towns to be kept, for the better observing of peace and quietness amongst his people.

And further, by the advice of them of Savoy, he ordained, that if any man chanced to be robbed, or by any means damnified by any thief or robber, he to whom the charge of keeping that country, city, or borough, chiefly appertained, where the robbery was done, should competently restore the loss. And this was after the use of Savoy, but yet thought more hard to be observed here than in those parts; and, therefore, leaving those laborious watches, I will speak of our pleasures and pastimes in watching by night.

In the months of June and July, on the vigils of festival days, and on the same festival days in the evenings after the sun setting, there were usually made bonfires in the streets, every man bestowing wood or labour towards them; the wealthier sort also, before their doors near to the said bonfires, would set out tables on the vigils, furnished with sweet bread and good drink, and on the festival days with meats and drinks plentifully, whereunto they would invite their neighbours and passengers also to sit and be merry with them in great familiarity, praising God for His benefits bestowed on them. These were called bonfires as well of good amity amongst neighbours that being before at controversy, were there, by the labour of others, reconciled, and made of bitter enemies loving friends; and also for the virtue that a great fire hath to purge the infection of the air. On the vigil of St. John the Baptist, and on St. Peter and Paul the Apostles, every man's door being shadowed with green birch, long fennel, St. John's wort, orpin, white lilies, and such like, garnished upon with garlands of beautiful flowers, had also lamps of glass, with oil burning in them all the night; some hung out branches of iron curiously wrought, containing hundreds of lamps alight at once, which made a goodly show, namely, in New Fish Street, Thames Street, &c. Then had ye besides the standing watches all in bright harness, in every ward and street of this city and suburbs, a marching watch, that passed through the principal streets thereof, to wit, from the little conduit by Paul's Gate to West Cheap, by the stocks through Cornhill, by Leadenhall to Aldgate, then back down Fenchurch Street, by Grass Church, about Grass Church conduit, and up Grass Church Street into Cornhill, and through it into West Cheap again. The whole way for this marching watch extendeth to three thousand two hundred tailor's yards of assize; for the furniture whereof with lights, there were appointed seven hundred cressets, five hundred of them being found by the companies, the other two hundred by the Chamber of London. Besides the which lights every constable in London, in number more than two hundred and forty, had his cresset: the charge of every cresset was in light two shillings and fourpence, and every cresset had two men, one to bear or hold it, another to bear a bag with light, and to serve it, so that the poor men pertaining to the cressets, taking wages, besides that every one had a straw hat, with a badge painted, and his breakfast in the morning, amounted in number to almost two thousand. The marching watch contained in number about two thousand men, part of them being old soldiers of skill, to be captains, lieutenants, sergeants, corporals, &c., whifflers, drummers, and fifes, standard and ensign bearers, sword players, trumpeters on horseback, demilances on great horses, gunners with hand guns, or half hakes, archers in coats of white fustian, signed on the breast and back with the arms of the city, their bows bent in their hands, with sheaves of arrows by their sides, pikemen in bright corslets, burganets, &c., halberds, the like billmen in almaine rivets, and aprons of mail in great number; there were also divers pageants, morris dancers, constables, the one-half, which was one hundred and twenty, on St. John's Eve, the other half on St. Peter's Eve, in bright harness, some overgilt, and every one a jornet of scarlet thereupon, and a chain of gold, his henchman following him, his minstrels before him, and his cresset light passing by him, the waits of the city, the mayor's officers for his guard before him, all in a livery of worsted or say jackets party-coloured, the mayor himself well mounted on horseback, the swordbearer before him in fair armour well mounted also, the mayor's footmen, and the like torch-bearers about him, henchmen twain upon great stirring horses, following him. The sheriff's watches came one after the other in like order, but not so large in number as the mayor's; for where the mayor had besides his giant three pageants, each of the sheriffs had besides their giants but two pageants, each their morris dance, and one henchman, their officers in jackets of worsted or say party-coloured, differing from the mayor's, and each from other, but having harnessed men a great many, &c.

This midsummer watch was thus accustomed yearly, time out of mind, until the year 1539, the 31st of Henry VIII., in which year, on the 8th of May, a great muster was made by the citizens at the Mile's End, all in bright harness, with coats of white silk, or cloth and chains of gold, in three great battles, to the number of fifteen thousand, which passed through London to Westminster, and so through the Sanctuary, and round about the park of St. James, and returned home through Oldbourne. King Henry, then considering the great charges of the citizens for the furniture of this unusual muster, forbade the marching watch provided for at Midsummer for that year, which being once laid down was not raised again till the year 1548, the second of Edward VI., Sir John Gresham then being mayor, who caused the marching watch, both on the eve of St. John the Baptist and of St. Peter the Apostle, to be revived and set forth in as comely order as it hath been accustomed, which watch was also beautified by the number of more than three hundred demilances and light horsemen, prepared by the citizens to be sent into Scotland for the rescue of the town of Haddington, and others kept by the Englishmen. Since this mayor's time, the like marching watch in this city hath not been used, though some attempts have been made thereunto; as in the year 1585, a book was drawn by a grave citizen, and by him dedicated to Sir Thomas Pullison. then lord mayor, and his brethren the aldermen, containing the manner and order of a marching watch in the city upon the evens accustomed; in commendation whereof, namely, in times of peace to be used, he hath words to this effect : "The artificers of sundry sorts were thereby well set a-work, none but rich men charged, poor men helped, old soldiers, trumpeters, drummers, fifes, and ensign-bearers, with such like men, meet for princes' service, kept in ure, wherein the safety and defence of every common weal consisteth. Armour and weapon being yearly occupied in this wise, the citizens had of their own readily prepared for any need ; whereas by intermission hereof, armourers are out of work, soldiers out of pay, weapons overgrown with foulness, few or none good being provided," &c.

In the month of August, about the feast of St. Bartholomew the Apostle, before the Lord Mayor, aldermen, and sheriffs of London, placed in a large tent near unto Clerkenwell, of old time, were divers days spent in the pastime of wrestling, where the officers of the city, namely, the sheriffs, sergeants, and yeomen, the porters of the king's beam or weigh-house, now no such men, and other of the city, were challengers of all men in the suburbs, to wrestle for games appointed, and on other days, before the said mayor, aldermen, and sheriffs, in Finsbury field, to shoot the standard, broad arrow, and flight, for games ; but now of late years the wrestling is only practised on Bartholomew's Day in the afternoon, and the shooting some three or four days after, in one afternoon, and no more. What should I speak of the ancient daily exercises in the long bow by citizens of this city, now almost clean left off and forsaken ?—I overpass it ; for by the mean of closing in the common grounds, our archers, for want of room to shoot abroad, creep into bowling-alleys and ordinary dicing houses nearer home, where they have room enough to hazard their money at unlawful games ; and there I leave them to take their pleasures.

Honour of Citizens, and Worthiness of Men in the Same.

"THIS city," saith Fitzstephen, "is glorious in manhood : furnished with munitions, populous with inhabitants ; insomuch, that in the troublesome time of King Stephen, it hath showed at a muster twenty thousand armed horsemen, and three score thousand foot-men, serviceable for the wars. Moreover, saith he, the citizens of London, wheresoever they become, are notable before all other citizens in civility of manners, attire, table, and talk. The matrons of this city are the very modest Sabine ladies of Italy. The Londoners, sometime called Trinobantes, repelled Cæsar, which always made his passage by shedding blood; whereupon Lucan sung:

> ' Territa quæsitis ostendit terga Britannis.'

"The city of London hath bred some which have subdued many kingdoms, and also the Roman Empire. It hath also brought forth many others, whom virtue and valour hath highly advanced; according to Apollo, in his Oracle to Brute, ' *Sub occasu solis,*' &c. In the time of Christianity, it brought forth that noble emperor, Constantine, which gave the city of Rome and all the imperial ensigns to God, St. Peter, and Pope Silvester; choosing rather to be called a defender of the Church than an emperor; and, lest peace might be violated, and their eyes troubled by his presence, he retired from Rome, and built the city of Constantinople. London also in late time hath brought forth famous kings: Maude the Empress, King Henry, son to Henry II., and Thomas the Archbishop, &c."

This Thomas, surnamed Becket, born in London, brought up in the Priory of Marton, student at Paris, became the sheriff's clerk of London for a time, then parson of St. Mary Hill, had a prebend at London, another at Lincoln, studied the law at Bologna, &c., was made Chancellor of England, and Archbishop of Canterbury, &c. Unto this might be added innumerable persons of honour, wisdom, and virtue, born in London; but of actions done by worthy citizens I will only note a few, and so to other matters.

The citizens of London, time out of mind, founded an hospital of St. James in the fields for leprous women of their city.

In the year 1197, Walter Brune, a citizen of London, and Rosia, his wife, founded the hospital of our Lady, called Domus Dei, or St. Mary Spital, without Bishopsgate of London; a house of such relief to the needy, that there was found standing at the surrender thereof nine score beds, well furnished for receipt of poor people.

In the year 1216, the Londoners sending out a navy, took ninety-five ships of pirates and sea-robbers, besides innumerable others that they drowned, which had robbed on the river of Thames.

In the year 1247, Simon Fitzmary, one of the sheriffs of London, founded the hospital of St. Mary called Bethlem, and without Bishopsgate.

In the year 1283, Henry Wallace, then mayor, built the Tun upon Cornhill, to be a prison for night-walkers, and a market-house called the Stocks, both for fish and flesh, standing in the midst of the city. He also built divers houses on the west and north side of Paul's Churchyard; the profits of all which buildings are to the maintenance of London Bridge.

In the year 1332, William Elsing, mercer of London, founded Elsing Spital within Cripplegate, for sustentation of an hundred poor blind men, and became himself the first prior of that hospital.

Sir John Poultney, draper, four times mayor, in 1337 built a fair chapel in Paul's Church, wherein he was buried. He founded a college in the parish church of St. Laurence, called Poultney: he built the parish church called Little Alhallows, in Thames Street; the Carmelite Friars Church in Coventry: he gave relief to prisoners in Newgate and in the Fleet, and ten shillings a year to St. Giles' Hospital by Oldborne for ever, and other legacies long to rehearse.

John Stodie, vintner, mayor 1358, gave to the vintners all the quadrant wherein the Vintners' Hall now standeth, with all the tenements round about, from Stadies Lane, wherein is founded thirteen almshouses for so many poor people, &c.

Henry Picard, vintner, mayor 1357, in the year 1363, did in one day sumptuously feast Edward III., King of England, John, King of France, David, King of Scots, the King of Cyprus, then all in England, Edward, Prince of Wales, with many other noblemen, and after kept his hall for all comers that were willing to play at dice and hazard. The Lady Margaret, his wife, kept her chamber to the same effect, &c.

John Lofken, fishmonger, four times mayor, 1367, built an hospital called Magdalen's, in Kingston-upon-Thames; gave thereunto nine tenements, ten shops, one mill, one hundred and twenty-five acres of land, ten acres of meadow, one hundred and twenty acres of pasture, &c.; more, in London, he built the fair parish church of St. Michael in Crooked Lane, and was there buried.

John Barnes, mayor 1371, gave a chest with three locks, and one thousand marks therein, to be lent to young men upon sufficient pawn, and for the use thereof, to say *De profundis*, or *Pater noster*, and no more: he also was a great builder of St. Thomas Apostle's parish church, as appeareth by his arms there, both in stone and glass.

In the year 1378, John Philpot, sometime mayor, hired with his own money one thousand soldiers, and defended the realm from incursions of the enemy, so that in small time his hired men took John Mercer, a sea-rover, with all his ships, which he before had taken from Scarborough, and fifteen Spanish ships, laden with great riches.

In the year 1380, Thomas of Woodstock, Thomas Percy, Hugh Calverley, Robert Knowles, and others, being sent with a great power to aid the Duke of Brytaine, the said John Philpot hired ships for them of his own charges, and released the armour, which the soldiers had pawned for their battels, more than a thousand in number. "This most noble citizen," saith Thomas Walsingham, "that had travailed for the commodity of the whole realm more than all other of his time, had often relieved the king by lending him great sums of money and otherwise, deceased in A.D. 1384, after that he had assured lands to the city for the relief of thirteen poor people for ever."

In the year 1381, William Walworth, then mayor, a most provident, valiant, and learned citizen, did by his arrest of Wat Tyler (a presumptuous rebel, upon whom no man durst lay hands), deliver the king and kingdom from the danger of most wicked traitors, and was for his service knighted in the field.

Nicholas Brember, John Philpot, Robert Laund, Nicholas Twiford, and Adam Francis, aldermen, were then for their service likewise knighted ; and Sir Robert Knowles, for assisting of the mayor, was made free of this city.

This Sir Robert Knowles, thus worthily infranchised a citizen, founded a college with an hospital at Pontefract : he also built the great stone bridge at Rochester, over the river of Medway, &c.

John Churchman, grocer, one of the sheriffs 1386, for the

quiet of merchants, built a certain house upon Wool Wharf, in Tower Ward, to serve for tronage or weighing of wools, and for the customer, comptroller, clerks, and other officers to sit, &c.

Adam Bamme, goldsmith, mayor 1391, in a great dearth, procured corn from parts beyond the seas to be brought hither in such abundance as sufficed to serve the city, and the countries near adjoining; to the furtherance of which good work he took out of the orphans' chest in the Guildhall two thousand marks to buy the said corn, and each alderman laid out twenty pounds to the like purpose.

Thomas Knowles, grocer, mayor 1400, with his brethren the aldermen, began to new build the Guildhall in London, and instead of an old little cottage in Aldermanbury Street, made a fair and goodly house, more near unto St. Laurence Church in the Jewry: he re-edified St. Anthony's Church, and gave to the grocers his house near unto the same, for relief of the poor for ever. More, he caused sweet water to be conveyed to the gates of Newgate and Ludgate, for relief of the prisoners there.

John Hinde, draper, mayor 1405, newly built his parish church of St. Swithin by London Stone: his monument is defaced, save only his arms in the glass windows.

Thomas Falconer, mercer, mayor 1414, lent to King Henry VI., towards maintenance of his wars in France, ten thousand marks upon jewels. More, he made the postern called Moorgate, caused the ditches of the city to be cleansed, and did many other things for good of the same city.

William Sevenoke, grocer, mayor 1419, founded in the town of Sevenoke, in Kent, a free school for poor men's children, and thirteen almshouses: his testament saith, twenty poor men and women.

Richard Whittington, mercer, three times mayor, in the year 1421 began the library of the Grey Friars in London, to the charge of four hundred pounds: his executors with his goods founded and built Whittington College, with almshouses for thirteen poor men, and divinity lectures to be read there for ever. They repaired St. Bartholomew's Hospital in Smithfield; they bare some charges to the glazing and paving of the Guildhall; they bare half the charges of building the library there, and they built the west gate of London, of old time called Newgate, &c.

John Carpenter, town clerk of London, in the reign of Henry V., caused with great expense to be curiously painted upon board, about the north cloister of Paul's, a monument of Death leading all estates, with the speeches of Death, and answer of every state. This cloister was pulled down 1549. He also gave tenements to the city, for the finding and bringing up of four poor men's children with meat, drink, apparel, learning at the schools in the universities, &c., until they be preferred, and then other in their places for ever.

Robert Chicheley, grocer, mayor 1422, appointed by his testament, that on his mind day,* a competent dinner should be ordained for two thousand four hundred poor men, householders of this city, and every man to have twopence in money. More, he gave one large plot of ground, thereupon to build the new parish church of St. Stephen, near unto Walbrook, &c.

John Rainwell, fishmonger, mayor 1427, gave tenements to discharge certain wards of London of fifteenths and other payments.

John Wells, grocer, mayor 1433, a great builder of the chapel or college of the Guildhall, and was there buried. He caused fresh water to be conveyed from Tybourne to the standard in West Cheap for service of the city.

William Eastfield, mercer, 1438, appointed his executors of his goods to convey sweet water from Tybourn, and to build a fair conduit, by Aldermanbury Church, which they performed, as also made a standard in Fleet Street by Shoe Lane end; they also conveyed water to Cripplegate, &c.

Stephen Browne, grocer, mayor 1439, sent into Prussia, causing corn to be brought from thence; whereby he brought down the price of wheat from three shillings the bushel to less than half that money.

Philip Malpas, one of the sheriffs 1440, gave by his testament one hundred and twenty-five pounds, to relieve poor prisoners, and every year for five years, four hundred shirts and smocks, forty pairs of sheets, and one hundred and fifty gowns of frieze, to the poor; to five hundred poor people in London six shillings and eightpence; to poor maids' marriages one hundred marks; to highways one hundred marks; twenty marks the year to a

* *Mind day*, day of remembrance, anniversary of death.

graduate to preach; twenty pounds to preachers at the Spital the three Easter holidays, &c.

Robert Large, mercer, mayor 1440, gave to his parish church of St. Olave in Surrey two hundred pounds; to St. Margaret's in Lothbury twenty-five pounds; to the poor twenty pounds; to London Bridge one hundred marks; towards the vaulting over the watercourse of Walbrook two hundred marks; to poor maids' marriages one hundred marks; to poor householders one hundred pounds, &c.

Richard Rich, mercer, one of the sheriffs 1442, founded almshouses at Hoddesdon in Hertfordshire.

Simon Eyre, draper, mayor 1346, built the Leaden Hall for a common garner of corn for the use of this city, and left five thousand marks to charitable uses.

Godfrey Bollein, mayor of London, 1458, by his testament, gave liberally to the prisons, hospitals, and lazar-houses, besides a thousand pounds to poor householders in London, and two hundred pounds to poor householders in Norfolk.

Richard Rawson, one of the sheriffs 1477, gave by testament large legacies to the prisoners, hospitals, lazar-houses, to other poor, to highways, to the water conduits, besides to poor maids' marriages three hundred and forty pounds, and his executors to build a large house in the churchyard of St. Mary Spital, wherein the mayor and his brethren do use to sit and hear the sermons in the Easter holidays.

Thomas Ilam, one of the sheriffs 1480, newly built the great conduit in Cheap, of his own charges.

Edward Shaw, goldsmith, mayor 1483, caused the Cripplegate of London to be newly built of his goods, &c.

Thomas Hill, grocer, mayor 1485, caused of his goods the conduit of Grass Street to be built.

Hugh Clopton. mercer, during his life a bachelor, mayor 1492, built the great stone-arched bridge at Stratford-upon-Avon in Warwickshire, and did many other things of great charity, as in my Summary.

Robert Fabian, alderman, and one of the sheriffs 1494, gathered out of divers good authors, as well Latin as French, a large Chronicle of England and of France, which he published in English, to his great charges, for the honour of this city, and common utility of the whole realm.

Sir John Percivall, merchant taylor, mayor 1498, founded a grammar school at Macclesfield in Cheshire, where he was born ; he endowed the same school with sufficient lands for the finding of a priest master there, to teach freely all children thither sent, without exception.

The Lady Thomasine his wife founded the like free school, together with fair lodgings for the schoolmasters, scholars, and other, and added twenty pounds of yearly revenue for supporting the charges, at St. Mary Wike in Devonshire, where she was born.

Stephen Gennings, merchant taylor, mayor 1509, founded a fair grammar school at Ulfrimhampton * in Staffordshire, left good lands, and also built a great part of his parish church, called St. Andrew's Undershaft, in London.

Henry Keble, grocer, mayor 1511, in his life a great benefactor to the new building of old Mary Church, and by his testament gave a thousand pounds towards the finishing thereof; he gave to highways two hundred pounds ; to poor maids' marriages one hundred marks ; to poor husbandmen in Oxford and Warwick shires one hundred and forty ploughshares and one hundred and forty coulters of iron ; and in London, to seven almsmen sixpence the week for ever.

John Colet, a citizen of London by birth and dignity, Dean of Paul's, Doctor of Divinity, erected and built one free school in Paul's Churchyard, 1512, for three hundred and fifty-three poor men's children to be taught free in the same school, appointing a master, a surmaster, and a chaplain, with sufficient stipends to endure for ever, and committed the oversight thereof to the mercers in London, because himself was son to Henry Colet, mercer, mayor of London, and endowed the mercers with lands to the yearly value of one hundred and twenty pounds or better.

John Tate, brewer, then a mercer, mayor 1514, caused his brewhouse, called the Swan, near adjoining to the hospital of St. Anthony in London, to be taken down for the enlarging of the said church, then newly built, a great part of his charge. This was a goodly foundation, with almshouses, free school, &c.

George Monox, draper, mayor 1515, re-edified the decayed

* *Ulfrimhampton*, Wolverhampton.

parish church of Waltonstow, or Walthamstow, in Essex; he founded there a free school, and almshouses for thirteen alms-people, made a causeway of timber over the marshes from Walthamstow to Lock Bridge, &c.

Sir John Milborne, draper, mayor 1522, built almshouses, fourteen in number, by the Crossed Friars Church * in London, there to be placed fourteen poor people; and left to the drapers certain messuages, tenements, and garden plots, in the parish of St. Olave in Hart Street, for the performance of stipends to the said almspeople, and other uses. Look more in Aldgate Ward.

Robert Thorne, merchant taylor, deceased a bachelor in the year 1532, gave by his testament to charitable actions more than four thousand four hundred and forty pounds, and legacies to his poor kindred more five thousand one hundred and forty-two pounds, besides his debts forgiven, &c.

Sir John Allen, mercer, mayor of London, and of council to King Henry VIII., deceased 1544, buried in St. Thomas of Acres in a fair chapel by him built. He gave to the city of London a rich collar of gold to be worn by the mayor, which was first worn by Sir W. Laxton. He gave five hundred marks to be a stock for sea-coal; his lands purchased of the king, the rent thereof to be distributed to the poor in the wards of London for ever. He gave besides to the prisons, hospitals, lazar-houses, and all other poor in the city, or two miles without, very liberally and long to be recited.

Sir William Laxton, grocer, mayor 1545, founded a fair free school at Oundle in Northamptonshire, with six almshouses for the poor.

Sir John Gresham, mercer, mayor 1548, founded a free school at Holt, a market-town in Norfolk.

Sir Rowland Hill, mercer, mayor 1550, caused to be made divers causeways both for horse and man; he made four bridges, two of stone, containing eighteen arches in them both; he built one notable free school at Drayton in Shropshire; he gave to Christ's Hospital in London five hundred pounds, &c.

Sir Andrew Jud, skinner, mayor 1551, erected one notable free

* *Crossed* or *Crutched Friars*, Cruciati, named from a cross embroidered on their dress.

school at Tunbridge in Kent, and almshouses nigh St. Helen's Church in London, and left to the Skinners lands to the value of sixty pounds three shillings and eightpence the year; for the which they be bound to pay twenty pounds to the schoolmaster, eight pounds to the usher, yearly, for ever, and four shillings the week to the six almspeople, and twenty-five shillings and four-pence the year in coals for ever.

Sir Thomas White, merchant taylor, mayor 1554, founded St. John's College, Oxford, and gave great sums of money to divers towns in England for relief of the poor, as in my Summary.

Edward Hall, gentleman, of Gray's Inn, a citizen by birth and office, as common sergeant of London, and one of the judges in the Sheriffs' Court; he wrote and published a famous and eloquent chronicle, entitled, "The Uniting of the Two Noble Families, Lancaster and York."

Richard Hills, merchant taylor, 1560, gave five hundred pounds towards the purchase of a house called the manor of the Rose, wherein the merchant taylors founded their free school in London; he also gave to the said merchant taylors one plot of ground, with certain small cottages on the Tower Hill, where he built fair alms-houses for fourteen sole women.

About the same time William Lambert, Esq., born in London, a justice of the peace in Kent, founded a college for the poor, which he named of Queen Elizabeth, in East Greenwich.

William Harper, merchant taylor, mayor 1562, founded a free school in the town of Bedford, where he was born, and also buried.

Sir Thomas Gresham, mercer, 1566, built the Royal Exchange in London, and by his testament left his dwelling-house in Bishopsgate Street to be a place for readings, allowing large stipends to the readers, and certain almshouses for the poor.

William Patton, gentleman, a citizen by birth, a customer of London outward, justice of peace in Middlesex, the parish church of Stoke Newington being ruinous, he repaired, or rather new built.

Sir Thomas Roo, merchant taylor, mayor 1568, gave to the merchant taylors lands or tenements, out of them to be given to ten poor men, clothworkers, carpenters, tilers, plasterers, and armourers, forty pounds yearly, namely, four pounds to each;

also one hundred pounds to be lent to eight poor men. Besides he enclosed with a wall of brick nigh one acre of ground, pertaining to the hospital of Bethlem, to be a burial for the dead.

Ambrose Nicholas, salter, mayor 1576, founded twelve almshouses in Monkswell Street, near unto Cripplegate, wherein he placed twelve poor people, having each of them sevenpence the week, and once every year five sacks of coals, and one quarter of a hundred faggots, all of his gift for ever.

William Lambe, gentleman and clothworker, in the year 1577 built a water conduit at Oldborne Cross to his charges of fifteen hundred pounds, and did many other charitable acts, as in my Summary.

Sir T. Offley, merchant taylor, mayor, deceased 1580, appointed by his testament the one half of all his goods, and two hundred pounds deducted out of the other half given to his son Henry, to be given and bestowed in deeds of charity by his executors, according to his confidence and trust in them.

John Haydon, sheriff 1583, gave large legacies, more than three thousand pounds, for the relief of the poor, as in my Summary.

Barnard Randolph, common sergeant of London 1583, gave and delivered with his own hand, nine hundred pounds towards the building of water conduits, which was performed. More, by testament he gave one thousand pounds to be employed in charitable actions; but that money being in holdfast hands, I have not heard how it was bestowed, more than of other good men's testaments—to be performed.

Sir Wolston Dixie, skinner, mayor 1586, founded a free school at Bosworth, and endowed it with twenty pounds land by year.

Richard May, merchant taylor, gave three hundred pounds toward the new building of Blackwell Hall in London, a market-place for woollen cloths.

John Fuller, Esq., one of the judges in the Sheriffs' Court of London, by his testament, dated 1592, appointed his wife, her heirs and assigns, after his decease, to erect one almshouse in the parish of Stikoneth,* for twelve poor single men, aged fifty years or upwards, and one other almshouse in Shoreditch, for twelve poor aged widow women of like age, she to endow them with one hundred pounds the year, to wit, fifty pounds to each

* *Stikoneth*, a corruption of Stebonhithe, Stepney.

for ever, out of his lands in Lincolnshire, assured ever unto certain fiefs in trust, by a deed of feoffment. Item : more, he gave his messuages, lands, and tenements, lying in the parishes of St. Benet and St. Peter, by Paul's Wharf in London, to feoffees in trust, yearly for ever, to disburse all the issues and profits of the said lands and tenements, to the relieving and discharge of poor prisoners in the Hole, or twopenny wards in the two compters in London, in equal portions to each compter, so that the prisoners exceed not the sum of twenty-six shillings and eightpence for every one prisoner at any one time.

Thus much for famous citizens have I noted their charitable actions, for the most part done by them in their lifetime. The residue left in trust to their executors, I have known some of them hardly, or never, performed ; wherefore I wish men to make their own hands their executors, and their eyes their over-seers, not forgetting the old proverb :—

> " Women be forgetful, children be unkind,
> Executors be covetous, and take what they find.
> If any body ask where the dead's goods became,
> They answer, So God me help, and holy dome, he died a poor man."

One worthy citizen merchant taylor, having many years considered this proverb foregoing, hath therefore established to twelve poor aged men, merchant taylors, six pounds two shillings to each yearly for ever. He hath also given them gowns of good broad cloth, lined thoroughly with bays, and are to receive every three years' end the like new gowns for ever.

And now of some women, citizens' wives, deserving memory, for example to posterity shall be noted.

Dame Agnes Foster, widow, sometime wife to Stephen Foster, fishmonger, mayor 1455, having enlarged the prison of Ludgate in 1463, procured in a common council of this city certain articles to be established for the ease, comfort, and relief of poor prisoners there, as in the Chapter of Gates I have set down.

Avice Gibson, wife unto Nicholas Gibson, grocer, one of the sheriffs 1539, by license of her husband, founded a free school at Radcliff, near unto London, appointing to the same, for the instruction of sixty poor men's children, a schoolmaster and usher with fifty pounds ; she also built almshouses for fourteen poor aged persons, each of them to receive quarterly six shillings and eightpence the piece for ever; the government of which free school and almshouses she left in confidence to the Coopers in London. This virtuous gentlewoman was after joined in marriage with Sir Anthony Knevet, knight, and so called the Lady Knevet; a fair painted table of her picture was placed in the chapel which she had built there, but of late removed thence, by the like reason as the Grocers' arms fixed on the outer wall of the school-house are pulled down, and the Coopers set in place.*

Margaret Danne, widow to William Danne, ironmonger, one of the sheriffs of London, gave by her testament to the iron-mongers, two thousand pounds, to be lent to young men of that company, paying after the rate of five pounds in the year for every hundred; which one hundred pounds so rising yearly, to be employed on charitable actions, as she then appointed, but not performed in more than thirty years after.

Dame Mary Ramsey, wife to Sir Thomas Ramsey, mayor about the year 1577, being seised of lands in fee simple of her inherit-ance to the yearly value of two hundred and forty-three pounds, by his consent gave the same to Christ's Hospital in London towards the relief of poor children there, and other ways, as in my Summary and Abridgment I have long since expressed; which gift she in her widowhood confirmed and augmented, as is showed by monuments in Christ's Hospital erected.

Thus much for the worthiness of citizens in this city, touching whom John Lydgate, a monk of Bury, in the reign of Henry VI., made, amongst other, these verses following:—

> " Of seaven things I prayse this citty.
> Of true meaning and faithful observance;
> Of righteousnes, truth, and equity;
> Of stablenes aye kept in legiance;
> And for of vertue thou hast suffisance,
> In this lond here and other londs all
> The kinges chamber of custome men thee call."

Having thus in generality handled the original, the walls, gates, ditches, and fresh waters, the bridges, towers, and castles, the

---

* "Cursed is hee that removeth his neighbors mark, have I read."—*Stow's sidenote.*

schools of learning and houses of law, the orders and customs, sports and pastimes, watchings and martial exercises, and lastly, the honour and worthiness of the citizens, I am now to set down the distribution of this city into parts ; and more especially to declare the antiquities noteworthy in every of the same ; and how both the whole and parts have been from time to time ruled and governed.

The City of London divided into Parts.

THE ancient division of this city was into wards or aldermanries. And therefore I will begin at the east, and so proceed through the high and most principal street of the city to the west, after this manner.

First, through Aldgate Street to the west corner of St. Andrew's Church, called Undershaft, on the right hand, and Lime Street corner on the left—all which is of Aldgate Ward ; from thence through Cornhill Street to the west corner of Leaden Hall—all which is of Lime Street Ward. From thence, leaving the street that leadeth to Bishopsgate on the right hand, and the way that leadeth into Grass Street on the left, still through Cornhill Street, by the conduit to the west corner against the Stocks—all which is in Cornhill Ward. Then by the said Stocks (a market-place both of fish and flesh standing in the midst of the city) through the Poultry (a street so-called) to the great conduit in West Cheap, and so through Cheap to the Standard, which is of Cheap Ward, except on the south side from Bow Lane to the said Standard, which is of Cordwainer Street Ward. Then by the Standard to the Great Cross, which is in Cripplegate Ward on the north side, and in Bread Street Ward on the south side. And to the little conduit by Paul's Gate, from whence of old time the said High Street stretched straight to Ludgate, all in the ward of Farringdon within, then divided truly from east to west ; but since by means of the burning of Paul's Church, which was in the reign of William I., Mauritius, then Bishop of London, laid the foundation of a new church, so far in largeness exceeding the old, that the way towards Ludgate was thereby greatly straitened, as before I have discoursed.

Now from the north to the south this city was of old time

divided, not by a large highway or street, as from east to west, but by a fair brook of sweet water, which came from out the north fields through the wall and midst of the city into the river of Thames; which division is till this day constantly and without change maintained. This water was called, as I have said, Walbrook, not Galus brook of a Roman captain slain by Asclepiodatus, and thrown therein, as some have fabled, but of running through, and from the wall of this city; the course whereof, to prosecute it particularly, was and is from the said wall to St. Margaret's Church in Lothbury; from thence beneath the lower part of the Grocers' Hall, about the east part of their kitchen, under St. Mildred's Church, somewhat west from the said Stocks' Market; from thence through Bucklesbury, by one great house built of stone and timber called the Old Barge, because barges out of the river of Thames were rowed up so far into this brook, on the backside of the houses in Walbrook Street (which street taketh the name of the said brook) by the west end of St. John's Church upon Walbrook, under Horseshoe Bridge, by the west side of Tallowchandlers' Hall, and of the Skinners' Hall, and so behind the other houses to Elbow Lane, and by a part thereof down Greenwich Lane, into the river of Thames.

This is the course of Walbrook, which was of old time bridged over in divers places, for passage of horses and men, as need required; but since, by means of encroachment on the banks thereof, the channel being greatly straitened, and other noyances done thereunto, at length the same by common consent was arched over with brick, and paved with stone, equal with the ground wherethrough it passed, and is now in most places built upon, that no man may by the eye discern it, and therefore the trace thereof is hardly known to the common people.

This city was divided from east to west, and from north to south. I am further to show how the same was of old time broken into divers parts called wards, whereof Fitzstephen, more than four hundred years since, writeth thus:—"This city, saith he, even as Rome, is divided into wards; it hath yearly sheriffs instead of consuls. It hath the dignity of senators in aldermen," &c. The number of these wards in London was, both before and in the reign of Henry III., twenty-four in all; whereof thirteen lay on the east side of the said Walbrook, and eleven on the west. Notwithstanding these eleven grew much more large than those on the east; and therefore in the year of Christ 1393, in the 17th of Richard II., Farringdon Ward, which was then one entire ward, but mightily increased of buildings without the gates, was by Act of Parliament appointed to be divided into twain, and to have two aldermen, to wit, Farringdon within, and Farringdon without, which made up the number of twelve wards on the west side of Walbrook, and so the whole number of twenty-five on both sides. Moreover, in the year 1550, the mayor, commonalty, and citizens of London, purchasing the liberties of the borough of Southwark, appointed the same to be a ward of London, and so became the number of thirteen wards on the east, twelve on the west, and one south of the river Thames, in the said borough of Southwark, in the county of Surrey, which in all arise to the number of twenty-six wards, and twenty-six aldermen of London.

Wards on the east part of Walbrook are these :—

1. Portsoken Ward without the walls.
2. Tower Street Ward.
3. Aldgate Ward.
4. Lime Street Ward.
5. Bishopsgate Ward, within the walls and without.
6. Broad Street Ward.
7. Cornhill Ward.
8. Langbourne Ward.
9. Billingsgate Ward.
10. Bridge Ward within.
11. Candlewick Street Ward.
12. Walbrook Ward.
13. Downgate Ward.

Wards on the west side of Walbrook are these :—

14. Vintry Ward.
15. Cordwainer Street Ward.
16. Cheap Ward.
17. Coleman Street Ward.
18. Basinghall Ward.
19. Cripplegate Ward, within and without.
20. Aldersgate Ward, within and without.
21. Farringdon Ward within.

22. Bread Street Ward.
23. Queenhithe Ward.
24. Castle Baynard Ward.
25. Farringdon Ward without the walls.

One ward south the river Thames, in the borough of Southwark, by the name of

26. Bridge Ward without.

Portsoken Ward.

SEEING that of every of these wards I have to say somewhat, I will begin with Portsoken Ward without Aldgate.

This Portsoken, which soundeth the franchise at the gate, was sometime a guild, and had beginning in the days of King Edgar, more than six hundred years since. There were thirteen knights or soldiers, well-beloved to the king and realm, for service by them done, which requested to have a certain portion of land on the east part of the city, left desolate and forsaken by the inhabitants, by reason of too much servitude. They besought the king to have this land, with the liberty of a guild for ever. The king granted to their request, with conditions following : that is, that each of them should victoriously accomplish three combats, one above the ground, one under ground, and the third in the water ; and after this, at a certain day in East Smithfield, they should run with spears against all comers ; all which was gloriously performed ; and the same day the king named it Knighten Guild, and so bounded it, from Aldgate to the place where the bars now are, toward the east, on both the sides of the street, and extended it towards Bishopsgate in the north, unto the house then of William Presbiter, after of Geffrey Tanner, and then of the heirs of Colver, after that of John Easeby, but since of the Lord Bourchier, &c. And again towards the south unto the river of Thames, and so far into the water, as a horseman, entering the same, may ride at a low water, and throw his spear ; so that all East Smithfield, with the right part of the street that goeth to Dodding Pond into the Thames, and also the hospital of St. Katherine's, with the mills that were founded in King Stephen's days, and the outward stone wall, and the new ditch of the Tower, are of the said fee and liberty ; for the said wall and ditch of the Tower were made in the time of King Richard, when he was in the Holy Land, by William Longchamp, Bishop of Ely, as before I have noted unto you.

These knights had as then none other charter by all the days of Edgar, Ethelred, and Cnutus, until the time of Edward the

Confessor, whom the heirs of those knights humbly besought to confirm their liberties ; whereunto he graciously granting, gave them a deed thereof, as appeareth in the book of the late house of the Holy Trinity. The said charter is fair written in the Saxon letter and tongue. After this, King William, the son of William the Conqueror, made a confirmation of the same liberties, unto the heirs of those knights, in these words :—

"William, king of England, to Maurice Bishop, and Godffrey de Magum, and Richard de Parre, and to his faithfull people of London, greeting : Know ye me to have granted to the men of Knighten Guilde, the guilde that belonged to them, and the land that belonged thereunto, with all customes, as they had the same in the time of King Edward, and my father. Witnesse, Hugh de Buche, at Rething."

After him, King Henry I. confirmed the same by his charter to the like effect, the recital whereof I pretermit for brevity. After which time, the Church of the Holy Trinity, within Aldgate of London, being founded by Queen Matilda, wife to the said Henry, the multitude of brethren, praising God day and night therein, in short time so increased, that all the city was delighted in the beholding of them : insomuch, that in the year 1115, certain burgesses of London, of the progeny of those noble English knights—to wit, Radulphus Fitalgod, Wilmarde le Deuereshe, Orgare le Prude, Edward Hupcornehill, Blackstanus, and Alwine his kinsman, and Robert his brother, the sons of Leafstanus the goldsmith, Wiso his son, Hugh Fitzvulgar, Algare Secusme—coming together into the chapter-house of the said Church of the Holy Trinity, gave to the same church and canons serving God therein, all the lands and soke called in English Knighten Guild, which lieth to the wall of the city, without the same gate, and stretcheth to the river of Thames ; they gave it, I say, taking upon them the brotherhood and participation of the benefits of that house, by the hands of Prior Norman. And the better to confirm this their grant, they offered upon the altar there the charter of Edward, together with the other charters which they had thereof ; and afterward they did put the foresaid prior in seisin thereof, by the Church of St. Botolph's, which is built thereon, and is the head of that land. These things were thus done before Bernard, prior of Dunstable, John, prior of Derland, Geffrey Clinton, chamberlain, and many other clerks and laymen, French and English. Orgar le Prude, one of their company, was sent to King Henry, beseeching him to confirm their gift, which the king gladly granted by his deed :

"Henrie, king of England, to Richard Bishop of London, to the shireffes and provost, and to all his barons and faithfull people, French and English, of London and Middlesex, greeting : Know ye mee to have graunted and confirmed to the church and canons of the Holy Trinitie of London, the soke of the English Knighten Guilde, and the land which pertaineth thereunto, and the church of St. Buttolph, as the men of the same guilde have given and granted unto them: and I will and straightly commaund, that they may hold the same well and honourably and freely, with sake and soke, toll and team, infangthefe, and all customs belonging to it, as the men of the same Guild in best sort had the same in the time of K. Edward, and as King William, my father and brother, did grant it to them by their writs. Witnesse, A. the queene, Geffrey the chauncellor, Geoffrey of Clinton, and William of Clinton, at Woodstocke."

All these prescribed writings, saith my book, which sometime belonged to the priory of the Holy Trinity, are registered in the end of the Book of Remembrances, in the Guildhall of London, marked with the letter C, folio 134. The king sent also his sheriffs, to wit, Aubrey de Vere, and Roger, nephew to Hubert, which upon his behalf should invest this church with the possessions thereof, which the said sheriffs accomplished coming upon the ground; Andrew Buchevite, and the fore-named witnesses, and other, standing by; notwithstanding, Othowerus Acolivillus, Otto, and Geffrey, Earl of Essex, constables of the Tower by succession, withheld by force a portion of the said land, as I have before delivered.

The prior and canons of the Holy Trinity, being thus seised of the said land and soke of Knighten Guild, a part of the suburb without the wall, but within the liberties of the city, the same prior was, for him and his successors, admitted as one of the aldermen of London, to govern the same land and soke. According to the customs of the city, he did sit in court, and rode with the mayor and his brethren the aldermen, as one of them, in scarlet or other livery as they used, until the year 1531, at the which time the said priory, by the last prior there, was surrendered to King Henry VIII., in the 23rd of his reign, who gave this priory to Sir Thomas Audley, knight, Lord Chancellor of England, and he pulled down the church. Since the which dissolution of that house, the said ward of Portsoken hath been governed by a temporal man, one of the aldermen of London, elected by the citizens, as the aldermen of other wards. Thus much for the out-bounds of Knighten Guild, or Portsoken Ward, and for the antiquity and government thereof.

Now, of the parts therein, this is specially to be noted. First, the east part of the Tower standeth there, then an hospital of St. Katherine's, founded by Matilda the queen, wife to King Stephen, by license of the priory and convent of the Holy Trinity in London, on whose grounds he founded it. Eleanor the queen, wife to King Edward I., a second foundress, appointed there to be a master, three brethren chaplains, and three sisters, ten poor women, and six poor clerks; she gave to them the manor of Carlton in Wiltshire, and Upchurch in Kent, &c. Queen Philippa, wife to King Edward III.,

1351, founded a chantry there, and gave to that hospital ten pounds land by year; it was of late time called a free chapel, a college, and an hospital for poor sisters. The choir, which of late years was not much inferior to that of Paul's, was dissolved by Dr. Wilson, a late master there, the brethren and sisters remaining. This house was valued at £315, 14s. 2d., being now of late years inclosed about, or pestered * with small tenements and homely cottages, having inhabitants, English and strangers, more in number than in some city in England. There lie buried in this church the Countess of Huntington, Countess of the March in her time, 1429; John Holland, Duke of Exeter and Earl of Huntington, 1447, and his two wives, in a fair tomb on the north side the choir; Thomas Walsingham, esquire, and Thomas Ballarde, esquire, by him, 1465; Thomas Flemming, knight, 1466, &c.

On the east and by north of the Tower, lieth East Smithfield and Tower Hill, two plots of ground so called, without the wall of the city; and east from them both was sometime a monastery, called New Abbey, founded by King Edward III. in the year 1359, upon occasion as followeth :—

In the year 1348, the 23rd of Edward III., the first great pestilence in his time began, and increased so sore, that for want of room in churchyards to bury the dead of the city and of the suburbs, one John Corey, clerk, procured of Nicholas, prior of the Holy Trinity within Aldgate, one toft † of ground near unto East Smithfield, for the burial of them that died, with condition that it might be called the churchyard of the Holy Trinity; which ground he caused, by the aid of divers devout citizens, to be inclosed with a wall of stone. Robert Elsing, son of William Elsing, gave five pounds thereunto; and the same was dedicated by Ralph Stratford, Bishop of London, where innumerable bodies of the dead were afterwards buried, and a chapel built in the same place to the honour of God : to the which King Edward setting his eye (having before, in a tempest on the sea, and peril of drowning, made a vow to build a monastery to the honour of God, and our lady of grace, if God would grant him grace to come safe to land), built there a monastery, placing an abbot, and monks of the Cistercian, or White order. The bounds of this plot of ground, together with a decree for tithes thereof, are expressed in the charter, the effect whereof I have set down in another place, and have to show. This house, at the late general suppression, was valued at £546, 0s. 10d. yearly; it was surrendered in the year 1539, the 30th of Henry VIII.; since the which time, the said

---

* *Pestered*, clogged, encumbered, Fr. *empêtrer*, which originally meant to hobble a horse turned out to pasture.

† *Toft*, clear space.

monastery being clean pulled down by Sir Arthur Darcie, knight, and others, of late time in place thereof is built a large storehouse for victuals; and convenient ovens are built there, for baking of biscuits to serve her majesty's ships. The grounds adjoining, belonging to the said abbey, are employed in building of small tenements.

For Tower Hill, as the same is greatly diminished by building of tenements and garden-plots, &c., so it is of late, to wit, in the year of Christ 1593, on the north side thereof, and at the west end of Hog Street, beautified by certain fair almshouses, strongly built of brick and timber, and covered with slate for the poor, by the merchant taylors of London, in place of some small cottages given to them by Richard Hills, sometime a master of that company, one thousand loads of timber for that use, being also given by Anthony Radcliff, of the same society, alderman. In these almshouses, fourteen charitable brethren of the said merchant taylors, yet living, have placed fourteen poor sole women, which receive each of them of their founder sixteen pence, or better, weekly, besides £8, 15s. yearly, paid out of the common treasury of the same corporation for fuel.

From the west part of this Tower Hill, towards Aldgate, being a long continual street, amongst other smaller buildings in that row, there was sometime an abbey of nuns of the order of St. Clare, called the Minories, founded by Edmond, Earl of Lancaster, Leicester, and Derby, brother to King Edward III., in the year 1293; the length of which abbey contained fifteen perches and seven feet, near unto the King's Street or highway, &c., as appeareth by a deed, dated 1303.

A plague of pestilence being in this city, in the year 1515, there died in this house of nuns professed to the number of twenty-seven, besides other lay people, servants in their house. This house was valued to dispend £418, 8s. 5d. yearly, and was surrendered by Dame Elizabeth Salvage, the last abbess there, unto King Henry VIII. in the 30th of his reign, the year of Christ 1539.

In place of this house of nuns is now built divers fair and large storehouses for armour and habiliments of war, with divers workhouses, serving to the same purpose: there is a small parish church for inhabitants of the close, called St. Trinities.

Near adjoining to this abbey, on the south side thereof, was sometime a farm belonging to the said nunnery; at the which farm I myself in my youth have fetched many a halfpenny worth of milk, and never had less than three ale pints for a halfpenny in the summer, nor less than one ale quart for a halfpenny in the winter, always hot from the kine, as the same was milked and strained. One Trolop, and afterwards Goodman, were the farmers there, and had thirty or forty kine to the pail. Goodman's son, being heir to his father's purchase, let out the ground first for grazing of horses, and then for garden-plots, and lived like a gentleman thereby.

On the other side of that street lieth the ditch without the walls of the city, which of old time was used to be open, always from time to time cleansed from filth and mud, as need required; of great breadth, and so deep, that divers, watering horses where they thought it shallowest, were drowned, both horse and man. But now of later time the same ditch is inclosed, and the banks thereof let out for garden-plots, carpenters' yards, bowling alleys, and divers houses thereon built, whereby the city wall is hidden, the ditch filled up, a small channel left, and that very shallow.

From Aldgate, east, lieth a large street and highway, sometime replenished with few but fair and comely buildings; on the north side whereof, the first was the parish church of St. Botolph, in a large cemetery or churchyard. This church hath been lately new built at the special charges of the priors of the Holy Trinity; patrons thereof, as it appeareth by the arms of that house, engraven on the stone work. The parishioners of this parish being of late years mightily increased, the church is pestered with lofts and seats for them. Monuments in this church are few: Henry Jorden founded a chantry there; John Romany Ollarie, and Agnes his wife, were buried there about 1408; Richard Chester, alderman, one of the sheriffs, 1484; Thomas Lord Darcie of the north, Knight of the Garter, beheaded 1537; Sir Nicholas Carew, of Bedington, in Surrey, Knight of the Garter, beheaded 1538; Sir Arthur Darcie, youngest son to Thomas Lord Darcie, deceased at the new abbey on the Tower Hill, was buried there. East from this parish church, there were certain fair inns for receipt of travellers repairing to the city; up towards Hog Lane end, somewhat within the bars, a mark showing how far the liberties of the city do extend.

This Hog Lane stretcheth north towards St. Mary Spital without Bishopsgate, and within these forty years had on both sides fair hedge rows of elm trees, with bridges and easy stiles to pass over into the pleasant fields, very commodious for citizens therein to walk, shoot, and otherwise to recreate and refresh their dull spirits in the sweet and wholesome air, which is now within a few years made a continual building throughout of garden-houses and small cottages; and the fields on either sides be turned into garden-plots, tenter yards, bowling alleys, and such like from Hounsditch in the west, as far as Whitechapel, and further towards the east.

On the south side of the highway from Aldgate were some few tenements, thinly scattered here and there, with many void spaces between them, up to the bars; but now that street is not only fully replenished with buildings outward, and also pestered with divers alleys on either side to the bars, but also even to Whitechapel and beyond. Among the which late buildings, one memorable for the commodity of that east part of this city is a fair water conduit, hard without the gate ; at the building whereof in the year 1535, Sir John Allen being mayor, two fifteens were granted by the citizens for the making and laying of pipes, to convey water from Hackney to that place ; and so that work was finished.

From Aldgate, north-west to Bishopsgate, lieth the ditch of the city called Hounsditch ; for that in old time, when the same lay open, much filth, conveyed forth of the city, especially dead dogs, were there laid or cast ; wherefore of latter time a mud wall was made, inclosing the ditch, to keep out the laying of such filth as had been accustomed. Over against this mud wall, on the other side of the street, was a fair field, sometime belonging to the priory of the Trinity, and since by Sir Thomas Audley given to Magdalen College in Cambridge : this field, as all other about the city, was enclosed, reserving open passage thereinto for such as were disposed. Towards the street were some small cottages, of two storeys high, and little garden-plots backward, for poor bed-rid people, for in that street dwelt none other, built by some prior of the Holy Trinity, to whom that ground belonged.

In my youth, I remember, devout people, as well men as women of this city, were accustomed oftentimes, especially on Fridays, weekly to walk that way purposely there to bestow their charitable alms ; every poor man or woman lying in their bed within their window, which was towards the street, open so low that every man might see them, a clean linen cloth lying in their window, and a pair of beads, to show that there lay a bed-rid body, unable but to pray only. This street was first paved in the year 1503.

About the latter reign of Henry VIII., three brethren that were gunfounders, surnamed Owens, got ground there to build upon, and to enclose for casting of brass ordnance. These occupied a good part of the street on the field side, and in a short time divers others also built there, so that the poor bed-rid people were worn out, and, in place of their homely cottages, such houses built as do rather want room than rent ; which houses be for the most part possessed by brokers, sellers of old apparel, and such like. The residue of the field was for the most part made into a garden by a gardener named Cawsway, one that served the markets with herbs and roots ; and in the last year of King Edward VI. the same was parcelled into gardens, wherein are now many fair houses of pleasure built.

On the ditch side of this street the mud wall is also by little and little all taken down, the bank of the ditch being raised, made level ground, and turned into garden-plots and carpenters' yards, and many large houses are there built ; the filth of which houses, as also the earth cast out of their vaults, is turned into the ditch, by which means the ditch is filled up, and both the ditch and wall so hidden that they cannot be seen of the passers-by. This Portsoken Ward hath an alderman and his deputy, common councillors six, constables four, scavengers four, for the wardmote inquest eighteen, and a beadle. To the fifteen it is cessed at four pounds ten shillings.

Tower Street Ward.

THE first ward in the east part of this city within the wall is called Tower Street Ward, and extendeth along the river of Thames from the said Tower in the east almost to Belinsgate in the west. One half of the Tower, the ditch on the west side, and bulwarks adjoining, do stand within that part where the wall of the city of old time went straight from the postern gate south to the river of Thames, before that the Tower was built. From and without the Tower ditch, west and by north, is the said Tower Hill, sometime a large plot of ground, now greatly straitened by encroachments, unlawfully made and suffered, for gardens and houses ; some on the bank of the Tower ditch, whereby the Tower ditch is marred, but more near unto the wall of the city from the postern north, till over against the principal fore-gate of the Lord Lumley's house, &c. ; but the Tower Ward goeth no further that way.

Upon this hill is always readily prepared, at the charges of the city, a large scaffold and gallows of timber, for the execution of such traitors or transgressors as are delivered out of the Tower, or otherwise, to the sheriffs of London by writ, there to be executed. I read, that in the fifth of King Edward IV. a scaffold and gallows was there set up by other the king's officers, and not of the city's charges, whereupon the mayor and his brethren complained, but were answered by the king that the Tower Hill was of the liberty of the city ; and whatsoever was done in that point was not in derogation of the city's liberties, and therefore commanded proclamation to be made, as well within the city as in the suburbs, as followeth :—

"Forasmuch as, the seventh day of this present month of November, gallows were erect and set up besides our Tower of London, within the liberties and franchises of our city of London, in derogation and prejudice of the liberties and franchises of this city, the king our sovereign lord would it be certainly understood that the erection and setting up of the said gallows was not done by his commandment ; wherefore the king our sovereign lord willeth, that the erection and setting up the said gallows be not any precedent or example thereby hereafter to be taken, in hurt, prejudice, or derogation of the franchises, liberties, and privileges of the said city, which he at all times hath had, and hath in his benevolence, tender favour, and good grace, &c. Apud Westminst. 9 die Novemb. anno regni nostri quinto."

On the north side of this hill is the said Lord Lumley's house, and on the west side divers houses lately built, and other encroachments along south to Chick Lane, on the east of Barking Church, at the end whereof you have Tower Street stretching from the Tower Hill, west to St. Margaret Patten's Church Parsonage.

Now therefore, to begin at the east end of the street, on the north side thereof, is the fair parish church called Allhallows Barking, which standeth in a large, but sometime far larger, cemetery or churchyard; on the north side whereof was sometime built a fair chapel, founded by King Richard I.: some have written that his heart was buried there under the high altar. This chapel was confirmed and augmented by King Edward I. Edward IV. gave license to his cousin John, Earl of Worcester, to found there a brotherhood for a master and brethren; and he gave to the custos of that fraternity, which was Sir John Scot, knight, Thomas Colte, John Tate, and John Croke, the priory of Tootingbrook, and advowson of the parish church of Streatham, in the county of Surrey, with all the members and appurtenances, and a part of the priory of Okeburn in Wiltshire, both priors aliens, and appointed it to be called the king's chapel or chantry, *In capella Beatæ Mariæ de Barking.* King Richard III. new built and founded therein a college of priests, &c. Hamond de Lega was buried in that chapel. Robert Tate. mayor of London, 1488, and other, were there buried. This chapel and college were suppressed and pulled down in the year 1548, the 2nd of King Edward VI. The ground was employed as a garden-plot during the reigns of King Edward, Queen Mary, and part of Queen Elizabeth, till at length a large strong frame of timber and brick was set thereon, and employed as a storehouse of merchants' goods brought from the sea by Sir William Winter, &c.

Monuments in the parish church of Allhallows Barking, not defaced, are these:—Sir Thomas Studinham, of Norwich diocess, knight, 1469; Thomas Gilbart, draper and merchant of the staple, 1483; John Bolt, merchant of the staple, 1459; Sir John Stile, knight, draper, 1500; William Thynne, Esq., one of the clerks of the Green Cloth, and master of the household to King Henry VIII., 1546; Humfrey Monmouth, draper, one of the sheriffs, 1535; Henry Howard, Earl of Surrey, beheaded 1546; Sir Richard Devereux, son and heir to the Lord Ferrers of Chartley; Richard Browne, Esq., 1546; Philip Dennis, Esq., 1556; Andrew Evenger, salter; William Robinson, mercer, alderman, 1552; William Armorer, clothworker, esquire, governor of the pages of honour, or master of the heance men,* servant to Henry VIII., Edward VI., and Queen Mary, buried 1560. Besides which there be divers tombs without

* *Heance men*, henchmen.

inscription. John Crolys and Thomas Pike, citizens of London, founded a chantry there, 1388.

By the west end of this parish church and chapel lieth Sidon Lane, now corruptly called Sything Lane, from Tower Street up north to Hart Street. In this Sidon Lane divers fair and large houses are built, namely, one by Sir John Allen, sometime mayor of London, and of council unto King Henry VIII.; Sir Francis Walsingham, knight, principal secretary to the queen's majesty that now is, was lodged there, and so was the Earl of Essex, &c. At the north-west corner of this lane standeth a proper parish church of St. Olave, which church, together with some houses adjoining, as also others over against it in Hart Street, are of the said Tower Street Ward. Monuments in this parish church of St. Olave be these :——Richard Cely and Robert Cely, fellmongers, principal builders and benefactors of this church; Dame Johan, wife to Sir John Zouch, 1439; John Clarenciaulx, king of arms, 1427; Thomas Sawle; Sir Richard Haddon, mercer, mayor 1512; Thomas Burnell, mercer, 1548; Thomas Morley, gentleman, 1566; Sir John Radcliffe, knight, 1568; and Dame Anne his wife, 1585; Chapone, a Florentine gentleman, 1582; Sir Hamond Vaughan, knight; George Stoddard, merchant, &c.

Woodroffe Lane towards the Tower is in this parish. Then have ye out of Tower Street, also on the north side, one other lane, called Marte Lane, which runneth up towards the north, and is for the most part of this Tower Street Ward; which lane is about the third quarter thereof divided from Aldgate Ward, by a chain to be drawn athwart the said lane, above the west end of Hart Street. Cokedon Hall, sometime at the south-west end of Marte Lane, I read of.

A third lane out of Tower Street, on the north side, is called Mincheon Lane, so called of tenements there sometime pertaining to the Minchuns or nuns of St. Helen's in Bishopsgate Street.* This lane is all of the said ward, except the corner house towards Fenchurch Street. In this lane of old time dwelt divers strangers, born of Genoa and those parts; these were commonly called galley men, as men that came up in the galleys brought up wines and other merchandises, which they landed in Thames Street, at a place called Galley Quay. They had a certain coin of silver amongst themselves, which were halfpence of Genoa, and were called Galley halfpence; these halfpence were forbidden in the 13th of Henry IV., and again by parliament in the 4th of Henry V. It was, that if any person

* *Minchuns or nuns*, " Minchin " seems to be a Teutonic feminine formed from " Monk," and perhaps derived from German use of such a feminine from *Mönch Mönchinn*. The French word so formed was *Moinesse*. The *in* was sometimes dropped, leaving Minch for a nun. A nunnery at Littlemore was called the Mincheries. The Minchins in the text left their name to Mincing Lane.

bring into this realm halfpence, suskinges, or dodkins,* he should be
punished as a thief; and he that taketh or payeth such money shall
lose a hundred shillings, whereof the king shall have the one half,
and he that will sue the other half.   Notwithstanding, in my youth,
I have seen them pass current, but with some difficulty, for that the
English halfpence were then, though not so broad, somewhat thicker
and stronger.

The Clothworkers' Hall is in this lane.   Then at the west end of
Tower Street have ye a little turning towards the north to a fair
house sometime belonging to one named Griste, for he dwelt there
in the year 1449.   And Jack Cade, captain of the rebels in Kent,
being by him in this his house feasted, when he had dined, like an
unkind guest, robbed him of all that was there to be found worth the
carriage.   Next to this is one other fair house, sometime built by
Angell Dune, grocer, alderman of London, since possessed by Sir
John Champneis, alderman, and mayor of London.   He built in this
house a high tower of brick, the first that I ever heard of in any
private man's house, to overlook his neighbours in this city.   But
this delight of his eye was punished with blindness some years before
his death.   Since that time, Sir Percevall Hart, a jolly courtier,
and knight-harbinger † to the queen, was lodged there, &c.   From
this house, somewhat west, is the parish church of St. Margaret
Patten's; to the which church and house, on the north side, and
as far over against on the south, stretcheth the farthest west part
of this ward.

And, therefore, to begin again at the east end of Tower Street, on
the south side, have ye Bear Lane, wherein are many fair houses,
and runneth down to Thames Street.   The next is Spurrier Lane, of
old time so called, but since and of later time named Water Lane,
because it runneth down to the water gate by the Custom House in
Thames Street.   Then is there Hart Lane for Harp Lane, which
likewise runneth down into Thames Street.   In this Hart Lane is
the Bakers' Hall, sometime the dwelling-house of John Chichley,
chamberlain of London, who was son to William Chichley, alderman of London, brother to William Chichley, Archdeacon of Canterbury, nephew to Robert Chichley, mayor of London, and to Henry
Chichley, Archbishop of Canterbury.   This John Chichley, saith
John Leland, had twenty-four children.   Sir Thomas Kirrioll, of
Kent, after he had been long prisoner in France, married Elizabeth,
one of the daughters of this Chichley, by whom he had this Chichley's
house.   This Elizabeth was secondly married to Sir Ralfe Ashton,

---

* *Suskinges or dodkins*, little sous and doits, small French and Dutch money.

† *Harbinger*, formerly *herbergour*, was one who went before to secure fit lodging,
in this case for the Queen and her retinue, when they were on a journey.

knight-marshal, and thirdly, to Sir John Burchier, uncle to the late Burchier, Earl of Essex, but she never had child. Edward Poynings made part with Burchier and Elizabeth to have Ostenhanger in Kent after their death, and entered into it, they living.

In Tower Street, between Hart Lane and Church Lane, was a quadrant called Galley Row, because galley men dwelt there. Then have ye two lanes out of Tower Street, both called Church Lanes, because one runneth down by the east end of St. Dunstan's Church, and the other by the west end of the same; out of the west lane turneth another lane west towards St. Mary Hill, and is called Fowle Lane, which is for the most part in Tower Street Ward.

This church of St. Dunstan is called, in the east, for difference from one other of the same name in the west; it is a fair and large church of an ancient building, and within a large churchyard; it hath a great parish of many rich merchants, and other occupiers of divers trades, namely,* salters and ironmongers.

The monuments in that church be these :—In the choir, John Kenington, parson, there buried, 1374; Willim Islip, parson, 1382; John Kryoll, Esq., brother to Thomas Kryoll, 1400; Nicholas Bond, Thomas Barry, merchant, 1445; Robert Shelly, Esq., 1420; Robert Pepper, grocer, 1445; John Norwich, grocer, 1390; Alice Brome, wife to John Coventry, sometime mayor of London, 1433; William Isaack, draper, alderman, 1508; Edward Skales, merchant, 1521; John Ricroft, Esq., sergeant of the larder to Henry VII. and Henry VIII., 1532; Edwaters, Esq., sergeant-at-arms, 1558; Sir Bartholomew James, draper, mayor, 1479, buried under a fair monument with his lady; Ralfe Greenway, grocer, alderman, put under the stone of Robert Pepper, 1559; Thomas Bledlow, one of the sheriffs, 1472; James Bacon, fishmonger, sheriff, 1573; Sir Richard Champion, draper, mayor, 1568; Henry Herdson, skinner, alderman, 1555; Sir James Garnado, knight; William Hariot, draper, mayor, 1481, buried in a fair chapel by him built, 1517; John Tate, son to Sir John Tate, in the same chapel in the north wall; Sir Christopher Draper, ironmonger, mayor, 1566, buried 1580. And many other worshipful personages besides, whose monuments are altogether defaced.

Now for the two Church Lanes, they meeting on the south side of this church and churchyard, do join in one, and running down to the Thames Street, the same is called St. Dunstan's Hill, at the lower end whereof the said Thames Street towards the west on both sides almost to Belinsgate, but towards the east up to the water gate, by the bulwark of the Tower, is all of Tower Street Ward. In this street, on the Thames side, are divers large landing-places called

* *Namely*, especially.

wharfs or quays, for craneage up of wares and merchandise, as also for shipping of wares from thence to be transported. These wharfs and quays commonly bear the names of their owners, and are therefore changeable. I read, in the 26th of Henry VI., that in the parish of St. Dunstan in the East, a tenement called Passeke's Wharf, and another called Horner's Quay, in Thames Street, were granted to William Harindon, Esq. I read also that in the 6th of Richard II., John Churchman, grocer, for the quiet of merchants, did newly build a certain house upon the quay, called Wool Wharf, in the Tower Street Ward, in the parish of Allhallows Barking, betwixt the tenement of Paul Salisberrie on the east part, and the lane called the Water Gate on the west, to serve for tronage, or weighing of wools in the port of London; whereupon the king granted that during the life of the said John, the aforesaid tronage should be held and kept in the said house, with easements there for the balances and weights, and a counting place for the customer, controllers, clerks, and other officers of the said tronage, together with ingress and egress to and from the same, even as was had in other places, where the said tronage was wont to be kept, and that the king should pay yearly to the said John during his life forty shillings at the terms of St. Michael and Easter, by even portions, by the hands of his customer, without any other payment to the said John, as in the indenture thereof more at large appeareth.

Near unto this Customer's Quay towards the east, is the said water gate, and west from it Porter's Quay, then Galley Quay, where the galleys were used to unlade and land their merchandises and wares; and that part of Thames Street was therefore of some called Galley Row, but more commonly Petty Wales.

On the north side, as well as on the south of this Thames Street, are many fair houses large for stowage, built for merchants; but towards the east end thereof, namely, over against Galley Quay, Wool Quay, and the Custom House, there have been of old time some large buildings of stone, the ruins whereof do yet remain, but the first builders and owners of them are worn out of memory, wherefore the common people affirm Julius Cæsar to be the builder thereof, as also of the Tower itself. But thereof I have spoken already. Some are of another opinion, and that a more likely, that this great stone building was sometime the lodging appointed for the Princes of Wales, when they repaired to this city, and that therefore the street in that part is called Petty Wales, which name remaineth there most commonly until this day, even as where the Kings of Scotland were used to be lodged betwixt Charing Cross and Whitehall, it is likewise called Scotland, and where the Earls of Brittany were lodged without Aldersgate, the street is called Britain Street, &c.

The said building might of old time pertain to the Princes of Wales, as is aforesaid, but is since turned to other use.

It is before noted of Galley Quay, that the galleys of Italy, and other parts, did there discharge their wines and merchandises brought to this city. It is like, therefore, that the merchants and owners procured the place to build upon for their lodgings and storehouses, as the merchants of the Hanse of Almaine were licensed to have a house, called *Gilda Teutonicorum*, the Guildhall of the Germans. Also the merchants of Bordeaux were licensed to build at the Vintry, strongly with stone, as may be yet seen, and seemeth old, though often repaired; much more cause have these buildings in Petty Wales, though as lately built, and partly of the like stone brought from Caen in Normandy, to seem old, which for many years,—to wit, since the galleys left their course of landing there,—hath fallen to ruin, and been let out for stabling of horses, to tipplers of beer, and such like. Amongst others, one Mother Mampudding, as they termed her, for many years kept this house, or a great part thereof, for victualling. And it seemeth that the builders of the hall of this house were shipwrights, and not house carpenters. For the frame thereof, being but low, is raised of certain principal posts of main timber, fixed deep in the ground, without any groundsell, boarded close round about on the inside, having none other wall from the ground to the roof; those boards not exceeding the length of a clap board, about an inch thick, every board ledging over other as in a ship or galley, nailed with ship nails called rough and clench, to wit, rough nails with broad round heads, and clenched on the other side with square plates of iron. The roof of this hall is also wrought of the like board, and nailed with rough and clench, and seemeth as it were a galley, the keel turned upwards; and I observed that no worm or rottenness is seen to have entered either board or timber of that hall, and therefore, in mine opinion, of no great antiquity.

I read, in 44th of Edward III., that a hospital in the parish of Barking Church was founded by Robert Denton, chaplain, for the sustentation of poor priests, and other both men and women, that were sick of the frenzy, there to remain till they were perfectly whole, and restored to good memory. Also I read, that in the 6th of Henry V. there was in the Tower Ward a messuage, or great house, called Cobham's Inn; and in the 37th of Henry VI. a messuage in Thames Street pertaining to Richard Longvile, &c. Some of the ruins before spoken of may seem to be of the foresaid hospital, belonging peradventure to some prior alien, and so suppressed among the rest in the reign of Edward III. or Henry V., who suppressed them all. Thus much for the bounds and antiquities of this ward, wherein is noted the Tower of London, three parish churches, the custom-house, and two halls of companies, to wit, the Clothworkers and the Bakers. This ward hath an alderman, his deputy, common councillors eight, constables thirteen, scavengers twelve, wardmote men thirteen, and a beadle; it is taxed to the fifteenth at six and twenty pounds.

Aldgate Ward.

THE second ward within the wall, on the east part, is called Aldgate Ward, as taking name of the same gate. The principal street of this ward beginneth at Aldgate, stretching west to sometime a fair well, where now a pump is placed. From thence the way being divided into twain, the first and principal street is called Aldgate Street, runneth on the south side to Lime Street corner, and half that street down on the left hand is also of that ward. In the midway on that south side, betwixt Aldgate and Lime Street, is Harthorn Alley, a way that goeth through into Fenchurch Street over against Northumberland House. Then have ye the Bricklayers' Hall, and another alley called Sprinckle Alley, now named Sugar-loaf Alley, of the like sign. Then is there a fair house, with divers tenements near adjoining, sometime belonging to a late dissolved priory, since possessed by Mistress Cornewallis, widow, and her heirs, by gift of Henry VIII., in reward of fine puddings, as it was commonly said, by her made, wherewith she had presented him. Such was the princely liberality of those times. Of later time Sir Nicholas Throgmorton, knight, was lodged there. Then, somewhat more west, is Belzettar's Lane, so called of the first builder and owner thereof, now corruptly called Billiter Lane. Betwixt this Belzettar Lane and Lime Street was of later time a frame of three fair houses, set up in the year 1590, in place where before was a large garden-plot, enclosed from the high street with a brick wall, which wall being taken down, and the ground dug deep for cellarage, there was found right under the said brick wall another wall of stone, with a gate arched of stone, and gates of timber to be closed in the midst towards the street; the timber of the gates was consumed, but the hinges of iron still remained on their staples on both the sides. Moreover, in that wall were square windows, with bars of iron on either side of the gate. This wall was under ground about two fathoms deep, as I then esteemed it, and seemeth to be the ruins of some houses burned in the reign of King Stephen, when the fire began in the house of one Alewarde, near London Stone, and consumed east to Aldgate, whereby it appeareth how greatly the ground of this city hath been in that place raised.

On the north side this principal street stretcheth to the west corner of St. Andrew's Church, and then the ward turneth towards the north by St. Mary Street, on the east side to St. Augustine's Church in the wall, and so by Buries Markes * again, or about by the wall to Aldgate.

The second way from Aldgate, more towards the south, from the pump aforesaid, is called Fenchurch Street, and is of Aldgate Ward till ye come to Culver Alley, on the west side of Ironmongers' Hall, where sometime was a lane which went out of Fenchurch Street to the middest of Lime Street, but this lane was stopped up for suspicion of thieves that lurked there by night. Again to Aldgate, out of the principal street, even by the gate and wall of the city, runneth a lane south to Crowched Friars, and then Woodroffe Lane to the Tower Hill, and out of this lane west a street called Hart Street, which of that ward stretcheth to Sidon Lane by St. Olave's Church. One other lane more west from Aldgate goeth by Northumberland House toward the Crossed Friars ; then have ye on the same side the north end of Mart Lane and Blanch Apleton, where that ward endeth.

Thus much for the bounds ; now for monuments, or places most ancient and notable.

I am first to begin with the late dissolved priory of the Holy Trinity, called Christ's Church, on the right hand within Aldgate. This priory was founded by Matilda, queen, wife to Henry I., in the same place where Siredus sometime began to erect a church in honour of the Cross and of St. Mary Magdalen, of which the Dean and Chapter of Waltham were wont to receive thirty shillings. The queen was to acquit her church thereof, and in exchange gave unto them a mill. King Henry confirmed her gift. This church was given to Norman, first canon regular in all England. The said queen also gave unto the same church, and those that served God therein, the plot of Aldgate, and the soke thereunto belonging, with all customs so free as she had held the same, and twenty-five pound blankes, which she had of the city of Exeter, as appeareth by her deed, wherein she nameth the house Christ's Church, and reporteth Aldgate to be of her domains, which she granteth, with two parts of the rent of the city of Exeter. Norman took upon him to be prior of Christ's Church, in the year of Christ 1108, in the parishes of St. Mary Magdalen, St. Michael, St. Katherine, and the Blessed Trinity, which now was made but one parish of the Holy Trinity, and was in old time of the Holy Cross or Holy Rood parish. The priory was built on a piece of ground in the parish of St. Katherine towards Aldgate, which lieth in length betwixt the King's Street, by the which men go towards Aldgate, near to the chapel of St. Michael towards the north, and containeth in length eighty-three ells, half, quarter,

---

* Bevis Marks.

and half-quarter of the king's iron eln, and lieth in breadth, &c. The soke and ward of Aldgate was then bounded as I have before showed. The queen was a means also that the land and English Knighten Guild was given unto the prior Norman: the honourable man, Geffrey de Glinton, was a great helper therein, and obtained that the canons might enclose the way betwixt their church and the wall of the city, &c. This priory, in process of time, became a very fair and large church, rich in lands and ornaments, and passed all the priories in the city of London or shire of Middlesex; the prior whereof was an alderman of London, to wit, of Portsoken Ward.

I read, that Eustacius, the eighth prior, about the year 1264, because he would not deal with temporal matters, instituted Theobald Fitz Ivonis, alderman of Portsoken Ward under him, and that William Rising, prior of Christ's Church, was sworn alderman of the said Portsoken Ward in the first of Richard II. These priors have sitten and ridden amongst the aldermen of London, in livery like unto them, saving that his habit was in shape of a spiritual person, as I myself have seen in my childhood; at which time the prior kept a most bountiful house of meat and drink, both for rich and poor, as well within the house as at the gates, to all comers, according to their estates.

These were the monuments in this church:—Sir Robert Turke, and Dame Alice his wife; John Tirell, esquire; Simon Kempe, esquire; James Manthorpe, esquire; John Ascue, esquire; Thomas Fauset, of Scalset, esquire; John Kempe, gentleman; Robert Chirwide, esquire; Sir John Heningham, and Dame Isabel his wife; Dame Agnes, wife first to Sir William Bardolph, and then to Sir Thomas Mortimer; John Ashfield, esquire; Sir John Dedham, knight; Sir Ambrose Charcam; Joan, wife to Thomas Nuck, gentleman; John Husse, esquire; John Beringham, esquire; Thomas Goodwine, esquire; Ralph Walles, esquire; Dame Margaret, daughter to Sir Ralph Chevie, wife to Sir John Barkeley, to Sir Thomas Barnes, and to Sir W. Bursire; William Roofe; Simon Francis; John Breton, esquire; Helling, esquire; John Malwen and his wife; Anthonie Wels, son to John Wels; Nicholas de Avesey, and Margarie his wife; Anthonie, son to John Milles; Baldwine, son to King Stephen, and Mathilde, daughter to King Stephen, wife to the Earl of Meulan; Henry Fitzalwine, mayor of London, 1213; Geffrey Mandevile, 1215; and many other. But to conclude of this priory: King Henry VIII., minding to reward Sir Thomas Audley, speaker of the parliament against Cardinal Wolsey, as ye may read in Hall, sent for the prior, commending him for his hospitality, promised him preferment, as a man worthy of a far greater dignity, which promise surely he performed, and compounded with him, though in what sort I never heard, so that the prior surrendered all that priory, with the appurtenances, to the king, in the month of July, in the year 1531, the 23rd of the said king's reign. The canons were sent to other houses of the same order, and the priory, with the appurtenances, King Henry gave to Sir Thomas Audley, newly knighted, and after made Lord Chancellor.

Sir Thomas Audley offered the great church of this priory, with a ring of nine bells well tuned (whereof four the greatest were since sold to the parish of Stebunhithe,* and the five lesser to the parish of St. Stephen in Coleman Street), to the parishioners of St. Katherine Christ Church, in exchange for their small parish church, minding to have pulled it down, and to have built there towards the street; but the parishioners having doubts in their heads of after-claps, refused the offer. Then was the priory church and steeple proffered to whomsoever would take it down, and carry it from the ground, but no man would undertake the offer; whereupon Sir Thomas Audley was fain to be at more charges than could be made of the stones, timber, lead, iron, &c. For the workmen, with great labour, beginning at the top, loosed stone from stone, and threw them down, whereby the most part of them were broken, and few remained whole; and those were sold very cheap, for all the buildings then made about the city were of brick and timber. At that time any man in the city might have a cartload of hard stone for paving brought to his door for sixpence or sevenpence, with the carriage. The said Thomas Lord Audley built and dwelt on this priory during his life, and died there in the year 1544; since the which time the said priory came by marriage of the Lord Audley's daughter and heir unto Thomas, late Duke of Norfolk, and was then called the Duke's place.

The parish church of St. Katherine standeth in the cemetery of the late dissolved priory of the Holy Trinity, and is therefore called St. Katherine Christ Church. This church seemeth to be very old, since the building whereof the high street hath been so often raised by pavements, that now men are fain to descend into the said church by divers steps, seven in number. But the steeple, or bell-tower thereof, hath been lately built, to wit, about the year 1504; for Sir John Percivall, merchant tailor, then deceasing, gave money towards the building thereof. There be the monuments of Sir Thomas Fleming, knight, of Rowles, in Essex, and Margaret his wife, 1464; Roger Marshall, esquire; Jane Horne, wife to Roger Marshall; William Multon, *alias* Bordeaux herald; John Goad, esquire, and Joan his wife; Beatrix, daughter to William Browne; Thomas Multon, esquire, son to Bordeaux herald; John Chitcroft, esquire;

* *Stebunhithe*, Stepney.

John Wakefield, esquire; William Criswick; Anne and Sewch,* daughters to Ralph Shirley, esquire; Sir John Rainsford, knight of Essex; Sir Nicholas Throkmorton, chief butler of England, one of the chamberlains of the exchequer, ambassador, &c., 1570, and other.

At the north-west corner of this ward, in the said high street, standeth the fair and beautiful parish church of St. Andrew the Apostle; with an addition, to be known from other churches of that name, of the knape † or undershaft; and so called St. Andrew Undershaft, because that of old time every year on May-day in the morning, it was used, that an high or long shaft, or May-pole, was set up there, in the midst of the street, before the south side of the said church: which shaft, when it was set on end and fixed in the ground, was higher than the church steeple. Geffrey Chaucer, writing of a vain boaster, hath these words, meaning of the said shaft :—

> " Right well aloft, and high ye beare your heade,
> The weather cocke, with flying, as ye would kill,
> When ye be stuffed, bet of wine then brede,
> Then looke ye, when your wombe doth fill,
> As ye would beare the great shaft of Cornehill,
> Lord, so merrily crowdeth then your croke,
> That all the streete may heare your body cloke." ‡

This shaft was not raised at any time since evil May-day (so called of an insurrection made by apprentices and other young persons against aliens in the year 1517); but the said shaft was laid along over the doors, and under the pentises of one row of houses and alley gate, called of the shaft Shaft Alley, being of the possessions of Rochester Bridge, in the ward of Lime Street. It was there, I say, hung on iron hooks many years, till the third of King Edward VI., that one Sir Stephen, curate of St. Katherine Christ's Church, preaching at Paul's Cross, said there that this shaft was made an idol, by naming the Church of St. Andrew with the addition of "under that shaft." He persuaded therefore that the names of churches might be altered; also that the names of days in the week might be changed; the fish days to be kept any days except Friday and Saturday, and the Lent any time, save only betwixt Shrovetide and Easter. I have oft times seen this man, forsaking the pulpit of his said parish church, preach out of a high elm tree in the midst of the churchyard, and then entering the church, forsaking the altar, to have sung his high mass in English upon a tomb of the dead towards the north. I heard his sermon at Paul's Cross, and I saw the effect that followed;

* *Sewch*, Suke, Susan.
† *Knape*, knob or bunch of flowers on top of the May-pole.
‡ Stow's sidenote is " Chaucer, Chance of Dice."

for in the afternoon of that present Sunday, the neighbours and
tenants to the said bridge, over whose doors the said shaft had lain,
after they had well dined, to make themselves strong, gathered more
help, and with great labour raising the shaft from the hooks, whereon
it had rested two-and-thirty years, they sawed it in pieces, every man
taking for his share so much as had lain over his door and stall, the
length of his house ; and they of the alley divided among them so
much as had lain over their alley gate.   Thus was this idol, as he
termed it, mangled, and after burned.

Soon after was there a commotion of the commons in Norfolk,
Suffolk, Essex, and other shires ; by means whereof, strait * orders
being taken for the suppression of rumours, divers persons were
apprehended and executed by martial law ; amongst the which the
bailiff of Romford, in Essex, was one, a man very well beloved.   He
was early in the morning of Mary Magdalen's day, then kept holiday,
brought by the sheriffs of London and the knight-marshal to the
well within Aldgate, there to be executed upon a gibbet set up that
morning, where, being on the ladder, he had words to this effect :—

"Good people, I am come hither to die, but know not for what offence, except
for words by me spoken yesternight to Sir Stephen, curate and preacher of this
parish, which were these.   He asked me, 'What news in the country?'   I
answered, 'Heavy news.'   'Why?' quoth he.   'It is said,' quoth I, 'that many
men be up in Essex, but, thanks be to God, all is in good quiet about us :' and
this was all, as God be my judge," &c.

Upon these words of the prisoner, Sir Stephen, to avoid reproach
of the people, left the city, and was never heard of since amongst
them to my knowledge.   I heard the words of the prisoner, for he
was executed upon the pavement of my door where I then kept
house.   Thus much by digression : now again to the parish church
of St. Andrew Undershaft, for it still retaineth the name, which hath
been new built by the parishioners there since the year 1520 ; every
man putting to his helping hand, some with their purses, other with
their bodies.   Steven Gennings, merchant tailor, sometime mayor
of London, caused at his charges to be built the whole north side
of the great middle aisle, both of the body and choir, as appeareth
by his arms over every pillar graven, and also the north aisle, which
he roofed with timber and ceiled ; also the whole south side of the
church was glazed, and the pews in the south chapel made of his
costs, as appeareth in every window, and upon the said pews.   He
deceased in the year 1524, and was buried in the Greyfriars Church.
John Kerkbie, merchant tailor, sometime one of the sheriffs, John
Garlande, merchant tailor, and Nicholas Levison, mercer, executor
to Garlande, were great benefactors to this work ; which was finished

* *Strait*, strict.

to the glazing in the year 1529, and fully finished 1532. Buried in this church : Philip Malpas, one of the sheriffs, 1439 ; Sir Robert Dennie, knight, and after him Thomas Dennie, his son, in the year 1421 ; Thomas Stokes, gentleman, grocer, 1496. In the new church : John Nichell, merchant tailor, 1537 ; William Draper, esquire, 1537 ; Isabell and Margaret, his wives ; Nicholas Levison, mercer, one of the sheriffs, 1534 ; John Gerrarde, woolman, merchant of the staple, 1546 ; Henry Man, Doctor of Divinity, Bishop of Man, 1550 ; Stephen Kyrton, merchant tailor, alderman, 1553 ; David Woodroffe, haberdasher, one of the sheriffs, 1554 ; Stephen Woodroffe, his son, gave one hundred pounds in money, for the which the poor of that parish receive two shillings in bread weekly for ever ; Sir Thomas Offley, merchant tailor, mayor, 1556 ; he bequeathed the one-half of all his goods to charitable actions, but the parish received little benefit thereby ; Thomas Starkey, skinner, one of the sheriffs, 1578 ; Hugh Offley, leatherseller, one of the sheriffs, 1588 ; William Hanbury, baker.

Now down St. Mary Street, by the west end of the church towards the north, stand divers fair houses for merchants and other ; namely, one fair great house, built by Sir William Pickering the father, possessed by Sir William his son, and since by Sir Edward Wootton of Kent. North from this place is the Fletchers' Hall, and so down to the corner of that street, over against London wall, and against eastwards to a fair house lately new built, partly by Master Robert Beale, one of the clerks of the council.

Then come you to the Papey, a proper house, wherein sometime was kept a fraternity or brotherhood of St. Charity and St. John Evangelist, called the Papey, for poor impotent priests (for in some language priests are called papes) founded in the year 1430 by William Oliver, William Barnaby, and John Stafford, chaplains or chantry priests in London, for a master, two wardens, &c., chaplains, chantry priests, conducts, and other brethren and sisters, that should be admitted into the Church of St. Augustine Papey in the wall. The brethren of this house becoming lame, or otherwise into great poverty, were here relieved, as to have chambers, with certain allowance of bread, drink, and coal, and one old man and his wife to see them served and to keep the house clean. This brotherhood, among others, was suppressed in the reign of Edward VI. ; since the which time in this house hath been lodged Master Moris of Essex; Sir Francis Walsingham, principal secretary to her majesty ; Master Barret of Essex, &c.

Then next is one great house, large of rooms, fair courts, and garden-plots ; sometimes pertaining to the Bassets, since that to the abbots of Bury in Suffolk, and therefore called Buries Markes, corruptly Bevis Marks, and since the dissolution of the abbey of Bury, to Thomas Henage the father, and to Sir Thomas his son. Then next unto it is the before-spoken priory of the Holy Trinity; to wit, the west and north part thereof, which stretcheth up to Aldgate, where we first began.

Now in the second way from Aldgate, more toward the south from the well or pump aforesaid, lieth Fenchurch Street; on the right hand whereof, somewhat west from the south end of Belzetter's Lane, is the Ironmongers' Hall; which company was incorporated in the 3rd of Edward IV. Richard Fleming was their first master; Nicholas Marshall and Richard Cox were custos, or wardens. And on the left hand, or south side, even by the gate and wall of the city, runneth down a lane to the Tower Hill; the south part whereof is called Woodroffe Lane, and out of this lane toward the west a street called Hart Street. In this street, at the south-east corner thereof, sometime stood one house of Crouched (or crossed) Friars, founded by Ralph Hosiar and William Sabernes about the year 1298. Stephen, the tenth prior of the Holy Trinity in London, granted three tenements for 13s. 8d. by the year unto the said Ralph Hosiar and William Sabernes, who afterwards became friars of St. Cross; Adam was the first prior of that house. These friars founded their house in place of certain tenements purchased of Richard Wimbush, the twelfth prior of the Holy Trinity, in the year 1319, which was confirmed by Edward III. the 17th of his reign, valued at £52, 13s. 4d., surrendered the twelfth of November, the 30th of Henry VIII. In this house was buried Master John Tirres; Nicholas, the son of William Kyriell, esquire; Sir Thomas Mellington, baron of Wemesse, and Dame Elizabeth his wife, daughter and heir of William Botelar, baron of Wome; Robert Mellington, esquire, and Elizabeth his wife, daughter to Ferris of Ousley; Henry Lovell, son to William Lord Lovell; Dame Isabel, wife to William Edwarde, mayor of London, 1471; William Narborough, and Dame Elizabeth his wife; William Narborough, and Dame Beatrix his wife; William Brosked, esquire; William Bowes; Lionel Mollington, esquire, son of Robert Mollington; Nicholas Couderow, and Elizabeth his wife; Sir John Stratford, knight; Sir Thomas Asseldy, knight, clerk of the crown, sub-marshal of England, and justice of the shire of Middlesex; John Rest, grocer, mayor of London, 1516; Sir John Skevington, knight, merchant tailor, sheriff, 1520; Sir John Milborne, draper, mayor in the year 1520, was buried there, but removed since to St. Edmondes in Lombard Street; Sir Rice Grifith, beheaded on the Tower Hill, 1531.

In place of this church is now a carpenters' yard, a tennis court, and such like. The friars' hall was made a glass-house, or house wherein was made glass of divers sorts to drink in; which house in the year 1575, on the 4th of September, burst out into a terrible fire, where being practised all means possible to quench, notwithstanding as the same house in a small time before had consumed a great quantity of wood by making of glasses, now itself having within it about forty thousand billets of wood, was all consumed to the stone walls, which nevertheless greatly hindered the fire from spreading any further.

Adjoining unto this Friars' Church, by the east end thereof in Woodroffe Lane towards the Tower Hill, are certain proper almshouses, fourteen in number, built of brick and timber, founded by Sir John Milborne, draper, sometime mayor, 1521, wherein he placed thirteen aged poor men and their wives, if they have wives. These have their dwellings rent free, and 2s. 4d. the piece, the first day of every month, for ever. One also is to have his house over the gate, and 4s. every month. More, he appointed every Sunday for ever, thirteen penny loaves of white bread, to be given in the parish church of St. Edmund in Lombard Street, to thirteen poor people of that parish; and the like thirteen loaves to be given in the parish church of St. Michael upon Cornhill, and in either parish every year one load of charcoal, of thirty sacks in the load; and this gift to be continued for ever. For performance whereof, by the master and wardens of the drapers in London, he assured unto them and their successors twenty-three messuages and tenements, and eighteen garden-plots, in the parish of St. Olave in Hart Street; with proviso, that if they perform not those points above mentioned, the said tenements and gardens to remain to the mayor and commonalty of the city of London.

Next to these almshouses is the Lord Lumley's house, built in the time of King Henry VIII. by Sir Thomas Wyat the father, upon one plot of ground of late pertaining to the foresaid Crossed Friars, where part of their house stood: and this is the farthest part of Aldgate Ward towards the south, and joineth to the Tower Hill. The other side of that line, over against the Lord Lumley's house, on the wall side of the city, is now for the most part, or altogether, built even to Aldgate.

Then have you on the south side of Fenchurch Street, over against the well or pump, amongst other fair and large built houses, one that sometime belonged to the prior of Monte Joves, or Monastery Cornute, a cell to Monte Joves beyond the seas, in Essex: it was the prior's inn, when he repaired to this city. Then a lane that leadeth down by Northumberland House towards the Crossed Friars, as is afore showed.

This Northumberland House, in the parish of St. Katherine Coleman, belonged to Henry Percy, Earl of Northumberland, in the 33rd of Henry VI., but of late being left by the earls, the gardens thereof were made into bowling alleys, and other parts into dicing houses, common to all comers for their money, there to bowl and hazard; but now of late so many bowling alleys, and other houses for unlawful gaming, hath been raised in other parts of the city and suburbs, that this their ancient and only patron of misrule, is left and forsaken of her gamesters, and therefore turned into a number of great rents, small cottages, for strangers and others.

At the east end of this lane, in the way from Aldgate toward the Crossed Friars, of old time were certain tenements called the poor Jewry, of Jews dwelling there.

Next unto this Northumberland House is the parish church of St. Katherine, called Coleman; which addition of Coleman was taken of a great haw-yard, or garden, of old time called Coleman Haw, in the parish of the Trinity, now called Christ's Church, and in the parish of St. Katherine and All Saints called Coleman Church.

Then have you Blanch Apleton; whereof I read, in the 13th of Edward I., that a lane behind the said Blanch Apleton was granted by the king to be enclosed and shut up. This Blanch Apleton was a manor belonging to Sir Thomas Roos of Hamelake, knight, the 7th of Richard II., standing at the north-east corner of Mart Lane, so called of a privilege sometime enjoined to keep a mart there, long since discontinued, and therefore forgotten, so as nothing remaineth for memory but the name of Mart Lane, and that corruptly termed Mark Lane. I read that, in the third of Edward IV., all basket-makers, wire-drawers, and other foreigners, were permitted to have shops in this manor of Blanch Apleton, and not elsewhere, within this city or suburbs thereof; and this also being the farthest west part of this ward on that south side, I leave it, with three parish churches, St. Katherine Christ Church, St. Andrew Undershaft, and St. Katherine Coleman's; and three halls of companies, the Brick-layers' Hall, the Fletchers' Hall, and the Ironmongers' Hall. It hath an alderman, his deputy, common councillors six, constables six, scavengers nine, wardmote men for inquest eighteen, and a beadle. It is taxed to the fifteen in London at five pounds.

Lime Street Ward.

THE next is Lime Street Ward, and taketh the name of Lime Street of making or selling of lime there, as is supposed. The east side of this Lime Street, from the north corner thereof to the midst, is of Aldgate Ward, as is aforesaid; the west side, for the most part from the said north corner, southward, is of this Lime Street Ward; the south end on both sides is of Langborne Ward; the body of this Lime Street Ward is of the high street called Cornhill Street, which stretcheth from Lime Street on the south side to the west corner of Leadenhall, and on the north side from the south-west corner of St. Mary Street to another corner over against Leadenhall. Now for St. Mary Street; the west side thereof is of this Lime Street Ward, and also the street which runneth by the north end of this St. Mary Street, on both sides, from thence west to an house called the Wrestlers, a sign so called, almost to Bishopsgate. And these are the bounds of this small ward.

Monuments, or places notable, in this ward be these:—In Lime Street are divers fair houses for merchants and others; there was sometime a mansion-house of the kings, called the King's Artirce,* whereof I find record in the 14th of Edward I., but now grown out of knowledge. I read also of another great house in the west side of Lime Street, having a chapel on the south and a garden on the west, then belonging to the Lord Nevill, which garden is now called the Green Yard of the Leadenhall. This house, in the 9th of Richard II., pertained to Sir Simon Burley, and Sir John Burley his brother; and of late the said house was taken down, and the forefront thereof new built of timber by Hugh Offley, alderman. At the north-west corner of Lime Street was of old time one great messuage called Benbrige's Inn. Ralph Holland, draper, about the year 1452, gave it to John Gill, master, and to the wardens and fraternity of tailors and linen-armourers of St. John Baptist in London, and to their successors for ever. They did set up in place thereof a fair large frame of timber, containing in the high street one great house, and before it to the corner of Lime Street three other tenements, the corner house being the largest, and then down Lime Street divers proper tenements; all which the merchant tailors, in the reign of Edward VI., sold to Stephen Kirton, merchant tailor and alderman. He gave with his daughter, Grisild, to Nicholas Woodroffe, the said great house, with two tenements before it, in lieu of a hundred pounds, and made it up in money £366, 13s. 4d. This worshipful man, and the gentlewoman his widow after him, kept those houses down Lime Street in good reparations, never put out but one tenant, took no fines, nor raised rents of them, which was ten shillings the piece yearly: but whether that favour did overlive her funeral, the tenants now can best declare the contrary.

Next unto this, on the high street, was the Lord Sowche's †

---

* *Artirce*, old French *artiers*, *artiiers*, skilled workmen. Probably the house had been used by men engaged on the king's palaces, or other public works.

† *Sowche*, Zouch.

messuage or tenement, and other; in place whereof, Richard Wethell, merchant tailor, built a fair house, with a high tower, the second in number, and first of timber, that ever I learnt to have been built to overlook neighbours in this city.

This Richard, then a young man, became in a short time so tormented with gouts in his joints, of the hands and legs, that he could neither feed himself nor go further than he was led; much less was he able to climb and take the pleasure of the height of his tower.* Then is there another fair house, built by Stephen Kirton, alderman; Alderman Lee doth now possess it, and again new buildeth it.

Then is there a fair house of old time called the Green Gate; by which name one Michael Pistoy Lombard held it, with a tenement and nine shops in the reign of Richard II., who in the 15th of his reign gave it to Roger Crophull and Thomas Bromeflet, esquires, by the name of the Green Gate, in the parish of St. Andrew upon Cornhill, in Lime Street Ward; since the which time Philip Malpas, some time alderman, and one of the sheriffs, dwelt therein, and was there robbed and spoiled of his goods to a great value by Jack Cade, and other rebels, in the year 1449.

Afterwards, in the reign of Henry VII., it was seized into the king's hands, and then granted, first, unto John Alston, after that unto William de la Rivers, and since by Henry VIII. to John Mutas, a Picarde or Frenchman, who dwelt there, and harboured in his house many Frenchmen, that kalendred wolsteds,† and did other things contrary to the franchises of the citizens; wherefore on evil May-day, which was in the year 1517, the apprentices and others spoiled his house; and if they could have found Mutas, they would have stricken off his head. Sir Peter Mutas, son to the said John Mutas, sold this house to David Woodroffe, alderman, whose son, Sir Nicholas Woodroffe, alderman, sold it over to John Moore, alderman, that now possesseth it.

Next is a house called the Leaden Porch, lately divided into two tenements; whereof one is a tavern, and then one other house for a merchant, likewise called the Leaden Porch, but now turned to a cook's house. Next is a fair house and a large, wherein divers mayoralties have been kept, whereof twain in my remembrance; to wit, Sir William Bowyer and Sir Henry Huberthorne.

The next is Leadenhall, of which I read, that in the year 1309

---

* It will be remembered that the first man who built in London so high as to overlook his neighbour, became blind (p. 155), and could see nothing if he climbed. The second we are now told was so lamed that he could not climb.

† *Kalendred wolsteds*, pressed and smoothed worsteds. A calender was the cylinder or roller used. Stow elsewhere writes wolsted, the early form of the word.

it belonged to Sir Hugh Nevill, knight, and that the Lady Alice his widow made a feoffment thereof, by the name of Leadenhall, with the advowsons of the Church of St. Peter upon Cornhill, and other churches, to Richard, Earl of Arundell and Surrey, 1362. More, in the year 1380, Alice Nevill, widow to Sir John Nevill, knight, of Essex, confirmed to Thomas Gogshall and others the said manor of Leadenhall, the advowsons, &c. In the year 1384, Humfrey de Bohun, Earl of Hereford, had the said manor. And in the year 1408, Robert Rikeden, of Essex, and Margaret his wife, confirmed to Richard Whittington, and other citizens of London, the said manor of Leadenhall, with the appurtenances, the advowsons of St. Peter's Church, St. Margaret Patten's, &c. And in the year 1411, the said Whittington and other confirmed the same to the mayor and commonalty of London, whereby it came to the possession of the city. Then in the year 1443, the 21st of Henry VI., John Hatherley, mayor, purchased license of the said king to take up two hundred fother of lead, for the building of water conduits, a common granary, and the cross in West Cheap, more richly, for the honour of the city. In the year next following, the parson and parish of St. Dunstan, in the east of London, seeing the famous and mighty man (for the words be in the grant, *cum nobilis et potens vir*), Simon Eyre, citizen of London, among other his works of piety, effectually determined to erect and build a certain granary upon the soil of the same city at Leadenhall, of his own charges, for the common utility of the said city, to the amplifying and enlarging of the said granary, granted to Henry Frowicke, then mayor, the aldermen and commonalty, and their successors for ever, all their tenements, with the appurtenances, sometime called the Horsemill, in Grass Street, for the annual rent of four pounds, &c. Also, certain evidences of an alley and tenements pertaining to the Horsemill adjoining to the said Leadenhall in Grass Street, given by William Kingstone, fishmonger, unto the parish church of St. Peter upon Cornhill, do specify the said granary to be built by the said honourable and famous merchant, Simon Eyre, some time an upholsterer, and then a draper,* in the year 1419. He built it of squared stone, in form as now it showeth, with a fair and large chapel in the east side of the quadrant, over the porch of which he caused to be written, *Dextra Domini exaltavit me* (The Lord's right hand exalted me). Within the said church, on the north wall, was written, *Honorandus famosus mercator Simon Eyre hujus operis, &c.* In English thus :—" The honourable and famous merchant, Simon

---

* The city tradition of Simon Eyre as *potens vir* is playfully preserved in Dekker's merry comedy of "The Shoemaker's Holiday." But Simon Eyre was not a shoemaker.

Eyre, founder of this work, once mayor of this city, citizen and draper of the same, departed out of this life, the 18th day of September, the year from the Incarnation of Christ 1459, and the 38th year of the reign of King Henry VI." He was buried in the parish church of St. Mary Woolnoth, in Lombard Street. He gave by his testament, which I have read, to be distributed to all prisons in London, or within a mile of that city, somewhat to relieve them. More, he gave two thousand marks, upon a condition, which not performed, was then to be distributed to maids' marriages, and other deeds of charity; he also gave three thousand marks to the drapers, upon condition they should, within one year after his decease, establish perpetually a master or warden, five secular priests, six clerks, and two choristers, to sing daily Divine service by note for ever, in his chapel of the Leadenhall; also, one master, with an usher, for grammar, one master for writing, and the third for song, with housing there newly built for them for ever; the master to have for his salary ten pounds, and every other priest eight pounds, every other clerk five pounds six shillings and eight-pence, and every other chorister five marks; and if the drapers refused this to do, within one year after his decease, then the three thousand marks to remain to the prior and convent of Christ's Church in London, with condition to establish, as is aforesaid, within two years after his decease; and if they refused, then the three thousand marks to be disposed by his executors, as they best could devise, in works of charity. Thus much for his testament, not performed by establishing of Divine service in his chapel, or free schools for scholars; neither how the stock of three thousand marks, or rather five thousand marks, was employed by his executors, could I ever learn. He left issue, Thomas, who had issue, Thomas, &c. True it is, that in one year, 1464, the 3rd of Edward IV., it was agreed by the mayor, aldermen, and commonalty of London, that notwithstanding the king's letters patent, lately before granted unto them, touching the tronage * or weighing of wares to be holden at the Leadenhall, yet suit should be made to the king for new letters patent to be granted to the mayor of the staple for the tronage of wools to be holden there, and order to be taken by the discretion of Thomas Cooke, then mayor, the council of the city, Geoffrey Filding, then mayor of the staple at West-minster, and of the king's council, what should be paid to the mayor and aldermen of the city, for the laying and housing of the wools there, that so they might be brought forth and weighed, &c.

---

* *Tronage* was weighing, from the old French *trone*, a weighing-machine. Tron was more especially applied to the machine for weighing wool. The Tron Church at Edinburgh had its name from being built near such a weighing-machine.

Touching the chapel there, I find that in the year 1466, by license obtained of King Edward IV., in the 6th of his reign, a fraternity of the Trinity, of sixty priests, besides other brethren and sisters, in the same chapel, was founded by William Rouse, John Risbie, and Thomas Ashby, priests, some of the which sixty priests, every market-day in the forenoon, did celebrate Divine service there to such market-people as repaired to prayer; and once every year they met all together and had solemn service, with procession of the brethren and sisters. This foundation was in the year 1512, by a common council, confirmed to the sixty Trinity priests, and to their successors, at the will of the mayor and commonalty.

In the year 1484, a great fire happened upon this Leadenhall, by what casualty I know not, but much housing was there destroyed, with all the stocks for guns, and other provision belonging to the city, which was a great loss, and no less charge to be repaired by them.

In the year 1503, the 18th of Henry VII., a request was made by the commons of the city, concerning the usage of the said Leadenhall, in form as followeth :—

" Please it, the lord mayor, and common council, to enact, that all Frenchmen bringing canvass, linen cloth, and other wares to be sold, and all foreigners bringing wolsteds, sayes, staimus,* coverings, nails, iron work, or any other wares, and also all manner of foreigners bringing lead to the city to be sold, shall bring all such their wares aforesaid to the open market of the Leadenhall, there and nowhere else to be sold and uttered, like as of old time it hath been used, upon pain of forfeiture of all the said wares showed or sold in any other place than aforesaid ; the show of the said wares to be made three days in the week, that is to say, Monday, Tuesday, and Wednesday ; it is also thought reasonable that the common beam be kept from henceforth in the Leadenhall, and the farmer to pay therefore reasonable rent to the chamber ; for better it is that the chamber have advantage thereby than a foreign person ; and also the said Leadenhall, which is more chargeable now by half than profitable, shall better bear out the charges thereof; also the common beam for wool at Leadenhall, may yearly pay a rent to the chamber of London, toward supportation and charges of the same place ; for reason it is, that a common office, occupied upon a common ground, bear a charge to the use of the commonalty ; also, that foreigners bringing wools, felts, or any other merchandises or wares to Leadenhall, to be kept there for the sale and market, may pay more largely for the keeping of their goods than free men."

Thus much for the request of the Commons at this time.

Now to set down some proof that the said Hall hath been employed and used as a granary for corn and grain, as the same was first appointed, leaving all former examples, this one may suffice : Roger Achley, mayor of London in the year 1512, the 3rd of Henry VIII., when the said mayor entered the mayoralty, there was not

---

* *Wolsteds, sayes, staimus.* Worsteds, or woollen goods, silks, and fabrics of thread, tammies. *Staimus* is probably a misprint for *stamins* (Latin, *stamineus*, made of threads).

found one hundred quarters of wheat in all the garners of the city, either within the liberties, or near adjoining; through the which scarcity, when the carts of Stratford came laden with bread to the city, as they had been accustomed, there was such press about them, that one man was ready to destroy another in striving to be served for their money. But this scarcity did not last long; for the mayor in short time made such provision of wheat, that the bakers, both of London and Stratford, were weary of taking it up, and were forced to take up much more than they would, and for the rest the mayor laid out the money, and stored it up in Leadenhall, and other garners of the city. This mayor also kept the market so well, that he would be at the Leadenhall by four o'clock in the summer's mornings; and from thence he went to other markets, to the great comfort of the citizens.

I read also that in the year 1528, the 20th of Henry VIII., surveyors were appointed to view the garners of the city, namely, the Bridgehouse and the Leadenhall, how they were stored of grain for the service of the city. And because I have here before spoken of the bread carts coming from Stratford-at-the-Bow, ye shall understand that of old time the bakers of bread at Stratford were allowed to bring daily, except the Sabbath and principal feasts, divers long carts laden with bread, the same being two ounces in the penny wheat loaf heavier than the penny wheat loaf baked in the city, the same to be sold in Cheap, three or four carts standing there, between Gutheron's Lane and Fauster's Lane end, one cart on Cornhill, by the conduit, and one other in Grass Street. And I have read, that in the 4th year of Edward II., Richard Reffeham being mayor, a baker named John of Stratford, for making bread less than the assize, was with a fool's hood on his head, and loaves of bread about his neck, drawn on a hurdle through the streets of this city. Moreover, on the 44th of Edward III., John Chichester being mayor of London, I read in the Visions of Pierce Plowman, a book so called, as followeth :—

> " At Londone, I leve,
> Liketh wel my wafres;
> And louren whan thei lakken hem.
> It is noght longe y passed,
> There was a careful commune,
> Whan no cart com to towne
> With breed fro Stratforde;
> Tho gonnen beggaris wepe,
> And werkmen were agast a lite;
> This wole be thoughte longe.
> In the date of oure Drighte,*
> In a drye Aprille,

---

* *Drighte,* Lord.

> A thousand and thre hundred
> Twies thretty and ten,
> My wafres there were gesene *
> Whan Chichestre was maire."

I read also in the 20th of Henry VIII., Sir James Spencer being mayor, six bakers of Stratford were amerced in the Guildhall of London for baking under the size appointed. These bakers of Stratford left serving of this city, I know not upon what occasion, about thirty years since.

In the year 1519 a petition was exhibited by the Commons to the Common Council, and was by them allowed, concerning the Leadenhall, how they would have it used, viz. :—

"Meekly beseeching, showeth unto your good lordship and masterships, divers citizens of this city, which under correction think, that the great place called the Leadenhall should nor ought not to be letten to farm to any person or persons, and in especial to any fellowship or company incorporate, to have and hold the same Hall for term of years, for such inconveniences as thereby may ensue, and come to the hurt of the common weal of the said city in time to come, as somewhat more largely may appear in the articles following.

"First, If any assembly or hasty gathering of the commons of the said city, for suppressing or subduing of misruled people within the said city, hereafter shall happen to be called or commanded by the mayor, aldermen, and other governors and councillors of the said city for the time being, there is none so convenient, meet, and necessary a place, to assemble them in, within the said city, as the said Leadenhall, both for largeness of room, and their sure defence in time of their counselling together about the premises. Also, in that place hath been used the artillery, guns, and other armours of the said city to be safely kept in a readiness for the safeguard, wealth, and defence of the said city, to be had and occupied at times when need required. As also the store of timber for the necessary reparations of the tenements belonging to the chamber of the said city, there commonly hath been kept. Item, If any triumph or nobleness were to be done, or shown by the commonalty of the city, for the honour of our sovereign lord the king and realm, and for the worship of the said city, the said Leadenhall is most meet and convenient place to prepare and order the said triumph therein, and from thence to issue forth to the places therefore appointed. Item, at any largess or dole of any money made unto the poor people of this city, it hath been used to be done and given in the said Leadenhall, for that the said place is most meet therefore. Item, the honourable father, that was maker of the said Hall, had a special will, intent, and mind, that (as it is commonly said) the market men and women that came to the city with victuals and other things, should have their free standing within the said Leadenhall in wet weather, to keep themselves and their wares dry, and thereby to encourage them, and all other, to have the better will and desire the more plenteously to resort to the said city, to victual the same. And if the said Hall should be letten to farm, the will of the said honourable father should never be fulfilled nor take effect. Item, if the said place, which is the chief fortress, and most necessary place within all the city for the tuition and safeguard of the same, should be letten to farm out of the hands of the chief heads of the same city, and especially to another body politic, it might at length by likelihood be occasion of discord and debate between the said bodies politic, which God defend

"For these and many other great and reasonable causes, which hereafter shall

---

* *Gesene*, scarce, rare. In Poor Robin's Almanac, the word is used as late as 1712—

> " Still oysters and fresh herrings are in season,
> But strawberries, cherries and green pease are geason."

be showed to this honourable court, your said beseechers think it much necessary that the said Hall be still in the hands of this city, and to be surely kept by sad* and discreet officers, in such wise, that it may alway be ready to be used and occupied for the common weal of the said city when need shall require, and in no wise to be letten to any body politic.

Thus much for the petition.

About the year 1534, great means were made about the Leadenhall to have the same made a bourse, for the assembly of merchants, as they had been accustomed in Lombard Street. Many common councils were called to that end; but in the year 1535, John Champneys being mayor, it was fully concluded that the bourse should remain in Lombard Street as afore, and Leadenhall no more to be spoken of concerning that matter.

The use of Leadenhall in my youth was thus:—In a part of the north quadrant, on the east side of the north gate, were the common beams for weighing of wool and other wares, as had been accustomed; on the west side the gate were the scales to weigh meal; the other three sides were reserved for the most part to the making and resting of the pageants showed at Midsummer in the watch; the remnant of the sides and quadrants was employed for the stowage of wool sacks, but not closed up; the lofts above were partly used by the painters in working for the decking of pageants and other devices for beautifying of the watch and watchmen; the residue of the lofts were letten out to merchants, the wool winders and packers therein to wind and pack their wools. And thus much for Leadenhall may suffice.

Now on the north of Lime Street Ward in the high street are divers fair houses for merchants, and proper tenements for artificers, with an alley also called Shaft Alley, of the shaft or May-pole sometime resting over the gate thereof, as I have declared in Aldgate Ward. In the year 1576, partly at the charges of the parish of St. Andrew, and partly at the charges of the chamber of London, a water-pump was raised in Lime Street Ward, near unto Lime Street corner; for the placing of the which pump, having broken up the ground, they were forced to dig more than two fathom deep before they came to any main ground, where they found a hearth made of Briton, or rather Roman tile, every tile half a yard square, and about two inches thick. They found coal lying there also, for that lying whole will never consume; then digging one fathom into the main, they found water sufficient, made their prall,† and set up the pump; which pump, with oft repairing and great charges to the parish, continued not four-and-twenty years, but being rotted, was taken up and a new set in place in the year 1600. Thus much for the high street.

---

* _Sad_, firm, serious. Grief was not connected with the word in its earlier use.
† _Prall_, or prill, a small spring of water.

In St. Mary Street had ye of old time a parish church of St. Mary the Virgin, St. Ursula and the eleven thousand virgins, which church was commonly called St. Mary at the Axe, of the sign of an axe, over against the east end thereof, or St. Mary Pellipar,* of a plot of ground lying on the north side thereof, pertaining to the Skinners in London. This parish, about the year 1565, was united to the parish church of St. Andrew Undershaft, and so was St. Mary at the Axe suppressed and letten out to be a warehouse for a merchant. Against the east end of this church was sometime a fair well, now turned to a pump. Also against the north end of this St. Mary Street, was sometime one other parish church of St. Augustine, called St. Augustine in the Wall, for that it stood adjoining to the wall of the city, and otherwise called St. Augustine's Papey, or the poor, as I have read in the reign of Edward III. About the year 1430, in the reign of Henry VI., the same church was allowed to the brethren of the Papey, the house of poor priests, whereof I have spoken in Aldgate Ward. The parishioners of this church were appointed to the parish church of Allhallows in the Wall, which is in Broad Street Ward. This brotherhood called Papey, being suppressed, the Church of St. Augustine was pulled down, and in place thereof one Grey an apothecary built a stable, hayloft, &c. It is now a dwelling-house. Those two parish churches, both lying in the ward of Lime Street, being thus suppressed, there is not any one parish church or place for Divine service in that ward, but the inhabitants thereof repair to St. Peter in Cornhill Ward, St. Andrew in Aldgate Ward, Allhallows in the Wall in Broad Street Ward, and some to St. Denis in Langborne Ward.

Now because of late there hath been some question to what ward this Church of St. Augustine Papey should of right belong, for the same hath been challenged by them of Aldgate Ward, and without reason taken into Bishopsgate Ward from Lime Street Ward, I am somewhat to touch it. About thirty years since the chamber of London granted a lease of ground, in these words : "Lying near London wall in the ward of Lime Street, from the west of the said church or chapel of St. Augustine Papey towards Bishopsgate," &c. On the which plot of ground the lease built three fair tenements, and placed tenants there ; these were charged to bear scot and lot, and some of them to bear office in Lime Street Ward ; all which they did willingly without grudging. And when any suspected or disordered persons were by the landlord placed there, the officers of Lime Street Ward fetched them out of their houses, committed them to ward, procured their due punishments, and banished them from thence ; whereby in short time that place was reformed, and brought

* *Pellipar*, skin preparer, skinner.

into good order; which thing being noted by them of Aldgate Ward, they moved their alderman, Sir Thomas Offley, to call in those houses to be of his ward; but I myself showing a fair ledger book, sometime pertaining to the late dissolved priory of the Holy Trinity within Aldgate, wherein were set down the just bounds of Aldgate Ward, before Sir Thomas Offley, Sir Rowland Heyward, the Common Council, and wardmote inquest of the same Lime Street Ward, Sir Thomas Offley gave over his challenge. And so that matter rested in good quiet until the year 1579, that Sir Richard Pype being mayor, and alderman of Bishopsgate Ward, challenged those houses to be of his ward, whereunto, without reason showed, Sir Rowland Heyward yielded. And thus is that side of the street, from the north corner of St. Mary Street almost to Bishopsgate, wherein is one plot of ground, letten by the chamberlain of London to the parish of St. Martin's Oteswich, to be a churchyard or burying-place for the dead of that parish, &c., unjustly drawn and withholden from the ward of Lime Street. Divers other proofs I could set down, but this one following may suffice. The mayor and aldermen of London made a grant to the fraternity of Papey in these words :—

"Be it remembered, that where now of late the master and wardens of the fraternity of the Papey have made a brick wall, closing in the chapel of St. Augustine called Papey Chapel, situate in the parish of All Saints in the Wall, in the ward of Lime Street, of the city of London; from the south-east corner of the which brick wall is a scutcheon of twenty-one feet of assize from the said corner eastward. And from the same scutcheon there to a messuage of fifty-five feet and a half westward, the said scutcheon breaketh out of line right southward betwixt the measures aforesaid three feet and five inches of assize, upon the common ground of the said city aforesaid, Ralph Verney, mayor, and the aldermen of the same city, the 22nd day of October, the 6th year of Edward IV., granted to John Hod, priest, and to Master John Bolte, and Thomas Pachet, priests, wardens of the fraternity of Papey aforesaid, and to their successors for ever, &c., yielding fourpence sterling yearly at Michaelmas."

And this is, saith my book, enrolled in the Guildhall of London; which is a sufficient proof the same plot of ground to be of Lime Street Ward, and never otherwise accounted or challenged.

On the south side of this street, stretching west from St. Mary Street towards Bishopsgate Street, there was of old time one large messuage built of stone and timber, in the parish of St Augustine in the Wall, now the parish of Allhallows in the same wall, belonging to the Earl of Oxford, for Richard de Vere, Earl of Oxford, possessed it in the 4th of Henry V.; but in process of time the lands of the earl fell to females, amongst the which, one being married to Wing-field of Suffolk, this house with the appurtenances fell to his lot, and was by his heir, Sir Robert Wingfield, sold to Master Edward Coke, at this time the queen's attorney-general. This house being greatly ruinated of late time, for the most part hath been letten out to poulterers, for stabling of horses and stowage of poultry, but now lately new built into a number of small tenements, letten out to strangers, and other mean people.

One note more of this ward, and so an end. I find of record that in the year 1371, the 45th of Edward III., a great subsidy of one hundred thousand pounds was granted towards the king's wars in France, whereof the clergy paid fifty thousand pounds, and the laity fifty thousand pounds, to be levied to thirty-nine shires of England, containing parishes eight thousand six hundred, of every parish five pounds sixteen shillings, the greater to help the lesser. This city, as one of the shires, then containing twenty-four wards, and in them one hundred and ten parishes, was therefore assessed to six hundred and thirty-five pounds twelve shillings, whereof Lime Street Ward did bear thirty-four shillings and no more, so small a ward it was, and so accounted, as having no one whole parish therein, but small portions only of two parishes in that ward. This ward hath an alderman, his deputy, common councillors four, constables four, scavengers two, wardmote inquest sixteen, and a beadle ; and is taxed to the fifteenth at one pound nineteen shillings and twopence three farthings.

Bishopsgate Ward.

THE next is Bishopsgate Ward ; whereof a part is without the gate and of the suburbs, from the bars by St. Mary Spital to Bishopsgate, and a part of Hounsditch ; almost half thereof, also without the wall, is of the same ward. Then within the gate is Bishopsgate Street, so called of the gate, to a pump, where sometime was a fair well, with two buckets, by the east end of the parish church of St. Martin Oteswich, and then winding by the west corner of Leadenhall down Grass Street to the corner over against Grass Church ; and this is the bounds of that ward.

Monuments most to be noted are these :—The parish church of St. Botolph without Bishopsgate, in a fair churchyard, adjoining to the town ditch, upon the very bank thereof, but of old time enclosed with a comely wall of brick, lately repaired by Sir William Allen, mayor, in the year 1571, because he was born in that parish, where also he was buried. An anchoress received 40s. the year of the sheriffs of London.

Now without this churchyard wall is a causey,* leading to a quadrant, called Petty France, of Frenchmen dwelling there, and to other dwelling-houses, lately built on the bank of the said ditch by some

---

* *Causey,* modern French *chaussée,* from *calciata,* a way made firm with lime or mortar, a paved way. The modern change to causeway is a corruption like the change of pentice into penthouse.

citizens of London, that more regarded their own private gain than the common good of the city ; for by means of this causey raised on the bank, and soilage of houses, with other filthiness cast into the ditch, the same is now forced to a narrow channel, and almost filled up with unsavoury things, to the danger of impoisoning the whole city.

Next unto the parish church of St. Botolph is a fair inn for receipt of travellers ; then an hospital of St. Mary of Bethlem, founded by Simon Fitz Mary, one of the sheriffs of London, in the year 1246. He founded it to have been a priory of canons, with brethren and sisters ; and King Edward III. granted a protection, which I have seen, for the brethren, *Milicia beata Maria de Bethlem*, within the city of London, the 14th year of his reign. It was an hospital for distracted people. Stephen Geninges, merchant tailor, gave £40 towards purchase of the patronage by his testament, 1523; the mayor and commonalty purchased the patronage thereof, with all the lands and tenements thereunto belonging, in the year 1546. The same year King Henry VIII. gave this hospital unto the city ; the church and chapel whereof were taken down in the reign of Queen Elizabeth, and houses built there by the governors of Christ's Hospital in London. In this place people that be distraight in wits are, by the suit of their friends, received and kept as afore, but not without charges to their bringers in. In the year 1569, Sir Thomas Roe, merchant tailor, mayor, caused to be enclosed with a wall of brick about one acre of ground, being part of the said hospital of Bethlem ; to wit, on the west, on the bank of Deep Ditch, so called, parting the said hospital of Bethlem from the Moor field. This he did for burial and ease of such parishes in London as wanted ground convenient within their parishes. The lady his wife was there buried (by whose persuasion he enclosed it), but himself, born in London, was buried in the parish church of Hackney.

From this hospital northward, upon the street's side, many houses have been built with alleys backward, of late time too much pestered with people (a great cause of infection) up to the bars.

The other side of this high street from Bishopsgate and Hounsditch, the first building a large inn for receipt of travellers, and is called the Dolphin, of such a sign. In the year 1513, Margaret Ricroft, widow, gave this house, with the gardens and appurtenances, unto William Gam, R. Clye, their wives, her daughters, and to their heirs, with condition they yearly do give to the warden or governors of the Grey Friars Church within Newgate forty shillings, to find a student of divinity in the university for ever. Then is there a fair house, of late built by John Paulet. Next to that, a far more large and beautiful house, with gardens of pleasure, bowling alleys, and such like, built by Jasper Fisher, free of the goldsmiths, late one of the six clerks of the chancery and a justice of the peace. It hath since for a time been the Earl of Oxford's place. The queen's majesty Elizabeth hath lodged there. It now belongeth to Sir Roger Maners. This house, being so large and sumptuously built by a man of no greater calling, possessions, or wealth, for he was indebted to many, was mockingly called Fisher's Folly, and a rhythm was made of it, and other the like, in this manner:—

> " Kirkebyes Castell, and Fishers Follie,
> Spinolas pleasure, and Megses glorie."

And so of other like buildings about the city by citizens, men have not letted to speak their pleasure.

From Fisher's Folly up to the west end of Bearward's Lane, of old time so called, but now Hogge Lane, because it meeteth with Hogge Lane, which cometh from the bars without Aldgate, as is afore showed, is a continual building of tenements, with alleys of cottages, pestered, &c. Then is there a large close, called Tasel Close, sometime for that there were tassels * planted for the use of clothworkers, since letten to the cross-bow makers, wherein they used to shoot for games at the popinjay. Now the same being enclosed with a brick wall, serveth to be an artillery yard, whereunto the gunners of the Tower do weekly repair, namely, every Thursday ; and there levelling certain brass pieces of great artillery against a butt of earth, made for that purpose, they discharge them for their exercise.

Then have you the late dissolved priory and hospital, commonly called St. Mary Spital, founded by Walter Brune and Rosia his wife, for canons regular. Walter, Archdeacon of London, laid the first stone in the year 1197. William, of St. Mary Church, then Bishop of London, dedicated to the honour of Jesus Christ and his mother, the perpetual Virgin Mary, by the name of *Domus Dei*, and *Beatæ Mariæ*, extra Bishopsgate, in the parish of St. Botolph ; the bounds whereof, as appeareth by composition betwixt the parson and prior of the said hospital concerning tithes, beginneth at Bearward's Lane towards the south, and extendeth in breadth to the parish of St. Leonard of Shoreditch towards the north ; and in length, from the King's Street on the west to the Bishop of London's field, called Lollesworth, on the east. The prior of this St. Mary Spital, for the emortising † and propriation of Bikenacar, in Essex, to his said house of St. Mary Spital, gave to Henry VII. £400 in the 22nd of his reign. This hospital, surrendered to Henry VIII., was valued to dispend £478 ;

---

* *Tassels*, teasels. The modern word *tassel* is of different origin.
† *Emortising*, redemption. French *amortissement*. The old French verb was *esmortir*.

wherein was found, besides ornaments of the church, and other goods pertaining to the hospital, one hundred and eighty beds, well furnished, for receipt of the poor; for it was an hospital of great relief. Sir Henry Plesington, knight, was buried there 1452.

In place of this hospital, and near adjoining, are now many fair houses built for receipt and lodging of worshipful persons. A part of the large churchyard pertaining to this hospital, and severed from the rest with a brick wall, yet remaineth as of old time, with a pulpit cross therein, somewhat like to that in Paul's Churchyard. And against the said pulpit on the south side, before the charnel and chapel of St. Edmund the Bishop and Mary Magdalen,—which chapel was founded about the year 1391 by William Eneshan, citizen and paperer of London, who was there buried,—remaineth also one fair built house, of two storeys in height, for the mayor and other honourable persons, with the aldermen and sheriffs, to sit in, there to hear the sermons preached in the Easter holidays. In the loft over them stood the Bishop of London, and other prelates; now the ladies and aldermen's wives do there stand at a fair window, or sit at their pleasure. And here is to be noted, that, time out of mind, it hath been a laudable custom, that on Good Friday, in the afternoon, some especial learned man, by appointment of the prelates, hath preached a sermon at Paul's Cross, treating of Christ's Passion; and upon the three next Easter holidays, Monday, Tuesday, and Wednesday, the like learned men, by the like appointment, have used to preach on the forenoons at the said Spital, to persuade the article of Christ's Resurrection; and then on Low Sunday, one other learned man at Paul's Cross, to make rehearsal of those four former sermons, either commending or reproving them, as to him by judgment of the learned divines was thought convenient. And that done, he was to make a sermon of his own study, which in all were five sermons in one. At these sermons, so severally preached, the mayor, with his brethren the aldermen, were accustomed to be present in their violets at Paul's on Good Friday, and in their scarlets at the Spital in the holidays, except Wednesday in violet, and the mayor with his brethren on Low Sunday in scarlet, at Paul's Cross, continued until this day.

Touching the antiquity of this custom, I find, that in the year 1398, King Richard having procured from Rome confirmation of such statutes and ordinances as were made in the parliament begun at Westminster and ended at Shrewsbury, he caused the same confirmation to be read and pronounced at Paul's Cross, and at St. Mary Spital, in the sermons before all the people. Philip Malpas, one of the sheriffs in the year 1439, gave twenty shillings by the year to the three preachers at the Spital. Stephen Forster, mayor in the year 1454, gave forty pounds to the preachers at Paul's Cross and Spital. I find also that the aforesaid house, wherein the mayor and aldermen do sit at the Spital, was built for that purpose of the goods, and by the executors, of Richard Lawson, alderman, and Isabell his wife, in the year 1488. In the year 1594, this pulpit, being old, was taken down, and a new set up ; the preacher's face turned towards the south, which was before toward the west ; also a large house, on the east side of the said pulpit, was then built for the governors and children of Christ's Hospital to sit in, and this was done of the goods of William Elkens, alderman, late deceased ; but within the first year the same house decaying, and like to have fallen, was again with great cost repaired at the city's charge.

On the east side of this churchyard lieth a large field, of old time called Lollesworth, now Spitalfield, which about the year 1576 was broken up for clay to make brick ; in the digging whereof many earthen pots, called *urnæ*, were found full of ashes, and burnt bones of men, to wit, of the Romans that inhabited here ; for it was the custom of the Romans to burn their dead, to put their ashes in an urn, and then bury the same, with certain ceremonies, in some field appointed for that purpose near unto their city. Every of these pots had in them with the ashes of the dead one piece of copper money, with the inscription of the emperor then reigning : some of them were of Claudius, some of Vespasian, some of Nero, of Antoninus Pius, of Trajanus, and others. Besides those urns, many other pots were there found, made of a white earth, with long necks and handles, like to our stone jugs : these were empty, but seemed to be buried full of some liquid matter long since consumed and soaked through ; for there were found divers phials and other fashioned glasses, some most cunningly wrought, such as I have not seen the like, and some of crystal ; all which had water in them, nothing differing in clearness, taste, or savour from common spring water, whatsoever it was at the first. Some of these glasses had oil in them very thick, and earthy in savour ; some were supposed to have balm in them, but had lost the virtue. Many of those pots and glasses were broken in cutting of the clay, so that few were taken up whole. There were also found divers dishes and cups of a fine red-coloured earth, which showed outwardly such a shining smoothness as if they had been of coral ; those had in the bottoms Roman letters printed. There were also lamps of white earth and red, artificially wrought with divers antiques about them, some three or four images made of white earth, about a span long each of them : one I remember was of Pallas, the rest I have forgotten. I myself have reserved, among divers of those antiquities there, one urn, with the ashes and bones, and one pot of white earth very small, not exceeding the quantity of a quarter of a wine pint, made in shape of a hare squatted upon her legs, and between her ears is the mouth of the pot. There hath also been found in the same field divers coffins of stone, containing the bones of men : these I suppose to be the burials of some especial persons in time of the Britons or Saxons, after that the Romans had left to govern here. Moreover, there were also found the skulls and bones of men without coffins, or rather whose coffins, being of great timber, were consumed. Divers great nails of iron were there found, such as are used in the wheels of shod carts, being each of them as big as a man's finger, and a quarter of a yard long, the heads two inches over. Those nails were more wondered at than the rest of things there found, and many opinions of men were there uttered of them ; namely, that the men there buried were murdered by driving those nails into their heads—a thing unlikely, for a smaller nail would more aptly serve to so bad a purpose, and a more secret place would likely be employed for their burial. But to set down what I have observed concerning this matter, I there beheld the bones of a man lying, as I noted, the head north, the feet south, and round about him, as thwart his head, along both his sides, and thwart his feet, such nails were found, wherefore I conceived them to be the nails of his coffin, which had been a trough cut out of some great tree, and the same covered with a plank, of a great thickness, fastened with such nails ; and therefore I caused some of the nails to be reached up to me, and found under the broad heads of them the old wood, skant turned into earth, but still retaining both the grain and proper colour. Of these nails, with the wood under the head thereof, I reserved one, as also the nether jawbone of the man, the teeth being great, sound, and fast fixed, which, among other many monuments there found, I have yet to show ; but the nail lying dry, is by scaling greatly wasted. And thus much for this part of Bishopsgate Ward, without the gate ; for I have in another place spoken of the gate, and therefore I am to speak of that other part of this ward which lieth within the gate.

And first to begin on the left hand of Bishopsgate Street, from the gate you have certain tenements of old time pertaining to a brotherhood of St. Nicholas, granted to the parish clerks of London, for two chaplains to be kept in the chapel of St. Mary Magdalen, near unto the Guildhall of London, in the 27th of Henry VI. The first of these houses towards the north, and against the wall of the city, was sometime a large inn or court called the Wrestlers, of such a sign ; and the last in the high street towards the south was sometime also a fair inn called the Angel, of such a sign. Among these said tenements was on the same street side a fair entry, or court, to the common hall of the said parish clerks, with proper almshouses, seven in number, adjoining, for poor parish clerks, and their wives and their widows, such as were in great years, not able to labour. One of these, by the said brotherhood of parish clerks, was allowed sixteen pence the week; the other six had each of them ninepence the week, according to the patent thereof granted. This brotherhood, amongst other, being suppressed in the reign of Edward VI., the said hall, with the other buildings there, was given to Sir Robert Chester, a knight of Cambridgeshire; against whom the parish clerks commencing suit, in the reign of Queen Mary, and being like to have prevailed, the said Sir Robert Chester pulled down the hall, sold the timber, stone, and lead, and thereupon the suit was ended. The almshouses remain in the queen's hands, and people are there placed, such as can make best friends; some of them, taking the pension appointed, have let forth their houses for great rent, giving occasion to the parson of the parish to challenge tithes of the poor, &c.

Next unto this is the small parish church of St. Ethelburge Virgin, and from thence some small distance is a large court called Little St. Helen's, because it pertained to the nuns of St. Helen's, and was their house: there are seven alms rooms or houses for the poor, belonging to the company of Leathersellers. Then, somewhat more west, is another court with a winding lane, which cometh out against the west end of St. Andrew Undershaft Church. In this court standeth the Church of St. Helen, sometime a priory of black nuns, and in the same a parish church of St. Helen.

This priory was founded before the reign of Henry III. William Basing, Dean of Paul's, was the first founder, and was there buried; and William Basing, one of the sheriffs of London, in the 2nd year of Edward II. was holden also to be a founder, or rather a helper there. This priory being valued at £314, 2s. 6d. was surrendered the 25th of November, the 30th of Henry VIII. The whole church, the partition betwixt the nuns' church and parish church being taken down, remaineth now to the parish, and is a fair parish church, but wanteth such a steeple as Sir Thomas Gresham promised to have built, in recompense of ground in their church filled up with his monument. The nuns' hall, and other houses thereunto appertaining, was since purchased by the company of the Leathersellers, and is their common hall; which company was incorporate in the 21st year of Richard II.

In the Church of St. Helen have you these monuments of the dead:—Thomas Langton, chaplain, buried in the choir, 1350; Adam Frances, mayor, 1354; Elizabeth Vennar, wife to William Vennar, alderman, one of the sheriffs of London, 1401; Joan, daughter to Henry Seamer, wife to Richard, son and heir to Robert Lord Poynings, died a virgin, 1420; John Swinflat, 1420; Nicholas

Marshall, ironmonger, alderman, 1474; Sir John Crosby, alderman, 1475, and Ann his wife; Thomas Williams, gentleman, 1495; Joan Cocken, wife to John Cocken, esquire, 1509; Marie Orrell, wife to Sir Lewis Orrell, knight; Henry Sommer, and Katherine his wife; Walter Huntington, esquire; John Langthorpe, esquire, 1510; John Gower, steward of St. Helen's, 1512; Robert Rochester, esquire, sergeant of the pantry to Henry VIII.; Sir William Sanctlo, and Sir William Sanctlo, father and son; Eleanor, daughter to Sir Thomas Butler; Lord Sudley; John Southworth; Nicholas Harpsfield, esquire; Thomas Sanderford, or Sommerford, alderman; Alexander Cheyney; Walter Dawbeney; George Fastolph, son to Hugh Fastolph; Robert Liade; Thomas Benolt, *alias* Clarenciaulx, king at arms, 1534; William Hollis, mayor, 1540; John Fauconbridge, esquire. 1545; Hacket, gentleman of the king's chapel; Sir Andrew Jud, mayor, 1551; Sir William Pickering, and Sir William Pickering, father and son; William Bond, alderman, 1567; Sir Thomas Gresham, mercer, 1579; William Skegges, sergeant poulter; Richard Gresham, son to Sir Thomas Gresham, 1564.

Then have you one great house called Crosby Place, because the same was built by Sir John Crosby, grocer and woolman, in place of certain tenements, with their appurtenances, letten to him by Alice Ashfed, prioress of St. Helen's, and the convent for ninety-nine years, from the year 1466 unto the year 1565, for the annual rent of £11, 6s. 8d. This house he built of stone and timber, very large and beautiful, and the highest at that time in London. He was one of the sheriffs, and an alderman in the year 1470, knighted by Edward IV. in the year 1471, and deceased in the year 1475; so short a time enjoyed he that his large and sumptuous building. He was buried in St. Helen's, the parish church; a fair monument of him and his lady is raised there. He gave towards the reforming of that church five hundred marks, which was bestowed with the better, as appeareth by his arms, both in the stone work, roof of timber, and glazing. I hold it a fable said of him to be named Crosby, of being found by a cross, for I have read of other to have that name of Crosby before him; namely, in the year 1406, the 7th of Henry IV., the said king gave to his servant John Crosby the wardship of Joan, daughter and sole heir to John Jordaine, fishmonger, &c. This Crosby might be the father or grandfather to Sir John Crosby.

Richard, Duke of Gloucester, and lord protector, afterward king, by the name of Richard III., was lodged in this house. Since the which time, among other, Anthony Bonvice, a rich merchant of Italy, dwelt there. After him, Germain Cioll. Then William Bond, alderman, increased this house in height, with building of a turret on the top thereof. He deceased in the year 1576, and was buried in St. Helen's Church. Divers ambassadors have been lodged there; namely, in the year 1586, Henry Ramelius, chancellor of Denmark, ambassador unto the queen's majesty of England from Frederick II., the king of Denmark; an ambassador of France, &c. Sir John Spencer, alderman, lately purchased this house, made great reparations, kept his mayoralty there, and since built a most large warehouse near thereunto.

From this Crosby Place up to Leadenhall corner, and so down Grass Street, amongst other tenements, are divers fair and large built houses for merchants, and such like.

Now for the other side of this ward, namely, the right hand, hard by within the gate, is one fair water conduit, which Thomas Knesworth, mayor, in the year 1505, founded. He gave £60, the rest was furnished at the common charges of the city. This conduit hath since been taken down and new built. David Woodrooffe, alderman, gave £20 towards the conveyance of more water thereunto. From this conduit have you, amongst many fair tenements, divers fair inns, large for receipt of travellers, and some houses for men of worship; namely, one most spacious of all other thereabout, built of brick and timber by Sir Thomas Gresham, knight, who deceased in the year 1579, and was buried in St. Helen's Church, under a fair monument, by him prepared in his life. He appointed by his testament this house to be made a college of readers, as before is said in the chapter of schools and houses of learning.

Somewhat west from this house is one other very fair house, wherein Sir William Hollies kept his mayoralty, and was buried in the parish church of St. Helen. Sir Andrew Jud also kept his mayoralty there, and was buried at St. Helen's. He built almshouses for six poor almspeople near to the said parish church, and gave lands to the Skinners, out of the which they are to give 4s. every week to the six poor almspeople, 8d. the piece, and 25s. 4d. the year in coals amongst them for ever.

Alice Smith, of London, widow, late wife of Thomas Smith, of the same city, esquire, and customer of the port of London, in her last will and testament, bequeathed lands to the value of £15 by the year for ever, to the company of Skinners, for the augmenting of the pensions of certain poor, inhabiting in eight almshouses, erected by Sir Andrew Jud, knight, her father, in the parish of Great St. Helen's, in Bishopsgate Street, in London. She hath also given in her said last will and testament, in other charitable uses, as to the hospitals and to the poor of other parishes and good preachers, the sum of £300; as also to the poor scholars in the two universities of Oxford and Cambridge the sum of £200. Of which, her last will and testament, she made her sons, Thomas

Smith, late sheriff of London, and Richard and Robert Smith, her executors, who have performed the same according to her godly and charitable mind.

Then in the very west corner, over against the east end of St. Martin's Oteswich, from whence the street windeth towards the south, you had of old time a fair well, with two buckets, so fastened that the drawing up of the one let down the other; but now of late that well is turned into a pump.

From this to the corner over against the Leadenhall, and so down Grass Street, are many fair houses for merchants and artificers, and many fair inns for travellers, even to the corner where that ward endeth, over against Grass Street. And thus much for this Bishopsgate Ward shall suffice; which hath an alderman, two deputies, one without the gate, another within, common councillors six, constables seven, scavengers seven, for wardmote inquest thirteen, and a beadle. It is taxed to the fifteen at £13.

Broad Street Ward.

THE next is Broad Street Ward, which beginneth within Bishopsgate, from the water conduit westward on both sides of the street, by Allhallows Church, to an iron grate on the channel which runneth into the watercourse of Walbrook, before you come to the postern called Moorgate; and this is the farthest west part of that ward.

Then have you Broad Street, whereof the ward taketh name, which stretcheth out of the former street from the east corner of Allhallows Churchyard, somewhat south to the parish church of St. Peter the Poor on both sides, and then by the south gate of the Augustine friars west, down Throgmorton Street by the Drapers' Hall into Lothbury, to another grate of iron over the channel there, whereby the water runneth into the course of Walbrook, under the east end of St. Margaret's Church, certain posts of timber are there set up; and this is also the farthest west part of this ward, in the said street. Out of the which Street runneth up Bartholomew Lane south to the north side of the Exchange; then more east, out of the former street from over against the Friars Augustine's Church south gate, runneth up another part of Broad Street south to a pump over against St. Bennet's Church. Then have you one other street called Threadneedle Street, beginning at the west, with two buckets, by St. Martin's Oteswich Church wall. This street runneth down on both sides to Finkes Lane, and half way up that lane to a gate of a merchant's house on the west side, but not so far on the east; then the foresaid street, from this Finkes Lane, runneth down by the Royal Exchange to the Stocks, and to a place formerly called

Scalding House, or Scalding Wick, but now Scalding Alley; by the west side whereof, under the parish church of St. Mildred, runneth the course of Walbrook; and these be the bounds of this ward.

Special monuments therein are these :—First, the parish church of Allhallows in the Wall, so called of standing close to the wall of the city, in which have been buried Thomas Durrem, esquire, and Margaret his wife; Robert Beele, esquire, 1601. On the other side of that street, amongst many proper houses possessed for the most part by curriers, is the Carpenters' Hall, which company was incorporated in the 17th year of King Edward IV.

Then east from the Curriers' Row is a long and high wall of stone, enclosing the north side of a large garden adjoining to as large an house, built in the reign of King Henry VIII. and of Edward VI. by Sir William Paulet, lord treasurer of England. Through this garden, which of old time consisted of divers parts, now united, was sometimes a fair footway, leading by the west end of the Augustine Friars Church straight north, and opened somewhat west from Allhallows Church against London wall towards Moorgate, which footway had gates at either end, locked up every night. But now the same way being taken into those gardens, the gates are closed up with stone; whereby the people are forced to go about by St. Peter's Church, and the east end of the said Friars Church, and all the said great place and garden of Sir William Paulet, to London wall, and so to Moorgate.

This great house, adjoining to the garden aforesaid, stretcheth to the north corner of Broad Street, and then turneth up Broad Street all that side to and beyond the east end of the said Friars Church. It was built by the said lord treasurer in place of Augustine friars house, cloister, and gardens, &c. The Friars Church he pulled not down, but the west end thereof, enclosed from the steeple and choir, was in the year 1550 granted to the Dutch nation in London, to be their preaching place : the other part, namely, the steeple, choir, and side aisles to the choir adjoining, he reserved to household uses, as for stowage of corn, coal, and other things. His son and heir, Marquis of Winchester, sold the monuments of noblemen there buried in great number, the paving stone and whatsoever, which cost many thousands, for one hundred pounds, and in place thereof made fair stabling for horses. He caused the lead to be taken from the roofs, and laid tile in place whereof, which exchange proved not so profitable as he looked for, but rather to his disadvantage.

On the east side of this Broad Street, amongst other buildings, on the back part of Gresham House, which is in Bishopsgate Street, be placed eight proper almshouses, built of brick and timber by

Sir Thomas Gresham, knight, for eight almsmen, which be now there placed rent free, and receive each of them by his gift £6, 13s. 4d. yearly for ever.

Next unto Paulet House is the parish church of St. Peter the Poor, so called for a difference from other of that name, sometime peradventure a poor parish, but at this present there be many fair houses, possessed by rich merchants and other. Buried in this church: Richard Fitzwilliams, merchant tailor, 1520; Sir William Roch, mayor, 1540; Martin Calthrope, mayor, 1588.

Then next have you the Augustine Friars Church and Churchyard; the entering thereunto by a south gate to the west porch, a large church, having a most fine spired steeple, small, high, and straight, I have not seen the like: founded by Humphrey Bohun, Earl of Hereford and Essex, in the year 1253. Reginald Cobham gave his messuage in London to the enlarging thereof, in the year 1344. Humphrey Bohun, Earl of Hereford and Essex, re-edified this church in the year 1354, whose body was there buried in the choir. The small spired steeple of this church was overthrown by a tempest of wind in the year 1362, but was raised of new, as now it standeth, to the beautifying of the city. This house was valued at £57, and was surrendered the 12th of November, the 30th of Henry VIII.

There lie buried in this Friars Church, amongst others, Edward, first son to Joan, mother to King Richard II.; Guy de Mericke, Earl of St. Paul; Lucy, Countess of Kent, and one of the heirs of Barnaby Lord of Millaine, with an epitaph; Dame Ide, wife to Sir Thomas West; Dame Margaret West; Stephen Lindericle, esquire: Sir Humphrey Bohun, Earl of Hereford and Essex, Lord of Brekenake; Richard, the great Earl of Arundell, Surrey, and Warren, beheaded, 1397; Sir Edward Arundell, and Dame Elizabeth his wife; Sir Francis Atcourt, Earl of Pembroke, which married Alice, sister to the Earl of Oxford; Dame Lucy Knowles, of Kent; Sir Peter Garinsers, of France; the Lord John Vere, Earl of Oxford, beheaded on the Tower Hill, 1463; Aubrey de Vere, son and heir to the Earl of Oxford; Sir Thomas Tudnam, knight; William Bourser; Lord Fitzwarren; Sir Thomas de la Lande, knight; Dame Joan Norris, the Lady of Bedford; Anne, daughter to John Viscount Welles; Walter Nevell, esquire; Sir John Manners, knight; the wife of Sir David Cradocke, knight; the mother to the Lord Spencer's wife; Sir Bartlemew Rodlegate; John, son to Sir John Wingfield; Sir Walter Mewes; Robert Newenton, esquire; Philip Spencer, son to Sir Hugh Spencer; Dame Isabel, daughter to Sir Hugh; The Lord Barons slain at Barnet field, buried there, 1471. In the body of the church: Dame Julian, wife to Sir Richard Lacy; Sir Thomas Courtney, son to the Earl of Devonshire, and by

him, his sister, wedded to Cheverstone; the daughter of the Lord
Beaumont; two sons of Sir Thomas Morley, to wit, William
and Ralph; Sir William Talmage, knight; Nicholas Blondell,
esquire; Sir Richard Chamberlain; John Halton, gentleman; Sir
John Gifford, knight; Thomas Manningham, esquire; Sir William
Kenude, knight; Sir William, son to Sir Thomas Terill; John Surell,
gentleman. In the east wing: Margaret Barentin, gentlewoman;
John Spicer, esquire, and Letis his wife; John le Percers, esquire;
Roger Chibary, esquire; Peter Morens, esquire; Thomas, son to Sir
William Beckland; James Cuthing, esquire; John Chorner, esquire;
William Kenley, esquire; Margery, wife to Thomas Band, and
daughter to John Hutch; the Lord William, Marquis of Barkeley
and Earl of Nottingham, and Dame Joan his wife. In the west
wing: Sir John Tirrill, and Dame Katherine his wife; Sir Walter of
Powle, knight; Sir John Blanckwell, and his wife Dame Jane Sayne,
daughter to Sir John Lee; Sir John Dawbeney, son and heir to Sir
Giles Dawbeney; William, son to Sir Roger Scroope; Dame Joan
Dawbeney, wife to Sir William Dawbeney; Thomas Charles, esquire;
Sir John Dawbeney, knight, and his son Robert; Sir James Bell,
knight; Sir Oliver Manny, knight; Henry Deskie, esquire; Sir
Diones Mordaske; Sir Bernard Rolingcort; Sir Peter Kayor;
Sir William Tirell; Sir William, his brother knights; William
Collingborne, esquire, beheaded, 1484; Sir Roger Clifford, knight;
Sir Thomas Coke, mayor in the year 1462; William Edward, mayor,
1471; Sir James Tirell, Sir John Windany, knights, beheaded, 1502;
Sir John Dawtry, knight, 1519; Dame Margaret Rede, 1510;
Edward, Duke of Buckingham, beheaded, 1521; Guiskard, Earl of
Huntington.

On the south side, and at the west end of this church, many fair
houses are built; namely, in Throgmorton Street, one very large and
spacious, built in the place of old and small tenements by Thomas
Cromwell, master of the king's jewel-house, after that master of the
rolls, then Lord Cromwell, knight, lord privy seal, vicar-general,
Earl of Essex, high chamberlain of England, &c. This house being
finished, and having some reasonable plot of ground left for a garden,
he caused the pales of the gardens adjoining to the north part thereof
on a sudden to be taken down; twenty-two feet to be measured forth
right into the north of every man's ground; a line there to be drawn,
a trench to be cast, a foundation laid, and a high brick wall to be
built. My father had a garden there, and a house standing close to
his south pale; this house they loosed from the ground, and bare
upon rollers into my father's garden twenty-two feet, ere my father
heard thereof. No warning was given him, nor other answer, when
he spake to the surveyors of that work but that their master Sir

Thomas commanded them so to do; no man durst go to argue the matter, but each man lost his land, and my father paid his whole rent, which was 6s. 6d. the year, for that half which was left. Thus much of mine own knowledge have I thought good to note, that the sudden rising of some men causeth them in some matters to forget themselves.

The company of the Drapers in London bought this house, and now the same is their common hall. This company obtained of King Henry VI., in the 17th of his reign, to be incorporate : John Gidney was chosen to be their first master, and the four wardens were, J. Wotton, J. Darby, Robert Breton, and T. Cooke. The arms granted to the said company by Sir William Bridges, knight, first garter king at arms, in blazon, are thus : Three sunbeams issuing out of three clouds of flame, crowned with three crowns imperial of gold, upon a shield azure. From this hall, on the same side down to the grates and course of Walbrook, have ye divers fair houses for merchants and other ; from the which grates back again on the other side in Lethbury, so called in record of Edward III., the 38th year, and now corruptly called Lothbury, are candlestick founders placed, till ye come to Bartholomew Lane, so called of St. Bartholomew's Church, at the south-east corner thereof. In this lane also are divers fair built houses on both sides, and so likewise have ye in the other street, which stretcheth from the Friars Augustine's south gate to the corner over against St. Bennet's Church. In this street, amongst other fair buildings, the most ancient was of old time a house pertaining to the Abbot of St. Albans ; John Catcher, alderman, now dwelleth there ; then is the free school pertaining to the late dissolved hospital of St. Anthony, whereof more shall be shown in another place, and so up to Threadneedle Street. On the south part of which street, beginning at the east, by the well with two buckets, now turned to a pump, is the parish church of St. Martin called Oteswich, of Martin de Oteswich, Nicholas de Oteswich, William Oteswich, and John Oteswich, founders thereof. There be monuments in this church of William Constantine, alderman, and Emme his wife ; Katherine, wife to Benedict Augustine ; Sir William Drifield, knight ; John Oteswich, and his wife, under a fair monument on the south side ; John Churchman, one of the sheriffs, in the year 1385 ; Richard Naylor, tailor, alderman, 1483 ; James Falleron ; John Melchborne ; Thomas Hey, and Hellis his wife ; William Clitherow and Margaret his wife ; Oliver and William, sons to John Woodroffe, esquire ; Hugh Pemberton, tailor, alderman, 1500, and Katherine his wife ; Matthew Pemberton, merchant tailor, about 1514 ; he gave £50 to the repairing of St. Lawrence Chapel. The aforesaid John Churchman, for William and John

Oteswich, by license of Henry IV., the 6th of his reign, gave the advowson or patronage of this church, four messuages, and seventeen shops, with the appurtenances in the parish of St. Martin's Oteswich, &c., to the master and wardens of tailors and linen armourers, keepers of the guild and fraternity of St. John Baptist in London, and to their successors, in perpetual alms, to be employed on the poor brethren and sisters. Whereupon, adjoining unto the west end of this parish church, the said master and wardens built about a proper quadrant or squared court, seven almshouses, wherein they placed seven almsmen of that company, and their wives, if they had wives. Each of these seven of old time had 13*d.* the week, but now of later time their stipend by the said master and wardens hath been augmented to the sum of 26*s.* the quarter, which is £5, 4*s.* the year to each of them, besides coals ; more, to each of them 20*s.* the year, by gift of Walter Fish, sometime master of that company, and tailor to her majesty.

Some small distance from thence is the Merchant Tailors' Hall, pertaining to the guild and fraternity of St. John Baptist, time out of mind called of tailors and linen armourers of London ; for I find that Edward I., in the 28th of his reign, confirmed this guild by the name of Tailors and Linen Armourers, and also gave to the brethren thereof authority every year at Midsummer to hold a feast, and to choose unto them a governor, or master, with wardens ; whereupon the same year, 1300, on the feast day of the nativity of St. John Baptist, they chose Henry de Ryall to be their pilgrim for the master of this mystery, as one that travelled for the whole company was then so called, until the 11th of Richard II. ; and the four wardens were then called purveyors of alms, now called quarterage, of the said fraternity. This Merchant Tailors' Hall, sometime pertaining to a worshipful gentleman named Edmond Creping, (Dominus Creping after some record), he in the year of Christ 1331, the first of Edward III., for a certain sum of money to him paid, made his grant thereof by the name of his principal messuage in the wards of Cornhill and Broad Street, which Sir Oliver Ingham, knight, did then hold, to John of Yakley, the king's pavilion maker. This was called the New Hall, or Tailors' Inn, for a difference from their old hall, which was about the back side of the Red Lion in Basing Lane, and in the ward of Cordwainer Street.

The 21st of Edward IV., Thomas Holme, *alias* Clarenciaulx, king of arms for the south part of England, granted by his parents to the said fraternity and guild of St. John Baptist, of tailors and linen armourers, to bear in a field silver, a pavilion between two mantels imperial purple garnished with gold, in a chief azure and holy Lamb, set within a sun, the crest upon the helm, a pavilion purple garnished with gold, &c. After this King Henry VII., being himself a brother of this fraternity or guild of St. John Baptist, of tailors or linen armourers, as divers other his predecessors kings before him had been, to wit, Richard III., Edward IV., Henry V., Henry IV., and Richard II. ; and for that divers of that fraternity had, time out of mind, been great merchants, and had frequented all sorts of merchandises into most parts of the world, to the honour of the king's realm, and to the great profit of his subjects, and of his progenitors ; and the men of the said mystery, during the time aforesaid, had exercised the buying and selling of all wares and merchandises, especially of woollen cloth, as well in gross, as by retail, throughout all this realm of England, and chiefly within the said city ; therefore he, of his especial grace, did change, transfer, and translate the guild aforesaid, and did incorporate them into the name of the Master and Wardens of the Merchant Tailors of the fraternity of of St. John Baptist, in the city of London.

Some distance west from this the Merchant Tailors' Hall is Finke's Lane, so called of Robert Finke, and Robert Finke his son, James Finke, and Rosamond Finke. Robert Finke the elder new built the parish church of St. Bennet, commonly called Finke, of the founder ; his tenements were both of St. Bennet's parish and St. Martin's Oteswich parish. The one half of this Finke Lane is of Broad Street Ward, to wit, on the west side up to the great and principal house wherein the said Finke dwelt ; but on the other side, namely the east, not so much towards Cornhill. Then without this lane in the aforesaid Threadneedle Street is the said parish church of St. Bennet, a proper church, in which are these monuments of the dead :—Robert Simson, and Elizabeth his wife ; Roger Strånge, esquire ; Trerisse ; William Coolby ; John Frey ; Thomas Briar, plumber, 1410, &c.

Some distance west is the Royal Exchange, whereof more shall be spoken in the ward of Cornhill, and so down to the little conduit, called the pissing conduit, by the Stocks Market, and this is the south side of Threadneedle Street.

On the north side of this street, from over against the east corner of St. Martin's Oteswich Church, have ye divers fair and large houses till ye come to the hospital of St. Anthony, sometime a cell to St. Anthony's of Vienna. For I read that King Henry III. granted to the brotherhood of St. Anthony of Vienna, a place amongst the Jews which was sometime their synagogue, and had been built by them about the year 1231 ; but the Christians obtained of the king that it should be dedicated to our Blessed Lady ; and since a hospital being there built, was called St. Anthony's in London. It was founded in the parish of St. Bennet Finke. for a master, two

priests, one schoolmaster, and twelve poor men. After which foundation, amongst other things, was given to this hospital, one messuage
and garden, whereon was built the fair large free school; and one
other parcel of ground, containing thirty-seven feet in length, and
eighteen feet in breadth, whereon was built the almshouses of hard
stone and timber, in the reign of Henry VI. Which said Henry VI.,
in the 20th of his reign, gave unto John Carpenter, D.D., master of
St. Anthony's Hospital, and to his brethren and their successors for
ever, his manor of Ponington, with the appurtenances, with certain
pensions and portions of Milburne, Burnworth, Charlton, and Up
Wimborne, in the county of Southampton, towards the maintenance
of five scholars in the university of Oxford, to be brought up in the
faculty of arts, after the rate of tenpence the week for every scholar,
so that the said scholars shall be first instructed in the rudiments of
grammar at the college of Eton, founded by the said king.

In the year 1474, Edward IV. granted to William Say, B.D.,
master of the said hospital, to have priests, clerks, scholars, poor
men, and brethren of the same, clerks, or laymen, choristers,
proctors, messengers, servants in household, and other things whatsoever, like as the prior and convent of St. Anthony's of Vienna, &c.
He also annexed, united, and appropriated the said hospital unto the
collegiate church of St. George in Windsor.

The proctors of this house were to collect the benevolence of
charitable persons towards the building and supporting thereof. And
amongst other things observed in my youth, I remember that the
officers charged with oversight of the markets in this city, did divers
times take from the market people, pigs starved, or otherwise un-
wholesome for man's sustenance; these they slit in the ear. One of
the proctors for St. Anthony's tied a bell about the neck, and let it
feed on the dunghills; no man would hurt or take them up, but if
any gave to them bread, or other feeding, such would they know,
watch for, and daily follow, whining till they had somewhat given
them; whereupon was raised a proverb, "Such an one will follow
such an one, and whine as it were an Anthony pig;" but if such a
pig grew to be fat, and came to good liking, as ofttimes they did,
then the proctor would take him up to the use of the hospital.

In the year 1499, Sir John Tate, sometime ale-brewer, then a
mercer, caused his brewhouse, called the Swan, near adjoining to
the said free chapel, college, or hospital of St. Anthony, to be taken
down for the enlarging of the church, which was then new built,
toward the building whereof the said Tate gave great sums of money,
and finished in the year 1501. Sir John Tate deceased 1514, and
was there buried under a fair monument by him prepared; Dr.
Tayler, master of the rolls, and other.

Walter Champion, draper, one of the sheriffs of London 1529, was buried there, and gave to the beadmen twenty pounds. The lands by year of this hospital were valued in the 37th year of Henry VIII. to be fifty-five pounds six shillings and eightpence.

One Johnson, a schoolmaster of the famous free-school there, became a prebend of Windsor, and then by little and little followed the spoil of this hospital. He first dissolved the choir, conveyed the plate and ornaments, then the bells, and lastly put out the almsmen from their houses, appointing them portions of twelvepence the week to each, but now I hear of no such matter performed. Their houses with other be letten out for rent, and the church is a preaching place for the French nation.

This school was commended in the reign of Henry VI., and sithence commended above other, but now decayed, and come to nothing, by taking that from it which thereunto belonged.

Next is the parish church of St. Bartholomew, at the end of Bartholomew Lane. Thomas Pike, alderman, with the assistance of Nicholas Yoo, one of the sheriffs of London, about the year 1438, new built this church. Sir John Fray, knight, was buried there; Margery his daughter and heir, wife to Sir John Lepington, knight, founded there a chantry the 21st of Edward IV. Alderban, a Gascoyne, was buried there; Sir Will. Capel, mayor 1509, added unto this church a proper chapel on the south side thereof, and was buried there; Sir Giles Cappell was also buried there; James Wilford, tailor, one of the sheriffs 1499, appointed by his testament a doctor of divinity, every Good Friday for ever, to preach there a sermon of Christ's passion, from six of the clock till eight before noon, in the said church. John Wilford, merchant tailor, alderman, 1544; Sir James Wilford, 1550; Sir George Barne, mayor 1552; John Dent; Miles Coverdale, Bishop of Excester; Thomas Dancer, and Anne his wife.

Then lower down towards the Stocks Market is the parish church of St. Christopher, but re-edified of new; for Richard Shore, one of the sheriffs 1506, gave money towards the building of the steeple. There lie buried Richard Sherington, 1392, who gave lands to that church; the Lady Margaret Norford, 1406; John Clavering, 1421, who gave lands thereunto; John Godnay, draper, mayor 1427. This Godnay, in the year 1444, wedded the widow of Robert Large, late mayor, which widow had taken the mantle and ring,* and the

---

* *The mantle and ring.* Widows' vows of chastity for the rest of life in honour of their dead husbands were made before the high altar during a celebration of mass, in this form, "I, —— heretofore wife to ——, vow to God and our Holy Lady St. Mary, and All Saints, in presence of our Reverend Father in God, that I will be chaste from henceforth during my life." Having made the vow, she was solemnly consecrated, and the mantle and the ring were put upon her in the presence of witnesses.

vow to live chaste to God during the term of her life ; for the breach whereof, the marriage done, they were troubled by the church, and put to penance, both he and she. William Hampton, mayor 1472, was a great benefactor, and glazed some of the church windows ; Sir William Martin, mayor 1492 ; Roger Achley, mayor 1511, he dwelt in Cornhill Ward, in a house belonging to Cobham College, rented by the year at twenty-six shillings and eightpence ; Robert Thorne, merchant tailor, a bachelor, 1532—he gave by his testament in charity more than four thousand four hundred and forty-five pounds ; John Norryholme ; Ralph Batte ; Alice Percivall ; Jane Drew ; William Borresbie ; John Broke ; Richard Sutton ; William Batte ; James Well ; Henry Beacher, alderman, 1570.

West from this church have ye Scalding Alley, of old time called Scalding House, or Scalding Wike, because that ground for the most part was then employed by poulterers that dwelt in the high street from the Stocks Market to the great conduit. Their poultry, which they sold at their stalls, was scalded there. The street doth yet bear the name of the Poultry, and the poulterers are but lately departed from thence into other streets, as into Grass Street, and the ends of St. Nicholas flesh shambles. This Scalding Wike is the farthest west part of Broad Street Ward, and is by the water called Walbrook parted from Cheap Ward. This Broad Street Ward hath an alderman, with his deputy, common councillors ten, constables ten, scavengers eight, wardmote inquest thirteen, and a beadle. It is taxed to the fifteenth in London at seven-and-twenty pounds, and accounted in the Exchequer after twenty-five pounds.

Cornhill Ward.

THE next ward towards the south is Cornhill Ward, so called of a corn market, time out of mind there holden, and is a part of the principal high street, beginning at the west end of Leadenhall, stretching down west on both the sides by the south end of Finke's Lane on the right hand, and by the north end of Birchovers Lane ; on the left part of which lanes, to wit, to the middle of them, is of this ward, and so down to the Stocks Market ; and this is the bounds.

The upper or east part of this ward, and also a part of Lime Street Ward, hath been, as I said, a market place, especially for corn, and since for all kind of victuals, as is partly showed in Lime Street Ward ; yet it appeareth of record, that in the year 1522, the rippers of Rye and other places sold their fresh fish in Leadenhall Market upon Cornhill, but foreign butchers were not admitted there to sell flesh till the year 1533 ; and it was enacted, that butchers should sell their beef not above a halfpenny the pound, and mutton a half-penny half-farthing. Which act being devised for the great commodity of the realm, as it was then thought, hath since proved far otherwise ; for before that time a fat ox was sold in London for six-and-twenty shillings and eightpence at the most, a fat wether for three shillings and fourpence, a fat calf the like price, a fat lamb for twelve pence, pieces of beef weighing two pounds and a half at the least, yea three pounds or better, for a penny, on every butcher's stall in this city, and of those pieces of beef thirteen or fourteen for twelve pence, fat mutton for eightpence the quarter, and one hundredweight of beef for four shillings and eightpence, at the dearest. What the price is now I need not to set down. Many men thought the same act to rise in price, by means that graziers knew or supposed what weight every their beasts contained, and so raising their price thereafter, the butcher could be no gainer, but by likewise raising his price. The number of butchers then in the city and suburbs was accounted six score, of which every one killed six oxen apiece weekly, which is in forty-six weeks thirty-three thousand one hundred and twenty oxen, or seven hundred and twenty oxen weekly. The foreign butchers for a long time stood in the high street of Lime Street Ward on the north side, twice every week, namely, Wednesday and Saturday, and were some gain to the tenants before whose doors they stood, and into whose houses they set their blocks and stalls ; but that advantage being espied, they were taken into Leadenhall, there to pay for their standing to the chamber of London. Thus much for the market upon Cornhill.

The chief ornaments in Cornhill Ward are these : first, at the east end thereof, in the middle of the high street, and at the parting of four ways, have ye a water standard, placed in the year 1582, in manner following. A certain German, named Peter Morris, having made an artificial forcier for that purpose, conveyed Thames water in pipes of lead over the steeple of St. Magnus Church, at the north end of London Bridge, and from thence into divers men's houses in Thames Street, New Fish Street, and Grass Street, up to the north-west corner of Leadenhall, the highest ground of all the city, where the waste of the main pipe rising into this standard, provided at the charges of the city, with four spouts did at every tide run, according to covenant, four ways, plentifully serving to the commodity of the inhabitants near adjoining in their houses, and also cleansed the channels of the street towards Bishopsgate, Aldgate, the Bridge, and the Stocks Market. But now no such matter, through whose default I know not.

Then have ye a fair conduit of sweet water castellated in the midst of that ward and street. This conduit was first built of stone in the year 1282, by Henry Walles, mayor of London, to be a prison for night-walkers and other suspicious persons, and was called the Tun upon Cornhill, because the same was built somewhat in fashion of a tun standing on the one end.

To this prison the night watches of this city committed not only night-walkers, but also other persons, as well spiritual as temporal, whom they suspected of incontinence, and punished them according to the customs of this city ; but complaint thereof being made about the year of Christ 1297, King Edward I. writeth to his citizens thus :—

"Edward, by the grace of God, &c. Whereas Richard Gravesend, Bishop of London, hath showed unto us, that by the Great Charter of England, the Church hath a privilege, that no clerk should be imprisoned by a layman without our commandment and breach of peace, which notwithstanding, some citizens of London, upon mere spite, do enter in their watches into clerks' chambers, and like felons carry them to the Tun, which Henry le Walleys, sometime mayor, built for night-walkers ; wherefore we will that this our commandment be proclaimed in full hustings, and that no watch hereafter enter into any clerk's chamber, under the forfeit of twenty pounds. Dated at Carlisle the 18th of March, the 25th of our reign."

More, I read that about the year of Christ 1299, the 27th of Edward I., certain principal citizens of London, to wit, T. Romane, Richard Gloucester, Nicholas Faringdon, Adam Helingburie, T. Saly, John Dunstable, Richard Ashwy, John Wade, and William Stortford, brake up this prison called the Tun, and took out certain prisoners, for which they were sharply punished by long imprisonment and great fines. It cost the citizens, as some have written, more than twenty thousand marks, which they were amerced in, before William le March, treasurer of the king's exchequer, to purchase the king's favour and confirmation of their liberties.

Also, that in the year 1383, the 7th of Richard II., the citizens of London, taking upon them the rights that belonged to their bishops, first imprisoned such women as were taken in fornication or adultery in the said Tun, and after bringing them forth to the sight of the world, they caused their heads to be shaven, after the manner of thieves, whom they named appellators, and so to be led about the city, in sight of all the inhabitants, with trumpets and pipes sounding before them, that their persons might be the more largely known. Neither did they spare such kind of men a whit the more, but used them as hardly, saying, they abhorred not only the negligence of their prelates, but also detested their avarice, that studying for money, omitted the punishment limited by law, and permitted those that were found guilty to live favourably in their sin. Wherefore, they would themselves, they said, purge their city from such filthiness, lest, through God's vengeance, either the pestilence or sword should happen to them, or that the earth should swallow them.

Last of all to be noted, I read in the charge of the wardmote inquest in every ward of the city, these words :—

" If there be any priest in service within the ward, which before time hath been set in the Tun in Cornhill for his dishonesty, and hath forsworn the city, all such shall be presented."

Thus much for the Tun in Cornhill have I read. Now for the punishment of priests in my youth : one note and no more. John Atwod, draper, dwelling in the parish of St. Michael upon Cornhill, directly against the church, having a proper woman to his wife, such an one as seemed the holiest among a thousand, had also a lusty chantry priest, of the said parish church, repairing to his house ; with the which priest the said Atwod would sometimes after supper play a game at tables for a pint of ale. It chanced on a time, having haste of work, and his game proving long, he left his wife to play it out, and went down to his shop, but returning to fetch a pressing-iron, he found such play to his misliking, that he forced the priest to leap out at a window over the penthouse into the street, and so to run to his lodging in the churchyard. Atwod and his wife were soon reconciled, so that he would not suffer her to be called in question ; but the priest being apprehended and committed, I saw his punishment to be thus :—He was on three market days conveyed through the high street and markets of the city with a paper on his head, wherein was written his trespass. The first day he rode in a carry, the second on a horse, his face to the horse tail, the third led betwixt twain, and every day rung with basons, and proclamations made of his fact at every turning of the street, as also before John Atwod's stall, and the church door of his service, where he lost his chantry of twenty nobles the year, and was banished the city for ever.

By the west side of the foresaid prison, then called the Tun, was a fair well of spring water, curbed round with hard stone ; but in the year 1401, the said prison house, called the Tun, was made a cistern for sweet water, conveyed by pipes of lead from Tybourne, and was from thenceforth called the conduit upon Cornhill. Then was the well planked over, and a strong prison made of timber called a cage, with a pair of stocks therein set upon it, and this was for night-walkers. On the top of which cage was placed a pillory, for the punishment of bakers offending in the assize of bread, for millers stealing of corn at the mill, for bawds, scolds, and other offenders. As in the year 1468, the 7th of Edward IV., divers persons being common jurors, such as at assizes were forsworn for rewards or favour of parties, were judged to ride from Newgate to the pillory in Cornhill, with mitres of paper on their heads, there to stand, and from thence again to Newgate, and this judgment was given by the mayor of London. In the year 1509, the 1st of Henry VIII., Darby, Smith, and Simson, ringleaders of false inquests in London, rode about the city with their faces to the horse tails, and papers on their heads, and were set on the pillory in Cornhill, and after brought again to Newgate, where they died for very shame, saith Robert Fabian. A ringleader of inquests, as I take it, is he that making a gainful occupation thereof, will appear on Nisi-priuses, or he be warned, or procure himself to be warned, to come on by a tales.* He will also procure himself to be foreman when he can, and take upon him to overrule the rest to his opinion ; such an one shall be laboured by plaintiffs and defendants, not without promise of rewards, and therefore to be suspected of a bad conscience. I would wish a more careful choice of jurors to be had ; for I have known a man carted, rung with basons, and banished out of Bishopsgate Ward, and afterward in Aldgate Ward admitted to be a constable, a grand juryman, and foreman of the wardmote inquest. What I know of the like, or worse men, preferred to the like offices, I forbear to write, but wish to be reformed.

The foresaid conduit upon Cornhill was in the year 1475 enlarged by Robert Drope, draper, mayor, that then dwelt in that ward. He increased the cistern of this conduit with an east end of stone, and castellated in comely manner.

In the year 1546, Sir Martin Bowes, mayor, dwelling in Lombard Street, and having his back gate opening into Cornhill against the said conduit, minded to have enlarged the cistern thereof with a west end, like as Robert Drope before had done towards the east. View and measure of the plot was taken for this work ; but the pillory and cage being removed, they found the ground planked, and the well aforesaid worn out of memory, which well they revived and restored to use. It is since made a pump. They set the pillory somewhat west from the well ; and so this work ceased.

On the north side of the street, from the east unto the west, have ye divers fair houses for merchants and other, amongst the which one large house is called the Weigh house, where merchandises brought from beyond the seas are to be weighed at the king's beam. This house hath a master, and under him four master porters, with porters under them : they have a strong cart, and four great horses, to draw and carry the wares from the merchants' houses to the beam and back again. Sir Thomas Lovell, knight, built this house. with a fair front of tenements towards the street ; all which he gave

---

* *By a tales.* By being called from among those standing around to supply the place of an absent juryman. Named from the first word in the provision made for such a case, "*Tales de circumstantibus.*"

to the Grocers of London, himself being free of the city, and a brother of that company.

Then have ye the said Finke's Lane, the south end of which lane on both sides is in Cornhill Ward.

Then next is the Royal Exchange, erected in the year 1566, after this order, namely, certain houses upon Cornhill, and the like upon the back thereof, in the ward of Broad Street, with three alleys, the first called Swan Alley, opening into Cornhill, the second New Alley, passing throughout of Cornhill into Broad Street Ward, over against St. Bartholomew Lane, the third St. Christopher's Alley, opening into Broad Street Ward, and into St. Christopher's parish, containing in all fourscore households, were first purchased by the citizens of London for more than three thousand five hundred and thirty-two pounds, and were sold for four hundred and seventy-eight pounds to such persons as should take them down and carry them thence ; also the ground or plot was made plain at the charges of the city ; and then possession thereof was by certain aldermen, in name of the whole citizens, given to Sir Thomas Gresham, knight, agent to the queen's highness, thereupon to build a bourse, or place for merchants to assemble, at his own proper charges. And he, on the 7th of June, laying the first stone of the foundation, being brick, accompanied with some aldermen, every of them laid a piece of gold, which the workmen took up, and forthwith followed upon the same with such diligence, that by the month of November, in the year 1567, the same was covered with slate, and shortly after fully finished.

In the year 1570, on the 23rd of January, the queen's majesty, attended with her nobility, came from her house at the Strand, called Somerset House, and entered the city by Temple Bar, through Fleet Street, Cheap, and so by the north side of the bourse, through Threadneedle Street, to Sir Thomas Gresham's in Bishopsgate Street, where she dined. After dinner her majesty returning through Cornhill, entered the bourse on the south side ; and after that she had viewed every part thereof above the ground, especially the pawn,* which was richly furnished with all sorts of the finest wares in the city, she caused the same bourse by an herald and trumpet to be proclaimed the Royal Exchange, and so to be called from thenceforth, and not otherwise.

Next adjoining to this Royal Exchange remaineth one part of a large stone house, and is now called the Castle of such a sign ; at

* *The pawn.* "You must to the pawn to buy lawn" (*Westward Ho,* 1607). Our modern word pawn, to pledge, is of the same origin, *pannus,* a cloth, because clothes are convenient for pledging. Their convenience to thieves caused the words "rob" and "reave" to arise from "robe" and the First English "reáf," clothing.

a tavern door there is a passage through out of Cornhill into Thread-needle Street; the other part of the said stone house was taken down for enlarging the Royal Exchange. This stone house was said of some to have been a church, whereof it had no proportion, of others a Jew's house, as though none but Jews had dwelt in stone houses; but that opinion is without warrant, for besides the strong building of stone houses against the invasion of thieves in the night, when no watches were kept, in the 1st year of Richard I., to pre-vent the casualties of fire, which often had happened in the city, when the houses were built of timber, and covered with reed or straw, Henry Fitz Alewine being mayor, it was decreed, that from henceforth no man should build within the city but of stone, until a certain height, and to cover the same building with slate or burnt tile; and this was the very cause of such stone buildings, whereof many have remained till our time, that for winning of ground they have been taken down, and in place of some one of them being low, as but two storeys above the ground, many houses of four or five storeys high are placed. From this stone house down to the Stocks are divers large houses, especially for height, for merchants and artificers.

On the south side of this high street is the parish church of St. Peter upon Cornhill, which seemeth to be of an ancient building, but not so ancient as fame reporteth, for it hath been lately repaired, if not all new built, except the steeple, which is ancient. The roof of this church and glazing were finished in the reign of Edward IV., as appeareth by arms of noblemen and aldermen of London then living. There remaineth in this church a table whereon it is written, I know not by what authority, but of a late hand, that King Lucius founded the same church to be an archbishop's see metropolitan, and chief church of his kingdom, and that it so endured the space of four hundred years, unto the coming of Augustin the monk.

Joceline of Furness writeth, that Thean, the first Archbishop of London, in the reign of Lucius, built the said church by the aid of Ciran, chief butler to King Lucius; and also that Eluanus, the second archbishop, built a library to the same adjoining, and converted many of the Druids, learned men in the Pagan law, to Christianity. True it is, that a library there was pertaining to this parish church of old time, built of stone, and of late repaired with brick by the executors of Sir John Crosby, alderman, as his arms on the south end doth witness.

This library hath been of late time, to wit, within these fifty years, well furnished of books; John Leland viewed and com-mended them; but now those books be gone, and the place is occupied by a schoolmaster and his usher, over a number of scholars learning their grammar rules, &c. Notwithstanding, before that time a grammar school had been kept in this parish, as appeareth in the year 1425, I read, that John Whitby was rector, and John Steward schoolmaster there; and in the 25th of Henry VI., it was enacted by parliament, that four grammar schools in London should be maintained, namely, in the parishes of Allhallows, in Thames Street, St. Andrew in Oldbourne, St. Peter's upon Cornhill, and St. Thomas of Acars.

Monuments of the dead in this church defaced: I read, that Hugh Waltham, Nicholas Pricot, mercer, alderman, Richard Manhall, 1503; William Kingston, fishmonger, gave his tenements called the Horsemill in Grass Street to this church, and was there buried about the year 1298; John Unisbrugh, poulterer, 1410; John Law. Also Peter Mason, tailor, gave to this church seven pounds sterling yearly for ever, out of his tenements in Colechurch parish, and deceased about the year 1416. John Foxton founded a chantry there. A brotherhood of St. Peter was in this church established by Henry IV., the 4th of his reign. William Brampton and William Askham, fishmongers and aldermen, were chief procurers thereof, for the fishmongers of late buried there; Sir William Bowyer, mayor 1543; Sir Henry Huberthorn, mayor 1546; Sir Christopher Morice, master-gunner of England to King Henry VIII.; Edward Elrington, esquire, chief butler to Edward VI.; Thomas Gardener, grocer; and Justice Smith, and other.

Then have ye the parish church of St. Michael the Archangel; for the antiquity whereof I find that Alnothus the priest gave it to the abbot and convent of Covesham, Reynold abbot, and the convent there did grant the same to Sperling the priest, in all measures as he and his predecessors before had held it; to the which Sperling also they granted all their lands which they there had, except certain lands which Orgar le Prowde had held of them, and paid two shillings yearly; for the which grant the said Sperling should yearly pay one mark of rent to the said abbot of Covesham, and find him and his lodging, salt, water, and fire, when he came to London. This was granted 1133, about the 34th of Henry I. Thus much for antiquity. Of later time I find that Elizabeth Peak, widow, gave the patronage or gift of this benefice to the Drapers in London. She lieth buried in the belfry, 1518: her monument yet remaineth.

This hath been a fair and beautiful church, but of late years, since the surrender of their lands to Edward VI., greatly blemished by the building of lower tenements on the north side thereof towards the high street, in place of a green churchyard, whereby the church is darkened, and other ways annoyed. The fair new steeple, or bell tower of this church, was begun to be built in the year 1421, which being finished, and a fair ring of five bells therein placed, a sixth bell * was added, and given by John Whitwell, Isabel his wife, and William Rus, alderman, and goldsmith, about the year 1430, which bell, named "Rus," nightly at eight of the clock, and otherwise for knells, and in peals, rung by one man, for the space of one hundred and sixty years, of late overhauled by four or five at once, hath been thrice broken, and new cast within the space of ten years, to the charges of that parish more than one hundred marks.

And here a note of this steeple : as I have oft heard my father report, upon St. James' night, certain men in the loft next under the bells, ringing of a peal, a tempest of lightning and thunder did arise, an ugly shapen sight appeared to them, coming in at the south window, and lighted on the north, for fear whereof they all fell down, and lay as dead for the time, letting the bells ring and cease of their own accord. When the ringers came to themselves, they found certain stones of the north window † to be razed and scratched, as if they had been so much butter, printed with a lion's claw. The same stones were fastened there again, and so remain till this day. I have seen them oft, and have put a feather or small stick into the holes where the claws had entered three or four inches deep. At the same time certain main timber posts at Queen Hithe were scratched and cleft from the top to the bottom ; and the pulpit cross in Paul's Churchyard was likewise scratched, cleft, and overturned. One of the ringers lived in my youth, whom I have oft heard to verify the same to be true.

But to return. William Rus was a special benefactor to this church ; his arms yet remain in the windows. William Comerton, Symon Smith, Walter Belingham, were buried there, and founded chantries there ; John Grace, 1439 ; Robert Drope, mayor, buried on the north side of the choir, under a fair tomb of grey marble, 1485, he gave to poor maids' marriages of that parish twenty pounds, to poor of that ward ten pounds, shirts and smocks three hundred, and gowns of broad cloth one hundred, &c. Jane his wife, matching with Edward Gray, Viscount Lisle, was buried by her first husband, 1500. She gave ninety pounds in money to the beautifying of that church, and her great messuage, with the appurtenance, which was by her executors, W. Caple and other, 1517, the 9th of Henry VIII., assured to John Wardroper, parson, T. Clearke, W. Dixson, and

---

* "This was accounted the best ring of six bells, to be rung by six men, that was in England, for harmony, sweetness of sound, and tune."—*Stow.*

† Struck by the lightning.

John Murdon, wardens of the said church, and their successors for ever, they to keep yearly for her an obite, or anniversary, to be spent on the poor, and otherwise, in all three pounds, the rest of the profits to be employed in reparation of the church. In the 34th year of Henry VIII., Edward Stephan, parson, T. Spencer, P. Guntar, and G. Grouch, churchwardens, granted to T. Lodge a lease for sixty years of the said great messuage, with the appurtenance, which were called the Lady Lisle's lands, for the rent of eight pounds thirteen shillings and fourpence the year. The parishioners since gave it up as chantry land, and wronged themselves. Also the said Robert Drope, and Lady Lisle, notwithstanding their liberality to that church and parish, their tomb is pulled down, no monument remaineth of them. Peter Hawton, late alderman, is laid in their vault, 1596. Robert Fabian, alderman, that wrote and published a Chronicle of England and of France, was buried there 1511, with this epitaph :—

> " Like as the day his course doth consume,
> And the new morrow springeth againe as fast,
> So man and woman, by Nature's custume,
> This life to pass, at last in earth are cast,
> In joy and sorrow which here their time do wast,
> Never in one state, but in course transitory,
> So full of change is of this world the glory."

His monument is gone. Richard Garnam, 1527, buried there ; Edmond Trindle and Robert Smith, my godfathers ; William Dickson and Margaret his wife, my godmother, buried in the cloister under a fair tomb now defaced ; Thomas Stow, my grandfather, about the year 1526, and Thomas Stow, my father, 1559 ; John Tolus, alderman, 1548. He gave to John Willowby, parson of that church, to Thomas Lodge, G. Hind, P. Bolde, churchwardens, and to their successors, towards the reparation of that church and relief of the poor for ever, his tenement with the appurtenances in the parish of St. Michael, which he had lately purchased of Alvery Randalph, of Badlesmeere in Kent ; but the parish never had the gift, nor heard thereof by the space of forty years after, such was the conscience of G. Barne and other the executors to conceal it to themselves ; and such is the negligence of the parishioners, that being informed thereof, make no claim thereunto. Philip Gonter, that was alderman for a time, and gave four hundred pounds to be discharged thereof, was buried in the cloister about the year 1582, and Anne his wife, &c. Thomas Houghton, father to the said Peter Houghton, Francis Beneson, and William Towersan.

This parish church hath on the south side thereof a proper cloister, and a fair churchyard, with a pulpit cross, not much unlike to that in Paul's Churchyard. Sir John Rudstone, mayor, caused the same pulpit cross in his lifetime to be built, the churchyard to be enlarged by ground purchased of the next parish, and also proper houses to be raised for lodging of choir men, such as at that time were assistants to divine service, then daily sung by note in that church. The said John Rudstone deceased 1531, and was buried in a vault under the pulpit cross. He appointed sermons to be preached there, not now performed. His tomb before the pulpit cross is taken thence, with the tomb of Richard Yaxley, Doctor of Physic to King Henry VIII. and other. The choir of that church dissolved, the lodgings of choir men were by the grave fathers of that time charitably appointed for receipt of ancient decayed parishioners, namely widows, such as were not able to bear the charge of greater rents abroad, which blessed work of harbouring the harbourless is promised to be rewarded in the kingdom of heaven.

Then have ye Birchover Lane, so called of Birchover, the first builder and owner thereof, now corruptly called Birchin Lane, the north half whereof is of the said Cornhill Ward; the other part is of Langborne Ward.

This lane, and the high street near adjoining, hath been inhabited for the most part with wealthy drapers. From Birchover's Lane, on that side the streets down to the Stocks, in the reign of Henry VI., had ye for the most part dwelling Fripperers or Upholders, that sold old apparel and household stuff.

I have read of a countryman, that then having lost his hood in Westminster Hall, found the same in Cornhill hanged out to be sold, which he challenged, but was forced to buy, or go without it, for their stall, they said, was their market. At that time also the wine drawer of the Pope's Head tavern, standing without the door in the high street, took the same man by the sleeve, and said, "Sir, will you drink a pint of wine?" whereunto he answered, "A penny spend I may;" and so drank his pint, for bread nothing did he pay, for that was allowed free.*

This Pope's Head tavern, with other houses adjoining, strongly built of stone, hath of old time been all in one, pertaining to some great estate, or rather to the king of this realm, as may be supposed both by the largeness thereof, and by the arms, to wit, three leopards passant, gardant, which were the whole arms of England before the reign of Edward III., that quartered them with the arms of France, three fleur-de-lis.

These arms of England, supported between two angels, are fair and largely graven in stone on the forefront towards the high street,

---

* Recollections of Lydgate's "London Lickpenny."

over the door or stall of one great house, lately for many years possessed by Mr. Philip Gunter. The Pope's Head tavern is on the back part thereof towards the south, as also one other house called the Stone House in Lombard Street. Some say this was King John's house, which might so be; for I find in a written copy of Matthew Paris' History, that in the year 1232, Henry III. sent Hubert de Burgh, Earl of Kent, to Cornhill in London, there to answer all matters objected against him, where he wisely acquitted himself. The Pope's Head tavern hath a footway through from Cornhill into Lombard Street. And down lower on the high street of Cornhill is there one other way through by the Cardinal's Hat tavern into Lombard Street. And so let this suffice for Cornhill Ward. In which be governors—an alderman, his deputy, common councillors four or six, constables four, scavengers four, wardmote inquest sixteen, and a beadle. It is charged to the fifteen * at sixteen pounds.

Langborne Ward and Fennie About.

LANGBORNE Ward, so called of a long bourne of sweet water, which of old time breaking out into Fenchurch Street, ran down the same street and Lombard Street to the west end of St. Mary Woolnoth's Church, where turning south, and breaking into small shares, rills, or streams, it left the name of Shareborne Lane, or Southborne Lane, as I have read, because it ran south to the river of Thames. This ward beginneth at the west end of Aldgate Ward in Fenchurch Street, by the Ironmongers' Hall, which is on the north side of that street, at a place called Culver Alley, where sometime was a lane, through the which men went into Lime Street, but that being long since stopped up for suspicion of thieves that lurked there by night, as is shown in Lime Street Ward, there is now this said alley, a tennis-court, &c.

Fenchurch Street took that name of a fenny or moorish ground, so made by means of this bourne which passed through it, and therefore until this day in the Guildhall of this city that ward is called by the name of Langborne and Fennie About, and not otherwise; yet others be of opinion that it took that name of *Fœnum*, that is, hay sold there, as Grass Street took the name of grass, or herbs, there sold.

In the midst of this street standeth a small parish church called St. Gabriel Fen Church, corruptly Fan Church.

---

* *Charged to the fifteen.* The tax of a fifteenth of all movables was first granted to Henry III. in February 1225 by the archbishops, bishops, abbots, priors, earls, barons, knights, freeholders, and all persons of the realm, on condition of a confirmation of Charters. The fifteenth had become under Elizabeth a recognised standard of taxation for the service of the country.

Helming Legget, esquire, by license of Edward III., in the 49th of his reign, gave one tenement, with a curtelage thereto belonging, and a garden, with an entry thereto leading, unto Sir John Hariot, parson of Fenchurch, and to his successors for ever ; the house to be a parsonage-house, the garden to be a churchyard or burying-place for the parish.

Then have ye Lombard Street, so called of the Longobards and other merchants, strangers of divers nations assembling there twice every day, of what original or continuance I have not read of record, more than that Edward II., in the 12th of his reign, confirmed a messuage, sometime belonging to Robert Turke, abutting on Lombard Street toward the south, and toward Cornhill on the north, for the merchants of Florence, which proveth that street to have had the name of Lombard Street before the reign of Edward II. The meeting of which merchants and others there continued until the 22nd of December, in the year 1568 ; on the which day the said merchants began to make their meetings at the bourse, a place then new built for that purpose in the ward of Cornhill, and was since by her majesty Queen Elizabeth named the Royal Exchange.

On the north side of this ward is Lime Street, one half whereof on both the sides is of this Langborne Ward, and therein on the west side is the Pewterers' Hall, which company were admitted to be a brotherhood in the 13th of Edward IV.

At the south-west corner of Lime Street standeth a fair parish church of St. Dionys called Backe Church, lately new built in the reign of Henry VI. John Budge, esquire, was a great benefactor to that work, as appeareth by his arms, three water budgets,* and his crest, a Morian's head, graven in the stone work of the choir, the upper end on the north side, where he was buried. Also John Darby, alderman, added thereunto a fair aisle, or chapel, on the south side, and was there buried about the year 1466. He gave, besides sundry ornaments, his dwelling-house and others unto the said church. The Lady Wich, widow to Hugh Wich, sometime mayor of London, was there buried, and gave lands for sermons, &c. John Master, gentleman, was by his children buried there 1444 ; Thomas Britaine ; Henry Travers, of Maidstone, in Kent, merchant, 1501 ; John Bond, about 1504 ; Robert Paget, merchant tailor, one of the sheriffs 1536 ; Sir Thomas Curteis, pewterer, then fishmonger, mayor 1557 ; Sir James Harvey, ironmonger, mayor 1581 ; William Paterson, esquire ; William Sherrington ; Sir Edward Osborne, clothworker, mayor, &c.

Then by the four corners, so called of Fenchurch Street in the

---

* *Water budgets,* small casks, originally water skins or bags. Bouge was commonly used in French as meaning a leather bag until the beginning of the seventeenth century.

east, Bridge Street on the south, Grass Street on the north, and Lombard Street on the west, in Lombard Street is one fair parish church called Allhallows Grass Church, in Lombard Street; I do so read it in the evidences of record, for that the grass market went down that way, when that street was far broader than now it is, being straitened by encroachments.

This church was lately new built. John Warner, armourer, and then grocer, sheriff 1494, built the south aisle; his son, Robert Warner, esquire, finished it in the year 1516. The pewterers were benefactors towards the north aisle, &c. The steeple or bell tower thereof was finished in the year 1544, about the 36th of Henry VIII. The fair stone porch of this church was brought from the late dissolved priory of St. John of Jerusalem by Smithfield, so was the frame for their bells, but the bells being bought, were never brought thither, by reason that one old Warner, draper of that parish, deceasing, his son Mark Warner would not perform what his father had begun and appointed, so that fair steeple hath but one bell, as friars were wont to use. The monuments of this church be these: The said Warners, and John Walden, draper.

Next is a common hostelry for travellers, called the George, of such a sign. This is said to have pertained to the Earl Ferrers, and was his London lodging in Lombard Street, and that in the year 1175, a brother of the said earl, being there privily slain in the night, was there thrown down into the dirty street, as I have afore shown in the chapter of night watches.

Next to this is the parish church of St. Edmund, the king and martyr, in Lombard Street, by the south corner of Birchover Lane. This church is also called St. Edmund Grass Church, because the said grass market came down so low. The monuments in this church are these: Sir John Milborne, draper, mayor, deceased, 1535, buried there by Dame Joan and Dame Margaret, his wives, under a tomb of touch; Humphrey Heyford, goldsmith, mayor 1477; Sir William Chester, draper, mayor 1560, with his wives, amongst his predecessors; Sir George Barne, mayor 1586; Matilde at Vine founded a chantry there, &c.

From this church down Lombard Street, by Birchover's Lane, the one half of which lane is of this ward, and so down, be divers fair houses, namely, one with a very fair forefront towards the street, built by Sir Martin Bowes, goldsmith, since mayor of London, and then one other, sometime belonging to William de la Pole, knight banneret, and yet the king's merchant, in the 14th of Edward III., and after him to Michael de la Pole, Earl of Suffolk, in the 14th of Richard II., and was his merchant's house, and so down towards the Stocks Market, lacking but some three houses thereof.

The south side of this ward beginneth in the east, at the chain to be drawn athwart Mart Lane up into Fenchurch Street, and so west by the north end of Minchin Lane to St. Margaret Patten's Street, or Rood Lane, and down that street to the midway towards St. Margaret's Church; then by Philpot Lane, so called of Sir John Philpot that dwelt there, and was owner thereof, and down that lane some six or eight houses on each side, is all of this ward.

Then by Grass Church corner into Lombard Street to St. Clement's Lane, and down the same to St. Clement's Church; then down St. Nicholas Lane, and down the same to St. Nicholas Church, and the same church is of this ward. Then to Abchurch Church Lane, and down some small portion thereof; then down Sherborne Lane, a part thereof, and a part of Bearebinder Lane, be of this ward; and then down Lombard Street to the sign of the Angel, almost to the corner over against the Stocks Market.

On the south side of this ward, somewhat within Mart Lane, have you the parish church of Allhallows, commonly called Stane Church, as may be supposed, for a difference from other churches of that name in this city, which of old time were built of timber, and since were built of stone. In this church have been divers fair monuments of the dead, namely, of John Costin, girdler, a great benefactor: he deceased 1244. His name remaineth painted in the church roof: if it had been set in brass, it would have been fetched down. He gave out of certain tenements to the poor of that parish a hundred quarters of charcoals yearly for ever. Sir Robert Test, knight of the holy sepulchre, and Dame Joan his wife, about 1486; Robert Stone; Sir John Steward, and Dame Alice his wife; John Bostocke, esquire; Christopher Holt; Sir Richard Tate, knight, ambassador to King Henry VIII., buried there 1554. His monument remaineth yet; the rest being all pulled down and swept out of the church, the churchwardens were forced to make a large account, 12*s.* that year for brooms, besides the carriage away of stone and brass of their own charge. And here I am to note, that being informed of the Writhsleys to be buried there, I have since found them and other to be buried at St. Giles without Cripplegate, where I mind to leave them.

By this church sometime passed a lane, called Cradock's Lane, from Mart Lane, winding by the north side of the said church into Fenchurch Street, the which lane being straitened by encroachments, is now called Church Alley.

Then is the parish church of St. Nicholas Acon, or Hacon, for so have I read it in records, in Lombard Street. Sir John Bridges, draper, mayor 1520, newly repaired this church, and embattled it, and was there buried. Francis Boyer, grocer, one of the sheriffs, was buried there 1580, with other of the Boyers: so was Julian, wife to John Lambart, alderman.

Then is there in the high street a proper parish church of St. Mary Woolnoth, of the Nativity, the reason of which name I have not yet learnt. This church is lately new built. Sir Hugh Brice, goldsmith, mayor in the first year of Henry VII., keeper of the king's exchange at London, and one of the governors of the king's mint in the Tower of London, under William Lord Hastings, the 5th of Edward IV., deceased 1496. He built in this church a chapel called the Charnell, as also part of the body of the church and of the steeple, and gave money toward the finishing thereof, besides the stone which he had prepared. He was buried in the body of the church. Guy Brice, or Boys, was buried there. Dame Joan, wife to Sir William Peach; Thomas Nocket, draper, 1396: he founded a chantry there. Simon Eyre, 1459: he gave the tavern called the Cardinal's Hat, in Lombard Street, with a tenement annexed on the east part of the tavern, and a mansion behind the east tenement, together with an alley from Lombard Street to Cornhill, with the appurtenances, all which were by him new built, toward a brotherhood of our Lady in St. Mary Woolnoth's Church. John Moager, pewterer, and Emma his wife, in St. John's Chapel; Sir John Percival, merchant tailor, mayor about 1504; Thomas Roch and Andrew Michael, vintners, and Joan their wife; William Hilton, merchant tailor, and tailor to King Henry VIII., was buried there 1519, under the chapel of St. George, which chapel was built by George Lufken, sometime tailor to the prince; Robert Amades, goldsmith, master of the king's jewels. Sir Martin Bowes, mayor, buried about 1569: he gave lands for the discharge of that Langborne Ward, of all fifteens to be granted to the king by parliament. George Hasken, Sir Thomas Ramsey, late mayor, &c. Thus have ye seven parishes in this ward, one hall of a company, divers fair houses for merchants, and other monuments none. It hath an alderman, his deputy, common councillors eight, constables fifteen, scavengers nine, men of the wardmote inquest seventeen, and a beadle. It is taxed to the fifteen, in the Exchequer, at £20, 9s. 8d.

Billingsgate Ward.

BILLINGSGATE Ward beginneth at the west end of Tower Street Ward in Thames Street, about Smart's Quay, and runneth down along that street on the south side to St. Magnus Church at the bridge foot, and on the north side of the said Thames Street, from over against Smart's Quay, till over against the north-west corner of St. Magnus Church aforesaid. On this north side of Thames Street, is

St. Mary Hill Lane, up to St. Margaret's Church, and then part of St. Margaret Patten's Street, at the end of St. Mary Hill Lane. Next out of Thames Street is Lucas Lane, and then Botolph Lane, and at the north end thereof Philpot Lane; then is Rother Lane, of old time so called, and thwart the same lane is Little East Cheap; and these be the bounds of Billingsgate Ward.

Touching the principal ornaments within this ward. On the south side of Thames Street, beginning at the east end thereof, there is first the said Smart's Quay, so called of one Smart sometime owner thereof; the next is Billingsgate, whereof the whole ward taketh name; the which, leaving out of the fable thereof, feigning it to be built by King Beline, a Briton, long before the incarnation of Christ, is at this present a large water-gate, port, or harborough, for ships and boats commonly arriving there with fish, both fresh and salt, shell-fishes, salt, oranges, onions, and other fruits and roots, wheat, rye, and grain of divers sorts, for service of the city and the parts of this realm adjoining. This gate is now more frequented than of old time, when the Queen's hithe was used, as being appointed by the kings of this realm to be the special or only port for taking up of all such kind of merchandises brought to this city by strangers and foreigners, and the drawbridge of timber at London Bridge was then to be raised or drawn up for passage of ships with tops thither.

Touching the ancient customs of Billingsgate in the reign of Edward III., every great ship landing there paid for standage two-pence, every little ship with oarlocks a penny, the lesser boat called a battle a halfpenny; of two quarters of corn measured the king was to have one farthing, of a combe of corn a penny, of every weight going out of the city a halfpenny, of two quarters of sea coal measured a farthing, and of every tun of ale going out of England beyond the seas by merchant strangers fourpence, of every thousand herrings a farthing, except franchises, &c.

Next to this is Sommer's Quay, which likewise took that name of one Sommer dwelling there, as did Lion Quay of one Lion, owner thereof, and since of the sign of a Lion.

Then is there a fair wharf, or quay, called Botolph's Gate, by that name so called in the times of William the Conqueror and of Edward the Confessor, as I have shown already in the description of the gates.

Next is the parish church of St. Botolph's, a proper church, and hath had many fair monuments therein, now defaced and gone: notwithstanding I find, by testimonies abroad, that these were buried there; to wit, Roger Coggar, 1384; Andrew Pikeman, and Joan his wife, 1391; Nicholas James, ironmonger, one of the sheriffs 1423; William Rainwell, fishmonger, and John Rainwell, his son,

fishmonger, mayor 1426, and deceasing 1445, buried there with
this epitaph :—

> " Citizens of London, call to your remembrance,
> The famous John Rainwell, sometime your Maior,
> Of the staple of Callis, so was his chance.
> Here lieth now his corps ; his soule bright and faire,
> Is taken to heaven's blisse, thereof is no dispaire.
> His acts beare witnes, by matters of recorde,
> How charitable he was, and of what accorde,
> No man hath beene so beneficiall as hee,
> Unto the Citie in giving liberallie," &c.

He gave a stone house to be a revestrie to that church for ever ;
more, he gave lands and tenements to the use of the commonalty,
that the mayor and chamberlain should satisfy unto the discharge
of all persons inhabiting the wards of Billingsgate, Downgate, and
Aldgate, as oft as it shall happen any fifteen by parliament of the
king to be granted, also to the Exchequer, in discharge of the sheriffs,
ten pounds yearly, which the sheriffs used to pay for the farm of
Southwark, so that all men of the realm, coming or passing with
carriage, should be free quitted and discharged of all toll and other
payments aforetime claimed by the sheriffs. Further, that the
mayor and chamberlain shall pay yearly to the sheriffs eight pounds,
so that the said sheriffs take no manner of toll or money of any
person of this realm for their goods, merchandises, victuals, and
carriages, for their passages at the great gate of the bridge of the
city, nor at the gate called the Drawbridge, &c.   The overplus of
money coming of the said lands and tenements, divided into even
portions ; the one part to be employed to instore the granaries of
the city with wheat for the release of the poor commonalty, and the
other moiety to clear and cleanse the shelves and other stoppages
of the river of Thames, &c.

Stephen Forstar, fishmonger, mayor in the year 1454, and Dame
Agnes his wife, lie buried there.   William Bacon, haberdasher, one
of the sheriffs 1480, was there buried, besides many other persons
of good worship, whose monuments are all destroyed by bad and
greedy men of spoil.

This parish of St. Botolph is no great thing, notwithstanding
divers strangers are there harboured, as may appear by a present-
ment not many years since made of strangers inhabitants in the
ward of Billingsgate, in these words : " In Billingsgate Ward were one
and fifty households of strangers, whereof thirty of these households
inhabited in the parish of St. Botolph, in the chief and principal
houses, where they give twenty pounds the year for a house lately
letten for four marks ; the nearer they dwell to the water-side the
more they give for houses, and within thirty years before there was

not in the whole ward above three Netherlanders; at which time there was within the said parish levied, for the help of the poor, seven and twenty pounds by the year; but since they came so plentifully thither, there cannot be gathered above eleven pounds, for the stranger will not contribute to such charges as other citizens do." Thus much for that south side of this ward.

On the north side is Boss Alley, so called of a boss of spring water continually running, which standeth by Billingsgate against this alley, and was sometime made by the executors of Richard Whittington.

Then is St. Mary Hill Lane, which runneth up north from Billingsgate to the end of St. Margaret Patten's, commonly called Rood Lane, and the greatest half of that lane is also of Billingsgate Ward. In this St. Mary Hill Lane is the fair parish church of St. Mary, called on the hill, because of the ascent from Billingsgate.

This church hath been lately built, as may appear by this that followeth. Richard Hackney, one of the sheriffs in the year 1322, and Alice his wife, were there buried, as Robert Fabian writeth, saying thus :—"In the year 1497, in the month of April, as labourers digged for the foundation of a wall, within the Church of St. Mary Hill, near unto Billingsgate, they found a coffin of rotten timber, and therein the corpse of a woman, whole of skin, and of bones undissevered, and the joints of her arms pliable, without breaking of the skin, upon whose sepulchre this was engraven : ' Here lieth the bodies of Richard Hackney, fishmonger, and Alice his wife.' " The which Richard was sheriff in the 15th of Edward II. Her body was kept above ground three or four days without nuisance, but then it waxed unsavoury, and so was again buried. John Mordand, stock-fishmonger, was buried there, 1387; Nicholas Exton, fishmonger, mayor 1387; William Cambridge, mayor 1420; Richard Goslin, sheriff 1422; William Philip, sergeant-at-arms, 1473; Robert Reuell, one of the sheriffs 1490, gave liberally toward the new building of this church and steeple, and was there buried; William Remington, mayor 1500; Sir Thomas Blanke, mayor 1582; William Holstocke, esquire, comptroller of the king's ships; Sir Cuthbert Buckle, mayor 1594.

This lane on both sides is furnished with many fair houses for merchants; and hath at the north end thereof one other lane, called St. Margaret Patten's, because of old time pattens were there usually made and sold; but of latter time this is called Rood Lane, of a rood there placed in the churchyard of St. Margaret, whilst the old church was taken down, and again newly built, during which time the oblations made to this rood were employed towards building of the church; but in the year 1538, about the 23rd of May, in the morning, the said rood was found to have been in the night preceding, by people unknown, broken all to pieces, together with the tabernacle wherein it had been placed. Also, on the 27th of the same month, in the same parish, amongst the basket-makers, a great and sudden fire happened in the night season, which within the space of three hours consumed more than a dozen houses, and nine persons were burnt to death there : and thus ceased that work of this church, being at that time nigh finished to the steeple.

The lane on both sides beyond the same church to the midway towards Fenchurch Street is of Billingsgate Ward.

Then again out of Thames Street, by the west end of St. Mary Hill Church, runneth up one other lane, of old time called Rope Lane, since called Lucas Lane, of one Lucas, owner of some part thereof, and now corruptly called Love Lane. It runneth up by the east end of a parish church of St. Andrew Hubbert, or St. Andrew in East Cheap. This church, and all the whole lane called Lucas Lane, is of this Billingsgate Ward.

Then have ye one other lane out of Thames Street, called Botolph Lane, because it riseth over against the parish church of St. Botolph, and runneth up north by the east end of St. George's Church to the west end of St. Andrew's Church, and to the south end of Philpot Lane.

This parish church of St. George in Botolph Lane is small, but the monuments for two hundred years past are well preserved from spoil, whereof one is of Adam Bamme, mayor 1397; Richard Bamme, esquire, his son, of Gillingham in Kent, 1452 ; John Walton, gentleman, 1401 ; Marpor, a gentleman, 1400 ; John St. John, merchant of Levant, and Agnes his wife, 1400 ; Hugh Spencer, esquire, 1424 ; William Combes, stock-fishmonger, one of the sheriffs 1452, who gave forty pounds towards the works of that church ; John Stoker, draper, one of the sheriffs 1477 ; Richard Dryland, esquire, and Katherine his wife, daughter to Morrice Brune, knight of Southuckenton in Essex, steward of household to Humphrey, Duke of Gloucester, 1487 ; Nicholas Patrich, one of the sheriffs 1519. In the churchyard : William Forman, mayor 1538 ; James Mumford, esquire, surgeon to King Henry VIII., buried 1544 ; Thomas Gayle, haberdasher, 1340 ; Nicholas Wilford, merchant tailor, and Elizabeth his wife, about the year 1551 ; Edward Heyward, 1573, &c. Roger Delakere founded a chantry there.

Then have ye one other lane called Rother Lane, or Red Rose Lane, of such a sign there, now commonly called Pudding Lane, because the butchers of East Cheap have their scalding house for hogs there, and their puddings, with other filth of beasts, are voided down that way to their dungboats on the Thames.

This lane stretcheth from Thames Street to Little East Cheap, chiefly inhabited by basket-makers, turners, and butchers, and is all of Billingsgate Ward. The Garland in Little East Cheap, sometime a brewhouse, with a garden on the back side, adjoining to the garden of Sir John Philpot, was the chief house in this East Cheap. It is now divided into sundry small tenements, &c.

This ward hath an alderman, and his deputy, common councillors, constables eleven, scavengers six, for the wardmote inquest fourteen, and a beadle. It is taxed to the fifteen in London at thirty-two pounds, and in the Exchequer at thirty-one pounds ten shillings.

Bridge Ward Within.

BRIDGE Ward Within, so called of London Bridge, which bridge is a principal part of that ward, and beginneth at the stulpes * on the south end by Southwark, runneth along the bridge, and north up Bridge Street, commonly called, of the fish market, New Fish Street, from Fish Street Hill, up Grass Street, to the north corner of Grass Church. All the bridge is replenished on both the sides with large, fair, and beautiful buildings, inhabitants for the most part rich merchants, and other wealthy citizens, mercers, and haberdashers.

In New Fish Street be fishmongers and fair taverns on Fish Street Hill and Grass Street, men of divers trades, grocers, and haberdashers.

In Grass Street have ye one fair conduit of sweet water castellated with crest and vent, made by the appointment of Thomas Hill, mayor 1484, who gave by his testament one hundred marks towards the conveyance of water to this place. It was begun by his executors in the year 1491, and finished of his goods whatsoever it cost.

On the east side of this Bridge Ward have ye the fair parish church of St. Magnus; in the which church have been buried many men of good worship, whose monuments are now for the most part utterly defaced. I find John Blund, mayor 1307; Henry Yeuele, freemason to Edward III., Richard II., and Henry IV., who deceased 1400— his monument yet remaineth; William Brampton; John Michell, mayor 1436; John French, baker, yeoman of the crown to Henry VII., 1510; Robert Clarke, fishmonger, 1521; Richard Turke, one of the sheriffs 1549; William Steede, alderman; Richard Morgan, knight, chief justice of the common pleas, 1556; Mauritius Griffeth, Bishop of Rochester, 1559; Robert Blanch, girdler, 1567; Robert

* "Stulpe or stake, *Paxillus*," Promptorium Parvulorum (1440). The stulpes were posts at the foot of the bridge. Hall the chronicler speaks of the stulpes on the Southwark side of the river, where there was a chain that might be used to bar the way. Palsgrave (1530) has "Stoulpe before a door, *Souche*," the French souche being a stump or stock.

Belgrave, girdler; William Brame; John Couper, fishmonger, alderman, who was put by his turn of mayoralty 1584; Sir William Garrard, haberdasher, mayor 1555, a grave, wise, and discreet citizen, equal with the best and inferior to none of our time, deceased 1571 in the parish of St. Christopher, but was buried in this church of St. Magnus as in the parish where he was born—a fair monument is there raised on him; Robert Harding, salter, one of the sheriffs 1568; Simon Low, merchant tailor, esquire, &c.

Then is the parish church of St. Margaret on Fish Street Hill, a proper church, but monuments it hath none. A footway passeth by the south side of this church from Fish Street Hill unto Rother Lane.

Up higher on this hill is the parish church of St. Leonard, Milk Church, so termed of one William Melker, an especial builder thereof, but commonly called St. Leonard's in East Cheap, because it standeth at East Cheap corner. Monuments there be of the Doggets, namely, Walter Dogget, vintner, one of the sheriffs 1380; John Dogget, vintner, and Alice his wife, about 1456—this John Dogget gave lands to that church; William Dogget, &c.

This church, and from thence into Little East Cheap to the east end of the said church, is of the Bridge Ward.

Then higher in Grass Street is the parish church of St. Bennet, called Grass Church,* of the herb market there kept. This church also is of the Bridge Ward, and the farthest north end thereof. Some monuments remain there undefaced, as of John Harding, salter, 1576; John Sturgeon, haberdasher, chamberlain of London; Philip Cushen, Florentine, a famous merchant, 1600.

The customs of Grass Church Market, in the reign of Edward III., as I have read in a book of customs, were these: Every foreign cart laden with corn or malt, coming thither to be sold, was to pay one halfpenny, every foreign cart bringing cheese twopence, every cart of corn and cheese together, if the cheese be more worth than the corn, twopence, and if the corn be more worth than the cheese, it was to pay a halfpenny; of two horses laden with corn or malt the bailiff had one farthing; the cart of the franchise of the Temple and of St. Martin le Grand paid a farthing; the cart of the hospital of St. John of Jerusalem paid nothing for their proper goods; and if the corn were brought by merchants to sell again, the load paid a halfpenny, &c.

On the west side of this ward, at the north end of London Bridge, is a part of Thames Street, which is also of this ward, to wit, so much as of old time was called Stock Fishmonger Row, of the stock fishmongers dwelling there, down west to a water-gate, of old time called Ebgate, since Ebgate Lane, and now the Old Swan,

* Now Gracechurch.

which is a common stair on the Thames, but the passage is very narrow by means of encroachments. On the south side of Thames Street, about the midway betwixt the bridge foot and Ebgate Lane, standeth the Fishmongers' Hall, and divers other fair houses for merchants.

These fishmongers were sometimes of two several companies, to wit, Stock-fishmongers and Salt-fishmongers, of whose antiquity I read, that by the name of fishmongers of London, they were, for forestalling, &c., contrary to the laws and constitutions of the city, fined to the king at five hundred marks, the 18th of King Edward I. More, that the said fishmongers, hearing of the great victory obtained by the same king against the Scots, in the 26th of his reign, made a triumphant and solemn show through the city, with divers pageants, and more than one thousand horsemen, &c., as in the chapter of sports and pastimes. These two companies of stock-fishmongers and salt-fishmongers of old time had their several halls; to wit, in Thames Street twain, in New Fish Street twain, and in Old Fish Street twain : in each place one for either company, in all six several halls, the company was so great, as I have read, and can prove by records, these fishmongers having been jolly citizens, and six mayors of their company in the space of twenty-four years ; to wit, Walter Turke, 1350; John Lofkin, 1359; John Wroth, 1361 ; John Pechie, 1362 ; Simon Morden, 1369 ; and William Walworth, 1374. It followed that in the year 1382, through the counsel of John Northampton, draper, then being mayor, William Essex, John More, mercer, and Richard Northbury, the said fishmongers were greatly troubled, hindered of their liberties, and almost destroyed by congregations made against them, so that in a parliament at London the controversy depending between the mayor and aldermen of London, and the fishmongers there, Nicholas Exton, speaker for the fishmongers, prayeth the king to receive him and his company into his protection, for fear of corporal hurt : whereupon it was commanded, either part to keep the peace, on pain of losing all they had. Hereupon, a fishmonger, starting up, replied that the complaint brought against them by the movers, &c., was but matter of malice, for that the fishmongers, in the reign of Edward III., being chief officers of the city, had, for their misdemeanours then done, committed the chief exhibitors of those petitions to prison. In this parliament the fishmongers, by the king's charter patents, were restored to their liberties. Notwithstanding, in the year next following, to wit, 1383, John Cavendish, fishmonger, craveth the peace against the chancellor of England, which was granted, and he put in sureties the Earls of Stafford and Salisbury. Cavendish challengeth the chancellor for taking of a bribe of ten pounds for favour of his case, which the chancellor by

oath upon the sacrament avoideth. In further trial it was found
that the chancellor's man, without his master's privity, had taken
it ; whereupon Cavendish was adjudged to prison, and to pay the
chancellor one thousand marks for slandering him.

After this, many of the nobles assembled at Reading to suppress
the seditious stirs of the said John Northampton, or Combarton,
late mayor, that had attempted great and heinous enterprises, of the
which he was convicted ; and when he stood mute, nor would utter
one word, it was decreed that he should be committed to perpetual
prison, his goods confiscate to the king's use, and that he should
not come within one hundred miles of London during his life. He
was therefore sent to the castle of Tintagell in the confines of Cornwall, and in the mean space the king's servants spoiled his goods.
John More, Richard Northbury, and other, were likewise there
convicted, and condemned to perpetual prison, and their goods
confiscate, for certain congregations by them made against the
fishmongers in the city of London, as is aforesaid ; but they obtained
and had the king's pardon, in the 14th of his reign, as appeareth
of record ; and thus were all these troubles quieted. Those stock-
fishmongers and salt-fishmongers were united in the year 1536, the
28th of Henry VIII. ; their hall to be but one, in the house given
unto them by Sir John Cornwall, Lord Fanhope, and of Ampthull,
in the parish of St. Michael in Crooked Lane, in the reign of Henry
VI. Thus much have I thought good to note of the fishmongers,
men ignorant of their antiquities, not able to show a reason why
or when they were joined in amity with the goldsmiths, do give part
of their arms, &c. Neither do say aught of Sir William Walworth,
the glory of their company, more than that he slew Jack Straw,
which is a mere fable, for the said Straw was, after overthrowing
of the rebels, taken, and by judgment of the mayor beheaded ;
whose confession at the gallows is extant in my Annals, where also
is set down the most valiant and praiseworthy act of William
Walworth against the principal rebel Wat Tyler. As, in reproof
of Walworth's monument in St. Michael's Church, I have declared,
and wished to be reformed there, as in other places.

On that south side of Thames Street have ye Drinkwater Wharf
and Fish Wharf, in the parish of St. Magnus. On the north side
of Thames Street is St. Martin's Lane ; a part of which lane is also
of this ward, to wit, on the one side to a well of water, and on the
other side as far up as against the said well. Then is St. Michael's
Lane, part whereof is also of this ward up to a well there, &c.
Then at the upper end of New Fish Street is a lane turning towards
St. Michael's Lane, and is called Crooked Lane, of the crooked
windings thereof.

Above this lane's end, upon Fish Street Hill, is one great house, for the most part built of stone, which pertained sometime to Edward the Black Prince, son to Edward III., who was in his lifetime lodged there. It is now altered to a common hostelry, having the Black Bell for a sign.

Above this house, at the Top of Fish Street Hill, is a turning into Great East Cheap, and so to the corner of Lombard Street, over against the north west corner of Grass Church ; and these be the whole bounds of this Bridge Ward within : the which hath an alderman and his deputy, for the common council sixteen, constables fifteen, scavengers six, for the wardmote inquest sixteen, and a beadle. It is taxed to the fifteen in London at forty-seven pounds.

Candlewick Street Ward.

CANDLEWICK STREET, or Candlewright Street Ward, beginneth at the east end of Great East Cheap ; it passeth west through East Cheap to Candlewright Street, and through the same, down to the north end of Suffolk Lane on the south side, and down that lane by the west end of St. Laurence Churchyard, which is the farthest west part of that ward. The street of Great East Cheap is so called of the market there kept in the east part of the city, as West Cheap is a market so called of being in the west.

This East Cheap is now a flesh market of butchers there dwelling on both sides of the street : it had sometime also cooks mixed amongst the butchers, and such other as sold victuals ready dressed of all sorts. For of old time, when friends did meet, and were disposed to be merry, they went not to dine and sup in taverns, but to the cooks, where they called for meat what they liked, which they always found ready dressed at a reasonable rate, as I have before showed.

In the year 1410, the 11th of Henry IV., upon the even of St. John Baptist, the king's sons, Thomas and John, being in East Cheap at supper, or rather at breakfast, for it was after the watch was broken up, betwixt two and three of the clock after midnight, a great debate happened between their men and other of the court, which lasted one hour, till the mayor and sheriffs, with other citizens, appeased the same ; for the which afterwards the said mayor, aldermen, and sheriffs were called to answer before the king, his sons and divers lords being highly moved against the city. At which time William Gascoyne, chief justice, required the mayor and aldermen, for the citizens, to put them in the king's grace ; whereunto they answered, that they had not offended, but, according to the law, had done their best in stinting debate and maintaining of the peace; upon which answer the king remitted all his ire, and dismissed them.　And to prove this East Cheap to be a place replenished with cooks, it may appear by a song called London Lickpenny, made by Lydgate, a monk of Bury, in the reign of Henry V., in the person of a countryman coming to London, and travelling through the same.　In West Cheap, saith the song, he was called on to buy fine lawn, Paris thread, cotton umble, and other linen clothes, and such like (he speaketh of no silks); in Cornhill, to buy old apparel and household stuff, where he was forced to buy his own hood, which he had lost in Westminster Hall; in Candlewright Street drapers proffered him cheap cloth; in East Cheap the cooks cried hot ribs of beef roasted, pies well baked, and other victuals: there was clattering of pewter-pots, harp, pipe, and sawtry, yea by cock, nay by cock, for greater oaths were spared; some sang of Jenken, and Julian, &c.; all which melody liked well the passenger, but he wanted money to abide by it, and therefore gat him into Gravesend barge, and home into Kent.

Candlewright, so called in old records of the Guildhall, of St. Mary Overies, and other, or Candlewick Street, took that name, as may be supposed, either of chandlers, or makers of candles, both of wax and tallow, for candlewright is a maker of candles; or of wick, which is the cotton or yarn thereof; or otherwise wike, which is the place where they used to work them, as Scalding Wike by the Stocks Market was called of the poulterers scalding and dressing their poultry there; and in divers countries, dairy houses, or cottages, wherein they make butter and cheese, are usually called wicks.　There dwelt also of old time divers weavers of woollen clothes, brought in by Edward III.　For I read, that in the 44th of his reign, the weavers, brought out of Flanders, were appointed their meetings to be in the churchyard of St. Laurence Poultney, and the weavers of Brabant in the churchyard of St. Mary Somerset. There were then in this city weavers of divers sorts; to wit, of drapery, or tapery, and napery.　These weavers of Candlewright Street being in short time worn out, their place is now possessed by rich drapers, sellers of woollen cloth, &c.

On the north side of this ward, at the west end of East Cheap, have ye St. Clement's Lane; a part whereof on both sides is of Candlewick Street Ward, to wit, somewhat north beyond the parish church of St. Clement in East Cheap.　This is a small church, void of monuments, other than of Francis Barnam, alderman, who deceased 1575, and of Benedick Barnam, his son, alderman also, 1598.　William Chartney and William Overie founded a chantry there.

Next is St. Nicholas Lane, for the most part on both sides of this ward, almost to St. Nicholas Church. Then is Abchurch Lane, which is on both the sides almost wholly of this ward, the parish church there, called of St. Mary Abchurch, Apechurch, or Upchurch, as I have read it, standeth somewhat near unto the south end thereof, on a rising ground. It is a fair church. Simon de Winch-comb founded a chantry there the 19th of Richard II. ; John Littleton founded another, and Thomas Hondon another ; and hath the monuments of J. Long, esquire, of Bedfordshire, 1442 ; William Wikenson, alderman, 1519 ; William Jawdrell, tailor, 1440 ; Sir James Hawes, mayor 1574 ; Sir John Branch, mayor 1580 ; John Miners ; William Kettle, &c.

On the south side of this ward, beginning again at the east, is St. Michael's Lane, which lane is almost wholly of this ward, on both sides down towards Thames Street, to a well or pump there. On the east side of this lane is Crooked Lane aforesaid, by St. Michael's Church, towards New Fish Street. One the most ancient house in this Lane is called the Leaden Porch, and belonged sometime to Sir John Merston, knight, the 1st of Edward IV. It is now called the Swan in Crooked Lane, possessed of strangers, and selling of Rhenish wine. The parish church of this St. Michael's was sometime but a small and homely thing, standing upon part of that ground wherein now standeth the parsonage house ; and the ground thereabout was a filthy plot, by reason of the butchers in East Cheap, who made the same their laystall. William de Burgo gave two messuages to that church in Candlewick Street, 1317. John Lofkin, stock-fishmonger, four times mayor, built in the same ground this fair church of St. Michael, and was buried there in the choir, under a fair tomb, with the images of him and his wife in alabaster. The said church hath been since increased with a new choir, and side chapels by Sir William Walworth, stock-fish-monger, mayor, sometime servant to the said John Lofkin : also the tomb of Lofkin was removed, and a flat stone of grey marble garnished with plates of copper laid on him, as it yet remaineth in the body of the church. This William Walworth is reported to have slain Jack Straw, but Jack Straw being afterward taken, was first adjudged by the said mayor, and then executed by the loss of his head in Smithfield.

True it is that this William Walworth, being a man wise, learned, and of an incomparable manhood, arrested Wat Tyler, a pre-sumptuous rebel, upon whom no man durst lay hand, whereby he delivered the king and kingdom from most wicked tyranny of traitors. The mayor arrested him on the head with a sound blow, whereupon Wat Tyler furiously struck the mayor with his dagger, but hurt him not, by reason he was well armed. The mayor, having received his stroke, drew his basiliard,* and grievously wounded Wat in the neck, and withal gave him a great blow on the head; in the which conflict, an esquire of the king's house, called John Cavendish, drew his sword, and wounded Wat twice or thrice even to the death; and Wat, spurring his horse, cried to the commons to revenge him : the horse bare him about eighty feet from the place, and there he fell down half dead; and by-and-by they which attended on the king environed him about, so as he was not seen of his company : many of them thrust him in divers places of his body, and drew him into the hospital of St. Bartholomew, from whence again the mayor caused him to be drawn into Smithfield, and there to be beheaded. In reward of this service, the people being dispersed, the king commanded the mayor to put a bascinet on his head; and the mayor requesting why he should do so, the king answered, he being much bound unto him, would make him knight. The mayor answered, that he was neither worthy nor able to take such estate upon him, for he was but a merchant, and had to live by his merchandise only. Notwithstanding, the king made him to put on his bascinet, and then with a sword in both his hands he strongly stroke him on the neck, as the manner was then ; and the same day he made three other citizens knights for his sake in the same place ; to wit, John Philpot, Nicholas Brember, and Robert Launde, alderman. The king gave to the mayor one hundred pounds land by year, and to each of the other forty pounds land yearly, to them and their heirs for ever.

After this, in the same year, the said Sir William Walworth founded in the said parish church of St. Michael a college of a master and nine priests, or chaplains, and deceased 1385, was there buried in the north chapel by the choir; but his monument being amongst other by bad people defaced in the reign of Edward VI., and again since renewed by the fishmongers, for lack of knowledge of what before had been written in his epitaph, they followed a fabulous book, and wrote Jack Straw instead of Wat Tyler, a great error meet to be reformed there and elsewhere ; and therefore have I the more at large discoursed of this matter.

It hath also been, and is now grown to a common opinion, that in reward of this service done by the said William Walworth against the rebel, King Richard added to the arms of this city, which was argent, a plain cross gules, a sword or dagger, for so they term it, whereof I have read no such record, but to the contrary. I find that in the 4th year of Richard II., in a full assembly made in the upper chamber of the Guildhall, summoned by this William Walworth, then mayor, as well of aldermen as of the common council, in

* *Basiliard*, baslard, a long dagger worn hanging from the girdle.

every ward, for certain affairs concerning the king, it was there by common consent agreed and ordained, that the old seal of the office of the mayoralty of the city being very small, old, unapt, and uncomely for the honour of the city, should be broken, and one other new should be had, which the said mayor commanded to be made artificially, and honourable for the exercise of the said office there, after, in place of the other; in which new seal, besides the images of Peter and Paul, which of old were rudely engraven, there should be under the feet of the said images a shield of the arms of the said city, perfectly graved, with two lions supporting the same, with two sergeants of arms; another part, one, and two tabernacles, in which above should stand two angels; between whom, above the said images of Peter and Paul, shall be set the glorious Virgin. This being done, the old seal of the office was delivered to Richard Odiham, chamberlain, who brake it, and in place thereof was delivered the new seal to the said mayor, to use in his office of mayoralty, as occasion should require. This new seal seemeth to be made before William Walworth was knighted, for he is not here entitled Sir, as afterwards he was; and certain it is that the same new seal then made is now in use, and none other in that office of the mayoralty; which may suffice to answer the former fable, without showing of any evidence sealed with the old seal, which was the cross and sword of St. Paul, and not the dagger of William Walworth.

Now of other monuments in that church. Simon Mordon, mayor 1368, was buried there; John Olney, mayor 1446; Robert March, stock-fishmonger, gave two pieces of ground to be a churchyard; John Radwell, stock-fishmonger, buried 1415; George Gowre, esquire, son to Edward Gowre, stock-fishmonger, esquire, 1470; Alexander Purpoynt, stock-fishmonger, 1373; Andrew Burel, gentleman of Gray's Inn, 1487; John Shrow, stock-fishmonger, 1487, with this epitaph:—

> "Farewell, my friends, the tide abideth no man,
> I am departed hence, and so shall ye.
> But in this passage the best song that I can,
> Is *requiem æternam*, now Jesus grant it me:
> When I have ended all mine adversitie,
> Grant me in Paradise to have a mansion,
> That sheddest thy blood for my redemption."

John Finkell, one of the sheriffs 1487, was knighted, and gave forty pounds to this church, the one half for his monument. John Pattesley, mayor 1441; Thomas Ewen, grocer, bare half the charges in building of the steeple, and was buried 1501; William Combes, gentleman, of Stoke, by Guildford in Surrey, 1502; Sir John Brudge, mayor 1530, gave fifty pounds for a house called the College in

Crooked Lane; he lieth buried in St. Nicholas Hacon. Walter Faireford; Robert Barre; Alexander Heyban; John Motte; John Gramstone; John Brampton; John Wood, stock-fishmonger, 1531; Sir Henry Amcots, mayor 1548, &c. Hard by this St. Michael's Church, on the south side thereof, in the year 1560, on the 5th of July, through the shooting of a gun, which brake in the house of one Adrian Arten, a Dutchman, and set fire on a firkin and barrel of gunpowder, four houses were blown up, and divers other sore shattered; eleven men and women were slain, and sixteen so hurt and bruised that they hardly escaped with life.

West from this St. Michael's Lane is St. Martin Orgar Lane, by Candlewick Street, which lane is on both sides down to a well, replenished with fair and large houses for merchants, and it is of this ward; one of which houses was sometime called Beachamp's Inn, as pertaining unto them of that family. Thomas Arundel, Archbishop of Canterbury, commonly for his time was lodged there.

The parish church of St. Martin Orgar is a small thing. William Crowmer, mayor, built a proper chapel on the south side thereof, and was buried there 1533; John Mathew, mayor 1490; Sir William Huet, mayor 1559, with his lady and daughter, wife to Sir Edward Osburne; Ralph Tabinham, alderman; Alice, wife to Thomas Winslow; Thorudon; Benedicke Reding; Thomas Harding; James Smith; Richard Gainford, esquire; John Bold, &c.

Then is there one other lane called St. Laurence, of the parish church there. This lane, down to the south side of the churchyard, is of Candlewick Street Ward. The parish church of St. Laurence was increased with a chapel of Jesus by Thomas Cole, for a master and chaplain; the which chapel and parish church was made a college of Jesus and of Corpus Christi, for a master and seven chaplains, by John Poultney, mayor, and was confirmed by Edward III., the 20th of his reign: of him was this church called St. Laurence Poultney, in Candlewick Street; which college was valued at £79, 17s. 11d., and was surrendered in the reign of Edward VI. Robert Ratcliffe, Earl of Essex, and Henry Ratcliffe, Earl of Sussex, were buried there; Alderman Beswicke was buried there; John Oliffe, alderman, Robert Browne, and others. Thus much for this ward, and the antiquities thereof. It hath now an alderman, his deputy, common councillors eight, constables eight, scavengers six, wardmote inquest men twelve, and a beadle. It is taxed to the fifteen at sixteen pounds.

Walbrook Ward.

WALBROOK WARD beginneth at the west end of Candlewick Street Ward. It runneth down Candlewick Street west towards Budge

Row. It hath on the north side thereof St. Swithin's Lane, so called of St. Swithin, a parish church by London Stone. This lane is replenished on both the sides with fair built houses, and is wholly of Walbrook Ward.

The said parish church of St. Swithin standeth at the south-west corner of this lane. License was procured to new build and increase the said church and steeple in the year 1420. Sir John Hend, draper, mayor, was an especial benefactor thereunto, as appeareth by his arms in the glass windows, even in the tops of them, which is in a field silver, a chief azure, a lion passant silver, a cheveron azure, three escalops silver. He lieth buried in the body of this church, with a fair stone laid on him, but the plates and inscriptions are defaced. Roger Depham, alderman, Thomas Aylesbourgh, William Neve, and Matilda Caxton, founded chantries, and were buried there ; John Butler, draper, one of the sheriffs 1420 ; Ralph Jecoline, mayor, a benefactor, buried in a fair tomb ; William White, draper, one of the sheriffs 1482, and other.

On the north side of this church and churchyard is one fair and large built house, sometime pertaining to the prior of Tortington in Sussex, since to the Earls of Oxford, and now to Sir John Hart, alderman ; which house hath a fair garden belonging thereunto, lying on the west side thereof. On the back side, of two other fair houses in Walbrook, in the reign of Henry VII., Sir Richard Empson, knight, Chancellor of the Duchy of Lancaster, dwelt in the one of them, and Edmund Dudley, esquire, in the other. Either of them had a door of intercourse into this garden, wherein they met and consulted of matters at their pleasures. In this Oxford Place Sir Ambrose Nicholas kept his mayoralty, and since him the said Sir John Hart.

On the south side of this high street, near unto the channel, is pitched upright a great stone called London Stone, fixed in the ground very deep, fastened with bars of iron, and otherwise so strongly set, that if carts do run against it through negligence, the wheels be broken, and the stone itself unshaken.

The cause why this stone was set there, the time when, or other memory hereof, is none, but that the same hath long continued there is manifest, namely, since, or rather before, the Conquest ; for in the end of a fair-written Gospel book given to Christ's Church in Canterbury, by Ethelstane, King of the West Saxons, I find noted of lands or rents in London belonging to the said church, whereof one parcel is described to lie near unto London Stone. Of later time we read, that in the year of Christ 1135, the 1st of King Stephen, a fire, which began in the house of one Ailward, near unto London Stone, consumed all east to Aldgate, in the which fire the priory of the Holy Trinity was burnt, and west to St. Erkenwald's shrine in Paul's Church. And these be the eldest notes that I read thereof.

Some have said this stone to be set as a mark in the middle of the city within the walls; but in truth it standeth far nearer unto the river of Thames than to the wall of the city. Some others have said the same to be set for the tendering and making of payment by debtors to their creditors at their appointed days and times, till of later time payments were more usually made at the font in Pont's Church, and now most commonly at the Royal Exchange. Some again have imagined the same to be set up by one John or Thomas Londonstone dwelling there against; but more likely it is, that such men have taken name of the stone than the stone of them as did John at Noke, Thomas at Stile, William at Wall, or at Well, &c.

Down west from this parish church, and from London Stone, have ye Walbrook corner; from whence runneth up a street north to the Stocks called Walbrook, because it standeth on the east side of the same brook, by the bank thereof, and the whole ward taketh the name of that street. On the east side of this street, and at the north corner thereof, is the Stocks Market, which had this beginning. About the year of Christ 1282, Henry Wales, mayor, caused divers houses in this city to be built towards the maintenance of London Bridge, namely, one void place near unto the parish church called Wool Church, on the north side thereof, where sometime, the way being very large and broad, had stood a pair of stocks for punishment of offenders. This building took name of these stocks, and was appointed by him to be a market-place for fish and flesh in the midst of the city. Other houses he built in other places, as by the patent of Edward I. it doth appear, dated the 10th of his reign. After this, in the year 1322, the 17th of Edward II., a decree was made by Hamond Chickwell, mayor, that none should sell fish or flesh out of the markets appointed, to wit, Bridge Street, East Cheap, Old Fish Street, St. Nicholas' Shambles, and the said Stocks, upon pain to forfeit such fish or flesh as were sold, for the first time, and the second time to lose their freedom; which act was made by commandment of the king under his letters patent, dated at the Tower the 17th of his reign, and then was this Stocks let to farm for £46, 13s. 4d. by year. This Stocks Market was again begun to be built in the year 1410, in the 11th of Henry IV., and was finished in the year next following. In the year 1507, the same was rented £56, 19s. 10d. And in the year 1543, John Cotes being mayor, there were in this Stocks Market,—for fishmongers twenty-five boards or stalls, rented yearly to £34, 13s. 4d.; there were for butchers eighteen boards or stalls, rented at £41, 16s. 4d.; and there were also chambers above, sixteen, rented at £5, 13s. 4d., in all £82, 3s.

Next unto this Stocks is the parish church of St. Mary Wool Church, so called of a beam placed in the churchyard, which was thereof called Wool Church Haw,* of the tronage or weighing of wool there used; and to verify this, I find amongst the customs of London written in French in the reign of Edward II., a chapter intituled *Les Customes de Wolchurch Haw*, wherein is set down what was there to be paid for every parcel of wool weighed. This tronage or weighing of wool, till the 6th of Richard II., was there continued. John Churchman then built the Custom House upon Wool Quay, to serve for the said tronage, as is before showed in Tower Street Ward. This church is reasonable fair and large, and was lately new built by license granted in the 20th of Henry VI., with condition to be built fifteen foot from the Stocks Market, for sparing of light to the same Stocks. The parson of this church is to have four marks the year for tithe of the said Stocks, paid him by the masters of the Bridge House, by special decree made the 2nd of Henry VII. John Winyar, grocer, mayor 1504, was a great helper to the building of this church, and was there buried 1505. He gave unto it by his testament two large basons of silver, and twenty pounds in money. Also Richard Shore, draper, one of the sheriffs 1505, was a great benefactor in his life, and by his testament gave twenty pounds to make a porch at the west end thereof, and was there buried. Richard Hatfield of Steplemorden in Cambridgeshire, lieth entombed there, 1467; Edward Deoly, esquire, 1467. John Handford, grocer, made the font of that church, very curiously wrought, painted, and gilded, and was there buried; John Archer, fishmonger, 1487; Anne Cawode founded a chantry there, &c.

From the Stocks Market and this parish church east up into Lombard Street, some four or five houses on a side, and also on the south side of Wool Church, have ye Bearbinder Lane, a part whereof is of this Walbrook Ward; then lower down in the street called Walbrook is one other fair church of St. Stephen, lately built on the east side thereof, for the old church stood on the west side, in place where now standeth the parsonage house, and therefore so much nearer the brook, even on the bank. Robert Chichley, mayor in the year 1428, the 6th of Henry VI., gave to this parish of St. Stephen one plot of ground, containing two hundred and eight feet and a half in length, and sixty-six feet in breadth, thereupon to build their new church, and for their churchyard; and in the 7th

---

* *Haw* was a yard or enclosure. Chaucer uses the word for a churchyard in the *Persones Tale:* "The holy place, as chirches or chirches hawes."

of Henry VI. the said Robert, one of the founders, laid the first stone for himself, the second for William Stoddon, mayor, with whose goods the ground that the church standeth on, and the housing, with the ground of the churchyard, was bought by the said Chichley for two hundred marks from the Grocers, which had been letten before for six-and-twenty marks the year ; Robert Whittingham, draper, laid the third stone, Henry Barton then mayor, &c. The said Chichley gave, more, one hundred pounds to the said work, and bare the charges of all the timber work on the procession way, and laid the lead upon it of his own cost. He also gave all the timber for the roofing of the two side aisles, and paid for the carriage thereof. This church was finished in the year 1439. The breadth thereof is sixty-seven feet, and length one hundred and twenty-five feet ; the churchyard ninety feet in length, and thirty-seven in breadth and more. Robert Whittingham, made Knight of the Bath, in the year 1432, purchased the patronage of this church from John Duke of Bedford, uncle to Henry VI. ; and Edward IV. in the 2nd of his reign, gave it to Richard Lee, then mayor. There be monuments in this church of Thomas Southwell, first parson of this new church, who lieth in the choir ; John Dunstable, master of astronomy and music, in the year 1453 ; Sir Richard Lee, mayor, who gave the said parsonage to the Grocers ; Rowland Hill, mayor 1549 ; Sir Thomas Pope, first treasurer of the augmentations, with his wife Dame Margaret ; Sir John Cootes, mayor 1542 ; Sir John Yorke, knight, merchant tailor, 1549 ; Edward Jackman, sheriff 1564 ; Richard Achley, grocer ; Dr. Owyn, physician to King Henry VIII. ; John Kirby, grocer, 1578 ; and others.

Lower down from this parish church be divers fair houses, namely, one wherein of late Sir Richard Baker, a knight of Kent, was lodged, and wherein dwelt Master Thomas Gore, a merchant famous for hospitality. On the west side of this Walbrook Street, over against the Stocks Market, is a part of the high street called the Poultry, on the south side west till over against St. Mildred's Church, and the Skalding Wike is of this ward. Then down again Walbrook Street some small distance is Bucklesbury, a street so called of Buckle, that sometime was owner thereof, part of which street on both sides, three or four houses, to the course of the brook, is of this ward, and so down Walbrook Street to the south corner ; from thence west down Budge Row some small distance to an alley, and through that alley south by the west end of St. John's Church upon Walbrook, by the south side and east end of the same again to Walbrook corner.

This parish church is called St. John upon Walbrook, because the west end thereof is on the very bank of Walbrook, by Horseshoe

Bridge, in Horseshoe Bridge Street. This church was also lately new built; for about the year 1412, license was granted by the mayor and commonalty to the parson and parish for enlarging thereof, with a piece of ground on the north part of the choir, twenty-one feet in length, seventeen feet and three inches in breadth, and on the south side of the choir one foot of the common soil. There be no monuments in this church of any account, only I have learned, William Cobarton, skinner, who gave lands to that church, was there buried 1410; and John Stone, tailor, one of the sheriffs 1464, was likewise buried there.

On the south side of Walbrook Ward, from Candlewick Street, in the midway betwixt London Stone and Walbrook corner, is a little lane with a turnpike in the midst thereof, and in the same a proper parish church, called St. Mary Bothaw, or Boatehaw by the Erber. This church being near unto the Downgate on the river of Thames, hath the addition of Boathaw or Boat Haw, of near adjoining to a haw or yard, wherein of old time boats were made, and landed from Downgate to be mended, as may be supposed, for other reason I find none why it should be so called. Within this church, and the small cloister adjoining, divers noblemen and persons of worship have been buried, as appeareth by arms in the windows, the defaced tombs, and print of plates torn up and carried away. There remain only of John West, esquire, buried in the year 1408; Thomas Huytley, esquire, 1539, but his monument is defaced since; Lancelot Bathurst, &c.

The Erber is an ancient place so called, but not of Walbrook Ward, and therefore out of that lane to Walbrook corner, and then down till over against the south corner of St. John's Church upon Walbrook. And this is all that I can say of Walbrook Ward. It hath an alderman, and his deputy, common councillors eleven, constables nine, scavengers six, for the wardmote inquest thirteen, and a beadle. It is taxed to the fifteen in London to £33, 5s.

Downgate Ward.

DOWNGATE Ward beginneth at the south end of Walbrook Ward over against the east corner of St. John's Church upon Walbrook, and descendeth on both the sides to Downgate on the Thames, and is so called of that down going or descending thereunto; and of this Downgate the ward taketh name. This ward turneth into Thames Street westward, some ten houses on a side to the course of Walbrook, but east in Thames Street on both sides to Ebgate Lane, or Old Swan, the land side whereof hath many lanes turning up, as shall be shown when I come to them.

But first to begin with the high street called Downgate. At the upper end thereof is a fair conduit of Thames water, castellated, and made in the year 1568, at charges of the citizens, and is called the conduit upon Downgate. The descent of this street is such, that in the year 1574, on the 4th of September, in the afternoon, there fell a storm of rain, wherethrough the channels suddenly arose, and ran with such a swift course towards the common shores, that a lad of eighteen years old, minding to have leapt over the channel near unto the said conduit, was taken with the stream, and carried from thence towards the Thames with such a violence, that no man with staves or otherwise could stay him, till he came against a cart wheel that stood in the said watergate, before which time he was drowned, and stark dead.

On the west side of this street is the Tallow Chandlers' Hall, a proper house, which company was incorporated in the 2nd year of Edward IV.

Somewhat lower standeth the Skinners' Hall, a fair house, which was sometime called Copped Hall, by Downgate, in the parish of St. John upon Walbrook. In the 19th year of Edward II., Ralph Cobham possessed it with five shops, &c.

This company of Skinners in London were incorporate by Edward III. in the 1st of his reign. They had two brotherhoods of Corpus Christi, viz., one at St. Mary Spital, the other at St. Mary Bethlem without Bishopsgate. Richard II., in the 18th of his reign, granted them to make their two brotherhoods one, by the name of the fraternity of Corpus Christi. Of Skinners, divers royal persons were named to be founders and brethren of this fraternity, to wit, kings six, dukes nine, earls two, lords one. Kings, Edward III., Richard II., Henry IV., Henry V., Henry VI., and Edward IV. This fraternity had also once every year, on Corpus Christi day afternoon, at procession passed through the principal streets of the city, wherein was borne more than one hundred torches of wax, costly garnished, burning light, and above two hundred clerks and priests, in surplices and copes, singing. After the which were the sheriffs' servants, the clerks of the compters, chaplains for the sheriffs, the mayor's sergeants, the council of the city, the mayor and aldermen in scarlet, and then the Skinners in their best liveries. Thus much to stop the tongues of unthankful men, such as used to ask, Why have ye not noted this, or that? and give no thanks for what is done.

Then lower down was a college of priests, called Jesus' Commons, a house well furnished with brass, pewter, napery, plate, &c., besides a fair library well stored with books, all which of old time was given to a number of priests that should keep commons there, and as one left his place, by death or otherwise, another should be admitted into his room, but this order within this thirty years being discontinued, the said house was dissolved, and turned to tenements.

Down lower have ye Elbow Lane; and at the corner thereof was one great stone house, called Old Hall. It is now taken down, and divers fair houses of timber placed there. This was sometime pertaining to William de Pont le Arch, and by him given to the priory of St. Mary Overy in Southwark, in the reign of Henry I. In this Elbow Lane is the Innholders' Hall, and other fair houses. This lane runneth west, and suddenly turneth south into Thames Street, and therefore of that bending is called Elbow Lane. On the east side of this Downgate Street is the great old house before spoken of, called the Erber, near to the Church of St. Mary Bothaw. Geoffrey Scroope held it by the gift of Edward III., in the 14th of his reign. It belonged since to John Nevell, Lord of Raby, then to Richard Nevell, Earl of Warwick; Nevell, Earl of Salisbury, was lodged there 1457; then it came to George Duke of Clarence, and his heirs male, by the gift of Edward IV., in the 14th of his reign. It was lately new built by Sir Thomas Pullison, mayor, and was afterwards inhabited by Sir Francis Drake, that famous mariner. Next to this great house is a lane turning to Bush Lane, of old time called Carter Lane, of carts and carmen having stables there, and now called Chequer Lane, or Chequer Alley, of an inn called the Chequer.

In Thames Street, on the Thames side, west from Downgate, is Greenwich Lane, of old time so called, and now Frier Lane, of such a sign there set up. In this lane is the Joiners' Hall, and other fair houses.

Then is Grantham's Lane, so called of John Grantham, sometime mayor, and owner thereof, whose house was very large and strong, built of stone, as appeareth by gates arched, yet remaining. Ralph Dodmer, first a brewer, then a mercer, mayor 1529, dwelt there, and kept his mayoralty in that house. It is now a brewhouse as it was afore.

Then is Downgate, whereof is spoken in another place. East from this Downgate is Cosin Lane, named of William Cosin that dwelt there in the 4th of Richard II., as divers his predecessors, father, grandfather, &c., had done before him. William Cosin was one of the sheriffs in the year 1306. That house standeth at the south end of the lane, having an old and artificial conveyance of Thames water into it, and is now a dyehouse called Lambard's Messuage. Adjoining to that house there was lately erected an engine to convey Thames water unto Downgate conduit aforesaid.

Next to this lane, on the east, is the Steelyard, as they term it, a place for merchants of Almaine, that used to bring hither as well wheat, rye, and other grain, as cables, ropes, masts, pitch, tar, flax, hemp, linen cloth, wainscots, wax, steel, and other profitable merchandises. Unto these merchants, in the year 1259, Henry III., at the request of his brother Richard, Earl of Cornwell, king of Almaine, granted that all and singular the merchants, having a house in the city of London, commonly called *Guilda Aula Teutonicorum*, should be maintained and upholden through the whole realm, by all such freedoms and free usages, or liberties, as by the king and his noble progenitors' time they had and enjoyed, &c. Edward I. renewed and confirmed that charter of liberties granted by his father. And in the 10th year of the same Edward, Henry Wales being mayor, a great controversy did arise between the said mayor and the merchants of the Hanse of Almaine about the reparations of Bishopsgate, then likely to fall, for that the said merchants enjoyed divers privileges in respect of maintaining the said gate, which they now denied to repair; for the appeasing of which controversy the king sent his writ to the treasurer and barons of his exchequer, commanding that they should make inquisition thereof; before whom the merchants being called, when they were not able to discharge themselves, sith they enjoyed the liberties to them granted for the same, a precept was sent to the mayor and sheriffs to distrain the said merchants to make reparations, namely, Gerard Marbod, alderman of the Hanse, Ralph de Cussarde, a citizen of Cologne, Ludero de Denevar, a burgess of Trivar, John of Aras, a burgess of Trivon,* Bartram of Hamburgh, Godestalke of Hundondale, a burgess of Trivon, John de Dele, a burgess of Munster, then remaining in the said city of London, for themselves and all other merchants of the Haunce, and so they granted two hundred and ten marks sterling to the mayor and citizens, and undertook that they and their successors should from time to time repair the said gate, and bear the third part of the charges in money and men to defend it when need were. And for this agreement the said mayor and citizens granted to the said merchants their liberties, which till of late they have enjoyed, as namely, amongst other, that they might lay up their grain which they brought into this realm, in inns, and sell it in their garners by the space of forty days after they had laid it up, except by the mayor and citizens they were expressly forbidden, because of dearth, or other reasonable occasions. Also they might have their aldermen as they had been accustomed, foreseeing always that he were of the city, and presented to the mayor and aldermen of the city, so oft as any should be chosen, and should take an oath before them to maintain justice in their courts, and to behave themselves in their office according to law, and as it stood with the customs of the city. Thus much for their privileges; whereby it appeareth that they were great

* *Trivar* and *Trivon*, Trier or Trèves.

merchants of corn brought out of the east parts hither, insomuch that
the occupiers of husbandry in this land were enforced to complain of
them for bringing in such abundance when the corn of this realm was
at such an easy price ; whereupon it was ordained by parliament,
that no person should bring into any part of this realm, by way of
merchandise, wheat, rye, or barley, growing out of the said realm,
when the quarter of wheat exceed not the price of 6s. 8d., rye 4s.
the quarter, and barley 3s. the quarter, upon forfeiture the one half
to the king, the other half to the seizor thereof. These merchants
of Hanse * had their Guildhall in Thames Street in place aforesaid
by the said Cosin Lane. Their hall is large, built of stone, with
three arched gates towards the street, the middlemost whereof is far
bigger than the other, and is seldom opened, the other two be mured
up. The same is now called the old hall.

Of later time, to wit, in the 6th of Richard II., they hired one house
next adjoining to their old hall, which sometime belonged to Richard
Lions, a famous lapidary, one of the sheriffs of London in the 49th
of Edward III., and in the 4th of Richard II., by the rebels of Kent,
drawn out of that house and beheaded in West Cheap. This also
was a great house with a large wharf on the Thames, and the way
thereunto was called Windgoose, or Wildgoose Lane, which is now
called Windgoose Alley, for that the same alley is for the most part
built on by the steelyard merchants.

The Abbot of St. Alban's had a messuage here with a quay, given
to him in the 34th of Henry VI. Then is one other great house,
which sometime pertained to John Rainwell, stock-fishmonger, mayor,
and it was by him given to the mayor and commonalty, to the end
that the profits thereof should be disposed in deeds of piety ; which
house, in the 15th of Edward IV., was confirmed unto the said merchants, in manner following, namely :—

"It is ordayned by our soveraigne lord and his parliament, that the said mar-
chants of Almaine, being of the companie called the *Guildhall Teutonicorum* (or
the Flemish gild), that now be, or hereafter shall be, shall have, hold, and enjoy,
to them and their successors for ever, the said place called the Steelhouse, yeelding
to the said mayor and communaltie an annuall rent of £70, 3s. 4d., &c."

In the year 1551, and the 5th of Edward VI., through complaint
of the English merchants, the liberty of the steelyard merchants was
seized into the king's hands, and so it resteth.

Then is Church Lane, at the west end of Allhallows Church, called
Allhallows the More in Thames Street, for a difference from Allhallows the Less in the same street. It is also called Allhallows *ad
fœnum* in the Ropery, because hay sold near thereunto at Hay Wharf,
and ropes of old time made and sold in the high street. This is a

* Stow's spelling throughout is "Haunce."

fair church, with a large cloister on the south side thereof about their churchyard, but foully defaced and ruinated.

The church also hath had many fair monuments, but now defaced. There remaineth in the choir some plates on grave stones—namely, of William Lichfield, D.D., who deceased the year 1447. He was a great student, and compiled many books, both moral and divine, in prose and in verse, namely, one intituled "The Complaint of God unto Sinful Man." He made in his time three thousand and eighty-three sermons, as appeared by his own handwriting, and were found when he was dead. One other plate there is of John Brickles, draper, who deceased in the year 1451. He was a great benefactor to that church, and gave by his testament certain tenements to the relief of the poor, &c. Nicholas Loven and William Peston founded chantries there.

At the east end of this church goeth down a lane called Hay Wharf Lane, now lately a great brewhouse, built there by one Pot. Henry Campion, esquire, a beer-brewer, used it, and Abraham his son now possesseth it. Then was there one other lane, sometime called Woolfe's Gate, now out of use ; for the lower part thereof upon the bank of Thames is built by the late Earl of Shrewsbury, and the other end is built on and stopped up by the chamberlain of London. John Butler, draper, one of the sheriffs in the year 1420, dwelt there. He appointed his house to be sold, and the price thereof to be given to the poor. It was of Allhallows parish the Less. Then is there the said parish church of Allhallows called the Less, and by some Allhallows on the Cellars, for it standeth on vaults. It is said to be built by Sir John Poultney, sometime mayor. The steeple and choir of this church standeth on an arched gate, being the entry to a great house called Cold Harbrough. The choir of late being fallen down, is now again at length, in the year 1594, by the parishioners new built. Touching this Cold Harbrough, I find, that in the 13th of Edward II., Sir John Abel, knight, demised or let unto Henry Stow, draper, all that his capital messuage called the Cold Harbrough, in the parish of All Saints *ad fœnum*, and all the appurtenances within the gate, with the quay which Robert Hartford, citizen, son to William Hartford, had, and ought ; and the foresaid Robert paid for it the rent of thirty-three shillings the year. This Robert Hartford being owner thereof, as also of other lands in Surrey, deceasing without issue male, left two daughters his co-heirs, to wit, Idonia, married to Sir Ralph Bigot, and Maude, married to Sir Stephen Cosenton, knights, between whom the said house and lands were parted. After the which, John Bigot, son to the said Sir Ralph, and Sir John Cosenton, did sell their moieties of Cold Harbrough unto John Poultney, son of Adam Poultney, the 8th of Edward III. This Sir

John Poultney dwelling in this house, and being four times mayor, the said house took the name of Poultney's Inn. Notwithstanding this, Sir John Poultney, the 21st of Edward III., by his charter, gave and confirmed to Humphrey de Bohun, Earl of Hereford and Essex, his whole tenement called Cold Harbrough, with all the tenements and quay adjoining, and appurtenances, sometime pertaining to Robert de Hereford, on the way called Hay Wharf Lane, &c., for one rose at midsummer, to him and to his heirs for all services, if the same were demanded. This Sir John Poultney deceased 1349, and left issue, by Margaret his wife, William Poultney, who died without issue, and Margaret his mother was married to Sir Nicholas Lovel, knight, &c. Philip S. Cleare gave two messuages pertaining to this Cold Harbrough in the Ropery, towards the enlarging of the parish church and churchyard of All Saints, called the Less, in the 20th of Richard II.

In the year 1397, the 21st of Richard II., John Holland, Earl of Huntington, was lodged there, and Richard II., his brother, dined with him. It was then counted a right fair and stately house; but in the next year following I find that Edmond, Earl of Cambridge, was there lodged, notwithstanding the said house still retained the name of Poultney's Inn, in the reign of Henry VI., the 26th of his reign. It belonged since to H. Holland, Duke of Excester, and he was lodged there in the year 1472. In the year 1485, Richard III., by his letters patent, granted and gave to John Writh, *alias* Garter, principal king of arms of Englishmen, and to the rest of the king's heralds and pursuivants of arms, all that messuage, with the appurtenances, called Cold Harbrough, in the parish of All Saints the Little in London, and their successors for ever, dated at Westminster the 2nd of March, *anno regni primo*, without fine or fee. How the said heralds departed therewith I have not read; but in the reign of Henry VIII., the Bishop of Durham's house near Charing Cross, being taken into the king's hand, Cuthbert Tunstall, Bishop of Durham, was lodged in this Cold Harbrough; since the which time it hath belonged to the Earls of Shrewsbury, by composition, as is supposed, from the said Cuthbert Tunstall. The last deceased earl took it down, and in place thereof built a great number of small tenements now letten out for great rents to people of all sorts.

Then is the Dyers' Hall, which company was made a brotherhood or guild, in the 4th of Henry VI., and appointed to consist of a guardian or warden, and a commonalty, the 12th of Edward IV. Then be there divers large brewhouses and others, till you come to Ebgate Lane, where that ward endeth in the east. On the north side of Thames Street be divers lanes also. The first is at the south end of Elbow Lane, before spoken of, west from Downgate, over against Greenwich Lane; then be divers fair houses for merchants and others all along that side. The next lane east from Downgate is called Bush Lane, which turneth up to Candlewick Street, and is of Downgate Ward. Next is Suffolk Lane, likewise turning up to Candlewick Street. In this lane is one notable grammar school, founded in the year 1561 by the master, wardens, and assistants of the merchant tailors, in the parish of St. Laurence Poultney; Richard Hilles, sometime master of that company, having before given £500 towards the purchase of a house, called the manor of the Rose, sometime belonging to the Duke of Buckingham, wherein the said school is kept. Then is there one other lane which turneth up to St. Laurence Hill, and to the south-west corner of St. Laurence Churchyard; then one other lane called Poultney Lane, that goeth up of this ward to the south-east corner of St. Laurence Churchyard, and so down again, and to the west corner of St. Martin Orgar Lane, and over against Ebgate Lane; and this is all of Downgate Ward, the thirteenth in number lying east from the watercourse of Walbrook, and hath not any one house on the west side of the said brook. It hath an alderman, his deputy, common councillors nine, constables eight, scavengers five, for the wardmote inquest fourteen, and a beadle. It is taxed to the fifteen eight and twenty pounds.

Wards on the West Side of Walbrook, and First of Vintry Ward.

Now I am to speak of the other wards, twelve in number, all lying on the west side of the course of Walbrook. And first of Vintry Ward, so called of vintners, and of the vintry, a part of the bank of the river of Thames, where the merchants of Bordeaux craned their wines out of lighters and other vessels, and there landed and made sale of them within forty days after, until the 28th of Edward I., at which time the said merchants complained that they could not sell their wines, paying poundage, neither hire houses or cellars to lay them in; and it was redressed by virtue of the king's writ, directed to the mayor and sheriffs of London, dated at Carlaveroke, or Carlisle, since the which time many fair and large houses, with vaults and cellars for stowage of wines, and lodging of the Bordeaux merchants, have been built in place where before time were cooks' houses; for Fitzstephen in the reign of Henry II., writeth, that upon the river's side, between the wine in ships, and the wine to be sold in taverns, was a common cookery or cooks' row, &c., as in another place I have set down; whereby it appeareth, that in those days, and till of late time, every man lived by his professed trade, not any one interrupting another : the cooks dressed meat, and sold no wine, and the taverner sold wine, but dressed no meat for sale, &c.

This ward beginneth in the east at the west end of Downgate Ward, as the watercourse of Walbrook parteth them, to wit, at Grantham's Lane, on the Thames side, and at Elbow Lane on the land side. It runneth along in Thames Street west some three houses beyond the Old Swan, a brewhouse, and on the land side some three houses west beyond St. James' at Garlick Hithe. In breadth this ward stretcheth from the Vintry north to the wall of the west gate of the Tower Royal ; the other north part is of Cordwainer Street Ward. Out of this Royal Street, by the south gate of Tower Royal, runneth a small street east to St. John's upon Walbrook, which street is called Horseshoe Bridge, of such a bridge sometime over the brook there, which is now vaulted over. Then from the said south gate west runneth one other street, called Knightriders' Street, by St. Thomas Apostle's Church on the north side, and Wringwren Lane by the said church, at the west end thereof, and to the east end of the Trinity Church in the said Knightriders' Street, where this ward endeth on that south side the street ; but on the north side it runneth no further than the corner against the new built tavern and other houses, in a plot of ground where sometime stood Ormond Place. Yet have ye one other lane lower down in Royal Street, stretching from over against St. Michael's Church to and by the north side of St. James' Church by Garlick Hithe ; this is called Kerion Lane. And thus much for the bounds of Vintry Ward. Now, on the Thames side, west from Grantham's Lane, have ye Herber Lane, or Brikels' Lane, so called of John Brikels, sometime owner thereof.

Then is Simpson's Lane, of one Simpson, or Emperor's Head Lane, of such a sign. Then the Three Cranes' Lane, so called not only of a sign of three cranes at a tavern door, but rather of three strong cranes of timber placed on the Vintry Wharf by the Thames side, to crane up wines there, as is afore showed. This lane was of old time, to wit, the 9th of Richard II., called The Painted Tavern Lane, of the tavern being painted.

Then next over against St. Martin's Church is a large house built of stone and timber, with vaults for the stowage of wines, and is called the Vintry. There dwelt John Gisers, vintner, mayor of London, and constable of the Tower, and then was Henry Picard, vintner, mayor. In this house Henry Picard feasted four kings in one day, as in my Summary I have showed. Then next is Vanner's Lane, so called of one Vanner that was owner thereof. It is now called Church Lane, of the coming up from the wharf to St. Martin's

Church. Next is Broad Lane, for that the same is broader for the passage of carts from the Vintry Wharf than be the other lanes. At the north-west corner of this lane is the Parish Clerks' Hall, lately by them purchased, since they lost their old hall in Bishopsgate Street. Next is Spital Lane, of old time so called, since Stodie's Lane, of the owner thereof named Stodie. Sir John Stodie, vintner, mayor in the year 1357, gave it with all the quadrant wherein Vintners' Hall now standeth, with the tenements round about unto the Vintners. The Vintners built for themselves a fair hall, and also thirteen almshouses there for thirteen poor people, which are kept of charity rent free.

The Vintners in London were of old time called Merchant-vintners of Gascoyne; and so I read them in the records of Edward II., the 11th year, and Edward III., the 9th year. They were as well Englishmen as strangers born beyond the seas, but then subjects to the kings of England, great Bordeaux merchants of Gascoyne and French wines, divers of them were mayors of this city, namely, John Adrian, vintner, Reginold at conduit, John Oxenford; Hen. Picard, that feasted the kings of England, France, Scotland, and Cypres; John Stodie, that gave Stodie's Lane to the vintners; which four last named were mayors in the reign of Edward III. And yet Gascoyne wines were then to be sold at London not above fourpence, nor Rhenish wine above sixpence the gallon. I read of sweet wines, that in the 50th of Edward III., John Peachie, fishmonger, was accused, for that he procured a license for the only sale of them in London; which notwithstanding he justified by law, he was imprisoned and fined. More, I read, that in the 6th of Henry VI., the Lombards corrupting their sweet wines, when knowledge thereof came to John Rainwell, mayor of London, he in divers places of the city commanded the heads of the butts and other vessels in the open streets to be broken, to the number of one hundred and fifty, so that the liquor running forth, passed through the city like a stream of rain water, in the sight of all the people, from whence there issued a most loathsome savour.

I read, in the reign of Henry VII., that no sweet wines were brought into this realm but Malmsies by the Longobards, paying to the king for his license six shillings and eightpence of every butt, besides twelvepence for bottle large. I remember within this fifty-four years Malmsey not to be sold more than one penny halfpenny the pint. For proof whereof, it appeareth in the church book of St. Andrew Undershaft, that in the year 1547 I. G. and S. K., then churchwardens, for eighty pints of Malmsey spent in the church, after one penny halfpenny the pint, paid at the year's end for the same ten shillings. More, I remember that no sacks were sold but

Rumney, and that for medicine more than for drink, but now many kinds of sacks * are known and used. And so much for wines.

For the Vintry, to end therewith, I read, that in the reign of Henry IV., the young prince Henry, Thomas Duke of Clarence, John Duke of Bedford, and Humphrey Duke of Gloucester, the king's sons, being at supper among the merchants of London in the Vintry, in the house of Lewes John, Henry Scogan sent to them a ballad beginning thus :—

> " My noble sonnes and eke my lordes deare,
> I your father, called unworthily,
> Send unto you this ballad following here,
> Written with mine own hand full rudely,
> Although it be that I not reverently
> Have written to your estates, I you pray
> Mine uncunning, taketh benignely,
> For Goddes sake, and hearken what I say."

Then follow in like metre twenty-three staves, containing a persuasion from losing of time follily in lust and vice, but to spend the same in virtue and godliness, as ye may read in Geoffrey Chaucer's works lately printed. The successors of those vintners and wine-drawers that retailed by the gallons, pottle, quart, and pint, were all incorporated by the name of Wine-tunners in the reign of Edward III., and confirmed in the 15th of Henry VI. Having thus much, not without travail and some charges, noted for the antiquity of the Vintners, about two years since or more I repaired to the common hall of that company, and there showed and read it in a court of assistance, requiring them, as being one of the principal companies in the city, of whom I meant therefore to write the more at large, that if they knew any more which might sound to their worship or commendation, at their leisure to send it me, and I would join it to my former collection. At which time I was answered by some that took upon them the speech, that they were none of the principal, but of the inferior companies ; and so willing me to leave them, I departed, and never since heard from them, which hath somewhat discouraged me any farther to travail amongst the companies to learn ought at their hands.

Next is Palmer's Lane, now called Anchor Lane. The Plumbers have their hall there, but are tenants to the Vintners. Then is Worcester House, sometime belonging to the Earls of Worcester, now divided into many tenements. The Fruiterers have their hall

---

* *Many kinds of sacks.* Sack was *sec*, a dry white wine. Falstaff praised "sherris sack," our amontillado, but had suspicions of the use of lime to give the dryness. Rumney was a hot Spanish wine. In the Promptorium Parvulorum its prevalent use in the fifteenth century is marked by the simple entry, " Rumneye, wine."

there. Then is the Old Swan, a great brewhouse. And this is all on the Thames side that I can note in this ward.

On the land side is the Royal Street and Paternoster Lane, I think of old time called Arches; for I read that Robert de Suffolk gave to Walter Darford his tenement with the appurtenance in the lane called Les Arches, in the parish of St. Michael de Paternoster Church, between the wall of the field called Winchester Field on the east, and the same lane on the west, &c. More, I read of a stone house called Sto da de Winton juxta Stenden Bridge, which in that lane was over Walbrook Water.

Then is the fair parish church of St. Michael called Paternoster Church in the Royal. This church was new built, and made a college of St. Spirit and St. Mary, founded by Richard Whittington, mercer, four times mayor, for a master, four fellows—masters of art, clerks, conducts, chorists, &c., and an almshouse called God's House, or hospital, for thirteen poor men, one of them to be tutor, and to have sixteen pence the week; the other twelve, each of them to have fourteen pence the week for ever, with other necessary provisions, a hutch with three locks, a common seal, &c. These were bound to pray for the good estate of Richard Whittington and Alice his wife, their founders; and for Sir William Whittington, knight, and Dame Joan his wife, and for Hugh Fitzwaren, and Dame Molde his wife, the fathers and mothers of the said Richard Whittington and Alice his wife; for King Richard II., and Thomas of Woodstock, Duke of Gloucester, special lords and promoters of the said Richard Whittington, &c. The license for this foundation was granted by King Henry IV., the 11th of his reign, and in the 12th of the same king's reign, the mayor and commonalty of London granted to Richard Whittington a vacant piece of ground, thereon to build his college in the Royal, all which was confirmed by Henry VI., the 3rd of his reign, to John Coventry, Jenkin Carpenter, and William Grove, executors to Richard Whittington. This foundation was again confirmed by parliament, the 10th of Henry VI., and was suppressed by the statute of Edward VI.

The almshouses, with the poor men, do remain, and are paid by the Mercers. This Richard Whittington was in this church three times buried: first by his executors under a fair monument; then in the reign of Edward VI., the parson of that church, thinking some great riches, as he said, to be buried with him, caused his monument to be broken, his body to be spoiled of his leaden sheet, and again the second time to be buried; and in the reign of Queen Mary the parishioners were forced to take him up, to lap him in lead as afore, to bury him the third time, and to place his monument, or the like, over him again, which remaineth, and so he resteth. Thomas Windford, alderman, was buried in this church 1448; Arnold Macknam, vintner, a merchant of Bordeaux, 1457; Sir Heere Tanke, or Hartancleux, knight of the garter, born in Almayne, a noble warrior in Henry V. and Henry VI. days; Sir Edmond Mulshew, knight, near to Thomas Cokham, recorder of London; the Lady Kyme; Sir William Oldhall, knight, 1460; William Barnocke; Sir John Yong, grocer, mayor 1466; Agnes, daughter to Sir John Yong, first married to Robert Sherington, after to Robert Mulleneux, then to William Cheyney, esquire; John Having, gentleman; William Roswell, esquire; William Postar, clerk of the crown, 1520; Sir William Bayly, draper, mayor 1533, with Dame Katherine his wife, leaving sixteen children; John Haydon, mercer, sheriff 1582, who gave legacies to the thirteen almsmen, and otherwise, for a lecture.

At the upper end of this street is the Tower Royal, whereof that street taketh name. This Tower and great place was so called of pertaining to the kings of this realm, but by whom the same was first built, or of what antiquity continued, I have not read more than that in the reign of Edward I., the 2nd, 4th, and 7th years, it was the tenement of Symon Beawmes; also, that in the 36th of Edward III., the same was called the Royal, in the parish of St. Michael de Paternoster, and that in the 43rd of his reign, he gave it by the name of his inn, called the Royal, in the city of London, in value twenty pounds by year, unto his college of St. Stephen at Westminster. Notwithstanding, in the reign of Richard II. it was called the Queen's Wardrobe, as appeareth by this that followeth:—King Richard having in Smithfield overcome and dispersed his rebels, he, his lords, and all his company, entered the city of London with great joy, and went to the lady princess his mother, who was then lodged in the Tower Royal, called the Queen's Wardrobe, where she had remained three days and two nights right sore abashed; but when she saw the king her son she was greatly rejoiced, and said, "Ah, son! what great sorrow have I suffered for you this day!" The king answered and said, "Certainly, madam, I know it well; but now rejoice, and thank God, for I have this day recovered mine heritage, and the realm of England, which I had near hand lost."

This Tower seemeth to have been at that time of good defence; for when the rebels had beset the Tower of London, and got possession thereof, taking from thence whom they listed, as in my Annals I have shown, the princess being forced to fly, came to this Tower Royal, where she was lodged, and remained safe, as ye have heard; and it may be also supposed that the king himself was at that time lodged there. I read, that in the year 1386, Lyon King of Armonie, being chased out of his realm by the Tartarians, received innumerable gifts of the king and of his nobles, the king then lying in the Royal, where he also granted to the said king of Armonie a charter of a thousand pounds by year during his life. This for proof may suffice that kings of England have been lodged in this Tower, though the same of later time have been neglected and turned into stabling for the king's horses, and now letten out to divers men, and divided into tenements.

In Horsebridge Street is the Cutlers' Hall. Richard de Wilehale, 1295, confirmed to Paul Butelar this house and edifices in the parish of St. Michael Paternoster Church and St. John's upon Walbrook, which sometime Lawrens Gisors and his son Peter Gisors did possess, and afterward Hugonis de Hingham, and lieth between the tenement of the said Richard towards the south, and the lane called Horseshoe Bridge towards the north, and between the way called Paternoster Church on the west, and the course of Walbrook on the east, paying yearly one clove of Gereflowers * at Easter, and to the prior and convent of St. Mary Overy six shillings. This house sometime belonged to Simon Dolesly, grocer, mayor 1359. They of this company were of old time divided into three arts or sorts of workmen : to wit, the first were smiths, forgers of blades, and therefore called bladers, and divers of them proved wealthy men, as namely, Walter Nele, blader, one of the sheriffs the 12th of Edward III., deceased 1352, and buried in St. James' Garlick Hithe. He left lands to the mending of highways about London, betwixt Newgate and Wycombe, Aldgate and Chelmsford, Bishopsgate and Ware, Southwark and Rochester, &c. The second were makers of hafts, and otherwise garnishers of blades. The third sort were sheathmakers, for swords, daggers, and knives. In the 10th of Henry IV. certain ordinances were made betwixt the bladers and the other cutlers ; and in the 4th of Henry VI. they were all three companies drawn into one fraternity or brotherhood by the name of Cutlers.

. Then is Knightriders' Street, so called, as is supposed, of knights well armed and mounted at the Tower Royal, riding from thence through that street west to Creed Lane, and so out at Ludgate towards Smithfield, when they were there to tourney, joust, or otherwise to show activities before the king and states of the realm.

In this street is the parish church of St. Thomas Apostle, by Wringwren Lane, a proper church, but monuments of antiquity be there none, except some arms in the windows, as also in the stone work, which some suppose to be of John Barns, mercer, mayor of

---

* *Gereflowers*, clove pinks. French *girofle*, from Latin *caryophyllum*, gave the name of gilofer, gilliflower, to pinks, carnations, and sweet-williams.

London in the year 1371, a great builder thereof; H. Causton, merchant, was a benefactor, and had a chantry there about 1396; T. Roman, mayor 1310, had also a chantry there 1319; Fitzwilliams, also a benefactor, had a chantry there. More, Sir William Littlesbery, *alias* Horne, for King Edward IV. so named him, because he was a most excellent blower in a horn. He was a salter and merchant of the staple, mayor of London in the year 1487, and was buried in this church, having appointed by his testament the bells to be changed for four new bells of good tune and sound, but that was not performed. He gave five hundred marks to the repairing of highways betwixt London and Cambridge; his dwelling-house with a garden and appurtenances in the said parish to be sold, and bestowed in charitable actions, as his executors would answer before God; his house called the George, in Bread Street, he gave to the Salters, they to find a priest in the said church, to have £6, 13s. 4d. the year, to every preacher at Paul's Cross and at the Spital fourpence for ever; to the prisoners of Newgate, Ludgate, Marshalsey, and King's Bench, in victuals, ten shillings at Christmas, and ten shillings at Easter for ever; which legacies are not performed. William Shipton, William Champneis, and John de Burford, had chantries there; John Martin, butcher, one of the sheriffs, was buried there 1533, &c. Then west from the said church, on the same side, was one great messuage, sometime called Ypres Inn, of William Ypres, a Fleming, the first builder thereof. This William was called out of Flanders, with a number of Flemings, to the aid of King Stephen against Maude the Empress, in the year 1138, and grew in favour with the said king for his services, so far that he built this his house near Tower Royal, in the which tower it seemeth the king was then lodged, as in the heart of the city, for his more safety.

Robert, Earl of Gloucester, brother to the empress, being taken, was committed to the custody of this William, to be kept in the castle of Rochester, till King Stephen was also taken, and then the one was delivered in exchange for the other, and both set free. This William of Ypres gave Edredes Hithe, now called the Queen's Hithe, to the prior and canons of the Holy Trinity in London: he founded the Abbey of Boxley in Kent, &c. In the 1st of Henry II., the said William, with all the other Flemings, fearing the indignation of the new king, departed the land; but it seemeth that the said William was shortly called back again, and restored both to the king's favour and to his old possessions here, so that the name and family continued long after in this realm, as may appear by this which followeth.

In the year 1377, the 51st of Edward III., the citizens of London, minding to have destroyed John of Gaunt, Duke of Lancaster, and Henry Percy, marshal, for cause shown in my Annals, sought up and down, and could not find them, for they were that day to dine with John of Ypres at his inn, which the Londoners wist not of, but thought the duke and marshal had been at the Savoy, and therefore posted thither; but one of the duke's knights seeing these things, came in great haste to the place where the duke was, and after that he had knocked and could not be let in, he said to Haveland the porter, "If thou love my lord and thy life, open the gate." With which words he gat entry, and with great fear he tells the duke, that without the gate were infinite numbers of armed men, and unless he took great heed, that day would be his last. With which words the duke leapt so hastily from his oysters, that he hurt both his legs against the form. Wine was offered, but he could not drink for haste, and so fled with his fellow Henry Percy out at a back gate, and entering the Thames, never stayed rowing until they came to a house near the manor of Kennington, where at that time the princess lay with Richard the young prince, before whom he made his complaint, &c.

On the other side, I read of a messuage called Ringed Hall. King Henry VIII., the 32nd of his reign, gave the same, with four tenements adjoining, unto Morgan Philip, *alias* Wolfe, in the parish of St. Thomas Apostles, in London, &c.

Over against Ypres Inn, in Knightriders' Street, at the corner towards St. James at Garlick Hithe, was sometime a great house built of stone, and called Ormond Place, for that it sometimes belonged to the Earls of Ormond. King Edward IV., in the 5th of his reign, gave to Elizabeth his wife the manor of Greenwich, with the tower and park, in the county of Kent. He also gave this tenement called Ormond Place, with all the appurtenances to the same, situate in the parish of St. Trinity in Knightriders' Street, in London. This house is now lately taken down, and divers fair tenements are built there, the corner house whereof is a tavern. Then lower down in Royal Street is Kerion Lane, of one Kerion sometime dwelling there. In this lane be divers fair houses for merchants, and amongst others is the Glaziers' Hall.

At the south corner of Royal Street is the fair parish church of St. Martin called in the Vintry, sometime called St. Martin de Beremand Church. This church was new built about the year 1399 by the executors of Mathew Columbars, a stranger born, a Bordeaux merchant of Gascoyne and French wines. His arms remain yet in the east window, and are between a cheveron, three columbins. There lie buried in this church—Sir John Gisors, mayor 1311; Henry Gisors, his son, 1343, and John Gisors, his brother, 1350.

He gave to his son Thomas his great mansion-house called Gisors Hall, in the parish of St. Mildred, in Bread Street. This Thomas had issue, John and Thomas. John made a feoffment, and sold Gisors Hall and other his lands in London, about the year 1386. Thomas deceased 1395. Henry Vennar; Bartholomew de la Vauch; Thomas Cornwalles, one of the sheriffs 1384; John Cornwalles, esquire, 1436; John Mustrell, vintner, 1424; William Hodson; William Castleton; John Gray; Robert Dalusse, barber, in the reign of Edward IV., with this epitaph :—

> " As flowers in the field thus passeth life,
>   Naked, then clothed, feeble in the end,
>   It sheweth by Robert Dalusse, and Alison his wife,—
>   Christ them save from the power of the fiend."

Sir Ralph Austrie, fishmonger, new roofed this church with timber, covered it with lead, and beautifully glazed it. He deceased 1494, and was there buried with his two wives. Ralph Austrie, his son, gentleman; William Austrie, and other of that name; Bartrand, wife to Grimond Descure, esquire, a Gascoyne and merchant of wines, 1494; Thomas Batson; Alice Fowler, daughter and heir to John Howton, wife to John Hulton; James Bartlet, and Alice his wife; William Fennor; Roger Cotton; Robert Stocker; John Pemberton; Philip de Plasse; John Stapleton; John Mortimer; William Lee; William Hamsteed; William Stoksbie, and Gilbert March, had chantries there.

Then is the parish church of St. James, called at Garlick Hithe, or Garlick Hive; for that of old time, on the bank of the river of Thames, near to this church, garlick was usually sold. This is a proper church, whereof Richard Rothing, one of the sheriffs 1326, is said to be the new builder, and lieth buried in the same. So was Walter Nele, blader, one of the sheriffs 1337; John of Oxenford, vintner, mayor 1341. I read, in the 1st of Edward III., that this John of Oxenford gave to the priory of the Holy Trinity in London two tofts of land, one mill, fifty acres of land, two acres of wood, with the appurtenances, in Kentish town, in value 20s. 3d. by year. Richard Goodcheape, John de Cressingham, and John Whitthorne, and before them, Galfrid Moncley, 1281, founded a chantry there.

Monuments remaining there: Robert Gabeter, esquire, mayor of Newcastle-upon-Tyne 1310; John Gisors; William Tiligham; John Stanley; Lord Strange, eldest son to the Earl of Derby, 1503; Nicholas Statham; Robert de Luton, 1361; Richard Lions, a famous merchant of wines, and a lapidary, sometime one of the sheriffs, beheaded in Cheap by Wat Tyler and other rebels in the year 1381. His picture on his grave-stone, very fair and large, is with his hair rounded by his ears, and curled; a little beard forked; a gown, girt to him down to his feet, of branched damask, wrought with the likeness of flowers; a large purse on his right side, hanging in a belt from his left shoulder; a plain hood about his neck, covering his shoulders, and hanging back behind him. Sir John Wrotch, fishmonger, mayor 1361, deceased 1407; Thomas Stonarde, of Oxfordshire; John Bromer, fishmonger, alderman 1474; the Lady Stanley, mother to the Lord Strange; the Countess of Huntington; the Lady Harbert; Sir George Stanley; Gilbert Bovet, 1398; a Countess of Worcester, and one of her children; William More, vintner, mayor 1395; William Venor, grocer, mayor 1389; Robert Chichley, mayor 1421; James Spencer, vintner, mayor 1543; Richard Plat, brewer, founded a free school there 1601.

And thus an end of Vintry Ward, which hath an alderman, with a deputy, common councillors nine, constables nine, scavengers four, wardmote inquest fourteen, and a beadle. It is taxed to the fifteen at £6, 13*s*. 4*d*.

Cordwainer Street Ward.

THE next is Cordwainer Street Ward, taking that name of cordwainers, or shoemakers, curriers, and workers of leather, dwelling there; for it appeareth in the records of Henry VI., the 9th of his reign, that an order was taken then for cordwainers and curriers in Corney Street and Sopar's Lane.

This ward beginneth in the east, on the west side of Walbrook, and turneth west through Budge Row, a street so called of the Budge fur, and of skinners dwelling there, then up by St. Anthony's Church through Aetheling, or Noble Street, as Leland termeth it, commonly called Wathling Street, to the Red Lion, a place so called of a great lion of timber placed there at a gate, entering a large court, wherein are divers fair and large shops, well furnished with broad cloths and other draperies of all sorts to be sold. And this is the farthest west part of this ward.

On the south side of this street from Budge Row lieth a lane turning down by the west gate of the Tower Royal, and to the south end of the stone wall beyond the said gate is of this ward, and is accounted a part of the Royal Street. Against this west gate of the Tower Royal is one other lane that runneth west to Cordwainer Street, and this is called Turnebase Lane; on the south side whereof is a piece of Wringwren Lane, to the north-west corner of St. Thomas Church the Apostle. Then again, out of the high street called Wathling, is one other street, which runneth thwart the same; and this is Cordwainer Street, whereof the whole ward taketh name.

This street beginneth by West Cheap, and St. Mary Bow Church is the head thereof on the west side, and it runneth down south through that part which of later time was called Hosier Lane, now Bow Lane, and then by the west end of Aldmary Church to the new built houses, in place of Ormond House, and so to Garlick Hill, or Hithe, to St. James' Church. The upper part of this street towards Cheap was called Hosier Lane, of hosiers dwelling there in place of shoe-makers; but now those hosiers being worn out by men of other trades, as the hosiers had worn out the shoemakers, the same is called Bow Lane of Bow Church. On the west side of Cordwainer Street is Basing Lane, right over against Turnebase Lane. This Basing Lane west to the back gate of the Red Lion, in Wathling Street, is of this Cordwainer Street Ward.

Now again, on the north side of the high street in Budge Row, by the east end of St. Anthony's Church, have ye St. Sithes Lane, so called of St. Sithes Church, which standeth against the north end of that lane, and this is wholly of Cordwainer Street Ward: also the south side of Needlers Lane, which reacheth from the north end of St. Sithes Lane west to Sopar's Lane; then west from St. Anthony's Church is the south end of Sopar's Lane, which lane took that name, not of soap-making, as some have supposed, but of Alen le Sopar, in the 9th of Edward II. I have not read or heard of soap-making in this city till within this fourscore years, that John Lame, dwelling in Grass Street, set up a boiling-house. For this city, of former time, was served of white soap in hard cakes, called Castell soap, and other, from beyond the seas, and of grey soap, speckled with white, very sweet and good, from Bristol, sold here for a penny the pound, and never above a penny farthing, and black soap for a halfpenny the pound. Then in Bow Lane, as they now call it, is Goose Lane, by Bow Church. William Essex, mercer, had tenements there in the 26th of Edward III.

Then from the south end of Bow Lane, by Wathling Street, till over against the Red Lion; and these be the bounds of Cordwainer Street Ward.

Touching monuments therein, first you have the fair parish church of St. Anthony's in Budge Row, on the north side thereof. This church was lately re-edified by Thomas Knowles, grocer, mayor, and by Thomas Knowles, his son, both buried there, with epitaphs, of the father thus :—

> " Here lieth graven vnder this stone,
> Thomas Knowles, both flesh and bone ;
> Grocer and alderman, yeares fortie,
> Shiriffe, and twice maior truly.
> And for he should not lie alone,
> Here lieth with him his good wife Joan.

> They were togither sixtie yeare,
> And ninteene children they had in feere," * &c.

Thomas Holland, mercer, was there buried 1456; Thomas Windent, mercer, alderman, and Katherine his wife; Thomas Hind, mercer, 1528. He was a benefactor to this church, to Aldermary Church, and to Bow. Hugh Acton, merchant tailor, buried 1520; he gave thirty-six pounds to the repairing of the steeple of this church. Simon Street, grocer, lieth in the church wall toward the south. His arms be three colts, and his epitaph thus :—

> " Such as I am, such shall you be,
> Grocer of London sometime was I,
> The king's wayer more then yeares twentie,
> Simon Streete called in my place,
> And good fellowship faine would trace ;
> Therefore in heaven, everlasting life,
> Jesu send me, and Agnes my wife :
> Kerlie Merlie† my words were tho,
> And *Deo gratias* I coupled thereto :
> I passed to God in the yeare of grace,
> A thousand foure hundred it was," &c.

William Dauntsey, mercer, one of the sheriffs, buried 1542. Henry Colet, mercer, mayor, a great benefactor to this church. The pictures of him, his wife, ten sons, and ten daughters, remain in the glass window on the north side of the church ; but the said Henry Colet was buried at Stebunhith.‡ Henry Halton, grocer, one of the sheriffs, deceased 1415 ; Thomas Spight, merchant tailor, 1533 ; and Roger Martin, mercer, mayor, deceased 1573. John Grantham and Nicholas Bull had chantries there.

Next on the south side of Budge Row, by the west corner thereof, and on the east side of Cordwainer Street, is one other fair church called Aldmary Church, because the same was very old, and elder than any church of St. Mary in the city, till of late years the foundation of a very fair new church was laid there by Henry Keble, grocer, mayor, who deceased 1518, and was there buried in a vault by him prepared, with a fair monument raised over him on the north side the choir, now destroyed and gone. He gave by his testament one thousand pounds towards the building up of that church, and yet not permitted a resting-place for his bones there. Thomas Roman, mayor 1310, had a chantry there. Richard Chaucer, vintner, gave to that church his tenement and tavern, with the appurtenance, in the Royal Street, the corner of Kerion Lane, and was there buried 1348. John Briton ; Ralph Holland, draper, one of the sheriffs, deceased 1452 ; William Taylor, grocer, mayor, deceased 1483. He

---

* *In feere*, in companionship, together.
† *Kerlie Merlie*, confused noise. In Ettrick "killie mahou."
‡ *Stebunhith*, Stepney.

discharged that ward of fifteens to be paid by the poor. Thomas Hinde, mercer, buried in St. Anthony's, gave ten fodder of lead to the covering of the middle aisle of this Aldmary Church. Charles Blunt, Lord Mountjoy, was buried there about the year 1545. He made or glazed the east window, as appeareth by his arms. His epitaph, made by him in his lifetime, thus :—

" Willingly have I fought, and willingly have I found
The fatall end that wrought thither as dutie bound :
Discharged I am of that I ought to my country by honest wound,
My soule departed Christ hath bought, the end of man is ground."

Sir William Laxton, grocer, mayor, deceased 1556, and Thomas Lodge, grocer, mayor 1583, were buried in the vault of Henry Keble, whose bones were unkindly cast out, and his monument pulled down ; in place whereof monuments are set up of the later buried. William Blunt, Lord Mountjoy, buried there 1594, &c.

At the upper end of Hosier Lane, toward West Cheap, is the fair parish church of St. Mary Bow. This church, in the reign of William Conqueror, being the first in this city built on arches of stone, was therefore called New Mary Church, of St. Mary de Arcubus, or Le Bow, in West Cheaping ; as Stratford Bridge being the first built, by Matilde the queen, wife to Henry I., with arches of stone, was called Stratford le Bow ; which names to the said church and bridge remaineth till this day. The Court of the Arches is kept in this church, and taketh name of the place, not the place of the court ; but of what antiquity or continuation that court hath there continued I cannot learn.

This church is of Cordwainer Street Ward, and for divers accidents happening there, hath been made more famous than any other parish church of the whole city or suburbs. First, we read, that in the year 1090, and the 3rd of William Rufus, by tempest of wind, the roof of the church of St. Mary Bow, in Cheap, was overturned, wherewith some persons were slain, and four of the rafters, of twenty-six feet in length, with such violence were pitched in the ground of the high street, that scantly four feet of them remained above ground, which were fain to be cut even with the ground, because they could not be plucked out, for the city of London was not then paved, and a marish ground.

In the year 1196, William Fitz Osbert, a seditious tailor, took the steeple of Bow, and fortified it with munitions and victuals, but it was assaulted, and William with his accomplices were taken, though not without bloodshed, for he was forced by fire and smoke to forsake the church ; and then, by the judges condemned, he was by the heels drawn to the Elms in Smithfield, and there hanged with nine of his fellows ; where, because his favourers came not to deliver him, he forsook Mary's son, as he termed Christ our Saviour, and called upon the devil to help and deliver him. Such was the end of this deceiver, a man of an evil life, a secret murderer, a filthy fornicator, a polluter of concubines, and, amongst other his detestable facts, a false accuser of his elder brother, who had in his youth brought him up in learning, and done many things for his preferment.

In the year 1271, a great part of the steeple of Bow fell down, and slew many people, men and women. In the year 1284, the 13th of Edward I., Laurence Ducket, goldsmith, having grievously wounded one Ralph Crepin in West Cheap, fled into Bow Church; into the which in the night time entered certain evil persons, friends unto the said Ralph, and slew the said Laurence lying in the steeple, and then hanged him up, placing him so by the window as if he had hanged himself, and so was it found by inquisition; for the which fact Laurence Ducket, being drawn by the feet, was buried in a ditch without the city; but shortly after, by relation of a boy, who lay with the said Laurence at the time of his death, and had hid him there for fear, the truth of the matter was disclosed; for the which cause, Jordan Goodcheape, Ralph Crepin, Gilbert Clarke, and Geoffrey Clarke, were attainted; a certain woman named Alice, that was chief causer of the said mischief, was burnt, and to the number of sixteen men were drawn and hanged, besides others that, being richer, after long imprisonment, were hanged by the purse.

The church was interdicted, the doors and windows were stopped up with thorns, but Laurence was taken up, and honestly buried in the churchyard.

The parish church of St. Mary Bow, by means of encroachment and building of houses, wanting room in their churchyard for burial of the dead, John Rotham, or Rodham, citizen and tailor, by his testament, dated the year 1465, gave to the parson and church-wardens a certain garden in Hosier Lane to be a churchyard, which so continued near a hundred years; but now is built on, and is a private man's house. The old steeple of this church was by little and little re-edified, and new built up, at the least so much as was fallen down, many men giving sums of money to the furtherance thereof; so that at length, to wit, in the year 1469, it was ordained by a common council that the Bow bell should be nightly rung at nine of the clock. Shortly after, John Donne, mercer, by his testament, dated 1472, according to the trust of Reginald Longdon, gave to the parson and churchwardens of St. Mary Bow two tenements, with the appurtenances, since made into one, in Hosier Lane, then so called, to the maintenance of Bow bell, the same to be rung as afore-said, and other things to be observed, as by the will appeareth.

This bell being usually rung somewhat late, as seemed to the young men 'prentices, and other in Cheap, they made and set up a rhyme against the clerk, as followeth :—

> " Clarke of the Bow bell with the yellow lockes,
>   For thy late ringing thy head shall have knocks."

Whereunto the clerk replying, wrote—

> " Children of Cheape, hold you all still,
>   For you shall have the Bow bell rung at your will."

Robert Harding, goldsmith, one of the sheriffs 1478, gave to the new work of that steeple forty pounds ; John Haw, mercer, ten pounds ; Doctor Allen, four pounds ; Thomas Baldry, four pounds ; and other gave other sums, so that the said work of the steeple was finished in the year 1512. The arches or bows thereupon, with the lanthorns, five in number, to wit, one at each corner, and one on the top in the middle upon the arches, were also afterward finished of stone, brought from Caen in Normandy, delivered at the Customers Quay for 4s. 8d. the ton ; William Copland, tailor, the king's merchant, and Andrew Fuller, mercer, being churchwardens 1515 and 1516. It is said that this Copland gave the great bell, which made the fifth in the ring, to be rung nightly at nine of the clock. This bell was first rung as a knell at the burial of the same Copland. It appeareth that the lanthorns on the top of this steeple were meant to have been glazed, and lights in them placed nightly in the winter, whereby travellers to the city might have the better sight thereof, and not to miss of their ways.

In this parish also was a grammar school, by commandment of King Henry VI., which school was of old time kept in a house for that purpose prepared in the churchyard ; but that school being decayed, as others about this city, the school-house was let out for rent, in the reign of Henry VIII., for four shillings the year, a cellar for two shillings the year, and two vaults under the church for fifteen shillings both.

The monuments in this church be these ; namely, of Sir John Coventry, mercer, mayor 1425 ; Richard Lambert, alderman ; Nicholas Alwine, mercer, mayor 1499 ; Robert Harding, goldsmith, one of the sheriffs 1478 ; John Loke, one of the sheriffs 1461 ; Edward Bankes, alderman, haberdasher, 1566 ; John Warde ; William Pierson, scrivener and attorney in the Common Pleas. In a proper chapel on the south side the church standeth a tomb, elevated and arched. Ade de Buke, hatter, glazed the chapel and most part of the church, and was there buried. All other monuments be defaced. Hawley and Southam had chantries there.

Without the north side of this church of St. May Bow, towards

West Cheap, standeth one fair building of stone, called in record Seldam, a shed, which greatly darkeneth the said church ; for by means thereof all the windows and doors on that side are stopped up. King Edward III. upon occasion, as shall be shown in the ward of Cheap, caused this seld or shed to be made, and to be strongly built of stone, for himself, the queen, and other estates to stand in, there to behold the joustings and other shows at their pleasures. And this house for a long time after served to that use, namely, in the reign of Edward III. and Richard II. ; but in the year 1410, Henry IV., in the 12th of his reign, confirmed the said shed or building to Stephen Spilman, William Marchford, and John Whately, mercers, by the name of one New Seldam, shed, or building, with shops, cellars, and edifices whatsoever appertaining, called Crounsilde or Tamersilde, situate in the mercery in West Cheap, and in the parish of St. Mary de Arcubus in London, &c. Notwithstanding which grant, the kings of England, and other great estates, as well of foreign countries, repairing to this realm, as inhabitants of the same, have usually repaired to this place, therein to behold the shows of this city passing through West Cheap, namely, the great watches accustomed in the night, on the even of St. John Baptist, and St. Peter at midsummer, the examples whereof were over long to recite, wherefore let it suffice briefly to touch one. In the year 1510, on St. John's even, at night, King Henry VIII. came to this place, then called the King's Head in Cheap, in the livery of a yeoman of the guard, with an halbert on his shoulder, and there beholding the watch, departed privily when the watch was done, and was not known to any but to whom it pleased him ; but on St. Peter's night next following, he and the queen came royally riding to the said place, and there with their nobles beheld the watch of the city, and returned in the morning.

This Church of St. Mary, with the said shed of stone, all the housing in or about Bow Churchyard, and without on that side the high street of Cheap to the Standard, be of Cordwainer Street Ward. These houses were of old time but sheds ; for I read of no housing otherwise on that side the street, but of divers sheds from Sopar's Lane to the Standard, &c. Amongst other, I read of three shops or sheds by Sopar's Lane, pertaining to the priory of the Holy Trinity within Aldgate ; the one was let out for twenty-eight shillings, one other for twenty shillings, and the third for twelve shillings, by the year. Moreover, that Richard Goodchepe, mercer. and Margery his wife, son to Jordaine Goodchepe, did let to John Dalinges the younger, mercer, their shed and chamber in West Cheap, in the parish of St. Mary de Arches, for three shillings and fourpence by the year. Also the men of Bread Street Ward contended with the men of Cordwainer Street Ward for a seld or shed opposite to the Standard, on the south side, and it was found to be of Cordwainer Street Ward; W. Waldorne being then mayor, the 1st of Henry VI. Thus much for Cordwainer Street Ward; which hath an alderman, his deputy, common councillors eight, constables eight, scavengers eight, wardmote inquest men fourteen, and a beadle. It standeth taxed to the fifteen in London at £52, 16s.; in the Exchequer at £52, 6s.

Cheap Ward.

NEXT adjoining is Cheap Ward, and taketh name of the market there kept, called West Cheping. This ward also beginneth in the east, on the course of Walbrook in Bucklesbury, and runneth up on both the sides to the great conduit in Cheap. Also on the south side of Bucklesbury, a lane turning up by St. Sithes Church, and by St. Pancrates Church, through Needler's Lane, on the north side thereof, and then through a piece of Sopar's Lane, on both sides up to Cheap, be all of Cheap Ward.

Then to begin again in the east upon the said course of Walbrook, is St. Mildred's Church in the Poultry, on the north side, and over against the said church gate, on the south, to pass up all that high street called the Poultry, to the great conduit in Cheap, and then Cheap itself, which beginneth by the east end of the said conduit, and stretcheth up to the north-east corner of Bow Lane on the south side, and to the Standard on the north side; and thus far to the west is of Cheap Ward.

On the south side of this high street is no lane turning south out of this ward, more than some portion of Sopar's Lane, whereof I have before written. But on the north side of this high street is Conyhope Lane, about one quarter of Old Jewry Lane on the west side, and on the east side almost as much, to the sign of the Angel. Then is Ironmonger's Lane, all wholly on both sides, and from the north end thereof through Catton Street, west to the north end of St. Lawrence Lane, and some four houses west beyond the same on that side, and over against Ironmonger's Lane end on the north side of Catton Street up by the Guildhall and St. Lawrence Church in the Jewry, is altogether of Cheap Ward. Then again in Cheap, more towards the west, is of St. Lawrence Lane before named, which is all wholly of this ward. And last of all is Honey Lane, and up to the Standard on the north side of Cheap. And so stand the bounds of Cheap Ward.

Now for antiquities there. First is Bucklesbury, so called of a manor and tenements pertaining to one Buckle, who there dwelt and kept his courts. This manor is supposed to be the great stone building, yet in part remaining on the south side of the street, which of late time hath been called the Old Barge, of such a sign hanged out near the gate thereof. This manor or great house hath of long time been divided and letten out into many tenements ; and it hath been a common speech, that when Walbrook did lie open, barges were rowed out of the Thames, or towed up so far, and therefore the place hath ever since been called the Old Barge.

Also on the north side of this street, directly over against the said Bucklesbury, was one ancient and strong tower of stone, the which tower King Edward III., in the 18th of his reign, by the name of the King's House, called Cornettes toure in London, did appoint to be his Exchange of money there to be kept. In the 29th he granted it to Frydus Guynysane and Landus Bardoile, merchants of Luke, for twenty pounds the year. And in the 32nd he gave the same tower to his college or free chapel of St. Stephen at Westminster, by the name of Cernet's Tower at Bucklesbury in London. This tower of late years was taken down by one Buckle, a grocer, meaning in place thereof to have set up and built a goodly frame of timber ; but the said Buckle greedily labouring to pull down the old tower, a part thereof fell upon him, which so sore bruised him that his life was thereby shortened, and another that married his widow set up the new prepared frame of timber, and finished the work.

This whole street called Bucklesbury on both the sides throughout is possessed of grocers and apothecaries towards the west end thereof : on the south side breaketh out one other short lane, called in records Peneritch Street ; it reacheth but to St. Sithes Lane, and St. Sithes Church is the farthest part thereof, for by the west end of the said church beginneth Needler's Lane, which reacheth to Sopar's Lane, as is aforesaid. This small parish church of St. Sith hath also an addition of Bennet Shorne, or Shrog or Shorehog, for by all these names have I read it, but the most ancient is Shorne, wherefore it seemeth to take that name of one Benedict Shorne, sometime a citizen and stock-fishmonger of London, a new builder, repairer, or benefactor thereof, in the reign of Edward II., so that Shorne is but corruptly called Shrog, and more corruptly Shorehog.

There lie buried in this church, John Froysh, mercer, mayor 1394 ; John Rochford and Robert Rochford ; John Hold, alderman ; Henry Froweke, mercer, mayor 1435 ; Edward Warrington ; John Morrice ; John Huntley ; Richard Lincoln, fellmonger, 1546 ; Sir Ralph Warren, mercer, mayor 1553 ; Sir John Lion, grocer, mayor 1554. These two last have monuments, the rest are all defaced. Edward Hall, gentleman of Gray's Inn, common sergeant of this city, and then under-sheriff of the same. He wrote the large chronicles from Richard II. till the end of Henry VIII., and was buried in this church.

Then in Needler's Lane have ye the parish church of St. Pancrate, a proper small church, but divers rich parishioners therein, and hath had of old time many liberal benefactors, but of late such as, not regarding the order taken by her majesty, the least bell in their church being broken, have rather sold the same for half the value than put the parish to charge with new casting; late experience hath proved this to be true, besides the spoil of monuments there. In this church are buried Sir Aker; John Aker; John Barens, mercer, mayor 1370; John Beston and his wife; Robert Rayland; John Hamber; John Gage; John Rowley; John Lambe; John Hadley, grocer, mayor 1379; Richard Gardener, mercer, mayor 1478; John Stockton, mercer, mayor 1470; John Dane, mercer; John Parker; Robert Marshall, alderman, 1439; Robert Corcheforde; Robert Hatfield; and Robert Hatfield; Nicholas Wilfilde, and Thomas his son; the monuments of all which be defaced and gone. There do remain of Robert Burley, 1360; Richard Wilson, 1525; Robert Packenton, mercer, slain with a gun shot at him in a morning, as he was going to morrow mass from his house in Cheap to St. Thomas of Acars, in the year 1536. The murderer was never discovered, but by his own confession made when he came to the gallows at Banbury to be hanged for felony. T. Wardbury, haberdasher, 1545; James Huish, grocer, 1590; Ambrose Smith, &c. Then is a part of Sopar's Lane turning up to Cheap.

By the assent of Stephen Abunden, mayor, the Pepperers in Sopar's Lane were admitted to sell all such spices and other wares as grocers now use to sell, retaining the old name of Pepperers in Sopar's Lane, till at length, in the reign of Henry VI., the same Sopar's Lane was inhabited by cordwainers and curriers, after that the Pepperers or Grocers had seated themselves in a more open street, to wit, Bucklesbury, where they yet remain. Thus much for the south wing of Cheap Ward.

Now to begin again on the bank of the said Walbrook, at the east end of the high street called the Poultry, on the north side thereof, is the proper parish church of St. Mildred, which church was new built upon Walbrook in the year 1457. John Saxton their parson gave thirty-two pounds towards the building of the new choir, which now standeth upon the course of Walbrook. Lovell and Puery, and Richard Keston, have their arms in the east window as benefactors. The roofing of that church is garnished with the arms of Thomas Archehull, one of the churchwardens in the year 1455, who was there buried. Thomas Morsted, esquire, and chirurgeon to

King Henry IV., V., and VI., one of the sheriffs of London in the year 1436, gave unto this church a parcel of ground, containing in length from the course of Walbrook toward the west forty-five feet, and in breadth from the church toward the north thirty-five feet, being within the gate called Scalding Wike, in the said parish, to make a churchyard wherein to bury their dead. Richard Shore, draper, one of the sheriffs 1505, gave fifteen pounds for making a porch to this church. Salomon Lanuare had a chantry there in the 14th of Edward II. Hugh Game had one other. Buried here, as appeareth by monuments, John Hildye, poulter, 1416; John Kendall, 1468; John Garland, 1476; Robert Bois, 1485, and Simon Lee, poulters, 1487; Thomas Lee of Essex, gentleman; William Hallingridge; Christopher Feliocke, 1494; Robert Draiton, skinner, 1484; John Christopherson, doctor of physic, 1524; William Turner, skinner, 1536; Blase White, grocer, 1558; Thomas Hobson, haberdasher, 1559; William Hobson, haberdasher, 1581; Thomas Tusser, 1580, with this epitaph :—

> " Here Thomas Tusser, clad in earth, doth lie,
> That sometime made the Poyntes of Husbandrie ;
> By him then learne thou maist, here learne we must,
> When all is done we sleepe and turne to dust,
> And yet through Christ to heaven we hope to go,
> Who reades his bookes shall find his faith was so."

On the north side of the churchyard remain two tombs of marble, but not known of whom, or otherwise than by tradition it is said, they were of Thomas Monshampe and William, brothers, about 1547, &c.

Some four houses west from this parish church of St. Mildred is a prison house pertaining to one of the sheriffs of London, and is called the Compter in the Poultry. This hath been there kept and continued time out of mind, for I have not read of the original thereof. West from this Compter was a proper chapel, called of Corpus Christi and St. Mary, at Conyhope Lane end, in the parish of St. Mildred, founded by one named Ion. Irunnes, a citizen of London, in the reign of Edward III., in which chapel was a guild or fraternity, that might dispend in lands better than twenty pounds by year. It was suppressed by Henry VIII., and purchased by one Thomas Hobson, haberdasher. He turned this chapel into a fair warehouse and shops towards the street, with lodgings over them.

Then is Conyhope Lane, of old time so called of such a sign of three conies hanging over a poulterer's stall at the lane's end. Within this lane standeth the Grocers' Hall, which company being of old time called Pepperers, were first incorporated by the name of Grocers in the year 1345, at which time they elected for custos, or guardian, of their fraternity, Richard Oswin and Laurence Haliwell, and twenty brethren were then taken in to be of their society. In the year 1411, the custos, or guardian, and the brethren of this company, purchased of the Lord Ro. Fitzwaters one plot of ground, with the building thereupon, in the said Conyhope Lane, for three hundred and twenty marks, and then laid the foundation of their new common hall.

About the year 1429, the Grocers had license to purchase five hundred marks land, since the which time, near adjoining unto the Grocers' Hall, the said company had built seven proper houses for seven aged poor almspeople. Thomas Knowles, grocer, mayor, gave his tenement in St Anthony's Churchyard to the Grocers, towards the relief of the poor brethren in that company. Also H. Keeble, grocer, mayor, gave to the seven almspeople sixpence the piece weekly for ever ; which pension is now increased by the masters, to some of them two shillings the piece weekly, and to some of them less, &c. Henry Adie, grocer, 1563, gave one thousand marks to the Grocers to purchase lands ; and Sir John Pechie, knight banneret, free of that company, gave them five hundred pounds to certain uses. He built almshouses at Ludingstone, in Kent, and was there buried.

West from this Conyhope Lane is the Old Jewry, whereof some portion is of Cheap Ward, as afore is showed. At the south end of this lane is the parish church of St. Mary Colechurch, named of one Cole that built it. This church is built upon a wall above ground, so that men are forced to go to ascend up thereunto by certain steps. I find no monuments of this church, more than that Henry IV. granted license to William Marshall and others to found a brotherhood of St. Katherine therein, because Thomas Becket, and St. Edmond, the archbishop, were baptized there. More, I read of Bordhangly Lane to be in that parish. And thus much for the north side of the Poultry. The south side of the said Poultry, beginning on the bank of the said brook over against the parish church of St. Mildred, passing up to the great conduit, hath divers fair houses, which were sometimes inhabited by poulters, but now by grocers, haberdashers, and upholsterers.

At the west end of this Poultry, and also of Bucklesbury, beginneth the large street of West Cheaping, a market-place so called, which street stretcheth west till ye come to the little conduit by Paul's Gate, but not all of Cheap Ward. In the east part of this street standeth the great conduit of sweet water, conveyed by pipes of lead under ground from Paddington for the service of this city, castellated with stone, and cisterned in lead, about the year 1285, and again new built and enlarged by Thomas Ilam, one of the sheriffs 1479.

About the midst of this street is the Standard in Cheap, of what antiquity the first foundation I have not read. But Henry VI. by his patent dated at Windsor the 21st of his reign, which patent was confirmed by parliament 1442, granted license to Thomas Knolles, John Chichle, and other, executors to John Wels, grocer, sometime mayor of London, with his goods to make new the highway which leadeth from the city of London towards the palace of Westminster, before and nigh the manor of Savoy, parcel of the Duchy of Lancaster, a way then very ruinous, and the pavement broken, to the hurt and mischief of the subjects, which old pavement then remaining in that way within the length of five hundred feet, and all the breadth of the same before and nigh the site of the manor aforesaid, they to break up, and with stone, gravel, and other stuff, one other good and sufficient way there to make for the commodity of the subjects.

And further, that the Standard in Cheap, where divers executions of the law before time had been performed, which Standard at the present was very ruinous with age, in which there was a conduit, should be taken down, and another competent standard of stone, together with a conduit in the same of new, strongly to be built, for the commodity and honour of the city, with the goods of the said testator, without interruption, &c.

Of executions at the Standard in Cheap, we read, that in the year 1293 three men had their right hands smitten off there, for rescuing of a prisoner arrested by an officer of the city. In the year 1326, the burgesses of London caused Walter Stapleton, Bishop of Excester, treasurer to Edward II., and other, to be beheaded at the Standard in Cheap (but this was by Paul's Gate); in the year 1351, the 26th of Edward III., two fishmongers were beheaded at the Standard in Cheap, but I read not of their offence. 1381, Wat Tyler beheaded Richard Lions and other there. In the year 1399, Henry IV. caused the blanck charters made by Richard II. to be burnt there. In the year 1450, Jack Cade, captain of the Kentish Rebels, beheaded the Lord Say there. In the year 1461, John Davy had his hand stricken off there, because he had stricken a man before the judges at Westminster, &c.

Then next is a great cross in West Cheap, which cross was there erected in the year 1290 by Edward I. upon occasion thus :—Queen Eleanor his wife died at Hardeby,* a town near unto the city of Lincoln ; her body was brought from thence to Westminster ; and the king, in memory of her, caused in every place where her body rested in the way, a stately cross of stone to be erected, with the queen's image and arms upon it, as at Grantham, Woburn, Nor-

* Harby in Nottinghamshire.

thampton, Stony Stratford, Dunstable, St. Alban's, Waltham, West Cheap, and at Charing, from whence she was conveyed to Westminster, and there buried.

This cross in West Cheap being like to those other which remain to this day, and being by length of time decayed, John Hatherly, mayor of London, procured, in the year 1441, license of King Henry VI. to re-edify the same in more beautiful manner for the honour of the city, and had license also to take up two hundred fodder of lead for the building thereof of certain conduits and a common granary. This cross was then curiously wrought at the charges of divers citizens: John Fisher, mercer, gave six hundred marks toward it. The same was begun to be set up 1484, and finished 1486, the 2nd of Henry VII. It was new gilt over in the year 1522, against the coming of Charles V., emperor; in the year 1553, against the coronation of Queen Anne; new burnished against the coronation of Edward VI.; and again new gilt 1554, against the coming in of King Philip. Since the which time the said cross having been presented by divers juries, or inquests of wardmote, to stand in the highway to the let of carriages, as they alleged, but could not have it removed, it followed that in the year 1581, the 21st of June, in the night, the lowest images round about the said cross, being of Christ's resurrection, of the Virgin Mary, King Edward the Confessor, and such like, were broken and defaced, proclamation was made, that whoso would bewray the doers, should have forty crowns, but nothing came to light. The image of the Blessed Virgin was at that time robbed of her Son, and her arms broken by which she stayed him on her knees; her whole body also was haled with ropes, and left likely to fall, but in the year 1595 was again fastened and repaired; and in the year next following a new misshapen son, as born out of time, all naked, was laid in her arms, the other images remaining broke as afore. But on the east side of the same cross, the steps taken thence, under the image of Christ's resurrection defaced, was then set up a curiously wrought tabernacle of grey marble, and in the same an image alabaster of Diana, and water conveyed from the Thames prilling from her naked breast for a time, but now decayed.

In the year 1599, the timber of the cross at the top being rotted within the lead, the arms thereof bending, were feared to have fallen to the harming of some people, and therefore the whole body of the cross was scaffolded about, and the top thereof taken down, meaning in place thereof to have set up a pyramis; but some of her majesty's honourable councillors directed their letters to Sir Nicholas Mosley, then mayor, by her highness' express commandment concerning the cross, forthwith to be repaired, and placed again as it formerly stood, &c. Notwithstanding, the said cross stood headless more than a year after; whereupon the said councillors, in greater number, meaning not any longer to permit the continuance of such a contempt, wrote to William Rider, then mayor, requiring him, by virtue of her highness' said former direction and commandment, without any further delay to accomplish the same her majesty's most princely care therein, respecting especially the antiquity and continuance of that monument, an ancient ensign of Christianity, &c. Dated the 24th of December 1600. After this a cross of timber was framed, set up, covered with lead, and gilded, the body of the cross downward cleansed of dust, the scaffold carried thence. About twelve nights following, the image of Our Lady was again defaced, by plucking off her crown, and almost her head, taking from her her naked child, and stabbing her in the breast, &c. Thus much for the cross in West Cheap.

Then at the west end of West Cheap Street was sometime a cross of stone called the Old Cross. Ralph Higden, in his *Policronicon*, saith, that Walter Stapleton, Bishop of Excester, treasurer to Edward II., was by the burgesses of London beheaded at this cross called the Standard, without the north door of St. Paul's Church; and so is it noted in other writers that then lived. This old cross stood and remained at the east end of the parish church called St. Michael in the corner by Paul's Gate, near to the north end of the old Exchange, till the year 1390, the 13th of Richard II., in place of which old cross then taken down, the said Church of St. Michael was enlarged, and also a fair water conduit built about the 9th of Henry VI.

In the reign of Edward III. divers joustings were made in this street, betwixt Sopar's Lane and the great cross, namely, one in the year 1331, the 21st of September, as I find noted by divers writers of that time. In the middle of the city of London, say they, in a street called Cheap, the stone pavement being covered with sand, that the horses might not slide when they strongly set their feet to the ground, the king held a tournament three days together, with the nobility, valiant men of the realm, and other some strange knights. And to the end the beholders might with the better ease see the same, there was a wooden scaffold erected across the street, like unto a tower, wherein Queen Philippa, and many other ladies, richly attired, and assembled from all parts of the realm, did stand to behold the jousts; but the higher frame, in which the ladies were placed, brake in sunder, whereby they were with some shame forced to fall down, by reason whereof the knights, and such as were underneath, were grievously hurt; wherefore the queen took great care to save the carpenters from punishment, and through her prayers, which she made upon her knees, pacified the king and council, and thereby purchased great love of the people. After which time the king caused a shed to be strongly made of stone, for himself, the queen, and other estates to stand on, and there to behold the joustings and other shows at their pleasure, by the Church of St. Mary Bow, as is showed in Cordwainer Street Ward. Thus much for the high street of Cheap.

Now let us return to the south side of Cheap Ward. From the great conduit west be many fair and large houses, for the most part possessed of mercers up to the corner of Cordwainer Street, corruptly called Bow Lane, which houses in former times were but sheds or shops, with solers * over them, as of late one of them remained at Sopar's Lane end, wherein a woman sold seeds, roots, and herbs ; but those sheds or shops, by encroachments on the high street, are now largely built on both sides outward, and also upward, some three, four, or five stories high.

Now of the north side of Cheap Street and ward, beginning at the great conduit, and by St. Mary Cole Church, where we left. Next thereunto westward is the Mercers' Chapel, sometime an hospital, intituled of St. Thomas of Acon, or Acars, for a master and brethren, " *Militia hospitalis*," &c., saith the record of Edward III., the 14th year. It was founded by Thomas Fitzthebald de Heili, and Agnes his wife, sister to Thomas Becket, in the reign of Henry II. They gave to the master and brethren the lands, with the appurtenances that sometime were Gilbart Becket's, father to the said Thomas, in the which he was born, there to make a church. There was a charnel, and a chapel over it, of St. Nicholas and St. Stephen. This hospital was valued to dispend £277, 3s. 4d., surrendered the 30th of Henry VIII., the 21st of October, and was since purchased by the Mercers, by means of Sir Richard Gresham, and was again set open on the eve of St. Michael, 1541, the 33rd of Henry VIII. It is now called the Mercers' Chapel. Therein is kept a free grammar school, as of old time had been accustomed, commanded by parliament. Here be many monuments remaining, but more have been defaced :—James Butler, Earl of Ormond, and Dame Joan his countess, 1428 ; John Norton, esquire ; Stephen Cavendish, draper, mayor 1362 ; Thomas Cavendish ; William Cavendish ; Thomas Ganon, called Pike, one of the sheriffs 1410 ; Hungate, of Yorkshire ; Ambrose Cresacre ; John Chester, draper ; John Trusbut, mercer, 1437 ; Tho. Norland, sheriff 1483 ; Sir Edmond Sha, goldsmith, mayor 1482 ; Sir Thomas Hill, mayor 1485 ; Thomas Ilam, sheriff 1479 ; Lancelot Laken, esquire ; Ralph Tilney, sheriff 1488 ; Garth, esquire ; John Rich ; Thomas Butler,

---

* *Solers*, upper rooms or lofts, from Latin *solarium*, a flat house-top or balcony, as being exposed to the sun.

Earl of Ormond, 1515; Sir W. Butler, grocer, mayor 1515; W. Browne, mercer, mayor 1513; John Loke, 1519; Sir T. Baldry, mercer, mayor 1523; Sir W. Locke, mercer, sheriff 1548; Sir John Allen, mercer, mayor 1525, deceased 1544; Sir Thomas Leigh, mercer, mayor 1558; Sir Richard Malory, mercer, mayor 1564; Humf. Baskervile, mercer, sheriff 1561; Sir G. Bond, mayor 1587, &c.

Before this hospital, towards the street, was built a fair and beautiful chapel, arched over with stone, and thereupon the Mercers' Hall, a most curious piece of work; Sir John Allen, mercer, being founder of that chapel, was there buried; but since his tomb is removed thence into the body of the hospital church, and his chapel, divided into shops, is letten out for rent.

These Mercers were enabled to be a company, and to purchase lands to the value of twenty pounds the year, the 17th of Richard II. They had three messuages and shops in the parish of St. Martin Oteswitch, in the ward of Bishopsgate, for the sustentation of the poor, and a chantry of the 22nd of Richard II. Henry IV., in the 12th of his reign, confirmed to Stephen Spilman, W. Marchford, and John Whatile, mercers, by the name of one new seldam, shed, or building, with shops, cellars, and edifices whatsoever appertaining called Crownsild, situate in the Mercery in West Cheap, in the parish of St. Mary de Arcubus in London, &c., to be holden in burgage, as all the city of London is, and which were worth by year in all issues, according to the true value of them, £7, 13s. 4d., as found by inquisition before T. Knolles, mayor, and escheator in the said city. Henry VI., in the 3rd of his reign, at the request of John Coventry, John Carpenter, and William Grove, granted to the Mercers to have a chaplain and a brotherhood, for relief of such of their company as came to decay by misfortune on the sea. In the year 1536, on St. Peter's night, King Henry VIII. and Queen Jane his wife stood in this Mercers' Hall, then new built, and beheld the marching watch of this city most bravely set out, Sir John Allen, mercer, one of the king's council, being mayor.

Next beyond the Mercers' Chapel and their hall is Ironmonger Lane, so called of ironmongers dwelling there, whereof I read, in the reign of Edward I., &c. In this lane is the small parish church of St. Martin called Pomary, upon what occasion I certainly know not. It is supposed to be of apples growing where houses are now lately built; for myself have seen large void places there. Monuments in that church none to be accounted of.

Farther west is St. Lawrence Lane, so called of St. Lawrence Church, which standeth directly over against the north end thereof. Antiquities in this lane I find none other, than that among many fair houses, there is one large inn for receipt of travellers called Blossoms Inn, but corruptly Bosoms Inn, and hath to sign St. Lawrence the Deacon, in a border of blossoms or flowers.

Then near to the Standard in Cheap is Honey Lane, so called, not of sweetness thereof, being very narrow, and somewhat dark, but rather of often washing and sweeping, to keep it clean. In this lane is the small parish church called Allhallows in Honey Lane. There be no monuments in this church worth the noting. I find that John Norman, draper, mayor 1453, was buried there. He gave to the Drapers his tenements on the north side the said church, they to allow for the beam light and lamp, 13s. 4d. yearly from this lane to the Standard. And thus much for Cheap Ward in the high street of Cheap, for it stretcheth no farther.

Now for the north wing of Cheap Ward have ye Catte Street, corruptly called Catteten Street, which beginneth at the north end of Ironmonger Lane, and runneth to the west end of St. Lawrence Church, as is afore showed.

On the north side of the street is the Guildhall, wherein the courts for the city be kept, namely, 1. The court of common council; 2. The court of the lord mayor and his brethren the aldermen; 3. The court of hustings; 4. The court of orphans; 5. The court of the sheriffs; 6. The court of the wardmote; 7. The court of hallmote; 8. The court of requests, commonly called the court of conscience; 9. The chamberlain's court for apprentices, and making them free. This Guildhall, saith Robert Fabian, was begun to be built new in the year 1411, the 12th of Henry IV., by Thomas Knoles, then mayor, and his brethren the aldermen: the same was made of a little cottage a large and great house, as now it standeth, towards the charges whereof the companies gave large benevolences; also offences of men were pardoned for sums of money towards this work, extraordinary fees were raised, fines, amercements, and other things employed during seven years, with a continuation thereof three years more, all to be employed to this building.

The 1st year of Henry VI., John Coventry and John Carpenter, executors to Richard Whittington, gave towards the paving of this great hall twenty pounds, and the next year fifteen pounds more to the said pavement with hard stone of Purbeck. They also glazed some windows thereof, and of the mayor's court; on every which window the arms of Richard Whittington are placed. The foundation of the mayor's court was laid in the 3rd year of the reign of Henry VI., and of the porch on the south side of the mayor's court, in the 4th of the said king. Then was built the mayor's chamber, and the council chamber with other rooms above the stairs. Last of all a stately porch entering the great hall was erected, the front thereof towards the south being beautified with images of stone, such as is showed by these verses following, made about some thirty years since by William Elderton, at that time an attorney in the sheriffs' courts there :—

> " Though most of the images be pulled down,
>   And none be thought remayne in towne,
>   I am sure there be in London yet,
>   Seven images in such and in such a place ;
>   And few or none I think will hit,
>   Yet every day they show their face,
>   And thousands see them every year,
>   But few I thinke can tell me where,
>   Where Jesu Christ aloft doth stand :
>   Law and Learning on eyther hand,
>   Discipline in the Devil's necke,
>   And hard by her are three direct,
>   There Justice, Fortitude, and Temperance stand,
>   Where find ye the like in all this land ?"

Divers aldermen glazed the great hall and other courts, as appeareth by their arms in each window. William Hariot, draper, mayor 1481, gave forty pounds to the making of two louvers in the said Guildhall, and towards the glazing thereof. The kitchens and other houses of office adjoining to this Guildhall were built of later time, to wit, about the year 1501, by procurement of Sir John Sha, goldsmith, mayor, who was the first that kept his feast there ; towards the charges of which work the mayor had of the fellowships of the city by their own agreement certain sums of money, as of the Mercers forty pounds, the Grocers twenty pounds, the Drapers thirty pounds, and so of the other fellowships through the city, as they were of power. Also widows and other well-disposed persons gave certain sums of money, as the Lady Hill ten pounds, the Lady Austrie ten pounds, and so of many other, till the work was finished, since the which time the mayor's feasts have been yearly kept there, which before time had been kept in the Tailors' Hall, and in the Grocers' Hall. Nicholas Alwyn, grocer, mayor 1499, deceased 1505, gave by his testament for a hanging of tapestry, to serve for principal days in the Guildhall, £73, 6s. 8d. How this gift was performed I have not heard, for executors of our time having no conscience (I speak of my own knowledge) prove more testaments than they perform.

Now for the chapel or college of our Lady Mary Magdalen, and of All Saints, by the Guildhall, called London College, I read that the same was built about the year 1299, and that Peter Fanelore, Adam Frauncis, and Henry Frowike, citizens, gave one messuage, with the appurtenances, in the parish of St. Fawstar, to William Brampton, custos of the chantry, by them founded in the said chapel with four chaplains, and one other house in the parish of St. Giles without

Cripplegate, in the 27th of Edward III., was given to them. Moreover, I find that Richard II., in the 20th of his reign, granted to Stephen Spilman, mercer, license to give one messuage, three shops, and one garden, with the appurtenances, being in the parish of St. Andrew Hubbard, to the custos and chaplains of the said chapel, and to their successors, for their better relief and maintenance for ever.

King Henry VI., in the 8th of his reign, gave license to John Barnard, custos, and the chaplains, to build of new the said chapel or college of Guildhall.; and the same Henry VI., in the 27th of his reign, granted to the parish clerks in London a guild of St. Nicholas, for two chaplains by them to be kept in the said chapel of St. Mary Magdalen, near unto the Guildhall, and to keep seven almspeople. Henry Barton, skinner, mayor, founded a chaplaincy there; Roger Depham, mercer, and Sir William Langford, knight, had also chaplaincies there. This chapel or college had a custos, seven chaplains, three clerks, and four choristers.

Monuments there have been sundry, as appeareth by the tombs of marble yet remaining, seven in number, but all defaced. The uppermost in the choir, on the south side thereof, above the revestry door, was the tomb of John Wells, grocer, mayor 1451. The likeness of wells are graven on the tomb on the revestry door, and other places on that side the choir. Also in the glass window over this tomb, and in the east window, is the likeness of wells, with hands elevated out of the same wells, holding scrolls, wherein is written "Mercy!"—the writing in the east window being broken, yet remaineth wells. I found his arms also in the south glass window. All which do show that the east end and south side the choir of this chapel, and the revestry, were by him both built and glazed. On the north side the choir the tomb of Thomas Knesworth, fishmonger, mayor 1505, who deceased 1515, was defaced, and within these forty-four years again renewed by the Fishmongers. Two other tombs lower there are; the one of a draper, the other of a haberdasher, their names not known. Richard Stomine is written in the window by the haberdasher. Under flat stones do lie divers custos of the chapel, chaplains and officers to the chamber. Amongst others, John Clipstone, priest, sometime custos of the library of the Guildhall, 1457; another of Edmond Alison, priest, one of the custos of the library, 1510, &c. Sir John Langley, goldsmith, mayor 1576, lieth buried in the vault, under the tomb of John Wells before-named. This chapel, or college, valued to dispend £15, 8s. 9d. by the year, was surrendered amongst other. The chapel remaineth to the mayor and commonalty, wherein they have service weekly, as also at the election of the mayor, and at the mayor's feast, &c.

Adjoining to this chapel, on the south side, was sometime a fair and large library, furnished with books, pertaining to the Guildhall and college. These books, as it is said, were in the reign of Edward VI. sent for by Edward, Duke of Somerset, lord protector, with promise to be restored. Men laded from thence three carries with them, but they were never returned. This library was built by the executors of Richard Whittington, and by William Bury. The arms of Whittington are placed on the one side in the stone work, and two letters, to wit, W. and B., for William Bury, on the other side. It is now lofted through, and made a storehouse for clothes.

South-west from this Guildhall is the fair parish church of St. Lawrence, called in the Jewry, because of old time many Jews inhabited thereabout. This church is fair and large, and hath some monuments, as shall be shown. I myself, more than seventy years since, have seen in this church the shank-bone of a man, as it is taken, and also a tooth, of a very great bigness, hanged up for show in chains of iron, upon a pillar of stone; the tooth, being about the bigness of a man's fist, is long since conveyed from thence; the thigh, or shank-bone, of twenty-five inches in length by the rule, remaineth yet fastened to a post of timber, and is not so much to be noted for the length as for the thickness, hardness, and strength thereof; for when it was hanged on the stone pillar it fretted, with moving, the said pillar, and was not itself fretted, nor, as seemeth, is not yet lightened by remaining dry; but where or when this bone was first found or discovered I have not heard, and therefore, rejecting the fables of some late writers, I overpass them. Walter Blundell had a chantry there, the 14th of Edward II. There lie buried in this church—Elizabeth, wife to John Fortescue; Katherine Stoketon; John Stratton; Philip Albert; John Fleming; Philip Agmondesham; William Skywith; John Norlong; John Baker; Thomas Alleyne; William Barton, mercer, 1410; William Melrith, mercer, one of the sheriffs 1425; Simon Bartlet, mercer, 1428; Walter Chartsey, draper, one of the sheriffs 1430; Richard Rich, esquire, of London, the father, and Richard Rich, his son, mercer, one of the sheriffs 1442, deceased 1469, with this epitaph:—

> " Respice quod ópus est præsentis temporis æuum,—
> Omne quod est, nihil est præter amare Deum."

This Richard was father to John, buried in St. Thomas Acars, which John was father to Thomas, father to Richard Lord Ritch, &c.; John Pickering, honourable for service of his prince and for the English merchants beyond the seas, who deceased 1448;

Godfrey Bollen, mercer, mayor 1457; Thomas Bollen, his son, esquire, of Norfolk, 1471; John Atkenson, gentleman; Dame Mary St. Maure; John Waltham; Roger Bonifant; John Chayhee; John Abbot; Geffrey Filding, mayor 1452, and Angell his wife; Simon Benington, draper, and Joan his wife; John Marshal, mercer, mayor 1493; William Purchat, mayor 1498; Thomas Burgoyne, gentleman, mercer, 1517; the wife of a master of defence, servant to the Princess of Wales, Duchess of Cornwall, and Countess of Chester; Sir Richard Gresham, mayor 1537; Sir Michell Dormer, mayor 1541; Robert Charsey, one of the sheriffs 1548; Sir William Row, ironmonger, mayor 1593; Samuel Thornhill, 1397. Thus much for Cheap Ward, which hath an alderman, his deputy, common councillors eleven, constables eleven, scavengers nine, for the wardmote inquest twelve, and a beadle. It is taxed to the fifteen at £72, 16s., and in the Exchequer at £52, 11s.

Coleman Street Ward.

NEXT to Cheap Ward, on the north side thereof, is Coleman Street Ward, and beginneth also in the east, on the course of Walbrook in Lothbury, and runneth west on the south side to the end of Ironmongers' Lane, and on the north side to the west corner of Bassinges Hall Street.

On the south side of Lothbury is the street called the Old Jewry; the one half, and better on both sides, towards Cheap, is of this ward. On the north side lieth Coleman Street, whereof the ward taketh name, wholly on both sides north to London Wall, and from that north end along by the wall, and Moorgate east, to the course of Walbrook; and again from Coleman Street west to the iron grates. And these be the bounds of this ward.

Antiquities to be noted therein are these: First, the street of Lothburie, Lathburie, or Loadburie, for by all these names have I read it, took the name, as it seemeth, of burie, or court of old time there kept, but by whom is grown out of memory. This street is possessed for the most part by founders, that cast candlesticks, chafing-dishes, spice mortars, and such like copper or latten works, and do afterward turn them with the foot, and not with the wheel, to make them smooth and bright with turning and scrating, as some do term it, making a loathsome noise to the by-passers that have not been used to the like, and therefore by them disdainfully called Lothburie.

On the south side of this street, amongst the founders, be some fair houses and large for merchants, namely, one that of old time was the Jews' synagogue, which was defaced by the citizens of

London, after that they had slain seven hundred Jews, and spoiled the residue of their goods, in the year 1262, the 47th of Henry III. And not long after, in the year 1291, King Edward I. banished the remnant of the Jews out of England, as is afore showed. The said synagogue being so suppressed, certain friars got possession thereof; "for in the year 1257," saith Matthew Paris, "there were seen in London a new order of friars, called *De Pœnitentia Jesu*, or *Fratres de Sacca*, because they were appareled in sackcloth, who had their house in London, near unto Aldersgate without the gate, and had license of Henry III., in the 54th of his reign, to remove from thence to any other place; and in the 56th he gave unto them this Jews' Synagogue. After which time, Eleanor the queen, wife to Edward I., took into her protection, and warranted unto the prior and brethren *De Penitentia Jesu Christi* of London, the said land and building in Colechurch Street, in the parish of St. Olave in the Jewry, and St. Margaret in Lothbury, by her granted, with consent of Stephen de Fulbaurne, under-warden of the Bridge House, and other brethren of that house, for sixty marks of silver, which they had received of the said prior and brethren of repentance, to the building of the said bridge." This order of friars gathered many good scholars, and multiplied in number exceedingly, until the council at Lyons, by the which it was decreed, that from that time forth there should be no more orders of begging friars permitted, but only the four orders; to wit, the Dominicke, or preacher, the Minorites, or grey friars, the Carmelites, or white friars, and the Augustines. And so from that time the begging friars deceased, and fell to nothing.

Now it followed, that in the year 1305, Robert Fitzwalter requested and obtained of the said King Edward I., that the same friars of the Sack might assign to the said Robert their chapel or church, of old time called the Synagogue of the Jews, near adjoining to the then mansion place of the same Robert, which was in place where now standeth the Grocers' Hall; and the said Synagogue was at the north corner of the Old Jewry. Robert Large, mercer, mayor in the year 1439, kept his mayoralty in this house, and dwelt there until his dying day. This house standeth, and is of two parishes, as opening into Lothbury, of St. Margaret's parish, and opening into the Old Jewry, of St. Olave's parish. The said Robert Large gave liberally to both these parishes, but was buried at St. Olave's. Hugh Clopton, mercer, mayor 1492, dwelt in this house, and kept his mayoralty there. It is now a tavern, and hath to sign a windmill. And thus much for this house, sometime the Jews' Synagogue, since a house of friars, then a nobleman's house after that, a merchant's house, wherein mayoralties have been kept, and now a wine tavern.

Then is the Old Jewry, a street so called of Jews sometime dwelling there, and near adjoining, in the parishes of St. Olave, St. Michael Basings Hall, St. Martin Ironmonger Lane, St. Lawrence, called the Jewry, and so west to Wood Street. William, Duke of Normandy, first brought them from Rouen to inhabit here.

William Rufus favoured them so far, that he sware by Luke's face, his common oath, if they could overcome the Christians, he would be one of their sect.

Henry II. grievously punished them for corrupting his coin.

Richard I. forbad Jews and women to be present at his coronation, for fear of enchantments ; for breaking of which commandment many Jews were slain, who being assembled to present the king with some gift, one of them was stricken by a Christian, which some unruly people perceiving, fell upon them, beat them to their houses, and burnt them therein, or slew them at their coming out. Also the Jews at Norwich, St. Edmondsbury, Lincoln, Stamford, and Lynne, were robbed and spoiled ; and at York, to the number of five hundred, besides women and children, entered a tower of the castle, proffered money to be in surety of their lives, but the Christians would not take it, whereupon they cut the throats of their wives and children, and cast them over the walls on the Christians' heads, and then entering the king's lodging, they burnt both the house and themselves.

King John, in the 11th of his reign, commanded all the Jews, both men and women, to be imprisoned and grievously punished, because he would have all their money. Some of them gave all they had, and promised more, to escape so many kinds of torments, for every one of them had one of their eyes at the least plucked out ; amongst whom there was one, which being tormented many ways, would not ransom himself, till the king had caused every day one of his great teeth to be plucked out by the space of seven days, and then gave the king ten thousand marks of silver, to the end they should pull out no more. The said king at that time spoiled the Jews of sixty-six thousand marks.

The 17th of this king, the barons brake into the Jews' houses, rifled their coffers, and with the stone of their houses repaired the gates and walls of London.

King Henry III., in the 11th of his reign, granted to Semayne, or Balaster, the house of Benomye Mittun the Jew, in the parish of St. Michael Bassinghaugh, in which the said Benomye dwelt, with the fourth part of all his land, in that parish which William Elie held of the fee of Hugh Nevell, and all the land in Coleman Street belonging to the said Benomye, and the fourth part of the land in the parish of St. Lawrence, which was the fee of T. Buckerell, and were escheated to the king for the murder which the said Benomye committed in the city of London, to hold to the said Semayne, and his heirs, of the king, paying at Easter a pair of gilt spurs, and to do the service thereof due unto the lord's court. In like manner, and for like services, the king granted to Guso for his homage the other part of the lands of the said Benomye in St. Michael's parish, which lands that Paynter held, and was the king's escheat, and the lands of the said Benomye in the said parish, which Walter Turner held, and fifteen feet of land, which Hugh Harman held, with fifteen iron ells of land, and half in the front of Ironmonger Lane, in the parish of St. Martin, which were the said Benomye's, of the fee of the hospital of St. Giles, and which Adam the smith held, with two stone houses, which were Moses', the Jew of Canterbury, in the parish of St. Olave, and which are of the fee of Arnold le Reus, and are the king's escheats as before said.

The 16th of the said Henry, the Jews in London built a synagogue, but the king demanded it should be dedicated to our Blessed Lady, and after gave it to the brethren of St. Anthony of Vienna, and so was it called St. Anthony's Hospital. This Henry founded a church and house for converted Jews in New Street, by the Temple, whereby it came to pass that in short time there was gathered a great number of converts. The 20th of this Henry, seven Jews were brought from Norwich, which had stolen a christened child, had circumcised, and minded to have crucified him at Easter, wherefore their bodies and goods were at the king's pleasure. The 26th, the Jews were constrained to pay to the king twenty thousand marks, at two terms in the year, or else to be kept in perpetual prison. The 35th, he taketh inestimable sums of money of all rich men, namely, of Aaron, a Jew, born at York, fourteen thousand marks for himself and ten thousand marks for the queen; and before he had taken of the same Jew as much as in all amounted to thirty thousand marks of silver, and two hundred marks of gold to the queen. In the 40th, were brought up to Westminster two hundred and two Jews from Lincoln, for crucifying of a child named Hugh; eighteen of them were hanged. The 43rd, a Jew at Tewkesbury fell into a privy on the Saturday, and would not that day be taken out for reverence of his Sabbath; wherefore Richard Clare, Earl of Gloucester, kept him there till Monday, that he was dead. The 47th, the barons slew the Jews at London seven hundred; the rest were spoiled, and their synagogue defaced, because one Jew would have forced a Christian to have paid more than twopence for the loan of twenty shillings a week.

The 3rd of Edward I., in a parliament at London, usury was forbidden to the Jews; and that all usurers might be known, the king commanded that every usurer should wear a table on his breast, the breadth of a paveline,* or else to avoid the realm. The 6th of the said King Edward a reformation was made for clipping of the king's coin, for which offence two hundred and sixty-seven Jews were drawn and hanged. Three were English Christians, and other were English Jews. The same year the Jews crucified a child at Northampton, for the which fact many Jews at London were drawn at horse-tails and hanged. The 11th of Edward I., John Peckham, Archbishop of Canterbury, commanded the Bishop of London to destroy all the Jews' synagogues in his diocese. The 16th of the said Edward, all the Jews in England were in one day apprehended by precept from the king, but they redeemed themselves for twelve thousand pounds of silver. Notwithstanding, in the 19th of his reign, he banished them all out of England, giving them only to bear their charge, till they were out of his realm. The number of Jews then expulsed were fifteen thousand and sixty persons. The king made a mighty mass of money of their houses, which he sold, and yet the Commons of England had granted and gave him a fifteenth of all their goods to banish them. And thus much for the Jews.

In this said street, called the Old Jewry, is a proper parish church of St. Olave Upwell, so called in record, 1320. John Brian, parson of St. Olave Upwell, in the Jewry, founded there a chantry, and gave two messuages to that parish, the 16th of Edward II., and was by the said king confirmed. In this church, to the commendation of the parsons and parishioners, the monuments of the dead remain less defaced than in many other: first, of William Dikman, ferreno or ironmonger, one of the sheriffs of London 1367 ; Robert Haveloke, ironmonger, 1390 ; John Organ, mercer, one of the sheriffs 1385 ; John Forest, vicar of St. Olave's, and of St. Stephen, at that time as a chapel annexed to St. Olave, 1399 ; H. Friole, tailor, 1400 ; T. Morsted, esquire, chirurgeon to Henry IV., V., and VI., one of the sheriffs 1436—he built a fair new aisle to the enlargement of this church, on the north side thereof, wherein he lieth buried, 1450 ; Adam Breakspeare, chaplain, 1411 ; William Kerkbie, mercer, 1465 ; Robert Large, mercer, mayor 1440—he gave to that church two hundred pounds ; John Belwine, founder, 1467 ; Gabriel Rave, fuller, 1511 ; Wentworth, esquire, 1510 ; Thomas Michell, ironmonger, 1527 ; Giles Dewes, servant to Henry VII. and to Henry VIII., clerk of their libraries, and schoolmaster for the French tongue to Prince Arthur and to the Lady Mary, 1535 ; Richard Chamberlaine, ironmonger, one of the sheriffs 1562 ; Edmond Burlacy, mercer, 1583 ; John Brian, &c.

From this parish church of St. Olave to the north end of the

* *Paveline* pennon

Old Jewry, and from thence west to the north end of Ironmongers' Lane, and from the said corner into Ironmongers' Lane almost to the parish church of St. Martin, was of old time one large building of stone, very ancient, made in place of Jews' houses, but of what antiquity, or by whom the same was built, or for what use, I have not learnt, more than that King Henry VI., in the 16th of his reign, gave the office of being porter or keeper thereof unto John Stent for term of his life, by the name of his principal palace in the Old Jewry. This was in my youth called the Old Wardrope, but of later time the outward stone wall hath been by little and little taken down, and divers fair houses built thereupon, even round about.

Now for the north side of this Lothbury, beginning again at the east end thereof, upon the watercourse of Walbrook, have ye a proper parish church called St. Margaret, which seemeth to be newly re-edified and built about the year 1440; for Robert Large gave to the choir of that church one hundred shillings and twenty pounds for ornaments. More, to the vaulting over the watercourse of Walbrook by the said church, for the enlarging thereof two hundred marks.

There be monuments in this church of Reginald Coleman, son to Robert Coleman, buried there 1483. This said Robert Coleman may be supposed the first builder or owner of Coleman Street, and that St. Stephen's Church, then built in Coleman Street, was but a chapel belonging to the parish church of St. Olave in the Jewry; for we read as afore that John Forest, vicar of St. Olave's, and of the chapel annexed of St. Stephen, deceased in the year 1399. Hugh Clotpon, mercer, mayor, deceased 1496; John Dimocke, Anselme Becker, John Julian, and William Ilford, chantries there; Sir Brian Tuke, knight, treasurer of the chamber to King Henry VIII., and Dame Grisilde his wife, that deceased after him, were there buried 1536; John Fetiplace, draper, esquire, 1464, and Joan his wife; Sir Hugh Witch, mercer, mayor, son to Richard Witch, entombed there 1466—he gave to his third wife three thousand pounds, and to maids' marriages five hundred marks; Sir John Leigh, 1564, with this epitaph :—

> "No wealth, no prayse, no bright renowne, no skill,
> No force, no fame, no princes loue, no toyle,
> Though forraigne land by trauell search ye will,
> No faithfull seruice of the country soyle,
> Can life prolong one minute of an houre,
> But death at length will execute his power;
> For Sir John Leigh to sundry countries knowne,
> A worthy knight well of his prince esteemde,
> By seeing much, to great experience growne,
> Though safe on seas, though sure on land he seemde,
> Yet here he lyes too soone by death opprest,
> His fame yet liues, his soule in heauen doth rest."

By the west end of this parish church have ye a fair water conduit, built at the charges of the city in the year 1546, Sir Martin Bowes being mayor. Two fifteens were levied of the citizens toward the charges thereof. This water is conveyed in great abundance from divers springs lying betwixt Hoxton and Iseldon.

Next is the Founders' Hall, a proper house, and so to the south-west corner of Basinghall Street have ye fair and large houses for merchants—namely, the corner house at the end of Basinghall Street, an old piece of work, built of stone, sometime belonging to a certain Jew named Mansere, the son of Aaron, the son of Coke the Jew, the 7th of Edward I.; since to Rahere de Sopar's Lane, then to Simon Francis. Thomas Bradbery, mercer, kept his mayoralty there; deceased 1509. Part of this house hath been lately employed as a market-house for the sale of woollen baize, wat-mols,* flannels, and such like. Alderman Bennet now possesseth it.

On this north side against the Old Jewry is Coleman Street, so called of Coleman, the first builder and owner thereof; as also of Colechurch, or Coleman Church, against the great conduit in Cheap. This is a fair and large street, on both sides built with divers fair houses, besides alleys, with small tenements in great number. On the east side of this street, almost at the north end thereof, is the Armourers' Hall, which company of armourers were made a fraternity or guild of St. George, with a chantry in the chapel of St. Thomas in Paul's Church, in the first of Henry VI. Also on the same side is King's Alley and Love Lane, both containing many tenements; and on the west side, towards the south end, is the parish church of St. Stephen, wherein the monuments are defaced. Notwithstanding, I find that William Crayhag founded a chantry there in the reign of Edward II., and was buried there; also John Essex, the 35th of Edward III.; Adam Goodman, the 37th of Edward III.; William King, draper, sometime owner of King's Alley, the 18th of Richard II.; John Stokeling, the 10th of Henry VI.; John Arnold, leather seller, the 17th of Henry VI.; Thomas Bradbery, mercer, mayor, the 1st of Henry VIII.—his tomb remaineth on the north side the choir; Richard Hamney, 1418; Kirnigham, 1468; Sir John Garme; Richard Colsel; Edmond Harbeke, currier. All these were benefactors, and buried there. This church was sometime a synagogue of the Jews, then a

---

* *Watmol*, wadmal, a coarse woollen stuff. The name is of northern origin. Its first syllable is equivalent to the "wad" in wadding. Icelandic vath is a piece of cloth rough from the loom, and the Icelandic compound "vathmál" (our wadmal) is the name of a coarse woollen stuff. Prof. Skeat suggests that our "wad" is a shortened form of "wadmal," and not from the old Swedish "wad" clothing. Wadmal was the name given also to a coarse tow used by horse-doctors.

parish church, then a chapel to St Olave's in the Jewry, until the 7th of Edward IV., and was then incorporated a parish church.

By the east end of this church is placed a cock of sweet water, taken of the main pipe that goeth into Lothbury. Also in London Wall, directly against the north end of Coleman Street, is a conduit of water, made at the charges of Thomas Exmew, goldsmith, mayor 1517. And let here be the end of this ward, which hath an alderman, his deputy, common councillors four, constables four, scavengers four, of the wardmote inquest thirteen, and a beadle. It is taxed to the fifteen at £15, 16s. 9d.

Basinghall Ward.

THE next adjoining to Coleman Street, on the west side thereof, is Basinghall Ward, a small thing, and consisteth of one street called Basinghall Street, of Basing Hall, the most principal house whereof the ward taketh name. It beginneth in the south by the late spoken market-house called the Bay Hall, which is the last house of Coleman Street Ward. This street runneth from thence north down to London Wall, and some little distance, both east and west, against the said hall; and this is the bound of Basinghall Ward.

Monuments on the east side thereof, amongst divers fair houses for merchants, have ye three halls of companies—namely, the Masons' Hall for the first, but of what antiquity that company is I have not read. The next is the Weavers' Hall, which company hath been of great antiquity in this city, as appeareth by a charter of Henry II., in these words, *Rex omnibus ad quos*, &c., to be Englished thus:—

" Henrie, king of England, duke of Normandie, and of Guien, Earl of Anjou, to the bishop, justices, shiriffes, barons, ministers, and all his true lieges of London, sendeth greeting : Know ye that we have granted to the weavers in London their guild, with all the freedomes and customes that they had in the time of King Henrie my grandfather, so that none but they intermit within the citie of their craft but he be of their guild, neither in Southwark, or other places pertaining to London, otherwise than it was done in the time of King Henrie my grandfather ; wherefore I will and straightly commaund that over all lawfully they may treate, and have all aforesaid, as well in peace, free, worshipfull, and wholy, as they had it, freer, better, worshipfullier, and wholier, than in the time of King Henrie my grandfather, so that they yeeld yearely to mee two markes of gold at the feast of St. Michaell ; and I forbid that any man to them do any unright, or disseise, upon paine of ten pound. Witnes, Thomas of Canterburie, Warwicke fili Gar, Chamberlaine at Winchester."

Also I read, that the same Henry II., in the 31st of his reign, made a confirmation to the weavers that had a guild or fraternity in London, wherein it appeareth that the said weavers made woollen cloth, and that they had the correction thereof; but amongst other articles in that patent, it was decreed, that if any man made cloth of Spanish wool, mixed with English wool, the portgrave, or principal magistrate of London, ought to burn it, &c.

Moreover, in the year 1197, King Richard I., at the instance of Hubert, Archbishop of Canterbury, and Justicier of England, ordained that the woollen cloths in every part of this realm should be in breadth two yards within the lists, and as good in the midst as in the sides, &c. King Henry III. granted that they should not be vexed, for the burels, or cloth listed, according to the constitution made for breadth of cloth the 9th of his reign, &c. Richard II., in the 3rd of his reign, granted an order of agreement between the weavers of London, Englishmen, and aliens, or strangers born, brought in by Edward III.

Lower down is the Girdlers' Hall, and this is all touching the east side of this ward.

On the west side, almost at the south end thereof, is Bakewell Hall, corruptly called Blackewall Hall, concerning the original whereof I have heard divers opinions, which I overpass as fables without colour of truth ; for though the same seemed a building of great antiquity, yet in mine opinion the foundation thereof was first laid since the conquest of William, Duke of Normandy ; for the same was built upon vaults of stone, which stone was brought from Caen in Normandy, the like of that of Paul's Church, built by Mauritius and his successors, bishops of London ; but that this house hath been a temple or Jewish synagogue (as some have fantasied) I allow not, seeing that it had no such form of round-ness or other likeness, neither had it the form of a church for the assembly of Christians, which are built east and west, but con-trariwise the same was built north and south, and in form of a nobleman's house ; and therefore the best opinion in my judgment is, that it was of old time belonging to the family of the Bassings, which was in this realm a name of great antiquity and renown, and that it bare also the name of that family, and was called therefore Bassings Haugh, or Hall. Whereunto I am the rather induced, for that the arms of that family were of old time so abundantly placed in sundry parts of that house, even in the stone-work, but more especially on the walls of the hall, which carried a continual paint-ing of them on every side, so close together as one escutcheon could be placed by another, which I myself have often seen and noted before the old building was taken down. These arms were a gyronny * of twelve points, gold and azure. Of the Bassings,

---

* *Gyronny, gyronnée*, divided after the manner of a gyron. And a gyron is defined in heraldry as "half of the first quarter of the shield, that quarter being divided diagonally by a line drawn from the dexter chief."

therefore, builders of this house and owners of the ground near adjoining, that ward taketh the name, as Coleman Street Ward of Coleman, and Farringdon Ward of William and Nicholas Farringdon, men that were principal owners of those places.

And of old time the most noble persons that inhabited this city were appointed to be principal magistrates there, as was Godfrey de Magun, or Magnavile, portgrave or sheriff in the reign of William Conqueror and of William Rufus; Hugh de Buch, in the reign of Henry I.; Aubery de Vere, Earl of Oxford; after him, Gilbert Becket, in the reign of King Stephen; after that, Godfrey de Magnavile, the son of William, the son of Godfrey de Magnavile, Earls of Essex, were portgraves or sheriffs of London and Middlesex. In the reign of Henry II., Peter Fitzwalter; after him, John Fitznigel, &c.; so likewise in the reign of King John, the 16th of his reign, a time of great troubles, in the year 1214, Salomon Bassing and Hugh Bassing, barons of this realm, as may be supposed, were sheriffs; and the said Salomon Bassing was mayor in the year 1216, which was the 1st of Henry III. Also Adam Bassing, son to Salomon, as it seemeth, was one of the sheriffs in the year 1243, the 28th of Henry III.

Unto this Adam de Bassing King Henry III., in the 31st of his reign, gave and confirmed certain messuages in Aldermanbury, and in Milk Street (places not far from Basinghall), the advowson of the church at Basinghall, with sundry liberties and privileges.

This man was afterwards mayor in the year 1251, the 36th of Henry III. Moreover, Thomas Bassing was one of the sheriffs 1269; Robert Bassing, sheriff 1279; and William Bassing was sheriff 1308, &c. For more of the Bassings in this city I need not note, only I read of this family of Bassings in Cambridgeshire, called Bassing at the Bourn, and more shortly Bassingbourn, and gave arms, as is afore showed, and was painted about this old hall. But this family is worn out, and hath left the name to the place where they dwelt. Thus much for this Basinghall.

Now how Bakewell Hall took that name is another question; for which I read that Thomas Bakewell dwelt in this house in the 36th of Edward III.; and that in the 20th of Richard II., the said king, for the sum of fifty pounds, which the mayor and commonalty had paid into the hanaper, granted license so much as was in him to John Frosh, William Parker, and Stephen Spilman, citizens and mercers, that they, the said messuage called Bakewell Hall, and one garden, with the appurtenances, in the parish of St. Michael of Basinghaugh, and of St. Laurence in the Jewry of London, and one messuage, two shops, and one garden in the said parish of St. Michael, which they held of the king in burgage, might give and assign to the mayor and commonalty for ever. This Bakewell Hall, thus established, hath been long since employed as a weekly market-place for all sorts of woollen cloths, broad and narrow, brought from all parts of this realm, there to be sold. In the 21st of Richard II., R. Whittington, mayor, and in the 22nd, Drengh Barringtine being mayor, it was decreed that no foreigner or stranger should sell any woollen cloth but in the Bakewell Hall, upon pain of forfeiture thereof.

This house of late years growing ruinous, and in danger of falling, Richard May, merchant tailor, at his decease gave towards the new building of the outward part thereof three hundred pounds, upon condition that the same should be performed within three years after his decease. Whereupon the old Bakewell Hall was taken down, and in the month of February next following, the foundation of a new, strong, and beautiful storehouse being laid, the work thereof was so diligently applied, that within the space of ten months after, to the charges of two thousand five hundred pounds, the same was finished in the year 1588.

Next beyond this house be placed divers fair houses for merchants and others, till ye come to the back gate of Guildhall, which gate and part of the building within the same is of this ward. Some small distance beyond this gate the Coopers have their common hall. Then is the parish church of St. Michael, called St. Michael at Basinghall, a proper church lately re-edified or new built, whereto John Barton, mercer, and Agnes his wife, were great benefactors, as appeareth by his mark placed throughout the whole roof of the choir and middle aisle of the church. He deceased in the year 1460, and was buried in the choir, with this epitaph:—

> " John Barton lyeth vnder here,
> Sometimes of London, citizen and mercere,
> And Ienet his wife, with their progenie,
> Beene turned to earth as ye may see:
> Friends free what so ye bee,
> Pray for vs we you pray,
> As you see vs in this degree,
> So shall you be another day."

Frances Cooke, John Martin, Edward Bromflit, esquire, of Warwickshire, 1460; Richard Barnes, Sir Roger Roe, Roger Velden, 1479; Sir James Yarford, mercer, mayor, deceased 1526, buried under a fair tomb with his lady in a special chapel by him built on the north side of the choir; Sir John Gresham, mercer, mayor, deceased 1554; Sir John Ailife, chirurgeon, then a grocer, one of the sheriffs 1548; Nicholas Bakhurst, one of the sheriffs 1577; Wolston Dixi, skinner, mayor 1585, &c. Thus have you noted one parish church of St. Michael; Bakewell Hall, a market-place for woollen cloths; the Masons' Hall, Weavers' Hall, Cordellers' Hall, and Coopers' Hall.   And thus I end this ward, which hath an alderman, his deputy, for common council four, constables two, scavengers two, for the wardmote inquest seventeen, and a beadle.   It is taxed to the fifteen in London at seven pounds, and likewise in the Exchequer at seven pounds.

Cripplegate Ward.

THE next ward is called of Cripplegate, and consisteth of divers streets and lanes, lying as well without the gate and wall of the city as within.   First within the wall, on the east part thereof, towards the north, it runneth to the west side of Basinghall Ward, and towards the south it joineth to the ward of Cheap.   It beginneth at the west end of St. Laurence Church in the Jewry, on the north side, and runneth west to a pump, where sometime was a well with two buckets, at the south corner of Aldermanbury Street; which street runneth down north to Gayspurre Lane, and so to London Wall, which street and lane are wholly on both sides of this ward, and so be some few houses on both the sides from Gayspurre Lane, by and against the wall of the city, east to the grates made for the watercourse of the channels, and west to Cripplegate.   Now on the south side, from over against the west end of St. Laurence Church to the pump, and then by Milk Street south unto Cheap, which Milk Street is wholly on both the sides of Cripplegate Ward, as also without the south end of Milk Street, a part of West Cheap, to wit, from the Standard to the Cross, is all of Cripplegate Ward. Then down Great Wood Street, which is wholly of this ward on both the sides thereof; so is Little Wood Street, which runneth down to Cripplegate.

Out of this Wood Street be divers lanes—namely, on the east side is Lad Lane, which runneth east to Milk Street corner; down lower in Wood Street is Love Lane, which lieth by the south side of St. Alban's Church in Wood Street, and runneth down to the Conduit in Aldermanbury Street.   Lower down in Wood Street is Addle Street, out of the which runneth Philip Lane down to London Wall.   These be the lanes on the east side.

On the west side of Wood Street is Huggen Lane, by the south side of St. Michael's Church, and goeth through to Gutheron's Lane.   Then lower is Maiden Lane, which runneth west to the north end of Gutheron's Lane, and up the said lane on the east side thereof, till against Kery Lane, and back again.   Then the said Maiden Lane on the north side goeth up to Staining Lane, and up a part thereof on the east side to the farthest north part of Haberdashers' Hall, and back again to Wood Street; and there lower down is Silver Street, which is of this ward, till ye come to the east end of St. Olave's Church on the south side, and to Monkswell Street on the north side; then down the said Monkswell Street on the east side thereof, and so to Cripplegate, do make the bounds of this ward within the walls.

Without Cripplegate, Fore Street runneth thwart before the gate, from against the north side of St. Giles' Church, along to Moor Lane end, and to a Postern Lane end that runneth betwixt the town ditch on the south and certain gardens on the north almost to Moorgate. At the east of which lane is a pot-maker's house, which house, with all other the gardens, houses, and alleys on that side the Moorfields, till ye come to a bridge and cow-house near unto Finsbury Court, is all of Cripplegate Ward. Then to turn back again through the said Postern Lane to Moor Lane, which Moor Lane, with all the alleys and buildings there, is of this ward. After that is Grub Street, more than half thereof to the straitening of the street. Next is Whitecross Street, up to the end of Bech Lane, and then Redcross Street wholly, with a part of Golding Lane, even to the posts there placed as a bounder.

There is Bech Lane before spoken of, on the east side of the Redcross and the Barbican Street, more than half thereof toward Aldersgate Street; and so have you all the bounds of Cripplegate Ward without the walls.

Now for antiquities and ornaments in this ward to be noted, I find first, at the meeting of the corners of the Old Jewry, Milk Street, Lad Lane, and Aldermanbury, there was of old time a fair well with two buckets, of late years converted to a pump. How Aldermanbury Street took that name many fables have been bruited, all which I overpass as not worthy the counting; but to be short, I say, this street took the name of Alderman's bury (which is to say a court), there kept in their bury, or court, but now called the Guildhall; which hall of old time stood on the east side of the same street, nor far from the west end of Guildhall, now used. Touching the antiquity of this old Alderman's bury or court, I have not read other than that Richard Renery, one of the sheriffs of London in the 1st of Richard I., which was in the year of Christ 1189, gave to the Church of St. Mary at Osney, by Oxford, certain ground and rents in Aldermanbury of London, as appeareth by the register of that church, as is also entered into the hoistings of the Guildhall in London. This old bury court or hall continued, and the courts of the mayor and aldermen were continually holden there, until the new bury court, or Guildhall that now is, was built and finished; which hall was first begun to be founded in the year 1411, and was not fully finished in twenty years after. I myself have seen the ruins of the old court hall in Aldermanbury Street, which of late hath been employed as a carpenter's yard, &c.

In this Aldermanbury Street be divers fair houses on both the sides, meet for merchants or men of worship, and in the midst thereof is a fair conduit, made at the charges of William Eastfield, sometime mayor, who took order as well for water to be conveyed from Tyborne, and for the building of this Conduit, not far distant from his dwelling-house, as also for a Standard of sweet water to be erected in Fleet Street, all which was done by his executors, as in another place I have showed.

Then is the parish church of St. Mary Aldermanbury, a fair church, with a churchyard and cloister adjoining, in the which cloister is hanged and fastened a shank-bone of a man, as is said, very great, and larger by three inches and a half than that which hangeth in St. Laurence Church in the Jewry, for it is in length twenty-eight inches and a half of assise, but not so hard and steel-like as the other, for the same is light, and somewhat pory and spongy. This bone is said to be found amongst the bones of men removed from the charnel-house of Paul's, or rather from the cloister of Paul's Church; of both which reports I doubt, for that the late Reyne Wolfe, stationer, who paid for the carriage of those bones from the charnel to the Moorfields, told me of some thousands of carry loads and more to be conveyed, whereof he wondered, but never told me of any such bone in either place to be found; neither would the same have been easily gotten from him if he had heard thereof, except he had reserved the like for himself, being the greatest preserver of antiquities in those parts for his time. True it is, that this bone, from whence soever it came, being of a man, as the form showeth, must needs be monstrous, and more than after the proportion of five shank-bones of any man now living amongst us.

There lie buried in this church—Simon Winchcombe, esquire, 1391; Robert Combarton, 1422; John Wheatley, mercer, 1428; Sir William Estfild, knight of the bath, mayor 1438, a great benefactor to that church, under a fair monument. He also built their steeple, changed their old bells into five tuneable bells, and gave one hundred pounds to other works of that church. Moreover, he caused the Conduit in Aldermanbury, which he had begun, to be performed at his charges, and water to be conveyed by pipes of lead from Tyborne to Fleet Street, as I have said; and also from Highbury to the parish of St. Giles without Cripplegate, where the inhabitants of those parts encastellated the same in sufficient cisterns. John Middleton, mercer, mayor 1472; John Tomes, draper, 1486; William Buckle, tailor, 1501; Sir William Browne, mayor 1507; Dame Margaret Jeninges, wife to Stephen Jeninges, mayor 1515; a widow named Starkey, sometime wife to Modie; Raffe Woodcock, grocer, one of the sheriffs 1586; Dame Mary Gresham, wife to Sir John Gresham, 1538; Thomas Godfrey, remembrancer of the office of the first fruits, 1577.

Beneath this church have ye Gayspur Lane, which runneth down to London Wall, as is afore showed. In this lane, at the north end thereof, was of old time a house of nuns; which house being in great decay, William Elsing, mercer, in the year of Christ 1329, the 3rd of Edward III., began in place thereof the foundation of an hospital for sustentation of one hundred blind men, towards the erection whereof he gave his two houses in the parishes of St. Alphage, and our Blessed Lady in Aldermanbury, near Cripplegate. This house was after called a priory, or hospital, of St. Mary the Virgin, founded in the year 1332 by W. Elsing, for canons regular; the which William became the first prior there. Robert Elsing, son to the said William, gave to the hospital twelve pounds by the year for the finding of three priests. He also gave one hundred shillings towards the enclosing of the new churchyard without Aldgate, and one hundred shillings to the enclosing of the new churchyard without Aldersgate; to Thomas Elsing, his son, eighty pounds; the rest of his goods to be sold and given to the poor. This house, valued £193, 15s. 5d., was surrendered the eleventh of May, the 22nd of Henry VIII.

The monuments that were in this church defaced:—Thomas Cheney, son to William Cheney; Thomas, John, and William Cheney; John Northampton, draper, mayor 1381; Edmond Hungerford; Henry Frowike; Joan, daughter to Sir William Cheney, wife to William Stoke; Robert Eldarbroke, esquire, 1460; Dame Joan Ratcliffe; William Fowler; William Kingstone; Thomas Swineley, and Helen his wife, &c. The principal aisle of this church towards the north was pulled down, and a frame of four houses set up in place. The other part, from the steeple upward, was converted into a parish church of St. Alphage; and the parish church which stood near unto the wall of the city by Cripplegate was pulled down, the plot thereof made a carpenter's yard, with saw-pits. The hospital itself, the prior and canons' house, with other lodgings, were made a dwelling-house. The churchyard is a garden plot, and a fair gallery on the cloister. The lodgings for the poor are translated into stabling for horses.

In the year 1541, Sir John Williams, master of the king's jewels, dwelling in this house, on Christmas even at night, about seven of the clock, a great fire began in the gallery thereof, which burned so sore that the flame firing the whole house and consuming it, was seen all the city over, and was hardly quenched, whereby many of the king's jewels were burnt, and more embezzled, as was said. Sir Rowland Heyward, mayor, dwelt in this Spital, and was buried there 1593; Richard Lee, *alias* Clarencieux king of arms, 1597.

Now to return to Milk Street, so called of milk sold there; there be many fair houses for wealthy merchants and other, amongst the which I read, that Gregory Rokesley, chief assay master of the king's mints, and mayor of London in the year 1275, dwelt in this Milk Street, in a house belonging to the priory of Lewes in Sussex, whereof he was tenant at will, paying twenty shillings by the year, without other charge: such were the rents of those times.

In this Milk Street is a small parish church of St. Mary Magdalen, which hath of late years been repaired. William Browne, mayor 1513, gave to this church forty pounds, and was buried there; Thomas Exmew, mayor 1528, gave forty pounds, and was buried there; so was John Milford, one of the sheriffs 1375; John Olney, mayor 1475; Richard Rawson, one of the sheriffs 1476; Henry Kelsey; Sir John Browne, mayor 1497; Thomas Muschampe, one of the sheriffs 1463; Sir William Cantilo, knight, mercer, 1462; Henry Cantlow, mercer, merchant of the Staple, who built a chapel, and was buried there 1495; John West, alderman, 1517; John Machell, alderman, 1558; Thomas Skinner, clothworker, mayor 1596.

Then next is Wood Street, by what reason so called I know not. True it is, that of old time, according to a decree made in the reign of Richard I., the houses in London were built of stone for defence of fire, which kind of building was used for two hundred years or more, but of later time, for the winning of ground, taken down and houses of timber set up in place. It seemeth therefore that this street hath been of the latter building, all of timber, for not one house of stone hath been known there, and therefore called Wood Street, otherwise it might take the name of some builder or owner thereof.

Thomas Wood, one of the sheriffs in the year 1491, dwelt there. He was an especial benefactor towards the building of St. Peter's Church at Wood Street end. He also built the beautiful front of houses in Cheap over against Wood Street end, which is called Goldsmiths' Row, garnished with the likeness of woodmen. His predecessors might be the first builders, owners, and namers of this street after their own name.

On the east side of this street is one of the prison houses pertaining to the sheriffs of London, and is called the Compter in Wood Street, which was prepared to be a prison house in the year 1555; and on the eve of St. Michael the Archangel, the prisoners that lay in the Compter in Bread Street were removed to this Compter in Wood Street. Beneath this Compter is Lad Lane, or Ladle Lane, for so I find it of record in the parish of St. Michael Wood Street; and beneath that is Love Lane, so called of wantons.

By this lane is the parish church of St. Alban, which hath the monuments of Sir Richard Illingworth, baron of the exchequer; Thomas Chatworth, grocer, mayor 1443; John Woodcocke, mayor 1405; John Colet, and Alice his wife; Ralph Thomas; Ralph and Richard, sons of Ralph Illingworth, which was son to Sir Richard Illingworth, baron of the exchequer; Thomas, son of Sir Thomas Fitzwilliams; Thomas Halton, mercer, mayor 1450; Thomas Ostrich, haberdasher, 1483; Richard Swetenham, esquire; and William Dunthorne, town-clerk of London, with this epitaph:—

> " *Fœlix prima dies postquam mortalibus ævi*
> *Cesserit, hic morbus subit, atque repente senectus.*
> *Tum mors, qua nostrum Dunthorn cecidisse Wilelmum,*
> *Haud cuiquam latuisse reor dignissimus (inquam),*
> *Artibus hic Doctor, necnon celeberrimus hujus*
> *Clericus Urbis erat, primus, nullique secundus,*
> *Moribus, ingenio, studio, nil dixeris illi,*
> *Quin dederit natura boni, pius ipse, modestus,*
> *Longanimus, solers, patiens, super omnia gratus,*
> *Quique sub immensas curas variosque labores,*
> *Anxius atteritur vitæ, dum carpserit auras,*
> *Hoc tetro in tumulo compostus pace quiescit.*"

Simon Morsted; Thomas Pikehurst, esquire; Richard Take; Robert Ashcombe; Thomas Lovet, esquire, sheriff of Northamptonshire 1491; John Spare; Katheren, daughter to Sir Thomas Mirley, knight; William Linchlade, mercer, 1392; John Penie, mercer, 1450; John Thomas, mercer, 1485; Christopher Hawse, mercer, one of the sheriffs 1503; William Scarborough, vintner; Simon de Berching; Sir John Cheke, knight, schoolmaster to King Edward VI., deceased 1557, do lie here.

Then is Adle Street, the reason of which name I know not, for at this present it is replenished with fair buildings on both sides, amongst the which there was sometime the Pinners' Hall, but that company being decayed, it is now the Plasterers' Hall.

Not far from thence is the Brewers' Hall, a fair house, which company of Brewers was incorporated by King Henry VI., in the 16th of his reign, confirmed by the name of St. Mary and St. Thomas the Martyr, the 19th of Edward IV.

From the west end of this Adle Street, Little Wood Street runneth down to Cripplegate; and somewhat east from the Sun Tavern, against the wall of the city, is the Curriers' Hall.

Now on the west side of Wood Street have ye Huggen Lane, so called of one Hugan that of old time dwelt there. He was called

Hugan in the Lane, as I have read in the 34th of Edward I. This lane runneth down by the south side of St. Michael's Church in Wood Street, and so growing very narrow by means of late encroachments to Gutheron's Lane.

The parish church of St. Michael in Wood Street is a proper thing, and lately well repaired. John Ive, parson of this church, John Forster, goldsmith, and Peter Fikelden, tailor, gave two messuages, and two shops, with solars, cellars, and other edifices, in the same parish and street, and in Ladle Lane, to the reparations of the church, chancel, and other works of charity, the 16th of Richard II.

The monuments here be of William Bambrough, the son of Henry Bambrough of Scarborough, 1392; William Turner, waxchandler, 1400; John Peke, goldsmith, 1441; William Taverner, girdler, 1454; William Mancer, ironmonger, 1465; John Nash, 1466, with an epitaph; John Allen, timbermonger, 1441; Robert Draper, 1500; John Lambarde, draper, alderman, one of the sheriffs of London, who deceased 1554, and was father to my loving friend William Lambarde, esquire, well known by sundry learned books that he hath published; John Medley, chamberlain of London; John Marsh, esquire, mercer, and common sergeant of London, &c. There is also, but without any outward monument, the head of James, the fourth king of Scots of that name, slain at Flodden field, and buried here by this occasion: After the battle the body of the said king being found, was enclosed in lead, and conveyed from thence to London, and so to the monastery of Shene in Surrey, where it remained for a time, in what order I am not certain; but since the dissolution of that house, in the reign of Edward VI., Henry Grey, Duke of Suffolk, being lodged, and keeping house there, I have been shown the same body so lapped in lead, close to the head and body, thrown into a waste room amongst the old timber, lead, and other rubble. Since the which time workmen there, for their foolish pleasure, hewed off his head; and Launcelot Young, master glazier to her majesty, feeling a sweet savour to come from thence, and seeing the same dried from all moisture, and yet the form remaining, with the hair of the head, and beard red, brought it to London to his house in Wood Street, where for a time he kept it for the sweetness, but in the end caused the sexton of that church to bury it amongst other bones taken out of their charnel, &c.

I read in divers records of a house in Wood Street, then called Black Hall, but no man at this day can tell thereof.

On the north side of this St. Michael's Church is Maiden Lane, now so called, but of old time Ingene Lane, or Ing Lane. In this lane the Wax-chandlers have their common hall, on the south side thereof; and the Haberdashers have their like hall on the north side, at Staining Lane end. This company of Haberdashers, or Hurrers, of old time so called, were incorporated a brotherhood of St. Katherine, the 26th of Henry VI., and so confirmed by Henry VII., the 17th of his reign, the Cappers and Hat Merchants, or Hurrers,* being one company of Haberdashers.

Down lower in Wood Street is Silver Street (I think of silver-smiths dwelling there), in which be divers fair houses.

And on the north side thereof is Monkswell Street, so called of a well at the north end thereof, where the Abbot of Garendon had a house, or cell, called St. James-in-the-Wall by Cripplegate, and certain monks of their house were the chaplains there, wherefore the well, belonging to that cell or hermitage, was called Monks' Well, and the street, of the well, Monkswell Street.

The east side of this street, down against London Wall, and the south side thereof to Cripplegate, be of Cripplegate Ward, as is afore shown. In this street, by the corner of Monkswell Street, is the Bowyers' Hall. On the east side of Monkswell Street be proper almshouses, twelve in number, founded by Sir Ambrose Nicholas, salter, mayor 1575, wherein be placed twelve poor and aged people rent free, having each of them sevenpence the week, and once the year each of them five sacks of charcoal, and one quarter of a hundred fagots, of his gift, for ever.

Then in Little Wood Street be seven proper chambers in an alley on the west side, founded for seven poor people therein to dwell rent free, by Henry Barton, skinner, mayor 1416. Thus much for the monuments of this ward within the walls.

Now without the postern of Cripplegate, first is the parish church of St. Giles, a very fair and large church, lately repaired, after that the same was burnt in the year 1545, the 37th of Henry VIII., by which mischance the monuments of the dead in this church are very few, notwithstanding I have read of these following :—Alice, William, and John, wife and sons to T. Clarell ; Agnes, daughter to Thomas Niter, gentleman ; William Atwell ; Felix, daughter to Sir Thomas Gisors, and wife to Thomas Travars ; Thomas Mason, esquire ; Edmond Wartar, esquire ; Joan, wife to John Chamberlaine, esquire, daughter to Roger Lewkner ; William Fryer ; John Hamberger, esquire ; Hugh Moresbye ; Gilbert Prince, alderman ; Oliver Cherley,

* *Hurrers.* "Hure," a hood, cap, or other head covering ; often a graduate's cap, or a cap of estate. In First English "hufe" was a head covering, in Piers Plowman "houve," in the Promptorium Parvulorum "howe," or "hure," and again as "hwyr, cappe." The source of the word, however, is the old French "hure," the hair covering the head of men or animals, their natural cap in the first instance.

gentleman ; Sir John Wright or Writhesley, *alias* Garter king-at-arms ; Joan, wife to Thomas Writhesley, Garter, daughter and heir to William Hal, esquire ; John Writhesley, the younger, son to Sir John Writhesley and Alianor ; Alianor, second wife to John Writhesley, daughter and heir to Thomas Arnold, sister and heir to Richard Arnold, esquire ; John, her son and heir ; Margaret, with her daughter ; John Brigget ; Thomas Ruston, gentleman ; John Talbot, esquire, and Katheren his wife ; Thomas Warfle, and Isabel his wife ; Thomas Lucie, gentleman, 1447 ; Ralph Rochford, knight, 1409 ; Edmond Watar, esquire ; Elizabeth, wife to Richard Barnes, sister and heir to Richard Malgrave, esquire, of Essex ; Richard Gowre, and John Gowre, esquires ; John Baronie, of Millain, 1546 ; Sir Henry Grey, knight, son and heir to George Grey, Earl of Kent, 1562, Reginald Grey, Earl of Kent ; Richard Choppin, tallow-chandler, one of the sheriffs 1530 ; John Hamber, esquire, 1573 ; Thomas Hanley, *alias* Clarenciaux king-at-arms ; Thomas Busby, cooper, who gave the Queen's Head Tavern to the relief of the poor in the parish, 1575 ; John Whelar, goldsmith, 1575 ; Richard Bolene, 1563 ; William Bolene, 1575 ; W. Bolene, physician, 1587 ; Robert Crowley, vicar there—all these four under one old stone in the choir ; the learned John Foxe, writer of the Acts and Monuments of the English Church, 1587 ; the skilful Robert Glover, *alias* Somerset herald, 1588.

There was in this church of old time a fraternity or brotherhood of Our Blessed Lady, or Corpus Christi, and St. Giles, founded by John Belancer, in the reign of Edward III., the 35th year of his reign.

Some small distance from the east end of this church is a water conduit, brought in pipes of lead from Highbury, by John Middleton, one of the executors to Sir William Eastfield, and of his goods. The inhabitants adjoining castellated it of their own cost and charges about the year 1483.

There was also a bosse of clear water in the wall of the church-yard, made at the charges of Richard Whittington, sometime mayor, and was like to that of Billingsgate. Of late the same was turned into an evil pump, and so is clean decayed.

There was also a fair pool of clear water near unto the parsonage, on the west side thereof, which was filled up in the reign of Henry VI. The spring was coped in, and arched over with hard stone, and stairs of stone to go down to the spring on the bank of the town ditch. And this was also done of the goods and by the executors of Richard Whittington.

In White Cross Street King Henry V. built one fair house, and founded there a brotherhood of St. Giles, to be kept, which house had sometime been an hospital of the French order, by the name of St. Giles without Cripplegate, in the reign of Edward I., the king having the jurisdiction and appointing a custos thereof for the precinct of the parish of St. Giles, &c., patent Richard II., the 15th year, which hospital being suppressed, the lands were given to the brotherhood for the relief of the poor.

One alley of divers tenements over against the north wall of St. Giles' Churchyard was appointed to be almshouses for the poor, wherein they dwelt rent free, and otherwise were relieved ; but the said brotherhood was suppressed by Henry VIII., since which time Sir John Gresham, Mayor, purchased the lands, aud gave part thereof to the maintenance of a free school which he had founded at Holt, a market town in Norfolk.

In Red Cross Street, on the west side from St. Giles' Churchyard up to the said cross, be many fair houses built outward, with divers alleys turning into a large plot of ground called the Jews' Garden, as being the only place appointed them in England wherein to bury their dead till the year 1177, the 24th of Henry II., that it was permitted to them, after long suit to the king and parliament at Oxford, to have a special place assigned them in every quarter where they dwelt. This plot of ground remained to the said Jews till the time of their final banishment out of England, and is now turned into fair garden plots and summer-houses for pleasure.

On the east side of this Red Cross Street be also divers fair houses up to the cross. And there is Beech Lane, peradventure so called of Nicholas de la Beech, lieutenant of the Tower of Lon- don, put out of that office in the 13th of Edward III. This lane stretcheth from the Red Cross Street to White Cross Street, re-plenished, not with beech trees, but with beautiful houses of stone, brick, and timber, amongst the which was of old time a great house, pertaining to the Abbot of Ramsey, for his lodging when he repaired to the city. It is now called Drewry House, of Sir Drewe Drewry, a worshipful owner thereof.

On the north side of this Beech Lane, towards White Cross Street, the Drapers of London have lately built eight almshouses of brick and timber, for eight poor widows of their own company, whom they have placed there rent free, according to the gift of Lady Askew, widow to Sir Christopher Askew, sometime draper, and mayor 1533.

Then in Golding Lane, Richard Gallard of Islington, esquire, citizen and painter-stainer of London, founded thirteen almshouses for so many poor people placed in them rent free. He gave to the poor of the same almshouses twopence the piece weekly, and a load of charcoal amongst them yearly for ever. He left fair lands about Islington to maintain his foundation. Thomas Hayes, sometime chamberlain of London, in the latter time of Henry VIII., married Elizabeth, his daughter and heir, which Hayes and Elizabeth had a daughter named Elizabeth, married to John Ironmonger of London, mercer, who now hath the order of the almspeople.

On the west side of the Red Cross is a street, called the Barbican, because sometime there stood on the north side thereof a burgh-kenning, or watch-tower of the city, called in some language a barbican, as a bikenning is called a beacon. This burgh-kenning, by the name of the Manor of Base Court, was given by Edward III. to Robert Ufford, Earl of Suffolk, and was lately appertaining to Peregrine Barty, Lord Willoughby of Eresby.

Next adjoining to this is one other great house, called Garter House, sometime built by Sir Thomas Writhe, or Writhesley, knight, *alias* Garter principal king of arms, second son of Sir John Writhe, knight, *alias* Garter, and was uncle to the first Thomas, Earl of Southampton, knight of the Garter, and chancellor of England. He built this house, and in the top thereof a chapel, which he dedicated by the name of St. Trinitatis in Alto.

Thus much for that part of Cripplegate Ward without the wall, whereof more shall be spoken in the suburb of that part. This ward hath an alderman and his deputy within the gate, common council eight, constables nine, scavengers twelve, for wardmote inquest fifteen, and a beadle. Without the gate it hath also a deputy, common council two, constables four, scavengers four, wardmote inquest seventeen, and a beadle. It is taxed in London to the fifteen at forty pounds.

Aldersgate Ward.

THE next is Aldersgate Ward, taking name of that north gate of the city. This ward also consisteth of divers streets and lanes, lying as well within the gate and wall as without. And first to speak of that part within the gate, thus it is.

The east part thereof joineth unto the west part of Cripplegate Ward in Engain Lane, or Maiden Lane. It beginneth on the north side of that lane, at Staining Lane end, and runneth up from the Haberdashers' Hall to St. Mary Staining Church, and by the church east winding almost to Wood Street, and west through Oate Lane, and then by the south side of Bacon House in Noble Street back again by Lilipot Lane, which is also of that ward, to Maiden Lane, and so on that north side west to St. John Zachary's Church, and to Foster Lane.

Now on the south side of Engain or Maiden Lane is the west side of Gutheron's Lane to Kery Lane, and Kery Lane itself, which is of this ward, and back again into Engain Lane, by the north side of the Goldsmiths' Hall to Foster Lane; and this is the east wing of this ward. Then is Foster Lane almost wholly of this ward, beginneth in the south toward Cheap, on the east side by the north side of St. Foster's Church, and runneth down north-west by the west end of Engain Lane, by Lilipot Lane and Oate Lane to Noble Street, and through that by Shelley House, of old time so called, as belonging to the Shelleys. Sir Thomas Shelley, knight, was owner thereof in the 1st of Henry IV. It is now called Bacon House, because the same was new built by Sir Nicholas Bacon, lord keeper of the great seal. Down on that side by Sergeant Fleetwood's House, recorder of London, who also new built it, to St. Olave's Church in Silver Street, which is by the north-west end of this Noble Street.

Then again in Foster Lane this ward beginneth on the west side thereof, over against the south-west corner of St. Foster's Church, and runneth down by St. Leonard's Church, by Pope Lane end, and by St. Ann's Lane end, which lane is also of this ward, north to the stone wall by the wall of the city, over against Bacon House, which stone wall, and so down north to Cripplegate on that side, is of Farringdon Ward.

Then have ye the main street of this ward, which is called St. Martin's Lane, including St. Martin, on the east side thereof, and so down on both the sides to Aldersgate. And these be the bounds of this ward within the wall and gate.

Without the gate the main street called Aldersgate Street runneth up north on the east side to the west end of Hounsditch, or Barbican Street, a part of which street is also of this ward; and on the west side to Long Lane, a part whereof is likewise of this ward. Beyond the which Aldersgate Street is Goswell Street up to the bars.

And on this west side of Aldersgate Street, by St. Botolph's Church, is Briton Street, which runneth west to a pump, and then north to the gate which entereth the churchyard sometime pertaining to the priory of St. Bartholomew on the east side; and on the west side towards St. Bartholomew's Spital, to a pair of posts there fixed. And these be the bounds of this Aldersgate Ward without.

The antiquities be these, first in Staining Lane, of old time so called, as may be supposed, of painter-stainers dwelling there.

On the east side thereof, adjoining to the Haberdashers' Hall, be ten almshouses, pertaining to the Haberdashers, wherein be placed ten almspeople of that company, every of them having eightpence the piece every Friday for ever, by the gift of Thomas Huntlow, haberdasher, one of the sheriffs in the year 1539. More, Sir George Baron gave them ten pounds by the year for ever.

Then is the small parish church of St. Mary, called Staining, because it standeth at the north end of Staining Lane. In the which church, being but newly built, there remains no monument worth the noting.

Then is Engain Lane, or Maiden Lane, and at the north-west corner thereof the parish church of St. John Zachary—a fair church, with the monuments well preserved, of Thomas Lichfield, who founded a chantry there in the 14th of Edward II. ; of Sir Nicholas Twiford, goldsmith, mayor 1388, and Dame Margery his wife, of whose goods the church was made and new built, with a tomb for them, and others of their race, 1390; Drugo Barentine, mayor 1398. He gave fair lands to the Goldsmiths. He dwelt right against the Goldsmiths' Hall, between the which hall and his dwelling-house he built a gallery thwarting the street, whereby he might go from one to the other. He was buried in this church, and Christian his wife, 1427. John Adis, goldsmith, 1400, and Margaret his wife; John Francis, goldsmith, mayor 1400, and Elizabeth his wife, 1450; I. Sutton, goldsmith, one of the sheriffs 1413; Bartholomew Seman, goldbeater, master of the king's mints within the Tower of London and the town of Calais, 1430; John Hewet, esquire, 1500; William Breakespere, goldsmith, 1461; Christopher Eliot, goldsmith, 1505; Bartholomew Reade, goldsmith, mayor 1502, was buried in the Charterhouse, and gave to this his parish church one hundred pounds. His wife was buried here with a fair monument, her picture in habit of a widow. Thomas Keyton Lorimar, 1522; William Potken, esquire, 1537; John Cornish, with an epitaph, 1470; Robert Fenruther, goldsmith, one of the sheriffs in the year 1512.

On the east side of this Foster Lane, at Engain Lane end, is the Goldsmiths' Hall, a proper house, but not large; and therefore to say that Bartholomew Read, goldsmith, mayor in the year 1502, kept such a feast in this hall, as some have fabled, is far incredible, and altogether impossible, considering the smallness of the hall, and number of the guests, which, as they say, were more than a hundred persons of great estate. For the messes and dishes of meats to them served, the paled park in the same hall furnished with fruitful trees, beasts of venery, and other circumstances of that pretended feast, well weighed, Westminster Hall would hardly have sufficed; and therefore I will overpass it, and note somewhat of principal goldsmiths.

First I read, that Leofstane, goldsmith, was provost of this city in the reign of Henry I. Also, that Henry Fitz Alewin Fitz Leafstane, goldsmith, was mayor of London in the first of Richard I., and continued mayor twenty-four years. Also that Gregory Rocksly, chief say-master * of all the king's mints within England, and there-fore by my conjecture a goldsmith, was mayor in the 3rd of Edward I., and continued mayor seven years together. Then William Farringdon, goldsmith, alderman of Farringdon Ward, one of the sheriffs 1231, the 9th of Edward I., who was a goldsmith, as appeareth in record, as shall be shown in Farringdon Ward. Then Nicholas Farringdon his son, goldsmith, alderman of Farringdon Ward, four times mayor in the reign of Edward II., &c. For the rest of latter time are more manifestly known, and therefore I leave them. The men of this mystery were incorporated or confirmed in the 16th of Richard II.

Then at the north end of Noble Street is the parish church of St. Olave in Silver Street, a small thing, and without any noteworthy monuments.

On the west side of Foster Lane is the small parish church of St. Leonard's, for them of St. Martin's le Grand. A number of tenements being lately built in place of the great collegiate church of St. Martin, that parish is mightily increased. In this church remain these monuments. First, without the church is graven in stone on the east end, John Brokeitwell, an especial re-edifier, or new builder thereof. In the choir, graven in brass, Robert Purfet, grocer, 1507; Robert Trapis, goldsmith, 1526, with this epitaph :—

> " When the bels be merily roong,
> And the masse devoutly sung,
> And the meat merily eaten,
> Then shall Robert Trips, his wives
> And children be forgotten."

Then in Pope Lane, so called of one Pope that was owner thereof, on the north side of the parish church of St. Anne in the Willows, so called, I know not upon what occasion, but some say of willows growing thereabouts ; but now there is no such void place for willows to grow, more than the churchyard, wherein do grow some high ash trees.

This church, by casualty of fire in the year 1548, was burnt, so far as it was combustible, but since being newly repaired, there remain a few monuments of antiquity : of Thomas Beckhenton, clerk of the pipe, was buried there 1499 ; Ralph Caldwell, gentleman, of Gray's Inn, 1527 ; John Lord Sheffelde ; John Herenden, mercer, esquire, 1572. These verses on an old stone : †—

> Qu an   tris   di   c   vul   stra
>   os   guis   ti   ro um nere   uit
>   h san   Chris mi t   mu   la

---

* *Say,* assay.
† " *Quos anguis tristi diro cum vulnere stravit,*
    Hos sanguis Christi miro tum munere lavit."

William Gregory, skinner, mayor of London in the year 1451, was there buried, and founded a chantry, but no monument of him remaineth.

Then in St. Martin's Lane was of old time a fair and large college of a dean and secular canons or priests, and was called St. Martin's le Grand, founded by Ingelricus and Edwardus his brother, in the year of Christ 1056, and confirmed by William the Conqueror, as appeareth by his charter dated 1068. This college claimed great privileges of sanctuary and otherwise, as appeareth in a book, written by a notary of that house about the year 1442, the 19th of Henry VI., wherein, amongst other things, is set down and declared, that on the 1st of September, in the year aforesaid, a soldier, prisoner in Newgate, as he was led by an officer towards the Guildhall of London, there came out of Panyer Alley five of his fellowship, and took him from the officer, brought him into sanctuary at the west door of St. Martin's Church, and took grith of that place; but the same day Philip Malpas and Rob. Marshall, then sheriffs of London, with many other, entered the said church, and forcibly took out with them the said five men thither fled, led them fettered to the Compter, and from thence, chained by the necks, to Newgate. Of which violent taking the dean and chapter in large manner complained to the king, and required him, as their patron, to defend their privileges, like as his predecessors had done, &c. All which complaint and suit the citizens by their counsel, Markam, sergeant at the law, John Carpenter, late common clerk of the city, and other, learnedly answered, offering to prove that the said place of St. Martin had no such immunity or liberty as was pretended; namely, Carpenter offered to lose his livelihood, if that church had more immunity than the least church in London. Notwithstanding, after long debating of this controversy, by the king's commandment and assent of his council in the starred chamber, the chancellor and treasurer sent a writ unto the sheriffs of London, charging them to bring the said five persons with the cause of their taking and withholding afore the king in his Chancery, on the vigil of Allhallows. On which day the said sheriffs, with the recorder and counsel of the city, brought and delivered them accordingly afore the said lords; whereas the chancellor, after he had declared the king's commandment, sent them to St. Martin's, there to abide freely, as in a place having franchises, whiles them liked, &c.

Thus much out of that book have I noted concerning the privilege of that place challenged in these days, since the which time, to wit, in the year 1457, the 36th of the said Henry VI., an ordinance was made by the king and his council concerning the said sanctuary men in St. Martin's le Grand, whereof the articles are set down in the book of K., within the chamber of the Guildhall, in the lease 299.

This college was surrendered to King Edward VI., the 2nd of his reign, in the year of Christ 1548; and the same year the college church being pulled down, in the east part thereof a large wine tavern was built, and withal down to the west, and throughout the whole precinct of that college, many other houses were built and highly prized, letten to strangers born, and other such as there claimed benefit of privileges granted to the canons serving God day and night, for so be the words in the charter of William the Conqueror, which may hardly be wrested to artificers, buyers and sellers, otherwise than is mentioned in the 21st of St. Matthew's Gospel.

Lower down on the west side of St. Martin's Lane, in the parish of St. Anne, almost by Aldersgate, is one great house, commonly called Northumberland House. It belonged to H. Percy. King Henry IV., in the 7th of his reign, gave this house, with the tenements thereunto appertaining, to Queen Jane his wife, and then it was called her Wardrobe. It is now a printing house.

Without Aldersgate, on the east side of Aldersgate Street, is the Cooks' Hall; which Cooks, or Pastelars, were admitted to be a company, and to have a master and wardens, in the 22nd of Edward IV. From thence along into Hounsditch, or Barbican Street, be many fair houses. On the west side also be the like fair buildings till ye come to Long Lane, and so to Goswell Street.

In Briton Street, which took that name of the Dukes of Brittany lodging there, is one proper parish church of St. Botolph, in which church was sometime a brotherhood of St. Fabian and Sebastian, founded in the year 1377, the 51st of Edward III., and confirmed by Henry IV., in the 6th of his reign. Then Henry VI., in the 24th of his reign, to the honour of the Trinity, gave license to Dame Joan Astley, sometime his nurse, to R. Cawod and T. Smith, to found the same a fraternity, perpetually to have a master and two custoses, with brethren and sisters, &c. This brotherhood was endowed with lands more than thirty pounds by the year, and was suppressed by Edward VI. There lie buried, John de Bath, weaver, 1390; Philip at Vine, capper, 1396; Benet Gerard, brewer, 1403; Thomas Bilsington founded a chantry there, and gave to that church a house, called the Helmet upon Cornhill; John Bradmore, chirurgeon, Margaret and Katheren his wives, 1411; John Michaell, sergeant-at-arms, 1415; Allen Bret, carpenter, 1425; Robert Malton, 1426; John Trigilion, brewer, 1417; John Mason, brewer, 1431; Rob. Cawood, clerk of the pipe in the king's exchequer, 1466; Ri. Emmessey; John Walpole; I. Hartshorne, esquire, servant to the king, 1400, and other of that family, great benefactors to that church ; W. Marrow, grocer, mayor, and Katherine his wife, were buried there about 1468. The Lady Ann Packington, widow, late wife to Jo. Packington, knight, chirographer of the court of the common pleas. She founded almshouses near unto the White Friars' Church in Fleet Street. The Clothworkers in London have oversight thereof.

And thus an end of this ward, which hath an alderman, his deputy, common councillors five, constables eight, scavengers nine, for the wardmote inquest fourteen, and a beadle. It is taxed to the fifteen in London seven pounds, and in the exchequer six pounds nineteen shillings.

Farringdon Ward, infra or within.

ON the south side of Aldersgate Ward lieth Farringdon Ward, called *infra* or within, for a difference from another ward of that name, which lieth without the walls of the city, and is therefore called Farringdon *extra*. These two wards of old time were but one, and had also but one alderman, till the 17th of Richard II., at which time the said ward, for the greatness thereof, was divided into twain, and by parliament ordered to have two aldermen, and so it continueth till this day. The whole great ward of Farringdon, both *infra* and *extra*, took name of W. Farringdon, goldsmith, alderman of that ward, and one of the sheriffs of London in the year 1281, the 9th of Edward I. He purchased the aldermanry of this ward, as by the abstract of deeds, which I have read thereof, may appear.

"Thomas de Arderne, son and heir to Sir Ralph Arderne, knight, granted to Ralph le Fevre, citizen of London, one of the sheriffs in the year 1277, all the aldermanry, with the appurtenances within the city of London, and the suburbs of the same between Ludgate and Newgate, and also without the same gates. Which aldermanry Ankerinus de Averne held during his life, by the grant of the said Thomas de Arderne, to have and to hold to the said Ralph, and to his heirs, freely without all challenge, yielding therefore yearly to the said Thomas and his heirs one clove or slip of gilliflowers, at the feast of Easter, for all secular service and customs, with warranty unto the said Ralph le Fevre and his heirs, against all people, Christians and Jews, in consideration of twenty marks, which the said Ralph le Fevre did give beforehand, in name of a gersum * or fine, to the said Thomas, &c., dated the 5th of Edward I. Witness, G. de Rokesley, mayor ; R. Arrar, one of the sheriffs ; H. Wales,

---

* *Gersum.* First English "gersuma," treasure, riches, compensation. Icelandic "gör-semi," usually "ger-semi," from "gör," a prefix meaning quite, and perhaps "sama" to beseem, befit.

P. le Taylor, T. de Basing, I. Horne, N. Blackthorn, aldermen of London." After this, John le Fevre, son and heir to the said Ralph le Fevre, granted to William Farringdon, citizen and goldsmith of London, and to his heirs, the said aldermanry, with the appurtenances, for the service thereunto belonging, in the 7th of Edward I., in the year of Christ 1279. This aldermanry descended to Nicholas Farringdon, son to the said William, and to his heirs ; which Nicholas Farringdon, also a goldsmith, was four times mayor, and lived many years after, for I have read divers deeds, whereunto he was a witness, dated the year 1360. He made his testament 1361, which was fifty-three years after his first being mayor, and was buried in St. Peter's Church in Cheap. So this ward continued under the government of William Farringdon the father, and Nicholas his son, by the space of eighty-two years, and retaineth their name until this present day.

This ward of Farringdon within the walls is bounded thus : Beginning in the east, at the great cross in West Cheap, from whence it runneth west. On the north side from the parish church of St. Peter, which is at the south-west corner of Wood Street, on to Gutheron's Lane, and down that lane to Hugon Lane on the east side, and to Kery Lane on the west.

Then again into Cheap and to Foster Lane, and down that lane on the east side to the north side of St. Foster's Church, and on the west till over against the south-west corner of the said church, from whence down Foster Lane and Noble Street is all of Aldersgate Street Ward, till ye come to the stone wall, in the west side of Noble Street, as is afore showed. Which said wall, down to Nevil's Inn or Windsor House, and down Monkswell Street, on that west side, then by London wall to Cripplegate, and the west side of that same gate, is all of Farringdon Ward.

Then back again into Cheap, and from Foster Lane end to St. Martin's Lane end, and from thence through St. Nicholas Shambles, by Pentecost Lane and Butchers' Alley, and by Stinking Lane through Newgate Market to Newgate. All which is the north side of Farringdon Ward.

On the south, from against the said great cross in Cheap west to Friday Street, and down that street on the east side till over against the north-east corner of St. Matthew's Church ; and on the west side till the south corner of the said church.

Then again along Cheap to the Old Exchange, and down that lane on the east side to the parish church of St. Augustine, which church, and one house next adjoining in Watheling Street, be of this ward, and on the west side of this lane, to the east arch or gate by St. Augustine's Church, which entereth the south churchyard of St.

Paul's, which arch or gate was built by Nicholas Farringdon about the year 1361, and within that gate, on the said north side, to the gate that entereth the north churchyard, and all the north churchyard is of this Farringdon Ward.

Then again into Cheap, and from the north end of the Old Exchange, west by the north gate of Paul's Churchyard, by Paternoster Row, by the two lanes out of Paul's Church, and to a sign of the Golden Lion, which is some twelve houses short of Ave Mary Lane, the west side of which lane is of this ward.

Then at the south end of Ave Mary Lane is Creed Lane, the west side whereof is also of this ward.

Now betwixt the south end of Ave Mary Lane and the north end of Creed Lane is the coming out of Paul's Churchyard on the east, and the high street called Bowier Row to Ludgate on the west, which way to Ludgate is of this ward. On the north side whereof is St. Martin's Church, and on the south side a turning into the Blackfriars.

Now to turn up again to the north end of Ave Mary Lane, there is a short lane which runneth west some small distance, and is there closed up with a gate into a great house; and this is called Amen Lane.

Then on the north side of Paternoster Row, beginning at the Conduit over against the Old Exchange Lane end, and going west by St. Michael's Church, at the west end of which church is a small passage through towards the north; and beyond this church some small distance is another passage, which is called Paniar Alley, and cometh out against St. Martin's Lane end.

Then further west in Paternoster Row is Ivy Lane, which runneth north to the west end of St. Nicholas Shambles; and then west Paternoster Row, till over against the Golden Lion, where the ward endeth for that street.

Then about some dozen houses, which is of Baynard's Castle Ward, to Warwick Lane end, which Warwick Lane stretcheth north to the high street of Newgate Market. And the west side of Warwick Lane is of this Farringdon Ward; for the east side of Warwick Lane, of Ave Mary Lane, and of Creed Lane, with the west end of Paternoster Row, are all of Baynard's Castle Ward.

Yet to begin again at the said Conduit by the Old Exchange, on the north side thereof is a large street that runneth up to Newgate, as is aforesaid, the first part or south side whereof, from the Conduit to the shambles, is called Bladder Street. Then on the back side of the shambles be divers slaughterhouses, and such like, pertaining to the shambles; and this is called Mount Godard Street. Then is the shambles itself, and then Newgate Market; and so the whole street, on both sides up to Newgate, is of this ward; and thus it is wholly bounded.

Monuments in this ward be these: First, the great cross in West Cheap Street, but in the ward of Farringdon; the which cross was first erected in that place by Edward I., as before is showed in West Cheap Street.

At the south-west corner of Wood Street is the parish church of St. Peter the Apostle by the said cross, a proper church lately new built. John Sha, goldsmith, mayor, deceased 1508, appointed by his testament the said church and steeple to be newly built of his goods, with a flat roof; notwithstanding, Thomas Wood, goldsmith, one of the sheriffs 1491, is accounted principal benefactor, because the roof of the middle aisle is supported by images of woodmen. I find to have been buried on this church—Nicholas Farringdon, mayor; Richard Hadley, grocer, 1592; John Palmer, fishmonger, 1500; William Rus, goldsmith, sheriff 1429; T. Atkins, esquire, 1400; John Butler, sheriff 1420; Henry Warley, alderman, 1524; Sir John Monday, goldsmith, mayor, deceased 1537; Augustine Hinde, clothworker, one of the sheriffs in the year 1550, whose monument doth yet remain, the others be gone; Sir Alexander Auenon, mayor 1570.

The long shop, or shed, encroaching on the high street before this church wall was licensed to be made in the year 1401, yielding to the chamber of London thirty shillings and fourpence yearly for the time, but since thirteen shillings and fourpence. Also the same shop was letten by the parish for three pounds at the most, many years since.

Then is Gutheron's Lane, so called of Gutheron, sometime owner thereof. The inhabitants of this lane of old time were goldbeaters, as doth appear by records in the exchequer; for the easterling money was appointed to be made of fine silver, such as men made into foil, and was commonly called silver of Gutheron's Lane, &c. The Embroiderers' Hall is in this lane. John Throwstone, embroiderer, then goldsmith, sheriff, deceased 1519, gave forty pounds towards the purchase of this hall. Hugon Lane on the east side, and Kery Lane, called of one Kery, on the west.

Then in the high street on the same north side is the Saddlers' Hall, and then Fauster Lane, so called of St. Fauster's, a fair church lately new built. Henry Coote, goldsmith, one of the sheriffs, deceased 1509, built St. Dunstan's Chapel there. John Throwstone, one of the sheriffs, gave to the building thereof one hundred pounds by his testament. John Browne, sergeant painter, alderman, deceased 1532, was a great benefactor, and was there buried. William Trist, cellarer to the king, 1425, John Standelfe, goldsmiths, lie buried there; Richard Galder, 1544; Agnes, wife to William Milborne, chamberlain of London, 1500, &c.

Then down Foster Lane and Noble Street, both of Aldersgate street Ward, till ye come to the stone wall which encloseth a garden plot before the wall of the city, on the west side of Noble Street, and is of this Farringdon Ward. This garden-plot, containing ninety-five ells in length, nine ells and a half in breadth, was by Adam de Bury, mayor, the aldermen, and citizens of London, letten to John de Nevil, Lord of Raby, Radulph and Thomas his sons, for sixty years, paying 6s. 8d. the year, dated the 48th of Edward III., having in a seal pendant on the one side the figure of a walled city and of St. Paul, a sword in his right hand, and in the left a banner; three leopards about that seal, on the same side, written, *Sigillum Baronium Londoniarum.* On the other side, the like figure of a city, a bishop sitting on an arch; the inscription, *Me : quae : te : peperi : ne : cesses : Thoma : tueri.* Thus much for the barons of London, their common seal at that time. At the north end of this garden-plot is one great house built of stone and timber, now called the Lord Windsor's house, of old time belonging to the Nevils, as in the 19th of Richard II. it was found by inquisition of a jury, that Elizabeth Nevil died, seised of a great messuage in the parish of St. Olave, in Monkswell Street in London, holding of the king in free burgage, which she held of the gift of John Nevil of Raby, her husband, and that John Latimer was next son and heir to the said Elizabeth.

In this west side is the Barbers-Chirurgeons' Hall. This company was incorporated by means of Thomas Morestede, esquire, one of the sheriffs of London 1436, chirurgeon to the kings of England, Henry IV., V., and VI. He deceased 1450. Then Jaques Fries, physician to Edward IV., and William Hobbs, physician and chirurgeon for the same king's body, continuing the suit the full time of twenty years, Edward IV., in the 2nd of his reign, and Richard, Duke of Gloucester, became founders of the same corporation in the name of St. Cosme and St. Damiane. The first assembly of that craft was Roger Strippe, W. Hobbs, T. Goddard, and Richard Kent, since the which time they built their hall in that street, &c.

At the north corner of this street, on the same side, was sometime an hermitage or chapel of St. James, called in the wall, near Cripplegate. It belonged to the abbey and convent of Garadon, as appeareth by a record, the 27th of Edward I., and also the 16th of Edward III. William de Lions was hermit there, and the abbot and convent of Geredon found two chaplains, Cistercian monks of their house, in this hermitage—one of them for Aymer de Valence, Earl of Pembroke, and Mary de Saint Paule, his countess.

Of these monks, and of a well pertaining to them, the street took that name, and is called Monkswell Street. This hermitage, with the appurtenances, was in the reign of Edward VI. purchased from the said king by William Lambe, one of the gentlemen of the king's chapel, citizen and clothworker of London. He deceased in the year 1577, and then gave it to the Clothworkers of London, with other tenements to the value of fifty pounds the year, to the intent they shall hire a minister to say divine service there, &c.

Again to the high street of Cheap, from Fauster Lane end to St. Martin's, and by that lane to the shambles or flesh-market, on the north side whereof is Pentecost Lane, containing divers slaughter-houses for the butchers.

Then was there of old time a proper parish church of St. Nicholas, whereof the said fleshmarket took the name, and was called St. Nicholas' Shambles. This church, with the tenements and ornaments, was by Henry VIII. given to the mayor and commonalty of the city, towards the maintenance of the new parish church then to be erected in the late dissolved church of the Grey Friars. So was this church dissolved and pulled down. In place whereof, and of the churchyard, many fair houses are now built in a court with a well, in the midst whereof the church stood.

Then is Stinking Lane, so called, or Chick Lane, at the east end of the Grey Friars Church, and there is the Butchers' Hall.

In the 3rd of Richard II. motion was made that no butcher should kill no flesh within London, but at Knightsbridge, or such like distance of place from the walls of the city.

Then the late dissolved church of the Grey Friars, the original whereof was this :—

The first of this order of friars in England, nine in number, arrived at Dover. Five of them remained at Canterbury ; the other four came to London, were lodged at the Preaching Friars in Oldborne for the space of fifteen days, and then they hired a house in Cornhill of John Trevers, one of the sheriffs of London. They built there little cells, wherein they inhabited ; but shortly after, the devotion of citizens towards them, and the number of the friars so increased, that they were by the citizens removed to a place in St. Nicholas' Shambles, which John Ewin, mercer, appropriated unto the commonalty, to the use of the said friars, and himself became a lay brother amongst them. About the year 1225, William Joyner built their choir, Henry Walles the body of the church, Walter Potter, alderman, the chapter-house, Gregory Rokesley their dorter ; Bartholomew of the Castle made the refectory, Peter de Heliland made the infirmitory, Bevis Bond, king of heralds, made the study, &c.

Margaret, queen, second wife to Edward I., began the choir of their new church in the year 1306 ; to the building whereof, in her lifetime, she gave two thousand marks, and one hundred marks by her testament. John Britaine, Earl of Richmond, built the body of the church to the charges of three hundred pounds, and gave many rich jewels and ornaments to be used in the same ; Marie, Countess of Pembroke, seventy pounds. Gilbert de Clare, Earl of Gloucester, bestowed twenty great beams out of his forest of Tunbridge, and twenty pounds sterling. Lady Helianor le Spencer, Lady Elizabeth de Burgh, sister to Gilbert de Clare, gave sums of money; and so did divers citizens, as Arnald de Tolinea, one hundred pounds; Robert, Baron Lisle, who became a friar there, three hundred pounds; Bartholomew de Almaine, fifty pounds. Also Philippa, queen, wife to Edward III., gave sixty-two pounds; Isabel, queen, mother to Edward III., gave threescore and ten pounds. And so the work was done within the space of twenty-one years, 1337. This church was furnished with windows made at the charges of divers persons. The Lady Margaret Segrave, Countess of Norfolk, bare the charges of making the stalls in the choir, to the value of three hundred and fifty marks, about the year 1330. Richard Whittington, in the year 1429, founded the library, which was in length one hundred and twenty-nine feet, and in breadth thirty-one, all ceiled with wainscot, having twenty-eight desks and eight double settles of wainscot, which in the next year following was altogether finished in building, and within three years after furnished with books, to the charges of five hundred and fifty-six pounds ten shillings. Whereof Richard Whittington bare four hundred pounds. The rest was borne by Doctor Thomas Winchelsey, a friar there; and for the writing out of D. Nicholas de Lira, his works, in two volumes, to be chained there, one hundred marks, &c. The ceiling of the choir at divers men's charges, two hundred marks, and the painting at fifty marks; their conduit head and watercourse given them by William Tailor, tailor to Henry III., &c.

The whole church containeth in length three hundred feet, of the feet of St. Paul; in breadth eighty-nine feet; and in height from the ground to the roof sixty-four feet and two inches, &c. It was consecrated 1325, and at the general suppression was valued at thirty-two pounds nineteen shillings, surrendered the 12th of November 1538, the 30th of Henry VIII., the ornaments and goods being taken to the king's use. The church was shut up for a time, and used as a storehouse for goods taken prizes from the French; but in the year 1546, on the 3rd of January, was again set open. On the which day preached at Paul's Cross the Bishop of Rochester, where he declared the king's gift thereof to the city for the relieving of the poor. Which gift was by patent—of St. Bartholomew's Spital, lately valued at three hundred and five pounds six shillings and sevenpence, and surrendered to the king; of the said church of the Grey Friars, and of two parish churches, the one of St. Nicholas in the shambles, and the other of St. Ewines in Newgate Market, which were to be made one parish church in the said Friars Church;

and in lands he gave for maintenance for the said church, with divine service, reparations, &c., five hundred marks by year for ever.

The 13th of January, the 38th of Henry VIII., an agreement was made betwixt the king and the mayor and commonalty of London, dated the 27th of December, by which the said gift of the Grey Friars Church, with all the edifices and ground, the fratry, the library, the dorter, and chapter-house, the great cloister and the lesser, tenements, gardens, and vacant grounds, lead, stone, iron, &c., the hospital of St. Bartholomew in West Smithfield, the church of the same, the lead, bells, and ornaments of the same hospital, with all the messuages, tenements, and appurtenances; the parishes of St. Nicholas and of St. Ewin, and so much of St. Sepulchre's parish as is within Newgate, were made one parish church in the Grey Friars Church, and called Christ's Church, founded by Henry VIII.

The vicar of Christ's Church was to have twenty-six pounds thirteen shillings and fourpence the year; the vicar of St. Bartholomew thirteen pounds six shillings and eightpence; the visitor of Newgate, being a priest, ten pounds; and other five priests in Christ's Church, all to be helping in Divine service, ministering the sacraments and sacramentals; the five priests to have eight pounds the piece, two clerks six pounds each, a sexton four pounds. Moreover, he gave them the hospital of Bethelem, with the laver of brass in the cloister, by estimation eighteen feet in length, and two feet and a half in depth; and the watercourse of lead, to the said Friar House belonging, containing by estimation in length eighteen acres.

In the year 1552 began the repairing of the Grey Friars House for the poor fatherless children; and in the month of November the children were taken into the same, to the number of almost four hundred. On Christmas Day, in the afternoon, while the lord mayor and aldermen rode to Paul's, the children of Christ's Hospital stood, from St. Lawrence Lane end in Cheap towards Paul's, all in one livery of russet cotton, three hundred and forty in number; and in Easter next they were in blue at the Spital, and so have continued ever since.

The defaced monuments in this church were these: First in the choir, of the Lady Margaret, daughter to Philip, king of France, and wife to Edward I., foundress of this new church, 1317; of Isabel, queen, wife to Edward II., daughter to Philip, king of France, 1358; John of the Tower; Queen of Scots, wife to David Bruce, daughter to Edward II., died in Hartford Castle, and was buried by Isabel her mother 1362; William Fitzwarren, baron, and Isabel his wife, sometime Queen of Man; Isabel, daughter to Edward III., wedded

to the Lord Courcy of France, after created Earl of Bedford ; Elianor,
wife to John, Duke of Britaine ; Beatrix, Duchess of Britaine, daughter
to Henry III. ; Sir Robert Lisle, baron ; the Lady Lisle, and Margaret de Rivers, Countess of Devon, all under one stone ; Roger
Mortimer, Earl of March, beheaded 1329 ; Peter, Bishop of Cardon
in Hungary, 1331 ; Gregory Rocksley, mayor 1282 ; Sir John
Devereux, knight, 1385 ; John Hastings, Earl of Pembroke, 1389 ;
Margaret, daughter to Thomas Brotharton, Earl Marshal. She was
Duchess of Norfolk, and Countess Marshal and Lady Segrave, 1389.
Richard Havering, knight, 1388 ; Robert Trisilian, knight justice,
1308 ; Geffrey Lucy, son to Geffrey Lucy ; John Anbry, son to John,
mayor of Norwich, 1368 ; John Philpot, knight, mayor of London,
and the Lady Jane Samford his wife, 1384 ; John, Duke of Bourbon,
and Anjou, Earl of Claremond, Montpensier, and Baron Beaujeu,
who was taken prisoner at Agincourt, kept prisoner eighteen years,
and deceased 1433 ; Robert Chalons, knight, 1439 ; John Chalons ;
Margaret, daughter to Sir John Philpot, first married to T. Santlor,
esquire, and after to John Neyband, esquire ; Sir Nicholas Brimbar,
mayor of London, buried 1386 ; Elizabeth Nevel, wife to John, son
and heir to Ralph, Earl of Westmoreland, and mother to Ralph, Earl
of Westmoreland, and daughter to Thomas Holland, Earl of Kent,
1423 ; Edward Burnell, son to the Lord Burnell. In Allhallows
Chapel : James Fines, Lord Say, 1450, and Helinor his wife, 1452 ;
John Smith, Bishop of Landafe, 1478 ; John, Baron Hilton ; John,
Baron Clinton ; Richard Hastings, knight, Lord of Willowby and
Welles ; Thomas Burdet, esquire, beheaded 1477 ; Robert Lisle,
son and heir to the Lord Lisle. In our Lady's Chapel : John Gisors,
of London, knight ; Humphrey Stafford, esquire, of Worcestershire,
1486 ; Robert Bartram, Baron of Bothell ; Ralph Barons, knight ;
William Apleton, knight ; Reynold de Cambrey, knight ; Thomas
Beaumont, son and heir to Henry Lord Beaumont ; John Butler,
knight ; Adam de Howton, knight, 1417 ; Bartholomew Caster,
knight of London ; Reinfride Arundele, knight, 1460 ; Thomas Covil,
esquire, 1422. In the 'Postles Chapel : Walter Blunt, knight of the
Garter, and Lord Mountjoy, treasurer of England, son and heir to
T. Blunt, knight, treasurer of Normandy, 1474 ; E. Blunt, Lord
Mountjoy, 1475 ; Alice Blunt Mountjoy, sometime wife to William
Brown, mayor of London, and daughter to H. Kebel, mayor 1521 ;
Anne Blunt, daughter to John Blunt, knight ; Lord Mountjoy, 1480 ;
Sir Allen Cheinie, knight, and Sir T. Greene, knight ; William Blunt,
esquire, son and heir to Walter Blunt, captain of Gwins, 1492 ;
Elizabeth Blunt, wife to Robert Curson, knight, 1494 ; Bartholomew
Burwashe, and John Burwashe his son ; John Blunt, Lord Mountjoy,
captain of Gwins and Hams, 1485 ; John Dinham, baron, sometime

treasurer of England, knight of the Garter, 1501; Elianor, Duchess of Buckingham, 1530; John Blunt, knight, 1531; Rowland Blunt, esquire, 1509; Robert Bradbury, 1489; Nicholas Clifton, knight; Francis Chape; two sons of Allaine Lord Cheinie, and John, son and heir to the same; Lord Allaine Cheinie, knight; John Robsart, knight of the Garter, 1450; Allaine Cheinie, knight; Thomas Malory, knight, 1470; Thomas Young, a justice of the bench, 1476; John Baldwin, fellow of Gray's Inn, and common sergeant of London, 1469; Walter Wrotsley, knight of Warwickshire, 1473; Steven Jenins, mayor 1523; Thomas a Par, and John Wiltwater, slain at Barnet, 1471; Nicholas Poynes, esquire, 1512; Robert Elkenton, knight, 1460; John Water, *alias* York herald, 1520; John More, *alias* Norroy king of arms, 1491; George Hopton, knight, 1489. Between the choir and the altar: Ralph Spiganel, knight: John Moyle, gentleman, of Gray's Inn, 1495; William Huddy, knight, 1501; John Cobham, a baron of Kent; John Mortain, knight; John Deyncort, knight; John Norbery, esquire, high treasurer of England; Henry Norbery, his son, esquire; John Southlee, knight; Thomas Sakvile; Thomas Lucy, knight, 1525; Robert de la Rivar, son to Mauricius de la Rivar, Lord of Tormerton, 1457; John Malmaynas, esquire, and Thomas Malmaynas, knight; Hugh Acton, tailor, 1530; Nicholas Malmains; Hugh Parsal, knight, 1490; Alexander Kirketon, knight, &c. In the body of the church: William Paulet, esquire of Somersetshire, 1482; John Moyle, gentleman, 1530; Peter Champion, esquire, 1511; John Hart, gentleman, 1449; Alice Lat Hungerford, hanged at Tyborne for murdering her husband, 1523; Edward Hall, gentleman, of Gray's Inn, 1470; Richard Churchyard, gentleman, fellow of Gray's Inn, 1498; John Bramre, gentleman, of Gray's Inn, 1498; John Mortimar, knight, beheaded 1423; Henry Frowike, alderman; Renauld Frowike; Philip Pats, 1518; William Porter, sergeant at arms, 1515; Thomas Grantham, gentleman, 1511; Edmond Rotheley, gentleman, 1470; Henry Roston, gentleman, of Gray's Inn, 1485; Nicholas Montgomery, gentleman, son to John Montgomery, of Northamptonshire, 1485; Sir Bartholomew Emfield, knight; Sir Barnard St. Peter, knight; Sir Ralph Sandwich, knight, custos of London; Sir Andrew Sakevile, knight; John Treszawall, gentleman and tailor of London, 1520. All these and five times so many more have been buried there, whose monuments are wholly defaced; for there were nine tombs of alabaster and marble, environed with strikes of iron in the choir, and one tomb in the body of the church, also coped with iron, all pulled down, besides seven score gravestones of marble, all sold for fifty pounds, or thereabouts, by Sir Martin Bowes, goldsmith and alderman of London. Of late time buried there, Walter Hadden, doctor, &c. From this church west to New-gate is of this ward.

Now for the south side of this ward, beginning again at the cross in Cheap, from thence to Friday Street, and down that street on the west side till over against the north-west corner of St. Matthew's Church; and on the west side, to the south corner of the said church, which is wholly in the ward of Farringdon. This church hath these few monuments : Thomas Pole, goldsmith, 1395 ; Robert Johnson, goldsmith, alderman ; John Twiselton, goldsmith, alderman, 1525 ; Ralph Allen, grocer, one of the sheriffs, deceased 1546 ; Anthony Gamage, ironmonger, one of the sheriffs, deceased 1579 ; Anthony Cage ; John Mabbe, chamberlain of London, &c. Allen at Condit, and Thomas Warlingworth, founded a chantry there. Sir Nicholas Twiford, goldsmith, mayor, gave to that church a house, with the appurtenances, called the Griffon on the Hope, in the same street.

From this Friday Street, west to the Old Exchange, a street so called of the King's Exchange there kept, which was for the receipt of bullion to be coined. For Henry III., in the 6th year of his reign, wrote to the Scabines and men of Ipre, that he and his council had given prohibition, that none, Englishmen or other, should make change of plate or other mass of silver, but only in his Exchange at London, or at Canterbury. Andrew Bukerell then had to farm the Exchange of England, and was mayor of London in the reign of Henry III. John Somercote had the keeping of the King's Exchange over all England. In the 8th of Edward I., Gregory Rockesly was keeper of the said Exchange for the king. In the 5th of Edward II., William Hausted was keeper thereof; and in the 18th, Roger de Frowicke, &c.

These received the old stamps, or coining-irons, from time to time, as the same were worn, and delivered new to all the mints in London, as more at large in another place I have noted.

This street beginneth by West Cheap in the north, and runneth down south to Knightriders' Street, that part thereof which is called Old Fish Street, but the very housing and office of the Exchange and coinage was about the midst thereof, south from the east gate that entereth Paul's Churchyard, and on the west side in Baynard's Castle Ward.

On the east side of this lane, betwixt West Cheap and the Church of St. Augustine, Henry Walles, mayor, by license of Edward I., built one row of houses, the profits rising of them to be employed on London Bridge.

The parish church of St. Augustine, and one house next adjoining in Watheling Street, is of this ward called Farringdon. This is a fair church, and lately well repaired, wherein be monuments remaining—of H. Reade, armourer, one of the sheriffs 1450 ; Robert Bellesdon, haberdasher, mayor 1491 ; Sir Townley William Dere, one of the sheriffs 1450 ; Robert Raven, haberdasher, 1500 ; Thomas Apleyard, gentleman, 1515 ; William Moncaster, merchant tailor, 1524 ; William Holte, merchant tailor, 1544, &c.

Then is the north churchyard of Paul's, in the which standeth the cathedral church, first founded by Ethelbert, king of Kent, about the year of Christ 610. He gave thereto lands as appeareth :—

"*Ædelbertus Rex, Deo inspirante, pro animæ suæ remedio dedit episcopo Melito terram quæ appellatur Tillingeham ad monasterii sui solatium, scilicet monasterium Sancti Pauli : et ego Rex Æthelbertus ita firmiter concedo tibi presuli Melito potestatem ejus habendi & possidendi ut in perpetuum in monasterii utilitate permaneat,*" &c. Athelstan, Edgar, Edward the Confessor, and others, also gave lands thereunto. William the Conqueror gave to the Church of St. Paul, and to Mauricius, then bishop, and his successors, the castle of Stortford, with the appurtenances, &c. He also confirmed the gifts of his predecessors in these words : "*W. Rex Angl. concedo Deo et S. Paulo in perpetuum,* 24 *Hidas quas Rex Æthelbert dedit S. Paulo juxta London,*" &c. The charter of King William the Conqueror, exemplified in the Tower, Englished thus :—

"William, by the grace of God, king of Englishmen, to all his welbeloued French and English people, greeting : Know ye that I do giue vnto God and the church of S. Paule of London, and to the rectors and seruitors of the same, in all their lands which the church hath, or shall have, within borough and without, sack and sock, thole and theam, infangthefe and grithbriche, and all freeships, by strand and by land, on tide and off tide, and all the rights that into them christendome byrath, on morth sprake, and on unright hamed, and on unright work, of all that bishoprick on mine land, and on each other man's land. For I will that the church in all things be as free as I would my soul to be in the day of judgement. Witnesses : Osmund, our Chancellor ; Lanfrank, the Archbishop of Canterbury ; and T. Archbishop of York ; Roger, Earle of Shrewesbury ; Alane, the county ; Geffrey de Magnavilla ; and Ralph Peuerel."

In the year 1087, this Church of St. Paul was burnt with fire, and therewith the most part of the city ; which fire began at the entry of the west gate, and consumed the east gate. Mauricius the bishop began therefore the foundation of a new Church of St. Paul, a work that men of that time judged would never have been finished, it was to them so wonderful for length and breadth ; and also the same was built upon arches or vaults of stone, for defence of fire, which was a manner of work before that time unknown to the people of this nation, and then brought in by the French ; and the stone was fetched from Caen in Normandy.

This Mauricius deceased in the year 1107. Richard Beamor succeeded him in the bishopric, who did wonderfully increase the said church, purchasing of his own cost the large streets and lanes about it, wherein were wont to dwell many lay people, which ground he began to compass about with a strong wall of stone and gates. King Henry I. gave to the said Richard so much of the moat or wall of the castle on the Thames side, to the south, as should be needful to make the said wall of the church, and so much as should suffice to make a wall without the way on the north side, &c.

It should seem that this Richard enclosed but two sides of the said church or cemetery of St. Paul, to wit, the south and north side; for King Edward II., in the 10th of his reign, granted that the said churchyard should be enclosed with a wall where it wanted, for the murders and robberies that were there committed. But the citizens then claimed the east part of the churchyard to be the place of assembly to their folkemotes, and that the great steeple there situate was, to that use, their common bell, which being there rung, all the inhabitants of the city might hear and come together. They also claimed the west side, that they might there assemble themselves together, with the lord of Baynard's Castle, for view of their armour, in defence of the city. This matter was in the Tower of London referred to Harvius de Stanton, and his fellow-justices itinerants; but I find not the decision or judgment of that controversy.

True it is, that Edward III., in the 17th of his reign, gave commandment for the finishing of that wall, which was then performed, and to this day it continueth; although now on both the sides, to wit, within and without, it be hidden with dwelling-houses. Richard Beamor deceased in the year 1127, and his successors in process of time performed the work begun.

The steeple of this church was built and finished in the year 1222. The cross on the said steeple fell down, and a new was set up in the year 1314. The new work of Paul's, so called, at the east end above the choir, was begun in the year 1251.

Henry Lacy, Earl of Lincoln, constable of Chester, and custos of England, in his time was a great benefactor to this work, and was there buried in the year 1310. Also Ralph Baldock, Bishop of London, in his lifetime gave two hundred marks to the building of the said new work, and left much by his testament towards the finishing thereof. He deceased in the year 1313, and was buried in the Lady Chapel. Also the new work of Paul's, to wit, the cross aisles, were begun to be new built in the year 1256.

The 1st of February, in the year 1444, about two of the clock in the afternoon, the steeple of Paul's was fired by lightning, in the midst of the shaft or spire, both on the west side and on the south;

but by labour of many well-disposed people the same to appearance
was quenched with vinegar, so that all men withdrew themselves
to their houses, praising God; but between eight and nine of the
clock in the same night the fire burst out again more fervently than
before, and did much hurt to the lead and timber, till by the great
labour of the mayor and people that came thither it was thoroughly
quenched.

This steeple was repaired in the year 1462, and the weathercock
again erected. Robert Godwin winding it up, the rope brake, and
he was destroyed on the pinnacles, and the cock was sore bruised;
but Burchwood, the king's plumber, set it up again. Since the which
time, needing reparation, it was both taken down and set up in
the year 1553. At which time it was found to be of copper, gilt
over; and the length from the bill to the tail being four feet, and
the breadth over the wings three feet and a half, it weighed forty
pounds; the cross from the bowl to the eagle, or cock, was fifteen
feet and six inches of assize; the length thereof overthwart was
five feet and ten inches, and the compass of the bowl was nine
feet and one inch.

The inner body of this cross was oak, the next cover was lead,
and the uttermost was of copper, red varnished. The bowl and
eagle, or cock, were of copper, and gilt also.

The height of the steeple was five hundred and twenty feet,
whereof the stone work is two hundred and sixty feet, and the spire
was likewise two hundred and sixty feet. The length of the whole
church is two hundred and forty tailors' yards, which make seven
hundred and twenty feet; the breadth thereof is one hundred and
thirty feet; and the height of the body of that church is one hundred and fifty feet. This church hath a bishop, a dean, a precentor,
chancellor, treasurer, and five archdeacons; to wit, of London,
Middlesex, Essex, Colchester, and St. Albans. It hath prebendaries
thirty, canons twelve, vicars choral six, &c.

The college of petty canons there was founded by King Richard
II. in honour of Queen Anne his wife, and of her progenitors, in the
17th of his reign. Their hall and lands were then given unto them,
as appeareth by the patent, Master Robert Dokesworth then being
master thereof. In the year 1408, the petty canons then building
their college, the mayor and commonalty granted them their water-
courses and other easements.

There was also one great cloister, on the north side of this
church, environing a plot of ground, of old time called Pardon
Churchyard, whereof Thomas More, Dean of Paul's, was either the
first builder, or a most especial benefactor, and was buried there.
About this cloister was artificially and richly painted the Dance of

Machabray, or Dance of Death, commonly called the Dance of Paul's, the like whereof was painted about St. Innocent's cloister at Paris, in France. The metres, or poesy of this dance, were translated out of French into English by John Lidgate, monk of Bury, and with the picture of death leading all estates, painted about the cloister, at the special request and at the dispence of Jenkin Carpenter, in the reign of Henry VI. In this cloister were buried many persons, some of worship, and others of honour, the monuments of whom, in number and curious workmanship, passed all other that were in that church.

Over the east quadrant of this cloister was a fair library, built at the costs and charges of Walter Sherrington, Chancellor of the Duchy of Lancaster, in the reign of Henry VI., which hath been well furnished with fair written books in vellum, but few of them now do remain there. In the midst of this Pardon Churchyard was also a fair chapel, first founded by Gilbert Becket, portgrave and principal magistrate of this city, in the reign of King Stephen, who was there buried.

Thomas More, Dean of Paul's beforenamed, re-edified or new built this chapel, and founded three chaplains there, in the reign of Henry V.

In the year 1549, on the 10th of April, the said chapel, by commandment of the Duke of Somerset, was begun to be pulled down, with the whole cloister, the Dance of Death, the tombs and monuments, so that nothing thereof was left but the bare plot of ground, which is since converted into a garden for the petty canons. There was also a chapel at the north door of Paul's, founded by the same Walter Sherrington, by license of Henry VI., for two, three, or four chaplains, endowed with forty pounds by the year. This chapel was also pulled down in the reign of Edward VI., and in place thereof a fair house built.

There was furthermore a fair chapel of the Holy Ghost in Paul's Church, on the north side, founded in the year 1400 by Roger Holmes, chancellor and prebendary of Paul's, for Adam Berie, alderman, mayor of London 1364, John Wingham, and others, for seven chaplains, and called Holme's College. Their common hall was in Paul's Churchyard, on the south side, near unto a carpenter's yard. This college was, with others, suppressed in the reign of Edward VI. Then under the choir of Paul's is a large chapel, first dedicated to the name of Jesu, founded, or rather confirmed, the 37th of Henry VI., as appeareth by his patent thereof, dated at Croydon, to this effect :—

"Many liege men, and Christian people, having begun a fraternitie and guild, to the honour of the most glorious name of Jesus Christ our Saviour, in a place called the shrowdes of the cathedrall church of Paul's in London, which hath continued long time peaceably till now of late ; whereupon they have made request, and we have taken upon us the name and charge of the foundation, to the laud of Almightie God, the Father, the Sonne, and the Holy Ghost, and especially to the honour of Jesu, in whose honour the fraternitie was begun," &c.

The king ordained William Say, then Dean of Paul's, to be the rector, and Richard Ford, a remembrancer in the Exchequer, and Henry Bennis, clerk of his privy seal, the guardians of those brothers and sisters. They and their successors to have a common seal, license to purchase lands or tenements to the value of forty pounds by the year, &c.

This foundation was confirmed by Henry VII., the 22nd of his reign, to Doctor Colet, then Dean of Paul's, rector there, &c. ; and by Henry VIII., the 27th of his reign, to Richard Pace, then Dean of Paul's, &c.

At the west end of this Jesus' Chapel, under the choir of Paul's, also was a parish church of St. Faith, commonly called St. Faith under Paul's, which served for the stationers and others dwelling in Paul's Churchyard, Paternoster Row, and the places near adjoining. The said Chapel of Jesus being suppressed in the reign of Edward VI., the parishioners of St. Faith's Church were removed into the same, as to a place more sufficient for largeness and lightsomeness, in the year 1551, and so it remaineth.

Then was there on the north side of this churchyard a large charnel house for the bones of the dead, and over it a chapel of an old foundation, such as followeth :—In the year 1282, the 10th of Edward I., it was agreed, that Henry Walles, mayor, and the citizens, for the cause of shops by them built without the wall of the churchyard, should assign to God and to the Church of St. Paul ten marks of rent by the year for ever, towards the new building of a chapel of the Blessed Virgin Mary, and also to assign five marks of yearly rent to a chaplain to celebrate there.

Moreover, in the year 1430, the 8th of Henry VI., license was granted to Jenkin Carpenter, executor to Richard Whittington, to establish upon the said charnel a chaplain, to have eight marks by the year. Then was also in this chapel two brotherhoods. In this chapel were buried Robert Barton, Henry Barton, mayor, and Thomas Mirfin, mayor, all skinners, and were entombed with their images of alabaster over them, grated or coped about with iron before the said chapel, all which were pulled down in the year 1549. The bones of the dead, couched up in a charnel under the chapel, were conveyed from thence into Finsbury field, by report of him who paid for the carriage, amounting to more than one thousand cart-loads, and there laid on a moorish ground, in short space after raised, by soilage of the city upon them, to bear three windmills. The chapel and charnel were converted into dwelling-houses, warehouses, and sheds before them, for stationers, in place of the tombs.

In the east part of this churchyard standeth Paul's School, lately new built, and endowed in the year 1512 by John Colet, Doctor of Divinity and Dean of Paul's, for one hundred and fifty-three poor men's children, to be taught free in the same school, for which he appointed a master, a surmaster, or usher, and a chaplain, with large stipends for ever, committing the oversight thereof to the masters, wardens, and assistants of the mercers in London, because he was son to Henry Colet, mercer, sometime mayor. He left to these mercers lands to the yearly value of one hundred and twenty pounds, or better.

Near unto this school, on the north side thereof, was of old time a great and high clochiard, or bell-house, four square, built of stone, and in the same a most strong frame of timber, with four bells, the greatest that I have heard. These were called Jesus' bells, and belonged to Jesus' Chapel, but I know not by whose gift. The same had a great spire covered with lead, with the image of St. Paul on the top, but was pulled down by Sir Miles Partridge, knight, in the reign of Henry VIII. The common speech then was, that he did set a hundred pounds upon a cast of dice against it, and so won the said clochiard and bells of the king ; and then causing the bells to be broken as they hung, the rest was pulled down. This man was afterward executed on the Tower Hill for matters concerning the Duke of Somerset, the 5th of Edward VI.

In place of this clochiard, of old times the common bell of the city was used to be rung for the assembly of the citizens to their folkemotes, as I have before showed.

About the midst of this churchyard is a pulpit cross of timber, mounted upon steps of stone, and covered with lead, in which are sermons preached by learned divines every Sunday in the forenoon, the very antiquity of which cross is to me unknown. I read, that in the year 1259, King Henry III. commanded a general assembly to be made at this cross, where he in proper person commanded the mayor, that on the next day following, he should cause to be sworn before the alderman every stripling of twelve years of age or upward, to be true to the king and his heirs, kings of England. Also, in the year 1262, the same king caused to be read at Paul's Cross a bull, obtained from Pope Urban IV., as an absolution for him, and for all that were sworn to maintain the articles made in parliament at Oxford. Also in the year 1299, the Dean of Paul's accursed at Paul's Cross all those which had searched in the Church of St. Martin in the Field for a hoard of gold, &c. This pulpit cross was by tempest of light-

ning and thunder defaced. Thomas Kempe, Bishop of London,
new built it in form as it now standeth.

In the year 1561, the 4th of June, betwixt the hours of three and
four of the clock in the afternoon, the great spire of the steeple of
St. Paul's Church was fired by lightning, which brake forth, as it
seemed, two or three yards beneath the foot of the cross ; and from
thence it went downward the spire to the battlements, stone-work,
and bells so furiously, that within the space of four hours the same
steeple, with all the roofs of the church, were consumed, to the great
sorrow and perpetual remembrance of the beholders. After this
mischance, the queen's majesty directed her letters to the mayor,
willing him to take order for the speedy repairing of the same ; and
she, of her gracious disposition, for the furtherance thereof, did presently give and deliver in gold one thousand marks, with a warrant
for a thousand loads of timber, to be taken out of her woods or elsewhere.

The citizens also gave first a great benevolencee, and after that
three fifteens, to be speedily paid. The clergy of England likewise,
within the province of Canterbury, granted the fortieth part of the
value of their benefices, charged with first fruits, the thirtieth part
of such as were not so charged ; but the clergy of London diocese
granted the thirtieth part of all that paid first fruits, and the twentieth
part of such as had paid their fruits.

Six citizens of London, and two petty canons of Paul's Church,
had charge to further and oversee the work, wherein such expedition
was used, that within one month next following the burning thereof,
the church was covered with boards and lead, in manner of a false
roof, against the weather ; and before the end of the said year, all
the said aisles of the church were framed out of new timber, covered
with lead, and fully finished. The same year also the great roofs
of the west and east ends were framed out of great timber in Yorkshire, brought thence to London by sea, and set up and covered with
lead. The north and south ends were framed of timber and covered
with lead before April 1566. Concerning the steeple, divers models
were devised and made, but little else was done, through whose default, God knoweth. It was said that the money appointed for new
building of the steeple was collected.

Monuments in this church be these : first, as I read, of Erkenwalde,
Bishop of London, buried in the old church about the year of Christ
700, whose body was translated into the new work in the year 1140,
being richly shrined above the choir behind the high altar.

Sebba, or Seba, king of the East Saxons, first buried in the old
church, since removed into the new, and laid in a coffin of stone,
on the north side without the choirs ; Ethelred, king of the West

Saxons, was likewise buried and removed; William Norman, Bishop of London in the reigns of Edward the Confessor and of William the Conqueror, deceased 1070, and is new buried in the body of the church, with an epitaph, as in my Summary I have shown; Eustauchius de Fauconbridge, Bishop of London, 1228, buried in the south aisle above the choir; Martin Pateshull, Dean of Paul's, 1239; W. Havarhul, canon; the king's treasurer, Hugh Pateshull, 1240; Roger Nigar, Bishop of London, 1241, buried in the north side of the choir; Fulco Basset, Bishop of London, 1259, and his brother, Philip Basset, knight, 1261; Henry Wingham, Bishop of London, buried in the south aisle above the choir, 1262; Geffrey de Acra, chaplain, in the chapel of St. James, under the rood at north door, 1264; Alexander de Swarford, 1273; John Grantham, 1273; John Braynford and Richard Umframuile, 1275; Roger de Iale, Archdeacon of Essex, 1280; Ralph Donion, canon, 1382; Godfrey S. Donstan, 1274; Fulke Lovell, 1298; William Harworth, clerk, 1302; Reginald Brandon, in the new Lady Chapel, 1305; Richard Newport, Archdeacon of Middlesex, 1309; Henry Lacie, Earl of Lincoln, in the new work of Paul's betwixt the Lady Chapel and St. Dunstan's Chapel, where a fair monument was raised for him, with his picture in armour, cross-legged, as one professed for defence of the Holy Land against the infidels, 1310. His monument is foully defaced. Ralph Baldoke, Bishop of London, 1313, in the said Lady Chapel, whereof he was founder.

Some have noted, that in digging the foundation of this new work, namely, of a chapel on the south side of Paul's Church, there were found more than a hundred scalps of oxen or kine, in the year 1316. Which thing, say they, confirmed greatly the opinion of those which have reported, that of old time there had been a temple of Jupiter, and that there was daily sacrifices of beasts.

Othersome, both wise and learned, have thought the buck's head, borne before the procession of Paul's on St. Paul's day, to signify the like. But true it is, I have read an ancient deed to this effect.

Sir William Baud, knight, the 3rd of Edward I., in the year 1274, on Candlemas day, granted to Harvey de Borham, Dean of Paul's, and to the chapter there, that in consideration of twenty-two acres of ground or land by them granted, within their manor of Westley in Essex, to be enclosed into his park of Curingham, he would for ever, upon the feast day of the Conversion of St. Paul in winter, give unto them a good doe, seasonable and sweet, and upon the feast of the commemoration of St. Paul in summer, a good buck, and offer the same upon the high altar, the same to be spent amongst the canons residents. The doe to be brought by one man at the hour of procession, and through the procession to the high altar; and the bringer to have nothing. The buck to be brought by all his men in like manner, and they to have paid unto them by the chamberlain of the church twelve pence only, and no more to be required. This grant he made, and for performance bound the lands of him and his heirs to be distrained on; and if the lands should be evicted, that yet he and his heirs should accomplish the gift. Witnesses: Richard Tilberie, William de Wokendon, Richard de Harlow, knights, Peter of Stanforde, Thomas of Waldon, and some others.

Sir Walter Baud, son to William, confirmed this gift, in the 30th of the said king, and the witnesses thereunto were Nicholas de Wokendon, Richard de Rokely, Thomas de Mandevile, John de Rochford, knights, Richard de Broniford, William de Markes, William de Fulham, and other. Thus much for the grant.

Now what I have heard by report, and have partly seen, it followeth. On the feast day of the commemoration of St. Paul, the buck being brought up to the steps of the high altar in Paul's Church, at the hour of procession, the dean and chapter being apparelled in copes and vestments, with garlands of roses on their heads, they sent the body of the buck to baking, and had the head fixed on a pole, borne before the cross in their procession, until they issued out of the west door, where the keeper that brought it blowed the death of the buck, and then the horners that were about the city presently answered him in like manner; for the which pains they had each one of the dean and chapter fourpence in money, and their dinner, and the keeper that brought it was allowed during his abode there, for that service, meat, drink, and lodging, at the dean and chapter's charges, and five shillings in money at his going away, together with a loaf of bread, having the picture of St. Paul upon it, &c.

There was belonging to the Church of St. Paul, for both the days, two special suits of vestments, the one embroidered with bucks, the other with does, both given by the said Bauds, as I have heard. Thus much for the matter.

Now to the residue of the monuments:—Sir Ralph Hingham, chief justice of both Benches successively, buried in the side of the north walk against the choir, 1308; Henry Guildford, clerk at the altar of the Apostles, 1313; Richard Newport, Bishop of London, 1318; William Chateslehunt, canon, in the new work, 1321, had a chantry there; Sir Nicholas Wokenden, knight, at the altar of St. Thomas in the new work, 1323; John Cheshull, Bishop of London, 1279; Roger Waltham, canon, 1325; Hamo Chikewell, six times mayor of London, 1328; Robert Monden and John Monden his brother, canons, in the new work, 1332; Walter Thorpe, canon, in the new work, 1333; John Fable, 1334; James Fisil, chaplain, 1341; William Melford, Archdeacon of Colchester, 1345; Richard de Placeto, Archdeacon of Colchester, 1345, before St. Thomas' Chapel; Geffrey Eton, canon, 1345; Nicholas Husband, canon, 1347; Sir John Poultney, mayor, 1348, in a fair chapel by him built on the north side of Paul's, wherein he founded three chaplains; William Eversden, canon, in the crowds, 1349; Alan Hotham, canon, in the new crowds, 1351; Henry Etesworth, under the rood at north door, 1353; John Beauchampe, constable of Dover, warden of the ports, knight of the Garter, son to Guy Beauchampe, Earl of Warwick, and brother to Thomas, Earl of Warwick, in the body of the church, on the south side, 1358, where a proper chapel and fair monument remaineth of him. He is by ignorant people misnamed to be Humphrey, Duke of Gloucester, who lieth honourably buried at St. Albans, twenty miles from London, and therefore such as merrily or simply profess themselves to serve Duke Humphrey in Paul's, are to be punished here, and sent to St. Albans, there again to be punished for their absence from their lord and master, as they call him. Michael Norborow, Bishop of London, 1361; Walter Nele, blader, and Avis his wife, 1361; Gilbert Brewer, Dean of Paul's, 1366; Richard Wendover, 1366; John Hiltoft, goldsmith, and Alice his wife, in the new works, St. Dunstan's Chapel, 1368; Adam de Bery, mayor in the year 1364, buried in a chapel of St. Mary Magdalen, or of the Holy Ghost, called Holmes' College, behind the rood at the north door of Paul's, 1390; Roger Holmes, chancellor and prebend of Paul's, was buried there 1400; John of Gaunt, Duke of Lancaster, 1399, buried on the north side the choir, beside Blanch his first wife, who deceased 1368; Sir Richard Burley, knight of the Garter, under a fair monument in the side of the north walk against the choir. A chantry was there founded for him, 1409. Beatrix his wife, after his death, married to Thomas Lord Rouse, was buried in the Chapel of St. John Baptist (or Poultney's Chapel), near the north door of Paul's, 1409; Thomas Evers, dean of Paul's, in St. Thomas' Chapel, the new work, 1411; Thomas More, dean of Paul's, in the chapel of St. Anne and St. Thomas, by him new built in Pardon Churchyard, 1419; Thomas Ston, dean of Paul's, by the tomb of John Beauchampe, 1423; the Duchess of Bedford, sister to Philip, Duke of Burgoyne, 1433; Robert Fitzhugh, Bishop of London, in the choir, 1435; Walter Sherington, in a chapel without the north door by him built, 1457; John Drayton, goldsmith, in Allhallows Chapel, 1456; William Say, dean of Paul's, in the Crowds, or Jesus' Chapel, 1468; Margaret, Countess of Shrewsbury, in the Crowds, or Jesus' Chapel, as appeareth by an inscription on a pillar there.

Here before the image of Jesus lieth the worshipful and right noble lady, Margaret Countess of Shrewsbury, late wife of the true and victorious knight and redoubtable warrior, John Talbot, Earl of Shrewsbury, which worship died in Guien for the right of his land. The first daughter, and one of the heirs of the right famous and renowned knight, Richard Beauchamp, late Earl of Warwick, which died in Rouen, and Dame Elizabeth his wife, the which Elizabeth was daughter and heir to Thomas, late Lord Berkeley, on his side, and of her mother's side, Lady Lisle and Tyes, which countess passed from this world the 14th day of June, in the year of our Lord 1468, on whose soul Jesus have mercy. Amen.

John Wenlock, by his last will, dated 1477, appointed there should be dispended upon a monument over the Lady of Shrewsbury where she is buried afore Jesus, one hundred pounds. He left Sir Humphrey Talbot his supervisor. This Sir Humphrey Talbot, knight, Lord Marshal of the town of Calais, made his will the year 1492. He was younger son of John Earl of Shrewsbury, and Margaret his wife; he appointed a stone to be put in a pillar before the grave of his lady mother in Paul's, of his portraiture and arms, according to the will of John Wenlock, but for want of room and lightsomeness in that place, it was concluded, the image of Jesus to be curiously painted on the wall of Paul's Church, over the door that entereth into the said chapel of Jesus, and the portraiture also of the said Lady Margaret, Countess of Shrewsbury, kneeling in her mantle of arms, with her progeny; all which was so performed, and remaineth till this day.

In the chapel of Jesus, Thomas Dowcrey, William Lamb, 1578, and many other, have been interred; John of London, under the north rood, 1266; John Lovell, clerk; John Romane; John of St. Olave; Walter Bloxley; Sir Alen Boxhull, knight of the Garter, constable of the Tower, custos of the forest and park of Clarendon, the forest of Brokholt, Grovell, and Melchet, buried beside St. Erkenwald's shrine, and of later time Thomas Kemp, Bishop of London, in a proper chapel of the Trinity by him founded in the body of the church, on the north side, 1489: Thomas Linacre, doctor of physic; John Collet, dean of Paul's, on the south side without the choir, 1519; John Dowman, canon of Paul's, 1525; Richard Fitz-James, Bishop of London, hard beneath the north-west pillar of Paul's steeple, under a fair tomb, and a chapel of St. Paul, built of timber, with stairs mounting thereunto over his tomb, of grey marble, 1521. His chapel was burned by fire falling from the steeple, his tomb was taken thence. John Stokesley, Bishop of London, in our Lady Chapel, 1539; John Nevill, Lord Latimer, in a chapel by the north door of Paul's, about 1542; Sir John Mason, knight, in the north walk, against the choir, 1566; William Herbert, Earl of Pembroke, knight of the Garter, on the north side of the choir, 1569; Sir Nicholas Bacon, lord-keeper of the great seal, on the south side of the choir, 1578; Sir Philip Sidney, above the choir on the north side, 1586; Sir Frances Walsingham, knight, principal secretary, and chancellor of the Duchy of Lancaster, 1590; Sir Christopher Hatton, lord chancellor of England, knight of the Garter, above the choir, 1591, under a most sumptuous monument, where a merry poet wrote thus :—

> " Philip and Francis have no tombe,
> For *great* Christopher takes all the roome." *

John Elmer, Bishop of London, before St. Thomas' Chapel, 1594; the Lady Heneage, and her husband, Sir Thomas Heneage, chancellor of the duchy, 1595; Richard Fletcher, Bishop of London, 1596. These, as the chief, have I noted to be buried there.

Without the north gate of Paul's Church from the end of the Old Exchange, west up Paternoster Row, by the two lanes out of Paul's Church, the first out of the cross aisle of Paul's, the other out of the body of the church, about the midst thereof, and so west to the Golden Lion, be all of this ward, as is aforesaid. The houses in this street, from the first north gate of Paul's Churchyard unto the next gate, was first built without the wall of the churchyard by Henry Walles, mayor in the year 1282. The rents of those houses go to the maintenance of London Bridge. This street is now called Paternoster Row, because of stationers or text writers that dwelt there, who wrote and sold all sorts of books then in use, namely, A. B. C. with the Pater Noster, Ave, Creed, Graces, &c.

There dwelt also turners of beads, and they were called paternoster makers, as I read in a record of one Robert Nikke, paternoster maker and citizen, in the reign of Henry IV., and so of other. At the end of Paternoster Row is Ave Maria Lane, so called upon the like occasion of text writers and bead makers then dwelling there; and at the end of that lane is likewise Creed Lane, late so called, but sometime Spurrier Row, of spurriers dwelling there; and Amen Lane is added thereunto betwixt the south end of Warwick Lane and the north end of Ave Maria Lane. At the north end of Ave Maria Lane is one great house, built of stone and timber, of old time pertaining to John, Duke of Britain, Earl of Richmond, as appeareth by the records of Edward II., since that it is called Pembrook's Inn, near unto Ludgate, as belonging to the earls of Pembrook, in the times of Richard II., the 18th year, and of Henry

* Of Saint Christopher, says an old romance, "Four and twenty feet he was long and thick and broad enough."

VI. the 14th year. It is now called Burgaveny House, and belongeth to Henry, late Lord of Burgaveny.

Betwixt the south end of Ave Maria Lane, and the north end of Creed Lane, is the coming out of Paul's Churchyard on the east, and the high street on the west, towards Ludgate, and this is called Bowyer Row, of bowyers dwelling there in old time, now worn out by mercers and others. In this street, on the north side, is the parish church of St. Martin, a proper church, and lately new built; for in the year 1437, John Michael, mayor, and the commonalty, granted to William Downe, parson of St. Martin's at Ludgate, a parcel of ground, containing in length twenty-eight feet, and in breadth four feet, to set and build their steeple upon, &c. The monuments here have been of William Sevenoake, mayor 1418; Henry Belwase and John Gest, 1458; William Taverner, gentleman, 1466; John Barton, esquire, 1439; Stephen Peacock, mayor 1533; Sir Roger Cholmley, John Went, and Roger Paine, had chantries there.

On the south side of this street is the turning into the Blackfriars, which order sometime had their houses in Holborn, where they remained for the space of fifty-five years, and then in the year 1276, Gregorie Roksley, mayor, and the barons of this city, granted and gave to Robert Kilwarby, Archbishop of Canterbury, two lanes or ways next the street of Baynard's Castle, and also the tower of Mountfitchit, to be destroyed; in place of which the said Robert built the late new church of the Blackfriars, and placed them therein. King Edward I. and Eleanor his wife, were great benefactors thereunto. This was a large church, and richly furnished with ornaments, wherein divers parliaments, and other great meetings, hath been holden; namely, in the year 1450, the 28th of Henry VI. a parliament was begun at Westminster, and adjourned to the Blackfriars in London, and from thence to Leicester. In the year 1522, the Emperor Charles V. was lodged there. In the year 1524, the 15th of April, a parliament was begun at the Blackfriars, wherein was demanded a subsidy of eight hundred thousand pounds to be raised of goods and lands, four shillings in every pound, and in the end was granted two shillings of the pound of goods or lands that were worth twenty pounds, or might dispend twenty pounds by the year, and so upward, to be paid in two years. This parliament was adjourned to Westminster amongst the black monks, and ended in the king's palace there, the 14th of August, at nine of the clock in the night, and was therefore called the Black Parliament. In the year 1529, Cardinal Campeius, the legate, with Cardinal Wolsey, sat at the said Blackfriars, where before them, as legates and judges, was brought in question the king's marriage with Queen Katherine, as unlawful, before whom the king and queen were cited and summoned to appear, &c., whereof more at large in my Annals I have touched.

The same year, in the month of October, began a parliament in the Blackfriars, in the which Cardinal Wolsey was condemned in the premunire ; this house, valued at £104, 15s. 5d., was surrendered the 12th of November, the 30th of Henry VIII. There were buried in this church, Margaret Queen of Scots ; Hubert de Burgh, Earl of Kent, translated from their old church by Holborn ; Robert de Atta-beto, Earl of Bellimon ; Dame Isabel, wife to Sir Roger Bygot, earl marshal ; William and Jane Huse, children to Dame Ellis, Countess of Arundell ; and by them lieth Dame Ellis, daughter to the Earl Warren, and after Countess of Arundell ; Dame Ide, wife to Sir Walter ——, daughter to Ferrers of Chartley ; Richard de Brewes ; Richard Strange, son to Roger Strange ; Elizabeth, daughter to Sir Barthol. Badlesmere, wife to Sir William Bohun, Earl of Northampton ; Marsh ; the Earls of Marsh and Hereford ; and Elizabeth Countess of Arundell ; Dame Joan, daughter to Sir John Carne, first wife to Sir Gwide Brian ; Hugh Clare, knight, 1295 ; the heart of Queen Eleanor, the foundress ; the heart of Alfonce, her son ; the hearts of John and Margaret, children to W. Vallence ; Sir William Thorpe, justice ; the Lord Lioth of Ireland ; Maude, wife to Geffrey Say, daughter to the Earl of Warwick ; Dame Sible, daughter to Wil. Pattehulle, wife to Roger Beauchampe ; and by her, Sir Richard or Roger Beauchampe ; Lord St. Amand, and Dame Elizabeth his wife, daughter to the Duke of Lancaster ; Sir Stephen Collington, knight ; Sir William Peter, knight ; the Countess of Huntingdon ; Duchess of Exeter, 1425 ; Sir John Cornwall ; Lord Fanhope, died at Amphill in Bedfordshire, and was buried here in 1443 ; Sir John Triptoste, Earl of Worcester, beheaded 1470 ; and by him in his chapel, James Touchet, Lord Audley, beheaded 1497 ; William Paston, and Anne, daughter to Edmond Lancaster ; the Lord Beamount ; Sir Edmond Cornewall, Baron of Burford ; the Lady Nevell, wedded to Lord Douglas, daughter to the Duke of Exeter ; Richard Scrope, esquire ; Dame Katheren Vaux, *alias* Cobham ; Sir Thomas Browne, and Dame Elizabeth his wife ; Jane Powell ; Thomas Swinforth ; John Mawsley, esquire, 1432 ; John de la Bere, Nicholas Eare, Geffrey Spring, William Clifford, esquires ; Sir Thomas Brandon, knight of the Garter, 1509 ; William Stalworth, merchant-tailor, 1518 ; William Courtney, Earl of Devonshire nominate, but not created, the 3rd of Henry VIII., &c.

There is a parish of St. Anne within the precinct of the Blackfriars, which was pulled down with the Friars' Church, by Sir Thomas Carden ; but in the reign of Queen Mary, he being forced to find a church to the inhabitants, allowed them a lodging chamber above a stair, which since that time, to wit, in the year 1597, fell down, and was again by collection therefore made, new built and enlarged in the same year, and was dedicated on the 11th of December.

Now to turn again out of the Blackfriars through Bowyer Row, Ave Maria Lane, and Paternoster Row, to the church of St. Michael *ad Bladum,* or at the corn (corruptly at the querne), so called, because in place thereof was sometime a corn-market, stretching by west to the shambles. It seemeth that the church was new built about the reign of Edward III. Thomas Newton, first parson there, was buried in the choir the year 1461. At the east end of this church stood a cross, called the old cross in West Cheap, which was taken down in the year 1390; since the which time the said parish church was also taken down, but new built and enlarged in the year 1430, the 8th of Henry VI. William Eastfield, mayor, and the commonalty, granted of the common soil of the city three feet and a half in breadth on the north part, and four feet in breadth towards the east. This is now a proper church, and hath the monuments of Thomas Newton, first parson; Roger Woodcocke, hatter, 1475; Thomas Rossel, brewer, 1473; John Hulton, stationer, 1475; John Oxney; Roger North, merchant-haberdasher, 1509; John Leiland, the famous antiquary; Henry Pranell, vintner, one of the sheriffs 1585; William Erkin, one of the sheriffs 1586; Thomas Bankes, barber-chirurgeon, 1598, &c. John Mundham had a chantry there in the reign of Edward II.

At the east end of this church, in place of the old cross, is now a water-conduit placed. W. Eastfield, mayor the 9th of Henry VI., at the request of divers common councils, granted it so to be; whereupon, in the 19th of the same Henry, one thousand marks were granted by a common council towards the works of this conduit, and the reparations of other; this is called the little conduit in West Cheap by Paul's Gate. At the west end of this parish church is a small passage for people on foot through the same church; and west from the said church, some distance, is another passage out of Paternoster Row, and is called, of such a sign, Panyar Alley, which cometh out into the north over against St. Martin's Lane. Next is Ivy Lane, so called of ivy growing on the walls of the prebend houses; but now the lane is replenished on both sides with fair houses, and divers offices be there kept by registers, namely, for the Prerogative Court of the Archbishop of Canterbury, the probate of wills, and for the lord treasurer's remembrance of the exchequer, &c.

This lane runneth north to the west end of St. Nicholas' Shambles. Of old time was one great house sometime belonging to the Earls of Britain, since that to the Lovels, and was called Lovels' Inn; for

Mathild, wife to John Lovell, held it in the 1st of Henry VI. Then is Eldenese Lane, which stretcheth north to the high street of Newgate Market. The same is now called Warwick Lane, of an ancient house there built by an Earl of Warwick, and was since called Warwick Inn. It is in record called a messuage in Eldenese Lane, in the parish of St. Sepulchre, the 28th of Henry the VI. Cicille Duchess of Warwick possessed it. Now again from the conduit by Paul's Gate on the north side is a large street running west to Newgate, the first part whereof, from the conduit to the shambles, is of selling bladders there, called Bladder Street. Then behind the butchers' shops be now divers slaughter-houses inward, and tippling houses outward. This is called Mountgodard Street of the tippling houses there, and the godards mounting from the tap to the table, from the table to the mouth, and sometimes over the head. This street goeth up to the north end of Ivy Lane.

Before this Mountgodard Street stall boards were of old time set up by the butchers to show and sell their flesh meat upon, over the which stall boards they first built sheds to keep off the weather ; but since that, encroaching by little and little, they have made their stall boards and sheds fair houses, meet for the principal shambles. Next is Newgate Market, first of corn and meal, and then of other victuals, which stretcheth almost to Eldenese Lane. A fair, new, and strong frame of timber, covered with lead, was therefore set up at the charges of the city, near to the west corner of St. Nicholas' Shambles, for the meal to be weighed, in the 1st of Edward VI., Sir John Gresham being then mayor. On this side the north corner of Eldenese Lane stood sometime a proper parish church of St. Ewine, as is before said, given by Henry VIII. towards the erecting of Christ's Church ; it was taken down, and in place thereof a fair strong frame of timber erected, wherein dwell men of divers trades. And from this frame to Newgate is all of this ward, and so an end thereof.

It hath an alderman, his deputy, common council twelve, constables seventeen, scavengers eighteen, wardmote inquest eighteen, and a beadle. And is taxed to the fifteen fifty pounds.

Bread Street Ward.

BREAD STREET WARD beginneth in the high street of West Cheap, to wit, on the south side from the standard to the great cross. Then is also a part of Watling Street of this ward, to wit, from over against the Lion on the north side up almost to Paul's gate, for it lacketh but one house of St. Augustine's Church. And on the south side, from the Red Lion Gate to the Old

Exchange, and down the same exchange on the east side by the west end of Maiden Lane, or Distar Lane, to Knightrider Street, or, as they call that part thereof, Old Fish Street. And all the north side of the said Old Fish Street to the south end of Bread Street, and by that still in Knightrider Street till over against the Trinity Church and Trinity Lane. Then is Bread Street itself, so called of bread in old time there sold; for it appeareth by records, that in the year 1302, which was the 30th of Edward I. the bakers of London were bound to sell no bread in their shops or houses, but in the market, and that they should have four hall-motes in the year, at four several terms, to determine of enormities belonging to the said company.

This street, giving the name to the whole ward, beginneth in West Cheap, almost by the Standard, and runneth down south through or thwart Watling Street to Knightrider Street aforesaid, where it endeth. This Bread Street is wholly on both sides of this ward. Out of the which street, on the east side, is Basing Lane, a piece whereof, to wit, to and over against the back gate of the Red Lion in Watling Street, is of this Bread Street Ward.

Then is Friday Street, beginning also in West Cheap, and runneth down south through Watling Street to Knightrider Street, or Old Fish Street. This Friday Street is of Bread Street Ward on the east side from over against the north-east corner of St. Matthew's Church, and on the west side from the south corner of the said church, down as aforesaid.

In this Friday Street, on the west side thereof, is a lane, commonly called Maiden Lane, or Distaff Lane, corruptly for Distar Lane, which runneth west into the Old Exchange; and in this lane is also one other lane, on the south side thereof, likewise called Distar Lane, which runneth down to Knightrider Street, or Old Fish Street; and so be the bounds of this whole ward.

Monuments to be noted here, first at Bread Street corner, the north-east end, 1595, of Thomas Tomlinson, causing in the high street of Cheap a vault to be digged and made, there was found, at fifteen feet deep, a fair pavement like unto that above ground, and at the further end at the channel was found a tree sawed into five steps, which was to step over some brook running out of the west towards Walbrook; and upon the edge of the said brook, as it seemeth, there were found lying along the bodies of two great trees, the ends whereof were then sawed off, and firm timber as at the first when they fell, part of the said trees remain yet in the ground undigged. It was all forced ground until they went past the trees aforesaid, which was about seventeen feet deep or better; thus much hath the ground of this city in that place been raised from the main.

Next to be noted, the most beautiful frame of fair houses and shops that be within the walls of London, or elsewhere in England, commonly called Goldsmith's Row, betwixt Bread Street end and the cross in Cheap, but is within this Bread Street Ward; the same was built by Thomas Wood, goldsmith, one of the sheriffs of London, in the year 1491. It containeth in number ten fair dwelling-houses and fourteen shops, all in one frame, uniformly built four stories high, beautified towards the street with the Goldsmiths' arms and the likeness of woodmen, in memory of his name, riding on monstrous beasts, all which is cast in lead, richly painted over and gilt. These he gave to the goldsmiths, with stocks of money, to be lent to young men having those shops, &c. This said front was again new painted and gilt over in the year 1594; Sir Richard Martin being then mayor, and keeping his mayoralty in one of them, serving out the time of Cuthbert Buckle in that office from the 2nd of July till the 28th of October.

Then for Watling Street, which Leyland called Atheling or Noble Street; but since he showeth no reason why, I rather take it to be so named of the great highway of the same calling. True it is, that at this present the inhabitants thereof are wealthy drapers, retailers of woollen cloths, both broad and narrow, of all sorts, more than in any one street of this city.

Of the Old Exchange, I have noted in Farringdon Ward; wherefore I pass down to Knightrider Street, whereof I have also spoken in Cordwainers Street Ward; but in this part of the said Knightrider Street is a fish-market kept, and therefore called Old Fish Street for a difference from New Fish Street.

In this Old Fish Street is one row of small houses, placed along in the midst of Knightrider Street, which row is also of Bread Street Ward: these houses, now possessed by fishmongers, were at the first but moveable boards, or stalls, set out on market-days, to show their fish there to be sold; but procuring licence to set up sheds, they grew to shops, and by little and little to tall houses, of three or four stories in height, and now are called Fish Street. Walter Turke, fishmonger, mayor 1349, had two shops in Old Fish Street, over against St. Nicholas' Church; the one rented five shillings the year, the other four shillings.

Bread Street, so called of bread sold there, as I said, is now wholly inhabited by rich merchants; and divers fair inns be there, for good receipt of carriers and other travellers to the city.

On the east side of this street, at the corner of Watling Street, is the proper church of Allhallows in Bread Street, wherein are the monuments of James Thame, goldsmith; John Walpole, goldsmith, 1349; Thomas Beamount, alderman, one of the sheriffs 1442;

Robert Basset, salter, mayor 1476; Sir Richard Chaury, salter, mayor 1509; Sir Thomas Pargitar, salter, mayor 1530; Henry Sucley, merchant-tailor, one of the sheriffs 1541; Richard Read, alderman, that served and was taken prisoner in Scotland, 1542; Robert House, one of the sheriffs 1589; William Albany, Richard May, and Roger Abde, merchant-tailors.

In the 23rd of Henry VIII., the 17th of August, two priests of this church fell at variance, that the one drew blood of the other; wherefore the same church was suspended, and no service sung or said therein for the space of one month after; the priests were committed to prison, and the 15th of October, being enjoined penance, went before a general procession, bare-headed, bare-footed, and bare-legged, before the children, with beads and books in their hands, from Paul's, through Cheap, Cornhill, &c.

More to be noted of this church, which had sometime a fair spired steeple of stone. In the year 1559, the 5th of September, about mid-day, fell a great tempest of lightning, with a terrible clap of thunder, which struck the said spire about nine or ten feet beneath the top; out of the which place fell a stone that slew a dog, and overthrew a man that was playing with the dog. The same spire being but little damnified thereby, was shortly after taken down, for sparing the charges of reparation.

On the same side is Salters' Hall, with six almshouses in number, built for poor decayed brethren of that company. This hall was burnt in the year 1539, and again re-edified.

Lower down on the same side is the parish church of St. Mildred the Virgin. The monuments in this church be—of the Lord Trenchaunt of St. Albans, knight, who was supposed to be either the new builder of this church, or best benefactor to the works thereof, about the year 1300; and Odde Cornish, gentleman, 1312; William Palmer, blader, a great benefactor also, 1356; John Shadworth, mayor 1401, who gave the parsonage-house, a revestry, and churchyard to that parish, in the year 1428; notwithstanding, his monument is pulled down; Stephen Bugg, gentleman; his arms be three water-bugs, 1419; Henry Bugg founded a chantry there 1419; Roger Ford, vintner, 1440; Thomas Barnwell, fishmonger, one of the sheriffs 1434; Sir John Hawlen, clerk, parson of that church, who built the parsonage-house newly after the same had been burnt to the ground, together with the parson and his man also, burnt in that fire, 1485; John Parnell, 1510; William Hurstwaight, pewterer to the king, 1526; Christopher Turner, chirurgeon to King Henry VIII., 1530; Ralph Simonds, fishmonger, one of the sheriffs in the year 1527; Thomas Langham gave to the poor of that parish four tenements 1575; Thomas Hall, salter, 1582; Thomas Collins, salter, alderman; Sir Ambrose Nicholás, salter, mayor 1575, was buried in Sir John Shadworth's vault.

Out of this Bread Street, on the same side, is Basing Lane; a part whereof, as is afore showed, is of this ward, but how it took the name of Basing I have not read: in the 20th year of Richard II. the same was called the bakehouse, whether meant for the king's bakehouse, or of bakers dwelling there, and baking bread to serve the market in Bread Street, where the bread was sold, I know not; but sure I am, I have not read of Basing, or of Gerrard the Giant, to have anything there to do.

On the south side of this lane is one great house, of old time built upon arched vaults, and with arched gates of stone, brought from Caen in Normandy. The same is now a common hostrey for receipt of travellers, commonly and corruptly called Gerrard's Hall, of a giant said to have dwelt there. In the high-roofed hall of this house sometime stood a large fir pole, which reached to the roof thereof, and was said to be one of the staves that Gerrard the Giant used in the wars to run withal. There stood also a ladder of the same length, which, as they say, served to ascend to the top of the staff. Of later years this hall is altered in building, and divers rooms are made in it. Notwithstanding, the pole is removed to one corner of the hall, and the ladder hanged broken upon a wall in the yard. The hostler of that house said to me, "the pole lacketh half a foot of forty in length;" I measured the compass thereof, and found it fifteen inches. Reason of the pole could the master of the hostelry give me none, but bade me read the great chronicles, for there he heard of it: which answer seemed to me insufficient, for he meant the description of Britain, for the most part drawn out of John Leyland his commentaries, borrowed of myself, and placed before Reyne Wolfe's Chronicle, as the labours of another, who was forced to confess he never travelled further than from London to the university of Oxford; he writing a chapter of giants or monstrous men, hath set down more matter than truth, as partly against my will I am enforced here to touch. R. G., in his brief collection of histories, as he termeth it, hath these words: "I, the writer hereof, did see, the 10th day of March, in the yeare of our Lord 1564, and had the same in my hand, the tooth of a man, which weighed ten ounces of troy weight; and the skull of the same man is extant, and to be seene, which will hold five pecks of wheat; and the shin-bone of the same man is six foote in length, and of a marvellous greatness." Thus far of R. G. The error thereof is thus; He affirmeth a stone to be the tooth of a man, which stone, so proved, having no shape of a tooth, had neither skull or shin-bone. Notwithstanding, it is added in the said description, that by conjectural symetry of those parts the body to be twenty-eight feet long, or more. From this he goeth to another like matter, of a man with a mouth sixteen feet wide, and so to Gerrard the Giant and his staff. But to leave these fables, and return where I left, I will note what myself hath observed concerning that house.

I read that John Gisors, mayor of London in the year 1245, was owner thereof, and that Sir John Gisors, knight, Mayor of London, and constable of the Tower 1311, and divers others of that name and family, since that time owned it. William Gisors was one of the sheriffs 1329. More, John Gisors had issue, Henry and John; which John had issue, Thomas; which Thomas deceasing in the year 1350, left unto his son Thomas his messuage called Gisor's Hall, in the parish of St. Mildred in Bread Street: John Gisors made a feoffment thereof, 1386, &c. So it appeareth that this Gisor's Hall of late time by corruption hath been called Gerrard's Hall for Gisor's Hall; as Bosom's Inn for Blossom's Inn, Bevis Marks for Buries Marks, Mark Lane for Mart Lane, Belliter Lane for Belsetter's Lane, Gutter Lane for Gutheron's Lane, Cry Church for Christ's Church, St. Mihel in the Quorn for St. Mihel at Corne, and sundry such others. Out of this Gisor's Hall, at the first building thereof, were made divers arched doors, yet to be seen, which seem not sufficient for any great monster or other than man of common stature to pass through. The pole in the hall might be used of old time, as then the custom was in every parish, to be set up in the summer as May-pole, before the principal house in the parish or street, and to stand in the hall before the screen, decked with holm and ivy, all the feast of Christmas. The ladder served for the decking of the May-pole and roof of the hall. Thus much for Gisor's Hall, and for that side of Bread Street, may suffice.

Now on the west side of Bread Street, amongst divers fair and large houses for merchants, and fair inns for passengers, had ye one prison-house pertaining to the sheriffs of London, called the compter in Bread Street; but in the year 1555 the prisoners were removed from thence to one other new compter in Wood Street, provided by the city's purchase, and built for that purpose. The cause of which remove was this: Richard Husband, pasteler,* keeper of this compter in Bread Street, being a wilful and headstrong man, dealt, for his own advantage, hard with the prisoners under his charge, having also servants such as himself liked best for their bad usage, and would not for any complaint be reformed; whereupon, in the year 1550, Sir Rowland Hill being mayor, by the assent of a court of aldermen, he was sent to the gaol of Newgate, for the cruel handling

---

* *Pasteler*, French "pasteleur" and "pastier," confectioner. Another English form was "pasterer."

of his prisoners; and it was commanded to the keeper to set those irons on his legs which are called the widow's alms. These he ware from Thursday to Sunday in the afternoon, and being by a court of aldermen released on the Tuesday, was bound in a hundred marks to observe from thenceforth an act made by the Common Council, for the ordering of prisoners in the compters. All which notwithstanding, he continued as afore, whereof myself am partly a witness; for being of a jury to inquire against a sessions of gaol delivery, in the year 1552, we found the prisoners hardly dealt withal, for their achates * and otherwise; as also that thieves and strumpets were there lodged for fourpence the night, whereby they might be safe from searches that were made abroad. For the which enormities, and other not needful to be recited, he was indicted at that session, but did rub it out, and could not be reformed till this remove of prisoners, for the house in Bread Street was his own by lease, or otherwise, so that he could not be put from it. Note, that gaolers buying their offices will deal hardly with pitiful prisoners.

Now in Friday Street, so called of fishmongers dwelling there, and serving Friday's Market, on the east side, is a small parish church, commonly called St. John Evangelist. The monuments therein be of John Dogget, merchant-tailor, one of the sheriffs in the year 1509; Sir Christopher Askew, draper, mayor 1533; William de Avinger, farrier, was buried there in the 34th of Edward III. Then lower down is one other parish church of St. Margaret Moyses, so called, as seemeth, of one Moyses, that was founder or new builder thereof. The monuments there be of Sir Richard Dobbes, skinner, mayor 1551; William Dane, ironmonger, one of the sheriffs 1569; Sir John Allet, fishmonger, mayor 1591. There was of older time buried, Nicholas Stanes, and Nicholas Braye. They founded chantries there.

On the west side of this Friday Street is Maiden Lane, so named of such a sign, or Distaffe Lane, for Distar Lane, as I read in the record of a brewhouse called the Lamb, in Distar Lane, the 16th of Henry VI. In this Distar Lane, on the north side thereof, is the Cordwainers, or Shoemakers' Hall, which company were made a brotherhood or fraternity in the 11th of Henry IV. Of these Cordwainers I read, that since the fifth of Richard II., when he took to wife Anne, daughter to Vesalaus, King of Boheme,† by her example, the English people had used peaked shoes, tied to their knees with silken laces, or chains of silver or gilt, wherefore in

---

* *Achates*, also "acates," contracted into "cates," provisions bought. Old French "achat." To cater has for its first meaning to buy provisions.

† *Vesalaus* means Wenceslaus, who was brother, not father, to Anne of Bohemia. Her father was the Emperor Charles IV., and she was eldest daughter of his fourth wife, Elizabeth of Pomerania.

the 4th of Edward IV. it was ordained and proclaimed that beaks of shoon * and boots should not pass the length of two inches, upon pain of cursing by the clergy, and by parliament to pay twenty shillings for every pair. And every cordwainer that shod any man or woman on the Sunday to pay thirty shillings.

On the south side of this Distar Lane is also one other lane, called Distar Lane, which runneth down to Knightriders' Street, or Old Fish Street, and this is the end of Bread Street Ward, which hath an alderman, his deputy, common council ten, constables ten, scavengers eight, wardmote inquest thirteen, and a beadle. It standeth taxed to the fifteen in London at £37, and in the Exchequer at £36, 18s. 2d.

Queen Hithe Ward.

NEXT unto Bread Street Ward, on the south side thereof, is Queen Hithe Ward, so called of a water gate, or harbour for boats, lighters, and barges; and was of old time for ships, at what time the timber bridge of London was drawn up, for the passage of them to the said hithe, as to a principal strand for landing and unlading against the midst and heart of the city.

This ward beginneth in the east, in Knightriders' Street, on the south side thereof, at the east end of the parish church called the Holy Trinity, and runneth west on the south side to a lane called Lambert Hill, which is the length of the ward in Knightriders' Street, out of the which street are divers lanes running south to Thames Street, and are of this ward. The first is Trinity Lane, which runneth down by the west end of Trinity Church; then is Spuren Lane, or Spooner's Lane, now called Huggen Lane; then Bread Street Hill; then St. Mary Mounthaunt, out of the which lane, on the east side thereof, is one other lane, turning east, through St. Nicholas Olave's Churchyard to Bread Street Hill. This lane is called Finimore Lane, or Fivefoot Lane, because it is but five feet in breadth at the west end. In the midst of this lane runneth down one other lane broader south to Thames Street. I think the same to be called Desbourne Lane, for I read of such a lane to have been in the parish of Mary Somerset, in the 22nd year of Edward III., where there is said to lie between the tenement of Edward de Montacute, knight, on the east part, and the tenement some time pertaining to William Gladwine on the west, one plot of ground, containing in length towards Thames Street twenty-five feet, &c.

Last of all, have you Lambert Hill Lane, so called of one Lambert, owner thereof; and this is the furthest west part of this ward.

---

* *Beaks of shoon.* Beak and peak are of the same origin. In the different forms of the Celtic from which they come there were " peac " and " beac."

On the north side coming down from Knightriders' Street, the east side of Lambert Hill is wholly of this ward; and the west side, from the north end of the Blacksmiths' Hall, which is about the midst of this lane, unto Thames Street; then part of Thames Street is also of this ward, to wit, from a cook's house called the sign of King David, three houses west from the Old Swan brewhouse in the east, unto Huntington House, over against St. Peter's Church in the west, near unto Paul's Wharf; and on the land side, from a cook's house called the Blue Boar, to the west end of St. Peter's Church, and up St. Peter's Hill, two houses north above the said church. And these be the bounds of this ward, in which are parish churches seven, halls of companies two, and other ornaments as shall be showed.

First in Knightriders' Street is the small parish church of the Holy Trinity, very old, and in danger of down falling. Collections have been made for repairing thereof, but they will not stretch so far, and therefore it leaneth upon props or stilts. Monuments as followeth :—

John Brian, alderman in the reign of Henry V., a great benefactor; John Chamber had a chantry there; Thomas Rishby, esquire, and Alice his wife, within the chancel; John Mirfin, auditor of the exchequer, 1471 ; Sir Richard Fowler, of Ricks in Oxfordshire, 1528 ; George Cope, second son to Sir John Cope of Copasashby in Northamptonshire, 1572.

Towards the west end of Knightriders' Street is the parish church of St. Nicholas Cold Abbey, a proper church, somewhat ancient, as appeareth by the ways raised thereabout, so that men are forced to descend into the body of the church. It hath been called of many Golden Abbey, of some, Gold Abbey, or Cold Bey, and so hath the most ancient writings, as standing in a cold place, as Cold Harbour, and such like. The steeple or tall tower of this church, with the south aisle, have been of a later building : to wit, the 1st of Richard II., when it was meant the whole old church should have been new built, as appeareth by the arching begun on the east side the steeple, under the which, in the stone work, the arms of one Buckland, esquire, and his wife, daughter to Beaupere, are cut in stone, and also are in the glass windows, whereby it appeareth he was the builder of the steeple and repairer of the residue. The 26th of Edward III., An. Aubrey being mayor, T. Frere, fishmonger, gave one piece of ground to the said parish church of St. Nicholas, containing eighty-six feet in length, and forty-three feet at one end, and thirty-four at the other, in breadth, for a cemetery or churchyard. The 20th of Richard II., Thomas Barnard Castle, clerk, John Sonderash, clerk, and John Nouncy, gave to the parson and churchwardens of the said church and their successors one messuage and one shop, with the appurtenances, in Distaffe Lane and Old Fish Street, for the reparation of the body of the said church, the belfry or steeple, and ornaments.

Buried in this church—John Calfe, and William Cogeshall, 1426; Walter Turke, fishmonger, mayor 1349; Richard Esastone, fishmonger, 1330; Nicholas Wolberge, fishmonger, 1407; Thomas Padington, fishmonger, 1485; Robert Hary, fishmonger, John Suring, 1490; Roger Darlington, fishmonger, 1557; Richard Lacty, parson, under a fair tomb on the north side the choir, 1491; Richard Bradbrudge, 1497; William Clarke, 1501; James Picman, 1507; Richard Farneford, 1525; Thomas Nicholas, fishmonger, 1527; William Barde, fishmonger, 1528.

On the north side of this church, in the wall thereof, was of late built a convenient cistern of stone and lead for receipt of Thames water, conveyed in pipes of lead to that place, for the ease and commodity of the fishmongers and other inhabitants in and about Old Fish Street. Barnard Randolph, common sergeant of the city of London, did in his lifetime deliver to the company of Fishmongers the sum of nine hundred pounds, to be employed towards the conducting of the said Thames water, and cisterning the same, &c.; in the parishes of St. Mary Magdalen, and St. Nicholas Cold Abbey, near unto Fish Street, seven hundred pounds; and other two hundred pounds to charitable deeds. He deceased 1583, and shortly after this conduit with the other was made and finished.

In Trinity Lane, on the west side thereof, is the Painterstainers' Hall, for so of old time were they called, but now that workmanship of staining is departed out of use in England. Lower down in Trinity Lane, on the east side thereof, was sometime a great messuage pertaining unto John, Earl of Cornwall, in the 14th of Edward III. On Bread Street Hill, down to the Thames on both sides, be divers fair houses, inhabited by fishmongers, cheesemongers, and merchants of divers trades. On the west side whereof is the parish church of St. Nicholas Olive, a convenient church, having the monuments of W. Newport, fishmonger, one of the sheriffs 1375; Richard Willowes, parson, 1391; Richard Sturges, fishmonger, 1470; Thomas Lewen, ironmonger, one of the sheriffs 1537, who gave his messuage, with the appurtenances, wherein he dwelt, with fourteen tenements in the said parish of St. Nicholas, to be had after the decease of Agnes his wife, to the Ironmongers, and they to give stipends appointed to almsmen, in five houses by them built in the churchyard of that parish, more to poor scholars in Oxford and Cambridge, &c. Blitheman, an excellent organist of the Queen's Chapel, lieth buried there with an epitaph, 1591, &c.

The next is Old Fish Street Hill, a lane so called, which also runneth down to Thames Street.   In this lane, on the east side thereof, is the one end of Finimore, or Five Foot Lane.   On the west side of this Old Fish Street Hill is the Bishop of Hereford's Inn or lodging, an ancient house and large rooms, built of stone and timber, which sometime belonged to the Mounthaunts in Norfolk. Radulphus de Maydenstone, Bishop of Hereford, about 1234, bought it of the Mounthaunts, and gave it to the Bishops of Hereford, his successors.   Charles, both Bishop of Hereford and Chancellor of the Marches, about the year 1517 repaired it, since the which time the same is greatly ruinated, and is now divided into many small tenements. The hall and principal rooms are a house to make sugar-loaves, &c.

Next adjoining is the parish church of St. Mary de Monte Alto, or Mounthaunt.   This is a very small church, and at the first built to be a chapel for the said house of the Mounthaunts, and for tenements thereunto belonging.   The Bishop of Hereford is patron thereof. Monuments in this church of John Glocester, alderman 1345, who gave Salt Wharf for two chantries there; John Skip, Bishop of Hereford, 1539, sate twelve years, died at London in time of parliament, and was buried in this church.   There was sometime a fair house in the said parish of St. Mary Mounthaunt, belonging to Robert Belkenape, one of the king's justices, but the said Belkenape being banished this realm, King Richard II., in the 12th of his reign, gave it to William Wickham, Bishop of Winchester.

On the east side of this Old Fish Street Hill is one great house, now let out for rent, which house sometime was one of the halls pertaining to the company of Fishmongers, at such time as they had six hallmotes or meeting-places : namely, two in Bridge Street, or New Fish Street ; two in Old Fish Street, whereof this was one ; and two in Stockfishmonger Row, or Thames Street, as appeareth by a record, the 22nd of Richard II.

Next westward is one other lane called Lambert Hill, the east side whereof is wholly of this ward, and but half the west side, to wit, from the north end of the Blacksmiths' Hall.

Then in Thames Street of this ward, and on the north side over against the Queen's Hithe, is the parish church of St. Michael, a convenient church, but all the monuments therein are defaced.

I find that Stephen Spilman, gentleman, of that family in Norfolk, sometime mercer, chamberlain of London, then one of the sheriffs, and alderman in the year 1404, deceasing without issue, gave his lands to his family the Spilmans, and his goods to the making or repairing of bridges and other like godly uses ; and amongst others in this church he founded a chantry, and was buried in the choir.

Also Richard Marlowe, ironmonger, mayor 1409. gave twenty pounds to the poor of that ward, and ten marks to the church.

Richard Gray, ironmonger, one of the sheriffs 1515, gave forty pounds to that church, and was buried there. At the west end of that church goeth up a lane called Pyel Lane. On the same north side, at the south end of St. Mary Mounthaunt Lane, is the parish church of St. Mary Somerset, over against the Broken Wharf. It is a proper church, but the monuments are all defaced. I think the same to be of old time called Somer's Hithe, of some man's name that was owner of the ground near adjoining, as Edred's Hithe was so called of Edred owner thereof, and thence called Queen Hithe as pertaining to the queen, &c.

Then is a small parish church of St. Peter, called *parva*, or little, near unto Paul's Wharf. In this church no monuments do remain. At the west end thereof is a lane called St. Peter's Hill, but two houses up that lane on the east side is of this ward, and the rest is of Castle Baynard Ward.

On the south side of Thames Street, beginning again in the east among the cooks, the first in this ward is the sign of David the King. Then is Towne's End Lane, turning down to the Thames. Then is Queen Hithe, a large receptacle for ships, lighters, barges, and such other vessels.

Touching the antiquity and use of this gate and hithe, first, I find the same belongeth to one named Edred, and was then called Edred's Hithe, which since falling to the hands of King Stephen, it was by his charter confirmed to William de Ypre. The farm thereof in fee and in heritage, William de Ypre gave unto the prior and convent of the Holy Trinity within Aldgate, as appeareth by this charter:—

"To Theobalde, by the grace of God, Archbishop of Canterbury, primate of England, and Legate Apostolike, to the Bishoppe of London, and to all faithful people, clarkes and layemen, William de Ypre sendeth greeting.

"Know ye me to have given and graunted to God, and to the church of the Holy Trinitie of London, to the prior and canons there serving God in perpetuall almes, Edred's hith, with the appurtenances, with such devotion, that they shall send every yeare twentie pound unto the maintenance of the hospital of St. Katherens, which hospitall they have in their hands, and one hundred shillinges to the monkes of Bermondsey, and sixty shillings to the brethren of the hospitall of St. Giles, and that which remayneth, the said prior and canons shall enjoy to themselves. Witnesses, Richard de Lucie, Raph Picot, &c.

This Edred's Hithe, after the aforesaid grants, came again to the king's hands, by what means I have not read, but it pertained unto the queen, and therefore was called *Ripa Reginæ*, the Queen's Bank, or Queen's Hithe, and great profit thereof was made to her use, as may appear by this which followeth.

King Henry III., in the 9th of his reign, commanded the constables of the Tower of London to arrest the ships of the Cinque Ports on the river of Thames, and to compel them to bring their corn to no other place but to the Queen's Hithe only. In the eleventh of his reign he charged the said constable to distrain all fish offered to be sold in any place of this city but at the Queen Hithe. Moreover, in the 28th of the said king's reign, an inquisition was made before William of York, provost of Beverley, Henry of Bath, and Hierome of Caxton, justices itinerant, sitting in the Tower of London, touching the customs of Queen Hithe, observed in the year last before the wars between the king and his father and the barons of England ; and of old customs of other times, and what customs had been changed, at what time the tax and payment of all things coming together, and between Woore Path and Anede Hithe were found and ceased, according to the old order, as well corn and fish as other things. All which customs were as well to be observed in the part of Downgate as in Queen Hithe, for the king's use. When also it was found that the corn arriving between the gate of the Guildhall of the merchants of Cologne, and the soke of the Archbishop of Canterbury, for he had a house near unto the Blackfriars, was not to be measured by any other quarter than by that of the Queen's soke.

After this, the bailiff of the said hithe complained that since the said recognition, fourteen foreign ships laden with fish arrived at Billingsgate, which ships should have arrived at the same hithe. And therefore it was ordered that if any foreign ship laden with fish should in form aforesaid arrive elsewhere than at this hithe, it should be at the king's pleasure to amerce them at forty shillings. Notwithstanding, the ships of the citizens of London were at liberty to arrive where the owners would appoint them.

After this, the said Henry III. confirmed the grant of Richard, Earl of Cornwall, for the farm of the Queen Hithe unto John Gisors, then mayor, and to the commonalty of London, and their successors for ever, as by this his charter appeareth :—

"Henry, by the grace of God, King of England, Lord of Ireland, Duke of Guienne, and Earl of Anjou, to all archbishops, &c. Be it known, that we have seen the covenant between our brother, Richard Earl of Cornwall, on the one part, and the mayor and commonalty on the other part, which was in this sort. In the 30th year of Henry, the son of King John, upon the feast of the Translation of St. Edward, at Westminster, this covenant was made between the honourable Lord Richard Earl of Cornwall, and John Gisors, then mayor of London, and the commons thereof, concerning certain ex- actions and demands pertaining to the Queen Hithe of London. The said earl granted for himself and his heirs, that the said mayor, and all mayors ensuing, and all the commons of the city, should have and hold the Queen Hithe, with all the liberties, customs, and other appurtenances, repaying yearly to the said earl, his heirs and assigns, fifty pounds, at Clerkenwell, at two several terms ; to wit, the Sunday after Easter twenty-five pounds, and at Michaelmas twenty-five pounds. And for more surety hereof the said earl hath set thereunto his seal, and left it with the mayor, and the mayor and commonalty have set to their seal, and left it with the earl. Wherefore we confirm and establish the said covenant for us, and for our heirs. Witnesses, Raph Fitz Nichol, Richard Gray, John and Wil. Brithem, Paulin Painter, Raph Wancia, John Cumbaud, and other, at Windsor, 26th of February, in the 31st of our reign."

The charge of this Queen Hithe was then committed to the sheriffs, and so hath continued ever since; the profits whereof are sore diminished, so that, as writeth Robert Fabian, it was worth in his time little above twenty marks, or fifteen pounds, one year with another. Now for customs of this Queen Hithe. In the year 1302, the 30th of Edward I., it was found by the oath of divers men, that bakers, brewers, and others, buying their corn at Queen Hithe, should pay for measuring, portage, and carriage, for every quarter of corn whatsoever, from thence to West Cheap, to St. Anthony's Church, to Horseshoe Bridge, and to Woolsey Street, in the parish of Allhallows the Less, and such like distances, one halfpenny farthing; to Fleet Bridge, to Newgate, Cripplegate, to Birchovers Lane, to East Cheap, and Billingsgate, one penny. Also, that the measure, or the meter, ought to have eight chief master-porters, every master to have three porters under him, and every one of them to find one horse and seven sacks; and he that so did not to lose his office. This hithe was then so frequented with vessels bringing thither corn, besides fish, salt, fuel, and other merchandises, that all these men, to wit, the meter and porters, thirty-seven in number, for all their charges of horses and sacks and small stipend, lived well of their labours; but now the bakers of London and other citizens travel into the countries, and buy their corn of the farmers, after the farmers' price.

King Edward II., in the 1st of his reign, gave to Margaret, wife to Piers de Gavestone, forty-three pounds twelve shillings and ninepence halfpenny farthing out of the rent of London, to be received of the Queen's Hithe. Certain impositions were set upon ships and other vessels coming thither, as upon corn, salt, and other things, toward the charge of cleansing Roomeland there, the 41st of Edward III.

The 3rd of Edward IV., the market at Queen Hithe being hindered by the slackness of drawing up London Bridge, it was ordained that all manner of vessels, ships or boats, great or small, resorting to the city with victual, should be sold by retail; and that if there came but one vessel at a time, were it salt, wheat, rye, or other corn, from beyond the seas, or other grains, garlic, onions, herrings, sprats, eels, whiting, plaice, cods, mackerel, &c., then that one vessel should come to Queen Hithe, and there to make sale; but if two vessels come, the one should come to Queen Hithe, the other to Billingsgate; if three, two of them should come to Queen Hithe, the third to Billingsgate, &c., always the more to Queen Hithe. If the vessel being great, coming with salt from the Bay, and could not come to these quays, then the same to be conveyed by lighters, as before is meant.

One large house for stowage of corn craned out of lighters and barges is there lately built. Sir John Lion, grocer, mayor 1554, by his testament gave a hundred pounds towards it, but since increased and made larger at the charges of the city, in the year 1565.

Against this Queen Hithe, on the river Thames, of late years, was placed a corn mill, upon or betwixt two barges or lighters, and there ground corn, as water mills in other places, to the wonder of many that had not seen the like; but this lasted not long without decay, such as caused the same barges and mill to be removed, taken asunder, and soon forgotten. I read of the like to have been in former time, as thus :—In the year 1525, the 16th of Henry VIII., Sir William Bayly being mayor, John Cooke of Gloucester, mercer, gave to the mayor and commonalty of London, and theirs for ever, one great barge, in the which two corn mills were made and placed, which barge and mills were set in and upon the stream of the river of Thames, within the jurisdiction and liberty of the said city of London.

And also he gave to the city all such timber, boards, stones, iron, &c., provided for making, mending, and repairing of the said barge and mills, in reward whereof the mayor gave him fifty pounds presently, and fifty pounds yearly during his life; and if the said Cooke deceased before Johan his wife, then she to have forty marks the year during her life.

Next adjoining to this Queen Hithe, on the west side thereof, is Salt Wharf, named of salt taken up, measured, and sold there. The next is Stew Lane, of a stew or hothouse there kept. After that is Timber Hithe, or Timber Street, so called of timber or boards there taken up and wharfed. It is in the parish of St. Mary Somershithe, as I read in the 56th of Henry III., and in the 9th of Edward II. Then is Brookes Wharf and Broken Wharf, a water gate or quay, so called of being broken and fallen down into the Thames. By this Broken Wharf remaineth one large old building of stone, with arched gates, which messuage, as I find, in the reign of Henry III., the 43rd year, pertaining unto Hugh de Bigot; and in the 11th of Edward III., to Thomas Brotherton, the king's brother, Earl of Norfolk, Marshal of England; in the 11th of Henry VI., to John Mowbray, Duke of Norfolk, &c.

Within the gate of this house, now belonging to the city of London, is lately, to wit, in the years 1594 and 1595, built one large house of great height, called an engine, made by Bevis Bulmar, gentleman, for the conveying and forcing of Thames water to serve in the middle and west parts of the city. The ancient great hall of this messuage is yet standing, and pertaining to a great brewhouse for beer. West from this is Trigg Lane, going down to Thames. Next is called Boss Lane, of a boss of water, like unto that of Billingsgate, there placed by the executors of Richard Whittington. Then is one great messuage, sometime belonging to the abbots of Chertsey in Surrey, and was their inn, wherein they were lodged when they repaired to the city. It is now called Sandie House, by what reason I have not heard. I think the Lord Sands * have been lodged there.

And this is an end of this Queen Hithe Ward, which hath an alderman and his deputy, common council six, constables nine, scavengers eight, wardmote inquest thirteen, and a beadle. It is taxed to the fifteen in London twenty pounds, and in the Exchequer at nineteen pounds sixteen shillings and twopence.

Castle Baynard Ward.

THE next is Castle Baynard Ward, so named of an old castle there. This ward beginneth in the east on the Thames side, at a house called Huntington House, and runneth west by Paul's Wharf, by Baynard's Castle, Puddle Wharf, and by the south side of Black-friars, then turning by the east wall of the said Friars to the south-west end of Creed Lane. Then on the north side of Thames Street, over against Huntington House, by St. Peter's Church and Lane, called Peter Hill, along till over against Puddle Wharf, and then north up by the great Wardrobe to the west end of Carter Lane, then up Creed Lane, Ave Mary Lane, and a piece of Paternoster Row to the sign of the Golden Lion, and back again up Warwick Lane, and all the east side thereof, to the sign of the Crown by Newgate Market ; and this is the farthest north part of this ward.

Then out of Thames Street be lanes ascending north to Knight-riders' Street. The first is Peter Hill Lane, all of that ward, two houses excepted, adjoining to St. Peter's Church. The next is Paul's Wharf Hill, which thwarting Knightriders' Street and Carter Lane, goeth up to the south chain of Paul's Churchyard.

Then is Adle Street, over against the west part of Baynard's Castle, going up by the west end of Knightriders' Street and to Carter Lane. Thus much for lanes out of Thames Street. The one half of the west side of Lambert Hill Lane being of this ward, at the north-west end thereof, on the south side, and at the west end of

---

* Lord Sands is spelt Sandys. The travels of George Sandys in Turkey and Palestine, begun in 1610, have been almost invariably labelled by the binders Sandy's Travels. Like confusion of the "s" with a case ending would turn Sandys into Sandy House.

St. Mary Magdalen's Church on the north side beginneth Knight-riders' Street to be of this ward, and runneth west on both sides to the parish church of St. Andrew by the Wardrobe.

Then at the east end of St. Mary Magdalen's Church goeth up the Old Exchange, all the west side whereof up to the south-east gate of Paul's Churchyard, and by St. Austen's Church, is of this ward. About the midst of this Old Exchange, on the west side thereof, is Carter Lane, which runneth west to the east entry of the Blackfriars, and to the south end of Creed Lane, out of the which Carter Lane descendeth a lane called Do-little Lane, and cometh into Knightriders' Street by the Boar's Head Tavern; and more west is Sermon Lane, by an inn called the Paul Head. Then out of Carter Lane, on the north side thereof, the south chain of Paul's Churchyard, and the churchyard itself on that south side of Paul's Church, and the church of St. Gregory, the bishop's palace, and the dean's lodging, be all of this ward; and such be the bounds thereof. The ornaments in this ward be parish churches four. Of old time a castle, divers noblemen's houses, halls of companies twain, and such others, as shall be shown.

In Thames Street, at the south-east end, is an ancient messuage, of old time called Beaumount's Inn, as belonging to that family of noblemen of this realm in the 4th of Edward III. Edward IV., in the 5th of his reign, gave it to W. Hastings, lord chamberlain, master of his mints. It is now called Huntington House, as belonging to the earls of Huntington. Next is Paul's Wharf, a large landing-place, with a common stair upon the river of Thames, at the end of a street called Paul's Wharf Hill, which runneth down from Paul's Chain. Next is a great messuage, called Scropes Inn, sometime belonging to Scropes, in the 31st of Henry VI.

Then is one other great messuage, sometime belonging to the Abbey of Fiscampe, beyond the sea, and by reason of the wars, it coming to the hands of King Edward III., the same was given to Sir Simon Burley, Knight of the Garter, and, therefore, called Burley House in Thames Street, between Baynard's Castle and Paul's Wharf. Then have you Baynard's Castle, whereof this whole ward taketh the name. This castle banketh on the river Thames, and was called Baynard's Castle, of Baynard, a nobleman that came in with William the Conqueror, of the which castle, and of Baynard himself, I have spoken in another place.

There was also another tower by Baynard's Castle, built by King Edward II. Edward III., in the 2nd of his reign, gave it to William Duke of Hamelake, in the county of York, and his heirs, for one rose yearly, to be paid for all service, the same place, as seemeth to me, was since called Legate's Inn, in the 7th of Edward IV., where be now divers wood wharfs in place. Then is there a great brew-house, and Puddle Wharf, a watergate into the Thames, where horses use to water, and therefore being defiled with their trampling, and made puddle, like as also of one Puddle dwelling there, it is called Puddle Wharf. Then is there a lane between the Blackfriars and the Thames, called in the 26th of Edward III. Castle Lane.

In this lane also is one great messuage, of old time belonging to the priory of Okeborne in Wiltshire, and was the prior's lodging when he repaired to London. This priory being of the French order, was suppressed by Henry V., and with other lands and tene-ments pertaining to the said priory, was by Henry VI. given to his college in Cambridge, called now the King's College. About this Castle Lane was sometime a mill or mills belonging to the Templars of the New Temple, as appeareth of record ; for King John, in the 1st year of his reign, granted a place in the Fleet, near unto Bay-nard's Castle, to make a mill, and the whole course of water of the Fleet to serve the said mill.

I read also, that in the year 1247, the 2nd of Edward I., Ri. Raison, and Atheline his wife, did give to Nicho. de Musely, clerk, ten shillings of yearly free and quiet rent, out of all his tenements, with the houses thereupon built, and their appurtenances, which they had of the demise of the master and brethren of Knights Templars, in England, next to their mill of Fleet, over against the houses of Laurence de Brooke, in the parish of St. Andrew, next to Baynard's Castle, which tenements lie between the way leading towards the said mill on the west part. Also in the rights belonging to Robert Fitz-water, and to his heirs, in the city of London, in the time of peace, it was declared in the year 1303, that the said Robert, castellan of London, and banner-bearer, had a soke, or ward, in the city, that was by the wall of St. Paul, as men go down the street before the brewhouse of St. Paul unto the Thames, and so to the side of the mill, which is in the water that cometh down from Fleet Bridge, and goeth by London Walls, betwixt Friars Preachers Church and Lud-gate. And so that ward turned back by the house of the said Friars unto the said common wall of the said canonry of St. Paul ; that is, all of the parish of St. Andrew, which is in the gift of his ancestors by seniority, as more I have shown in the Castles. Now here is to be noted, that the wall of London at that time went straight south from Ludgate down to the river of Thames ; but for building of the Blackfriars Church, the said wall in that place was by commandment taken down, and a new wall made straight west from Ludgate to Fleet Bridge, and then by the water of Fleet to the river of Thames, &c.

In the year 1307, the 35th of Edward I., in a parliament at Carlisle, Henry Lacy, Earl of Lincoln, complained of noyances done to the water of the Fleet ; whereupon it was granted that the said mill should be removed and destroyed.

This ward ascendeth up by the east wall of the Blackfriars to the south-west end of Creed Lane, where it endeth on that side.

Then to begin again on the north side of Thames Street, over against Huntington House, by St. Peter's Church and Lane, called Peter Hill, and so to St. Benet Hude, or Hithe, over against Paul's Wharf, a proper parish church, which hath the monuments of Sir William Cheiny, knight, and Margaret his wife, 1442, buried there ; Doctor Caldwell, physician ; Sir Gilbert Dethik, knight, *alias* Garter king at arms. West from this church, by the south end of Adle Street, almost against Puddle Wharf, there is one ancient building of stone and timber, built by the lords of Barkley, and therefore called Barklies Inn. This house is all in ruin, and letten out in several tenements, yet the arms of the Lord Barkley remain in the stonework of an arched gate, gules, between a cheveron, crosses ten— three, three, and four. Richard Beauchampe, Earl of Warwick, was lodged in this house, then called Barklies Inn, in the parish of St. Andrew, in the reign of Henry VI.

Then turning up towards the north is the parish church of St. Andrew in the Wardrobe, a proper church, but few monuments hath it. John Parnt founded a chantry there. Then is the king's Great Wardrobe. Sir John Beauchamp, knight of the Garter, constable of Dover, warden of the Cinque Ports, son to Guido de Beauchampe, Earl of Warwick, built this house, was lodged there, deceased in the year 1359, and was buried on the south side of the middle aisle of Paul's Church. His executors sold the house to King Edward III., unto whom the parson of St. Andrew's complaining that the said Beauchampe had pulled down divers houses, in their place to build the same house, wherethrough he was hindered of his accustomed tithes, paid by the tenants of old time, granted him forty shillings by year out of that house for ever. King Richard III. was lodged there in the second of his reign.

In this house of late years is lodged Sir John Fortescue, knight, master of the wardrobe, chancellor and under-treasurer of the exchequer, and one of her Majesty's most honourable privy council. The secret letters and writings touching the estate of the realm were wont to be enrolled in the king's wardrobe, and not in the chancery, as appeareth by the records. Claus. 18. E. 4. 1. Memb. 13. Claus. 33. E. 1. Memb. 3. Et liberat. 1. E. 2. Memb. 4, &c. From this wardrobe, by the west end of Carter Lane, then up Creed Lane, Ave Mary Lane, a piece of Paternoster Row, up Warwick Lane all the east side, to a brewhouse called the Crown, as I said is of this ward. Touching lanes ascending out of Thames Street to Knightriders'

Street, the first is Peter's Hill, wherein I find no matter of note, more than certain almshouses, lately founded on the west side thereof by David Smith, embroiderer, for six poor widows, whereof each to have twenty shillings by the year.

On the east side of this lane standeth a large house, of ancient building, sometime belonging to the abbot of St. Mary in York, and was his abiding house when he came to London. Thomas Randolfe, esquire, hath lately augmented and repaired it.

At the upper end of this lane, towards the north, the corner houses there be called Peter's Key, but the reason thereof I have not heard. Then is Paul's Wharf Hill, on the east side whereof is Woodmonger's Hall. And next adjoining is Darby House, sometime belonging to the Stanleys, for Thomas Stanley, first Earl of Derby of that name, who married the Lady Margaret, Countess of Richmond, mother to Henry VII., in his time built it.

Queen Mary gave it to Gilbert Dethick, then Garter principal king of arms of Englishmen ; Thomas Hawley, Clarenceaux king of arms of the south parts ; William Harvy, *alias* Norroy king of arms of the north parts, and the other heralds and pursuivants of arms, and to their successors, all the same capital messuage or house called Derby House, with the appurtenances, situate in the parish of St. Benet and St. Peter, then being in the tenure of Sir Richard Sackville, knight, and lately parcel of the lands of Edward, Earl of Derby, &c., to the end that the said king of arms, heralds, and pursuivants of arms, and their successors, might at their liking dwell together, and at meet times to congregate, speak, confer, and agree among themselves for the good government of their faculty, and their records might be more safely kept, &c. Dated the 18th of July, 1555, Philip and Mary I., and third year.

Then higher up, near the south chain of Paul's Churchyard, is the Paul Head Tavern, which house, with the appurtenances, was of old time called Paul's brewhouse, for that the same was so employed, but been since left off, and let out.

On the west side of this street is one other great house, built of stone, which belongeth to Paul's Church, and was sometime let to the Blunts, Lords Mountjoy, but of latter time to a college in Cambridge, and from them to the doctors of the civil law and Arches, who keep a commons there ; and many of them being there lodged, it is called the Doctors' Commons. Above this, on the same side, was one other great building over against Paul's brewhouse, and this was called Paul's bakehouse, and was employed in baking of bread for the Church of Paul's.

In Addle Street, or Lane, I find no monuments.

In Lambert Hill Lane, on the west side thereof, is the Blacksmiths' Hall, and adjoining to the north side thereof have ye one plot of ground, enclosed with a brick wall for a churchyard, or burying-plot for the dead of St. Mary Magdalen's by Old Fish Street, which was given to that use by John Iwarby, an officer in the receipt of the exchequer, in the 26th of King Henry VI., as appeareth by patent. John Iwarby, &c., gave a piece of land lying void in the parish of St. Mary Magdalen, nigh to Old Fish Street, between the tenement of John Philpot on the south and the tenement of Bartholomew Burwash on the west, and the tenement pertaining to the convent of the Holy Well on the north and the way upon Lambert Hill on the east, for a churchyard, to the parson and churchwardens, &c.

Over against the north-west end of this Lambert Hill Lane in Knightriders' Street is the parish church of St. Mary Magdalen, a small church, having but few monuments, Richard Woodroffe, merchant tailor, 1519; Barnard Randolph, esquire, 1853.

On the west side of this church, by the porch thereof, is placed a conduit or cistern of lead, castellated with stone, for receipt of Thames water, conveyed at the charges of the before-named Barnard Randolph, esquire. By the east end of St. Mary Magdalen's Church runneth up the Old Exchange Lane, by the west end of Carter Lane, to the south-east gate or chain of Paul's Churchyard, as is before shown. And in this part was the Exchange kept, and bullion was received for coinage, as is noted in Farringdon Ward within. In this parish church of St. Mary Magdalen, out of Knightriders' Street up to Carter Lane, be two small lanes, the one of them called Do Little Lane, as a place not inhabited by artificers or open shopkeepers, but serving for a near passage from Knightriders' Street to Carter Lane.

The other, corruptly called Sermon Lane for Sheremoniars' Lane, for I find it by that name recorded in the 14th of Edward I., and in that lane, a place to be called the Black Loft, of melting silver, with four shops adjoining. It may, therefore, be well supposed that lane to take name of Sheremoneyers, such as cut and rounded the plates to be coined or stamped into sterling pence; for the place of coining was the Old Exchange, near unto the said Sheremoniars' Lane. Also I find that in the 13th of Richard II. William de la Pole had a house there. In Knightriders' Street is the College of Physicians, wherein was founded in the year 1582 a public lecture in surgery, to be read twice every week, &c., as is shown elsewhere.

In the south churchyard of Paul's is the south side and west end of the said church; in the which west end be three stately gates or entries, curiously wrought of stone: namely, the middle gate, in the midst whereof is placed a massy pillar of brass, whereunto the leaves of the said great gate are closed and fastened with locks, bolts, and bars of iron; all which, notwithstanding, on the 24th of December in the year 1565, by a tempest of wind then rising from the west, these gates were blown open, the bars, bolts, and locks broken in sunder, or greatly bended. Also on the 5th of January in the year 1589, by a like tempest of wind, then in the south-west, the lesser west gate of the said church, next to the bishop's palace, was broken, both bolts, bars, and locks, so that the same was blown over.

At either corner of this west end is, also of ancient building, a strong tower of stone, made for bell towers; the one of them, to wit, next to the palace, is at this present to the use of the same palace; the other, towards the south, is called the Lollardes' Tower, and hath been used as the bishop's prison, for such as were detected for opinions in religion contrary to the faith of the Church.

The last prisoner which I have known committed thereto was in the year 1573, one Peter Burcher, gentleman, of the Middle Temple, for having desperately wounded, and minding to have murdered, a serviceable gentleman named John Hawkins, esquire, in the high street near unto the Strand, who, being taken and examined, was found to hold certain opinions erroneous, and therefore committed thither, and convicted; but in the end, by persuasion, he promised to abjure his heresies, and was, by commandment of the council, removed from thence to the Tower of London, &c., where he committed as in my Annals I have expressed.

Adjoining to this Lollardes' Tower is the parish church of St. Gregory, appointed to the petty canons of Pauls. Monuments of note I know none there. The rest of that south side of St. Paul's Church, with the chapter-house, a beautiful piece of work, built about the reign of Edward III., is now defaced by means of licenses granted to cutlers, budget makers, and others, first to build low sheds, but now high houses, which do hide that beautiful side of the church, save only the top and south gate.

On the north-west side of this churchyard is the bishop's palace, a large thing for receipt, wherein divers kings have been lodged, and great household hath been kept, as appeareth by the great hall, which of late years, since the rebatement of bishops' livings, hath not been furnished with household menie and guests, as was meant by the builders thereof, and was of old time used.

The dean's lodging, on the other side, directly against the palace, is a fair old house, and also divers large houses are on the same side builded, which yet remain, and of old time were the lodgings of prebendaries and residentiaries, which kept great households and liberal hospitality, but now either decayed, or otherwise converted.

Then is the Stationers' Hall on the same side, lately built for them in place of Peter College, where in the year 1549, the 4th of January, five men were slain by the fall of earth upon them, digging for a well. And let this be an end of Baynard's Castle Ward, which hath an alderman, his deputy, common council nine, constables ten, scavengers seven, wardmote inquest fourteen, and a beadle. And to the fifteen is taxed at £12, in the exchequer £11, 13s.

The Ward of Farringdon Extra, or Without.

THE farthest west ward of this city, being the twenty-fifth ward of London, but without the walls, is called Farringdon Without, and was of old time part of the other Farringdon Within, until the 17th of Richard II., that it was divided and made twain, by the names of Farringdon *infra* and Farringdon *extra*, as is afore shown.

The bounds of which ward without Newgate and Ludgate are these : first, on the east part thereof, is the whole precinct of the late priory of St. Bartholomew, and a part of Long Lane on the north, towards Aldersgate Street and Ducke Lane, with the hospital of St. Bartholomew on the west, and all Smithfield to the bars in St. John Street. Then out of Smithfield, Chick Lane, toward Turmill Brook, and over that brook by a bridge of timber into the field, then back again by the pens, or folds, in Smithfield, by Smithfield Pond to Cow Lane, which turneth toward Oldborne, and then Hosier Lane out of Smithfield, also toward Oldborne, till it meet with a part of Cow Lane. Then Cock Lane out of Smithfield, over against Pye Corner, then also is Giltspur Street, out of Smithfield to Newgate, then from Newgate west by St. Sepulchre's Church to Turnagain Lane, to Oldborne Conduit, on Snow Hill, to Oldborne Bridge, up Oldborne Hill to the bars on both sides. On the right hand or north side, at the bottom of Oldborne Hill, is Gold Lane, sometime a filthy passage into the fields, now both sides built with small tenements. Then higher is Lither Lane, turning also to the field, lately replenished with houses built, and so to the bar.

Now on the left hand or south side from Newgate lieth a street called the Old Bailey, or court of the chamberlain of this city ; this stretcheth down by the wall of the city unto Ludgate, on the west side of which street breaketh out one other lane, called St. George's Lane, till ye come to the south end of Seacole Lane, and then turning towards Fleet Street it is called Fleet Lane. The next out of the high street from Newgate turning down south is called the Little Bailey, and runneth down to the east of St. George's Lane. Then is Seacole Lane, which turneth down into Fleet Lane. Near unto this Seacole Lane, in the turning towards Oldborne conduit, is another lane, called in records Wind Again Lane; it turneth down to Turnemill brook, and from thence back again, for there is no way over. Then beyond Oldborne Bridge to Shoe Lane, which runneth out of Oldborne unto the Conduit in Fleet Street. Then also is Fewtar's Lane,* which likewise stretcheth south into Fleet Street by the east end of St. Dunstan's Church, and from this lane to the bars be the bounds without Newgate.

Now without Ludgate, this ward runneth by from the said gate to Temple Bar, and hath on the right hand or north side the south end of the Old Bailey, then down Ludgate Hill to the Fleet Lane over Fleet Bridge, and by Shoe Lane and Fewtar's Lane, and so to New Street, or Chancery Lane, and up that lane to the house of the Rolls, which house is also of this ward, and on the other side to a lane over against the Rolls, which entereth Ficquets' field.

Then hard by the bar is one other lane called Shire Lane, because it divideth the city from the shire, and this turneth into Ficquets' field.

From Ludgate again on the left hand, or south side, to Fleet Bridge, to Bride Lane, which runneth south by Bridewell, then to Water Lane, which runneth down to the Thames.

Then by the Whitefriars and by the Temple, even to the bar aforesaid, be the bounds of this Farringdon Ward Without.

Touching ornaments and antiquities in this ward, first, betwixt the said Newgate and the parish church of St. Sepulchre's is a way towards Smithfield, called Gilt Spurr, or Knightriders' Street of the knights and others riding that way into Smithfield, replenished with buildings on both sides up to Pie Corner, a place so called of such a sign, sometimes a fair inn for receipt of travellers, but now divided into tenements, and over against the said Pie Corner lieth Cock Lane, which runneth down to Oldborne conduit.

Beyond this Pie Corner lieth West Smithfield, compassed about with buildings, as first on the south side following the right hand, standeth the fair parish church and large hospital of St. Bartholomew, founded by Rahere, the first prior of St. Bartholomew's thereto near adjoining, in the year 1102.

Alfune, that had not long before built the parish church of St. Giles without Cripplegate, became the first hospitaller, or proctor, for the poor of this house, and went himself daily to the shambles and other markets, where he begged the charity of devout people for their relief, promising to the liberal givers, and that by

---

* *Fewtar's Lane*, now corrupted into Fetter Lane. "Feultre," felt, anything set close, when "feutre" or "fewtar," also "fautre," was the name of a spear rest. Probably spear rests had been made there, as is suggested by the neighbourhood of Knightrider or Giltspur Street. But Stow takes Fewtars in the sense of loiterers, and afterwards names the lane as from loiterers hanging about the way to gardens.

alleging testimonies of the Holy Scripture, reward at the hands of God. Henry III. granted to Catherine, late wife to W. Hardell, twenty feet of land in length and breadth in Smithfield, next to the chapel of the hospital of St. Bartholomew, to build her a recluse or anchorage, commanding the mayor and sheriffs of London to assign the said twenty feet to the said Catherine, Carta 11 of Henry III. The foundation of this hospital, for the poor and diseased their special sustentation, was confirmed by Edward III. the 26th of his reign. It was governed by a master and eight brethren, being priests, for the church, and four sisters to see the poor served. The executors of R. Whittington, sometime mayor of London, of his goods repaired this hospital about the year 1423. Sir John Wakering, priest, master of this house in the year 1463, amongst other books, gave to their common library the fairest Bible that I have seen, written in large vellum by a brother of that house named John Coke, at the age of sixty-eight years, when he had been priest forty-three years. Since the spoil of that library, I have seen this book in the custody of my worshipful friend, Master Walter Cope.

Monuments in this church of the dead, benefactors thereunto, be these : Elizabeth, wife to Adam Hone, gentleman ; Bartholomew Bildington ; Jane, wife to John Cooke ; Dame Alis, wife to Sir Richard Isham ; Alice, wife to Nicholas Bayly ; John Woodhouse, esquire ; Robert Palmar, gentleman ; Idona, wife to John Walden, lying by her husband on the north side, late newly built, 1424 ; Sir Thomas Malifant, or Nanfant, Baron of Winnow, Lord St. George in Glamorgan, and Lord Ockeneton and Pile in the county of Pembroke, 1438 ; Dame Margaret his wife, daughter to Thomas Astley, esquire, with Edmond and Henry his children ; William Markeby, gentleman, 1438 ; Richard Shepley, and Alice his wife ; Thomas Savill, serjeant-at-arms ; Edward Beastby, gentleman, and Margaret his wife ; Waltar Ingham, and Alienar his wife ; Robert Warnar, and Alice Lady Carne ; Robert Caldset, Johan and Agnes his wives ; Sir Robert Danvars, and Dame Agnes his wife, daughter to Sir Richard Delaber ; William Brookes, esquire ; John Shirley, esquire, and Margaret his wife, having their pictures of brass, in the habit of pilgrims, on a fair flat stone, with an epitaph thus :—

> " Beholde how ended is our poore pilgrimage,
> Of John Shirley, esquier, with Margaret his wife,
> That xii. children had together in marriage,
> Eight sonnes and foure daughters withouten strife,
> That in honor, nurtur, and labour flowed in fame,
> His pen reporteth his lives occupation,
> Since Pier his life time, John Shirley by name,
> Of his degree, that was in Brutes Albion,

> That in the yeare of grace deceased from hen,
> Foureteene hundred winter, and sixe and fiftie,
> In the yeare of his age, fourescore and ten,
> Of October moneth, the day one and twenty."

This gentleman, a great traveller in divers countries, amongst other his labours, painfully collected the works of Geoffrey Chaucer, John Lidgate, and other learned writers, which works he wrote in sundry volumes to remain for posterity. I have seen them, and partly do possess them. Jane, Lady Clinton, gave ten pounds to the poor of this house, was there buried, 1458; Agnes, daughter to Sir William St. George; John Rogerbrooke, esquire; Richard Sturgeon; Thomas Burgan, gentleman; Elizabeth, wife to Henry Skinard, daughter to Chincroft, esquire; William Mackley, gentleman, and Alice his wife; W. Fitzwater, gentleman, 1466.

This hospital was valued at the suppression in the year 1539, the 31st of Henry VIII., to thirty-five pounds five shillings and sevenpence yearly. The church remaineth a parish-church to the tenants dwelling in the precinct of the hospital; but in the year 1546, on the 13th of January, the bishop of Rochester, preaching at Paul's Cross, declared the gift of the said king to the citizens for relieving of the poor, which contained the church of the Greyfriars, the church of St. Bartholomew, with the hospital, the messuages, and appurtenances in Giltspurre, *alias* Knightriders' Street, Breton Street, Peter Quay, in the parish of St. Mary Magdalen, in Old Fish Street, and in the parish of St. Benet Buda, Lymehurst, or Limehost, in the parish of Stebunheth, &c. Then also were orders devised for relief of the poor, the inhabitants were all called to their parish-churches, whereby Sir Richard Dobbes, then mayor, their several aldermen, or other grave citizens, they were by eloquent orations persuaded how great and how many commodities would ensue unto them and their city if the poor of divers sorts, which they named, were taken from out their streets, lanes, and alleys, and were bestowed and provided for in hospitals abroad, &c. Therefore was every man moved liberally to grant what they would impart towards the preparing and furnishing of such hospitals, and also what they would contribute weekly towards their maintenance for a time, which they said should not be past one year, or twain, until they were better furnished of endowment. To make short, every man granted liberally, according to his ability; books were drawn of the relief in every ward of the city towards the new hospitals, and were delivered by the mayor to the king's commissioners, on the 17th of February, and order was taken therein; so as the 26th of July in the year 1552 the repairing of the Greyfriars' house, for poor fatherless children was taken in hand; and also in the

latter end of the same month began the repairing of this hospital
of St. Bartholomew, and was of new endowed and furnished at
the charges of the citizens.

On the east side of this hospital lieth Duck Lane, which runneth
out of Smithfield south to the north end of Little Britain Street.
On the east side of this Duck Lane, and also of Smithfield, lieth
the late dissolved priory of St. Bartholomew, founded also by
Rahere, a pleasant - witted gentleman, and therefore in his time
called the king's minstrel, about the year of Christ 1102. He
founded it in a part of the oft before-named morish ground,
which was therefore a common laystall of all filth that was to
be avoided out of the city; he placed canons there, himself became
their first prior, and so continued till his dying day, and was there
buried in a fair monument, of late renewed by Prior Bolton.

Amongst other memorable matters touching this priory, one is
of an archbishop's visitation, which Matthew Paris hath thus :—
" Boniface," saith he, " Archbishop of Canterbury, in his visitation
came to this priory, where being received with procession in the most
solemn wise, he said that he passed not upon the honour, but came
to visit them; to whom the canons answered, that they having
a learned bishop, ought not in contempt of him to be visited by
any other : which answer so much offended the archbishop, that
he forthwith fell on the subprior, and smote him on the face, saying,
' Indeed, indeed, doth it become you English traitors so to answer
me.' Thus raging, with oaths not to be recited, he rent in pieces
the rich cope of the subprior, and trod it under his feet, and thrust
him against a pillar of the chancel with such violence, that he had
almost killed him ; but the canons, seeing their subprior thus almost
slain, came and plucked off the archbishop with such force, that
they overthrew him backwards, whereby they might see that he
was armed and prepared to fight. The archbishop's men seeing their
master down, being all strangers, and their master's countrymen,
born at Provence, fell upon the canons, beat them, tare them, and
trod them under feet. At length the canons getting away as well
as they could, ran bloody and miry, rent and torn, to the Bishop
of London to complain, who bade them go to the king at Westminster, and tell him thereof. Whereupon four of them went thither,
the rest were not able, they were so sore hurt ; but when they came
to Westminster, the king would neither hear nor see them, so they
returned without redress. In the mean season the whole city was
in an uproar, and ready to have rung the common bell, and to have
hewn the archbishop into small pieces, who was secretly crept to
Lambhith, where they sought him, and not knowing him by sight,
said to themselves, ' Where is this ruffian ? that cruel smiter ! He

is no winner of souls, but an exactor of money, whom neither God nor any lawful or free election did bring to this promotion, but the king did unlawfully intrude him, being utterly unlearned, a stranger born, and having a wife,' &c. But the archbishop conveyed himself over, and went to the king with a great complaint against the canons, whereas himself was guilty." This priory of St. Bartholomew was again new built in the year 1410.

Bolton was the last prior of this house, a great builder there; for he repaired the priory church, with the parish church adjoining, the offices and lodgings to the said priory belonging, and near adjoining. He built anew the manor of Canonbery at Islington, which belonged to the canons of this house, and is situate in a low ground, somewhat north from the parish church there; but he built no house at Harrow on the Hill, as Edward Hall hath written, following a fable then on foot. "The people," saith he, "being feared by prognostications, which declared, that in the year of Christ 1524 there should be such eclipses in watery signs, and such conjunctions, that by waters and floods many people should perish, people victualled themselves, and went to high grounds for fear of drowning, and especially one Bolton, which was prior of St. Bartholomew's in Smithfield, built him a house upon Harrow on the Hill, only for fear of this flood. Thither he went, and made provision of all things necessary within him for the space of two months," &c.; but this was not so indeed, as I have been credibly informed. True it is, that this Bolton was also parson of Harrow, and therefore bestowed some small reparations on the parsonage house, and built nothing there more than a dove house, to serve him when he had foregone his priory.

To this priory King Henry II. granted the privilege of fair, to be kept yearly at Bartholomew Tide for three days, to wit, the eve, the day, and next morrow, to the which the clothiers of all England and drapers of London repaired, and had their booths and standings within the churchyard of this priory, closed in with walls, and gates locked every night and watched for safety of men's goods and wares. A court of pie powders was daily during the fair holden for debts and contracts. But now, notwithstanding all proclamations of the prince, and also the act of parliament, in place of booths within this churchyard, only let out in the fair time, and closed up all the year after, be many large houses built, and the north wall towards Long Lane taken down, a number of tenements are there erected for such as will give great rents.

Monuments of the dead in this priory are these: of Rahere, the first founder; Roger Walden, Bishop of London, 1406; John Warton, gentleman, and Elizabeth his wife, daughter to William

Scott, esquire; John Louth, gentleman; Robert Shikeld, gentleman; Sir —— Bacon, knight; John Ludlow, and Alice his wife; W. Thirlewall, esquire; Richard Lancaster, herald-at-arms; Thomas Torald; John Royston; John Watforde; John Carleton; Robert, son to Sir Robert Willowby; Gilbert Halstocke; Eleanor, wife to Sir Hugh Fen, mother to Margaret Lady Burgavenie; William Essex, esquire; Richard Vancke, baron of the exchequer, and Margaret his wife, daughter to William de la Rivar; John Winderhall; John Duram, esquire, and Elizabeth his wife; John Malwaine; Alice, wife to Balstred, daughter to Kniffe; William Scarlet, esquire; John Golding; Hugh Walter, gentleman; and the late Sir Walter Mildmay, knight, chancellor of the exchequer, &c.

This priory at the late surrender, the 30th of Henry VIII., was valued at £653, 15s. by year.

This church having in the bell-tower six bells in a tune, those bells were sold to the parish of St. Sepulchre's; and then the church being pulled down to the choir, the choir was, by the king's order, annexed for the enlarging of the old parish church thereto adjoining, and so was used till the reign of Queen Mary, who gave the remnant of the priory church to the Friars Preachers, or Black Friars, and was used as their conventual church until, the 1st of our sovereign lady Queen Elizabeth, those friars were put out, and all the said church, with the old parish church, was wholly as it stood in the last year of Edward VI., given by parliament to remain for ever a parish church to the inhabitants within the close called Great St. Bartholomew's. Since the which time that old parish church is pulled down, except the steeple of rotten timber ready to fall of itself. I have oft heard it reported, that a new steeple should be built with the stone, lead, and timber of the old parish church, but no such thing was performed. The parish have lately repaired the old wooden steeple to serve their turn. On the north side of this priory is the lane truly called Long, which reacheth from Smithfield to Aldersgate Street. This lane is now lately built on both the sides with tenements for brokers, tipplers, and such like; the rest of Smithfield from Long Lane end to the bars is enclosed with inns, brewhouses, and large tenements; on the west side is Chicken Lane down to Cowbridge. Then be the pens or folds, so called, of sheep there parted, and penned up to be sold on the market-days.

Then is Smithfield Pond, which of old time in records was called Horse Pool, for that men watered horses there, and was a great water. In the 6th of Henry V. a new building was made in this west part of Smithfield betwixt the said pool and the river of the Wells, or Turnmill Brook, in a place then called the Elms, for that there grew many elm-trees; and this had been the place of execution for offenders. Since the which time the building there hath been so increased that now remaineth not one tree growing.

Amongst these new buildings is Cowbridge Street, or Cow Lane, which turneth toward Oldborne, in which lane the prior of Semperingham had his inn, or London lodging.

The rest of that west side of Smithfield hath divers fair inns and other comely buildings up to Hosier Lane, which also turneth down to Oldborne till it meet with Cowbridge Street. From this lane to Cock Lane, over against Pie Corner.

And thus much for encroachments and enclosure of this Smithfield, whereby remaineth but a small portion for the old uses ; to wit, for markets of horses and cattle, neither for military exercises, as joustings, turnings, and great triumphs, which have been there performed before the princes and nobility both of this realm and foreign countries. For example to note :—In the year 1357, the 31st of Edward III., great and royal jousts were there holden in Smithfield ; there being present, the King of England, France, and Scotland, with many other nobles and great estates of divers lands.

1362, the 36th of Edward III., on the first five days of May, in Smithfield, were jousts holden, the king and queen being present, with the most part of the chivalry of England, and of France, and of other nations, to the which came Spaniards, Cyprians, and Arminians, knightly requesting the King of England against the pagans that invaded their confines.

The 48th of Edward III., Dame Alice Perrers, the king's concubine, as Lady of the Sun, rode from the Tower of London, through Cheap, accompanied of many lords and ladies, every lady leading a lord by his horse-bridle, till they came into West Smithfield, and then began a great joust, which endured seven days after.

Also, the 9th of Richard II., was the like great riding from the Tower to Westminster, and every lord led a lady's horse-bridle ; and on the morrow began the joust in Smithfield, which lasted two days. There bare them well, Henry of Darby, the Duke of Lancaster's son, the Lord Beaumont, Sir Simon Burley, and Sir Paris Courtney.

In the 14th of Richard II., after Froissart, royal jousts and tournaments were proclaimed to be done in Smithfield, to begin on Sunday next after the feast of St. Michael. Many strangers came forth of other countries, namely, Valerian, Earl of St. Paul, that had married King Richard's sister, the Lady Maud Courtney, and William, the young Earl of Ostervant, son to Albert of Baviere, Earl of Holland and Henault. At the day appointed there issued forth of the Tower, about the third hour of the day, sixty coursers, apparelled for the jousts, and upon every one an esquire of honour, riding a soft pace. Then came forth sixty ladies of honour, mounted upon palfreys, riding on the one side, richly apparelled, and every lady led a knight with a chain of gold. Those knights being on the king's party had their harness and apparel garnished with white harts, and crowns of gold about the harts' necks, and so they came riding through the streets of London to Smithfield, with a great number of trumpets and other instruments of music before them. The king and queen, who were lodged in the bishop's palace of London, were come from thence, with many great estates, and placed in chambers to see the jousts. The ladies that led the knights were taken down from their palfreys, and went up to chambers prepared for them. Then alighted the esquires of honour from their coursers, and the knights in good order mounted upon them; and after their helmets were set on their heads, and being ready in all points, proclamation made by the heralds, the jousts began, and many commendable courses were run, to the great pleasure of the beholders. These jousts continued many days, with great feasting, as ye may read in Froisart.

In the year 1393, the 17th of Richard II., certain lords of Scotland came into England to get worship by force of arms. The Earl of Mar challenged the Earl of Nottingham to joust with him, and so they rode together certain courses, but not the full challenge, for the Earl of Mar was cast both horse and man, and two of his ribs broken with the fall, so that he was conveyed out of Smithfield, and so towards Scotland, but died by the way at York. Sir William Darell, knight, the king's banner bearer of Scotland, challenged Sir Percy Courtney, knight, the king's banner bearer of England; and when they had run certain courses, gave over without conclusion of victory. Then Cookeborne, esquire, of Scotland, challenged Sir Nicholas Hawberke, knight, and rode five courses, but Cookeborne was borne over horse and man, &c.

In the year 1409, the 10th of Henry IV., a great play was played at the Skinners' Well, which lasted eight days, where were to see the same the most part of the nobles and gentles in England. And forthwith began a royal jousting in Smithfield between the Earl of Somerset, and the Seneschal of Henalt, Sir John Cornwall, Sir Richard Arundell, and the son of Sir John Cheiney, against certain Frenchmen. And the same year a battle was fought in Smithfield between two esquires, the one called Gloucester, appellant, and the other Arthur, defendant. They fought valiantly, but the king took up the quarrel into his hands, and pardoned them both.

In the year 1430, the 8th of Henry VI., the 14th of January, a battle was done in Smithfield, within the lists, before the king, between two men of Faversham in Kent, John Upton, notary, appellant, and John Downe, gentleman, defendant. John Upton put upon John Downe, that he and his compeers should imagine the king's death the day of his coronation. When these had fought long, the king took up the matter, and forgave both the parties.

In the year 1442, the 20th of Henry VI., the 30th of January, a challenge was done in Smithfield, within lists, before the king, there being Sir Philip la Beaufe of Aragon, knight, the other an esquire of the king's house, called John Ansley or Anstley. They came to the field all armed, the knight with his sword drawn, and the esquire with his spear, which spear he cast against the knight, but the knight avoided it with his sword, and cast it to the ground. Then the esquire took his axe, and smote many blows on the knight, and made him let fall his axe, and break up his umber * three times, and would have smote him on the face with his dagger, for to have slain him, but then the king cried hold, and so they were departed. The king made John Ansley knight, and the knight of Aragon offered his harness at Windsor.

In the year 1446, the 24th of Henry VI., John David appeached his master, Wil. Catur, of treason, and a day being assigned them to fight in Smithfield, the master being well-beloved, was so cherished by his friends, and plied with wine, that being therewith overcome, was also unluckily slain by his servant; but that false servant, for he falsely accused his master, lived not long unpunished, for he was after hanged at Tybourn for felony. Let such false accusers note this for example, and look for no better end without speedy repentance.

The same year Thomas Fitz-Thomas, Prior of Kilmaine, appeached Sir James Butler, Earl of Ormond, of treasons, which had a day assigned them to fight in Smithfield, the lists were made, and the field prepared; but when it came to the point, the king commanded they should not fight, and took the quarrel into his hands.

In the year 1467, the 7th of Edward IV., the Bastard of Burgoine challenged the Lord Scales, brother to the queen, to fight with him both on horseback and on foot. The king therefore caused lists to be prepared in Smithfield, the length of one hundred and twenty tailors' yards and ten feet, and in breadth eighty yards and twenty feet, double-barred, five feet between the bars, the timber-work whereof cost two hundred marks, besides the fair and costly galleries prepared for the ladies and other, at the which martial enterprise the king and nobility were present. The first day they ran together with spears, and departed with equal honour. The next day they

---

* *Umber* and "umbriere," the shade for the eyes over the sight of the helmet, sometimes attached to the visor, and often identified with it. So in Spencer's "Faerie Queene" Britomart

" would not disarmed be
But only vented up her umbriere
And so did let her goodly visage to appear."
Book III. 1, 42.

† *Chafron*, chaufrain, the headpiece of a barbed horse.

tourneyed on horseback, the Lord Scales horse having on his chafron a long spear pike of steel; and as the two champions coped together, the same horse thrust his pike into the nostrils of the Bastard's horse, so that for very pain he mounted so high that he fell on the one side with his master, and the Lord Scales rode about him with his sword dwran till the king commanded the marshal to help up the Bastard, who said, I cannot hold me by the clouds, for though my horse fail me, I will not fail an encounter companion; but the king would not suffer them to do any more that day.

The next morrow they came into the lists on foot with two pole-axes, and fought valiantly; but at the last the point of the pole-axe of the Lord Scales entered into the side of the Bastard's helm, and by force might have placed him on his knees; but the king cast down his warder, and the marshal severed them. The Bastard required that he might perform his enterprise; but the king gave judgment as the Bastard relinquished his challenge, &c. And this may suffice for jousts in Smithfield.

Now to return through Giltspur Street by Newgate, where I first began, there standeth the fair parish church, called St. Sepulchre's in the Bailey, or by Chamberlain gate, in a fair churchyard, though not so large as of old time, for the same is letten out for buildings and a garden plot.

This church was newly re-edified or built about the reign of Henry VI. or of Edward IV. One of the Pophames was a great builder there, namely, of one fair chapel on the south side of the choir, as appeareth by his arms and other monuments in the glass windows thereof, and also the fair porch of the same church towards the south. His image, fair graven in stone, was fixed over the said porch, but defaced and beaten down. His title by offices was this, Chancellor of Normandy, Captain of Vernoyle, Pearch, Susan, and Bayon,* and treasurer of the king's household. He died rich, leaving great treasure of strange coins, and was buried in the Charterhouse Church by West Smithfield. The first nobilitating of these Pophames was by Matilda the empress, daughter to Henry I., and by Henry her son. One Pophame, gentleman, of very fair lands in South-amptonshire, died without issue male, about Henry VI., and leaving four daughters, they were married to Fostar, Barentine, Wodham, and Hamden. Popham Dean, distant three miles from Clarendon, and three miles from Mortisham, was sometime the chief lordship or manor-house of these Pophames.

There lie buried in this church, William Andrew, Stephen Clamparde, Lawrence Warcam, John Dagworth, William Porter, Robert Scarlet, esquires.

* Verneuil, Perche, Suzanne, and Bayonne.

Next to this church is a fair and large inn for receipt of travellers, and hath to sign the Saracen's Head.

There lieth a street from Newgate west to the end of Turnagain Lane, and winding north to Oldborne Conduit. This conduit by Oldborn Cross was first built 1498. Thomasin, widow to John Percival, mayor, gave to the second making thereof twenty marks, Richard' Shore ten pounds. Thomas Knesworth and others also did give towards it.

But of late a new conduit was there built in place of the old, namely, in the year 1577, by William Lamb, sometime a gentleman of the chapel to King Henry VIII., and afterward a citizen and cloth-worker of London. The water thereof he caused to be conveyed in lead, from divers springs to one head, and from thence to the said conduit, and waste of one cock at Oldborne Bridge, more than two thousand yards in length. All of which was by him performed at his own charges, amounting to the sum of fifteen hundred pounds.

From the west side of this conduit is the highway, there called Snore Hill. It stretcheth out by Oldborne Bridge over the oft-named water of Turnmill Brook, and so up to Oldborne Hill, all replenished with fair building.

Without Oldborne Bridge, on the right hand, is Gold Lane, as is before shown. Up higher on the hill be certain inns, and other fair buildings, amongst the which of old time was a messuage called Scropes Inn, for so I find the same recorded in the 37th of Henry VI.

This house was sometime letten out to sergeants-at-the-law, as appeareth, and was found by inquisition taken in the Guildhall of London, before William Purchase, mayor, and escheator for the king, Henry VII., in the 14th of his reign, after the death of John Lord Scrope, that he died deceased in his demesne of fee, by the feoffment of Guy Fairfax, knight, one of the king's justices, made in the 9th of the same king, unto the said John Scrope, knight, Lord Scrope of Bolton, and Robert Wingfield, esquire, of one house or tenement, late called Sergeants' Inn, situate against the Church of St. Andrew in Oldborne, in the city of London, with two gardens and two messuages to the same tenement belonging in the said city, to hold in burgage, valued by the year in all reprises ten shillings.

Then is the Bishop of Ely's Inn, so called of belonging and per-taining to the Bishops of Ely. William de Luda, Bishop of Ely, deceased 1297, gave this house by the name of his manor, with the appurtenances in Oldborne, to his successors, with condition his next successor should pay one thousand marks to the finding of three chaplains in the chapel there. More, John Hotham, Bishop of Ely, did give by the name of six messuages, two cellars, and forty acres of land, in the suburbs of London, in the parish of St. Andrew in

Oldborne, to the prior and convent of Ely, as appeareth by patent, the 9th of Edward III. This man was Bishop of Ely twenty years, and deceased 1336.

Thomas Arundell, Bishop of Ely, beautifully built of new his palace at Ely, and likewise his manors in divers places, especially this in Oldborne, which he did not only repair, but rather new-built, and augmented it with a large port, gatehouse, or front towards the street or highway. His arms are yet to be discerned in the stone-work thereof. He sat Bishop of Ely fourteen years, and was translated to York. In this house, for the large and commodious rooms thereof, divers great and solemn feasts have been kept, especially by the sergeants-at-the-law, whereof twain are to be noted for posterity.

The first in the year 1464, the 4th of Edward IV., in Michaelmas term, the sergeants-at-law held their feast in this house, to the which, amongst other estates, Matthew Phillip, mayor of London, with the aldermen, sheriffs, and commons, of divers crafts, being invited, did repair; but when the mayor looked to keep the state in the hall, as it had been used in all places within the city and liberties, out of the king's presence, the Lord Gray of Ruthen, then lord treasurer of England, unwitting the sergeants, and against their wills, as they said, was first placed. Whereupon the mayor, aldermen, and commons departed home, and the mayor made the aldermen to dine with him. Howbeit he and all the citizens were wonderfully displeased that he was so dealt with; and the new sergeants and others were right sorry therefor, and had rather than much good, as they said, it had not so happened.

One other feast was likewise there kept in the year 1531, the 23rd of King Henry VIII. The sergeants then made were in number eleven; namely, Thomas Audeley, Walter Luke, I. Bawdwine, I. Hinde, Christopher Jennie, John Dowsell, Edward Mervine, Edmond Knightley, Roger Chomley, Edward Montague, and Robert Yorke.

These also held their feast in this Ely House for five days, to wit, Friday the 10th of November, Saturday, Sunday, Monday, and Tuesday. On Monday, which was their principal day, King Henry and Queen Katherine dined there, but in two chambers, and the foreign ambassadors in a third chamber. In the hall, at the high table, sat Sir Nicholas Lambard, mayor of London, the judges, the barons of the exchequer, with certain aldermen of the city. At the board on the south side sat the master of the rolls, the master of the chancery, and worshipful citizens. On the north side of the hall certain aldermen began the board, and then followed merchants of the city; in the cloister, chapel, and gallery, knights, esquires, and gentlemen were placed; in the halls the crafts of London. The sergeants-of-law and their wives kept in their own chambers.

It were tedious to set down the preparation of fish, flesh, and other victuals spent in this feast, and would seem almost incredible, and, as to me it seemeth, wanted little of a feast at a coronation ; nevertheless, a little I will touch, for declaration of the change of prices. There were brought to the slaughter-house twenty-four great beefs at twenty-six shillings and eightpence the piece from the shambles, one carcase of an ox at twenty-four shillings, one hundred fat muttons two shillings and tenpence the piece, fifty-one great veals at four shillings and eightpence the piece, thirty-four porks three shillings and eightpence the piece, ninety-one pigs sixpence the piece, capons of grese, of one poulterer (for they had three) ten dozens at twentypence the piece, capons of Kent nine dozens and six at twelvepence the piece, capons coarse nineteen dozen at six-pence the piece, cocks of grose seven dozen and nine at eightpence the piece, cocks coarse fourteen dozen and eight at threepence the piece, pullets, the best, twopence halfpenny, other pullets twopence, pigeons thirty-seven dozen at tenpence the dozen, swans fourteen dozen, larks three hundred and forty dozen at fivepence the dozen, &c. Edward Nevill was seneschal or steward, Thomas Ratcliffe, comptroller, Thomas Wildon, clerk of the kitchen.

Next beyond this manor of Ely House is Lither Lane, turning into the field. Then is Furnivall's Inn, now an inn of chancery, but sometime belonging to Sir William Furnivall, knight, and Thomasin his wife, who had in Oldborne two messuages and thirteen shops, as appeareth by record of Richard II., in the 6th of his reign.

Then is the Earl of Bath's Inn, now called Bath Place, of late for the most part new built, and so to the bars.

Now again, from Newgate, on the left hand, or south side, lieth the Old Bailey, which runneth down by the wall upon the ditch of the city, called Hounsditch, to Ludgate. I have not read how this street took that name, but is like to have risen of some court of old time there kept; and I find that in the year 1356, the 34th of Edward III., the tenement and ground upon Hounsditch, between Ludgate on the south and Newgate on the north, was appointed to John Cambridge, fishmonger, chamberlain of London, whereby it seemeth that the chamberlains of London have there kept their courts, as now they do by the Guildhall, and till this day the mayor and justices of this city kept their sessions in a part thereof, now called the Sessions Hall, both for the city of London and shire of Middlesex. Over against the which house, on the right hand, turneth down St. George's Lane towards Fleet Lane.

In this St. George's Lane, on the north side thereof, remaineth yet an old wall of stone, enclosing a piece of ground up Seacoal Lane, wherein by report sometime stood an inn of chancery. Which house being greatly decayed, and standing remote from other houses of that profession, the company removed to a common hostelry, called of the sign Our Lady Inn, not far from Clement's Inn, which they procured from Sir John Fineox, lord chief justice of the King's Bench, and since have held it of the owners by the name of the New Inn, paying therefor six pounds rent by the year, as tenants at their own will, for more, as is said, cannot be gotten of them, and much less will they be put from it.   Beneath this St. George's Lane, the lane called Fleet Lane, winding south by the prison of the Fleet into Fleet Street by Fleet Bridge.   Lower down in the Old Bailey is at this present a standard of timber, with a cock or cocks, delivering fair spring water to the inhabitants, and is the waste of the water serving the prisoners in Ludgate.

Next out of the high street turneth down a lane called the Little Bailey, which runneth down to the east end of St. George's Lane. The next is Seacoal Lane, I think called Limeburner's Lane, of burning lime there with seacoal.   For I read in record of such a lane to have been in the parish of St. Sepulchre, and there yet remaineth in this lane an alley called Limeburner's Alley.   Near unto this Seacoal Lane, in the turning towards Oldborne Conduit, is Turnagain Lane, or rather, as in a record of the 5th of Edward III., Windagain Lane, for that it goeth down west to Fleet Dike, from whence men must turn again the same way they came, for there it stopped.   Then the high street turneth down Snore Hill to Oldborne Conduit, and from thence to Oldborne Bridge, beyond the which bridge, on the left hand, is Shoe Lane, by the which men pass from Oldborne to Fleet Street by the conduit there.   In this Shoe Lane, on the left hand, is one old house called Oldborne Hall.   It is now letten out into divers tenements.

On the other side, at the very corner, standeth the parish church of St. Andrew, in the which church, or near thereunto, was sometime kept a grammar school, as appeareth in another place by a patent made, as I have shown, for the erection of schools.   There be monuments in this church of Thomas, Lord Wriothesley, Earl of Southampton, buried 1550; Ralph Rokeby of Lincoln's Inn, esquire, Master of St. Katherine's, and one of the masters of requests to the queen's majesty, who deceased the 14th of June 1596.   He gave by his testament to Christ's Hospital in London one hundred pounds, to the college of the poor of Queen Elizabeth in East Greenwich one hundred pounds, to the poor scholars in Cambridge one hundred pounds, to the poor scholars in Oxford one hundred pounds, to the prisoners in the two compters in London two hundred pounds, to the prisoners in the Fleet one hundred pounds, to the prisoners in Ludgate one hundred pounds, to the prisoners in Newgate one hundred pounds, to the prisoners in the King's Bench one hundred pounds, to the prisoners in the Marshalsea one hundred pounds, to the prisoners in the White Lion twenty pounds, to the poor of St. Katherine's twenty pounds, and to every brother and sister there forty shillings. William Sydnam founded a chantry there. There was also of old time, as I have read in the 3rd of Henry V., an hospital for the poor, which was a cell to the house of Cluny in France, and was therefore suppressed among the priories aliens.

From this church of St. Andrew, up Oldborne Hill be divers fair built houses, amongst the which, on the left hand, there standeth three inns of chancery, whereof the first adjoining unto Crookhorn Alley is called Thaves Inn, and standeth opposite or over against the said Ely House. Then is Fewter Lane, which stretcheth south into Fleet Street, by the east end of St. Dunstan's Church, and is so called of Fewters, or idle people, lying there, as in a way leading to gardens ; but the same is now of latter years on both sides built through with many fair houses.

Beyond this Fewter Lane is Barnard's Inn, *alias* Mackworth's Inn, which is of chancery, belonging to the Dean and Chapter of Lincoln, as saith the record of Henry VI., the 32nd of his reign, and was founded by inquisition in the Guildhall of London, before John Norman, mayor, the king's escheator. The jury said that it was not hurtful for the king to license T. Atkens, citizen of London, and one of the executors to John Mackworth, Dean of Lincoln, to give one messuage in Holborn in London, with the appurtenances called Mackworth's Inn, but now commonly known by the name of Barnard's Inn, to the Dean and Chapter of Lincoln, to find one sufficient chaplain to celebrate divine service in the chapel of St. George, in the cathedral church of Lincoln, where the body of the said John is buried, to have and to hold the said messuage to the said Dean and Chapter, and to their successors for ever, in part of satisfaction of twenty pounds lands and rents, which Edward III. licensed the said Dean and Chapter to purchase to their own use, either of their own fee or tenure, or of any other, so the lands were not holden of the king *in capite*.

Then is Staple Inn, also of Chancery, but whereof so named I am ignorant. The same of late is for a great part thereof fair built, and not a little augmented. And then at the bar endeth this ward without Newgate.

Without Ludgate, on the right hand, or north side from the said gate, lieth the Old Bailey, as I said, then the high street called Ludgate Hill down to Fleet Lane, in which lane standeth the Fleet, a prison house so called of the Fleet or water running by it, and sometime flowing about it, but now vaulted over.

I read that Richard I., in the 1st of his reign, confirmed to Osbert, brother to William Longchamp, Chancellor of England and elect of Ely, and to his heirs for ever, the custody of his house or palace at Westminster, with the keeping of his gaol of the Fleet at London; also King John, by his patent, dated the 3rd of his reign, gave to the Archdeacon of Wells the custody of the said king's house at Westminster, and of his gaol of the Fleet, together with the wardship of the daughter and heir of Robert Loveland, &c. Then is Fleet Bridge pitched over the said water, whereof I have spoken in another place.

Then also against the south end of Shoe Lane standeth a fair water conduit, whereof William Eastfield, sometime mayor, was founder; for the mayor and commonalty of London being possessed of a conduit head, with divers springs of water gathered thereinto in the parish of Paddington, and the water conveyed from thence by pipes of lead towards London unto Tybourn, where it had lain by the space of six years or more, the executors of Sir William Eastfield obtained license of the mayor and commonalty for them, in the year 1453, with the goods of Sir William to convey the said waters, first in pipes of lead into a pipe begun to be laid besides the great conduit head at Marylebone, which stretcheth from thence unto a separall, late before made against the Chapel of Rouncevall by Charing Cross, and no further; and then from thence to convey the said water into the city, and there to make receipt or receipts for the same unto the common weal of the commonalty, to wit, the poor to drink, the rich to dress their meats; which water was by them brought thus into Fleet Street to a standard, which they had made and finished 1471.

The inhabitants of Fleet Street, in the year 1478, obtained license of the mayor, aldermen, and commonalty to make at their own charges two cisterns, the one to be set at the said standard, the other at Fleet Bridge, for the receipt of the waste water. This cistern at the standard they built, and on the same a fair tower of stone, garnished with images of St. Christopher on the top, and angels round about lower down, with sweet sounding bells before them, whereupon, by an engine placed in the tower, they divers hours of the day and night chimed such an hymn as was appointed.

This Conduit, or standard, was again new built with a larger cistern, at the charges of the city, in the year 1582.

From this Conduit up to Fewter Lane, and further, is the parish church of St. Dunstan called in the West, for difference from St. Dunstan in the East, where lieth buried T. Duke, skinner, in St. Katherine's Chapel, by him built, 1421; Nicholas Coningstone, John Knape, and other, founded chantries there; Ralph Bane, Bishop of Coventry and Lichfield, 1559, and other.

Next beyond this church is Clifford's Inn, sometime belonging to Robert Clifford, by gift of Edward II. in these words :—" The king granteth to Robert Clifford that messuage, with the appurtenances, next the church of St. Dunstan in the West, in the suburbs of London, which messuage was sometime Malculines de Herley, and came to the hands of Edward I., by reason of certaine debts which the said Malculine was bound at the time of his death to our sayde father, from the time that hee was escaetor on this side Trent; which house John, Earle of Richmount, did holde of our pleasure, and is now in our possession."—Patent, the 3rd of Edward II.   After the death of this Robert Clifford, Isabel, his wife, let the same messuage to students of the law, as by the record following may appear :—

" *Isabel quæ fuit uxor Roberti Clifford, Messuagium unipartitum quod Robertus Clifford habuit in parochia sci. Dunstonis West. in suburbio Londini, &c., tenuit, et illud dimisit post mortem dict. Roberti, Apprenticiis de banco, pro x. li. annuatium, &c.   Anno 18 Eduardi Tertii, inquisitio post mortem Roberti Clifford.*"

This house hath since fallen into the king's hands, as I have heard, but returned again to the Cliffords, and is now let to the said students for four pounds by the year.

Somewhat beyond this Clifford's Inn is the south end of New Street, or Chancellor Lane, on the right hand whereof is Sergeants' Inn called in Chancery Lane.   And then next was sometime the house of the converted Jews, founded by King Henry III., in place of a Jew's house to him forfeited, in the year 1233, and the 17th of his reign, who built there for them a fair church now used, and called the chapel for the custody of the Rolls and Records of Chancery.   It standeth not far from the Old Temple, but in the midway between the Old Temple and the New, in the which house all such Jews and infidels as were converted to the Christian faith were ordained and appointed, under an honest rule of life, sufficient maintenance, whereby it came to pass that in short time there were gathered a great number of converts, which were baptized, instructed in the doctrine of Christ, and there lived under a learned Christian appointed to govern them.   Since the which time, to wit, in the year 1290, all the Jews in England were banished out of the realm, whereby the number of converts in this place was decayed; and therefore in the year 1377 this house was annexed by patent to William Burstall Clarke, custos rotulorum, or keeper of the Rolls of the Chancery, by Edward III., in the 5th year of his reign ; and this first Master of the Rolls was sworn in Westminster Hall, at the table of marble stone.   Since the which time that house hath been commonly called the Rolls in Chancery Lane.

Notwithstanding such of the Jews, or other infidels, as have in this realm been converted to Christianity, and baptized, have been relieved there; for I find in record that one William Piers, a Jew that became a Christian, was baptized in the 5th of Richard II., and had twopence the day allowed him during his life by the said king.

On the west side was sometime a house pertaining to the prior of Necton Park, a house of canons in Lincolnshire. This was commonly called Hereflete Inn, and was a brewhouse, but now fair built for the five clerks of the Chancery, and standeth over against the said house called the Rolls, and near unto the lane which now entereth Fickets Croft, or Fickets Field. Then is Shere Lane, opening also into Fickets Field, hard by the bars.

On this north side of Fleet Street, in the year of Christ 1595, I observed, that when the labourers had broken up the pavement, from against Chancery Lane end up toward St. Dunstan's Church, and had digged four feet deep, they found one other pavement of hard stone, more sufficient than the first, and therefore harder to be broken, under the which they found in the made ground piles of timber driven very thick, and almost close together, the same being as black as pitch or coal, and many of them rotten as earth, which proveth that the ground there, as sundry other places of the city, have been a marish, or full of springs.

On the south side from Ludgate, before the wall of the city, be fair built houses to Fleet Bridge, on which bridge a cistern for receipt of spring water was made by the men of Fleet Street, but the watercourse is decayed, and not restored.

Next is Bride Lane, and therein Bridewell, of old time the king's house, for the kings of this realm have been there lodged; and till the 9th of Henry III., the courts were kept in the king's house, wheresoever he was lodged, as may appear by ancient records, whereof I have seen many, but for example set forth one in the Chapter of Towers and Castles.

King Henry VIII. built there a stately and beautiful house of new, for receipt of the Emperor Charles V., who, in the year of Christ 1522, was lodged himself at the Blackfriars, but his nobles in this new built Bridewell, a gallery being made out of the house over the water, and through the wall of the city, into the emperor's lodging at the Blackfriars. King Henry himself oftentimes lodged there also, as, namely, in the year 1525, a parliament being then holden in the Blackfriars, he created estates of nobility there, to wit, Henry Fitz Roy, a child, which he had by Elizabeth Blunt, to be Earl of Nottingham, Duke of Richmond and of Somerset, Lieutenant-General from Trent northward, Warden of the East, Middle, and West Marches, for anenst Scotland; Henry Courtney, Earl of Devonshire, cousin-german to the king, to be Marquis of Exeter;

Henry Brandon, a child of two years old, son to the Earl of Suffolk, to be Earl of Lincoln; Sir Thomas Manners, Lord Rose, to be Earl of Rutland; Sir Henry Clifford, to be Earl of Cumberland; Sir Robert Ratcliffe, to be Viscount Fitzwater; and Sir Thomas Boloine, treasurer of the king's household, to be Viscount Rochford.

In the year 1528, Cardinal Campeius was brought to the king's presence, being then at Bridewell, whither he had called all his nobility, judges, and councillors, &c. And there, the 8th of November, in his great chamber, he made unto them an oration touching his marriage with Queen Katherine, as ye may read in Edward Hall.

In the year 1529, the same King Henry and Queen Katherine were lodged there, whilst the question of their marriage was argued in the Blackfriars, &c.

But now you shall hear how this house became a house of correction. In the year 1553, the 7th of King Edward VI., the 10th of April, Sir George Baron, being mayor of this city, was sent for to the court at Whitehall, and there at that time the king gave unto him for the commonalty and citizens, to be a workhouse for the poor and idle persons of the city, his house of Bridewell, and seven hundred marks land, late of the possessions of the house of the Savoy, and all the bedding and other furniture of the said hospital of the Savoy, towards the maintenance of the said workhouse of Bridewell, and the hospital of St. Thomas in Southwark.

This gift King Edward confirmed by his charter, dated the 26th of June next following; and in the year 1555, in the month of February, Sir William Gerarde, mayor, and the aldermen entered Bridewell, and took possession thereof according to the gift of the said King Edward, the same being confirmed by Queen Mary.

The Bishop of St. David's had his inn over against the north side of this Bridewell, as I have said.

Then is the parish church of St. Bridges, or Bride, of old time a small thing, which now remaineth to be the choir, but since increased with a large body and side aisles towards the west, at the charges of William Venor, esquire, warden of the Fleet, about the year 1480, all which he caused to be wrought about in the stone in the figure of a vine with grapes and leaves, &c. The partition betwixt the old work and the new, sometime prepared as a screen to be set up in the hall of the Duke of Somerset's house at Strand, was bought for eight score pounds, and set up in the year 1557. One wilful body began to spoil and break the same in the year 1596, but was by the high commissioners forced to make it up again, and so it resteth. John Ulsthorpe, William Evesham, John Wigan, and other founded chantries there.

The next is Salisbury Court, a place so called for that it belonged to the Bishops of Salisbury, and was their inn, or London house, at such time as they were summoned to come to the parliament, or came for other business. It hath of late time been the dwelling, first of Sir Richard Sackvile, and now of Sir Thomas Sackvile his son, Baron of Buckhurst, Lord Treasurer, who hath greatly enlarged it with stately buildings.

Then is Water Lane, running down, by the west side of a house called the Hanging Sword, to the Thames.

Then was the White Friars Church, called *Fratres beatæ Mariæ de Monte Carmeli*, first founded, saith John Bale, by Sir Richard Gray, knight, ancestor to the Lord Gray Codnor, in the year 1241. King Edward I. gave to the prior and brethren of that house a plot of ground in Fleet Street, whereupon to build their house, which was since re-edified or new built by Hugh Courtney, Earl of Devonshire, about the year 1350, the 24th of Edward III. John Lutken, mayor of London, and the commonalty of the city, granted a lane called Crockers Lane, reaching from Fleet Street to the Thames, to build in the west end of that church. Sir Robert Knoles, knight, was a great builder there also, in the reign of Richard II., and of Henry IV. He deceased at his manor of Scone Thorpe, in Norfolk, in the year 1407, and was brought to London, and honourably buried by the Lady Constance his wife, in the body of the said White Friars Church, which he had newly built.

Robert Marshall, Bishop of Hereford, built the choir, presbytery, steeple, and many other parts, and was there buried, about the year 1420. There were buried also in the new choir, Sir John Mowbery, Earl of Nottingham, 1398; Sir Edward Courtney; Sir Hugh Montgomery, and Sir John his brother; John Wolle, son to Sir John Wolle; Thomas Bayholt, esquire; Elizabeth, Countess of Athole; Dame Johan, wife to Sir Thomas Say of Alden: Sir Pence Castle, baron; John, Lord Gray, son to Reginald, Lord Gray of Wilton, 1418; Sir John Ludlow, knight; Sir Richard Derois, knight; Richard Gray, knight; John Ashley, knight; Robert Bristow, esquire; Thomas Perry, esquire; Robert Tempest, esquire; William Call; William Neddow.

In the old choir were buried: Dame Margaret, &c.; Eleanor Gristles; Sir John Browne, knight, and John his son and heir; Sir Simon de Berforde, knight; Peter Wigus, esquire; Robert Matthew, esquire; Sir John Skargell, knight; Sir John Norice, knight; Sir Geffrey Roose, knight; Matthew Hadocke, esquire; William Clarell, esquire; John Aprichard, esquire; William Wentworth, esquire; Thomas Wicham, esquire; Sir Terwit, knight; Sir Stephen Popham, knight; Bastard de Scales; Henry Blunt, esquire; Elizabeth Blunt; John Swan, esquire; Alice Foster, one of the heirs of Sir Stephen Popham; Sir Robert Brocket, knight; John Drayton, esquire; John, son to Robert Chanlowes, and his daughter Katherine; John Salvin, William Hampton, John Bampton, John Winter, Edmond Oldhall, William Appleyard, Thomas Dabby, esquires; Sir Hugh Courtney, knight; John Drury, son to Robert Drury; Elizabeth Gemersey, gentlewoman; Sir Thomas Townsend, knight; Sir Richard Green, knight; William Scott, esquire; Thomas Federinghey, I. Fulforde, esquire; Edward Eldsmere, gentleman; W. Hart, gentleman; Dame Mary Senclare, daughter to Sir Thomas Talbot, knight; Ancher, esquire; Sir William Moris, knight, and Dame Christian his wife; Sir Peter de Mota, knight; Richard Hewton, esquire; Sir I. Heron, knight; Richard Eton, esquire; Hugh Stapleton, gentleman; William Copley, gentleman; Sir Ralph Saintowen, knight; Sir Hugh Bromeflete, knight; Lord Vessey, principal founder of that order, the 6th of Edward IV., &c.

This house was valued at £62, 7s. 3d., and was surrendered the 10th of November, the 30th of Henry VIII.

In place of this Friars Church be now many fair houses built, lodgings for noblemen and others.

Then is the Sergeants' Inn, so called, for that divers judges and sergeants at the law keep a commons, and are lodged there in term time.

Next is the New Temple, so called because the Templars, before the building of this house, had their temple in Oldborne. This house was founded by the Knights Templars in England, in the reign of Henry II., and the same was dedicated to God and our Blessed Lady, by Heraclius, Patriarch of the church called the Holy Resurrection in Jerusalem, in the year of Christ 1185.

These Knights Templars took their beginning about the year 1118, in manner following. Certain noblemen, horsemen, religiously bent, bound by vow themselves in the hands of the Patriarch of Jerusalem, to serve Christ after the manner of regular canons in chastity and obedience, and to renounce their own proper wills for ever; the first of which order were Hugh Paganus, and Geffrey de S. Andromare. And whereas at the first they had no certain habitation, Baldwin, king of Jerusalem, granted unto them a dwelling-place in his palace by the Temple, and the canons of the same Temple gave them the street thereby to build therein their houses of office, and the patriarch, the king, the nobles, and prelates gave unto them certain revenues out of their lordships.

Their first profession was for safeguard of the pilgrims coming to visit the sepulchre, and to keep the highways against the lying in wait of thieves, &c. About ten years after they had a rule appointed unto them, and a white habit, by Honorius II., then Pope; and whereas they had but nine in number, they began to increase greatly. Afterward, in Pope Eugenius' time, they bare crosses of red cloth on their uppermost garments, to be known from others ; and in short time, because they had their first mansion hard by the Temple of our Lord in Jerusalem, they were called Knights of the Temple.

Many noble men in all parts of Christendom became brethren of this order, and built for themselves temples in every city or great town in England, but this at London was their chief house, which they built after the form of the temple near to the sepulchre of our Lord at Jerusalem. They had also other temples in Cambridge, Bristow, Canterbury, Dover, Warwick. This Temple in London was often made a storehouse of men's treasure, I mean such as feared the spoil thereof in other places.

Matthew Paris noteth that in the year 1232, Hubert de Burgh, Earl of Kent, being prisoner in the Tower of London, the king was informed that he had much treasure laid up in this New Temple, under the custody of the Templars. Whereupon he sent for the master of the Temple, and examined him straitly, who confessed that money being delivered unto him and his brethren to be kept, he knew not how much there was of it. The king demanded to have the same delivered, but it was answered, that the money being committed unto their trust, could not be delivered without the license of him that committed it to ecclesiastical protection, whereupon the king sent his Treasurer and Justiciar of the Exchequer unto Hubert, to require him to resign the money wholly into his hands, who answered that he would gladly submit himself, and all his, unto the king's pleasure ; and thereupon desired the knights of the Temple, in his behalf, to present all the keys unto the king, to do his pleasure with the goods which he had committed unto them. Then the king commanded the money to be faithfully told and laid up in his treasury, by inventory, wherein was found, besides ready money, vessels of gold and silver unpriceable, and many precious stones, which would make all men wonder if they knew the worth of them.

This Temple was again dedicated 1240, belike also newly re-edified then.

These Templars at this time were in so great glory, that they entertained the nobility, foreign ambassadors, and the prince himself very often, insomuch that Matthew Paris crieth out on them for their pride, who being at the first so poor, as they had but one horse to serve two of them, in token whereof they gave in their seal two men riding of one horse, yet suddenly they waxed so insolent, that they disdained other orders, and sorted themselves with noblemen.

King Edward I. in the year 1283, taking with him Robert

Waleran, and other, came to the Temple, where calling for the keeper of the treasure-house, as if he meant to see his mother's jewels, that were laid up there to be safely kept, he entered into the house, breaking the coffers of certain persons that had likewise brought their money thither, and he took away from thence to the value of a thousand pounds.

Many parliaments and great councils have been there kept, as may appear by our histories. In the year 1308, all the Templars in England, as also in other parts of Christendom, were apprehended and committed to divers prisons. In 1310, a provincial council was holden at London against the Templars in England, upon heresy and other articles whereof they were accused, but denied all except one or two of them, notwithstanding they all did confess that they could not purge themselves fully as faultless, and so they were condemned to perpetual penance in several monasteries, where they behaved themselves modestly.

Philip, king of France, procured their overthrow throughout the whole world, and caused them to be condemned by a general council to his advantage, as he thought, for he believed to have had all their lands in France, and therefore seized the same in his hands as I have read, and caused the Templars to the number of four and fifty, or after Fabian, threescore, to be burned at Paris.

Edward II. in the year 1313, gave unto Aymer de Valence, Earl of Pembroke, the whole place and houses called the New Temple at London, with the ground called Fickets Croft, and all the tenements and rents, with the appurtenances, that belonged to the Templars in the city of London and suburbs thereof.

After Aymer de Valence, sayeth some, Hugh Spencer, usurping the same, held it during his life, by whose death it came again to the hands of Edward III.; but in the meantime, to wit, 1324, by a council holden at Vienna, all the lands of the Templars, lest the same should be put to profane uses, were given to the knights hospitallers of the order of St. John Baptist, called St. John of Jerusalem, which knights had put the Turks out of the Isle of Rhodes, and after won upon the said Turks daily for a long time.

The said Edward III., therefore, granted the same to the said knights, who possessed it, and in the eighteenth year of the said king's reign, were forced to repair the bridge of the said Temple. These knights had their head house for England by West Smithfield, and they in the reign of the same Edward III. granted, for a certain rent of ten pounds by the year, the said Temple, with the appurtenances thereunto adjoining, to the students of the common laws of England, in whose possession the same hath ever since remained; and is now divided into two houses of several students, by the name of Inns of Court, to wit, the Inner Temple, and the Middle Temple, who kept two several halls, but they resort all to the said Temple Church, in the round walk whereof, which is the west part without the choir, there remaineth monuments of noblemen buried, to the number of eleven. Eight of them are images of armed knights—five lying cross-legged as men vowed to the Holy Land, against the infidels and unbelieving Jews; the other three straight-legged. The rest are coped stones all of grey marble. The first of the cross-legged was W. Marshall, the elder Earl of Pembroke, who died 1219; Will. Marshall, his son, Earl of Pembroke, was the second, he died 1231; and Gilbert Marshall, his brother, Earl of Pembroke, slain in a tournament at Hertford, beside Ware, in the year 1241.

After this Robert Rose, otherwise called Fursan, being made a Templar in the year 1245, died and was buried there, and these are all that I can remember to have read of. Sir Nicholas Hare, Master of the Rolls, was buried there in the year 1557.

In the year 1381, the rebels of Essex and of Kent destroyed and plucked down the houses and lodgings of this Temple, took out of the church the books and records that were in hutches of the apprentices of the law, carried them into the streets, and burnt them. The house they spoiled and burned for wrath that they bare Sir Robert Halles, Lord Prior of St. John's in Smithfield; but it was since again at divers times repaired, namely, the gate-house of the Middle Temple in the reign of Henry VIII., by Sir Amias Paulet, knight, upon occasion, as in my Annals I have shown. The great hall of the Middle Temple was newly built in the year 1572, in the reign of our Queen Elizabeth.

This Temple Church hath a master and four stipendiary priests, with a clerk. These for the ministration of divine service there have stipends allowed unto them out of the possessions and revenues of the late hospital and house of St. John's of Jerusalem in England, as it had been in the reign of Edward VI.; and thus much for the said New Temple, the farthest west part of this ward, and also of this city for the liberties thereof, which ward hath an alderman, and his deputies three. In Sepulchre's parish, common council six, constables four, scavengers four, wardmote inquest twelve; St. Bridget's parish, common councillors eight, constables eight, scavengers eight, wardmote inquest twenty; in St. Andrew's, common council two, constables two, scavengers three, wardmote inquest twelve. It is taxed to the fifteen at thirty-five pounds one shilling.

Bridge Ward without, the twenty-sixth in number, consisting of the Borough of Southwark, in the County of Surrey.

HAVING treated of wards in London on the north side the Thames, in number twenty-five, I am now to cross over the said river into the borough of Southwark, which is also a ward of London without the walls, on the south side thereof, as is Portsoken on the east, and Farringdon extra on the west.

This borough being in the county of Surrey, consisteth of divers streets, ways, and winding lanes, all full of buildings, inhabited; and first, to begin at the west part thereof, over against the west suburb of the city.

On the bank of the river Thames there is now a continual building of tenements, about half a mile in length to the bridge. Then from the bridge, straight towards the south, a continual street, called Long Southwark, built on both sides with divers lanes and alleys up to St. George's Church, and beyond it through Blackman Street towards New Town, or Newington, the liberties of which borough extend almost to the parish church of New Town aforesaid, distant one mile from London Bridge, and also south-west a continual building almost to Lambeth, more than one mile from the said bridge.

Then from the bridge along by the Thames eastward is St. Olave's Street, having continual building on both the sides, with lanes and alleys, up to Battle Bridge, to Horsedown, and towards Rotherhithe; also some good half mile in length from London Bridge.

So that I account the whole continual buildings on the bank of the said river, from the west towards the east, to be more than a large mile in length.

Then have ye, from the entering towards the said Horsedown, one other continual street called Bermondes high street, which stretcheth south, likewise furnished with buildings on both sides, almost half a mile in length, up to the late dissolved monastery of St. Saviour called Bermondsey. And from thence is one Long Lane, so called of the length, turning west to St. George's Church afore named. Out of the which lane mentioned, Long Lane, breaketh one other street towards the south, and by east, and this is called Kentish Street, for that is the way leading into that country; and so have you the bounds of this borough.

The antiquities most notable in this borough are these: First, for ecclesiastical, there was Bermondsey, an abbey of black monks; St. Mary Overy, a priory of canons regular; St. Thomas, a college or hospital for the poor; and the Lock, a lazar house in Kent Street. Parish churches there have been six, whereof five do remain, viz.,

St. Mary Magdalen, in the priory of St. Mary Overy, now the same St. Mary Overy is the parish church for the said Mary Magdalen, and for St. Margaret on the Hill, and is called St. Saviour.

St. Margaret on the Hill being put down is now a court for justice; St. Thomas in the hospital serveth for a parish church as afore; St. George a parish church as before it did; so doth St. Olave and St. Mary Magdalen, by the abbey of Bermondsey.

There be also these five prisons or gaols :—

> The Clink on the Banke.
> The Compter, in the late parish church of St. Margaret.
> The Marshalsey.
> The King's Bench.
> And the White Lion, all in Long Southwark.

Houses most notable be these :—

> The Bishop of Winchester's house.
> The Bishop of Rochester's house.
> The Duke of Suffolk's house, or Southwark Place.
> The Tabard, an hostelry or inn.
> The Abbot of Hyde, his house.
> The Prior of Lewes, his house.
> The Abbot of St. Augustine, his house.
> The Bridge House.
> The Abbot of Battaile, his house.
> Battaile Bridge.
> The Stewes on the bank of Thames.
> And the Bear-Gardens there.

Now, to return to the west bank, there be two bear-gardens, the old and new places, wherein be kept bears, bulls, and other beasts, to be baited; as also mastiffs in several kennels, nourished to bait them. These bears and other beasts are there baited in plots of ground, scaffolded about for the beholders to stand safe.

Next on this bank was sometime the Bordello, or Stewes, a place so called of certain stew-houses privileged there, for the repair of incontinent men to the like women; of the which privilege I have read thus :—

In a parliament holden at Westminster the 8th of Henry II. it was ordained by the commons, and confirmed by the king and lords, that divers constitutions for ever should be kept within that lordship or franchise, according to the old customs that had been there used time out of mind : amongst the which these following were some, viz. :—

"That no stew-holder or his wife should let or stay any single woman, to go and come freely at all times when they listed.

"No stew-holder to keep any woman to board, but she to board abroad at her pleasure.

"To take no more for the woman's chamber in the week than fourteen pence.

"Not to keep open his doors upon the holidays.

"Not to keep any single woman in his house on the holidays, but the bailiff to to see them voided out of the lordship.

"No single woman to be kept against her will that would leave her sin.

"No stew-holder to receive any woman of religion, or any man's wife.

" No single woman to take money to lie with any man, but she lie with him all night till the morrow.

" No man to be drawn or enticed into any stew-house.

" The constables, bailiff, and others, every week to search every stew-house.

" No stew-holder to keep any woman that hath the perilous infirmity of burning, not to sell bread, ale, flesh, fish, wood, coal, or any victuals, &c."

These and many more orders were to be observed upon great pain and punishment. I have also seen divers patents of confirmation, namely, one dated 1345, the 19th of Edward III. Also I find, that in the 4th of Richard II., these stew-houses belonging to William Walworth, then Mayor of London, were farmed by Froes of Flanders, and spoiled by Walter Tyler and other rebels of Kent. Notwithstanding, I find that ordinances for the same place and houses were again confirmed in the reign of Henry VI., to be continued as before. Also, Robert Fabian writeth, that in the year 1506, the 21st of Henry VII., the said stew-houses in Southwark were for a season inhibited, and the doors closed up, but it was not long, saith he, ere the houses there were set open again, so many as were permitted, for, as it was said, whereas before were eighteen houses, from thenceforth were appointed to be used but twelve only. These allowed stew-houses had signs on their fronts, towards the Thames, not hanged out, but painted on the walls, as a Boar's Head, the Cross Keys, the Gun, the Castle, the Crane, the Cardinal's Hat, the Bell, the Swan, &c. I have heard of ancient men, of good credit, report that these single women were forbidden the rites of the church so long as they continued that sinful life, and were excluded from Christian burial if they were not reconciled before their death. And therefore there was a plot of ground called the Single Woman's Churchyard, appointed for them far from the parish church.

In the year of Christ 1546, the 37th of Henry VIII., this row of stews in Southwark was put down by the king's commandment, which was proclaimed by sound of trumpet, no more to be privileged, and used as a common brothel, but the inhabitants of the same to keep good and honest rule, as in other places of this realm, &c.

Then next is the Clink, a jail or prison for the trespassers in those parts ; namely, in old time, for such as should brabble, fray, or break the peace on the said bank, or in the brothel-houses, they were by the inhabitants thereabout apprehended and committed to this jail, where they were straitly imprisoned.

Next is the Bishop of Winchester's house, or lodging, when he cometh to this city ; which house was first built by William Gifford, Bishop of Winchester, about the year 1107, the 7th of Henry I., upon a plot of ground pertaining to the prior of Bermondsey, as appeareth by a writ directed unto the barons of the Exchequer in the year 1366, the 41st of Edward III., the bishop's see being void, for eight pounds, due to the monks of Bermondsey for the Bishop of Winchester's lodging in Southwark. This is a very fair house, well repaired, and hath a large wharf and landing-place, called the Bishop of Winchester's Stairs.

Adjoining to this, on the south side the roof, is the Bishop of Rochester's inn or lodging, by whom first erected I do not now remember me to have read; but well I wot the same of long time hath not been frequented by any bishop, and lieth ruinous for lack of reparations. The abbot of Maverley had a house there.

East from the Bishop of Winchester's house, directly over against it, standeth a fair church called St. Mary over the Rie, or Overie; that is, over the water. This church, or some other in place thereof, was of old time, long before the Conquest, a house of sisters, founded by a maiden named Mary; unto the which house and sisters she left, as was left to her by her parents, the oversight and profits of a cross ferry, or traverse ferry over the Thames, there kept before that any bridge was built. This house of sisters was after by Swithen, a noble lady, converted into a college of priests, who in place of the ferry built a bridge of timber, and from time to time kept the same in good reparations; but lastly the same bridge was built of stone; and then in the year 1106 was this church again founded for canons regulars by William Pont de la Arche and William Dauncy, knights, Normans.

William Gifford, Bishop of Winchester, was a good benefactor also, for he, as some have noted, built the body of that church in the year 1106, the 7th of Henry I.

The canons first entered the said church then; Algodus was the first prior.

King Henry I. by his charter gave them the church of St. Margaret in Southwark.

King Stephen confirmed the gift of King Henry, and also gave the stone-house, which was William Pont de la Arche's, by Downgate.

This priory was burnt about the year 1207, wherefore the canons did found a hospital near unto their priory, where they celebrated until the priory was repaired; which hospital was after, by consent of Peter de la Roch, Bishop of Winchester, removed into the land of Anicius, Archdeacon of Surrey, in the year 1228, a place where the water was more plentiful and the air more wholesome, and was dedicated to St. Thomas.

This Peter de Rupibus, or de la Roch, founded a large chapel of St. Mary Magdalen, in the said church of St. Mary Overie; which chapel was after appointed to be the parish church for the inhabitants near adjoining.

This church was again newly built in the reign of Richard II. and King Henry IV.

John Gower, esquire, a famous poet, was then an especial benefactor to that work, and was there buried on the north side of the said church, in the chapel of St. John, where he founded a chantry. He lieth under a tomb of stone, with his image, also of stone, over him; the hair of his head, auburn, long to his shoulders, but curling up, and a small forked beard; on his head a chaplet, like a coronet of four roses; a habit of purple, damasked down to his feet; a collar of esses gold about his neck; under his head the likeness of three books which he compiled. The first, named *Speculum Meditantis*, written in French; the second, *Vox Clamantis*, penned in Latin; the third, *Confessio Amantis*, written in English, and this last is printed. *Vox Clamantis*, with his *Cronica Tripartita*, and other, both in Latin and French, never printed, I have and do possess, but *Speculum Meditantis* I never saw, though heard thereof to be in Kent. Beside on the wall where he lieth there was painted three virgins crowned; one of the which was named Charity, holding this device—

> "En toy qui es Fitz de dieu le pere,
> Sauve soit que gist souz cest piere."

The second writing, Mercy, with this device—

> "O bone Jesu, fait ta mercie
> Al alme dont le corps gist icy."

The third writing, Pity, with this device—

> "Pur ta pité Jesu regarde,
> Et met cest alme en sauve garde."

His arms a field argent, on a chevron azure, three leopards' heads gold, their tongues gules; two angels supporters, on the crest a talbot: his epitaph—

> "Armigeri scutum nihil a modo fert sibi tutum,
> Reddidit immolutum morti generale tributum,
> Spiritus exutum se gaudeat esse solutum,
> Est ubi virtutum regnum sine labe statutum."

The roof of the middle west aisle fell down in the year 1469. This priory was surrendered to Henry VIII., the 31st of his reign, the 27th of October, the year of Christ 1539, valued at £624, 6s. 6d. by the year.

About Christmas next following the church of the said priory was purchased of the king by the inhabitants of the borough, Doctor Stephen Gardiner, Bishop of Winchester, putting to his helping hand. They made thereof a parish church for the parish church of St. Mary

Magdalen, on the south side of the said choir, and of St. Margaret on-the-Hill, which were made one parish of St. Saviour.

There be monuments in this church of Robert Liliard, or Hiliard, esquire; Margaret, daughter to the Lady Audley, wife to Sir Thomas Audley; William Greville, esquire, and Margaret his wife; one of the heirs of William Spershut, esquire; Dame Katherine, wife to John Stoke, alderman; Robert Merfin, esquire; William Undall, esquire; Lord Ospay Ferar; Sir George Brewes, knight; John Browne; Lady Brandon, wife to Sir Thomas Brandon; William, Lord Scales; William, Earl Warren; Dame Maud, wife to Sir John Peach; Lewknor; Dame Margaret Elrington, one of the heirs of Sir Thomas Elrington; John Bowden, esquire; Robert St. Magil; John Sandhurst; John Gower; John Duncell, merchant tailor, 1516; John Sturton, esquire; Robert Rouse; Thomas Tong, first Norroy, and after Clarenceaux king-of-arms; William Wickham, translated from the see of Lincoln to the bishopric of Winchester in the month of March 1595, deceased the 11th of June next following, and was buried here; Thomas Cure, esquire, saddler to King Edward VI., Queen Mary, and Queen Elizabeth, deceased the 24th of May 1598, &c.

Now passing through St. Mary Overy's Close, in possession of the Lord Mountacute, and Pepper Alley, into Long Southwark, on the right hand thereof the market hill, where the leather is sold, there stood the late-named parish church of St. Margaret, given to St. Mary Overy by Henry I., put down and joined with the parish of St. Mary Magdalen, and united to the late dissolved priory church of St. Mary Overy.

A part of this parish church of St. Margaret is now a court, wherein the assizes and sessions be kept, and the court of admiralty is also there kept. One other part of the same church is now a prison, called the Compter in Southwark, &c.

Farther up on that side, almost directly over against St. George's Church, was sometime a large and most sumptuous house, built by Charles Brandon, late Duke of Suffolk, in the reign of Henry VIII., which was called Suffolk House; but coming afterwards into the king's hands, the same was called Southwark Place, and a mint of coinage was there kept for the king.

To this place came King Edward VI., in the second of his reign, from Hampton Court, and dined in it. He at that time made John York, one of the sheriffs of London, knight, and then rode through the city to Westminster.

Queen Mary gave this house to Nicholas Heath, Archbishop of York, and to his successors, for ever, to be their inn or lodging for their repair to London, in recompense of York House near to

Westminster, which King Henry, her father, had taken from Cardinal Wolsey, and from the see of York.

Archbishop Heath sold the same house to a merchant, or to merchants, that pulled it down, sold the lead, stone, iron, &c., and in place thereof built many small cottages of great rents, to the increasing of beggars in that borough. The Archbishop bought Norwich House, or Suffolk Place, near unto Charing Cross, because it was near unto the court, and left it to his successors.

Now on the south side to return back again towards the bridge, over against this Suffolk Place, is the parish church of St. George, sometime pertaining to the priory of Bermondsey, by the gift of Thomas Arderne and Thomas his son, in the year 1122. There lie buried in this church William Kirton, esquire, and his wives, 1464.

Then is the White Lion, a gaol so called, for that the same was a common hostelry for the receipt of travellers by that sign. This house was first used as a goal within these forty years last, since the which time the prisoners were once removed thence to a house in Newtown, where they remained for a short time, and were returned back again to the foresaid White Lion, there to remain as in the appointed gaol for the county of Surrey.

Next is the gaol or prison of the King's Bench, but of what antiquity the same is I know not. For I have read that the courts of the King's Bench and Chancery have ofttimes been removed from London to other places, and so hath likewise the goals that serve those courts; as in the year 1304 Edward I. commanded the courts of the King's Bench and the Exchequer, which had remained seven years at York, to be removed to their old places at London. And in the year 1387, the 11th of Richard II., Robert Tresilian, chief-justice, came to the city of Coventry, and there sate by the space of a month, as justice of the King's Benches, and caused to be indited in that court about the number of two thousand persons of that country.

It seemeth, therefore, that for that time the prison or gaol of that court was not far off. Also in the year 1392, the 16th of the same Richard, the Archbishop of York being lord chancellor, for goodwill that he bare to his city, caused the King's Bench and Chancery to be removed from London to York, but ere long they were returned to London.

Then is the Marshalsea, another gaol or prison, so called, as pertaining to the marshals of England. Of what continuance kept in Southwark I have not learned; but like it is, that the same hath been removable, at the pleasure of the marshals; for I find that in the year 1376, the 50th of Edward III., Henry Percy, being marshal, kept his prisoners in the city of London, where having committed one John Prendergast, of Norwich, contrary to the liberties of the city of London, the citizens, by persuasion of the Lord Fitzwalter, their standard-bearer, took armour and ran with great rage to the marshal's inn, brake up the gates, brought out the prisoner, and conveyed him away, minding to have burnt the stocks in the midst of their city, but they first sought for Sir Henry Percy to have punished him, as I have noted in my annals.

More, about the feast of Easter next following, John, Duke of Lancaster, having caused all the whole navy of England to be gathered together at London, it chanced a certain esquire to kill one of the shipmen, which act the other shipmen taking in ill part, they brought their suit into the king's court of the Marshalsea, which then, as chanced, saith mine author, was kept in Southwark. But when they perceived that court to be so favourable to the murderer, and further that the king's warrant was also gotten for his pardon, they in great fury ran to the house wherein the murderer was imprisoned, brake into it, and brought forth the prisoner with his gyves on his legs. They thrust a knife to his heart, and sticked him as if he had been a dog; after this they tied a rope to his gyves and drew him to the gallows, where when they had hanged him, as though they had done a great act, they caused the trumpets to be sounded before them to their ships, and there in great triumph they spent the rest of the day.

Also the rebels of Kent, in the year 1381, brake down the houses of the Marshalsea and King's Bench in Southwark, took from thence the prisoners, brake down the house of Sir John Immorth, then marshal of the Marshalsea and King's Bench, &c. After this, in the year 1387, the 11th of Richard II., the morrow after Bartholomew Day, the king kept a great council in the castle of Nottingham, and the Marshalsea of the king was then kept at Loughborough by the space of five days or more. In the year 1443 Sir Walter Manny was marshal of the Marshalsea, the 22nd of Henry VI. William Brandon, esquire, was marshal in the 8th of Edward IV. In the year 1504 the prisoners of the Marshalsea, then in Southwark, brake out, and many of them being taken were executed, especially such as had been committed for felony or treason.

From thence towards London Bridge, on the same side, be many fair inns, for receipt of travellers, by these signs, the Spur, Christopher, Bull, Queen's Head, Tabard, George, Hart, King's Head, &c. Amongst the which the most ancient is the Tabard, so called of the sign, which, as we now term it, is of a jacket, or sleeveless coat, whole before, open on both sides, with a square collar, winged at the shoulders; a stately garment of old time, commonly worn of noblemen and others, both at home and abroad in the wars, but then, to wit, in the wars, their arms embroidered, or otherwise depict upon them, that every man by his coat-of-arms might be known from others. But now these tabards are only worn by the heralds, and be called their coats-of-arms in service. For the inn of the Tabard Geoffrey Chaucer, esquire, the most famous poet of England, in commendation thereof, writeth thus :—

> " Befell that in that season, on a day,
> In Southwark at the Tabard, as I lay,
> Readie to wenden on my Pilgrimage
> To Canterburie with devout courage,
> At night was come into that hosterie,
> Well nine-and-twentie in a companie,
> Of sundrie folke, by adventúre yfalle,
> In fellowship, and pilgrimes were they all,
> That toward Canterburie wolden ride,
> The chambers and the stables weren wide,
> And well we weren eased at the best," &c.

Within this inn was also the lodging of the abbot of Hide, by the city of Winchester, a fair house for him and his train when he came to that city to parliament, &c.

And then Thieves' Lane, by St. Thomas's Hospital. The Hospital of St. Thomas, first founded by Richard Prior of Bermondsey, in the Cellarer's ground against the wall of the monastery, in the year 1213, he named it the Almerie, or house of alms for converts and poor children ; for the which ground the prior ordained that the almoner should pay ten shillings and fourpence yearly to the Cellarer at Michaelmas.

But Peter de Rupibus, Bishop of Winchester, in the year 1215, founded the same again more fully for canons regular in place of the first hospital. He increased the rent thereof to three hundred and forty-four pounds in the year. Thus was this hospital holden of the prior and abbot of Bermondsey till the year 1428, at which time a composition was made between Thomas Thetford, abbot of Bermondsey, and Nicholas Buckland, master of the said Hospital of St. Thomas, for all the lands and tenements which were holden of the said abbot and convent in Southwark, or elsewhere, for the old rent to be paid unto the said abbot.

There be monuments in this hospital church of Sir Robert Chamber, knight ; William Fines, Lord Say ; Richard Chaucer, John Gloucester, Adam Atwood, John Ward, Michael Cambridge, William West, John Golding, esquires ; John Benham, George Kirkes, Thomas Kninton, Thomas Baker, gentlemen ; Robert, son to Sir Thomas Fleming ; Agnes, wife to Sir Walter Dennis, knight, daughter, and one of the heirs of Sir Robert Danvars ; John Evarey, gentleman ; &c.

This hospital was by the visitors, in the year 1538, valued at two hundred and sixty - six pounds seventeen shillings and six- pence, and was surrendered to Henry VIII. in the 30th year of his reign.

In the year 1552, the citizens of London having purchased the void suppressed Hospital of St. Thomas in Southwark, in the month of July began the reparations thereof, for poor, impotent, lame, and diseased people, so that in the month of November next following the sick and poor people were taken in. And in the year 1553, on the 10th of April, King Edward VI., in the 7th of his reign, gave to the mayor, commonalty, and citizens of London, to be a workhouse for the poor and idle persons of this city, his house of Bridewell, and seven hundred marks lands of the Savoy rents, which hospital he had suppressed, with all the beds, bedding, and other furniture belonging to the same, towards the maintenance of the said workhouse of Bridewell and of this Hospital of St. Thomas in Southwark. This gift the king confirmed by his charter, dated the 26th of June next following, and willed it to be called the King's Hospital in Southwark.

The church of this hospital, which of old time served for the tenements near adjoining, and pertaining to the said hospital, re- maineth as a parish church.

But now to come to St. Olave's Street. On the bank of the river of Thames is the parish church of St. Olave, a fair and meet large church, but a far larger parish, especially of aliens or strangers, and poor people ; in which church there lieth entombed Sir John Burcettur, knight, 1466.

Over against this parish church, on the south side the street, was sometime one great house built of stone, with arched gates, per- taining to the prior of Lewes in Sussex, and was his lodging when he came to London. It was now a common hostelry for travellers, and hath to sign the Walnut Tree.

Then east from the said parish church of St. Olave is a quay. In the year 1330, by the license of Simon Swanlond, Mayor of London, built by Isabel, widow to Hammond Goodchepe. And next thereunto was then a great house of stone and timber, be- longing to the abbot of St. Augustine without the walls of Canter- bury, which was an ancient piece of work, and seemeth to be one of the first built houses on that side the river over against the city ; it was called the abbot's inn of St. Augustine in Southwark, and was sometime holden of the Earls of Warren and Surrey, as appeareth by a deed made 1281, which I have read, and may be Englished thus :—

To all whom this present writing shall come, John Earl Warren sendeth greeting. Know ye, that we have altogether remised and quit-claimed for us and our heirs for ever, to Nicholas, abbot of St. Augustine's of Canterbury, and the convent of the same, and their successors, suit to our court of Southwark, which they owe unto us, for all that messuage and houses thereon built, and all their appurtenances, which they have of our fee in Southwark, situate upon the Thames, between the Bridge House and the church of St. Olave. And the said messuage, with the buildings thereon built, and all their appurtenances, to them and their successors, we have granted in perpetual alms, to hold of us and our heirs for the same, saving the service due to any other persons, if any such be, then to us ; and for this remit and grant the said abbot and convent have given unto us five shillings of rent yearly in Southwark, and have received us and our heirs in all benefices which shall be in their church for ever."

This suit of court one William Graspeis was bound to do to the said earl for the said messuage, and heretofore to acquit in all things the church of St. Augustine against the said earl.

This house of late time belonged to Sir Anthony Sentlegar, then to Warham Sentlegar, &c., and is now called Sentlegar House, but divided into sundry tenements. Next is the Bridge House, so called as being a storehouse for stone, timber, or whatsoever pertaining to the building or repairing of London Bridge.

This house seemeth to have taken beginning with the first founding of the bridge either of stone or timber ; it is a large plot of ground, on the bank of the river Thames, containing divers large buildings for stowage of things necessary towards reparation of the said bridge.

There are also divers garners for laying up of wheat, and other grainers for service of the city, as need requireth. Moreover, there be certain ovens built, in number ten, of which six be very large, the other four being but half so big. These were purposely made to bake out the bread corn of the said grainers, to the best advantage for relief of the poor citizens, when need should require. Sir John Throstone, knight, sometime an embroiderer, then a goldsmith, one of the sheriffs 1516, gave by his testament towards the making of these ovens two hundred pounds, which thing was performed by his executors. Sir John Munday, goldsmith, then being mayor, there was of late, for the enlarging of the said Bridge House, taken in an old brewhouse, called Goldings, which was given to the city by George Monex, sometime mayor, and in place thereof is now a fair brewhouse new built, for service of the city with beer.

Next was the abbot of Battle's Inn, betwixt the Bridge House and Battle Bridge, likewise on the bank of the river of Thames ; the walks and gardens thereunto appertaining, on the other side of the way before the gate of the said house, and was called the Maze ; there is now an inn, called the Flower de Luce, for that the sign is three Flower de Luces. Much other buildings of small tenements are thereon builded, replenished with strangers and other, for the most part poor people.

Then is Battle Bridge, so called of Battaile Abbey, for that it standeth on the ground, and over a watercourse flowing out of Thames, pertaining to that abbey, and was, therefore, both built and repaired by the abbots of that house, as being hard adjoining to the abbot's lodging.

Beyond this bridge is Bermondsey Street, turning south, in the south end whereof was sometime a priory or abbey of St. Saviour, called Bermond's Eye in Southwark, founded by Alwin Childe, a citizen of London, in the year 1081.

Peter, Richard, Obstert, and Umbalde, monks de Caritate, came unto Bermondsey in the year 1089, and Peter was made first prior there, by appointment of the prior of the house, called Charity in France, by which means this priory of Bermondsey, being a cell to that in France, was accounted a priory of Aliens.

In the year 1094 deceased Alwin Childe, founder of this house. Then William Rufus gave to the monks his manor of Bermondsey, with the appurtenances, and built for them there a new great church.

Robert Blewet, Bishop of Lincoln, King William's chancellor, gave them the manor of Charlton, with the appurtenances. Also Geoffrey Martell, by the grant of Geoffrey Magnavile, gave them the land of Halingbury and the tithe of Alferton, &c.

More, in the year 1122, Thomas of Arderne, and Thomas his son, gave to the monks of Bermond's Eye the church of St. George in Southwark, &c.

In the year 1165 King Henry II. confirmed to them the hyde or territory of Southwark, and Laygham Wadden, with the land of Coleman, &c.

In the year 1371 the priors of Aliens throughout England being seized into the king's hands, Richard Denton, an Englishman, was made prior of Bermondsey, to whom was committed the custody of the said priory, by the letters patents of King Edward III., saving to the king the advowsons of churches.

In the year 1380, the 4th of Richard II., this priory was made a denison, or free English, for the fine of two hundred marks paid to the king's Hanaper in the chancery. In the year 1399 John Attelborough, prior of Bermondsey, was made the first abbot of that house by Pope Boniface IX., at the suit of King Richard II.

In the year 1417 Thomas Thetford, abbot of Bermondsey, held a plea in chancery against the king for the manors of Preston, Bermondsey, and Stone, in the county of Somerset, in the which suit the abbot prevailed and recovered against the king.

In the year 1539 this abbey was valued to dispend by the year four hundred and seventy-four pounds fourteen shillings and fourpence-haifpenny, and was surrendered to Henry VIII., the 31st of his reign; the abbey church was then pulled down by Sir Thomas Pope, knight, and in place thereof a goodly house built of stone and timber, now pertaining to the Earls of Sussex.

There are buried in that church, Leoftane, provost, shrive or domesman of London, 1115; Sir William Bowes, knight, and Dame Elizabeth his wife; Sir Thomas Pikeworth, knight; Dame Anne Audley; George, son to John Lord Audley; John Winkfield, esquire; Sir Nicholas Blonket, knight; Dame Bridget, wife to William Trussell; Holgrave, baron of the exchequer, &c.

Next unto this abbey church standeth a proper church of St. Mary Magdalen, built by the priors of Bermondsey, serving for resort of the inhabitants (tenants to the prior or abbots near adjoining), there to have their divine service. This church remaineth, and serveth as afore, and is called a parish church.

Then in Kent Street is a lazar-house for leprous people, called the Loke, in Southwark, the foundation whereof I find not. Now, having touched divers principal parts of this borough, I am to speak somewhat of its government, and so to end.

This borough, upon petition made by the citizens of London to Edward I., in the 1st year of his reign, was, for divers causes, by parliament granted to them for ever, yielding into the exchequer the feefirm of ten pounds by the year; which grant was confirmed by Edward III., who, in the 3rd of his reign, gave them license to take a toll towards the charge of paving the said borough with stone. Henry IV. confirmed the grant of his predecessors; so did Edward IV., &c.

But in the year 1550 King Edward VI., for the sum of six hundred and forty-seven pounds two shillings and one penny, paid into his court of augmentations and revenues of his crown, granted to the mayor and commonalty all his lands and tenements in Southwark, except, and reserved, the capital messuage, two mansions, called Southwark Place, late the Duke of Suffolk's, and all the gardens and lands to the same appertaining, the park, and the messuage called the Antelope. Moreover, he gave them the lordship and manor of Southwark, with all members and rights thereof, late pertaining to the monastery of Bermondsey. And all messuages, places, buildings, rents, courts, waifs and strays to the same appertaining in the county of Surrey, except as is before excepted. He also granted unto them his manor and borough of Southwark, with all the members, rights, and appurtenances, late of the possession of the Archbishop of Canterbury and his see in Southwark. Moreover, for the sum of five hundred marks, he granted to the said mayor and commonalty, and their successors, in and through the

borough and town of Southwark, and in all the parishes of St.
Saviour, St. Olave, and St. George, and the parish of St. Thomas's
Hospital, now called the King's Hospital, and elsewhere, in the said
town and borough of Southwark, and Kentish Street, Bermondsey
Street, in the parish of Newington, all waifs and strays, treasure-
trove, all felons' goods, &c., within the parishes and precinct aforesaid, &c. ; the return of writs, processes, and warrants, &c. ; together
with a fair in the whole town for three days, to wit, the 7th, 8th,
and 9th of September, yearly, with a court of pye powders. A view
of frank pledge, with attachments, arrests, &c. Also to arrest all
felons and other malefactors within their precinct, and send them
to ward and to Newgate. Provided that nothing in that grant
should be prejudicial to the stewards and marshal of the king's
house. The same premises to be holden of the manor of East
Greenwich, in the county of Kent, by fealty in free forage. Dated
at Westminster the 23rd of April, in the 4th of his reign. All
which was also confirmed by parliament, &c. And the same year,
in the Whitsun week, in a court of aldermen kept at the Guildhall
of London, Sir John Aylophe, knight, was sworn the first alderman
of Bridge Ward Without, and made up the number of twenty-six
aldermen of London.

This borough at a subsidy to the king yieldeth about one thousand
marks, or eight hundred pounds, which is more than any one city in
England payeth, except the city of London. And also the muster
of men in this borough doth likewise in number surpass all other
cities, except London. And thus much for the borough of Southwark, one of the twenty-six wards of London, which hath an alderman, deputies three, and a bailiff, common council none, constables
sixteen, scavengers six, wardmote inquest twenty ; and is taxed to
the fifteen at seventeen pounds seventeen shillings and eightpence.

The Suburbs without the Walls of the said City briefly touched. As also without the Liberties more at large described.

HAVING spoken of this city, the original, and increase, by degrees ;
the walls, gates, ditch, castles, towers, bridges, the schools and houses
of learning ; of the orders and customs, sports and pastimes ; of the
honour of citizens and worthiness of men ; and last of all, how the
same city is divided into parts and wards, and how the same be
bounded, and what monuments of antiquity or ornaments of building, in every of them, as also in the borough of Southwark ; I am
next to speak briefly of the suburbs, as well without the gates and
walls as without the liberties, and of the monuments in them.

Concerning the estate of the suburbs of this city in the reign of Henry II., Fitz-Stephen hath these words :—

"Upwards, on the west," saith he, "is the king's palace, which is an incomparable building, rising with a vawmure and bulwark aloft upon the river, two miles from the wall of the city, but yet conjoined with a continual suburb. On all sides, without the houses of the suburbs, are the citizens' gardens and orchards, planted with trees, both large, sightly, and adjoining together. On the north side are pastures and plain meadows, with brooks running through them, turning water-mills with a pleasant noise. Not far off is a great forest, a well-wooded chase, having good covert for harts, bucks, does, boars, and wild bulls. The corn-fields are not of a hungry sandy mould, but as the fruitful fields of Asia, yielding plentiful increase, and filling the barns with corn. There are near London, on the north side, especial wells in the suburbs, sweet, wholesome, and clear. Amongst which Holywell, Clarkenwell, and St. Clement's Well are most famous, and most frequented by scholars and youths of the city in summer evenings, when they walk forth to take the air."

Thus far out of Fitz-Stephen for the suburbs at that time.

The 2nd of King Henry III. the forest of Middlesex and the warren of Staines were disafforested ; since the which time the suburbs about London hath been also mightily increased with buildings ; for first, to begin in the east, by the Tower of London, is the Hospital of St. Katherine, founded by Matilda, the queen, wife to King Stephen, as is afore shown in Portsoken Ward. From this precinct of St. Katherine to Wapping in the west, the usual place of execution for hanging of pirates and sea-rovers, at the low-water mark, and there to remain till three tides had overflowed them, was never a house standing within these forty years ; but since the gallows being after removed farther off, a continual street, or filthy straight passage, with alleys of small tenements, or cottages, built, inhabited by sailors' victuallers, along by the river of Thames, almost to Ratcliffe, a good mile from the Tower.

On the east side, and by north of the Tower, lieth East Smithfield, Hogs' Street, and Tower Hill ; and east from them both was the new abbey called Grace, founded by Edward III. From thence Ratcliffe, up East Smithfield, by Nightingale Lane, which runneth south to the Hermitage, a brewhouse so called of a hermit sometime being there, beyond this lane to the manor of Bramley, called in record of Richard II. Villa East Smithfield and Villa de Bramley, and to the manor of Shadwell, belonging to the Dean of Paul's. There hath been of late, in place of elm-trees, many small tenements raised towards Ratcliffe ; and Ratcliffe itself hath been also increased in building eastward, in place where I have known a large highway, with fair elm-trees on both the sides, that the same hath now taken hold of Lime Hurst, or Lime Host, corruptly called Lime House, sometime distant a mile from Ratcliffe.

Having said this much for building at Wapping, East Smithfield, Bramley, and Shadwell, all on the south side of the highway to

Ratcliffe, now one note on the north side, also concerning pirates. I read that in the year 1440, in the Lent season, certain persons, with six ships, brought from beyond the seas fish to victual the city of London, which fish, when they had delivered and were returning homeward, a number of sea-thieves, in a barge, in the night came upon them, when they were asleep in their vessels, riding at anchor on the river Thames, and slew them, cut. their throats, cast them overboard, took their money, and drowned their ships, for that no man should espy or accuse them. Two of these thieves were after taken, and hanged in chains upon a gallows set upon a raised hill, for that purpose made, in the field beyond East Smithfield, so that they might be seen far into the river Thames. The first building at Ratcliffe in my youth, not to be forgotten, was a fair free school and almshouses, founded by Avice Gibson, wife to Nicholas Gibson, grocer, as before I have noted; but of late years shipwrights and, for the most part, other marine men, have built many large and strong houses for themselves, and smaller for sailors, from thence almost to Poplar, and so to Blackwall. Now for Tower Hill; the plain there is likewise greatly diminished by merchants for building of small tenements. From thence towards Aldgate was the Minories, whereof I have spoken.

From Aldgate east again lieth a large street, replenished with buildings; to wit, on the north side the parish church of St. Botolph, and so other buildings, to Hog Lane, and to the bars on both sides.

Also without the bars both the sides of the street be pestered with cottages and alleys, even up to Whitechapel Church, and almost half a mile beyond it, into the common field; all which ought to be open and free for all men. But this common field, I say, being sometime the beauty of this city on that part, is so encroached upon by building of filthy cottages, and with other purpressors, enclosures, and laystalls (notwithstanding all proclamations and acts of parliament made to the contrary), that in some places it scarce remaineth a sufficient highway for the meeting of carriages and droves of cattle. Much less is there any fair, pleasant, or wholesome way for people to walk on foot; which is no small blemish to so famous a city to have so unsavoury and unseemly an entrance or passage thereunto.

Now of Whitechapel Church somewhat, and then back again to Aldgate. This church is, as it were, a chapel of ease to the parish of Stebinhith, and the parson of Stebinhith hath the gift thereof; which, being first dedicated to the name of God and the Blessed Virgin, is now called St. Mary Matfellon. About the year 1428, the 6th of King Henry VI., a devout widow of that parish had long time cherished and brought up of alms a certain Frenchman, or Breton born, which most unkindly and cruelly in a night murdered the said widow sleeping in her bed, and after fled with such jewels and other stuff of hers as he might carry; but he was so freshly pursued, that for fear he took the church of St. George in Southwark, and challenged privilege of sanctuary there, and so abjured the king's land. Then the constables having charge of him brought him into London, intending to have conveyed him eastward; but so soon as he was come into the parish where before he had committed the murder the wives cast upon him so much filth and ordure of the street, that, notwithstanding the best resistance made by the constables, they slew him out of hand; and for this feat, it hath been said, that parish to have purchased that name of St. Mary Matfellon; but I find in record the same to be called Villa beatæ Mariæ de Matfellon, in the 21st of Richard II.

More, we read that in the year 1336, the 10th of Edward III., the Bishop of Alba, cardinal and parson of Stebinhith, procurator-general in England, presented a clerk to be parson in the church of the Blessed Mary called Matfellon, without Aldgate of London, &c.

Now again from Aldgate north-west to Bishopsgate lieth Houndsditch, and so to Bishopsgate.

North, and by east from Bishopsgate, lieth a large street or highway, having on the west side thereof the parish church of St. Botolph.

Then is the Hospital of St. Mary of Bethlehem, founded by a citizen of London, and as before is showed; up to the bars without the which is Norton Fall Gate, a liberty so called, belonging to the Dean of Paul's; thence up to the late dissolved priory of St. John Baptist, called Holywell, a house of nuns, of old time founded by a Bishop of London. Stephen Grausend, Bishop of London, about the year 1318, was a benefactor thereunto; re-edified by Sir Thomas Lovel, knight of the Garter, who built much there in the reigns of Henry VII. and of Henry VIII.; he endowed this house with fair lands, and was there buried in a large chapel by him built for that purpose. This priory was valued at the suppression to have of lands two hundred and ninety-three pounds by year, and was surrendered 1539, the 31st of Henry VIII. The church thereof being pulled down, many houses have been built for the lodgings of noblemen, of strangers born, and other.

From Holywell in the high street is a continual building of tenements to Shoreditch, having one small side of a field, already made a garden plot. Over against the north corner of this field, between it and the church of St. Leonard in Shoreditch, sometime stood a cross, now a smith's forge, dividing three ways; forth right the highway is built upon either side, more than a good flight shot, towards Kingsland, Newington, Tottenham, &c.

On the left hand is Galde Street, which reacheth west to a stone cross over against the north end of Golden Lane, and so to the end of Goswell Street. On the right hand of this Galde Street, not far from Shoreditch, but on the north side thereof, is Hoxton, a large street with houses on both sides, and is a prebend belonging to Paul's Church in London, but of Shoreditch parish.

On the right hand, beyond Shoreditch Church toward Hackney, are some late-built houses upon the common soil, for it was a laystall, but those houses belong to the parish of Stebinhith.

On the other side of the highway from Bishopsgate and Hounds-ditch is the Dolphin, a common inn for receipt of travellers; then a house built by the Lord John Powlet, then Fisher's Folly, and so up to the west end of Berwardes Lane is a continual building of small cottages; then the hospital called St. Mary Spittle, hard within the bars, whereof I have spoken in Bishopsgate Ward.

From the which bars towards Shoreditch on that side is all along a continual building of small and base tenements, for the most part lately erected.

Amongst the which, I mean of the ancientest building, was one row of proper small houses, with gardens for poor decayed people, there placed by the prior of the said hospital; every one tenant whereof paid one penny rent by the year at Christmas, and dined with the prior on Christmas Day; but after the suppression of the hospital these houses, for want of reparations, in few years were so decayed, that it was called Rotten Row, and the poor worn-out— for there came no new in their place—houses, for a small portion of money, were sold from Goddard to Russell, a draper, who new built them, and let them out for rent enough, taking also large fines off the tenants, near as much as the houses cost him purchase and building; for he made his bargains so hardly with all men, that both carpenter, bricklayer, and plasterer were by that work undone; and yet, in honour of his name, it is now called Russell's Row.

Now for the parish of St. Leonard at Shoreditch. The Archdeacon of London is always parson thereof, and the cure is served by a vicar. In this church have been divers honourable persons buried, as appeareth by monuments yet remaining:—Sir John Elrington, with Margaret his wife, daughter and heir to Thomas, Lord Itch-ingham, widow to William Blount, son and heir to Walter Blount, the first Lord Mountjoy, which Margaret died 1481; Sir Humphrey Starkie, recorder of London, baron of the Exchequer; John Gadde, shireman of London, and Anne his wife, 1480; Sir Thomas Seymore, Mayor of London, deceased 1535; Sir Thomas Ligh, doctor of law, 1545. Item, under one fair monument lieth buried the Lady Katherine, daughter to Edward, Duke of Buckingham, wife to

Ralph Nevell, Earl of Westmoreland, who died 1553; also Elianor, daughter to Sir William Paston, wife to Thomas Mannars, Earl of Rutland, 1551; Margaret, daughter to Ralph Nevell, Earl of Westmoreland, and wife to Henry Mannars, Earl of Rutland, 1560; Katherine, daughter to Henry Nevell, Earl of Westmoreland, and wife to Sir John Constable of Holderness, 1591; Anne, daughter to T. Mannars, Earl of Rutland; Sir T. Mannars, fourth son to Thomas, Earl of Rutland, 1591; Oliver Mannars, fifth son to Thomas, Earl of Rutland, 1563, all under one monument; Richard and Harry Young, 1545.

Notwithstanding that, of late one vicar there, for covetousness of the brass, which he converted into coined silver, plucked up many plates fixed on the graves, and left no memory of such as had been buried under them, a great injury both to the living and the dead, forbidden by public proclamation, in the reign of our sovereign lady Queen Elizabeth, but not forborne by many, that either of a preposterous zeal or of a greedy mind spare not to satisfy themselves by so wicked a means.

One note of Shoreditch, and so an end of that suburb. I read that in the year 1440, the 18th of Henry VI., a fuller of Shoreditch appeached of treason many worthy esquires and gentlemen of Kent, but he being proved false, was attainted, condemned, and had judgment to be drawn, hanged, and quartered, which was done; his head set on London Bridge, and his quarters on the gates. This justice was done according to the 16th of Deuteronomy; "The judges shall make diligent inquisition, and if the witness be found false, and to have given false witness against his brother, then shall they do unto him as he had thought to do unto his brother," &c. I read of the King's Manor vocatur Shoreditch Place, in the parish of Hackney, but how it took that name I know not, and therefore I will turn back from Shoreditch Cross to Bethlehem Cross, and so pass through that hospital into the Moorfield, which lieth without the postern called Moorgate.

This field of old time was called the Moor, as appeareth by the charter of William the Conqueror to the college of St. Martin, declaring a running water to pass into the city from the same Moor, Also Fitz-Stephen writeth of this Moor, saying thus:—"When the great fen, or moor, which watereth the walls on the north side, is frozen," &c. This fen, or moorfield, stretching from the wall of the city betwixt Bishopsgate and the postern called Cripplegate, to Finsbury and to Holywell, continued a waste and unprofitable ground a long time, so that the same was all letten for four marks the year, in the reign of Edward II. But in the year 1415, the 3rd of Henry V., Thomas Fawconer, mayor, as I have showed, caused the wall of the city to be broken toward the said moor, and built the postern called Moorgate, for the ease of the citizens to walk that way upon causeways towards Iseldon and Hoxton. Moreover, he caused the ditches of the city, and other the ditches from Shoreditch to Deepditch by Bethlehem into the Moorditch, to be new cast and cleansed; by means whereof the said fen or moor was greatly drained and dried. But shortly after, to wit, in 1477, Ralph Joceline, mayor, for repairing of the wall of the city, caused the said moor to be searched for clay, and brick to be burnt there, &c., by which means this field was made the worse for a long time.

In the year 1498 all the gardens which had continued time out of mind without Moorgate, to wit, about and beyond the lordship of Finsbury, were destroyed, and of them was made a plain field for archers to shoot in. And in the year 1512 Roger Archley, mayor, caused divers dikes to be cast, and made to drain the waters of the said Moorfield, with bridges arched over them, and the grounds about to be levelled, whereby the said field was made somewhat more commodious, but yet it stood full of noisome waters; whereupon, in the year 1527, Sir Thomas Semor, mayor, caused divers sluices to be made to convey the said waters over the Town Ditch into the course of Walbrook, and so into the Thames. And by these degrees was this fen or moor at length made main and hard ground, which before being overgrown with flags, sedges, and rushes, served to no use; since the which time also the further grounds beyond Finsbury Court have been so overheightened with laystalls of dung, that now three windmills are thereon set, the ditches be filled up, and the bridges overwhelmed.

And now concerning the enclosures of common grounds about this city, whereof I mind not much to argue, Edward Hall setteth down a note of his time, to wit, in the 5th, or rather 6th of Henry VIII. :—

"Before this time," saith he, "the inhabitants of the towns about London, as Iseldon, Hoxton, Shoreditch, and others, had so inclosed the common fields with hedges and ditches, that neither the young men of the city might shoot, nor the ancient persons walk for their pleasures in those fields, but that either their bows and arrows were taken away or broken, or the honest persons arrested or indicted; saying, 'that no Londoner ought to go out of the city, but in the highways.' This saying so grieved the Londoners, that suddenly this year a great number of the city assembled themselves in a morning, and a turner, in a fool's coat, came crying through the city, 'Shovels and spades! shovels and spades!' So many of the people followed, that it was a wonder to behold; and within a short space all the hedges about the city were cast down, and the ditches filled up, and everything made plain, such was the diligence of these workmen. The king's council hearing of this assembly, came to the Gray Friars, and sent for the mayor and council of the city to know the cause, which declared to them the injury and annoying done to the citizens and to their liberties, which though they would not seek disorderly to redress, yet the commonalty and young persons could not be stayed thus to remedy the same. When the king's council had heard their answer, they dissimuled the matter, and commanded the mayor to see that no other thing were attempted, but that they should forthwith call home the younger sort; who having speedily achieved their desire, returned home before the king's council, and the mayor departed without more harm: after which time," saith Hall, "these fields were never hedged, but now we see the thing in worse case than ever, by means of inclosure for gardens, wherein are built many fair summer-houses; and, as in other places of the suburbs, some of them like Midsummer pageants, with towers, turrets, and chimney-tops, not so much for use of profit as for show and pleasure, betraying the vanity of men's minds, much unlike to the disposition of the ancient citizens, who delighted in the building of hospitals and almshouses for the poor, and therein both employed their wits, and spent their wealths in preferment of the common commodity of this our city."

But to come back again to Moorgate, and from thence west through a narrow lane called the Postern, because it hath at either end a door to be shut in the night season, betwixt the Moor Ditch enclosed with brick for tenter-yards, and the gardens of the said Moorfield, to Moor Lane; a part of the suburb without Cripplegate, without this Postern, called Cripplegate, also lay a part of the said Moor even to the river of the Wells, as in another place I have showed; and no houses were there built till the latter end of the reign of William the Conqueror, and of his son William Rufus; about which times some few houses being there built along east and west, thwart before the said gate, one Alfune built for the inhabitants a parish church, which is of St. Giles, somewhat west from the said gate, and is now on the bank of the Town Ditch; and so was there a street, since called Fore Street, as standing before the gate.

This Alfune, in the reign of Henry I., became the first hospitaller of St. Bartholomew's Hospital in Smithfield, as in another place I have noted. And this parish church of St. Giles, being at the first a small thing, stood in place where now standeth the vicarage-house, but hath been since at divers times much enlarged, according as the parish hath increased, and was at the length newly built in place where now it standeth. But the same new church being large, strongly built, and richly furnished with ornaments, was in the year 1545, by casualty of fire, sore burnt and consumed, notwithstanding it was again within a short space of time repaired, as now it showeth.

Some little distance from the east end of this church standeth a fair conduit, castellated, in Fore Street. Then have ye a boss of sweet water in the wall of the churchyard, lately made a pump, but already decayed.

Then have ye a fair pool of sweet water near to the church of St. Giles, wherein Anne of Lothbury was drowned, as I have before declared.

In the east end of Fore Street is More Lane; then next is Grub Street, of late years inhabited, for the most part, by bowyers, fletchers, bow-string makers, and such like occupations, now little occupied; archery giving place to a number of bowling-alleys and dicing-houses, which in all places are increased, and too much frequented.

This street stretcheth north to Guerades Well Street, which thwarteth it to White Cross Street; the next from Fore Street north is White Cross Street, likewise extending itself up to the west end of Guerades Well Street, and from the end thereof to Eald Street.

From the west end of Fore Street lieth Red Cross Street; from the which cross on the right hand east lieth Beech Lane, and reacheth to the White Cross Street. From Red Cross north lieth Golding Lane, which stretcheth up to a cross in Eald Street, which Golding Lane on both the sides is replenished with many tenements of poor people.

On the left hand, and west of the Red Cross, lieth a street of old time called Houndsditch, and of later time named Barbican, of such cause as I have before noted. And thus have you all the suburb without Cripplegate, being almost altogether in the parish of St. Giles, which hath more than eighteen hundred householders and above four thousand communicants.

Without Aldersgate on the left hand is the parish church of St. Botolph; on the north side of the which church lieth a way called Little Britain Street, towards the priory of St. Bartholomew in Smithfield; but the highway without Aldersgate runneth straight north from the said gate unto Houndsditch, or Barbican Street, on the right hand, and Long Lane on the left hand, which runneth into Smithfield.

Then from the farther end of Aldersgate Street, straight north to the bar, is called Goswell Street, replenished with small tenements, cottages, and alleys, gardens, banqueting-houses, and bowling-places.

Beyond these bars, leaving the Charterhouse on the left hand, or the west side, the way stretcheth up towards Iseldon, and on the right hand, or east side, at a red cross, turneth into Eald Street, so called for that it was the old highway from Aldersgate for the north-east parts of England, before Bishopsgate was built, which street runneth east to a smith's forge, sometime a cross before Shoreditch Church, from whence the passengers and carriages were to turn north to King's Land, Tottenham, Waltham, Ware, &c.

There was sometime in this suburb without Aldersgate an hospital for the poor, but an alien of Cluny, a French order, and therefore suppressed by King Henry V., who gave the house, with lands and goods, to the parish of St. Botolph, and a brotherhood of the Trinity was there founded, which was afterward suppressed by Henry VIII. or Edward VI.

There is at the farthest north corner of this suburb a windmill, which was sometime by a tempest of wind overthrown, and in place thereof a chapel was built by Queen Katherine, first wife to Henry VIII., who named it the Mount of Calvary, because it was of Christ's Passion, and was in the end of Henry VIII. pulled down, and a windmill newly set up as afore.

Without Newgate lieth the west and by north suburb ; on the right hand, or north side whereof, betwixt the said gate and the parish of St. Sepulchre, turneth a way towards West Smithfield, called, as I have showed, Giltspur Street, or Knightriders' Street. Then is Smithfield itself compassed about with buildings, as I have before declared, in Farringdon Ward Without.

And without the bar of West Smithfield lieth a large street or way, called of the house of St. John there St. John's Street, and stretcheth toward Iseldon, on the right hand whereof stood the late dissolved monastery called the Charterhouse, founded by Sir Walter Manny, knight, a stranger born, lord of the town of Manny, in the diocese of Cambray, beyond the seas, who for service done to King Edward III. was made knight of the Garter. So his house he founded upon this occasion. A great pestilence entering this island, began first in Dorsetshire, then proceeded into Devonshire, Somersetshire, Gloucestershire, and Oxfordshire, and at length came to London, and overspread all England, so wasting the people that scarce the tenth person of all sorts was left alive, and churchyards were not sufficient to receive the dead, but men were forced to choose out certain fields for burials ; whereupon Ralph Stratford, Bishop of London, in the year 1348, bought a piece of ground called No Man's Land, which he enclosed with a wall of brick, and dedicated for burial of the dead, building thereupon a proper chapel, which is now enlarged and made a dwelling-house ; and this burying-plot is become a fair garden, retaining the old name of Pardon Churchyard.

About this, in the year 1349, the said Sir Walter Manny, in respect of danger that might befall in this time of so great a plague and infection, purchased thirteen acres and a rod of ground adjoining to the said No Man's Land, and lying in a place called Spittle Cross, because it belonged to St. Bartholomew's Hospital, since that called the New Church Haw, and caused it to be consecrated by the said bishop of London to the use of burials.

In this plot of ground there were in that year more than fifty thousand persons buried, as I have read in the charters of Edward III. ; also, I have seen and read an inscription fixed on a stone cross sometime standing in the same churchyard, and having these words :—

" *Anno Domini* 1349, *regnante magna pestilentia consecratum fuit hoc Cœmiterium, in quo et infra septa presentis monasterii, sepulta fuerunt mortuorum corpora plusquam quinquaginta millia, præter alia multa abhinc usque ad presens, quorum animabus propitietur Deus. Amen.*"

In consideration of the number of Christian people here buried, the said Sir Walter Manny caused first a chapel to be built, where for the space of twenty-three years offerings were made; and it is to be noted that above one hundred thousand bodies of Christian people had in that churchyard been buried; for the said knight had purchased that place for the burial of poor people, travellers, and other that were deceased, to remain for ever; whereupon an order was taken for the avoiding of contention between the parsons of churches and that house; to wit, that the bodies should be had unto the church where they were parishioners, or died, and, after the funeral service done, had to the place where they should be buried. And in the year 1371 he caused there to be founded a house of Carthusian monks, which he willed to be called the Salutation, and that one of the monks should be called prior; and he gave them the said place of thirteen acres and a rod of land, with the chapel and houses there built, for their habitation. He also gave them the three acres of land lying without the walls on the north part, betwixt the lands of the abbot of Westminster and the lands of the prior of St. John, which three acres were purchased, enclosed, and dedicated by Ralph Stratford, Bishop of London, as is afore showed, and remained till our time by the name of Pardon Churchyard, and served for burying of such as desperately ended their lives, or were executed for felonies, who were fetched thither usually in a close cart, bailed over and covered with black, having a plain white cross thwarting, and at the fore end a St. John's cross without, and within a bell ringing by shaking of the cart, whereby the same might be heard when it passed; and this was called the friary cart, which belonged to St John's, and had the privilege of sanctuary.

In this Charterhouse were the monuments of the said Sir Walter Manny, and Margaret his wife; Marmaduke Lumley; Laurence Brumley, knight; Sir Edward Hederset, knight; Sir William Manny, knight; Dame Joan Borough; John Dore; Want Water, knight; Robert Olney, esquire; Katherine, daughter to Sir William Babington, knight; Blanch, daughter to Hugh Waterton; Katherine, wife to John at Poote, daughter and heir to Richard de Lacy; William Rawlin; Sir John Lenthaine, and Dame Margaret his wife, daughter to John Fray; John Peake, esquire; William Baron, and William Baron, esquire; Sir Thomas Thawites, knight; Philip Morgan, Bishop of Ely, 1434.

In the cloister :—Bartholomew Rede, knight, Mayor of London, buried 1505; Sir John Popham, &c.

This monastery, at the suppression in the 29th of Henry VIII., was valued at six hundred and forty-two pounds and fourpence-half-penny yearly.

A little without the bars of West Smithfield is Charterhouse Lane, so called for that it leadeth to the said plot of the late dissolved monastery ; in place whereof, first the Lord North, but since Thomas Howard, late Duke of Norfolk, have made large and sumptuous buildings both for lodging and pleasure. At the gate of this Charterhouse is a fair water-conduit, with two cocks, serving the use of the neighbours to their great commodity.

St. John's Street, from the entering this lane, is also on both the sides replenished with buildings up to Clerkenwell ; on the left hand of which street lieth a lane called Cow Cross, of a cross sometime standing there ; which lane turneth down to another lane called Turnemill Street, which stretcheth up to the west of Clerkenwell, and was called Turnemill Street for such cause as is afore declared.

One other lane there is called St. Peter's Lane, which turneth from St. John's Street to Cow Cross.

On the left hand also stood the late dissolved priory of St. John of Jerusalem in England, founded about the year of Christ 1100 by Jorden Briset, baron, and Muriell his wife, near unto Clarkeswell, beside West Smithfield ; which Jorden having first founded the priory of nuns at Clarkeswell, bought of them ten acres of land, giving them in exchange ten acres of land in his lordship of Welling Hall, in the county of Kent. St. John's Church was dedicated by Eraclius, patriarch of the holy resurrection of Christ at Jerusalem, in the year 1185, and was the chief seat in England of the religious knights of St. John of Jerusalem, whose profession was, besides their daily service of God, to defend Christians against pagans, and to fight for the Church, using for their habit a black upper garment, with a white cross on the fore-part thereof ; and for their good service was so highly esteemed, that when the order of Templars was dissolved, their lands and possessions were by parliament granted unto these who, after the loss of Jerusalem, recovered the isle of Rhodes from the Turks, and there placed themselves, being called thereof for many years knights of the Rhodes ; but after the loss thereof, 1523, they removed to the isle of Malta, manfully opposing themselves against the Turkish invasions.

The rebels of Essex and of Kent, 1381, set fire on this house, causing it to burn by the space of seven days together, not suffering any to quench it ; since the which time the priors of that house have new built both the church and houses thereunto appertaining ; which church was finished by Thomas Docwrey, late lord prior there, about the year 1504, as appeareth by the inscription over the gate-house, yet remaining. This house, at the suppression in the 32nd of Henry VIII., was valued to dispend in lands three thousand three hundred and eighty-five pounds nineteen shillings and eightpence yearly. Sir

W. Weston, being then lord prior, died on the same 7th of May, on which the house was suppressed; so that great yearly pensions being granted to the knights by the king, and namely to the lord prior during his life one thousand pounds, he never received a penny.

The king took into his hands all the lands that belonged to that house and that order, wheresoever in England and Ireland, for the augmentation of his crown.

This priory church and house of St. John was preserved from spoil or down-pulling so long as King Henry VIII. reigned, and was employed as a storehouse for the king's toils and tents, for hunting, and for the wars, &c.; but in the 3rd of King Edward VI., the church, for the most part, to wit, the body and side aisles, with the great bell tower, a most curious piece of workmanship, graven, gilt, and enamelled, to the great beautifying of the city, and passing all other that I have seen, was undermined and blown up with gunpowder. The stone thereof was employed in building of the Lord Protector's house at the Strand. That part of the choir which remaineth, with some side chapels, was by Cardinal Pole, in the reign of Queen Mary, closed up at the west end, and otherwise repaired; and Sir Thomas Tresham, knight, was then made lord prior there, with restitution of some lands, but the same was again suppressed in the first year of Queen Elizabeth.

There were buried in this church brethren of that house and knights of that order: John Botell; William Bagecore; Richard Barrow; John Vanclay; Thomas Launcelen; John Mallory; William Turney; William Hulles, Hils, or Hayles; John Weston; Redington; William Longstrother; John Longstrother; William Tong; John Wakeline. Then of other: Thomas Thornburgh, gentleman; William West, gentleman; John Fulling and Adam Gill, esquires; Sir John Mortimor, and Dame Elianor his wife; Nicholas Silverston; William Plompton, esquire; Margaret Tong and Isabel Tong; Walter Bellingham, *alias* Ireland, king-of-arms of Ireland; Thomas Bedle, gentleman; Katherine, daughter of William Plompton, esquire; Richard Turpin, gentleman; Joan, wife to Alexander Dikes; John Bottle and Richard Bottle, esquires; Rowland Darcy; Richard Sutton, gentleman; Richard Bottill, gentleman; Sir W. Harpden, knight; Robert Kingston, esquire, and Margery his wife; John Roch; Richard Cednor, gentleman; Simon Mallory, 1442; William Mallory, Robert Longstrother, Ralph Asteley, William Marshall, Robert Savage, Robert Gondall, esquires, and Margery his wife; William Bapthorpe, baron of the Exchequer, 1442.

North from the house of St. John's was the priory of Clarkenwell, so called of Clarkeswell adjoining; which priory was also founded about the year 1100 by Jorden Briset, baron, the son of Ralph, the son of Brian Briset, who gave to Robert, a priest, fourteen acres of land lying in the field next adjoining to the said Clarkeswell, thereupon to build a house of religious persons, which he founded to the honour of God and the Assumption of Our Lady, and placed therein black nuns. This Jorden Briset gave also to that house one piece of ground thereby, to build a windmill upon, &c. He and Muriell his wife were buried in the Chapterhouse there. More buried in this church: John Wikes, esquire, and Isabel his wife; Dame Agnes Clifford; Ralph Timbleby, esquire; Dame Jahan, baroness of Greystocke; Dame Jahan, Lady Ferrars. And of later time in the parish church, Constances Bennet, a Greek born. He gave two houses, the one in St. John's Street, the other in Turnemill Street; the rents of them to be distributed in coals every year against Christmas to the poor of that parish.

William Herne, a master of defence and yeoman of the guard, 1580, gave lands and tenements to the clothworkers in London; they to pay yearly for ever fourteen pounds to the churchwardens of Clarkenwell, and fourteen pounds to the churchwardens of St. Sepulchre's, towards reparations of these churches, and relief of the poor men. More, he gave after the death of one man, yet living, eight pounds the year for ever to the mending of highways.

Thomas Sackeford, esquire, one of the Masters of Requests, gave to the poor of that parish forty shillings the year for ever out of his almshouse at Woodbridge in Suffolk, where he is buried. Henry Stoke, gardener, buried there, gave twenty shillings the year for ever towards reparation of that church. This priory was valued to dispend two hundred and sixty-two pounds nine shillings by the year, and was surrendered the 31st of Henry VIII. Many fair houses are now built about the priory, namely, by the highway towards Iseldon.

So much of the church which remaineth, for one great aisle thereof fell down, serveth as a parish church of St. John, not only for the tenements and near inhabitants, but also, as is aforesaid, for all up to Highgate, Muswell, &c.

Near unto this church, beside Clarkeswell Lane, divers other wells, namely, Skinners' Well, Fag's Well, Tode Well, Loder's Well, Rede Well, &c., now dammed up.

Now to return again to Giltspur Street, where I first began with this suburb, there standeth the parish church of St. Sepulchre in the Bailey, as is before showed; from this street to Turnagain Lane, by Hosier Lane, Cow Lane, and Holborn Conduit, down Snore Hill to Oldborne Bridge, and up Oldborne Hill, by Gold Lane on the right hand, and Lither Lane beyond it, to the bars; beyond the which bars on the same side is Port Pool, or Gray's Inn Lane, so called of the inn of court named Gray's Inn, a goodly house there situate, by whom built or first begun I have not yet learned, but seemeth to be since Edward III.'s time, and is a prebend to Paul's Church in London.

This lane is furnished with fair buildings and many tenements on both the sides, leading to the fields towards Highgate and Hampstead.

On the high street have ye many fair houses built, and lodgings for gentlemen, inns for travellers, and such like up almost (for it lacketh but little) to St. Giles-in-the-Felds; amongst the which buildings, for the most part being very new, one passeth the rest in largeness of rooms, lately built by a widow, sometime wife to Richard Alington, esquire; which Richard Alington deceased in the year 1561. And thus much for that north side of Oldborne.

Now from Newgate, on the left hand or south side, lieth the Old Bailey, and so down by Seacole Lane End to Oldborne Bridge, up Oldborne Hill, by Shoe Lane and Fewter's Lane, to the bars.

Beyond the bars had ye in old time a temple built by the Templars, whose order first began in the year of Christ 1118, in the 19th of Henry I. This temple was left and fell to ruin since the year 1184, when the Templars had built them a new temple in Fleet Street, near to the river of Thames. A great part of this old temple was pulled down but of late in the year 1595. Adjoining to this old Temple was sometime the Bishop of Lincoln's Inn, wherein he lodged when he repaired to this city. Robert de Curars, Bishop of Lincoln, built it about the year 1147. John Russell, Bishop of Lincoln, chancellor of England, in the reign of Richard III., was lodged there. It hath of late years belonged to the Earls of Southampton, and therefore called Southampton House. Master Ropar hath of late built much there; by means whereof part of the ruins of the old Temple were seen to remain built of Caen stone, round in form as the new Temple, by Temple Bar, and other temples in England. Beyond this old Temple and the Bishop of Lincoln's house is New Street, so called in the reign of Henry III., when he of a Jew's house founded the House of Converts, betwixt the old Temple and the new.

The same street hath since been called Chancery Lane, by reason that King Edward III. annexed the house of Converts by patent to the office of Custos Rotulorum, or master of the Rolls, in the 15th of his reign.

In this street the first fair building to be noted on the east side is called the Coursitors' Office, built with divers fair lodgings for gentlemen, all of brick and timber, by Sir Nicholas Bacon, late lord keeper of the Great Seal.

Near unto this Coursitors' Office be divers fair houses and large gardens, built and made in a ground sometime belonging to one great house on the other side the street, there made by Ralph Nevel, Bishop of Chichester. This ground he had by the gift of Henry III., as appeareth. The king granteth to Ralph, Bishop of Chichester, chancellor, that place, with the garden, which John Herlirum forfeited in that street, called New Street, over against the land of the said bishop in the same street ; which place, with the garden and appurtenance, was the king's escheat by the liberty of the city of London, as it was acknowledged before the king in his court at the Tower of London, in the last pleas of the crown of that city, Cart. II. Henry III.

Then was the house of Converts, wherein now the rolls of Chancery be kept ; then the Sergeants' Inn, &c.

On the west side of New Street, towards the north end thereof, was of old time the church and house of the Preaching Friars ; concerning the which house I find, that in the year of Christ 1221, the Friars Preachers, thirteen in number, came into England, and having to their prior one named Gilbert de Fraxineto, in company of Peter de la Roche, Bishop of Winchester, came to Canterbury, where presenting themselves before the Archbishop Steven, he commanded the said prior to preach, whose sermon he liked so well that ever after he loved that order. These friars came to London, and had their first house without the wall of the city by Oldborne, near unto the Old Temple.

Hubert de Burgh, Earl of Kent, was a great benefactor unto these friars, and deceasing at his manor of Banstead in Surrey, or, after some writers, at his castle of Barkhamstead in Hertfordshire, in the year 1242, was buried in their church ; unto the which church he had given his place at Westminster, which the said friars afterwards sold to Walter Grey, Archbishop of York ; and he left it to his successors in that see for ever, to be their house when they should repair to the city of London. And therefore the same was called York Place ; which name so continued until the year 1529, that King Henry VIII. took it from Thomas Wolsey, Cardinal and Archbishop of York, and then gave it to name Whitehall.

Margaret, sister to the king of Scots, widow to Geoffrey, earl marshal, deceased 1244, and was buried in this church.

In the year 1250 the friars of this order of preachers, through Christendom and from Jerusalem, were by a convocation assembled together at this their house by Oldborne, to entreat of their estate, to the number of four hundred, having meat and drink found them of alms, because they had no possessions of their own. The first day the king came to their chapter, found them meat and drink, and dined with them ; another day the queen found them meat and drink ; afterward the Bishop of London, then the abbot of Westminster, of St. Alban's, Waltham, and others. In the year 1276 Gregory Rokesley, mayor, and the barons of London granted and gave to Robert Kilwarbie, Archbishop of Canterbury, two lanes or ways next the street of Baynard's Castle, and the tower of Mountfichet, to be destroyed ; on the which place the said Robert built the late new church, with the rest of the stones that were left of the said tower ; and thus the Black Friars left their church and house by Oldborne, and departed to their new. This old friar-house (juxta Holborne, saith the patent) was by King Edward I., in the 16th of his reign, given to Henry Lacy, Earl of Lincoln.

Next to this house of friars was one other great house, sometime belonging to the Bishop of Chichester, whereof Matthew Paris writeth thus :—

"Ralph de Nova Villa, or Nevill, Bishop of Chichester and chancellor of England, sometime built a noble house, even from the ground, not far from the New Temple and house of Converts, in the which place he deceased in the year 1244. In this place, after the decease of the said bishop, and in place of the house of Black Friars before spoken of, Henry Lacy, Earl of Lincoln, constable of Chester and custos of England, built his inn, and for the most part was lodged there. He deceased in this house in the year 1310, and was buried in the new work, whereunto he had been a great benefactor, of St. Paul's Church betwixt Our Lady Chapel and St. Dunstan's Chapel. This Lincoln's Inn, sometime pertaining to the Bishops of Chichester, as a part of the said great house, is now an inn of court, retaining the name of Lincoln's Inn as afore, but now lately increased with fair buildings, and replenished with gentlemen studious in the common laws. In the reign of Henry VIII. Sir Thomas Lovell was a great builder there ; especially he built the gate-house and fore-front towards the east, placing thereon as well the Lacys' arms as his own. He caused the Lacys' arms to be cast and wrought in lead, on the louer of the hall of that house, which was, in the three escutcheons, a lion rampant for Lacy, seven mascules voided for Quincy, and three wheatsheafs for Chester. This louer being of late repaired, the said escutcheons were left out. The rest of that side, even to Fleet Street, is replenished with fair buildings."

Now the High Oldborne Street, from the north end of New Street, stretcheth on the left hand in building lately framed, up to St. Giles in the Field, which was an hospital founded by Matilda the queen, wife to Henry I., about the year 1117. This hospital, saith the record of Edward III., the 19th year, was founded without the bar : *Veteris Templi London, et conversorum.*

This hospital was founded as a cell to Burton Lager of Jerusalem, as may appear by a deed dated the 24th of Henry VII. in these words :—

"Thomas Norton, knight, master of Burton Lager of Jerusalem in England, and the brethren of the same place, keepers of the hospital of St. Giles, without the bars of the Old Temple of London, have sold to Goeffrey Kent, citizen and draper of London, a messuage or house, with two cellars above, edified in the parish of Allhallows, Honey Lane in West Cheap, adjoining to the west part of a tenement called the Cote on the Hope, pertaining to the drapers of London, for thirty-one pounds."

At this hospital the prisoners conveyed from the city of London towards Tyburn, there to be executed for treasons, felonies, or other trespasses, were presented with a great bowl of ale, thereof to drink at their pleasure, as to be their last refreshing in this life.

Now without Ludgate lieth the south end of the Old Bailey, then down Ludgate Hill by Fleet Lane, over Fleet Bridge, up Fleet Street, by Shoe Lane, Fewter's Lane, New Street, or Chancery Lane, and to Shire Lane, by the bar on the right hand ; and from Ludgate on the left hand, or south side, by Bride Lane, Water Lane, Croker's Lane, Sergeants' Inn, and the New Temple, by the bar ; all which is of Farringdon Ward, as is afore showed.

Liberties of the Duchy of Lancaster.

NEXT without the bar is the New Temple, and liberties of the city of London. In the suburbs, is a liberty pertaining to the Duchy of Lancaster, which beginneth in the east, on the south side or left hand, by the river Thames, and stretcheth west to Ivy Bridge, where it endeth ; and again on the north side, or right hand, some small distance without Temple Bar, in the high street, from a pair of stocks there standing, stretcheth one large middle row, or troop of small tenements, partly opening to the south, partly towards the north, up west to a stone cross, now headless, over against the Strand ; and this is the bounds of that liberty which sometime belonged to Brian Lisle, since to Peter of Savoy, and then to the house of Lancaster, as shall be showed. Henry III., in the 30th year of his reign, did grant to his uncle Peter of Savoy all those houses upon the Thames which sometime pertained to Brian de Insula, or Lisle, without the walls of his city of London, in the way or street called the Strand, to hold to him and to his heirs, yielding yearly in the Exchequer, at the feast of St. Michael the Archangel, three barbed arrows, for all services, dated at Reading, &c. This Peter of Savoy built the Savoy.

But first amongst other buildings memorable for greatness on the river of Thames, Excester House, so called for that the same belonged to the Bishops of Excester, and was their inn or London lodging. Who was first builder thereof I have not read, but that Walter Stapleton was a great builder there in the reign of Edward II. is manifest ; for the citizens of London, when they had beheaded him in Cheap, near unto the cathedral church of St. Paul, they buried him in a heap of sand or rubbish in his own house without Temple Bar, where he had made great building. Edmond Lacy, Bishop of Excester, built the great hall in the reign of Henry VI., &c. The same hath since been called Paget House, because William Lord Paget enlarged and possessed it. Then Leicester House, because Robert Dudley, Earl of Leicester, of late new built there, and now Essex House, of the Earl of Essex lodging there.

Then west was a chapel dedicated to the Holy Ghost, called St. Sprite, upon what occasion founded I have not read. Next is Milford Lane down to the Thames, but why so called I have not read as yet.

Then was the Bishop of Bath's Inn, lately new built, for a great part thereof, by the Lord Thomas Seymour, admiral; which house came since to be possessed by the Earl of Arundel, and thereof called Arundel House.

Next beyond the which, on the street side, was sometime a fair cemetery or churchyard, and in the same a parish church called of the Nativity of Our Lady, and the Innocents of the Strand, and of some, by means of a brotherhood kept there, called St. Ursula at the Strand. And near adjoining to the said church, betwixt it and the river of Thames, was an inn of Chancery commonly called Chester's Inn, because it belonged to the Bishop of Chester, by others, named of the situation, Strand Inn.

Then was there a house belonging to the Bishop of Llandaff; for I find in record, the 4th of Edward II., that a vacant place lying near the church of Our Lady at Strand, the said bishop procured it of Thomas, Earl of Lancaster, for the enlarging of this house. Then had ye in the high street a fair bridge called Strand Bridge, and under it a lane or way down to the landing-place on the bank of Thames.

Then was the Bishop of Chester's, commonly called of Lichfield and Coventry, his inn or London lodging. This house was first built by Walter Langton, Bishop of Chester, treasurer of England in the reign of Edward I.

And next unto it adjoining was the Bishop of Worcester's Inn; all which, to wit, the parish of St. Mary at Strand, Strand Inn, Strand Bridge, with the lane under it, the Bishop of Chester's Inn, the Bishop of Worcester's Inn, with all the tenements adjoining, were by commandment of Edward, Duke of Somerset, uncle to Edward VI., and lord protector, pulled down and made level ground in the year 1549; in place whereof he built that large and goodly house now called Somerset House.

In the high street, near unto the Strand, sometime stood a cross of stone against the Bishop of Coventry or Chester his house;

whereof I read that in the year 1294, and divers other times, the justices itinerants sate without London, at the stone cross over against the Bishop of Coventry's house, and sometime they sate in the Bishop's house, which was hard by the Strand, as is aforesaid.

Then next is the Savoy, so called of Peter, Earl of Savoy, and Richmond, son to Thomas, Earl of Savoy, brother to Boniface, Archbishop of Canterbury, and uncle unto Eleanor, wife to King Henry III.

He first built this house in the year 1245 ; and here is occasion offered me for satisfying of some deniers thereof, to prove that this Peter of Savoy was also Earl of Savoy ; wherefore, out of a book of the genealogies of all the whole house of Savoy, compiled by Phillebert Pingonio, Baron of Guzani, remaining in the hands of W. Smith, *alias* Rougedragon, officer of arms, I have gathered this :—

Thomas, Earl of Savoy, had issue by Beatrix, daughter to Aimon, Earl of Geneva, nine sons and three daughters. Amades, his first son, succeeded Earl of Savoy in the year 1253 ; Peter, his second son, Earl of Savoy and of Richmond, in 1268 ; Philip, his third son, Earl of Savoy and Burgundie, 1284 ; Thomas, the fourth, Earl of Flanders and Prince of Piemont ; Boniface, the eighth, Archbishop of Canterbury ; Beatrix, his daughter, married to Raymond Beringarius of Aragon, Earl of Province and Narbone, had issue, and was mother to five queens. The first, Margaret, wife to Louis, King of France ; the second, Eleanor, wife to Henry III., King of England ; the third, Sanctia, wife to Richard, King of the Romans ; the fourth, Beatrix, wife to Charles, King of Naples ; the fifth, Johanna, wife to Philip, King of Navarre.

To return again to the house of Savoy. Queen Eleanor, wife to King Henry III., purchased this place afterwards of the fraternity or brethren of Montjoy ; unto whom Peter of Savoy, as it seemeth, had given it, for her son, Edmond, Earl of Lancaster, as M. Camden hath noted out of a register-book of the Dukes of Lancaster. Henry, Duke of Lancaster, repaired, or rather new built it, with the charges of fifty-two thousand marks, which money he had gathered together at the town of Bridgerike. John, the French king, was lodged there in the year 1357, and also in the year 1363 ; for it was at that time the fairest manor in England.

In the year 1381 the rebels of Kent and Essex burnt this house ; unto the which there was none in the realm to be compared in beauty and stateliness, saith mine author. They set fire on it round about, and made proclamation that none, on pain to lose his head, should convert to his own use anything that there was, but that they should break such plate and vessels of gold and silver as was found in that house, which was in great plenty, into small pieces, and throw the same into the river of Thames. Precious stones they should bruise in mortars, that the same might be to no use, and so it was done by them. One of their companions they burnt in the fire because he minded to have reserved one goodly piece of plate.

They found there certain barrels of gunpowder, which they thought had been gold or silver, and throwing them into the fire more suddenly than they thought, the hall was blown up, the houses destroyed, and themselves very hardly escaped away.

This house being thus defaced, and almost overthrown by these rebels for malice they bare to John of Gaunt, Duke of Lancaster, of latter time came to the king's hands, and was again raised and beautifully built for an hospital of St. John Baptist by King Henry VII. about the year 1509, for the which hospital, retaining still the old name of Savoy, he purchased lands to be employed upon the relieving of a hundred poor people. This hospital being valued to dispend five hundred and twenty-nine pounds fifteen shillings, &c., by year, was suppressed the 10th of June, the 7th of Edward VI. The beds, bedding, and other furniture belonging thereunto, with seven hundred marks of the said lands by year, he gave to the citizens of London, with his house of Bridewell, to the furnishing thereof, to be a workhouse for the poor and idle persons, and towards the furnishing of the Hospital of St. Thomas in Southwark, lately suppressed.

This hospital of Savoy was again new founded, erected, corporated, and endowed with lands by Queen Mary, the 3rd of November. In the 4th of her reign one Jackson took possession, and was made master thereof in the same month of November. The ladies of the court and maidens of honour,—a thing not to be forgotten,—stored the same of new with beds, bedding, and other furniture, in very ample manner, &c. ; and it was by patent so confirmed at Westminster the 9th of May, the 4th and 5th of Philip and Mary. The chapel of this hospital serveth now as a parish church to the tenements thereof near adjoining, and others.

The next was sometime the Bishop of Carlisle's inn, which now belongeth to the Earl of Bedford, and is called Russell or Bedford House. It stretcheth from the Hospital of Savoy west to Ivy Bridge, where Sir Robert Cecil, principal secretary to her Majesty, hath lately raised a large and stately house of brick and timber, as also levelled and paved the highway near adjoining, to the great beautifying of that street and commodity of passengers. Richard II., in the 8th of his reign, granted license to pave with stone the highway called Strand Street from Temple Bar to the Savoy, and toll to be taken towards the charges ; and again the like was granted in the 42nd of Henry VI.

Ivy Bridge, in the high street, which had a way under it leading down to the Thames, the like as sometime had the Strand Bridge, is now taken down, but the lane remaineth as afore, or better, and parteth the liberty of the duchy and the city of Westminster on that south side.

Now to begin again at Temple Bar, over against it. In the high street, as is afore showed, is one large middle row of houses and small tenements built, partly opening to the south, partly towards the north; amongst the which standeth the parish church of St. Clement Danes, so called because Harold, a Danish king, and other Danes were buried there. This Harold, whom King Canutus had by a concubine, reigned three years, and was buried at Westminster; but afterward Hardicanutus, the lawful son of Canutus, in revenge of a displeasure done to his mother, by expelling her out of the realm, and the murder of his brother Alured, commanded the body of Harold to be digged out of the earth, and to be thrown into the Thames, where it was by a fisherman taken up and buried in this churchyard. But out of a fair ledger-book, sometime belonging to the abbey of Chertsey, in the county of Surrey, is noted, as in Francis Thynne, after this sort:—In the reign of King Etheldred the monastery of Chertsey was destroyed: ninety monks of that house were slain by the Danes, whose bodies were buried in a place next to the old monastery. William Malmesbury saith :—

"They burnt the church, together with the monks and abbot; but the Danes continuing in their fury throughout the whole land, desirous at the length to return home into Denmarke, were by the just judgment of God all slain at London in a place which is called the church of the Danes."

This said middle row of houses stretching west to a stone cross, now headless, by or against the Strand, including the said parish church of St. Clement, is also wholly of the liberty and duchy of Lancaster.

Thus much for the bounds and antiquities of this liberty, wherein I have noted parish churches twain, sometime three, houses of name six; to wit, the Savoy or Lancaster House, now an hospital, Somerset House, Essex House, Arundel House, Bedford or Russell House, and Sir Robert Cecil's house; besides of Chester's Inn or Strand Inn, sometime an inn of Chancery, &c. This liberty is governed by the chancellor of that duchy at this present, Sir Robert Cecil, knight, principal secretary to her Majesty, and one of her Majesty's most honourable privy councillors. There is under him a steward that keepeth court and leet for the queen; giveth the charge and taketh the oaths of every under-officer. Then is there four burgesses and four assistants, to take up controversies; a bailiff, which hath two or three under-bailiffs, that make arrests within that liberty; four constables; four wardens, that keep the lands and stock for the poor; four wardens for highways; a jury or inquest of fourteen or sixteen, to present defaults; four ale-conners, which look to assize of weights and measures, &c.; four scavengers, and a beadle; and their common prison is Newgate. There is in this liberty fifty men, which is always to be at an hour's warning, with all necessary furniture, to serve the queen, as occasion shall require. Their charge at a fifteen is thirteen shillings and fourpence. Thus much for the suburb in the liberty of the duchy of Lancaster.

The City of Westminster, with the Antiquities, Bounds, and Liberties thereof.

Now touching the city of Westminster, I will begin at Temple Bar, on the right-hand or north side, and so pass up west through a back lane or street, wherein do stand three inns of chancery. The first is called Clement's Inn, because it standeth near to St. Clement's Church, but nearer to the fair fountain called Clement's Well. The second, New Inn, so called as latelier made, —of a common hostelry and the sign of Our Lady,—an inn of chancery for students than the other, to wit, about the beginning of the reign of Henry VII.; and not so late as some have supposed, to wit, at the pulling down of Strand Inn, in the reign of King Edward VI.; for I read that Sir Thomas More, sometime lord chancellor, was a student in this New Inn, and went from thence to Lincoln's Inn, &c. The third is Lyon's Inn, an inn of chancery also.

This street stretcheth up unto Drury Lane, so called for that here is a house belonging to the family of the Druries. This lane turneth north toward St. Giles in the Field. From the south end of this lane in the high street are divers fair buildings, hostelries, and houses for gentlemen and men of honour; amongst the which Cecil House is one, which sometime belonged to the parson of St. Martin's in the Field, and by composition came to Sir Thomas Palmer, knight, in the reign of Edward VI., who began to build the same of brick and timber, very large and spacious, but of later time it hath been far more beautifully increased by the late Sir William Cecil, Baron of Burghley, lord treasurer, and great councillor of the estate.

From thence is now a continual new building of divers fair houses, even up to the Earl of Bedford's house, lately built nigh to Ivy Bridge, and so on the north side to a lane that turneth to the parish church of St. Martin's in the Field, in the liberty of Westminster. Then had ye one house wherein sometime were distraught and lunatic people, of what antiquity founded or by whom I have not read, neither of the suppression; but it was said that sometime a king of England, not liking such a kind of people to remain so near his palace, caused them to be removed farther off, to Bethlem without Bishop's Gate of London, and to that hospital. The said house by Charing Cross doth yet remain.

Then is the Mews, so called of the king's falcons there kept by the king's falconer, which of old time was an office of great account, as appeareth by a record of Richard II., in the first year of his reign. Sir Simon Burley, knight, was made constable for the castles of Windsor, Wigmore, and Guilford, and of the manor of Kennington, and also master of the king's falcons at the Mews, near unto Charing Cross by Westminster; but in the year of Christ 1534, the 28th of Henry VIII., the king having fair stabling at Lomsbery (a manor in the farthest west part of Oldborne), the same was fired and burnt, with many great horses and great store of hay; after which time the fore-named house, called the Mews by Charing Cross, was new built, and prepared for stabling of the king's horses, in the reign of Edward VI. and Queen Mary, and so remaineth to that use; and this is the farthest building west on the north side of that high street.

On the south side of the which street, in the liberties of Westminster (beginning at Ivy Bridge), first is Durham House, built by Thomas Hatfield, Bishop of Durham, who was made bishop of that see in the year 1545, and sat bishop there thirty-six years.

Amongst matters memorable concerning this house, this is one:—In the year of Christ 1540, the 32nd of Henry VIII., on May-day, a great and triumphant jousting was holden at Westminster, which had been formerly proclaimed in France, Flanders, Scotland, and Spain, for all comers that would undertake the challengers of England; which were, Sir John Dudley, Sir Thomas Seymour, Sir Thomas Ponings, and Sir George Carew, knights, and Anthony Kingston and Richard Cromwell, esquires; all which came into the lists that day richly apparelled, and their horses trapped all in white velvet. There came against them the said day forty-six defendants or undertakers, viz., the Earl of Surrey, foremost, Lord William Howard, Lord Clinton, and Lord Cromwell, son and heir to Thomas Cromwell, Earl of Essex, and chamberlain of England, with other; and that day, after the jousts performed, the challengers rode unto this Durham House, where they kept open household, and feasted the King and Queen, with her ladies, and all the court. The second day Anthony Kingston and Richard Cromwell were made knights there. The third day of May the said challengers did tourney on horseback with swords, and against them came forty-nine defendants; Sir John Dudley and the Earl of Surrey running first, which at the first course lost their gauntlets; and that day Sir

Richard Cromwell overthrew Master Palmer and his horse in the field, to the great honour of the challengers. The fifth of May the challengers fought on foot at the barriers, and against them came fifty defendants, which fought valiantly; but Sir Richard Cromwell overthrew that day at the barriers Master Culpepper in the field; and the sixth day the challengers brake up their household.

In this time of their housekeeping they had not only feasted the king, queen, ladies, and all the court, as is afore shewed, but also they cheered all the knights and burgesses of the common house in the parliament, and entertained the Mayor of London, with the aldermen and their wives, at a dinner, &c. The king gave to every of the said challengers, and their heirs for ever, in reward of their valiant activity, one hundred marks and a house to dwell in, of yearly revenue, out of the lands pertaining to the hospital of St. John of Jerusalem.

Next beyond this Durham House is another great house, sometime belonging to the Bishop of Norwich, and was his London lodging, which now pertaineth to the Archbishop of York by this occasion. In the year 1529, when Cardinal Wolsey, Archbishop of York, was indicted in the Premunire, whereby King Henry VIII. was entitled to his goods and possessions, he also seized into his hands the said archbishop's house, commonly called York Place, and changed the name thereof into Whitehall; whereby the archbishops of York being dispossessed, and having no house of repair about London, Queen Mary gave unto Nicholas Heath, then Archbishop of York, and to his successors, Suffolk House in Southwark, lately built by Charles Brandon, Duke of Suffolk, as I have showed.

This house the said archbishop sold, and bought the aforesaid house of old time belonging to the bishops of Norwich, which of this last purchase is now called York House. The lord chancellors or lord keepers of the Great Seal of England have been lately there lodged.

Then was there an hospital of St. Marie Rouncivall by Charing Cross (a cell to the priory and convent of Roncesvalles in Navarre, in Pamplona diocese), where a fraternity was founded in the 15th of Edward IV., but now the same is suppressed and turned into tenements.

Near unto this hospital was a hermitage, with a chapel of St. Katherine, over against Charing Cross; which cross, built of stone, was of old time a fair piece of work, there made by commandment of Edward I., in the 21st year of his reign, in memory of Eleanor, his deceased queen, as is before declared.

West from this cross stood sometime an hospital of St. James, consisting of two hides of land, with the appurtenances, in the parish of St. Margaret in Westminster, and founded by the citizens of London, before the time of any man's memory, for fourteen sisters, maidens, that were leprous, living chastely and honestly in divine service.

Afterwards divers citizens of London gave five-and-fifty pounds rent thereunto, and then were adjoined eight brethren to minister divine service there. After this, also, sundry devout men of London gave to this hospital four hides of land in the field of Westminster; and in Hendon, Chalcote, and Hampstead eighty acres of land and wood, &c. King Edward I. confirmed those gifts, and granted a fair to be kept on the eve of St. James, the day, the morrow, and four days following, in the 18th of his reign.

This hospital was surrendered to Henry VIII. the 23rd of his reign. The sisters, being compounded with, were allowed pensions for the term of their lives; and the king built there a goodly manor, annexing thereunto a park, closed about with a wall of brick, now called St. James' Park, serving indifferently to the said manor, and to the manor or palace of Whitehall.

South from Charing Cross, on the right hand, are divers fair houses lately built before the park, then a large tilt-yard for noblemen and other, to exercise themselves in jousting, turning, and fighting at barriers.

On the left hand from Charing Cross be also divers fair tenements lately built, till ye come to a large plot of ground enclosed with brick, and is called Scotland, where great buildings have been for receipt of the kings of Scotland, and other estates of that country; for Margaret, Queen of Scots, and sister to King Henry VIII., had her abiding there, when she came into England after the death of her husband, as the kings of Scotland had in former times, when they came to the parliament of England.

Then is the said Whitehall, sometime belonging to Hubert de Burgh, Earl of Kent, and Justice of England, who gave it to the Black Friars in Oldborne, as I have before noted. King Henry VIII. ordained it to be called an honour, and built there a sumptuous gallery and a beautiful gate-house, athwart the high street to St. James' Park, &c.

In this gallery the princes, with their nobility, used to stand or sit, and at windows, to behold all triumphant joustings and other military exercises.

Beyond this gallery, on the left hand, is the garden or orchard belonging to the said Whitehall.

On the right hand be divers fair tennis-courts, bowling-alleys, and a cock-pit, all built by King Henry VIII. ; and then one other arched gate, with a way over it, thwarting the street from the king's gardens to the said park.

From this gate up King's Street to a bridge over Long Ditch (so called for that the same almost insulateth the city of Westminster), near which bridge is a way leading to Canon Row, so called for that the same belonged to the dean and canons of St. Stephen's Chapel, who were there lodged, as now divers noblemen and gentlemen be; whereof one is belonging to Sir Edward Hobbey, one other to John Thine, esquire, one stately built by Ann Stanhope, Duchess of Somerset, mother to the Earl of Hartford, who now enjoyeth that house. Next a stately house, now in building by William Earl of Derby ; over against the which is a fair house built by Henry Clinton, Earl of Lincoln.

From this way up to the Woolstaple and to the high tower, or gate which entereth the palace court, all is replenished with buildings and inhabitants.

Touching this Woolstaple, I read that in the reign of Edward I., the staple being at Westminster, the parishioners of St. Margaret and merchants of the staple built of new the said church, the great chancel excepted, which was lately before new built by the abbot of Westminster.

Moreover, that Edward III., in the 17th of his reign, decreed that no silver be carried out of the realm on pain of death ; and that whosoever transporteth wool should bring over for every sack four nobles of silver bullion.

In the 25th of his reign he appointed the staple of wool to be kept only at Canterbury, for the honour of St. Thomas ; but in the 27th of the same King Edward, the staple of wool, before kept at Bruges in Flanders, was ordained by parliament to be kept in divers places of England, Wales, and Ireland, as at Newcastle, York, Lincoln, Canterbury, Norwich, Westminster, Chichester, Winchester, Excester, Bristow, Carmardyn, &c., to the great benefit of the king and loss unto strangers and merchants ; for there grew unto the king by this means (as it was said) the sum of one thousand one hundred and two pounds by the year, more than any his predecessors before had received. The staple at Westminster at that time began on the next morrow after the feast of St. Peter ad vincula. The next year was granted to the king by parliament, towards the recovery of his title in France, fifty shillings of every sack of wool transported over seas, for the space of six years next ensuing ; by means whereof the king might dispend daily during those years more than a thousand marks sterling ; for by the common opinion there were more than one hundred thousand sacks of wool yearly transported into foreign lands, so that during six years the said grant extended to fifteen hundred thousand pounds sterling.

In the 37th of Edward III. it was granted unto him for two years to take five-and-twenty shillings and eightpence upon every sack of wool transported; and the same year the staple of wool (notwithstanding the king's oath and other great estates) was ordained to be kept at Calais, and six-and-twenty merchants, the best and wealthiest of all England, to be farmers there, both of the town and staple, for three years; every merchant to have six men of arms and four archers at the king's cost. He ordained there also two mayors, one for the town and one for the staple; and he took for *mala capta*, commonly called Maltorth, twenty shillings, and of the said merchants' guardians of the town forty pence, upon every sack of wool.

In the 44th of Edward III., Quinborough, Kingston-upon-Hull, and Boston were made staples of wool; which matter so much offended some, that in the 50th of his reign, in a parliament at London, it was complained that the staple of wool was so removed from Calais to divers towns in England, contrary to the statute appointing that citizens and merchants should keep it there, and that the king might have the profits and customs, with the exchange of gold and silver, that was there made by all the merchants in Christendom (esteemed to amount to eight thousand pounds by year), the exchange only; and the citizens and merchants so ordered the matter that the king spent nothing upon soldiers, neither upon defence of the town against the enemies; whereas now he spent eight thousand pounds by year.

In the 51st of Edward III., when the staple was sealed at Calais, the mayor of the staple did furnish the captain of the town upon any road with one hundred billmen, twelve hundred archers of merchants and their servants, without any wages.

In the year 1388, the 12th of Richard II., in a parliament at Cambridge, it was ordained that the staple of wools should be brought from Middleborough in Holland to Calais.

In the 14th of his reign there was granted forty shillings upon every sack of wool, and in the 21st was granted fifty shillings upon every sack transported by Englishmen, and three pounds by strangers, &c. It seemeth that the merchants of this staple be the most ancient merchants of this realm; and that all commodities of the realm are staple merchandises by law and charter, as wools, leather, wool fells, lead, tin, cloth, &c.

King Henry VI. had six wool-houses within the staple at Westminster; those he granted to the dean and canons of St.

Stephen at Westminster, and confirmed it the 21st of his reign.
Thus much for the staple have I shortly noted.

And now to pass to the famous monastery of Westminster.
At the very entrance of the close thereof is a lane that leadeth
toward the west, called Thieving Lane, for that thieves were
led that way to the gate-house, while the sanctuary continued
in force.

This monastery was founded and built by Sebert, king of the
East Saxons, upon the persuasion of Ethelbert, king of Kent,
who having embraced Christianity, and being baptized by Melitus,
Bishop of London, immediately (to show himself a Christian
indeed) built a church to the honour of God and St. Peter, on
the west side of the city of London, in a place which, because
it was overgrown with thorns and environed with water, the
Saxons called Thorney, and now of the monastery and west
situation thereof is called Westminster.

In this place, saith Sulcardus, long before was a temple of
Apollo, which being overthrown, King Lucius built therein a
church of Christianity.

Sebert was buried in this church, with his wife Athelgoda;
whose bodies many years after, to wit, in the reign of Richard
II., saith Walsingham, were translated from the old church to
the new, and there interred.

Edgar, king of the West Saxons, repaired this monastery about
the year of Christ 958. Edward the Confessor built it of new,
whereupon T. Clifford writeth thus:—

"Without the walls of London," saith he, "upon the river of Thames, there was
in times passed a little monastery, built to the honour of God and St. Peter, with
a few Benedict monks in it, under an abbot, serving Christ: very poor they were,
and little was given them for their relief. Here the king intended (for that it was
near to the famous city of London and the river of Thames, that brought in all
kind of merchandises from all parts of the world,) to make his sepulchre: he
commanded, therefore, that of the tenths of all his rents the work should be
begun in such sort as should become the prince of the Apostles.

"At this his commandment the work is nobly begun, even from the foundation,
and happily proceedeth till the same was finished: the charges bestowed, or to be
bestowed, are not regarded. He granted to this church great privileges, above
all the churches in this land, as partly appeareth by this his charter:—

"'Eѵpeanѵ Cynᵹ ᵹnæᴄ Willm biᵳceoᵽe ⁊ Leoᵳᵳᴄane ⁊ Alᵳᵳie Poɲ-
ᴄᵹeneᵳen ⁊ ealle minɲe buɲhþeᵹn on Lunѵen ᵳneonѵlice: Anѵ ic cyþe
e∙ᵽ ⁊ hæbbe ᵳ²o ᵹiᵽᴄa ᵹyᵳen ⁊ unnan Chᵳiᵳᴄ ⁊ ѵ. Peᴄeɲ þam haliᵹan
Aᵽoᵳᴄel inᴄo Weᵳᴄminᵳᴄeɲ, ᵳulɲa ᵳneoѵome oᵳeɲ ealle þa lanѵ þe lonᵹaþ
inᴄo þæɲe haliᵹan ᵳᴄoᵽ, &c.'

"'Edwarde, king, greets William, bishop, and Leofstane, and Aelsie Portreves,
and all my burgesses of London friendly, and I tell you, that I have this gift given
and granted to Christ and St. Peter the holy Apostle, at Westminster, full freedome
over all the land that belongeth to that holy place, &c.'"

He also caused the parish church of St. Margaret to be newly built without the abbey church of Westminster, for the ease and commodity of the monks, because before that time the parish church stood within the old abbey church in the south aisle, somewhat to their annoyance.

King Henry III., in the year of Christ 1220, and in the 5th of his reign, began the new work of Our Lady's Chapel, whereof he laid the first stone in the foundation; and in the year 1245 the walls and steeple of the old church (built by King Edward) were taken down, and enlarging the same church, caused them to be made more comely; for the furtherance whereof, in the year 1246, the same king (devising how to extort money from the citizens of London towards the charges) appointed a mart to be kept at Westminster, the same to last fifteen days, and in the mean space all trade of merchandise to cease in the city; which thing the citizens were fain to redeem with two thousand pounds of silver.

The work of this church, with the houses of office, was finished to the end of the choir, in the year 1285, the 14th of Edward I.; all which labour of sixty-six years was in the year 1299 defaced by a fire kindled in the lesser hall of the king's palace at Westminster; the same, with many other houses adjoining, and with the queen's chamber, were all consumed; the flame thereof also, being driven with the wind, fired the monastery, which was also with the palace consumed.

Then was this monastery again repaired by the abbots of that church; King Edward I. and his successors putting to their helping hands.

Edward II. appropriated unto this church the patronages of the churches of Kelveden and Sawbridgeworth in Essex, in the diocese of London.

Simon Langham, abbot (having been a great builder there in the year 1362), gave forty pounds to the building of the body of the church; but (amongst others) Abbot Islip was in his time a great builder there, as may appear in the stonework and glass windows of the church; since whose decease that work hath stayed as he left it, unperfected, the church and steeple being all of one height.

King Henry VII., about the year of Christ 1502, caused the chapel of Our Lady, built by Henry III., with a tavern also, called the White Rose, near adjoining, to be taken down; in which plot of ground, on the 24th of January, the first stone of the new chapel was laid by the hands of Abbot Islip, Sir Reginald Bray, knight of the Garter, Doctor Barnes, master of the Rolls,

Doctor Wall, chaplain to the king, Master Hugh Aldham, chaplain to the Countess of Derby and Richmond (the king's mother), Sir Edward Stanhope, knight, and divers other: upon the which stone was engraven the same day and year, &c.

The charges in building this chapel amounted to the sum of fourteen thousand pounds. The stone for this work (as I have been informed) was brought from Huddlestone Quarry in Yorkshire.

The altar and sepulture of the same King Henry VII., wherein his body resteth in this his new chapel, was made and finished in the year 1519 by one Peter, a painter of Florence; for the which he received one thousand pounds sterling for the whole stuff and workmanship at the hands of the king's executors; Richard, Bishop of Winchester; Richard, Bishop of London; Thomas, Bishop of Durham; John, Bishop of Rochester; Thomas, Duke of Norfolk, treasurer of England; Charles, Earl of Worcester, the king's chamberlain; John Fineaux, knight, chief-justice of the King's Bench; Robert Reade, knight, chief-justice of the Common Pleas.

This monastery being valued to dispend by the year three thousand four hundred and seventy pounds, &c., was surrendered to Henry VIII. in the year 1539. Benson, then abbot, was made the first dean, and not long after it was advanced to a bishop's see in the year 1541; Thomas Thirlby being both the first and last bishop there, who, when he had impoverished the church, was translated to Norwich in the year 1550, the 4th of Edward VI., and from thence to Elie in the year 1554, the 2nd of Queen Mary. Richard Cox, doctor in divinity (late school-master to King Edward VI.), was made dean of Westminster, whom Queen Mary put out, and made Doctor Weston dean until the year 1556; and then he being removed from thence on the 21st of November, John Feckenham (late dean of Pauls) was made abbot of Westminster, and took possession of the same, being installed, and fourteen monks more received the habit with him that day of the order of St. Benedict; but the said John Feckenham, with his monks, enjoyed not that place fully three years, for in the year 1559, in the month of July, they were all put out, and Queen Elizabeth made the said monastery a college, instituting there a dean, twelve prebends, a schoolmaster, and usher, forty scholars, called commonly the Queen's scholars, twelve alms-men; and so it was named the Collegiate Church of Westminster, founded by Queen Elizabeth, who placed Doctor Bill, first dean of that new erection; after whom succeeded Doctor Gabriel Goodman, who governed that church forty years, and after Doctor Lancelot Andrewes.

Kings and queens crowned in this church :—William, surnamed the Conqueror, and Matilde his wife were the first, and since them all other kings and queens of this realm have been there crowned.

Kings and queens buried in this church are these :—Sebert, king of the East Saxons, with his wife Athelgede ; Harold, sur-named Harefoot, king of the West Saxons ; Edward the Simple, surnamed Confessor, sometime richly shrined in a tomb of silver and gold, curiously wrought by commandment of William the Conqueror ; Egitha his wife was there buried also ; Hugolyn, chamberlain to Edward the Confessor ; King Henry III., whose sepulture was richly garnished with precious stones of jasper, which his son Edward I. brought out of France for that purpose ; Eleanor, wife to Henry III. ; Edward I., who offered to the shrine of Edward the Confessor the chair of marble wherein the kings of Scotland were crowned, with the sceptre and crown also to the same king belonging.

He gave also to that church lands to the value of one hundred pounds by the year ; twenty pounds thereof yearly to be distri-buted to the poor for ever. Then there lieth Eleanor, his wife, daughter to Ferdinando, king of Castile, 1293 ; Edward III. by Queen Philippa of Henault his wife ; Richard II. and Anne his wife, with their images upon them, which cost more than four hundred marks for the gilding ; Henry V., with a royal image of silver and gilt, which Katherine his wife caused to be laid upon him, but the head of this image, being of massy silver, is broken off, and conveyed away with the plates of silver and gilt that covered his body ; Katherine his wife was buried in the old Lady chapel 1438, but her corpse being taken up in the reign of Henry VII., when a new foundation was to be laid, she was never since buried, but remaineth above ground in a coffin of boards behind the east end of the presbytery ; Henry VII. in a sumptuous sepulture and chapel before specified, and Elizabeth his wife ; Edward VI. in the same chapel, without any monument ; Queen Mary, without any monument, in the same chapel ; Matilde, daughter to Malcolm, king of Scots, wife to Henry I., died 1118, lieth in the revestry ; Anne, wife to Richard III. ; Margaret, Countess of Richmond and Derby, mother to Henry VII. ; Anne of Cleves, wife to Henry VIII. ; Edmond, second son to Henry III., first Earl of Lancaster, Derby, and Leicester, and Aveline his wife, daughter and heir to William de Fortibus, Earl of Albemarle. In St. Thomas' Chapel lie the bones of the children of Henry III. and of Edward I., in number nine. In the chapter-house :—Elianor, Countess of Barre, daughter to Edward I.; William of Windsor, and Blaunch his sister, children to Edward III.; John of Eltham, Earl of Cornwall, son to Edward II.; Elianor, wife to Thomas of Woodstock, Duke of Gloucester; Thomas of Woodstock by King Edward III., his father; Margaret, daughter to Edward IV.; Elizabeth, daughter to Henry VII.; William de Valence, Earl of Pembroke; Aymer de Valence, Earl of Pembroke; Margaret and John, son and daughter to William de Valence; John Waltham, Bishop of Sarum, treasurer of England; Thomas Ruthal, Bishop of Durham, 1522; Giles, Lord Dawbeny, lord lieutenant of Callis, chamberlain to King Henry VII., 1508, and Elizabeth his wife, of the family of the Arundels in Cornwall, 1500; John, Viscount Wells, 1498; the Lady Katherine, daughter to the Duchess of Norfolk; Sir Thomas Hungerford, knight, father to Sir John Hungerford of Downampney, knight; a son and daughter to Humphrey Bohun, Earl of Hereford and Essex, and Elizabeth his wife; Philippa, Duchess of York, daughter to the Lord Mohun, thrice married, to the Lord Fitzwalter, Sir John Golofer, and to the Duke of York; William Dudley, Bishop elect of Durham, son to John, Baron of Dudley; Nicholas, Baron Carew, 1470; Walter Hungerford, son to Edward Hungerford, knight; Sir John Burley, knight, and Anne his wife, daughter to Alane Buxull, knight, 1416; Sir John Golofer, knight, 1396; Humphrey Burcher, Lord Cromwell, son to Bourchier, Earl of Essex, slain at Barnet; Henry Bourchier, son and heir to John Bourchier, Lord Barners, also slain at Barnet, 1471; Sir William Trussell, knight; Sir Thomas Vaughan, knight; Frances Brandon, Duchess of Suffolk, 1560; Mary Gray, her daughter, 1578; Sir John Hampden, knight; Sir Lewis, Viscount Robsart, knight; Lord Bourchere of Henault, 1430, and his wife, daughter and heir to the Lord Bourchere; Robert Brown and William Browne, esquires; the Lady Johane Tokyne, daughter of Dabridge Court; George Mortimer, bastard; John Felbye, esquire; Ann, wife to John Watkins; William Southwike, esquire; William Southcot, esquire; Ralph Constantine, gentleman; Arthur Troffote, esquire; Robert Hawley, esquire, slain in that church; Sir Richard Rouse, knight; Sir Geoffrey Maundeville, Earl of Essex, and Athelarde his wife; Sir Foulke of Newcastle; Sir James Barons, knight; Sir John Salisbury, knight; Margaret Dowglas, Countess of Lennox, with Charles her son, Earl of Lennox; Henry Scogan, a learned poet in the cloister; Geoffrey Chaucer, the most famous poet of England, also in the cloister, 1400, but since Nicholas Brigham, gentleman, raised a monument for him in the south cross aisle of the church. His works were partly published in print by William Caxton, in the reign of Henry VI., increased by

William Thynne, esquire, in the reign of Henry VIII. ; corrected and twice increased, through mine own painful labours, in the reign of Queen Elizabeth, to wit, in the year 1561 ; and again beautified with notes by me, collected out of divers records and monuments, which I delivered to my loving friend, Thomas Speght ; and he having drawn the same into a good form and method, as also explained the old and obscure words, &c., hath published them in anno 1597.

Anne Stanhope, Duchess of Somerset, and Jane her daughter ; Anne Cecil, Countess of Oxford, daughter to the Lord Burghley, with Mildred Burghley, her mother ; Elizabeth Barkley, Countess of Ormond ; Frances Sydney, Countess of Sussex ; Frances Howard, Countess of Hertford, 1598 ; Thomas, Baron Wentworth ; Thomas, Baron Warton ; John, Lord Russell ; Sir Thomas Bromley, lord chancellor ; Sir John Puckering, lord keeper ; Sir Henry Cary, Lord Hunsdon, and lord chamberlain 1596, to whose memory his son, Sir George Cary, Lord Hunsdon, and lord chamberlain, hath created a stately monument.

This church hath had great privilege of sanctuary within the precinct thereof, to wit, the church, churchyard, and close, &c. ; from whence it hath not been lawful for any prince or other to take any person that fled thither for any cause ; which privilege was first granted by Sebert, king of the East Saxons, since increased by Edgar, king of the West Saxons, renewed and confimed by King Edward the Confessor, as appeareth by this his charter following :—

" Edward, by the grace of God, king of Englishmen : I make it to be known to all generations of the world after me, that by speciall commandement of our holy father, Pope Leo, I have renewed and honored the holy church of the blessed apostle St. Peter, of Westminster ; and I order and establish for ever, that what person, of what condition or estate soever he be, from whence soever he come, or for what offence or cause it be, either for his refuge into the said holy place, he be assured of his life, liberty, and limbs. And over this I forbid, under the paine of everlasting damnation, that no minister of mine, or of my successors, intermeddle them with any the goods, lands, or possessions of the said persons taking the said sanctuary ; for I have taken their goodes and livelode into my speciall protection, and therefore I grant to every each of them, in as much as my terrestriall power may suffice, all maner freedom of joyous libertie ; and whosoever presumes or doth contrary to this my graunt, I will hee lose his name, worship, dignity, and power, and that with the great traytor Judas that betraied our Saviour, he be in the everlasting fire of hell ; and I will and ordayne that this my graunt endure as long as there remayneth in England eyther love or dread of Christian name."

More of this sanctuary ye may read in our histories, and also in the statute of Henry VIII., the 32nd year.

The parish church of St. Margaret, sometime within the abbey, was by Edward the Confessor removed, and built without, for ease of the monks. This church continued till the days of Edward I., at which time the merchants of the staple and parishioners of Westminster built it all of new, the great chancel excepted, which was built by the abbots of Westminster; and this remaineth now a fair parish church, though sometime in danger of down-pulling. In the south aisle of this church is a fair marble monument of Dame Mary Billing, the heir of Robert Nesenham of Conington, in Huntingdonshire, first married to William Cotton, to whose issue her inheritance alone descended, remaining with Robert Cotton at this day, heir of her and her first husband's family; her second husband was Sir Thomas Billing, chief-justice of England; and her last, whom likewise she buried, was Thomas Lacy; erecting this monument to the memory of her three husbands, with whose arms she hath garnished it, and for her own burial, wherein she was interred in the year 1499.

Next to this famous monastery is the king's principal palace, of what antiquity it is uncertain; but Edward the Confessor held his court there, as may appear by the testimony of sundry, and, namely, of Ingulphus, as I have before told you. The said king had his palace, and for the most part remained there; where he also ended his life, and was buried in the monastery which he had built. It is not to be doubted but that King William I., as he was crowned there, so he built much at his palace, for he found it far inferior to the building of princely palaces in France; and it is manifest, by the testimony of many authors, that William Rufus built the great hall there about the year of Christ 1097. Amongst others, Roger of Wendover and Mathew Paris do write, that King William (being returned out of Normandy into England) kept his feast of Whitsuntide very royally at Westminster, in the new hall which he had lately built; the length whereof, say some, was two hundred and seventy feet, and seventy-four feet in breadth; and when he heard men say that this hall was too great, he answered and said, "This hall is not big enough by the one half, and is but a bed-chamber in comparison of that I mean to make." A diligent searcher, saith Paris, might find out the foundation of the hall which he was supposed to have built, stretching from the river of Thames even to the common highway.

This palace was repaired about the year 1163 by Thomas Becket, chancellor of England, with exceeding great celerity and speed, which before was ready to have fallen down. This hath been the principal seat and palace of all the kings of England since the Conquest; for here have they in the great hall kept their feasts of coronation especially, and other solemn feasts, as at Christmas and such like, most commonly ; for proof whereof, I find recorded that in the year 1236, and the 20th of Henry III., on the 29th of December, William de Haverhull, the king's treasurer, is commanded, that upon the day of circumcision of our Lord he caused six thousand poor people to be fed at Westminster, for the state of the king, the queen, and their children ; the weak and aged to be placed in the great hall and in the lesser ; those that were most strong, and in reasonable plight, in the king's chamber ; the children in the queen's ; and when the king knoweth the charge he would allow it in the accounts.

In the year 1238 the same King Henry kept his feast of Christmas at Westminster, in the great hall ; so did he in the year 1241, where he placed the legate in the most honourable place of the table, to wit, in the midst, which the noblemen took in evil part. The king sat on the right hand, and the archbishop on the left, and then all the prelates and nobles according to their estates ; for the king himself set the guests. The year 1242 he likewise kept his Christmas in the hall, &c. Also, in the year 1243, Richard, Earl of Cornwall, the king's brother, married Cincia, daughter to Beatrice, Countess of Provence, and kept his marriage-feast in the great hall at Westminster, with great royalty and company of noblemen ; insomuch that there were told (*triginta millia*) thirty thousand dishes of meats at that dinner.

In the year 1256 King Henry sate in the exchequer of this hall, and there set down order for the appearance of sheriffs, and bringing in of their accounts. There were five marks set on every sheriff's head for a fine, because they had not distrained every person that might dispend fifteen pounds land by the year to receive the order of knighthood, as the same sheriffs were commanded. Also, the mayor, aldermen, and sheriffs of London, being accused of oppression and wrongs done by them, and submitting themselves in this place before the king sitting in judgment upon that matter, they were condemned to pay their fines for their offences committed, and further, every one of them discharged of assize and ward.

In the years 1268 and 1269 the same king kept his Christmas feasts at Westminster as before ; and also in the same 1269 he translated with great solemnity the body of King Edward the Confessor into a new chapel, at the back of the high altar ; which chapel he had prepared of a marvellous workmanship, bestowing a new tomb or shrine of gold ; and on the day of his translation he kept a royal feast in the great hall of the palace. Thus much for the feasts of old time in this hall.

We read, also, that in the year 1236 the river of Thames overflowing the banks, caused the marshes about Woolwich to be all on a sea, wherein boats and other vessels were carried with the stream; so that, besides cattle, the greatest number of men, women, and children, inhabitants there, were drowned; and in the great palace of Westminster men did row with wherries in the midst of the hall, being forced to ride to their chambers.

Moreover, in the year 1242, the Thames overflowing the banks about Lambhithe, drowned houses and fields by the space of six miles, so that in the great hall at Westminster men took their horses, because the water ran over all. This palace was in the year 1299, the 27th of Edward I., burnt by a vehement fire, kindled in the lesser hall of the king's house. The same, with many other houses adjoining, and with the queen's chamber, were consumed, but after that repaired

In the year 1313, the 31st of Edward I., the king's treasury at Westminster was robbed; for the which, Walter, abbot of Westminster, with forty-nine of his brethren and thirty-two other, were thrown into the Tower of London, and indicted of the robbery of a hundred thousand pounds; but they affirming themselves to be clear of the fact, and desiring the king of speedy justice, a commission was directed for inquiry of the truth, and they were freed.

In the year 1316 Edward II. did solemnise his feast of Pentecost at Westminster, in the great hall; where sitting royally at the table, with his peers about him, there entered a woman adorned like a minstrel, sitting on a great horse, trapped as minstrels then used, who rode round about the tables, showing pastime, and at length came up to the king's table, and laid before him a letter, and forthwith turning her horse, saluted every one, and departed. The letter, being opened, had these contents :—

"Our soveraigne lord the king, hath nothing curteously respected his knights, that in his father's time, and also in his owne, have put forth their persons to divers perils, and have utterly lost, or greatly diminished their substance, for honor of the said king, and he hath inriched abundantly such as have not borne the waight as yet of the busines," &c.

This great hall was begun to be repaired in the year 1397 by Richard II., who caused the walls, windows, and roof to be taken down, and new made, with a stately porch, and divers lodgings of a marvellous work, and with great costs; all which he levied of strangers banished or flying out of their countries, who obtained license to remain in this land by the king's charters, which they had purchased with great sums of money; John Boterell being then clerk of the works.

This hall being finished in the year 1398, the same king kept a most royal Christmas there, with daily joustings and runnings at tilt; whereunto resorted such a number of people, that there was every day spent twenty-eight or twenty-six oxen and three hundred sheep, besides fowl without number. He caused a gown for himself to be made of gold, garnished with pearl and precious stones, to the value of three thousand marks. He was guarded by Cheshire men, and had about him commonly thirteen bishops, besides barons, knights, esquires, and other more than needed; insomuch, that to the household came every day to meat ten thousand people, as appeareth by the messes told out from the kitchen to three hundred servitors.

Thus was this great hall, for the honour of the prince, oftentimes furnished with guests, not only in this king's time (a prodigal prince), but in the time of other also, both before and since, though not so usually noted. For when it is said the king held his feast of Christmas, or such a feast, at Westminster, it may well be supposed to be kept in this great hall, as most sufficient to such a purpose.

I find noted by Robert Fabian, sometime an alderman of London, that King Henry VII., in the 9th of his reign, holding his royal feast of Christmas at Westminster, on the twelfth day feasted Ralph Austry, then Mayor of London, and his brethren the aldermen, with other commoners in great number, and after dinner dubbing the mayor knight, caused him with his brethren to stay and behold the disguisings and other disports in the night following, showed in the great hall, which was richly hanged with arras, and staged about on both sides. Which disports being ended in the morning, the king, the queen, the ambassadors, and other estates being set at a table of stone, sixty knights and esquires served sixty dishes to the king's mess, and as many to the queen's (neither flesh nor fish), and served the mayor with twenty-four dishes to his mess, of the same manner, with sundry wines, in most plenteous wise; and finally, the king and queen being conveyed with great lights into the palace, the mayor with his company in barges returned and came to London by break of the next day. Thus much for building of this great hall and feasting therein.

It moreover appeareth that many parliaments have been kept there; for I find noted that in the year 1397, the great hall at Westminster being out of reparations, and therefore, as it were, new built by Richard II. (as is afore showed), the same Richard, in the meantime having occasion to hold a parliament, caused for that purpose a large house to be built in the midst of the palace-court, betwixt the clock-tower and the gate of the old great hall. This house was very large and long, made of timber, covered with tile, open on both the sides and at both the ends, that all men might see and hear what was both said and done.

The king's archers, in number four thousand Cheshire men, compassed the house about with their bows bent and arrows knocked in their hands, always ready to shoot. They had bouche of court (to wit, meat and drink), and great wages of sixpence by the day.

The old great hall being new built, parliaments were again there kept as before; namely, one in the year 1399, for the deposing of Richard II. A great part of this palace at Westminster was once again burnt in the year 1512, the 4th of Henry VIII. ; since the which time it hath not been re-edified : only the great hall, with the offices near adjoining, are kept in good reparations, and serveth as afore for feasts at coronations, arraignments of great persons charged with treasons, keeping of the courts of justice, &c. But the princes have been lodged in other places about the city, as at Baynard's Castle, at Bridewell, at Whitehall, sometime called York Place, and sometime at St. James'.

This great hall hath been the usual place of pleadings and ministration of justice, whereof somewhat shortly I will note. In times past the courts and benches followed the king wheresoever he went, as well since the Conquest as before; which thing at length being thought cumbersome, painful, and chargeable to the people, it was in the year 1224, the 9th of Henry III., agreed that there should be a standing-place appointed, where matters should be heard and judged, which was in the great hall at Westminster.

In this hall he ordained three judgment-seats ; to wit, at the entry on the right hand, the Common Pleas, where civil matters are to be pleaded, specially such as touch lands or contracts; at the upper end of the hall, on the right hand, or south-east corner, the King's Bench, where pleas of the crown have their hearing ; and on the left hand, or south-west corner, sitteth the lord chancellor, accompanied with the master of the Rolls and other men, learned for the most part in the civil law, and called masters of the chancery, which have the king's fee. The times of pleading in these courts are four in the year, which are called terms : the first is Hilary term, which beginneth the 23rd of January, if it be not Sunday, and endeth the 12th of February ; the second is Easter term, and beginneth seventeen days after Easter-day, and endeth four days after Ascension-day ; the third term beginneth six or seven days after Trinity Sunday, and endeth the Wednesday fortnight after ; the fourth is Michaelmas term, which beginneth the 9th of October, if it be not Sunday, and endeth the 28th of November.

And here it is to be noted that the kings of this realm have used sometimes to sit in person in the King's Bench; namely, King Edward IV., in the year 1462, in Michaelmas term, sat in the King's Bench three days together, in the open court, to understand how his laws were ministered and executed.

Within the port, or entry into the hall, on either side are ascendings up into large chambers, without the hall adjoining thereunto, wherein certain courts be kept; namely, on the right hand is the court of the Exchequer, a place of account for the revenues of the crown. The hearers of the account have auditors under them; but they which are the chief for accounts of the prince are called barons of the Exchequer, whereof one is called the chief baron. The greatest officer of all is called the high treasurer. In this court be heard those that are delators, or informers, in popular and penal actions, having thereby part of the profit by the law assigned unto them.

In this court, if any question be, it is determined after the order of the common law of England by twelve men, and all subsidies, taxes, and customs by account; for in this office the sheriffs of the shire do attend upon the execution of the commandments of the judges, which the earl should do if he were not attending upon the princes in the wars, or otherwise about him. For the chief office of the earl was to see the king's justice to have course, and to be well executed in the shire, and the prince's revenues to be well answered and brought into the treasury.

If any fines or amerciaments be extracted out of any of the said courts upon any man, or any arrearages of accounts of such things as is of customs, taxes, and subsidies, or other such like occasions, the same the sheriff of the shire doth gather, and is answerable therefor in the Exchequer. As for other ordinary rents of patrimonial lands, and most commonly of taxes, customs, and subsidies, there be particular receivers and collectors, which do answer it into the Exchequer. This court of the Exchequer hath of old time, and, as I think, since the Conquest, been kept at Westminster, notwithstanding sometimes removed thence by commandment of the king, and after restored again, as, namely, in the year 1209, King John commanded the Exchequer to be removed from Westminster to Northampton, &c.

On the left hand, above the stair, is the Duchy chamber, wherein is kept the court for the duchy of Lancaster by a chancellor of that duchy, and other officers under him. Then is there in another chamber the office of the receipts of the queen's revenues for the crown; then is there also the Star chamber, where in the term time, every week once at the least, which is commonly on Fridays and Wednesdays, and on the next day after the term endeth, the lord chancellor and the lords, and other of the Privy Council, and the chief-justices of England, from nine of the clock till it be eleven, do sit.

This place is called the Star chamber because the roof thereof is decked with the likeness of stars gilt. There be plaints heard of riots, routs, and other misdemeanours; which if they be found by the king's council, the party offender shall be censured by these persons, which speak one after another, and he shall be both fined and commanded to prison.

Then at the upper end of the great hall, by the King's Bench, is a going up to a great chamber, called the White hall, wherein is now kept the court of Wards and Liveries, and adjoining thereunto is the Court of Requests. Then is St. Stephen's Chapel, of old time founded by King Stephen. King John, in the 7th of his reign, granted to Baldwinus de London, clerk of his Exchequer, the chapelship of St. Stephen's at Westminster, &c. This chapel was again since, of a far more curious workmanship, new built by King Edward III. in the year 1347, for thirty-eight persons in that church to serve God; to wit, a dean, twelve secular canons, thirteen vicars, four clerks, five choristers, two servitors, to wit, a verger and a keeper of the chapel. He built for those from the house of Receipt, along nigh to the Thames, within the same palace, there to inhabit; and since that there was also built for them, betwixt the clock-house and the Woolstaple, called the Weighhouse. He also built to the use of this chapel, though out of the palace court, some distance west, in the little sanctuary, a strong clochard of stone and timber, covered with lead, and placed therein three great bells, since usually rung at coronations, triumphs, funeral of princes, and their obits. Of those bells men fabled that their ringing soured all the drink in the town: more, that about the biggest bell was written—

> " King Edward made me,
> Thirtie thousand and three;
> Take me downe and wey me,
> And more shall ye find me."

But these bells being taken down, indeed, were found all three not to weigh twenty thousand. True it is, that in the city of Rouen, in Normandy, there is one great bell that hath such inscription as followeth :—

> " Je suis George de Ambois,
> Qui trente cinq mil a pois,

Mes lui qui me pesera,
Trente six mil me trouera."

" I am George of Ambois,
Thirty-five thousand in poise ;
But he that shall weigh me,
Thirty-six thousand shall find me."

The said King Edward endowed this chapel with lands to the yearly value of five hundred pounds. Doctor John Chambers, the king's physician, the last dean of this college, built thereunto a cloister of curious workmanship, to the charges of eleven thousand marks. This chapel, or college, at the suppression, was valued to dispend in lands by the year one thousand and eighty-five pounds ten shillings and fivepence, and was surrendered to Edward VI. ; since the which time the same chapel hath served as a parliament house.

By this chapel of St. Stephen was sometime one other smaller chapel, called Our Lady of the Pew, to the which lady great offerings were used to be made ; amongst other things, I have read that Richard II., after the overthrow of Wat Tyler and other his rebels, in the 4th of his reign, went to Westminster, and there giving thanks to God for his victory, made his offering in this chapel ; but as divers have noted, namely, John Piggot, in the year 1252, on the 17th of February, by negligence of a scholar appointed by his schoolmaster to put forth the lights of this chapel, the image of Our Lady, richly decked with jewels, precious stones, pearls, and rings, more than any jeweller could judge the price for, so saith mine author, was, with all this apparel, ornaments, and chapel itself, burnt ; but since again re-edified by Anthony, Earl Rivers, Lord Scales, and of the Isle of Wight, uncle and governor to the Prince of Wales, that should have been King Edward V., &c.

The said palace, before the entry thereunto, hath a large court and in the same a tower of stone, containing a clock, which striketh every hour on a great bell, to be heard into the hall in sitting-time of the courts, or otherwise ; for the same clock, in a calm, will be heard into the city of London. King Henry VI. gave the keeping of this clock, with the tower called the clock-house and the appurtenances, unto William Walsby, dean of St. Stephens, with the wages of sixpence the day out of his Exchequer. By this tower standeth a fountain, which at coronations and great triumphs is made to run with wine out of divers spouts.

On the east side of this court is an arched gate to the river of Thames, with a fair bridge and landing-place for all men that have occasion. On the north side is the south end of St.

Stephen's Alley, or Canon Row, and also a way into the old Wool-staple; and on the west side is a very fair gate, begun by Richard III. in the year 1484, and was by him built a great height, and many fair lodgings in it, but left unfinished, and is called the high tower at Westminster. Thus much for the monastery and palace may suffice. And now will I speak of the gate-house, and of Tothill Street, stretching from the west part of the close.

The gate-house is so called of two gates, the one out of the College court towards the north, on the east side whereof was the Bishop of London's prison for clerks' convict; and the other gate, adjoining to the first, but towards the west, is a jail or prison for offenders thither committed. Walter Warfield, cellarer to the monastery, caused both these gates, with the appurtenances, to be built in the reign of Edward III.

On the south side of this gate King Henry VII. founded an almshouse for thirteen poor men; one of them to be a priest, aged forty-five years, a good grammarian, the other twelve to be aged fifty years, without wives; every Saturday the priest to receive of the abbot. or prior, fourpence by the day, and each other twopence-halfpenny by the day for ever, for their sustenance, and every year to each one a gown and a hood ready made; and to three women that dressed their meat, and kept them in their sickness, each to have every Saturday sixteenpence, and every year a gown ready made. More, to the thirteen poor men yearly eighty quarters of coal and one thousand of good faggots to their use, in the hall and kitchen of their mansion; a discreet monk to be overseer of them, and he to have forty shillings by the year, &c.; and hereunto was every abbot and prior sworn.

Near unto this house westward was an old chapel of St. Anne; over against the which the Lady Margaret, mother to King Henry VII., erected an almshouse for poor women, which is now turned into lodgings for the singing-men of the College. The place wherein this chapel and almshouse standeth was called the Elemosynary, or Almonry, now corruptly the Ambry, for that the alms of the abbey were there distributed to the poor. And therein Islip, abbot of Westminster, erected the first press of book printing that ever was in England, about the year of Christ 1471. William Caxton, citizen of London, mercer, brought it into England, and was the first that practised it in the said abbey; after which time the like was practised in the abbeys of St. Augustine at Canterbury, St. Alban's, and other monasteries.

From the west gate runneth along Tothill Street, wherein is a house of the Lord Gray of Wilton; and on the other side, at the entry into Tothill Field, Stourton House, which Gyles, the last

Lord Dacre of the south, purchased and built new, whose lady and wife Anne, sister to Thomas, the Lord Buckhurst, left money to her executors to build an hospital for twenty poor women, and so many children, to be brought up under them, for whose maintenance she assigned lands to the value of one hundred pounds by the year, which hospital her executors have new begun in the field adjoining. From the entry into Tothill Field the street is called Petty France, in which, and upon St. Hermit's Hill, on the south side thereof, Cornelius Van Dun, a Brabanter born, yeoman of the guard to King Henry VIII., King Edward VI., Queen Mary, and Queen Elizabeth, built twenty houses for poor women to dwell rent-free; and near hereunto was a chapel of Mary Magdalen, now wholly ruinated.

In the year of Christ 1256, the 40th of Henry III., John Mansell, the king's councillor and priest, did invite to a stately dinner the kings and queens of England and Scotland, Edward the king's son, earls, barons, and knights, the Bishop of London, and divers citizens, whereby his guests did grow to such a number that his house at Totehill could not receive them, but that he was forced to set up tents and pavilions to receive his guests, whereof there was such a multitude that seven hundred messes of meat did not serve for the first dinner.

The city of Westminster for civil government is divided into twelve several wards; for the which the dean of the collegiate church of Westminister, or the high-steward, do elect twelve burgesses and as many assistants; that is, one burgess and one assistant for every ward; out of the which twelve burgesses two are nominated yearly, upon Thursday in Easter week, for chief burgesses to continue for one year next following, who have authority given them by the Act of parliament, 27th Elizabeth, to hear, examine, determine, and punish, according to the laws of the realm, and lawful customs of the city of London, matters of incontinency, common scolds, inmates, and common annoyances; and likewise to commit such persons as shall offend against the peace, and thereof to give knowledge within four-and-twenty hours to some justice of peace in the county of Middlesex.

Governors of the City of London; and first of Ecclesiastical Bishops, and other Ministers, there.

HAVING thus run through the description of these cities of London and Westminster, as well in their original foundations as in their increases of buildings and ornaments, together with such incidents of sundry sorts as are before, both generally and particularly, discoursed, it remaineth that somewhat be noted by me, touching the policy and government, both ecclesiastical and civil, of London, as I have already done for Westminster, the order whereof is appointed by the late statute, even as that of London is maintained by the customs thereof, most laudably used before all the time of memory.

And first, to begin with the ecclesiastical jurisdiction : I read that the Christian faith was first preached in this island, then called Britain, by Joseph of Arimathea, and his brethren, disciples of Christ, in the time of Aruiragus, then governor here under the Roman Emperor ; after which time, Lucius, king of the Britons, sent his ambassadors, Eluanus and Meduvanus, two men learned in the Scriptures, with letters to Eleutherius, Bishop of Rome, desiring him to send some devout and learned men, by whose instruction he and his people might be taught the faith and religion of Christ. Eleutherius baptized those messengers, making Eluanus a bishop, and Meduvanus a teacher, and sent over with them into Britain two other famous clerks, Faganus and Deruvianus, by whose diligence Lucius and his people of Britain were instructed in the faith of Christ and baptized, the temples of idols were converted into cathedral churches, and bishops were placed where Flamines before had been ; at London, York, and Carleon upon Usk, were placed archbishops, saith some. The epistle said to be sent by Eleutherius to King Lucius, for the establishing of the faith, ye may read in my Annals, Summaries, and Chronicles, truly translated and set down as mine author hath it, for some hath curtailed and corrupted it, and then fathered it upon reverend Bede, who never wrote word thereof, or otherwise to that effect, more than this as followeth :—

In the year 156 Marcus Aurelius Verus, the fourteenth emperor after Augustus, governed the empire with his brother, Aurelius Commodus ; in whose time Glutherius, a holy man, being Pope of the Church of Rome, Lucius, king of Britain, wrote unto him, desiring that by his commandment he might be made Christian ; which his request was granted him ; whereby the Britons receiving then the faith, kept it sound and undefiled in rest and peace until Dioclesian the emperor's time. Thus far Bede, which may suffice to prove the Christian faith there to be received here. And now of the London bishops as I find them.

There remaineth in the parish church of St. Peter upon Cornhill in London a table wherein is written that Lucius founded the same **church to be an archbishop's see** and metropolitan or chief church of his kingdom, and that it so endured the space of four hundred years, until the coming of Augustine the monk, and others, from Rome, in the reign of the Saxons. The archbishops' names I find only to be set down by Joceline of Furness, in his book of British bishops, and not elsewhere. Thean, saith he, was the first Archbishop of London, in the time of Lucius, who built the said church of St. Peter, in a place called Cornhill in London, by the aid of Ciran, chief butler to King Lucius.

2. Eluanus was the second, and he built a library to the same church adjoining, and converted many of the Druids, learned men in the pagan law, to the Christian faith. 3. Cadar was the third. Then followed.—4. Obinus. 5. Conan. 6. Paludius. 7. Stephen. 8. Iltute. 9. Dedwin. 10. Thedred. 11. Hilary. 12. Guidelium. 13. Vodimus, slain by the Saxons. 14. Theanus, the fourteenth, fled with the Britons into Wales, about the year of Christ 587.

This much out of Joceline of the archbishops, the credit whereof I leave to the judgment of the learned; for I read of a bishop of London, not before named, in the year of Christ 326, to be present at the second council, holden at Arles, in the time of Constantine the Great, who subscribed thereunto in these words, *Ex provinciæ Britanniæ Civitate Londiniensi Restitutus Episcopus*, as plainly appeareth in the first tome of the Councils, he writeth not himself archbishop, and therefore maketh the matter of archbishops doubtful, or rather, overfloweth that opinion.

The Saxons being pagans, having chased the Britons, with the Christian preachers, into the mountains of Wales and Cornwall, and having divided this kingdom of the Britons amongst themselves, at the length, to wit, in the year 596, Pope Gregory, moved of a godly instinction, sayeth Bede, in the 147th year after the arrival of the Angles or Saxons in Britain, sent Augustine, Melitus, Justus, and John, with other monks, to preach the Gospel to the said nation of the Angles. These landed in the isle of Thanet, and were first received by Ethelbert, king of Kent, whom they converted to the faith of Christ, with divers other of his people, in the 34th year of his reign, which Ethelbert gave unto Augustine the city of Canterbury.

This Augustine, in the year of Christ 604, consecrated Melitus and Justus bishops, appointing Melitus to preach unto the East Saxons, whose chief city was London; and there King Sebert, nephew to Ethelbert, by preaching of Melitus, received the Word of Life; and then Ethelbert, king of Kent, built in the city of London St. Paul's Church, wherein Melitus began to be bishop in the year 619, and sat five years. Ethelbert, by his charter, gave lands to this church of St. Paul, so did other kings after him. King Sebert, through the good life and like preaching of Melitus, having received baptism, to show himself a Christian, built a church to the honour of God and St. Peter on the west side of London, which church is called Westminster. But the successors of Sebert, being pagans, expelled Melitus out of their kingdoms.

Justus, the second bishop for a time, and then Melitus again ; after whose decease the seat was void for a time. At length Sigebert, son to Sigebert, brother to Sebert, ruled in Essex ; he became a Christian, and took to him a holy man named Cedde, or Chadde, who won many by preaching and good life to the Christian religion.

Cedde, or Chadde, was by Finan consecrated bishop of the East Saxons, and he ordered priests and deacons in all the parts of Essex, but especially at Ithancaster and Tilbury.

This city of Ithancaster, saith Ralph Cogshall, stood on the bank of the river Pant, that runneth by Maldon, in the hundred of Danesey, but now is drowned in Pant, so that nothing remaineth but the ruin of the city in the river Tilbury, both the west and east, standeth on the Thames side, nigh over against Gravesend.

Wina, expelled from the church of Winchester by Cenewalche, the king, was adopted to be the fourth bishop of London, in the reign of Wolferus, king of Mercia, and sat nine years.

Erkenwalde, born in the castle or town of Stallingborough in Lindsey, first abbot of Crotesey, was by Theodore, Archbishop of Canterbury, appointed to be bishop of the East Saxons, in the city of London. This Erkenwalde, in the year of Christ 677, before he was made bishop, had built two monasteries, one for himself, being a monk, in the isle of Crote in Surrey, by the river of Thames, and another for his sister Edilburge, being a nun, in a certain place called Berching in Essex. He deceased at Berching in the year 697, and was then buried in Paul's Church, and translated into the new church of St. Paul in the year 1148.

Waldhere was Bishop of London. Sebba, king of the East Saxons, at his hands received the habit of monk, for at that time there were monks in Paul's Church, as writeth Radulphus de Diceto and others. To this bishop he brought a great sum of money, to be bestowed and given to the poor, reserving nothing to himself, but rather desired to remain poor in goods as in spirit, for the kingdom of heaven. When he had reigned thirty years he deceased at Paul's, and was there buried, and lieth now in a coffin of stone, on the north side of the aisle next the choir.

Ingwaldus, bishop of London, was at the consecration of Tatwine, archbishop of Canterbury ; he confirmed the foundation of Crowland in the year 716, saith Ingulfus, and deceased in the year 744, as saith Hoveden.

746. Engulfe, bishop of London.

754. Wicket, or Wigerus, bishop of London.

761. Eaderightus, or Edbrithe, bishop of London.

768. Eadgain, or Eadgarus, bishop of London.

773. Kenewallth, bishop of London.

784. Eadbaldus, bishop of London.

795. Heatbright, bishop of London, deceased 802, saith Hoveden.

813. Osmond, bishop of London; he was witness to a charter made to Crowland in the year 833, saith Ingulphus.

835. Ethelmothe, bishop of London.

838. Elbertus, or Celbertus, bishop of London.

841. Caulfe, bishop of London.

850. Swithulfus, bishop of London; he likewise was witness to a charter of Crowland 851.

860. Edstanus, bishop of London; witness to a charter to Crowland 860.

870. Ulsius, bishop of London.

878. Ethelwardus, bishop of London.

886. Elstanus, bishop of London, died in the year 900, saith Asser; and all these, saith the author of *Flores Historiarum*, were buried in the old church of St. Paul, but there remaineth now no memory of them.

900. Theodricus, bishop of London; this man confirmed King Edred's charter made to Winchester in the year 947, whereby it seemeth that he was bishop of London of a later time than is here placed.

922. Welstanus, bishop of London.

941. Brithelme, bishop of London.

958. Dunstanus, abbot of Glastonberie, then bishop of Worcester, and then bishop of London; he was afterwards translated to Canterbury 960.

960. Ealfstanus, bishop of London; the 28th in number.

981. Edgare, bishop of London; he confirmed the grants made to Winchester and to the Crowland 966, and again to Crowland 970, the charter of Ethelred, concerning Ulfrunhampton, 996.

1004. Elphinus, bishop of London.

1010. Alwinus, bishop of London; he was sent into Normandy in the year 1013, saith Asser.

1044. Robert, a monk of Gemerisins in Normandy, bishop of London seven years, afterwards translated from London to Canterbury.

1050. Specgasius, elected, but rejected by the king.

1051. William, a Norman chaplain to Edward the Confessor, was made bishop of London 1051, sate nineteen years, and deceased 1070. He obtained of William the Conqueror the charter of liberties for the city of London, as I have set down in my Summary, and appeareth by his epitaph in Paul's Church.

1070. Hugh de Orwell, bishop of London; he died of a leprosy when he had sitten fifteen years.

1085. Maurice, bishop of London; in whose time, to wit, in the year 1086, the church of St. Paul was burnt, with the most part of this city; and therefore he laid the foundation of a new large church; and having sat twenty-two years he deceased 1107, saith Paris.

1108. Richard Beame, or Beamor, bishop of London, did wonderfully increase the work of this church begun, purchasing the streets and lanes adjoining with his own money; and he founded the monastery of St. Osyth in Essex. He sat bishop nineteen years, and deceased 1127.

1127. Gilbertus Universalis, a canon of Lyons, elected by Henry I.; he deceased 1141, when he had sat fourteen years.

1142. Robert de Segillo, a monk of Reading, whom Maude, the empress, made bishop of London, where he sat eleven years. Geoffrey de Magnavile took him prisoner at Fulham, and he deceased 1152.

1153. Richard Beames, archdeacon of Essex, bishop of London ten years, who deceased 1162.

1163. Gilbert Foliot, bishop of Hereford, from whence translated to London, sat twenty-three years, and deceased 1186.

1189. Richard Fitz Nele, the king's treasurer, archdeacon of Essex, elected bishop of London at Pipwel, 1189. He sate nine years, and deceased 1198. This man also took great pains about the building of Paul's Church, and raised many other goodly buildings in his diocese.

1199. William S. Mary Church, a Norman, bishop of London, who was one of the three bishops that, by the Pope's commandment, executed his interdiction, or curse, upon the whole realm of England; but he was forced, with the other bishops, to flee the realm in 1208; and his castle at Stratford in Essex was by command-ment of King John overthrown, 1210. This William, in company of the arch-bishop of Canterbury, and of the bishop of Ely, went to Rome, and there com-plained against the king, 1212, and returned, so as in the year 1215 King John, in the church of St. Paul, at the hands of this William, took upon him the cross for the Holy Land. He resigned his bishopric of his own voluntarily in the year 1221, saith Cogshall.

1221. Eustachius de Fauconbridge, treasurer of the exchequer (saith Paris) chancellor of the exchequer (saith Textor and Cogshall), bishop of London, 1223, whilst at Chelmesford he was giving holy orders, a great tempest of wind and rain annoyed so many as came thither, whereof it was gathered how highly God was displeased with such as came to receive orders, to the end that they might live a more easy life of the stipend appointed to the Churchmen, giving themselves to banqueting; and so with unclean and filthy bodies (but more unclean souls) presume to minister unto God, the author of purity and cleanness. Falcatius de Brent was delivered to his custody in the year 1224. This Eustachius deceased in the year 1228, and was buried in Paul's church, in the south side, without, or above, the choir.

1229. Roger Niger, archdeacon of Colchester, made bishop of London. In the year 1230, saith Paris, upon the feast-day of the Conversion of St. Paul, when he was at mass in the cathedral church of St. Paul, a great multitude of people being there present, suddenly the weather waxed dark, so as one could scantily see another and a horrible thunder-clap lighted on the church, which so shook it, that it was like to have fallen, and therewithal out of a dark cloud proceeded a flash of light-ning, that all the church seemed to be on fire, whereupon such a stench ensued, that all men thought they should have died; thousands of men and women ran out of the church, and being astonished, fell upon the ground void of all sense and understanding. None of all the multitude tarried in the church save the bishop and one deacon, which stood still before the high altar, awaiting the will of God. When the air was cleansed, the multitude returned into the church, and the bishop ended the service.

This Roger Niger is commended to have been a man of worthy life, excellently well learned, a notable preacher, pleasant in talk, mild of countenance, and liberal at his table. He admonished the usurers of his time to leave such enormities as they tendered the salvation of their souls, and to do penance for that they had committed. But when he saw they laughed him to scorn, and also threatened him, the bishop generally excommunicated and accursed all such, and commanded straitly that such usurers should depart farther from the city of London, which hithertowards had been ignorant of such mischief and wickedness, lest his diocese should be infected therewithal. He fell sick and died at his manor of Bishopshall, in the lordship and parish of Stebinhith, in the year 1241, and was buried in Paul's Church, on the north side of the presbytery, in a fair tomb, coped, of grey marble.

1241. Fulco Basset, dean of York, by the death of Gilbert Basset, possessed his lands, and was then made bishop of London, deceased on the 21st of May, in the year 1259, as saith John Textor, and was buried in Paul's Church.

1259. Henry Wingham, chancellor of England, made bishop of London, deceased in the year 1262, saith Textor, and was buried in Paul's Church, on the south side, without or above the choir, in a marble monument, close at the head of Faucon-bridge.

1262. Richard Talbot, bishop of London, straightways after his consecration deceased, saith Eversden.

1262. Henry Sandwich, bishop of London, deceased in the year 1273, as the same author affirmeth.

1273. John Cheshul, dean of Paul's, treasurer of the Exchequer and keeper of the Great Seal, was bishop of London, and deceased in the year 1279, saith Eversden.

1280. Fulco Lovel, archdeacon of Colchester, elected bishop of London, but refused that place.

1280. Richard Gravesend, archdeacon of Northampton, bishop of London. It appeareth, by the charter-warren granted to this bishop, that in his time there were two woods in the parish of Stebinhith pertaining to the said bishop. I have since I kept house for myself known the one of them by Bishop's hall; but now they are both made plain of wood, and not to be discerned from other grounds. Some have fabuled that this Richard Gravesend, bishop of London, in the year 1392, the 16th of Richard II., purchased the charter of liberties to this city; which thing hath no possibility of truth, as I have proved, for he deceased in the year 1303, almost ninety years before that time.

1307. Ralph Baldocke, dean of Paul's, bishop of London, consecrated at Lyons by Peter, bishop of Alba, in the year 1307; he was a great furtherer of the new work of Paul's; to wit, the east end, called our Lady chapel, and other adjoining. This Ralph deceased in the year 1313, and was buried in the said Lady chapel, under a flat stone.

1313. Gilbert Seagrave was consecrated bishop of London, and sat three years.

1317. Richard Newport, bishop of London, sat two years, and was buried in Paul's church.

1318. Stephen Gravesend, bishop of London, sat twenty years.

1338. Richard Wentworth, bishop of London, and chancellor of England, and deceased the year 1339.

1339. Ralph Stratford, bishop of London; he purchased the piece of ground called No Man's land, beside Smithfield, and dedicated it to the use of burial, as before hath appeared. He was born at Stratford upon Avon, and therefore built a chapel to St. Thomas there: he sat fourteen years, deceased at Stebunhith.

1354. Michael Norbroke, bishop of London, deceased in the year 1361, saith Mirimouth, sat seven years.

1362. Simon Sudbery, bishop of London, sat thirteen years, translated to be archbishop of Canterbury in the year 1375.

1375. William Courtney, translated from Hereford to the bishopric of London, and after translated from thence to the archbishopric of Canterbury in the year 1381.

1381. Robert Breybrook, canon of Lichfield, bishop of London, made chancellor in the 6th of Richard II., sat bishop twenty years, and deceased in the year 1404: he was buried in the said Lady chapel at Paul's.

1405. Roger Walden, treasurer of the exchequer, archbishop of Canterbury, was deposed, and after made bishop of London; he deceased in the year 1406, and was buried in Paul's church, Allhallowes altar.

1406. Richard Bubwith, bishop of London, treasurer of the exchequer, translated to Salisbury, and from thence to Bath, and lieth buried at Wells.

1407. Richard Clifford, removed from Worcester to London, deceased 1422, as saith Thomas Walsingham, and was buried in Paul's.

1422. John Kempe, fellow of Martin College in Oxford, was made bishop of Rochester, from whence removed to Chichester, and thence to London; he was made the King's chancellor in the year 1425, the 4th of Henry VI., and was removed from London to York in the year 1426: he sat archbishop there twenty-five years, and was translated to Canterbury; he was afterwards made cardinal in the year 1452. In the bishop of London's house at Fulham he received the cross, and the next day the pall, at the hands of Thomas Kempe, bishop of London. He deceased in the year 1454.

1426. William Gray, dean of York, consecrated bishop of London, who founded a college at Thele in Hartfordshire, for a master and four canons, and made it a cell to Elsing spittle in London; it had of old time been a college, decayed, and therefore newly founded. He was translated to Lincoln 1431.

1431. Robert Fitzhugh, archdeacon of Northampton, consecrated bishop of London, sat five years, deceased 1435, and was buried on the south side of the choir of Paul's.

1435. Robert Gilbert, doctor of divinity, dean of York, consecrated bishop of London, sat twelve years, deceased 1448.

1449. Thomas Kempe, archdeacon of Richmond, consecrated bishop of London at York house (now Whitehall), by the hands of his uncle John Kemp, archbishop of York, the 8th of February 1449; he founded a chapel of the Trinity in the body of St. Paul's church, on the north side; he sat bishop of London thirty-nine years and forty-eight days, and then deceased in the year 1489, was there buried.

1489. John Marshal, bishop of London, deceased in the year 1493.

1493. Richard Hall, bishop of London, deceased 1495, and was buried in the body of St. Paul's church.

1496. Thomas Savage, first bishop of Rochester, then bishop of London five years, was translated to York 1501, where he sat archbishop seven years, and was there buried in the year 1507.

1502. William Warrham, bishop of London, made keeper of the Great Seal, sat two years, was translated to Canterbury.

1504. William Barons, bishop of London, sat ten months and eleven days, deceased in the year 1505.

1505. Richard Fitz James, fellow of Merton College in Oxford, in the reign of Henry VI., was made bishop of Rochester, after bishop of Chichester, then bishop of London; he deceased 1521, and lieth buried hard beneath the north-west pillar of the steeple in St. Paul's, under a fair tomb of marble, over the which was built a fair chapel of timber, with stairs mounting thereunto: this chapel was burned with fire from the steeple 1561, and the tomb was taken down.

1521. Cuthbert Tunstal, doctor of law, master of the rolls, lord privy seal, and bishop of London, was thence translated to the bishopric of Durham in the year 1529.

1529. John Stokeley, bishop of London, sat thirteen years, deceased in the year 1539, and was buried in the Lady chapel in Paul's.

1539. Edmond Bonner, doctor of the civil law, archdeacon of Leicester, then bishop of Hereford, was elected to London in the year 1539, whilst he was beyond the seas, ambassador to King Henry VIII. On the 1st of September 1549, he preached at Paul's Cross; for the which sermon he was charged before the Council of King Edward VI., by William Latimer, parson of St. Lawrence Poultney, and John Hooper, sometime a white monk, and being convented before certain commissioners at Lambeth, was for his disobedience to the king's order, on the 20th day of the same month sent to the Marshalsea, and deprived from his bishopric.

1550. Nicholas Ridley, bishop of Rochester, elected bishop of London, was installed in Paul's Church on the 12th of April. This man by his deed, dated the 12th day after Christmas, in the 4th year of Edward VI., gave to the king the manors of Branketrie and Southminster, and the patronage of the church of Cogshall in Essex, the manors of Stebunheth and Hackney, in the county of Middlesex, and the marsh of Stebunheth, with all and singular messuages, lands, and tenements, to the said manors belonging, and also the advowson of the vicarage of the parish church of Cogshall in Essex aforesaid; which grant was confirmed by the dean and chapter of Paul's, the same day and year, with exception of such lands in Southminster, Stebunheth, and Hackney, as only pertained to them. The said King Edward, by his letters patents, dated the 16th of April, in the said

4th year of his reign, granted to Sir Thomas Wentworth, Lord Wentworth, lord chamberlain of the king's household, for, and in consideration of his good and faithful service before done, a part of the late received gift, to wit, the lordships of Stebunheth and Hackney, with all the members and appurtenances thereunto belonging, in Stebunheth, Hackney way, Shoreditch, Holywell Street, Whitechapel, Stratford at Bow, Poplar, North Street, Limehouse, Ratcliffe, Cleve Street, Brock Street, Mile End, Bletenhall Green, Oldford, Westheth, Kingsland, Shakelwell, Newington Street, *alias* Hackney Street, Clopton, Church Street, Well Street, Humbarton, Grove Street, Gunston Street, *alias* More Street, in the county of Middlesex, together with the march of Stebunheth, &c. The manor of Hackney was valued at sixty-one pounds nine shillings and four-pence, and the manor Stebunheth at one hundred and forty pounds eight shillings and eleven pence, by year, to be holden in chief, by the service of the twentieth part of a knight's fee. This bishop, Nicholas Ridley, for preaching a sermon at Paul's Cross, on the 16th of July, in the year 1553, was committed to the Tower of London, where he remained prisoner till the 10th of April 1554, and was thence sent to Oxford there to dispute with the divines and learned men of the contrary opinion; and on the 16th of October, 1555, he was burned at Oxford for opinions against the Romish order of sacraments, &c.

1553. Edmond Bonner aforesaid, being released out of the Marshal-sea, was restored to the bishopric of London by Queen Mary, on the 5th of August, in the year 1553, and again deposed by Queen Elizabeth, in the month of July 1559, and was eftsoones committed to the Marshalsea, where he died on the 5th of September 1569, and was at midnight buried amongst other prisoners in St. George's churchyard.

1559. Edmond Grindal, bishop of London, being consecrated the 21st of December 1559, was translated to York in the year 1570, and from thence removed to Canterbury in the year 1575. He died blind 1583, on the 6th of July, and was buried at Croydon in Surrey.

1570. Edwin Sandys, being translated from Worcester to the bishopric of London, in the year 1570, was thence translated to York in the year 1576, and died in the year 1588.

1576. John Elmere, bishop of London, deceased in the year 1594, on the 3rd of June at Fulham, and was buried in Paul's Church, before St. Thomas' Chapel.

1594. Richard Fletcher, bishop of Worcester, was on the 30th of December in Paul's Church elected bishop of London, and deceased on the 15th of June 1596. He was buried in Paul's Church without any solemn funeral.

1597. Richard Bancroft, doctor of divinity, consecrated at Lambeth on Sunday, the 8th of May, now sitteth bishop of London, in the year 1598, being installed there.

This much for the succession of the bishops of London, whose diocese containeth the city of London, the whole shires of Middlesex and Essex, and part of Hertfordshire. These bishops have for assistants in the cathedral church of St. Paul, a dean, a chaunter, a chancellor, a treasurer, five archdeacons—to wit, London, Middlesex, Essex, Colchester, and St. Alban's, and thirty prebendaries. There appertaineth also to the said churches for furniture of the choir in divine service, and ministration of the sacraments, a college of twelve petty canons, six vicars choral, and choristers, &c.

This diocese is divided into parishes, every parish having its parson, or vicar at the least, learned men for the most part, and sufficient preachers, to instruct the people. There were in this city, and within the suburbs thereof, in the reign of Henry II., as writeth Fitzstephen, thirteen great conventual churches, besides the lesser sort called parish churches, to the number of one hundred and twenty-six, all which conventual churches, and some others since that time founded, are now suppressed and gone, except the cathedral church of St. Paul in London, and the college of St. Peter at Westminster; of all which parish churches, though I have spoken, yet for more ease to the reader I will here again set them down.

[*This list is omitted.*]

Thus have ye in the wards of London, and in the suburbs of the same city, the borough of Southwark, and the city of Westminster, a cathedral church of St. Paul, a collegiate church of St. Peter in Westminster, and parish churches one hundred and twenty-three.

Hospitals in this City, and Suburbs thereof, that have been of old Time, and now presently are, I read of these as followeth:

HOSPITAL of St. Mary, in the parish of Barking Church, that was provided for poor priests and others, men and women in the city of London, that were fallen into frenzy or loss of their memory, until such time as they should recover, was since suppressed and given to the hospital of St. Katherine, by the Tower.

St. Anthony's, an hospital of thirteen poor men, and college, with a free school for poor men's children, founded by the citizens of London, lately by John Tait, first a brewer and then a mercer, in the ward of Broad Street, suppressed in the reign of Edward VI., the school in some sort remaining, but sore decayed.

St. Bartholomew, in Smithfield, an hospital of great receipt and relief for the poor, was suppressed by Henry VIII., and again by him given to the city, and is endowed by the citizens' benevolence.

St. Giles in the Fields was an hospital for leprous people out of the city of London and shire of Middlesex, founded by Matilda the queen, wife to Henry I., and suppressed by King Henry VIII.

St. John of Jerusalem, by West Smithfield, an hospital of the Knights of the Rhodes, for maintenance of soldiers against the Turks and infidels, was suppressed by King Henry VIII.

St. James in the Field was an hospital for leprous virgins of the city of London, founded by citizens for that purpose, and suppressed by King Henry VIII.

St. John, at Savoy, an hospital for relief of one hundred poor people, founded by Henry VII., suppressed by Edward VI. ; again new founded, endowed, and furnished by Queen Mary, and so remaineth.

St. Katherine, by the Tower of London, an hospital with a master, brethren, and sisters, and alms women, founded by Matilda, wife to King Stephen; not suppressed, but in force as before.

St. Mary within Cripplegate, an hospital founded by William Elsing, for a hundred blind people of the city, was suppressed by King Henry VIII.

St. Mary Bethlehem, without Bishopsgate, was an hospital, founded by Simon Fitzmary, a citizen of London, to have been a priory, and remaineth for lunatic people, being suppressed and given to Christ's Hospital.

St. Mary, without Bishopsgate, was an hospital and priory, called St. Mary Spittle, founded by a citizen of London for relief of the poor, with provision of one hundred and eighty beds there for the poor; it was suppressed in the reign of King Henry VIII.

St. Mary Rouncevall, by Charing Cross, was an hospital, suppressed with the priories aliens in the reign of King Henry V.; then was it made a brotherhood in the 15th of Edward IV., and again suppressed by King Edward VI.

St. Thomas of Acres, in Cheap, was an hospital for a master and brethren, in the record called Militia; it was surrendered and sold to the mercers.

St. Thomas, in Southwark, being an hospital of great receipt for the poor, was suppressed, but again newly founded and endowed by the benevolence and charity of the citizens of London.

An hospital there was without Aldersgate, a cell to the house of Cluny, of the French order, suppressed by King Henry V.

An hospital without Cripplegate, also a like cell to the said house of Cluny, suppressed by King Henry V.

A third hospital in Oldborne, being also a cell to the said house of Cluny, suppressed by King Henry V.

The hospital or almshouse called God's House, for thirteen poor men, with a college, called Whittington College, founded by Richard Whittington, mercer, and suppressed; but the poor remain, and are paid their allowance by the mercers.

Christ's Hospital, in Newgate Market, of a new foundation in the Grey Friars Church by King Henry VIII.; poor fatherless children be there brought up and nourished at the charges of the citizens.

Bridewell, now an hospital, or house of correction, founded by King Edward VI., to be a workhouse for the poor and idle persons of the city, wherein a great number of vagrant persons be now set a-work, and relieved at the charges of the citizens. Of all these hospitals, being twenty in number, you may read before in their several places, as also of good and charitable provisions made for the poor by sundry well-disposed citizens.

Now of Leprous People, and Lazar Houses.

IT is to be observed that leprous persons were always, for avoiding the danger of infection, to be separated from the sound, &c.; God himself commanding to put out of the host every leper. Whereupon I read, that in a provincial synod holden at Westminster by Hubert, Archbishop of Canterbury, in the year of Christ 1200, the 2nd of King John, it was decreed, according to the institution of the Lateran Council, that when so many leprous people were assembled, that might be able to build a church, with a churchyard for themselves, and to have one especial priest of their own, that they should be permitted to have the same without contradiction, so they be not injurious to the old churches, by that which was granted to them for pity's sake. And further, it was decreed that they be not compelled to give any tithes of their gardens or increase of cattle.

I have moreover heard that there is a writ in our law, *de leproso amovendo;* and I have read that King Edward III., in the 20th year of his reign, gave commandment to the mayor and sheriffs of London, to make proclamation in every ward of the city and suburbs, that all leprous persons inhabiting there should avoid within fifteen days next, and that no man suffer any such leprous person to abide within his house, upon pain to forfeit his said house, and to incur the king's further displeasure; and that they should cause the said lepers to be removed into some out places of the fields, from the haunt or company of sound people, whereupon certain lazar-houses, as may be supposed, were then built without the city some good distance, to wit, the Lock without Southwark in Kent Street; one other betwixt the Miles End and Stratford, Bow; one other at Kingsland, betwixt Shoreditch and Stoke Newington; and another at Knight's Bridge, west from Charing Cross. These four I have noted to be erected for the receipt of leprous people sent out of the city. At that time also the citizens required of the guardian of St. Giles' Hospital to take from them, and to keep continually, the number of fourteen persons leprous, according to the foundation of Matilda the queen, which was for leprous persons of the city of London and the shire of Middlesex, which was granted. More, the wardens, or keepers of the ports, gates, or posterns of this city, were sworn in the mayor's court before the recorder, &c., that they should well and faithfully keep the same ports and posterns, and not to suffer any leprous person to enter the said city.

John Gardener, porter of the postern by the Tower, his oath before the mayor and recorder of London, on Monday, after the feast of St. Bartholomew, the 49th of Edward III.: That the gates and postern be well and faithfully kept in his office and bailiwick, and that he should not suffer any lepers or leper to enter the city, or to remain in the suburbs; and if any leper or lepers force themselves to enter by his gates or postern, he to bind them fast to horses, and send them to be examined of the superiors, &c.

Finally, I read that one William Pole, yeoman of the crown to King Edward IV., being stricken with a leprosy, was also desirous to build an hospital, with a chapel, to the honour of God and St. Anthony, for the relief and harbouring of such leprous persons as were destitute in the kingdom, to the end they should not be offensive to other in their passing to and fro: for the which cause Edward IV. did by his charter, dated the 12th of his reign, give unto the said William for ever a certain parcel of his land lying in his highway of Highgate and Holloway, within the county of Middlesex, containing sixty feet in length and thirty-four in breadth.

The Temporal Government of this City, somewhat in brief manner.

THIS city of London, being under the government of the Britons, Romans, and Saxons, the most ancient and famous city of the whole realm, was at length destroyed by the Danes, and left desolate, as may appear by our histories. But Alfred, king of the West Saxons, having brought this whole realm, from many parts, into one monarchy, honourably repaired this city, and made it again habitable, and then committed the custody thereof to his son-in-law Adhered, Earl of Mercia; after whose decease the city, with all other possessions pertaining to the said earl, returned to King Edward, surnamed the Elder, &c. : and so remained in the king's hands, being governed under him by portgraves, or portreves, which name is compounded of the two Saxon words, *porte* and *gerefe*, or *reve*. *Porte* betokeneth a town, and *gerefe* signifieth a guardian, ruler, or keeper of the town.

These governors of old time, saith Robert Fabian, with the laws and customs then used within this city, were registered in a book called the Doomsday, written in the Saxon tongue; but of later days, when the said laws and customs were changed, and for that also the said book was of a small hand, sore defaced, and hard to be read or understood, it was less set by, so that it was embezzled and lost. Thus far Fabian.

Notwithstanding, I have found, by search of divers old registers and other records abroad, namely, in a book sometime appertaining to the monastery of St. Alban's, of the portgraves, and other governors of this city, as followeth :—

First, that in the reign of King Edward, the last before the Conquest, Wolfegare was portgrave, as may appear by the charter of the same king, in these words: "Edward, king, greeteth Alfward, bishop, and Wolfegare, my portgrave, and all the burgesses in London." And afterward that, in another charter, "King Edward greeteth William, bishop, and Sweetman, my portgrave." And after that, in another charter to the Abbey of Chertsey, to William, bishop, and Leofstane and Alsy, portgraves. In the reign of William the Conqueror, William, Bishop of London, procured of the said Conqueror his charter of liberties, to the same William, bishop, and Godfrey, portgrave, in Saxon tongue, and corrected in English thus :—

"William, king, greet William, bishop, and Godfrey, portgrave, and all the burgesses within London, French and English. And I graunt that they be all their law worth, that they were in Edward's dayes the king. And I will that each child bee his father's heire. And I will not suffer that any man do you wrong, and God you keepe." And then in the reign of the said Conqueror and of William Rufus, Godfrey de Magnavile was portgrave, or sheriff, as may appear by their charters, and Richard de Par was provost.

In the reign of King Henry I., Hugh Buche was portgrave, and Leofstanus, goldsmith, provost, buried at Bermondsey.

After them Aubrey de Vere was portgrave, and Robert Bar Querel provost. This Aubrey de Vere was slain in the reign of King Stephen. It is to be noted, also, that King Henry I. granted to the citizens of London the shrivewick thereof, and of Middlesex, as in another place is showed.

In the reign of King Stephen, Gilbert Becket was portgrave, and Andrew Buchevet provost.

After him, Godfrey Magnavile, the son of William, the son of Godfrey Magnavile, by the gift of Maude, the empress, was portgrave, or sheriff of London and Middlesex, for the yearly farm of three hundred pounds, as appeareth by the charter.

In the time of King Henry II., Peter Fitzwalter was portgrave; after him John Fitznigel was portgrave; after him Ernulfus Buchel became portgrave; and after him William Fitz Isabel. These portgraves are also in divers records called vicecounties, vicounties, or sheriffs, as being under an earl; for that they then, as since, used that office as the sheriffs of London do till this day. Some authors do call them domesmen, aldermen, or judges of the king's court.

William Fitzstephen, noting the estate of this city, and government thereof in his time, under the reign of King Stephen and of Henry II., hath these words :—

"This city," saith he, "even as Rome, is divided into wards. It hath yearly sheriffs instead of consuls ; it hath the dignity of senators and alderman ; it hath under-officers, and, according to the quality of laws, it hath several courts and general assemblies upon appointed days." Thus much for the antiquity of sheriffs, and also of aldermen, in several wards of this city, may suffice. And now for the name of bailiffs, and after that of mayors, as followeth :

In the first year of King Richard I., the citizens of London obtained to be governed by two bailiffs, which bailiffs are in divers ancient deeds called sheriffs, according to the speech of the law, which called the shire Balliva, for that they, like as the portgraves, used the same office of shrivewick, for the which the city paid to fee farm three hundred pounds yearly as before, since the reign of Henry I., which also is yet paid by the city into the Exchequer until this day.

They also obtained to have a mayor, to be their principal governor and lieutenant of the city, as of the king's chamber.

1180. The names of the first bailiffs, or officers, entering into their office at the feast of St. Michael the Archangel, in the year of Christ 1189, were named Henry Cornhill and Richard Reynere, bailiffs or sheriffs.

Their first mayor was Henry Fitz Alwin Fitz Liefstane, goldsmith, appointed by the said king, and continued mayor from the 1st of Richard I. until the 15th of King John, which was twenty-four years and more.

[*The list of mayors and sheriffs from* 1190 *to* 1602 *is omitted.*]

Thus much for the chief and principal governors of this famous city; of whose public government, with the assistance of inferior officers, their charges for keeping of the peace, service of the prince, and honour of this city, much might have been said, and I had thought to have touched more at large; but being informed that a learned gentleman, James Dalton, a citizen born, minded such a labour, and promised to perform it, I have forborne and left the same to his good leisure, but he being now lately deceased without finishing any such work, a common fault to promise more than to perform, and I hear not of any other that taketh it in hand, I have been divers times minded to add certain chapters to this book, but being, by the good pleasure of God, visited with sickness,—such as my feet, which have borne me many a mile, have of late years refused, once in four or five months, to convey me from my bed to my study,—and therefore could not do as I would.

At length, remembering I had long since gathered notes to have chaptered, am now forced to deliver them unperfected, and desire the readers to pardon me, that want not will to pleasure them.

Aldermen and Sheriffs of London.

THERE be in this city, according to the number of wards, twenty-six Aldermen; whereof yearly, on the feast day of St. Michael the Archangel, one of them is elected to be mayor for the year following, to begin on the 28th of October: the other aldermen, his brethren, are to him assistants in councils, courts, &c.

More, there is a Recorder of London, a grave and learned lawyer, skilful in the customs of this city, also assistant to the lord mayor: he taketh place in councils and in courts before any man that hath not been Mayor, and learnedly delivereth the sentences of the whole court.

The Sheriffs of London, of old time chosen out of the commonalty, commoners, and oftentimes never came to be aldermen, as many aldermen were never sheriffs, and yet advanced to be mayor, but of late, by occasion, the sheriffs have been made aldermen before or presently after their election.

Nicholas Faringdon was never sheriff, yet four times mayor of this city, and so of other, which reproveth a bye-word, such a one will be mayor, or he be sheriff, &c.

Then is there a Chamberlain of London.

A Common Clerk, or town clerk.

A Common Sergeant.

Officers belonging to the Lord Mayor's House.

Sword-bearer,
Common hunt,
Common crier,   } esquires, four.
Water bailiff.
Coroner of London.
Sergeant carvers, three.
Sergeants of the chamber, three.
Sergeant of the channel.
Yeoman of the channel.
Yeomen of the water side, four.
Under water-bailiff.
Yeomen of the chamber, two.
Meal weighers, three.
Yoeman of the wood wharfs, two.
The sword-bearer's man.
Common hunt's men, two.
Common crier's man.   } gentlemen's men, seven.
Water bailiff men, two.
The carver's man.

Whereof nine of these have liveries of the lord mayor, viz., the sword-bearer and his man, the three carvers, and the four yeomen of the water side ; all the rest have their liveries from the chamber of London.

Thus far after my notes delivered by an officer of the lord mayor's house, but unperfected ; for I remember a crowner, an under-chamberlain, and four clerks of the mayor's court and others.

The Sheriffs of London; their Officers.

THE Sheriffs of London, in the year 1471, were appointed each of them to have sixteen sergeants, every sergeant to have his yeoman, and six clerks ; to wit, a secondary, a clerk of the papers, and four other clerks, besides the under-sheriffs' clerks, their stewards, butlers, porters, and other in household many.

Of the Mayor's and Sheriffs' Liveries somewhat.

TO follow precedent of former time, the clerks of companies were to inquire for them of their companies that would have the mayor's livery, their money as a benevolence given, which must be twenty shillings at the least put in a purse, with their names that gave it, and the wardens to deliver it to the mayor by the first of December ; for the which every man had then sent him four yards of broadcloth, rowed or striped athwart, with a different colour to make him a gown, and these were called ray gowns, which was then the livery of the mayor, and also of the sheriffs, but each differing from others in the colours.

Of older times I read, that the officers of this city wore gowns of party colours, as the right side of one colour and the left side of another ; as, for example, I read in books of accounts in the Guildhall, that in the 19th year of Henry VI. there was bought for an officer's gown two yards of cloth, coloured mustard villars, a colour now out of use, and two yards of cloth, coloured blue, price two shillings the yard, in all eight shillings. More, paid to John Pope, draper, for two gown cloths, eight yards of two colours, *eux ombo deux de rouge* (or red), *medle brune*, and *porre* (or purple) colour, price the yard two shillings. These gowns were for Piers Rider and John Buckles, clerks of the chamber.

More, I read that in the year 1516, in the 7th of Henry VIII., it was agreed by a common council in the Guildhall that the sheriffs of London should (as they had been accustomed) give yearly rayed gowns to the recorder, chamberlain, common sergeant, and common clerk, the sword-bearer, common hunt, water-bailiff, common crier, like as to their own offices, &c.

1525. More, in the 16th of Henry VIII., Sir William Bayly, then being mayor, made a request, for that clothes of ray (as he alleged) were evil wrought, his officers might be permitted, contrary to custom, for that year to wear gowns of one colour ; to the which, in a Common Council, one answered and said, " Yea, it might be permitted," and no man said, " Nay," and so it passed. Thus much for party coloured and ray gowns have I read : but for benevolence to the mayor, I find that of later time that each man giving forty shillings towards his charges, received four yards of broad cloth to make him a gown, for Thomas White performed it in the 1st of Queen Mary ; but Sir Thomas Lodge gave instead of four yards of broad cloth, three yards of satin to make them doublets, and since that the three yards of satin is turned into a silver spoon, and so it holdeth.

The days of attendance that the fellowships do give to the Mayor at his going to Paul's were seven, as followeth :—1. Alhallowen day. 2. Christmas day. 3. St. Stephen's day. 4. St. John's day. 5. New Year's day. 6. Twelfth day. 7. Candlemas day.

The 23rd of Henry VIII., these companies had place at the mayor's feast in the Guildhall, in order as followeth. I speak by precedent, for I was never feast-follower :—

1. Mercers, the wardens, and seventeen persons, five messes.
2. Grocers, the wardens, and sixteen persons, four messes.
3. Drapers, the wardens, and twelve persons, four messes.
4. Fishmongers, the wardens, and twelve persons, four messes.
5. Goldsmiths, the wardens, and ten persons, three messes.
6. Skinners, the wardens, and eight persons, three messes.
7. Merchant-tailors, the wardens, and nine persons, three messes.
8. Vintners, the wardens, and six persons, two messes.
9. Ironmongers, the wardens, and four persons, four messes and a half.
10. Merchant-haberdashers, the wardens, and fourteen persons, four messes and a half.
11. Salters, the wardens, and eight persons, two messes and a half.
12. Dyers, the wardens, and six persons, two messes.
13. Leathersellers, the wardens, and eight persons, three messes.
14. Pewterers, the wardens, and five persons, two messes.
15. Cutlers, the wardens, and five persons, two messes.
16. Armourers, the wardens, and three persons, one mess.
17. Waxchandlers, the wardens, and six persons, two messes.
18. Tallow-chandlers, the wardens, and three persons, two messes.
19. Shiremen, the wardens, and five persons, two messes.
20. Fullers, the wardens, and nine persons, two messes.
21. Sadlers, the wardens, and four persons, two messes.
22. Brewers, the wardens, and twelve persons, four messes.
23. Scriveners, the wardens, and six persons, two messes.
24. Butchers, the wardens, and seven persons, three messes.
25. Bakers, the wardens, and four persons, two messes.
26. Poulterers, the wardens, and one person, one mess.
27. Stationers, the wardens, and two persons, one mess.
28. Inholders, the wardens, and four persons, two messes.
29. Girdlers, the wardens, and four persons, two messes.
30. Chirurgeons, the wardens, and two persons, one mess.
31. Founders, the wardens, and one person, one mess.
32. Barbers, the wardens, and four persons, two messes.
No Clothing. Upholders, the wardens, and two persons, one mess.
34. Broiderers, the wardens, and two persons, one mess.
35. Bowyers, the wardens, and two persons, one mess.
36. Fletchers, the wardens, and two persons, one mess.
No Clothing. Turners, the wardens, and two persons, one mess.
38. Cordwainers, the wardens, and four persons, two messes.
39. Painters-stainers, the wardens, and five persons, two messes.
40. Masons, the wardens, and one person, one mess.
41. Plumbers, the wardens, and two persons, one mess.
42. Carpenters, the wardens, and four persons, two messes.
43. Pouch-makers, the wardens, and two persons, one mess.
44. Joiners, the wardens, and two persons, one mess.
45. Coopers, the wardens, and one person, one mess.
No Clothing. Glaziers, the wardens, and two persons, one mess.
No Clothing. Linendrapers, the wardens, and two persons, one mess.
No Clothing. Woodmongers, the wardens, and two persons, one mess.
49. Curriers, the wardens, and two persons, one mess.
No Clothing. Foystors, the wardens, and two persons, one mess.
No Clothing. Grey Tanners, the wardens, and two persons, one mess.
52. Tilers, the wardens, and one person, one mess.
53. Weavers, the wardens, and one person, one mess.
54. Blacksmiths, the wardens, and one mess.
No Clothing. Lorimars, the wardens, and two persons, one mess.
56. Spurriers, the wardens, and two persons, one mess.
57. Wiresellers, the wardens, and two persons, one mess.
No Clothing. Fruiterers, the wardens, and two persons, one mess.
No Clothing. Farriers, the wardens, and two persons, one mess.
60. Bladesmiths, the wardens, and two persons, one mess.

These companies severally, at sundry times, purchased the king's favour and license by his letters patents, to associate themselves in brotherhoods, with Master and Wardens for their government. Many also have procured corporations, with privileges, &c. ; but I read not of license by them procured for liveries to be worn, but at their governor's discretion to appoint, as occasion asketh, some time in triumphant manner, some time more mourning like, and such liveries have they taken upon them, as well before, as since they were by license associated into brotherhoods, or corporations. For the first of these companies that I read of to be a guild, brotherhood, or fraternity, in this city, were the weavers, whose guild was confirmed by Henry II. The next fraternity, which was of St. John Baptist, time out of mind, called of tailors and linen-armourers of London ; I find that King Edward I. in the 28th of his reign, confirmed that guild by the name of tailors and linen-armourers, and gave to the brethren there of authority yearly to choose unto them a governor, or master, with wardens, &c. The other companies have since purchased license of societies, brotherhoods, or corporations, in the reigns of Edward III., Richard II., Henry IV., Henry V., Henry VI., and Edward IV., &c.

Somewhat of Liveries worn by Citizens of London, in Time of Triumphs and Otherways.

1236. The 20th of Henry III., the mayor, aldermen, sheriffs, and citizens of London, rode out to meet the king and his new wife, Queen Eleanor, daughter to Reymond Beringarius of Aragon, Earl of Provence and Narbone. The citizens were clothed in long garments, embroidered about with gold, and silk in divers colours, their horses finely trapped, to the number of three hundred and sixty, every man bearing a golden or silver cup in his hand, the king's trumpets before them sounding, &c., as ye may read in my Annales.

1300. The 29th of Edward I., the said king took to wife Margaret, sister to Philip Le Beau, king of France ; they were married at Canterbury. The queen was conveyed to London, against whom the citizens to the number of six hundred rode in one livery of red and white, with the cognizances of their mysteries embroidered upon their sleeves, they received her four miles out of London, and so conveyed her to Westminster.

1415. The 3rd of Henry V., the said king arriving at Dover, the mayor of London with the aldermen and crafts-men riding in red, with hoods red and white, met with the king on the Black heath, coming from Eltham with his prisoners out of France.

1432. The 10th of Henry VI., he being crowned in France, returning into England, came to Eltham towards London, and the mayor of London, John Welles, the aldermen, with the commonality, rode against him on horseback, the mayor in crimson velvet, a great velvet hat furred, a girdle of gold about his middle, and a bawdrike of gold about his neck trilling down behind him, his three henxemen, on three great coursers following him, in one suit of red, all spangled in silver, then the aldermen in gowns of scarlet, with sanguine hoods, and all the commonality of the city clothed in white gowns, and scarlet hoods, with divers cognizances embroidered on their sleeves, &c.

1485. The 1st of Henry VII., the mayor, aldermen, sheriffs, and commonality, all clothed in violet, as in a mourning colour, met the king at Shorditch, and conveyed him to Paul's Church, where he offered his banners.

Thus much for liveries of citizens in ancient times, both in triumphs and otherwise, may suffice, whereby may be observed, that the coverture of men's heads was then hoods, for neither cap nor hat is spoken of, except that John Welles, Mayor of London to wear a hat in time of triumph, but differing from the hats lately taken in use, and now commonly worn for noblemen's liveries. I read that Thomas, Earl of Lancaster in the reign of Edward II. gave at Christmas in liveries, to such as served him, a hundred and fifty-nine broad cloths, allowing to every garment furs to fur their hoods. More near our time, there yet remaineth the counterfeits and pictures of aldermen, and others that lived in the reigns of Henry VI. and Edward IV., namely aldermen Darby dwelling in Fenchurch Street, over against the parish Church of St. Diones, left his picture, as of an alderman, in a gown of scarlet on his back, a hood on his head, &c., as is in that house, and elsewhere, to be seen; for a further monument of those late times, men may behold the glass windows of the Mayor's Court in the Guildhall above the stairs, the mayor is there pictured sitting in habit, party-coloured, and a hood on his head, his swordbearer before him with a hat or cap of maintenance; the common clerk, and other officers bare-headed, their hoods on their shoulders; and therefore I take it, that the use of square bonnets worn by noblemen, gentlemen, citizens, and others, took beginning in this realm by Henry VII. and in his time, and of further antiquity, I can seen no counterfeit or other proof of use. Henry VIII., towards his latter reign, wore a round flat cap of scarlet or of velvet, with a brooch or jewel, and a feather; divers gentlemen, courtiers, and others, did the like. The youthful citizens also took them to the new fashion of flat caps, knit of woollen yarn black, but so light that they were obliged to tie them under their chins, for else the wind would be master over them. The use of these flat round caps so far increased, being of less price than the French bonnet, that in short time young aldermen took the wearing of them; Sir John White wore it in his mayoralty, and was the first that left example to his followers; but now the Spanish felt, or the like counterfeit, is most commonly of all men both spiritual and temporal taken to use, so that the French bonnet or square cap, and also the round or flat cap, have for the most part given place to the Spanish felt; but yet in London amongst the graver sort, (I mean the liveries of companies), remaineth a memory of the hoods of old time worn by their predecessors: these hoods were worn, the roundlets upon their heads, the skirts to hang behind in their necks to keep them warm, the tippet to lie on their shoulder, or to wind about their necks, these hoods were of old time made in colours according to their gowns, which were of two colours, as red and blue, or red and purple, murrey, or as it pleased their masters and wardens to appoint to the companies; but now of late time, they have used their gowns to be all of one colour, and those of the saddest, but their hoods being made the one half of the same cloth their gowns be of, the other half remaineth red as of old time.

And so I end, as wanting time to travel further in this work.

INDEX

AARON, son of Abraham, 65
Aaron of York, 272
Abbo Floriancensis, 63
Abbot, John, 269
Abbot of St Albans' House, 192
Abchurch Lane, 211, 223
Abde, Roger, 325
Able, Sir John, 236
Abunden, Stephen, 257
Achley, Rich., 230
Achley, Roger, 62, 173, 197
Acra, Geffrey de, 314
Acton, Hugh, 250, 305
Adam, prior of St Cross, 166
Addle St., 280, 285, 337, 341
Adie, Henry, 259
Adis, John, 292
Adrian, John, 240
Æneas, 33
Agmondesham, Philip, 268
Agricola, 36
Ailife, Sir John, 279
Ailward, 227
Aker, John, 257
Alba, Bishop of, 385
Albany, 325
Albert, Philip, 268
Alcestone Manor, 53
Aldborough, 37
Alderban, 196
Aldermanbury Church, 134
Aldermanbury St., 132, 281
Aldermen and Sheriffs, 440
Aldersgate, 41, 42, 63
Aldersgate Ward, 290-6
Aldgate, 41, 42
Aldgate Ward, 159-68
Aldham, Master Hugh, 412
Aldrich, 63
Ale for prisoners going to Tyburn, 399
Alectus, 37
Alewarde, 159
Alfonse, son of Ed. I., 320
Alfune, 83, 345, 389
Algodus, 372
Alhollen Eve, 122
Alien priory, 380
Aliens—
    Dutch, 214
    Flemings, 222
    French, 158, 170, 179, 238-40, 295

Aliens (continued)—
    Germans, 62, 70, 158, 233-5
    Italians, 154
    Jews, 41, 60, 65, 67, 168, 184, 203, 268-74, 288, 361, 368-7
Alington, Rich., 396
Alison, Edmond, 267
Allen, Dr., 253
Allen, John, 286
Allen, Ralph, 306
Allen, Sir John, 137, 151, 154, 264
Allen, Sir Will., 179
Allet, Sir John, 327
Alleyne, Thos., 268
All Hallows, Barking, 153, 157
All Hallows, Bread St., 324
All Hallows, the Great, 42, 100, 235
All Hallows, Honey Lane, 265
All Hallows, the Less, 71, 131, 236
All Saints at the Wall, 45
Almaine, Bartholomew de, 302
"Almerie," The, 376
"Almonry," The, 424
Almshouses, 139-43, 187, 189, 193, 195, 240, 242, 259, 287, 289, 296, 341, 384, 424, 425
Alnothus, 204
Alwin, Childe, 380
Alwine, 146
Alwine, Nicholas, 253, 266
Alwyne, Bishop of Helmsham, 63
Amades, Robert, 212
Amcotes, Sir Henry, 51, 226
Amen Lane, 298, 318
Anbry, John, 304
Ancalits, 34
Anchorage, 346
Andrew, Will., 354
Andrewes, Dr. Lancelot, 412
Androgeus, 33
Anede Hithe, 334
Angel, The, 184
Angels, 84
Angew, Bishop of, 112
Anicius, Archdeacon of Surrey, 372

Anne of Bohemia, 110, 309, 328, 413
Anne of Cleves, 413
Anne of Lothbury, 47
Anne of Warwick, 413
Ansley, John, 353
"Antelope," The, 381
Antoninus, 183
Apleton, Will., 304
Apleyard, Thos., 307
Appleton (Confessor to King), 86
Appleyard, Will., 365
Apprentices of the Law, 105
Aprichard, John, 364
Aras, John of, 234
Arcadius, 37
Archer, Esq., 365
Archer, John, 229
Archery, 129, 181, 388, 389
Arches, 242
Archley, Roger, 388
Archull, Thos., 257
Arden, Thos., 53
Arderne, Ralph de, 296
Arderne, Thos. de, 380
Arguings of Schoolboys, 89, 101
Arles, British Bishop at Council, 427
Armorer, Will., 153
Armourers' Hall, 275
Arms, 127
Arnold, John, 275
Arnold, Thos. and Rich., 288
Arrar, R., 296
Arundel, E. of, 171, 190
Arundel, Eliz., Countess, 320
Arundel House, 400
Arundell, Reinfride, 304
Arundell, Rich., 352
Arundell, Sir Edward, 190
Arundell, Thos., 356
Asclepiodatus, 143
Ascue, John, 161
Ascue, Lady, 50, 289
Ashby, Thos., 173
Ashcombe, Rob., 285
Ashfed, Alice, 186
Ashfield, John, 161
Ashley, John, 364
Ashton, Sir Ralfe, 155
Ashwy, Rich., 199
Askham, Will., 204

447

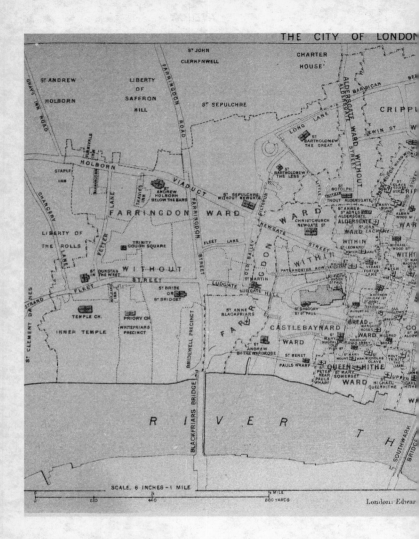

THE CITY OF LONDON

1

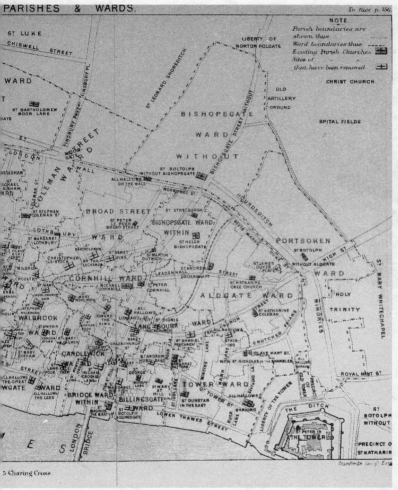

The City of London in Parishes and Wards from a map prepared in the nineteenth century. The later additions of Blackfriars and Southwark bridges were not contemporary with Stow's London. Reproduced by permission of the Guildhall Library, London

John Leland's Itinerary

Itinerary

Travels in Tudor England

John Chandler

The work of John Leland, a Tudor scholar who travelled the length of England during the 1530s and 1540s, is frequently cited and quoted in books about the places which he described, and is acknowledged to be one of the most important sources of information about English towns and countryside in the sixteenth century. But hitherto this fascinating work has been largely inaccessible to the general reader, available only in a five-volume edition which retained much of Leland's disjointed order and his frequent lapses into Latin.

For this new edition John Chandler has retained everything in the itinerary of historical or topographical interest, but has turned the text into modern English and rearranged it by historic county. Leland's descriptions are complemented by the county maps of the Tudor cartographer, Christopher Saxton, as well as by illustrations of many of the places and buildings which he mentioned. There are introductions to his accounts of each county, and an important reassessment of Leland's life and work.

ISBN 0 86299 957 X (hardback)

FOOD AND FEAST IN TUDOR ENGLAND

ALISON SIM

Popular representations of the Tudors at table have caricatured diners of the period as loud, gross and lacking any polite graces. This is far from the case, as Alison Sim shows in this lavishly illustrated and highly readable account of Tudor eating habits.

Tudor society went through vast changes, many of which were reflected in the food which people ate and in the way food and dining were used for social display by the upwardly mobile. For those with money, meals became extravagantly sophisticated, with a staggering number of courses and breathtaking table displays. Even those lower down the social scale enjoyed some of the benefits of increasing prosperity and the new markets which England's merchants exploited, bringing new foodstuffs into the country and new ideas about eating.

This is the first general overview of Tudor dining, and makes the case for regarding Tudor food and feast as different from its medieval counterpart. It brings alive the royal courts and great houses of the period, but considers also the lives of the poor, whose diet was so crucially dependent on the seasons. All those interested in daily life in Tudor times and in the way that food and eating have changed over the centuries will enjoy this book.

ISBN 0 7509 1476 9 (hardback)

HENRY VIII AND THE INVASION OF FRANCE

CHARLES CRUICKSHANK

In 1513 the young Henry VIII departed from Dover with a fleet 'the like of which Neptune had never seen before', carrying an army of about 28,000 troops as part of a concerted European effort to prevent France from gaining the ascendancy in Europe. This book chronicles the campaign which followed, including the establishment of a beach-head at the then English port of Calais, the bombardment and razing of Therouanne, the Battle of the Spurs, and the siege and capture of the city of Tournai, which was subsequently represented as an English town at the parliament in Westminster. The two people who gained most from the campaign were Thomas Wolsey, who became the Bishop of Tournai, and Emperor Maximilian I, who benefited from Henry's amateurish exploits since they successfully neutralized an enemy town on the borders of the Holy Roman Empire.

Supplemented by numerous illustrations, the book not only narrates and evaluates events but also draws upon contemporary sources to bring vividly to life the nature of the campaign and what conditions were like for those involved in it.

ISBN 0 7509 0678 2 (paperback)

INVISIBLE POWER

THE ELIZABETHAN SECRET SERVICES 1570–1603

ALAN HAYNES

An unrivalled and impeccably detailed account of the
'secret services' operated by the great men of Elizabethan
England. Kidnapping, surveillance, conspiracy, counter-
espionage, theft and lying were just a few of the methods
used to defeat the ever-present threat of regicide. This
book challenges many stale notions about espionage in
Renaissance England and throws a compellingly new and
bold light on the reign of Elizabeth I.

'a superb analysis' *The Mail on Sunday*
'recommended' *The Spectator*

ISBN 0 7509 0037 7 (hardback)
ISBN 0 7509 0676 6 (paperback)

SEX IN ELIZABETHAN ENGLAND

ALAN HAYNES

Some twenty years ago the historian A.L. Rowse wrote that the sex lives of the Elizabethans would need and merit a whole volume, 'one of far greater significance than most works of historical research'. This fully illustrated study finally fills that gap by examining sexual behaviour in the Elizabethan age, approached through the literature and literary personalities of the period.

Although there is much we will never know, poets and playwrights can provide valuable insights into our ancestors' sexual lives. Here, with help from the work of figures such as Shakespeare, Marlowe and Donne, Alan Haynes builds up a vivid picture of the sexual experiences of Elizabethans at all levels of society, from the 'virgin Queen' herself, who slept alone despite rumours that she was sexually promiscuous as her mother was alleged to have been, to characters such as Moll Cutpurse, a gutsy female transvestite who shocked and amused generations of Londoners in almost equal measure. There is a full examination of the Elizabethan court, which 'seethed with clandestine sexual activity' and revolved round sophisticated rituals of courtship and display, and chapters on love and marriage, prostitution, brothels and bawdy behaviour in the playhouses, as well as impotence, homosexuality and sexual diseases.

This book will intrigue and fascinate anyone with an interest in the very private lives of our forebears.

ISBN 0 7509 1071 2 (hardback)

THE GUNPOWDER PLOT

ALAN HAYNES

The people of Britain still celebrate annually the failure of an intended violent episode that was thwarted nearly four hundred years ago. The fireworks and bonfires are linked with one name and date – but who was Guy Fawkes and how did he come to be below the chamber of the House of Lords in the first hour of 5 November 1605? Who employed this taciturn mercenary soldier, and what desperation drove those involved to plan a horrific massacre of the Protestant royal family and government? In this fascinating book, the first general study of the plot in its historical context for many years, Alan Haynes recovers the truth about this Catholic conspiracy. His probing analysis offers the clearest, most balanced view yet of often conflicting evidence, as he disentangles the threads of disharmony, intrigue, betrayal, terror and retribution. It makes a remarkable story.

Illustrated throughout, this enthralling book will grip the general reader, while the scope of its detailed research will require historians of the period to consider again the commanding importance of the plot throughout the seventeenth century.

ISBN 0 7509 0332 5 (hardback)